DUNNINGER'S COMPLETE ENCYCLOPEDIA OF MAGIC

DUNNINGER'S COMPLETE ENCYCLOPEDIA OF MAGIC

SPRING BOOKS London New York Sydney Toronto

Published by
The Hamlyn Group Limited
London · New York · Sydney · Toronto
Hamlyn House, Feltham, Middlesex, England

Distributed in the U.S.A. by BONANZA BOOKS
a division of Crown Publishers, Inc.
419 Park Avenue South
New York, N. Y. 10016
Manufactured in the United States of America

F G H

Introduction

This, Dunninger's Encyclopedia of Magic, is the largest, the most complete, and undoubtedly the most important volume on magic and stage illusions ever published.

It contains more explanations and information than any other combined fifty books on magic.

Much of the material in this book has been originated by me, and this material has been the basis for hundreds of effects used this day by magicians on TV, in nightclubs, theaters and various branches of entertainment throughout the world.

Most of the material in these pages was originally published in three separate volumes under the title: "Dunninger's Popular Magic."

These books were published by Mr. Hugo Gernsback, one of the world's outstanding scientists and inventors.

Some contributors to the original "Popular Magic" publications were: Al Flosso, Dr. Jaks, Dr. Joseph Krauss, Walter B. Gibson, scientist H. Winfield Secor and numerous other important writers.

The three volumes of "Popular Magic" are today the most sought after magic books in the United States. An important New York book dealer has been paying forty to fifty dollars per volume, for each copy securable, of "Popular Magic" Volume two.

In addition to all the important material from these volumes, numerous outstanding effects have been added, thereby bringing the Encyclopedia up to date.

Many of the tricks and illusions herein explained have been sold separately by many dealers of magical equipment throughout the world. Were one to total the prices paid for these secrets, it would amount to many thousands of dollars.

Mr. Lyle Stuart, the eminent publisher of this work, has suggested that I include a modern brief autobiography.

To me, it seems rather difficult for any author to do this, without seeming to exaggerate his talents. Therefore, I have chosen to republish the original introduction and brief biography, as were first published in the previous volumes of "Popular Magic." You will find them at the end of this book.

To omit any part of the original publication would be to deprive this book of some of the flavor of the original work.

Since this material was first published I have made numerous theatrical strides such as presenting my performances in important theaters throughout the world. For many years I have appeared on the various networks, demonstrating programs of thought reading together with magic and illusionary effects. My television network shows received the highest ratings for any thirty minute show in all TV history.

In conclusion, may I sincerely add the hope that those who might choose magic and mystery as a hobby will find this volume most rewarding. To the many who may, on the other hand, decide to make this time-honored art the means of their profession, I trust that they may meet with successful recognition.

Respectfully yours,

JOSEPH DUNNINGER

NOTE: Thanks is herewith extended to Mr. Hugo Gernsback for permission to include the material in this Encyclopedia which originally appeared under the author's byline in "Science and Invention" and "Everyday Science and Mechanics."

Contents

Magic for Everybody

The Blocks of Yogi

PRIOR to beginning this series of articles upon popular conjuring, mind reading, telepathy and general mysteries purporting to be on the mental order, a few words of introduction will be in place. It is not my desire to expose the conjurers' greatest mysteries or to lay bare the secrets of famous illusions. To my thinking the general theatre-going public enjoy the mystification due to modern stage illusions and deciding for themselves how the trick is done, an explanation prior to witnessing a demonstration would be injurious to the interest supposed to be excited. The average theatre-goer would no more desire to know in advance how an illusion is accomplished, than he would care to be told the story of a play before seeing the same acted. The average stage effect such as produced by present day illusionists may involve an investment of thousands of dollars and the secret of an effect of this kind would be of no value to the readers of this paper because it is doubtful whether anyone not a professional would care to invest such a sum of money to duplicate the effect simply for one's amusement.

It is, therefore, my desire to expose a series of effects, which cost but little to construct and can be accomplished with little practice, yet will be such as to appear to be bordering upon the impossible and will have to all appearances as mysterious an effect as would be found in more costly and difficult experiments.

THE BLOCKS OF THE YOGI

This weird and startling effect is one that I originated some eight years ago and which has been the means of mystifying quite a number of professional magicians. Two small blocks of wood are passed around for thorough inspection. It is found that both are three inches long, one and one-half inches wide and about one-half inch in thickness. Closest inspection will reveal no difference other than the color. The one is painted a bright vermilion or red, the other block a dull black. The performer requests a subject from his audience to take these blocks into another room with him and to place the blocks in different side pockets. The subject re-enters the room and the performer is at once able to state which pocket holds the red block and which the black one. Still another test is made; while in another part of the house, the blocks are separately wrapped in sheets of paper and the performer is still able to indicate the packages containing the red and black respectively.

The Telephone Mystery

In spite of the weird and mystifying effect produced by the performance of this trick, the secret is extremely simple but still remarkably clever. With reference to the diagram, one will find that in the black block, which really consists of two pieces of wood

Prof. Joseph Dunninger, Master Magician, and Mind Reader, Author of the Series of Magic Articles Which Follow.

carefully glued together, is secreted a piece of magnetized steel. The red block is likewise treated but the metal (zinc or copper) therein concealed is not magnetic. Its purpose is only to give it the proper weight to be in positive harmony with the other block. The performer has a small compass concealed between the fingers of his hand. This compass has a plate case which is flesh colored so as not to be easily noticed. Naturally all that remains to be done in order to discover the package or pocket containing the black block is for the performer to pass his hand over such package or pocket, apparently only for effect, but in reality the reader will understand for the purpose of having the block indicate its presence as the magnetized steel will cause the compass needle to move. Many other experiments with the blocks will suggest themselves to

A Hindu Mystery

the readers as one will readily see that the array of possibilities is unlimited.

A HINDU MYSTERY

Several years ago a certain Hindu mystic was practicing his apparent powers of witchcraft and enchantment in one of our largest cities and succeeded in obtaining large sums of money from many of our foremost society leaders and business men by his illusions. This method of a get-rich-quick schemer became the talk of the town until his psychic power came to a sad ending through police detection. I will herewith lay bare a method which he employed which proved to be one of the best mechanical methods for weird impression that has ever been practiced. Briefly, here is the method of his operation. The subject would enter the mystic's parlor, which was found to be elaborately trimmed with an array of zodiac charts, ancient hierogliphics, incense pots, skulls and other weird uncanny objects to make the psychic's work more impressive. After waiting for five or ten minutes, the weird-looking gentleman would enter the room from behind a pair of antique portieres. The subject would be ushered to a chair directly in front of a table, upon which lay a pad, a candlestick containing a burning candle, two incense pots and several pencils. The Hindu wonder-worker would seat himself upon a chair directly opposite the subject. After a brief interview with reference to the month, day and year in which the subject was born and other apparently necessary questions relative to his horoscope, the Hindu would finally ask him to take a sheet of paper from his own pocket if necessary and to write upon it five or six questions, which he would wish to have answered. After these had been written he was requested to put this paper into his pocket or to burn it in the flame of the candle as his desire would dictate. After a few moments of ceremony, the Hindu would begin to call the subject's questions and in a low mysterious tone answer them to the subject's entire satisfaction. Not alone would this information be given to the spectator, but a series of questions and experiences with his friends who, while apparently unknown to the mystic were called by name. Following this, their addresses would be mentioned, naturally producing a bewildering and uncanny effect upon the subject, who could not possibly doubt the genuineness of the occult powers after a demonstration as convincing as this.

One Block of Wood is Red, the Other Black. Both are wrapped in Newspaper and Then Placed in the Vest Pockets. With a Slight Flourish of His Hand the Magician Informs the Holder of the Blocks in Which Pocket Each of the Colored Blocks is Located. A palmed Compass and a Magnet Concealed in One of the Blocks Solve the Mystery.

A Deck of Cards is Shuffled up, Placed Into the Magician's Pocket and One Withdrawn. The Holder of the Card Now Telephones to a Town Some Fifteen Miles Distant, Where the Individual Answering the Phone Correctly Informs Him of the Number of Spots on the Card and Its Suite. A Prepared Deck Containing Cards of But One Suit, a Double Pocket, and Some Friend Who Knows the Trick, Are the Sole Requirements.

Now for the explanation: As in all cases of the greatest apparent mysteries, the explanation is extremely simple. The table, apparently an innocent piece of furniture, is partly responsible for the success of this effect, as will be noted by the diagram. One of the legs of the table is hollow. Over the top of the table a sheet of thin white China silk has been previously placed, to one corner of which a string is affixed, which passes down the leg of this table through a tube leading into another room. On top of this silk is placed a large sheet of carbon paper, and above this affair a rim of wood with a thin oil cloth top. It is, therefore, noted that although the table appears to be nothing more than an unprepared card table, it is in reality a traveller for information. The paper upon which the subject writes naturally rests upon the top. As the writing is done, a secret carbon copy is produced on the silk through the cloth of the table top upon the sheet of silk exactly as in office practice. At the proper moment the sheet is drawn down through the table-leg and through the tube into the hands of the assistant hidden in the other room. The diagram will further disclose the fact that a telephone arrangement consisting of a receiving apparatus concealed in the turban of the Hindu's costume leads off to a transmitter in the assistant's room. All that now remains to be done is for the concealed assistant to transmit the information secured by reading the carbon copy on the silk sheet to the wizard. Other information has also been obtained unknown to the subject. When he entered this "palace of mystery" he was asked to hang his coat upon a rack in the hall leading to the den. This was done ostensibly so that he might wear a robe or mantel which was furnished him by the attendant. In reality, however, it was the means of supplying additional information to the Hindu. During the period of conversation between the subject and the wizard,

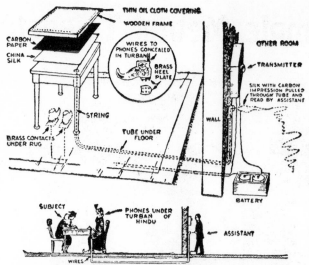

A Mystic for a Long Time Fooled His Followers by the Simple Trick Shown in the Diagram Above. A message written on a Sheet of Paper Produced a Carbon Copy on a China Silk Sheet Located Under the Oil Cloth Covering of the Table. This Carbon Copy Was Withdrawn by the Assistant Through the Hollow Leg of the Table to a Distant Room, Where the Questions Were Transmitted to the "Man of Mystery" in the Ordinary Telephonic Manner.

the assistant would go through the pockets of the subject's coat hanging upon the rack and read whatever letters, papers, addresses, visiting cards, and the like, might be contained therein. All this information naturally was transmitted to the Hindoo by this telephone contrivance. It will be noted that the magician has the freedom of walking about and can at the proper time secure the proper telephone connection by placing the heels of his shoes upon two (or more pairs) plates secreted under the carpet, thus forming the necessary connection. To the metal shoe heels, of course, are affixed a number of spikes which penetrate the fibres of the carpet and come in direct contact with the plates. The writer feels that the exposing of this weird and extremely clever method of fraud will operate as a form of education to those desirous of parting with large sums of money for a look-in upon the

boundary of the odd, fascinating, occult side of mystery.

THE TELEPHONE MYSTERY

This interesting method of proving the existence of mental telepathy has been used by some of our foremost mind-readers with signal success. A deck of cards is freely shown and inspected. The mind-reader places the deck of cards in his pocket and requests one of his subjects to remove one card therefrom. The subject is now asked to concentrate upon this card for several moments. Another member of the audience is directed to go to a telephone and call up the mind-reader's assistant, who, at a distance of some twenty miles or more, distinctly designates the correct suit of the card selected.

The explanation is simple. To begin with, two decks of cards are employed. For the one, an ordinary deck, purchasable anywhere, is used. The other deck consists of 52 cards of one suit and one denomination. For example's sake, we will say, all are jacks of diamonds. The pocket of the trousers in which the deck is afterward placed really consists of a pocket within a pocket. The original or unprepared deck descends into the lower pocket, as indicated in the diagram. It now will be seen by the reader that when the subject places his hand in the performer's pocket with the intent of removing one card, he is bound to remove the jack of diamonds, regardless of which of the 52 he may happen to draw. The assistant to the performer, who has been stationed at the other end of the 'phone, of course, understands that his part of the mystery consists in acting with hesitation for effect, and slowly repeats THE JACK OF DIAMONDS over the 'phone. The jack, of course, has been removed from the unprepared deck, so that when the same is again brought to view from out the performer's pocket, the secret of the trick would not be overthrown by the discovery of another jack of diamonds.

Sketch with Fire

A most novel method of entertainment is given in the above diagram. A simple design, without a great deal of detail, is drawn on a piece of heavy paper with a concentrated solution of potassium nitrate, which is given time to dry. Then the end of a lighted cigarette or piece of glowing string is touched to the starting point and the design burns itself out of the paper. The design should be one continuous line for best effect.

Ice in Boiling Water

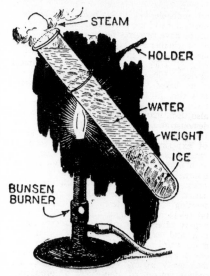

A very pretty experiment which illustrates the fact that heated water rises to the top of a container may be made as above. Drop a piece of ice in a test tube and weight it down with a leaden ball. Fill the tube with ice water and hold over a Bunsen burner at a 45° angle. The water will soon boil, but the ice will remain solid. The convection currents in the water keep the heat away from the ice.

Simple Mental Telepathy

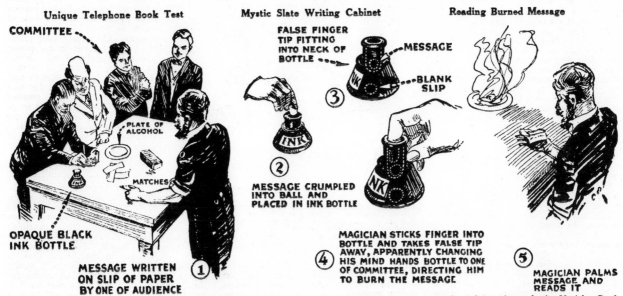

Unique Telephone Book Test

COMMITTEE

PLATE OF ALCOHOL

MATCHES

OPAQUE BLACK INK BOTTLE

MESSAGE WRITTEN ON SLIP OF PAPER BY ONE OF AUDIENCE ①

Mystic Slate Writing Cabinet

FALSE FINGER TIP FITTING INTO NECK OF BOTTLE

MESSAGE

BLANK SLIP

③

MESSAGE CRUMPLED INTO BALL AND PLACED IN INK BOTTLE

②

MAGICIAN STICKS FINGER INTO BOTTLE AND TAKES FALSE TIP AWAY, APPARENTLY CHANGING HIS MIND HANDS BOTTLE TO ONE OF COMMITTEE, DIRECTING HIM TO BURN THE MESSAGE ④

Reading Burned Message

⑤

MAGICIAN PALMS MESSAGE AND READS IT

Here is the Clever Ink Bottle Trick Described in this article by Professor Dunninger. You Write a Message on a Piece of Paper, and Place it in

What You Believe to be a Bottle of Ink; Afterwards the Magician Reads Your Message as the Paper is Burned in a Dish of Alcohol—But Does He?

MUCH has been said and written with reference to the truth of mental telepathy, mind reading, thought transference, etc. The writer herewith emphasizes the fact that in exposing problems bordering upon the psychic senses of the human mind, it is not his desire to belittle the truth and scientific value attached to the sincere demonstrations which are mentally possible. Mind reading is an absolute scientific fact, the fundamental principles of which have been sadly neglected, and as my scientific readers will no doubt agree, it is human nature to disbelieve anything which one does not thoroughly understand. It is the belief of the writer that there is nothing that the human mind can possibly conceive that is not probable, but, as his many genuine demonstrations in the past before men of prominence have proven, there is always a doubt as to whether effects of this kind are brought about by mental thought waves, clever methods of trickery or concealed mechanical devices. The study of mind reading is not alone based upon an education obtainable only through the reading of various volumes upon the subject, but the training depends also upon many years of practice and actual demonstration. As it is my desire to give the many readers of Popular Magic a series of experiments along this unique form of entertainment, that can be accomplished with a very small outlay of money and an unusually small amount of practice, I am opening this feature article with the explanation of one of the most interesting and seemingly difficult tests in so-called mental telepathy. I might further add that an expert after years of practical demonstration and experience could not produce a more weird and unbelievable result than the one I am about to describe. Yet, I know that many of my readers will receive an endless amount of amusement by producing this effect, and many comments and sincere congratulations from their friends, who will compliment them upon being possessed of a sixth sense. Briefly, the effect:

The mind reader and his associate enter a room together with a committee who have been invited to test the ability of the mind reader. A telephone book is inspected and is found to be of ordinary type and absolutely free from preparation of any kind.

It is explained that the mind reader is to leave the room and during his absence the committee are to select one name in the many thousands printed in the book. They are further asked to memorize the number of the page upon which the name appears. Prior to the performer's leaving the room, his eyes are bandaged and securely blindfolded, making it quite impossible for him to see. The effect may be heightened, if desired, by having strips of adhesive plaster

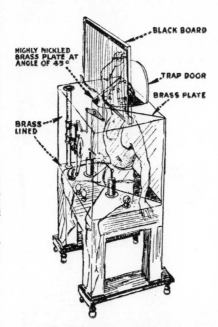

HIGHLY NICKLED BRASS PLATE AT ANGLE OF 45°

BLACK BOARD

TRAP DOOR

BRASS PLATE

BRASS LINED

The Mystic Spirit Slate or Blackboard and How the Trick is Done. The Man Inside the Cabinet Does the Writing on the Rear of the Slate or Blackboard Once it is Placed in Position, Extending the Hand Through the Little Trap Door on Top of the Cabinet. The Gears and Other "Works" Seen in the Front of the Cabinet Are Mere Camouflage to Mystify the Audience, and They Think They See All the Way Back Into the Cabinet, Owing to the Reflection Illusion Caused by the Two Polished Metal Plates or Mirrors Placed in Triangular Formation as Shown, with the Peak of the Triangle Toward the Audience and in the Center of the Cabinet.

placed over the bandages. After the name has been decided upon, the performer is led into the room and asks permission to hold a member of the committee by the wrist. This means of contact, he explains, will aid him in reading the mind of the subject. After a few moments of silence, in a low, slow tone of voice, he calls the number of the page decided upon, which, for example's sake, we will say was page 765. He now requests his subject to slowly run his finger down the columns of this page and the moment the subject's finger reaches the name thought of, the mind reader requests him to stop. It is naturally found to be correct, much to the amazement of the spectators.

Now, for the explanation. As in all mysteries that are most bewildering, the explanation is extremely simple. Before the test takes place, the mind reader provides himself with an apparatus, as is herewith illustrated. This consists of nothing more than a so-called plate lifter, purchasable in any of the many novelty shops. It consists of a small rubber bag, attached to a long piece of rubber tubing, to the free end of which is affixed a rubber ball. This apparatus is concealed beneath the carpet in the room where the demonstration takes place. The assistant, who seemingly is disinterested in everything, other than seeing that the mind readers' eyes are properly blindfolded, etc., is really the so-called "information bureau" for bringing about this effect. He secretly makes note of the name in the book selected, also the page upon which it appears. After the selection has been made, and the blindfolded wonder-worker is led into the room, the assistant sees that his foot rests upon the part of the carpet directly above the rubber bag. This is easily located, as the design of the rug discloses its hiding place. The assistant now moves to the opposite side of the table and stands with his foot directly on top of the concealed rubber ball. The interested spectators are asked to group around the table and to assist by concentration. Seven sharp taps upon the ball secretly advise the "mind reader" that the first digit to the page is number 7. Six taps and then five more and he, of course, knows where to request the spectator to turn. As the spectator's finger slowly passes over the various names, the assistant awaits the moment until the finger rests upon the proper name. Another tap upon the rubber ball, and the mind reader calls "that's the name decided upon." The miracle has been accomplished.

MESSAGES FROM THE GREAT BEYOND

Some years ago while traveling through the Middle West, I met a very interesting Hindu fakir, who specialized in what he termed East Indian spiritualism. In several weeks we became quite friendly and during the course of the conversations he explained

cated electrical mechanism. Four sets of cables were led from the apparatus to electric sockets. After an explanation to his spectators, in which he said that he had devised a machine for proving that we had absolute communication with the Great Beyond, a few switches were tampered with, the lights in the interior of the cabinet were lighted, and the machine became active. The dozens of wheels therein slowly revolved and a number of sparks and flashes played here and there upon various receiving posts. The

cealed in two of the legs of the cabinet, his body hidden from view by two highly polished nickel-plated brass plates, placed at an angle of 45 degrees. In front of these plates was affixed this array of mechanism, which consisted of nothing more than a high frequency apparatus, to produce a large display of spark effects, together with two electric motors which ran a series of wheels. This apparatus was naturally reflected in the highly polished plates, and gave the audience the effect of seeing clearly to the back of the cabinet, whereas in reality it was nothing more than an optical illusion. The two electric bulbs aided further in the deception, and were also reflected, giving the audience the impression that four globes were lighted. My readers will, of course, understand that all that remained to be done was for the Hindu High Priest to equip himself with information as to those departed, and to instruct his assistant in writing messages of an appropriate nature upon the blackboard. A small trap door in the top of the cabinet acted as a convenience through which the assistant's arm could easily project during the action of writing the messages.

A CLEVER PARLOR EXPERIMENT

The apparatus necessary to bring about this very interesting and mystifying effect apparently consists of nothing more than an empty ink-well and cork, a saucer containing a small quantity of alcohol, a box of matches, a few small slips of writing paper and several pencils.

The magician requests his subject to write a series of names, or numbers, upon one of the small slips of paper. The magician may, if necessary, leave the room during this procedure. The paper is now rolled into a small ball and dropped into the ink bottle. On second thought, however, the magician advises his subject to drop the paper from out of the bottle into the saucer and light the alcohol poured upon the paper which is permitted to burn to ashes. The subject is asked to concentrate and the magician mysteriously repeats the name and numbers that have been previously written, stating that he is able to do this reading through the flames of the burning paper.

Now for the explanation. A small metal finger tip, as illustrated in the diagram, is employed. This is painted black upon the inside. A small blank piece of paper is rolled into a ball and thrown into the bottle, which should be made of black non-transparent glass. This finger tip, which is naturally flesh colored upon the outer side, is placed in the mouth of the bottle flush with its top edge. You are now prepared to present the effect.

After the subject has written the names and numbers upon the paper which is rolled into a ball, and you request him to throw it into the bottle, he, in reality, throws it into the interior of the finger tip. The magician innocently thrusts his finger into the bottle, apparently forcing the paper down, but in reality he secretly carries the slip away with him unnoticed. The rest my reader will readily understand. The duplicate paper is burnt and the magician finds time to secretly remove the finger tip, and then read the original paper under cover of the table. The subject, of course, is seated at the side of the table opposite the conjurer. This performance will be found highly effective and is well worthy of the little practice necessary to bring it about impressively. In this instance, as in all similar effects, a bit of patter helps greatly.

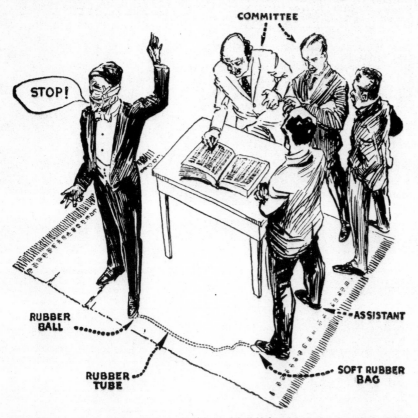

In the Telephone Book Number Trick, the Magician is Blindfolded, and Led Out of the Room Where the Committee Is. One of the Committee is Then Asked to Pick Out a Certain Page in the Telephone Book and to Run His Finger Down the Column and Stop at any, Name He Desires. These Facts He is Then Asked to Concentrate on, and He then Closes the Book. The Blindfolded Magician is Brought Back Into the Room, and in a Few Moments He Tells the Gentlemen to What Page Number to Turn, and After He Has Done This He Tells Him to Run His Finger Slowly Down the Column, and He Will Tell Him When to Stop. The Method of Performing This Remarkable Trick is Explained Clearly in This Article.

that he was the High Priest of a spiritualistic church, and although he claimed his methods were absolutely scientific and sincere, he felt the necessity of bringing trickery into his work to strengthen the effects of his teachings upon his many followers. He further asserted that, while many of his congregation were satisfied with simple tests and manifestations, he had constructed and invented a spirit machine, which he felt would truly be the means of leaving a positive impression upon the most skeptic. I was his guest one evening, and there beheld one of the cleverest mechanical devices it has ever been my good fortune to see. As will be seen by the diagram accompanying this article, it consisted of a mahogany cabinet, supported approximately 30″ off the floor upon four legs. The cabinet itself was about 30″ square and supported a metal framework upon the top, to which was affixed a slide which held a large blackboard. Two small doors in the front of the cabinet were opened, disclosing a large amount of wheels, mechanical devices, a few electric globes, in short, an apparently very compli-

blackboard was then taken from its stand and passed about for inspection. After having been found free from deception, it was again replaced. After a brief interval, the slate was removed and thereupon was found a message written in chalk addressed to a member of the gathering. The message was erased, the blackboard replaced, another brief interval, and another spirit communication was found thereupon. In this manner some 20 or 30 messages were produced upon the slate.

As it is my intention to discourage methods of fraud, practised by mediums, I will herewith expose the ingenious and unusual method used by the Hindu. It may be well to state that by this exposé I am not attacking the principles of spiritualism generally, as I believe there is much of scientific value in the study of spiritualism. But as to the spirit machine—a glance at my diagram explains all; although to all appearances the cabinet held nothing other than mechanism, it in reality concealed a trained assistant who did the writing. As the diagram discloses, the legs of the assistant were con-

Spectacular Innovations

X-ray Sight

The effect which I am about to describe is perhaps one of the most puzzling and mysterious parlor tricks ever created. It has its advantages over many tricks of a similar nature inasmuch as it is one that will bear repeating over and over again without any possible danger of its secret being detected.

STEEL SQUARES UNDER SURFACE OF BLOCKS

BOX PLACED INSIDE OF LARGER BOX

MAGIC X-RAY TUBE

COMPASS SLIPPED INTO TUBE UNOBSERVED

Four Blocks of Wood Are Placed in Any Order in a Box, Which Box Is Locked. This Box Is Again Placed Into a Still Larger One, Which Is Likewise Locked. The Performer Enters the Room and by Peering Through an Open Tube Tells His Audience the Order in Which the Blocks Appear. The Compass and Steel Plates Do the Trick.

THE EFFECT: Two small boxes are passed for thorough inspection. They are so constructed that one will nest conveniently into the other. In the smaller of these chests are found four small blocks of wood, each individually numbered with digits from one to four. The closest inspection of this apparatus is invited, but nothing can possibly be found to arouse the slightest suspicion as to any concealed trickery or mechanism. A small metal tube about two inches long and one-half inch in diameter is also exhibited and freely passed around. The magician explains that he possesses a weird power of concentration, and by the assistance of this tube can place himself in a cataleptic state by which he acquires the power of X-ray sight, and is able to look through solid objects. In order to demonstrate his marvelous power he explains that during his absence from the room the spectators may arrange the blocks in any position they desire in the smallest of the boxes. By this arrangement he suggests that the total number of combinations possible with an arrangement of four digits are considerable. He further explains that after this box has been locked it is to be placed in the second or larger box and this one also is to be securely locked and the key thereto retained by a member of the audience. The magician is then to re-enter the room, and will, by running the small tube over the top surface of the box, be able to penetrate the covers with his X-ray eyes and at once to state the exact arrangement of the numbers. The magician leaves the room and his skeptical spectators at once go to work to test the ability of the conjurer. The numbers are, we will state for example, arranged so as to indicate 4,132. The wizard re-enters, and as previously stated, mysteriously calls the total of the numbers, apparently doing nothing more than running the small tube or concentration instrument over the surface of the box.

Again and again the numbers are rearranged, and yet the performer states their arrangement with amazing ease and without

Walking Through a Rope

an error. All of the paraphernalia can be passed for thorough inspection at any period of the trick. Now for the explanation:

A glance at the diagram makes all clear. The boxes are unprepared, but the blocks are not as innocent as their appearance may suggest. It will be found that they are really composed of two layers of wood, between which in each respective block is placed a small piece of magnetized steel in different respective positions, as indicated in the diagram. Unknown to the spectators, the conjurer has secreted in his pocket a small tube, an exact duplicate of which he has passed about for inspection. In the lower end of this cylinder is affixed a compass. The tube otherwise is identical with the one examined. The workings of the trick are practically simple, as my readers will surmise. Regardless of the position of the blocks, the magnetized pieces of steel will register upon the compass point through the upper surfaces of the boxes. As the bars of steel are placed in different positions in the blocks, the indications of the compass will naturally divulge the number. The performer must, of course memorize the four positions, so that he will be in position to locate the individual digits during the test. The prepared tube is secretly exchanged for the one examined during the performer's absence from the room.

WALKING THROUGH A ROPE

This amazing and bewildering illusionary effect has for years baffled large audiences and has deceived magicians and those well up in the studies of the art of deception as well. I have presented this effect for a number of years, and have found it to be one of the most talked of sensational problems in any of my programs.

As the curtain rises, the stage is free from any paraphernalia of an unusual type with the possible exception of two posts, similar in appearance to those illustrated in Fig. 1. Two rows of chairs on either side of the stage and a table complete the stage furniture. The magician enters, clad in a costume of white flannel, the importance of which will afterward be understood. He states that he is about to present a miracle, and,

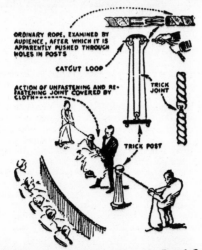

ORDINARY ROPE, EXAMINED BY AUDIENCE, AFTER WHICH IT IS APPARENTLY PUSHED THROUGH HOLES IN POSTS

CATGUT LOOP

ACTION OF UNFASTENING AND REFASTENING JOINT COVERED BY CLOTH

TRICK JOINT

TRICK POST

Walking Through a Rope Previously Passed Out for Examination. This is Pushed Through Holes in Both Posts. Two Men Hold the Ends of the Rope While the Performer Covering It in Front of His Body, Passes Right Through It. Note the Rope Concealed in the Post, Which is Fitted with the Trick Joint.

The Bank Note Trick

contrary to all natural laws, will demonstrate that it is possible to pass a *solid* through a *solid*. For the objects of his experiment he will use his own body and prove that there is nothing that can obstruct his passage through a solid substance. Upon

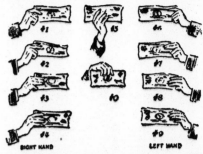

#1 #5 #6

#2 #7

#3 #10 #8

#4 #9

RIGHT HAND   LEFT HAND

The Method of Reading the Figures on a Bill from a Distance of Thirty or Forty Feet, is Illustrated in the Above Chart. The Performer, if Possible, Maintains an Almost Ceaseless Patter with His Spectators on Either Side. The Medium is Twenty or Thirty Feet Away. By Straightening the Bill Repeatedly, and Changing the Position of His Fingers, the Magician Informs the Medium of the Proper Figures in Their Correct Sequence.

the table, standing upon the stage, are several lengths of unprepared rope, each about ten yards long. To heighten the effect of the offering and to further convince his audience that the items of this experiment are absolutely without pre-arrangement, or preparation, he invites a committee from the spectators to go upon the stage, so they might partake in the offering and inspect all that is used.

After the committee has been secured, the ropes are passed for thorough inspection, and one is selected for the purpose of the test. This rope is passed through two holes in the top of the posts as indicated below, and the performer stations himself directly back of the rope at a point midway between these posts. The magician explains that the posts act as an obstruction should he be accused of lifting or lowering the rope at any time during the presentation of the trick. The opposite ends of the rope are held by two assistants, one on either side of the stage. Two attendants now come forth and hold a small cloth two feet wide and three and one-half feet long in front of the performer's body, so as to obstruct the view of the section of rope between the posts and that part of the performer's body from the sight of the audience. The upper part of the performer's body and his legs are in full view at all times. The performer is now seen to mysteriously walk forth and pass through the rope. The cloth is removed and the rope is found intact as before the presentation. The rope is now withdrawn from out the posts and passed for thorough inspection. Nothing can be found to help solve the mystery.

Now for the secret: One of the posts is genuine and entirely unprepared, the other not quite as innocent.

Referring to the diagram, it will be seen that in the hollow post is constructed an arrangement composed of a series of three wheels over which passes a duplicate piece of rope which is concealed from view prior to the performance. In a section of this rope is a trick-joint operated similarly to a screw-plug, which can be opened or closed by one or two twists. To one of the free ends of this rope is affixed a bayonet-catch, an to the other end a catgut loop.

After the genuine and inspected rope is passed through the opening of the post it is caught in the bayonet catch and carried down over the pulleys and into the post proper. The duplicate is drawn out of the post and carried through the unprepared post so that the trick-joint is brought to a point directly in front of the performer. When the cloth is held up before him so as to obstruct his action from view he has but to open the trick joint with his hands, pass before it and again close it behind him. He has to all appearances passed through the rope. As the rope is drawn out of the posts,

the mechanical action is reversed and the duplicate or trick rope is once more drawn into the post and the original one brought to view.

BANK-NOTE TRICK

The mind-reader and the assistant enter. The lecturer or the assistant requests a bill or bank-note from anyone of his many spectators. He explains that codes or forms of mechanical communication are out of the question as the mind-reader will call all the numbers upon the bill without one word of conversation prior to the calling. This, the lecturer asserts, eliminates all suspicion as

to verbal communication. The lecturer holds the bill between his fingers, and at once the mind-reader mysteriously calls the exact serial numbers thereupon. The mind-reader, of course, stands at a distance of some twenty or thirty feet away from his assistant.

Now for the explanation; the diagram makes all clear. A signal finger system is employed. The entire code is disclosed in the drawing. The reader will understand that the lecturer during the action of deep concentration is quite naturally handling the bill and is secretly signaling the information to the mind-reader unawares.

VANISHING TUMBLER

In the vanishing tumbler effect, the magician brings forth a large glass tumbler, containing a beverage which he drinks. After the glass has been emptied of its contents, it is placed, mouth

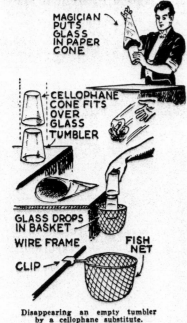

MAGICIAN PUTS GLASS IN PAPER CONE

CELLOPHANE CONE FITS OVER GLASS TUMBLER

GLASS DROPS IN BASKET

WIRE FRAME

CLIP

FISH NET

Disappearing an empty tumbler by a cellophane substitute.

down, upon a table top. A cone is now made from a sheet of newspaper and, holding the cone in one hand, the glass is removed from the table, and placed inside the cone. Without suspicious moves, and with arms bare to the elbow, the magician crushes the cone between his fingers, rolls it into a small ball, and carelessly tosses it aside. The glass has completely vanished.

Explanation: A cone, constructed of heavy cellophane, fits loosely over the glass tumbler. In the act of picking up the glass, the tumbler is secretly dropped into a bag supported upon a wire frame, which has been attached to the back of the table. Thus, the cellophane cone, (which in reality appears to be the tumbler), is slowly lowered into the mouth of the paper cone and, a moment later, is crushed between the performer's hands, and tossed aside.

DAGGER THROUGH CHEEK

Many are the tales of magic and mystery which come from the East. Reports recently arrived of a new mystery, in which the faker parades the streets of Calcutta, with a long, twenty-inch dagger, penetrating his cheeks. When a few coppers are dropped into his ever-open palm, he nonchalantly opens his mouth, displaying the remainder of the blade, which is clearly seen.

Explanation: In spite of the faker's spiritual countenance, the affair is but a clever deception. As illustrated, the dagger is of special construction. The two sections of the blade are held close to his cheeks, by a concealed metal loop, easily kept from view by his thick full-grown beard. A special piece of steel, constructed with two loops, is held between his jaws, and helps to complete the illusion when his mouth is opened wide.

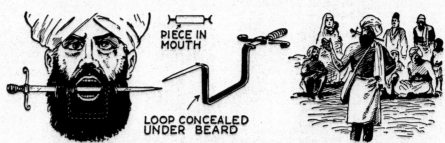

PIECE IN MOUTH

LOOP CONCEALED UNDER BEARD

In this illusion, the sword apparently pierces the jaws of the mystic; when he opens his mouth, the blade may be seen inside. Actually, the blade is made in two parts, as shown.

RISING CARD

● RISING-CARD tricks are ever popular in the program of the modern magician. The trick here described is perhaps the simplest in preparation, and the most effective of them all. Three cards are chosen (not forced) from a deck and, after being noted by the spectators, are returned individually to different parts of the pack. Holding the deck at arm's length, the magician calls upon the selected cards to rise; and they mysteriously obey his command, making their appearance in rotation, and rising slowly out of the

pack. As they are removed, they are passed to the spectators for identification and inspection.

Explanation: Half the deck has a section cut away from each respective card, as illustrated. This prepared half is on top of the pack, and in spreading them fanwise, in the act of having three cards selected, the magician takes care to see that this selection is made from the lower or unprepared part. (A plain card conceals the cut-away section of the top half.) When the cards are returned to the deck, the magician sees to it that they are placed

in the upper section; anywhere within the area of the prepared cards. His index finger secretly pushes the cards into view, one after another, while he holds the deck in his outstretched hand. Although exceedingly simple to operate, the reader will find this experiment extremely mystifying and completely deceptive.

CUT AWAY SECTION

The cut cards enable those selected to rise mysteriously.

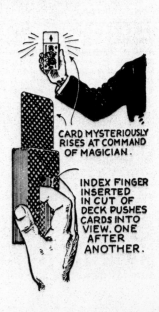

CARD MYSTERIOUSLY RISES AT COMMAND OF MAGICIAN.

INDEX FINGER INSERTED IN CUT OF DECK PUSHES CARDS INTO VIEW, ONE AFTER ANOTHER.

A Few Master Mysteries

The Vanishing Horse and Rider

THE effect I am herewith about to describe, although more of a joke than a pocket trick, is one of the most effective impromptu experiments in conjuring ever presented. It requires but little practice and although the method of presentation is extremely simple, it has been the means of mystifying some of the greatest magicians in the country, among whom I might mention the late Professor Harry Keller. Before the eyes of a spectator a handkerchief apparently disappears in thin air, having been rolled into a small ball between the palms of the hands. It may be well to emphasize that this trick is accomplished without any secret appliances of any nature, and with the performer's arms bared to his elbows.

It may be best to refer to the diagram to observe the position in which the spectator is seated. As the handkerchief is rolled into a ball between the conjurer's palms it is sent clear over the head of your observer with a sharp snap as indicated in the picture. In print this problem will appear extremely simple but the effect of bewilderment left upon the spectators will be amazing to my readers experimenting with this trick.

THE VANISHING HORSE

This extremely interesting and sensational stage illusion is one that I originated some six years ago and it has been included in the programs of prominent magicians throughout Europe and the United States. The curtain rises upon a bare stage, save for the fact that upon the center thereon stands a structure consisting of two trestles and a large plank resting thereupon. To this plank leads an additional board from the floor up to its edge, not indicated in my diagram. The performer enters and explains to his audience that he is about to present one of the most mystifying and daring effects ever presented before the public. He describes that he is about to vanish a horse and rider before their very eyes, and

Impromptu Handkerchief Vanish

emphasizes the fact that he will present this effect absolutely without the assistance of stage traps, or clumsy apparatus, and without employing deceptive cabinets such as are usually brought into play in an effect of this nature. After several other convincing and

The Horse On a Platform Vanishes Completely. It Cannot Pass Below the Stage Through a Trap Door, As the Audience's View Below the Platform Is Unobstructed. As Shown Above, What Actually Occurs Is That the Horse Is Lifted Bodily.

impressive remarks, a horse is led upon the stage bearing a rider. The horse is a snow white animal, beautifully and heavily draped with a spangled head-stall and body-piece. The rider is clad in the uniform of a knight of old and with a lance in hand adds much atmosphere to the picture. The horse is led up the inclined board to the structure. Two attendants now remove the board and carry it off the stage. A pole operated from two chains from the upper part of the stage is now let down. To this pole is affixed a roller-blind arrangement. This

A Handkerchief Is Rolled Up and Mysteriously Disappears Without Employing Mechanical Aid Or By Pulls. A Flip of the Fingers Shoots It Over the Head of the Observer.

Catching Fish in Mid-Air

roller-blind consists of a colored cloth drop and is sufficiently large to completely cover from view the horse and rider. It is let down in front of the horse but for a moment. Several shots are fired from the performer's pistol. The roller-blind flies back into place and the horse and rider have vanished. But where? That is hard to explain

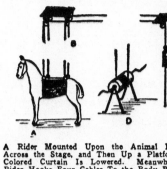

A Rider Mounted Upon the Animal Proceeds Across the Stage, and Then Up a Platform. A Colored Curtain Is Lowered. Meanwhile, the Rider Hooks Four Cables To the Body Belt, and the Stage Hands Raise the Horse, So That When the Roller Blind Is Released, the Animal Will Have Disappeared. Actually, the Animal Is In Back of a Black Velvet Curtain. Cut Shows Details.

—at least from the viewpoint of the audience. Inasmuch as two assistants now carry the platform and trestles from off the stage and the roller-blind and chain arrangement is drawn upward out of sight, the stage is left absolutely bare. The entire effect has been accomplished within a few seconds and there is no possible or prevailing clue remaining.

Now, as to the method by which this daring illusion is accomplished. The diagrams practically make all clear. Beneath the horse's blanket of spangles is a heavy leather harness permanently affixed around his body. To this harness four rings are attached. The chain and roller-blind arrangement is not quite as innocent as its appearance suggests, as in reality it is responsible for the effectiveness of the illusion. Between the set of chains is a curtain of black velvet of the same material as the back-drop and stage setting which is employed. It is behind this cloth of velvet that the horse is secretly hoisted out of sight by an arrangement of four cables working over a series of pulleys as are clearly described in the drawings. These cables are connected with the four rings of the horse-harness. A windlass concealed in the wings completes the necessary arrangement for hoisting the horse and rider out of view. It may be important to mention that although the stage is to all appearance brilliantly lighted when this effect is produced, all the lights are in reality only the border and footlights. The overhead lights are eliminated. With an arrangement of this kind complete illumination seems evident but the presence of the black velvet screen is entirely imperceptible to the audience, as they imagine they see through the back drop. The white horse and rider of course help to make the contrast impressive.

THE MYSTERIOUS FISHING TRICK

This is an improved form upon the ever popular experiment of catching live gold fish in mid-air. The effect: The performer comes forth holding a fishing rod about six feet long and of the average variety. Over his shoulder hangs a fishing-basket. On the side of the stage is a large glass fish-globe filled to the brim with water. The magician explains that fishing in water and making a successful catch depends largely upon the luck of the angler, and his ability as a fisherman. But fishing in mid-air is quite another thing. This, as he explains, depends upon the ability of the magician to see the invisible fish floating about in the atmosphere, as well as the faculty of being able to catch them at the end of his hook. In this case as in all others the conjurer explains a bit of bait is necessary and he at once proceeds to bait the end of his line by removing the necessary worm from out his basket and to all action and appearances attaches it to his hook. The line now dangles about in space for a number of seconds and behold! much to the amazement of the spectators, a small form of bright yellow is seen dangling from off the end of the line. The conjurer draws in the line and removes therefrom a small gold fish which he drops into the fish globe. The fish swims about quite actively beneath the glare of a spotlight which is thrown upon the bowl to assure the audience of the actual

presence of the gold fish. Again the performer rebaits his line, another moment or two of angling in mid-air and another fish

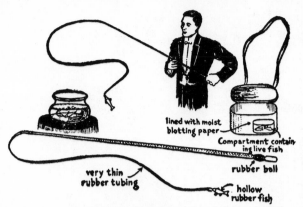

lined with moist blotting paper

Compartment containing live fish

rubber ball

very thin rubber tubing

hollow rubber fish

Details of the Champion Mystery Trick Catching Fish in Mid-Air.

appears to be dangling from the line.

The fishing line consists of very thin rubber tubing which leads clearly through the fishing rod down to the handle, where it is affixed to a rubber bulb. The fish that appears on the end of the line is an imitation, being nothing more than a small rubber bag shaped and colored to represent a fish. The bait which is permanently affixed to the line is a small piece of metal tubing. It will be seen that when the air in the apparatus is released the rubber fish is concealed in the bait and will not become visible until pressure is applied to the rubber ball. The air therein is forced through the thin piece of tubing into the rubber fish, and brings it to view.

The genuine, or live fish, are concealed in a compartment in the fishing basket. These fish are kept alive inasmuch as they are held in a nest consisting of moistened blotting paper. I believe my readers have guessed the method of presentation. The first fish is brought to view by a pressure on the rubber ball. In the act of removing it from the line it is in reality exchanged for one of the live fish which has been secretly held in the magician's hand. He has gotten possession of the fish under pretense of removing a bit of bait from the basket. It is this live fish that is naturally dropped into the globe.

Mystifying Juggler Tricks

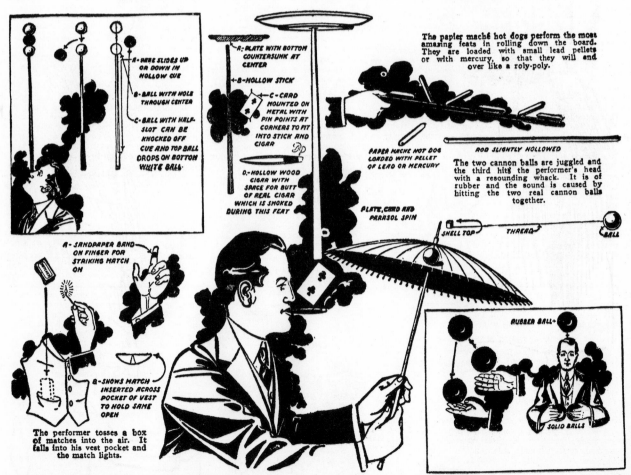

A - WIRE SLIDES UP OR DOWN IN HOLLOW CUE

B - BALL WITH HOLE THROUGH CENTER

C - BALL WITH HALF-SLOT CAN BE KNOCKED OFF CUE AND TOP BALL DROPS ON BOTTOM WHITE BALL

A - PLATE WITH BOTTOM COUNTERSUNK AT CENTER

B - HOLLOW STICK

C - CARD MOUNTED ON METAL WITH PIN POINTS AT CORNERS TO FIT INTO STICK AND CIGAR

D - HOLLOW WOOD CIGAR WITH SPACE FOR BUTT OF REAL CIGAR WHICH IS SMOKED DURING THIS FEAT

The papier maché hot dogs perform the most amazing feats in rolling down the board. They are loaded with small lead pellets or with mercury, so that they will end over like a roly-poly.

PAPER MACHE HOT DOG LOADED WITH PELLET OF LEAD OR MERCURY

ROD SLIGHTLY HOLLOWED

The two cannon balls are juggled and the third hits the performer's head with a resounding whack. It is of rubber and the sound is caused by hitting the two real cannon balls together.

PLATE, CARD AND PARASOL SPIN

SHELL TOP   THREAD   BALL

A - SANDPAPER BAND ON FINGER FOR STRIKING MATCH ON

B - SHOWS MATCH INSERTED ACROSS POCKET OF VEST TO HOLD SAME OPEN

The performer tosses a box of matches into the air. It falls into his vest pocket and the match lights.

RUBBER BALL

SOLID BALLS

The stunts illustrated here are all performed with the aid of apparatus, and when worked before an audience will be surprisingly mystifying if done with some degree of perfection. In balancing the billiard balls on the cuestick the stiff wire holds the balls in place. The center ball is slotted so it can fall out. In the stunt illustrated at the center the cigar is a hollow wood cylinder which takes a regular cigar stump. The card is backed with a piece of thin sheet iron and a pin extends from bottom and top. The stick upon which the plate spins is made of some tough light wood and the plate is countersunk at the bottom, to receive the stick. A little practice will be necessary before the three of them can be held perfectly straight.

H. R. H. Prince of Wales Astounded

Dunninger Gives Prince of Wales Cigarette Trick To Fool Home Folks.

A VERY simple trick as described and illustrated at the bottom of this page was responsible for the great amount of newspaper write-ups shown by the clippings on this page. The actors in the engagement were respectively His Royal Highness, the Prince of Wales, and Prof. Joseph Dunninger, known by some as "Dunninger." The trick was the cigarette levitation effect produced as shown below. Of course, "Dunninger" did some scientific mind reading at which he is adept. Then he offered the Prince a cigarette. Naturally the Prince had to pick it out of the box "even as you and I." "Dunninger," however, merely held his hand over the box and the cigarette slowly rose up to his finger tips. Now for the secret. Extending around the small of the back is a piece of elastic attached behind the right shoulder. At the other end a thin black silk thread is secured. This thread passes down to the palm of the hand and under a ring. A tiny button is secured to the far end of this thread, and this button coated with beeswax. Pressing the pellet of beeswax against the cigarette and holding the cigarette in place while the hand is lifted, it will be seen that the thread connected with the cigarette causes the elastic band to stretch. The finger is now bent downward, locking the thread beneath the ring until the crucial moment, when releasing the pressure the cigarette rises up to the hand. The button is slipped through the ring by means of the thumb and disappears up the coat sleeve.

EYELET THRU RING

BEESWAX

ELASTIC AROUND BACK

Nights of Mystery

The Mystic Fruit
Cutting Apple on Person's Neck

PERHAPS it would be impossible to find a more mystifying and effective experiment in the entire field of impromptu conjuring than the one I am about to describe. This experiment is not only exceedingly effective, but is one

The Secret: The number upon the paper is forced, as it is a simple matter for the conjurer to exchange the stack of sheets for a set of duplicates. This exchange is made quite unnoticed beneath the cover of the table cloth while the seated conjurer is di-

The Magnetic Cigarette
Striking Safety Matches on Shoes

The other end of the thread naturally is still in that hole.

It will be seen that in reality the magician has really threaded the piece of cotton all around the banana directly under the peal. The diagrams help to make this clear. The two ends of the thread are now taken and gently drawn out together, the thread cutting the banana. This process is repeated until the necessary cuts have been made, dividing the fruit into the required number of parts for bringing out the desired effect.

It is needless to remark that the holes made by the needle are so small that detection is quite impossible. Should the small hole, however, be discovered it would not be of any direct importance, inasmuch as no one could possibly suppose that it would be the means of tampering with the banana to bring about a complete cut in the fruit. My readers will, of course, understand that the prepared banana is forced upon the spectator when the selection is made. One or two unprepared bananas should be hidden well below a group of apples, oranges, grapes and other fruits contained in the fruit dish. The prearranged fruit on the top will naturally be the first to be taken when a request is made that a banana be selected.

Still another plan to heighten the effect of this trick would be to prepare two or three bananas, dividing them into a different number of pieces, let us say, for example, one banana into 4, another into 5, and still another into 7. In this event the fruits would have to be of three different sizes, the smallest of them divided into 4, the next size into the 5, and the largest into the 7 pieces. When the fruit is selected, the magician at once knows the number of pieces contained within the peel, the information being easily imparted to him by the various sizes. He, of course, has prearranged three duplicate sets of cigarette papers respectively numbered 4, 5 and 7, in different pockets about his clothing and secures the necessary set to force the desired number upon one of his spectators. A little practice in the preparing part of the trick will enable anyone to divide the banana in such a way that practically no trace or evidence of the action will be left upon the peel.

THE HINDU APPLE AND SWORD MYSTERY

Tourists passing through India cannot overlook many of the so-called startling

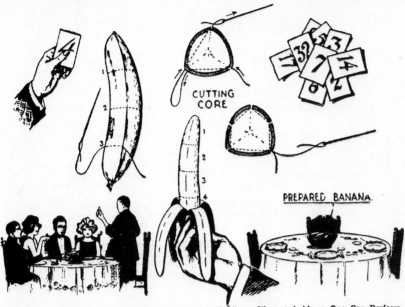

By Cutting a Banana With a Piece of Thread and a Needle as Illustrated Above One Can Perform a Very Surprising Feat. By Clever Manipulation of the Various Numbered Cards, it is Possible to Have One Draw a Certain Card and Then Peel a Banana and Find the Fruit to be Cut Into Just the Number of Parts Indicated on the Drawn Card.

that is of double value to the amateur conjurer inasmuch as it is an after-dinner trick, and is one of the few items in magic that can be presented with apparently no paraphernalia other than that of unprepared available objects.

The Effect: After the conjurer and his friends who have been gathered around the dinner table have feasted to their heart's content, the magician announces that he is about to present a trick which in his belief is little short of a miracle. A package of unprepared cigarette papers are passed about to various members of the audience with a request that they write a variety of numbers respectively on each of the sheets, numerated, we will say, from 1 to 20. These are collected by the magician, and after the stack of sheets have been shuffled he requests that one of the many be selected. The number chosen is now found to be, we will say for example, the digit 4. The wizard now passes a plate of fruit about with a request to someone in his audience that one of the bananas be selected therefrom and after the same is thoroughly inspected, it is to be used as the item for the experiment. The selected fruit is placed on a plate by itself and the others removed from the table.

The conjurer claims by a weird method of control he will perform a most unexplainable phenomenon. The magician takes up the selected banana and strips the peel from off the fruit which is found to have been mysteriously divided into four parts corresponding with the number upon the chosen cigarette paper. The audience is, of course, led to believe that if the number chosen had been 5 or 12, the banana would have been divided into whatever number of pieces would have been necessary for the success of the trick.

recting attention to the bananas upon the fruit tray. The duplicate set of papers have all been numbered 4's so it is quite impossible for the spectator to secure any other number when the selection is made. One banana is especially prepared for the trick. The magician takes a needle and thread and passes the needle through one side of the same, leaving the end of the thread hanging outside the fruit. He then passes the needle back through the same hole by which it was drawn out, and passes it across another side of the banana. This is repeated and so at the end the needle is brought out through the small hole in which it was first inserted.

It Would Seem that Our Hindu Friend on the Right is Contemplating Cold Blooded Murder and That the One on His Knees is Calmly Submitting to the Same. However, it is Only a Trick and We Find That the Wicked Looking Gentleman With the Sword is Merely Going to Cut the Apple in Half Without as Much as Touching the Neck of His Partner. The Trick Lies in an Ordinary Sewing Needle Passed Through the Apple as Illustrated on the Left.

effects in conjuring presented by the fakirs so plentiful in the Orient. As my readers undoubtedly know this land of mystery is credited with many problems or so-called unexplainable feats that have never been duplicated in America or Europe. Conjurers in this part of the globe, however, who have studied methods of East Indian magicians express disappointment, inasmuch as they state that their methods of mysticism are limited, and their truly impressive tricks are few and far between. Our magicians have found but little difficulty generally in duplicating the effects employed by these wizards, and the famous Hindu basket trick, turban trick, duck trick, and ball-on-string trick, have been discarded from many up-to-date programs of present day magicians. Still, as originally stated, there are a few mysteries presented in this land of enchantment that are still generally unsolved and have not been reproduced by European countries. The effect I am about to describe is one that is often referred to as one of the most daring and unbelievable feats of Oriental magic, and still to my knowledge has not been presented other than in the land of the Yogi, due to the fact that its secret is so little known.

The effect upon the spectator is as follows: The Hindu magician passes a large razor-edged sword or Oriental knife for inspection. It is found to be quite intact and its sharpness is demonstrated by slicing bits of paper. The conjurer's assistant, a rather indifferent seeming individual, whose body is bared from the waist up, is introduced to the audience. The attendant kneels to the ground and utters a short prayer to the spirit of the East. A plate of apples is now passed for thorough inspection and one of the fruit selected and freely inspected. It is found intact and apparently free from preparation. The fruit is placed upon the bare neck of the attendant in a position as indicated in the drawing. The fakir utters a few words in ceremony and with a quick sharp action brings the sharp edge of the knife down upon the surface of the apple, dividing it into two parts which drop to the floor. The attendant's neck, of course, is unharmed, much to the amazement of the onlookers. My readers will, of course, be led to believe that this is the work of a skilled performer who by years of practice is able to accomplish this seemingly impossible and unbelievable feat. It is this belief that has probably kept many of our aggressive magicians from duplicating this experiment.

Not so, however; merely a trick is responsible for the effect. A needle of good steel has been passed through the apple in a manner as indicated in the drawing. In fact, all of the apples which are passed for inspection have been treated in a similar way, so it matters not which one is selected, the result will still be the same. The razor-edged section does not extend throughout the entire blade of the knife, as a section of the edge nearest the handle is slightly dulled. It is this part of the blade that comes down and divides the apple, and, of course, is naturally prevented from passing further into the fruit than desired, as it stops mechanically when it strikes the needle. A certain amount of practice, of course, is necessary to prevent the performer from striking alongside the fruit, but even in this event results would not be serious inasmuch as the dullness of the blade and lack of sufficient force in bringing down the knife would prevent any serious accident. The fruit is permitted to remain in the sun as a rule for a short period of time prior to the performance which has a tendency of softening the apple considerably, thereby making the success of dividing the fruit with ease more positive.

LIGHTING SAFETY MATCHES ON YOUR SHOE

I am sure that the readers of Popular Magic will agree that a better experiment

that one can present impromptu with less preparation than the trick I am herewith about to offer, will be hard to find.

It is commonly supposed that a safety match cannot be struck other than on its original box. The magician, however, upon meeting a friend who requests a light, amazes his spectator by striking this match upon the sole of his shoe and then challenging anyone to duplicate the feat. Try as they will, they will find it impossible to do.

The secret is exceedingly simple. The striking side of a match box was previously rubbed against the performer's shoe at the instep. Some of the substance is in this manner transferred from the box to the shoe. One will, of course, understand that the striking of the match now becomes a simple matter. As the instep does not touch the ground in walking the application will not wear off for quite a time. Inasmuch as the conjurer knows that his friends had not previously prepared their shoes, he is free to challenge them without fear of the feat being duplicated.

THE MAGNETIC CIGARETTE TRICK

This is an excellent impromptu trick and an unusually effective pocket experiment. You offer a friend one of your cigarettes from your case and incidentally remove one yourself. After a few puffs the conjurer explains that he would like to demonstrate the power of mind over matter, and will demonstrate that in order to impress upon his audience the fact that he actually

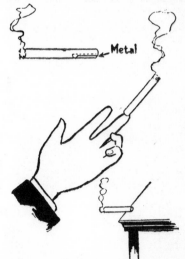

A Balancing Cigarette May be Made With the Aid of a Small Piece of Metal as shown in the Upper Left Hand Corner. It Will Balance Very Nicely on the Finger Tips or on the Edge of the Table.

possesses this weird quality, he will defy all laws of gravitation.

The cigarette is placed upon his fingertips, the longer end of the cigarette projecting and much to the amazement of his spectator it remains so suspended. To further prove that as the magician claims it is all mind-power and has no bearing upon digital dexterity, he places the cigarette with its end upon a table or any other flat object, and still it remains suspended.

As to the secret:—A small piece of metal has been previously placed in one end of the cigarette. The conjurer, of course, knows where this prepared cigarette has been placed in his case and is careful to see that it is retained when offering the cigarettes to his friend. The weight is responsible for the miracle. The weighted end is of course the one that rests upon the fingers or table edge.

The Reversing Colors

Effect: The Magician shows two wineglasses partially filled, one with a red and the other with a blue liquid. He stirs the contents of the first glass with a wand, whereupon they immediately turn blue. He then remarks, "Turn-about is fair play," and on stirring the blue liquid with the same wand, it assumes a red color.

Explanation: The first glass is filled about half full of water in which a tiny pinch of the dye, Congo red, has been dissolved. The blue liquid consists of a nearly saturated solution of litmus.

The wand is a specially prepared glass tube. When one end of a soft-glass tube is heated strongly in the flame of a burner or spirit lamp, it gradually softens and begins to close. If the heating is carried to a certain point, the end will appear entirely closed but in reality a tiny hole will remain. A foot length of glass tubing, treated in this manner at both ends and coated with black enamel, constitutes the wand.

Before working the trick, the wand is placed (out of sight of the audience) into a tall, narrow glass cylinder filled with hydrochloric acid. Then the palm is pressed tightly over the opening at the top and when the wand is withdrawn, a portion of the liquid remains in the tube. The principle is the same as that of the pipette. While stirring the first solution, the pressure of the palm is released momentarily and a small portion of the acid spills into the liquid, thus effecting the color change. The pressure is renewed, the rod transferred to the litmus solution and the rest of the acid is released.

There can be no hard and fast rules for preparing the solutions, but the strength should be adjusted so that the tints match.

Crystal Gazing

The Bon-Bon Box Candy Vanish

TOP EDGE OF FLAP COVERED SAME AS TABLE-TOP.

LOOSE-WORKING FLAP IN COVER OF CANDY BOX WHICH DROPS THRU BODY OF BOX FORMING TABLE-TOP.

CATCH HOLDING TRAY.

TRAY OF CANDIES

SIDE OF CANDY BOX.

TABLE TOP

SHOWING HOW SIDE-FLAPS DROP FORMING BOTTOM TO BOX.

Crystal Globe Visions All May See

Left—The Magician Opens a Box On the Table Which Is Brimful of Candy. Taking Out Several Pieces He Proceeds to Devour Them. Some Guests Remark On His Seeming Bad Manners In Not Offering the Candy to Others. They Are Told to Help Themselves, But When They Open the Box They Find It Completely Empty.

Right—Usually In the Art of Crystal Gazing Only the "Medium" Sees Visions, But With This New Type of Crystal All the Spectators May Distinctly See the Apparition. Pictures On An Endless Film Rotated By a Small Wheel Actuated By the Foot, Are Magnified By the Crystal Ball.

Cigarette Paper Trick

SMALL WHEELS   ROLL OF PICTURES TRAVELING AROUND   EXPOSED WHEEL

YEA, in the days of ancient Egypt, when enchantment and so-called witchcraft was in vogue, the ancient crystal was used by the wizards of old as a mystic mirror in which could be seen the reflection of the things to be. Much of Biblical importance and religious value has been attached in the centuries gone by, to the predictions which have been made by soothsayers after consulting the so-called mystic spheres of mysterious information. With the twentieth century and its many explanations of the many things at one time seemingly impossible, with achievements such as the radio, the submarine, the telephone, etc., has come a disbelief in the probabilities of forecasting through the focus of the mystic sphere, and yet there are many that claim that they can actually see things in the crystal.

Public wonder workers are to some extent using the crystal as an object of a most delightful form of entertainment, many of the society people whom I have entertained, have positive belief in the crystal as an information bureau. But as I have so frequently stated in my articles, it is merely my intention to offer in this series, tricks of a nature, such, as to prove of practical demonstrative value to my readers, and I will therefore not attempt to criticize the believers in the weird art of *crystal gazing*, nor will I attempt to deride or destroy the religious value that some have attached thereto.

I offer herewith an original method of crystal gazing which will be found to be of unique value to those caring to put themselves to the trouble of constructing the paraphernalia necessary. It has its advantages over the average so-called form of crystal gazing, inasmuch as the operator or wizard wonder, as you care to term him, has absolute control over the sphere, and therefore can cause his friends to actually see things in the enchanted globe.

HOW THE CRYSTAL GLOBE IS BUILT

Referring to the diagram one will find that the stand upon which the crystal rests is the responsible item for bringing about the necessary results. Passing over a series of small wheels will be found a roll of spirit

pictures. These pictures, which are rather small, should be painted upon a roll of black canvas cloth with phosphorous paint, the purpose of which will be readily explained. A small wheel with pointed edge is exposed, in the base of the stand, and also is a member of the series upon which the roll of pictures travel. It will not be necessary to explain that by turning the wheel, the pictures which are traveling upon an endless loop will be brought to view beneath the upper opening of the stand one at a time. The crystal ball being of solid glass (it may be an inverted fish aquarium) has magnifying qualities, and the subject looking into the crystal will therefore see the picture beneath, magnified many times, and as the basis of the cloth upon which the pictures are painted is a dull or dead black, the picture will to all appearances present itself apparently within the center of the sphere.

MAGIC CANDY

Smilingly the magician walks over to a table upon which is resting a candy box, and apparently carelessly opens the cover thereof and eats one, again closing the cover without offering any to his friends.

It Is not Generally Known That Cigarette Papers Are Cut On the Bias, and That If One Of Them Is Initialed and Placed Into the Pack, the Performer Can Find it With Ease, Even Though Blindfolded and Made to Hold the Package of Papers in Back of Him.

One of the spectators is sure to comment thereupon, and the magician with surprising apology for his seeming neglect at once makes his way to the table and offers the box and its entire contents to his friends to partake of the candy. Much to their surprise, however, when the cover is lifted, the box which a moment ago was brimful with the choicest of sugared goodies, is now entirely empty. The candies really consist of but one layer, which are contained in a tray, held to the upper edge of the box by a set of catches, which will not release until the cover of the box is shut down tightly. In this cover will be found a loose working flap the top side of which has been covered with material similar to the table top covering. When the cover of the box is closed down tight the catches holding this tray are released and the tray of candies travels down through the box, which is bottomless, and rests itself in a trap made to receive it in the table top. The flap also travels through the box and covers the candy and tray, so that when the box removed from the table no traces of the sweets can be found. A set of flaps working on small spring hinges are held in place to the sides of the box, as shown in the drawings, and then when released at the proper time, fall into place, forming a false bottom.

THE CIGARETTE PAPER TRICK

The Effect: A package of cigarette paper of the average kind and quality is passed about for thorough inspection.

One of the cigarette papers is taken from a package and is secretly marked while the performer has left the room. It is then mixed in with the rest so that it's direct location is unknown. The performer place the papers beneath a table, or behind his back, so that his audience is convinced that he cannot possibly see them and immediately draws out the marked one. How is it done?

Inspection will prove that most cigarette papers are cut on the bias, that is to say, instead of the corners being square, they are cut at an angle. While one paper is being marked the performer leaves the room. When the marking has been done, he is recalled and brings with him the balance of the sheets. The performer secretly sees that when the marked paper, which is turned mark side down, so that he cannot see it, is returned to the stack, the package is so turned that when the paper is replaced two of its corners will protrude slightly. The magician has but to feel for the projecting corners and draw out the marked slip.

Hypnotism as an Art

Angular Semi-Levitation   Reading Cards from Back   Empty and Full Wine Glass   The Knotting Handkerchiefs

ROD SLIPPING UP AND DOWN

WINDLASS

THUMB SCREW

CABLE

DESIGN IN RUG CONCEALING SLIT IN THE FLOOR

ROD

UNDER STAGE

CARD REFLECTED IN MIRROR

SMALL SPANGLE BEES-WAX

WINE GLASS HOLLOW STEM

RUBBER BALL CONTAINING WINE

RUBBER BAND

The Hypnotic Stunt (1) is Performed with Apparatus Shown. The Rod Slipped Through Tube, Operated by Windlass Beneath Stage, is Attached to the Lady's Legs. (2) To Read the Deck from the Back Use Small Mirror and Wax. (3) The Mystic Wineglass Fills as Soon as Emptied if Bulb is Pressed. (4) The Handkerchiefs Knot When Thrown, with the Aid of a Rubber Band. Operator Snaps Band Over Corners When He Drops Them.

Sleight of Hand

**Wine Bottle to Rabbit Change
Color Changing King Tut**

**Balancing Billiard Ball on Card Fan
A Simple Mind Reading Effect**

The magician pours liquid from the bottle, then wraps it in newspaper and tears it in two. A rabbit jumps out on the table. The Professor throws the crumpled wrapper off stage. It's all very simple when the apparatus used is explained. The shank of the bottle is made of lacquered paper. A false top is made of light metal laquered the same color. The top contains the liquid; the bottom the rabbit.

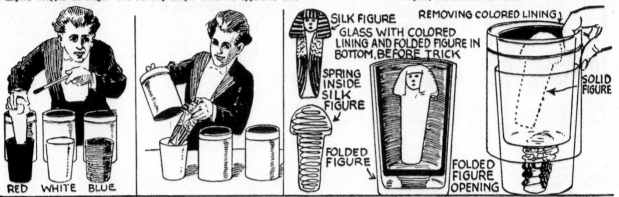

The magician has a solid King Tut figure examined. He then places it in a red colored glass, puts a paper cover over it and—Behold—the glass is clear and there is a red King Tut figure in it. The red figure is then placed in a blue glass—the glass becomes colorless and the figure blue. The color of the glass is imparted by a false celluloid tumbler inside. The colored figures are of cloth with a spring inside. They open up when the lining is removed.

Professor hands out a deck of cards to be examined, also a billiard ball. He then shuffles them, balances the ball on top and it rolls from side to side. Wonderful, his sense of equilibrium. But, look closely, the ball has a small hole and the professor depends on a small steel wire to hold the ball.

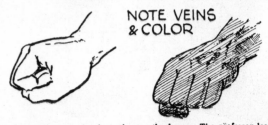

Two coins are held in the hands resting on the knees. The professor leaves the room. The observer is asked to hold one of the coins up in front of his eyes for a count of twenty. The Professor returns to the room and tells which coin was observed. While holding the coins on the knees the blood rushes to the hands and colors them slightly. In the hand that holds the coin in front of the eyes the blood recedes and leaves it lighter than the other. Try it.

The Mysterious Box

Passing Vase Through Glass
The Disappearing Candle

The Color Writing Pencil
Trick Match Box Holder

A wooden box open at both ends is shown to the audience and then placed upon a table. The open top is then covered with plate glass sheets. A vase is placed on the glass. This vase is covered with a duplicate box. A moment later the top box is removed and the vase has disappeared. The plate glass is taken away and the bottom box is picked up. The vase is found on the table. The boxes are made with a flap while the vases are of cloth opened by springs. When it is desired to disappear one of them, the wooden leaf is pressed to one side, folding and concealing the vase.

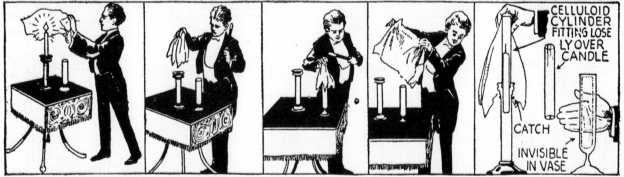

A lighted candle is seen in a candle-stick. A silk handkerchief is placed over it. The candle, whose shape can be easily seen beneath the handkerchief, is put into a tall glass. Snapping the kerchief away, it will be found that the candle has completely disappeared. A celluloid tube surrounds the candle in the candle-stick. A catch in the candle-stick holds the candle in position. When the magician covers the candle he releases the catch, permitting the tallow taper to slide into the candle-stick. The celluloid cylinder is removed and placed in a glass vase, where it is invisible.

Although not a magical trick, the above novelty if constructed, will repay the slight amount of work required. When one sees a choice box of cigars open and no one else looking, he will undoubtedly step over, extract one and then take a match. He strikes a match on the box, and then with a sudden snap the entire contents of the match box fly all over the table and floor. The construction of the device is made clear in the diagram. The side of the match box is hinged so that a catch on the bottom will be released when the striking surface is touched.

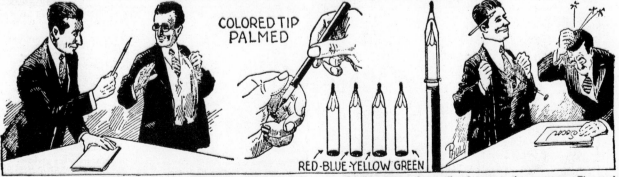

The magician passes an ordinary pencil to his audience for examination and tells them that the pencil will write in colors, and asks them to name a color in which he desires the writing to appear. One of the audience says "green." Grasping the pencil he writes a name in the chosen color on a sheet of paper and then returns the pencil and paper to the spectators. The magician has a series of colored crayon pencil-tips resembling the end of the regular pencil. The tip of the color requested is palmed, and when the pencil is returned to the magician the tip is put on the end.

A Miracle Man's Methods

Torn and Restored Card   The Vanishing Paper Matches   The Mystic Coin and Glass   A Flashlight Load

A sheet of paper is held up and then torn longitudinally in three pieces. These are placed in front of each other and then folded in thirds. Some one is requested to initial the paper, and when it is opened, the paper will be found whole again. Two papers of identical size are pasted together. One of them, however, has been folded up as shown in the illustration. When the paper is torn, the performer is careful not to show the folded piece. These torn parts are folded up. The whole sheet is opened.

A box of matches is removed from the pocket and the trickster lights his own cigarette. His friend is waiting for a light and asks for it. The book of matches is closed and handed to the waiting guest, so that he can light his own cigarette. When he opens the match book he finds it empty. This stunt is easily performed, it being necessary to tear two match books so that one will be complete, except for the cover, and the other will contain no matches. The group of matches is then placed within the cover, and after a light has been obtained, the matches are slipped out of the cover and the cover is closed and banded to the spectator.

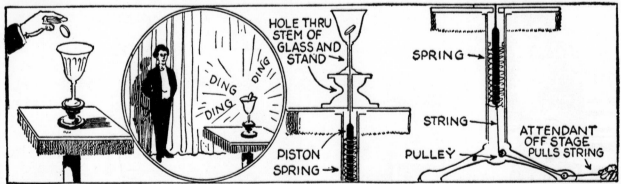

A glass may be seen resting on a small magician's table. Into this is thrown a borrowed coin. The glass will now answer any questions because of the fact that the coin jumps up and down in it. Two leaps signify "yes" and one "no." A knitting needle passes through a hole in a glass. An assistant off-stage, operates the mechanism.

The performer takes a sheet of paper and rolls it up to form a tube. To demonstrate that it is empty, he holds a flashlight at one end, and permits the beams of light to pass through the tube. He drops the flashlight through it, and removes vast quantities of flags and ribbons from this empty tube. The flashlight is fitted with but one section of the usual battery. When the flashlight is dropped through the paper tube, the handkerchief container remains within it. This is finally dropped into a "servante."

A Ball and a Sieve

Rising and Falling Ball   **Hands Dipped in Water Remain Dry**   **Gravity Defying Glass**   **A Sieve Full of Water**

A hollow brass rod secured to a stand is passed for examination, as is a wooden ball with a hole through it, allowing it to move freely on the rod. At the word of command, the ball can be made to rise or fall on the rod. An assistant below the stage is supplied with another rod sliding freely within the rod of the stand. To the upper end of this a magnet is secured which receives its energy from the batteries beneath the stage floor. The understage man causes the ball to rise and fall by sliding the rod up and down.

A polite spectator drops a ring into a fish bowl full of water. The magician washes and dries his hands thoroughly to prove that they are unprepared, and then plunges his hand into the water and withdraws the ring. To the spectator's astonishment, his hands are perfectly dry. Use lycopodium powder, sprinkled upon the water prior to the trick.

A ruler is placed on the edge of the table. A glass of water is balanced on the free end, while the other is held with a few books. The books are now removed, but the glass and rule still maintain their positions. Finally the rule is also taken away, but the glass remains suspended in mid-air. For holding the rule on the table, the tack in the table and the slot in the base of the rule are very effective. In suspending the glass in mid-air a thin thread is used. This drops off when the glass is passed out for examination.

The performer pours water into a sieve and it flows through freely. He repeats the operation, but this time the water remains in the sieve. The water is then poured out by tipping the sieve as though it were a dipper, and the sieve passed for examination. The performer slipped the invisible celluloid lining out of the sieve when he tipped it.

Tricks for Lyceum and Club

The Phantom Card Mystery   **The Spirit Colors**   **The Trained Goldfish**   **Whistle on String**

The above illustrations show Professor Dunninger demonstrating his new phantom card mystery. (The professor is seen holding the cards). Effect: Two cards are placed on a glass plate, one facing upward and the other downward. The card with its face up is passed half way beneath the other, and then both turned over. The spectator believes he sees two different cards. One of the cards is now placed beneath the glass plate and with a quick movement brought up toward the plate. It has changed its suit. By pasting two cards with their faces together, and two with their backs together, this trick is easily performed. One must try it to obtain the effect.

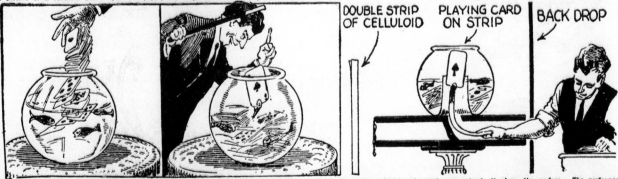

The magician becomes an artist. A frame with a glass center plate is passed out for examination, and on being returned, is covered with a piece of thin drawing paper. A lamp in back of the easel throws its beams of light through the paper. The artist draws a picture of a southern beach upon the paper, and steps aside. Presently the entire scene becomes vividly colored. Due to the celluloid screen, the colors appear. This screen is painted and rolls up at one end of the frame on a small curtain roller. The magician merely draws it across the back of the drawing board in order to obtain the colors.

You undoubtedly have heard of the educated gold fish. Every good magician must have one of these. A deck of cards each and every one different, is thrown into the water of a gold fish globe in which three or four fishes are swimming. One of the audience calls for a card. Instantly the gold fish dips down, grasps the card in his mouth and carries it to the surface of the water and even extends it above the surface. The performer thanks the fish and calls for another card. Note that the gold fish globe is a peculiar construction and an assistant manipulates the imitation fish on the end of a celluloid strip. The cards are obtained from a duplicated set.

A whistle on the end of a string answers any question, by whistling once for "yes" and twice for "no." One never suspects that the performer has a whistle concealed in each arm while a rubber ball connecting with the whistle by means of a small tube, causes the whistle to sound. This trick goes over better than you would think.

The Zodiac Mystery

The Iron Spider   **Coin Monte**   **The Dyeing Matchboxes**   **Cigarette Vanish**

On the table is found a zodiac with its signs painted thereon. The performer places an iron spider upon the wheel and immediately the spider moves around and around on the surface of the zodiac. He tells his audience that the spider is educated and to prove his statement he asks any of them when they were born. If one of the audience claims they were born in the month of March, the spider promptly stops at the sign for the date mentioned. Its manipulation and the secret of its education is seen above.

A coin is placed on the table and one of the audience instructed to place it under any of the three cups, while the performer turns his back. On looking at the cups he can tell instantly under which one the coin rests, thanks to a little hair glued to the coin. If blindfolded the performer looks at the covers from beneath the blindfold.

The magician takes two match boxes out of his pocket. Into one of them he stuffs a small red kerchief; into another a blue handkerchief is placed. Holding one in each hand, he closes the boxes, and on opening them again it will be found that the blue kerchief is now where the red one was, and vice versa. The match boxes are peculiarly constructed. Each has a diagonal partition with an opening on either side. The performer in closing the boxes, inverts them so as to bring the opposite side to the top.

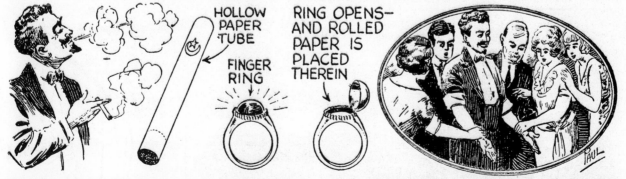

A puff of smoke escapes from the magician's lips. He rolls up his sleeves and requests that two spectators hold his wrists. The lit cigarette is now placed in his hand, one hand rolled upon the other, and presto! the whole cigarette has vanished. The cigarette is merely a thin paper tube with a small quantity of tobacco at the end. It can consequently be rolled into a very small space and be vanished into a finger ring, the stone of which may be lifted up. The above tricks are very mystifying.

The Mysterious Painting

The Vanishing Drawing   **Full to Empty Cigarette Box Change**   **Full and Empty Wine Glass**   **Rose Produced from Wand**

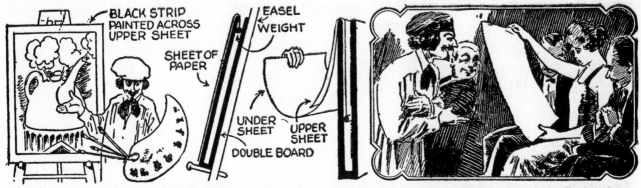

The magician becomes an artist. On an easel a pad of paper is secured. He draws a picture upon the top sheet, and then exhibiting his work to his audience he raises the sheet and tears it off. He walks toward one of his audience and hands her the sheet, which to her amazement is quite devoid of any sketch. The sheet of paper upon which the drawing is made is weighted and passes over the top of the easel. When the sheet of paper is lifted, the one upon which the drawing is made disappears.

The trickster raises the cover from a box of cigarettes, takes one, lights it and replaces the cover. One of his audience is bound to remark that he is rather stingy with his cigarettes, and he informs him to help himself. When the spectator raises the cover from the box, it is found to be empty. The box has a false cover to which cigarette stubs are glued, but contains one whole cigarette which the performer removes. This false top comes off with the cover when taken from the box by the spectator.

A glass apparently full of wine is raised to the magician's lips, but the happy grin of anticipation changes to a puzzled expression as the wine is seen to disappear before it reaches the performer's mouth. When he brings his hand down again the wine glass fills itself. The explanation is given in the illustration above.

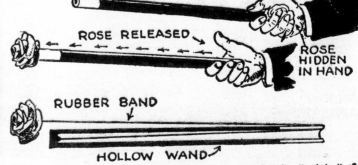

The performer tells one of the fairer members of his group of onlookers that she had better not crush the rose at her waist with her arm. She answers that there is no rose there, but he disagrees with her and passing the end of a wand forward, he withdraws it, which to her amazement now has a rose attached to it. He plucks it off and presents her with it. A rubber band passes out through an opening in the wand, and is then tied to a rose which is held in the performer's hand.

Off the Beaten Trail

Mysterious Beer Drinking Glasses   The Spirit Rapping Hand   Vanishing Ink from Bottle   Silk Production from Empty Glass

FALSE CENTER

BEER BETWEEN OUTER AND INNER GLASS.

The performer, after a rather long speech, tells his audience that prohibition has made him dry and asks for a glass of beer. His kind assistant brings out an immense glass full of the foaming liquid and continues to bring forth glass after glass while the performer downs their contents with remarkable rapidity. The way is shown in the sketch. The glass is double and the liquid fills the space between the two walls, making it appear that an immense quantity has been consumed.

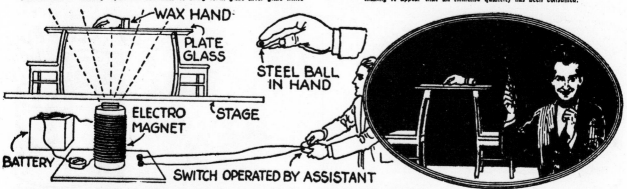

WAX HAND

PLATE GLASS

STEEL BALL IN HAND

ELECTRO MAGNET

STAGE

BATTERY

SWITCH OPERATED BY ASSISTANT

The mystery of the rapping hand is made plain in the above illustration. A large electromagnet placed under the floor attracts the steel ball in the hand and causes the hand to tip. At each tip a distinct click is heard. The hand is operated by an assistant located beneath the stage or behind the wings.

CORK

INK COMPARTMENT

EMPTY BOTTLE

INK

The performer dips his pen into an ink bottle and writes a short note. He then hands the pen to one of the spectators and requests that the paper be signed. Much to the spectator's surprise, the ink bottle is empty. The secret is a small false ink well which is slipped into the bottle and which is removed with the cork.

EMPTY GLASS

SILK APPEARS

BOX ATTACHED TO RING

SMALL HOLE IN BOTTOM OF TUMBLER

STRING ATTACHED TO PERFORMERS COAT

An empty glass is held by the performer. With a sudden lunge forward the glass will be found to contain a silk handkerchief. This is removed and the glass again held up for examination. The method by which this trick is performed is to attach to the back of the hand a small metallic box. This may be secured to a finger ring. A thread passes over the top of the glass through a hole in the bottom and is attached to performer's coat. Moving the hand forward produces the illusion.

Some Unique Effects

The Disappearing Table   Candle to Flag Change   The Red and White Pencil   Producing Wine from Paper Tube

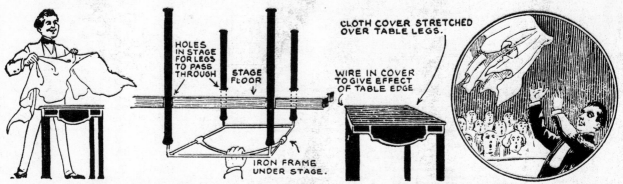

HOLES IN STAGE FOR LEGS TO PASS THROUGH

STAGE FLOOR

IRON FRAME UNDER STAGE.

CLOTH COVER STRETCHED OVER TABLE LEGS.

WIRE IN COVER TO GIVE EFFECT OF TABLE EDGE

The performer covers a large table with a cloth. With considerable effort he tosses the cloth into the air and the Table has completely disappeared. The legs of the table are solid and pass through holes in the floor. They are joined together by an iron frame so that but one movement is required to lower them, as shown. The table top is of cloth with a wire frame around the edges to give the effect of solidity. The cloth is disappeared into one of the legs or remains concealed in the covering. An assistant is needed.

A lighted candle is taken from its holder and immediately changes into an American flag. The candle is made of two metal parts and at its upper extremity a small piece of real candle is loosely fastened. The candle end is sewed to the back of the silk flag and is hidden by it from the audience. This trick is easily learned.

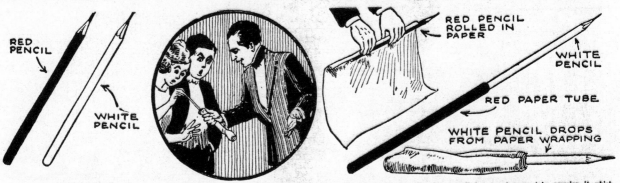

RED PENCIL

WHITE PENCIL

RED PENCIL ROLLED IN PAPER

WHITE PENCIL

RED PAPER TUBE

WHITE PENCIL DROPS FROM PAPER WRAPPING

A red pencil is rolled into a sheet of paper. One of the audience is then requested to draw it out. It miraculously changes to white. The paper is crumbled and thrown away. The secret is, that the white pencil has a red paper tube covering it which makes the audience think that the pencil is red. The red tube remains in the paper.

RUBBER TOY-BALLOON FILLED WITH WINE

PAPER.

BALLOON CONCEALED IN SLEEVE.

BALLOON SECRETLY INTRODUCED INTO PAPER AND ROLLED UP.

CUT IN TWO WITH SCISSORS.

A paper is rolled into the form of a tube. Both ends are then twisted up and the tube is cut through the center with a pair of shears. Wine flows out of the tube, filling two glasses, and the paper is then crumbled and thrown away. In the sleeve of the performer's coat, a rubber toy balloon filled with wine, either real or artificial, is to be found. This is secretly introduced into the paper roll while it is being formed. The balloon remains in the paper when it is thrown away.

A Sharpshooting Magician

Handkerchief Dyeing Bottle   **Coin Vanish**   **Torn and Restored Card**   **Bow and Arrow Technique**

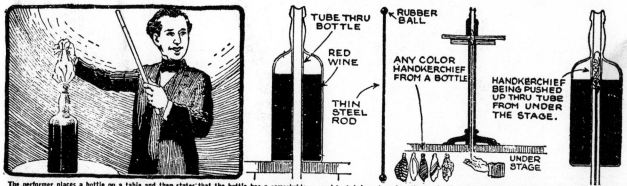

The performer places a bottle on a table and then states that the bottle has a remarkable dyeing solution in it, and will color a handkerchief in any color desired. A red, blue and orange kerchief are called forth, and each is removed from the bottle as requested. The assistant below stage has these colored, speckled and striped handkerchiefs all arranged on hooks and pushes those called for up through the bottle by means of a rod fitted with a rubber ball at the top. The bottle has an opening in the bottom.

A coin is held in the palm of the hand and is then rubbed between the fingers whereupon it immediately vanishes. No palming is required in this stunt. The coin is an imitation made of tin-foil by rubbing a tin-foil covering of a real coin with the side of a pencil. The tin-foil duplicate is easily rolled into a small pellet and concealed beneath a ring.

A torn card is put into a pistol which is then fired at a target. Without breaking the glass covering the target, the card will be found to have made its appearance. The card is specially prepared and concealed in the border of a frame. Two opposite corners of the card are connected together by means of an elastic band which passes over rollers, as indicated in the illustration. A pin holds the card in this position until the assistant off stage pulls the string releasing it. Details are given above.

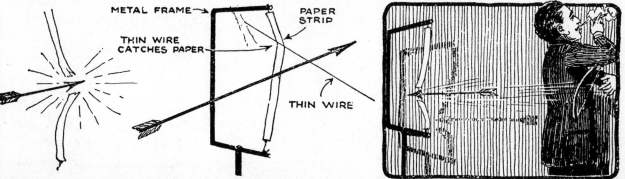

The magician is an expert marksman and regardless of how he holds his bow and arrow he always hits the target, which in this instance is a thin strip of paper. If the arrow itself does not cut the paper strip, then the thin wire projecting on either side of the arrow will do so. It is impossible to miss. The audience is completely mystified.

Simple Mysteries Thrill Many

| Reading Cards Face Down | The Hypnotized Teaspoons | The Vanishing Ring | The Disappearing Statue |

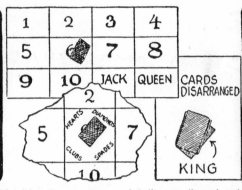

The magician requests that his assistant be blindfolded and leave the room. He now asks one of the audience to select a card from a pack, look at it and return it to the same. The cards are placed face downward on the table. The assistant returning, instantly names the card mentally selected. The magician placing the cards face downward on the table indicates the suit and value by their position on the table. The table is mentally divided up into sections as indicated. Disarranged cards mean a King.

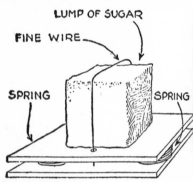

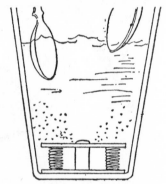

The magician puts two spoons into a glass, fills it with water and at his command the spoons fly upward into the air. The spring system used is illustrated above. A lump of sugar prevents it from acting until the sugar melts. The contents of the glass including the spring are then poured into the pitcher and the glass passed for examination.

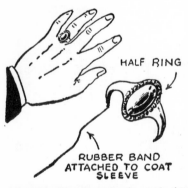

The performer's mystic ring has the property of vanishing at his command. A puff of smoke and presto! The ring is gone. The ring is really a half ring. A rubber band is attached to one end and a flip of the thumb releases it from the finger. The ring slips into the performer's coat sleeve under cover of the cloud of smoke.

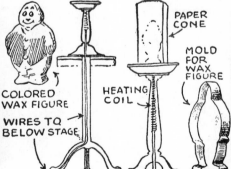

The figure shown above is solid and is passed around for examination. It is put on a stand and covered with a roll of paper. A little smoke indicates that the figure has vanished. Sh—the figure is wax and the heating coil in the stand melts it. The wiring is concealed in the candle-stick holder and passes down through a leg of the table.

The Magician Is the Life of the Party

Canary in Electric Light Bulb
Billiard Ball Balanced on Wand

Silk Handkerchief in Corked Bottle
Thimble Through Kerchief Effect

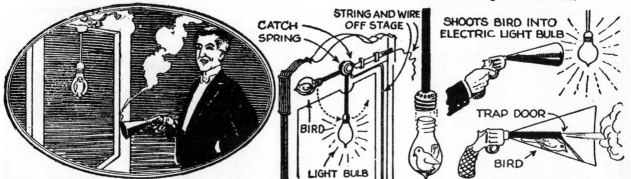

The magician places the bird in a prepared compartment in the pistol, fires at the bulb and behold, the bird is in the bulb. An assistant behind scene pulls a string which drops the bird into view with the device shown. The magician breaks the glass and the bird flies away.

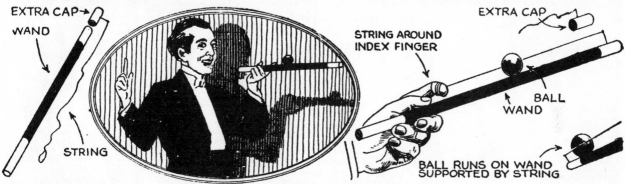

The conjurer becomes a juggler, the billiard ball rolls up and down his wand. An extra cap with a string attached and a billiard ball balanced between the string and wand make the stunt easy. The false tip of the wand is removed before passing the wand out for examination.

A magician forces a handkerchief into the barrel of a gun, and fires with the barrel pointing toward the bottle resting on a table and lo, the handkerchief is found in the corked bottle. The trick is explicable seeing the hollow cork holding a second handkerchief. The string passes to an assistant.

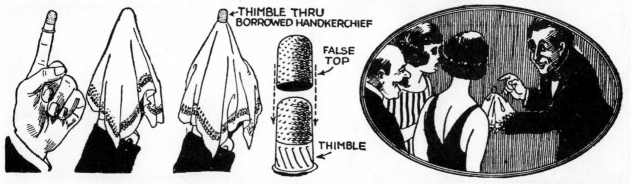

To pass a thimble through a handkerchief without making a hole in it is the magician's next stunt. However, it is quite simply performed if the thimble is equipped with a duplicate top, such as the one shown in the above illustration. Dexterity is all the magician needs for this performance.

Stage and Lyceum Tricks

Gold Fish Vanish from Bowl
The Vanishing Midget

Rabbit from Closed Opera Hat
Red to White Billiard Ball

A fish bowl is seen to be alive with gold fish. The performer seizes his gun and fires point-blank at the fish. Instantly they vanish. The bowl is specially constructed, and the fish are enclosed in a hair net. An assistant off stage pulls the string, which draws the fish down into the bottom of the bowl.

The performer comes forth, closed opera hat in hand. The hat is opened and the hand of the performer dives down into it and a rabbit is withdrawn from the inside. The accordion silk cloth closing an aperture in the back of the hat folds with the hat. The performer's hand passes into the hat through the opening and to a pocket inside the coat.

Below and to the left the performer places a midget upon a small stool well out on the stage. He brings down a cloth in front of the midget and suddenly snaps the cloth away. The midget has vanished. The secret is simple. Strapped to the performer's back is a rack which holds the midget.

In the color changing ball a double red shell fits around the ball. The ball is tossed into the air, and a pass causes the first half of the red shell to be swung around toward the back, making the ball appear white. The ball is then tossed into the air, but the double shell is retained in the hand, proving that the ball is white.

The Magic Wand

Cabinet for Vanishing Lady

In the cabinet disappearance shown here, the girl is to be seen within the cabinet which is mounted on four thin legs. The performer's wand passes under the cabinet, proving an entire absence of mirrors. The cabinet is closed, turned around and opened again, and the girl will be found to have disappeared. When the back of the cabinet is opened, the girl braces herself on the sloping ledge. After the front is opened, telescoping tubes permit the whole back to slide downward and the girl then slips beneath the stage floor.

Full to Empty Match Box Change

The Jumping Black Checker

The Clock Dial Mystery

A stack of checkers is placed upon the table. They are found to be all red, with the exception of one, which is black. This is put anywhere in the stack. A paper tube is then slid down over the checkers, and it will be found that the tube is barely large enough to encompass the stack. At the performer's command, the black checker shifts its position to a new location selected by any one of the audience. The secret lies in the fact that there is a black band which surrounds one of the red checkers. This black band slides up and down due to friction from the paper tube. Pins fastened to one red checker properly located beforehand stop the black band at the desired place.

The performer has a box of matches in his hand, and, extracting one match after offering a cigarette to his friend, he lights his own and makes sure that his pal sees that the box is full. He then extinguishes his own light and offers the box to his companion. When the box is opened it will be found to be empty. The secret lies in the arrangement of matches upon a small tin shelf, which slides between the cover and the drawer of the match box. An elastic band draws the fake into the sleeve of the performer.

The box has a cover rotating on one single screw, which is passed out to the audience. They are instructed to turn the hand of the clock to any hour they wish, then close the cover. The performer's X-ray eyes tell him exactly to what hour the hand has been turned. The secret lies in the fact that the hand and screw are connected together by means of a train of gears. The number of teeth in the gears does not matter, just as long as the blind screw gear and the hand gear are identical in size and in the number of teeth. The hand's position is read by looking at the screw.

The Conjurer's Art

Rising and Falling Skull   Producing Kerchief from Spool of Thread   Explosive Soap Bubbles   Visible Handkerchief Exchange

A papier maché skull rests inside of a cabinet made of glass on three of its sides. Front and top are open. The magician professes to be able to cause the skull to rise and fall at command, and the skull promptly obeys his orders. It can be made to answer questions by rising once for "no," twice for "yes." The secret lies in the fact that the skull is mounted upon a glass slab which is perfectly transparent. Attached to the bottom of the slab is a string passing over a pulley, and then to an assistant off stage. Naturally the bottom of the slab is concealed by the stand upon which the cabinet rests.

SKULL
GROOVE IN SKULL FOR GLASS SLAB
GLASS SLAB
PULLEY
GLASS SCREEN
STRING OFF STAGE

SOAP BUBBLE
SOAP WATER
GASOLINE SOAKED COTTON IN BOWL OF PIPE

The magician now changes the type of his performance. He becomes a child again and blows soap bubbles, but the remarkable thing about these soap bubbles is the fact that when they are held near the flame of the candle, they explode. This may or may not be due to the gas in the magician's body; at least, that is the way he explains it. Actually the construction of the pipe has much to do with the exploding soap bubbles. Inside of the pipe one will find a small sponge soaked in gasoline. When the bubble is blown, gas fumes permeate its interior. Holding a candle near the bubble ignites the fumes as they are released, when the bubble bursts.

GLASS SCREEN

BANG
EXPLOSION OF BUBBLE

SPOOLS OF SILK
RED
BLUE
GREEN
YELLOW

RED   BLUE
FINE SILK THREAD

WHEN ARMS PULL OUT
BLUE   RED
THREAD

To demonstrate that the magician is likewise an expert weaver, he places several spools on a stand. There are vari-colored threads on the spools one being red, another blue, a third green, etc. Picking up one of the spools, the magician proceeds to demonstrate how expertly he can weave the thread into a silk kerchief. He unwinds the thread from the spool slowly, curling it about his fingers, and finally withdraws a similarly colored kerchief. The secret lies in the construction of the spools, which contain the kerchiefs and which have a small lever and spring, permitting the kerchief to drop into the hand when it is released.

RED SILK
SPRING
SMALL LEVER
HINGE
CUP
RED SILK HANDKERCHIEF

BLUE HANDKERCHIEF   RED HANDKERCHIEF
RED   BLUE

The magician holds two glasses in his hands. One of these glasses contains a red handkerchief and the other a blue one. He now causes the kerchiefs to visibly jump from one glass to the other, exchanging places. He merely raises his hands slightly and draws them apart, and presto! the exchange is made before the very eyes of the onlookers. In preparation two holes are drilled in the bottoms of two tumblers, and a fine silk thread tied to the blue handkerchief is passed through the glass containing the red handkerchief, then through the glass containing the blue handkerchief, and finally tied to the red handkerchief, as illustrated.

The Magnetism of Magic

Invisible Billiard Ball Toss
A Non-Magnetic Magnet

Vanishing Card Spots
Handkerchief Appearance on Wand

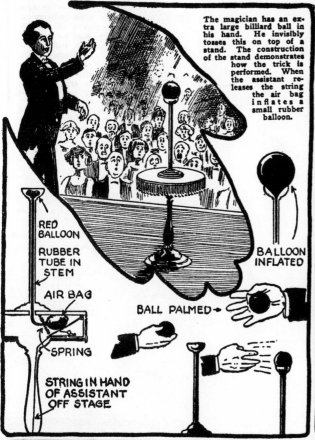

The magician has an extra large billiard ball in his hand. He invisibly tosses this on top of a stand. The construction of the stand demonstrates how the trick is performed. When the assistant releases the string the air bag inflates a small rubber balloon.

RED BALLOON

RUBBER TUBE IN STEM

AIR BAG

SPRING

STRING IN HAND OF ASSISTANT OFF STAGE

BALLOON INFLATED

BALL PALMED →

Three cards are shown. They are placed face downward on the table. On turning them over the center card has changed to a blank. A corner of any card is cut off and glued to another so that it forms an envelope-like corner for the blank card.

SMALL PIECE PALMED

BLANK CARD

30   ?   50

SPRING WHEELS

THIN THREAD

IN THE HANDS OF THE MAGICIAN

BALL FLOATS THRU —SPACE!

ASSISTANTS HAND

The magician holds a large magnet. His assistant walks off with a large ball. This is released in air and slowly floats toward the magnet. Actually the ball rolls along two thin threads.

WAND   HANDKERCHIEF

STRING TO FLOOR

IN HAND OF ASSISTANT OFF STAGE

The performer loads a handkerchief into a pistol. A wand is suspended in midair and the performer fires at the wand. The wand contains the handkerchief. An assistant pulls it into view.

Simple Deception

HAT EMPTY

HAT BRUSH

CATCH

LOAD OF HANDKERCHIEFS, FLAGS ETC., ETC.

SILK FLAGS ETC. PRODUCED FROM HAT

POCKET

VELVET COVERING

STOP

STRINGS

THIN ELASTIC

POCKET

BOTH SIDES SHOWN

ONE OF THE CARDS SELECTED

SELECTED CARD

① ② ③ ④

A very good method of loading materials into a hat is illustrated in Fig. 1. The performer borrows a hat, drops it; he brushes it off with the mechanical brush illustrated, and drops the load into the hat.

Fig. 2 illustrates the paddle selector. The performer forces a card upon one of the audience, then tosses a duplicate deck into the air. His assistant swats at the deck and the selected card appears upon the paddle. The paddle is covered with velvet and has a secret pocket holding a duplicate of the forced card.

A low stand which the magician covers with a cloth, as in Fig. 3, is placed in the center of the stage. On drawing the cloth away an immense flower pot full of flowers is visible. The flowers are concealed in the legs and pass down beneath the stage.

The string of the pull illustrated in Fig. 4 passes through the vest pocket and down the trouser leg. With its aid a coin may easily be vanished from a handkerchief.

EMPTY STAND

SPRING IN CLOTH-FOLDING-POT

MAGICIAN HOLDS CLOTH IN FRONT OF STAND

LOOP LOOP

BELOW STAGE

COIN IN CLIP

VEST

STRING

COIN SILK

WEIGHT

COIN IN HANDKERCHIEF

SMALL CLIP STRING & WEIGHT

Home Stunts for Amateurs

The Vanishing Radio Set
Reading Through Card Box

Matches to Handkerchief Change
Cut and Restored Handkerchief

The Vanishing Radio Set
Reading Through Card Box

Matches to Handkerchief Change
Cut and Restored Handkerchief

CLOTH TOP
CLOTH BACK
CATCH

SPRING ROLLER

SPRING HINGES

SPRING ROLLER

HORN

KEY

PHONOGRAPH RECORD

SPRING CLOCK ARRANGEMENT

MATCHES

HANDKERCHIEF

MATCHES

BLOCK OF MATCHES

HANDKERCHIEF

BLOCK OF HALF-MATCHES GLUED TOGETHER

A radio set is seen on the table, its loud speaker filling the air with music. The performer places a cloth over the set, removes both to the front of the stage and snapping the cloth away, the set has vanished. In reality the set vanished before he ever moved away from the table. The panel drops into the table, the sides fold on top of it and the back and top combined form a roller curtain. A phonograph is concealed in the table and a wire frame in the cloth.

Above and to the right a full box of matches is shown by the performer. He removes one of them, lights his pipe, then closes the box, and instantly the matches disappear and a handkerchief is found in their place. The matches are glued together in block form.

Below and to the left: A cigarette box which will snugly hold a deck of cards is opened, and the cards, thoroughly shuffled, are then dropped into the box. This is closed and opened again, whereupon the performer names the suit and face of each card just before he removes it. A duplicate set of cards are fixed in the cover of the box, and these drop down upon the shuffled deck when the cover is closed.

Lower right hand corner: A borrowed handkerchief is forced through the palm of the hand and a piece cut out of it with a pair of scissors. The ends are tucked back into the palm, and the handkerchief appears whole. The method is made clear in the diagram illustrating the trick.

PACK OF CARDS WELL SHUFFLED

PACK OF CARDS IN BOX

HAND MADE CIGARETTES

CARDS-ORDER OF WHICH ARE MEMORIZED

CARDS FACED WITH A CIGARETTE BOX LABEL

CARDS DROP FROM COVER WHEN BOX IS CLOSED

4-SPADES
6-DIAMONDS
10-CLUBS
8-HEARTS

BORROWED HANDKERCHIEF

SMALL PIECE OF CLOTH HELD IN PLACE BY RUBBER BAND

CUP

ELASTIC

EXTRA PIECE

CUP

ELASTIC UP SLEEVE

BORROWED HANDKERCHIEF

Seeing Is Believing

Three Coin Vanish and Appearance
Removing a Thumb

Stand for Changing Bran to Water
Rising Card Effect

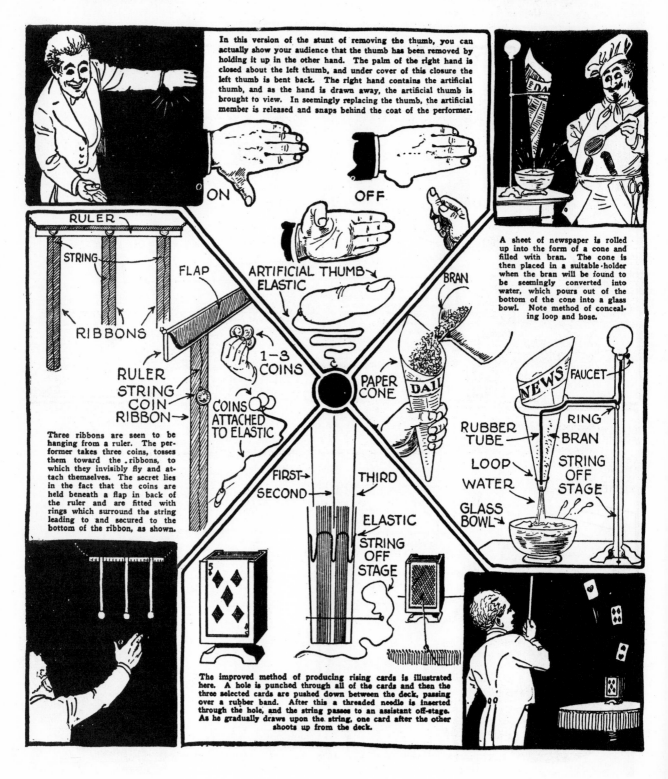

In this version of the stunt of removing the thumb, you can actually show your audience that the thumb has been removed by holding it up in the other hand. The palm of the right hand is closed about the left thumb, and under cover of this closure the left thumb is bent back. The right hand contains the artificial thumb, and as the hand is drawn away, the artificial thumb is brought to view. In seemingly replacing the thumb, the artificial member is released and snaps behind the coat of the performer.

A sheet of newspaper is rolled up into the form of a cone and filled with bran. The cone is then placed in a suitable holder when the bran will be found to be seemingly converted into water, which pours out of the bottom of the cone into a glass bowl. Note method of concealing loop and hose.

Three ribbons are seen to be hanging from a ruler. The performer takes three coins, tosses them toward the ribbons, to which they invisibly fly and attach themselves. The secret lies in the fact that the coins are held beneath a flap in back of the ruler and are fitted with rings which surround the string leading to and secured to the bottom of the ribbon, as shown.

The improved method of producing rising cards is illustrated here. A hole is punched through all of the cards and then the three selected cards are pushed down between the deck, passing over a rubber band. After this a threaded needle is inserted through the hole, and the string passes to an assistant off-stage. As he gradually draws upon the string, one card after the other shoots up from the deck.

Showing Them How

Flower Producing Cone
Unique Card Frame

The Educated Beetle
The Black Ace Change

The performer passes an empty cone for examination, and to prove that it is empty, he pushes his hand through it. He then places the cone on an empty flower pot and produces a blooming plant. The flowers were concealed in the sleeve and removed with the cone.

In the effect illustrated, a small "educated" beetle made of metal runs around the board and spells any name or word called for. The secret lies in the fact that a magnet moved by two assistants off stage, causes the bug to seemingly spell out the words.

A glass and frame is examined. A piece of cardboard is then inserted into the frame and upon firing a shot, the value of a forced card is shown in large figures in the frame. A roller curtain carries the figures which jump into view when the catch is released.

The face value of a card can be easily changed by the method illustrated.

Keeping Them Guessing

Production of Spirits for Mediums
Coin Shower from Finger Tips

Billiard Ball to Handkerchief Change
The Mystic Skull

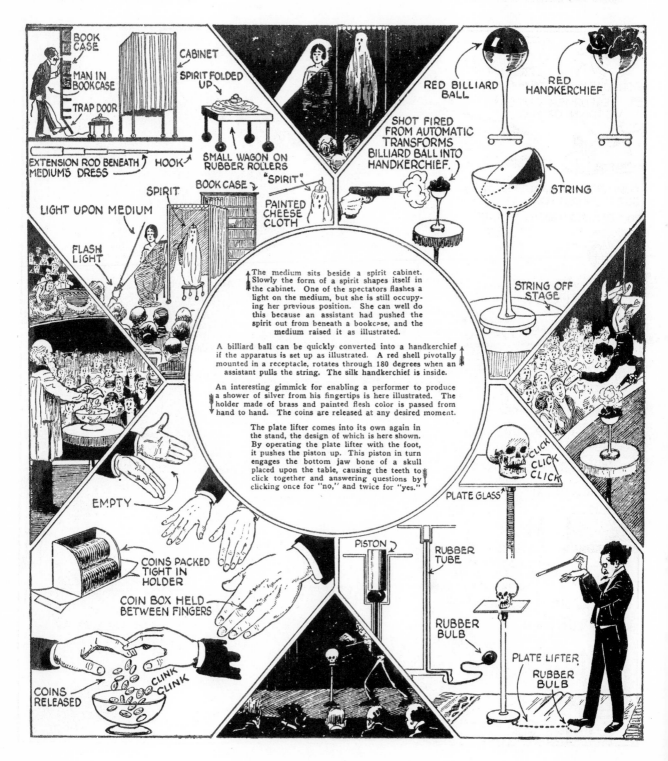

BOOK CASE

CABINET

MAN IN BOOK CASE

SPIRIT FOLDED UP

TRAP DOOR

EXTENSION ROD BENEATH MEDIUMS DRESS

HOOK

SMALL WAGON ON RUBBER ROLLERS

RED BILLIARD BALL

RED HANDKERCHIEF

SHOT FIRED FROM AUTOMATIC TRANSFORMS BILLIARD BALL INTO HANDKERCHIEF.

LIGHT UPON MEDIUM

SPIRIT

BOOK CASE

"SPIRIT"

PAINTED CHEESE CLOTH

STRING

FLASH LIGHT

STRING OFF STAGE

The medium sits beside a spirit cabinet. Slowly the form of a spirit shapes itself in the cabinet. One of the spectators flashes a light on the medium, but she is still occupying her previous position. She can well do this because an assistant had pushed the spirit out from beneath a bookcase, and the medium raised it as illustrated.

A billiard ball can be quickly converted into a handkerchief if the apparatus is set up as illustrated. A red shell pivotally mounted in a receptacle, rotates through 180 degrees when an assistant pulls the string. The silk handkerchief is inside.

An interesting gimmick for enabling a performer to produce a shower of silver from his fingertips is here illustrated. The holder made of brass and painted flesh color is passed from hand to hand. The coins are released at any desired moment.

The plate lifter comes into its own again in the stand, the design of which is here shown. By operating the plate lifter with the foot, it pushes the piston up. This piston in turn engages the bottom jaw bone of a skull placed upon the table, causing the teeth to click together and answering questions by clicking once for "no," and twice for "yes."

CLICK CLICK CLICK

PLATE GLASS

EMPTY

COINS PACKED TIGHT IN HOLDER

COIN BOX HELD BETWEEN FINGERS

PISTON

RUBBER TUBE

RUBBER BULB

PLATE LIFTER

RUBBER BULB

COINS RELEASED

CLINK CLINK

How Professionals Do It

Cut and Restored Derby with Load
Burned and Restored Bank-Note

Handkerchief Tying Cylinder
Liquid from Finger-Tips

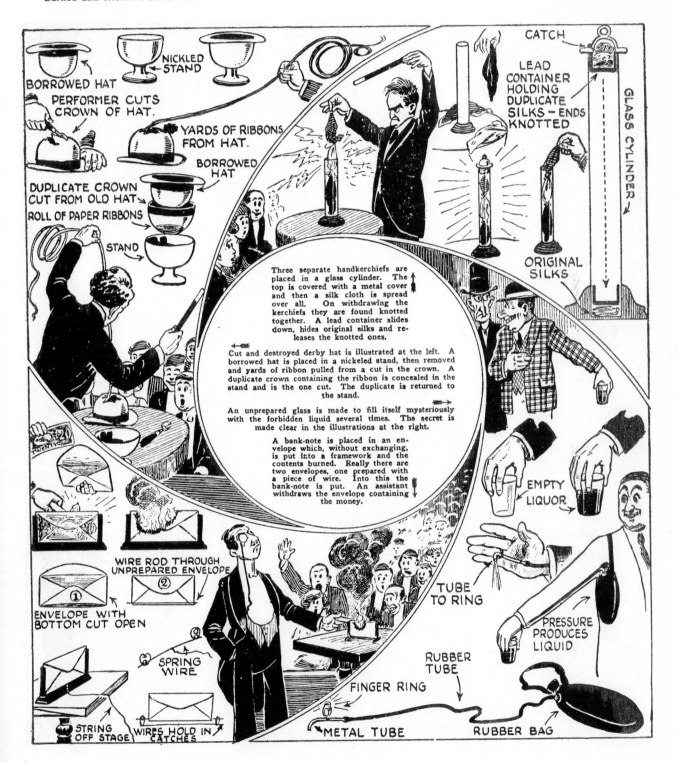

Three separate handkerchiefs are placed in a glass cylinder. The top is covered with a metal cover and then a silk cloth is spread over all. On withdrawing the kerchiefs they are found knotted together. A lead container slides down, hides original silks and releases the knotted ones.

Cut and destroyed derby hat is illustrated at the left. A borrowed hat is placed in a nickeled stand, then removed and yards of ribbon pulled from a cut in the crown. A duplicate crown containing the ribbon is concealed in the stand and is the one cut. The duplicate is returned to the stand.

An unprepared glass is made to fill itself mysteriously with the forbidden liquid several times. The secret is made clear in the illustrations at the right.

A bank-note is placed in an envelope which, without exchanging, is put into a framework and the contents burned. Really there are two envelopes, one prepared with a piece of wire. Into this the bank-note is put. An assistant withdraws the envelope containing the money.

Manipulating for Fun

The Spirit Medium's Chair
The Disappearing Coin

The Vanishing Table Lamp
The Sinking Ball

The medium is seated in a chair and her arms firmly secured by means of cords knotted and then sealed. The lights are turned out and tambourines, bells and horns are sounded. When the lights are turned on again, the medium is found tied in the same place. The secret lies in the construction of the chair, the arm of which comes out and permits of free movements. The latches for the arms are released when the medium is seated.

A large glass lamp which may be passed for examination is placed upon the table. This is covered with a cloth, which on being removed shows the lamp to have vanished. The lamp is then made to reappear. Under cover of the cloth, the magician fastens the lamp to his back and makes it reappear when he desires.

For the amateur trickster the coin illustrated here is of particular value. The coin is merely a rubber disk, silver colored on one side, and flesh colored on the other. Because of its flexibility, it can be passed around the finger, placed under a ring or concealed between the fingers. A coin of this nature saves many hours of practice and is very deceptive at a distance.

The celluloid ball is tossed into the air by the magician, and finally dropped into a glass globe containing water, to which a little ink has been added to color it. On command the ball sinks or rises. The secret lies in the beeswax pellet to which a hair is attached. The hair passes through a small lead weight, which acts as a pulley. Both weight and ball are dropped into the globe containing the colored water. The pellet is pressed to the ball which secures it in place.

Behind the Scenes with Magic

The Floating Ball (New Version)
Handkerchief in Glass Vanish

Table Rapper for Spirit Seances
Disappearance from Tank of Water

CYLINDER OF GAS ATTACHED TO HARNESS

The performer attired in an Oriental costume makes several passes over a large celluloid ball. Then, pointing his finger at the ball, the ball spins up into the air. He continues to point his finger at the ball, causing it to float before him as he walks among the audience. The secret lies in the compressed air harness hooked to his back, the hose from which terminates at his sleeve.

Mysterious table rappings can be easily produced by employing the harness shown here. A lead hammer secured to the harness as illustrated, is operated by the foot of the performer. The beauty of this trick is that the spirit raps may be produced at anyone's home, using any table and the performer need not be seated. The harness is turned around on the body when not in use.

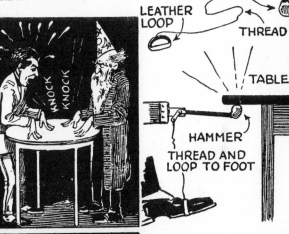

LEATHER BELT

LEAD HAMMER COVERED WITH FELT

LEATHER LOOP

THREAD

TABLE

HAMMER

THREAD AND LOOP TO FOOT

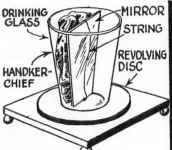

DRINKING GLASS

MIRROR

STRING

HANDKER-CHIEF

REVOLVING DISC

The performer demonstrates a remarkable "disappearing lady" act. A girl in a swimming suit leaps into a large tank made entirely of glass which contains enough water to come up to her neck. Spectators from the audience are invited to surround the tank and make sure that she cannot escape through the back or over the top of the tank. Curtains are now drawn, a shot is fired, the curtains are raised and the girl is gone. The details of the system are illustrated below.

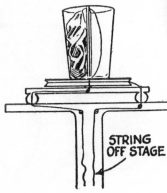

STRING OFF STAGE

A silk handkerchief is made to disappear from a glass and to reappear therein in the manner here shown. The glass contains a mirror partition. The silk is placed in front of the mirror. Pulling the string attached to the silk piece causes the kerchief to leap into the other half of the glass. Pulling the other string attached to the revolving disk, turns the glass, bringing the kerchief into view again.

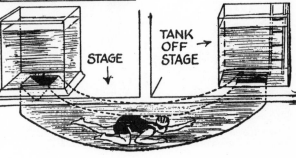

STAGE

TANK OFF STAGE

The Perfect Mysteries

Flower Growth in Tent
Vanishing Bottle

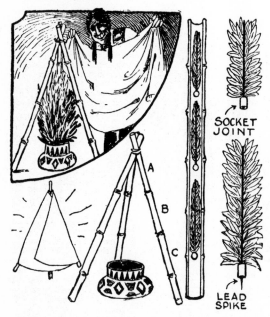

SOCKET JOINT

A
B
C

LEAD SPIKE

The illustrations at the left show an interesting stage effect easily produced. The Indian makes a tent of three bamboo rods and a cloth. The cloth has previously been passed around for examination. A flower pot is pushed into the tent, and when the cloth is removed, the pot will be found full of flowers. The secret lies in the fact that the bamboos which support the cloth, have holes drilled in them to accommodate feathered artificial flowers. The bottom flower section is equipped with a spike, and others are provided with sockets to make the bush seem large. The sections are pulled out through the holes.

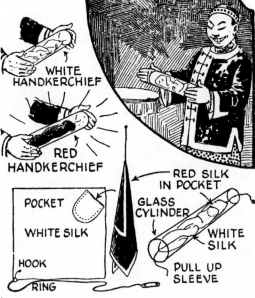

WHITE HANDKERCHIEF

RED HANDKERCHIEF

POCKET
WHITE SILK
HOOK
RING

RED SILK IN POCKET

GLASS CYLINDER

WHITE SILK

PULL UP SLEEVE

The illustration below shows the vanishing wine bottle. The wine bottle is covered with a cloth. Another bottle top palmed in the hand is then pushed over the cloth, making it appear as if the wine bottle actually passed through the cloth. Meanwhile the bottom portion of the bottle slides onto the performer's arm under his coatsleeve. The finger of the performer's hand inserted into the neck of the bottle wiggles the top around. The inside top is palmed off; the outer top likewise, and the cloth passed for examination.

The above illustration shows a unique color change. A white silk handkerchief is placed inside of a glass cylinder. The hand is moved up quickly as if making a pass and a red silk handkerchief will be found in place of the vanished white one. The cylinder and handkerchief are then passed for examination. The secret lies in the fact that the white handkerchief has a pocket sewed on it as illustrated. In this pocket a red silk handkerchief is concealed. Under cover of a movement of the hands, the white piece, being attached to an elastic band, vanishes up the sleeve. The red kerchief is left behind.

FINGER

LOWER PART OF BOTTLE IN SLEEVE

XXX

SPRINGS

BOTTLE TOP PALMED

A number of messages written on papers which are then folded and placed in heavy manila envelopes, are handed to the performer. The envelopes are very well sealed before he gets them. He retires to his cabinet and while there answers the questions asked in the messages, or gives the desired council. A few minutes later he emerges with the envelopes in his hand and permits the seals to be examined. They have not been tampered with. Nevertheless the messages have been removed. The tiny tool illustrated is slipped into the envelope, the message sheet is curled upon it, removed, read and again reinserted.

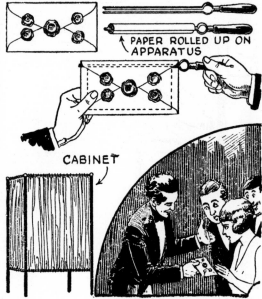

PAPER ROLLED UP ON APPARATUS

CABINET

Stage and Parlor Tricks

Shooting Through Plate Glass
The Magnetic Knife

Productions from an Opera Hat
The Magnetic Wand Tip

At the right is illustrated a new method of apparently shooting through a sheet of plate glass, and breaking a tumbler on the other side of it. It will be noted that on the table an ordinary drinking glass is to be seen. In front of this a sheet of plate glass is held by a suitable holder. The magician picks up an automatic revolver and fires directly at the tumbler, which is seen to burst. The plate glass remains undamaged. The effect is produced by having a specially prepared table arranged with a spring trigger as illustrated. At the end of the spring a pointed weight is to be found. The spring when released by the assistant, comes up and breaks the glass tumbler. The revolver is loaded with blank cartridges. The spring flies into a groove provided for it in the top of the table.

PLATE GLASS
DRINKING GLASS
STRING OFF STAGE
SPRING

Below we find a new method for securing a "load" from an ordinary opera hat. A load, as every magician knows, is anything which the magician desires to produce for use in future tricks or with which he is attempting to make a hit. It may be silks, flags, flowers, rabbits, baby's clothes, vegetables, ribbons, or anything else. The opera hat from which this load is produced has a specially hinged compartment, which slides from the inside to the outside of the hat, as can be seen by referring to the diagram below. In this hinged compartment the load is located. When the inside of the hat is shown, the load naturally is pushed to the outside, where it is hidden under cover of the hand of the performer. A flip of the hat transfers the load to the inside to be removed at will.

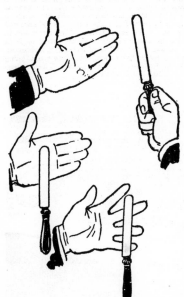

The illustration below shows a new type of magic wand. Any ordinary magic wand may be used in constructing a device of this nature. The performer should have a good selection of magic wands, and they should all be similar in appearance, so that he can employ one or the other whenever needed, and the change in the selection of wands will be scarcely apparent. Strange as it may seem, a great many tricks may be done with wands alone. Thus we have a type of wand which defies gravity and will remain suspended in almost any position from the edge of the table, chair or book. Then there is the disappearing wand and the rising and falling wand, and countless other styles which in themselves make a very pleasing exhibition. Here, however, we have a tip which may be added to any wand, and with which two or more interesting tricks may be added to the magician's repertoire. The metal tip of the wand below is fitted with a bar magnet of the permanent type. This causes cards specially prepared with strips of clock spring attached to their backs to cling to the wand. The magician may also put a silk kerchief into the pocket of his assistant and withdraw it with the wand to which the silk clings mysteriously.

AUDIENCE SEES EMPTY HAT
LID
HINGE

The above shows an interesting little parlor trick which may be performed around the dining table. The amateur picks up a knife, rubs it briskly on the palm of his hand and then suspends it from the finger tips, from the palm or from the back of the hand in a very mysterious manner. A very weak solution of seccotine and water is applied to the palms and fingers and allowed to dry. This is sticky enough to cause the knife to stay in any prescribed position.

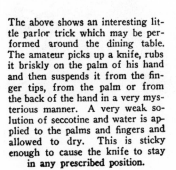

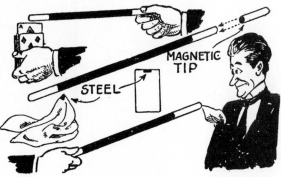

MAGNETIC TIP
STEEL

The hat illustrated in the drawing above may also be used for the production of eggs in one of two ways. Two or three real eggs may be placed in the compartment, and the others may be of a collapsible spring type, or the performer may drop the real eggs into the compartment on the outside of the hat, push the compartment into the hat, and extract the eggs from the inside. The eggs may be secured from the vest or from a "servante" attached to the back of a chair.

The Spooks of Magic

Production of Spirit Pictures
Vanishing Glass of Wine from Tray

The Ghost Frame for Messages
Reading Cards from Back

Spirit Pictures: The magician playing the rôle of a medium sits before a large canvas covered frame placed on an easel. A lamp with a powerful light is fixed directly behind the canvas, rendering it transparent. As the medium goes into a trance and the lights are lowered, a picture in colors gradually forms. This effect is produced by an assistant below the stage, who holds in his hand a bottle containing a solution of potassium prussiate. A tube leading from the bottle runs through the light stand through which the solution is sprayed upon the canvas. The canvas itself has been previously painted with solutions of iron sulphate, bismuth nitrate and copper sulphate for blue, yellow and brown colors respectively. When these solutions dry they are invisible. It is preferable to lightly outline with a pencil the picture to be painted before applying the solutions.

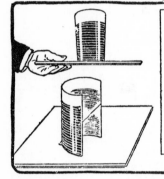
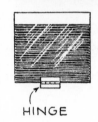

Magic Tumbler: The effect of this mysterious trick is attained by very simple apparatus. The magician's assistant comes forth with a thin metal tray holding a large tumbler of wine. The conjurer covers the glass with a silk handkerchief and removes it from the tray. Tossing the kerchief into the air the glass and its liquid contents have apparently vanished. The telltale diagrams accompanying disclose the secret. The glass itself is nothing more than a sheet of celluloid held in position as here illustrated in a semi-circular form by means of a thread. The celluloid is painted to resemble wine. When the thread is released the piece of celluloid falls flat upon the tray and is invisible. A metal ring of the same size as the supposed glass is placed in a pocket in a handkerchief to enhance the illusion.

The Ghost Frame: This particular offering has been used by the author for a number of years and holds the distinction of having mystified some of the cleverest and best posted magicians in the country. It consists of a large wooden frame in which is fixed a sheet of glass. A flap which opens up as illustrated is hinged to the affair. The flap being shown empty and the glass frame being exhibited, the affair is closed and placed face down upon the table, but in the act of closing, the "flap within a flap" is permitted to fall, exposing the secret contents. With a little practice the magician can manipulate the apparatus with such dexterity that the action of causing the second flap to fall is unobserved by the spectators.

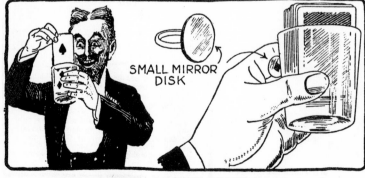

Twentieth Century Mind Reading: In this particular experiment an unprepared deck of cards bearing the closest of inspection is freely shuffled and placed into a glass tumbler, which is held at arm's length by the magician. In spite of the fact that the cards face the audience with their back to the performer, he mysteriously calls the exact rotation of the entire deck reading the cards in front first, and removing one at a time as he reads them. The magician does not have to have his own deck for this experiment as any deck will serve the purpose. Like most good effects the trick is extremely simple, the magician having merely provided himself with a small mirror disk, attached to a flesh colored band or a ring. The small dental mirrors serve the purpose admirably. One need merely look at the index of the card and name it.

Paper Tricks

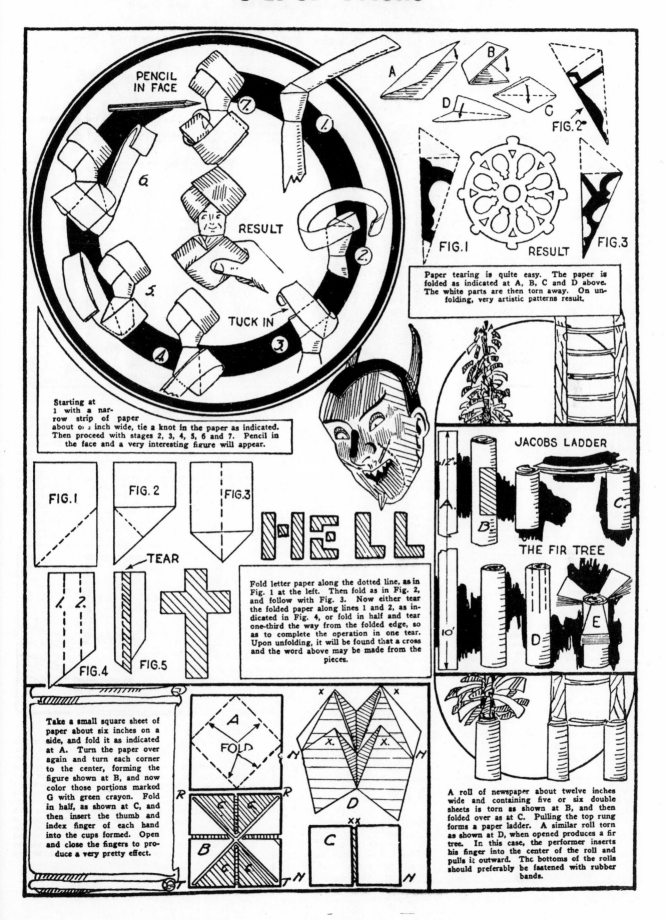

PENCIL IN FACE

RESULT

TUCK IN

Starting at 1 with a narrow strip of paper about one inch wide, tie a knot in the paper as indicated. Then proceed with stages 2, 3, 4, 5, 6 and 7. Pencil in the face and a very interesting figure will appear.

FIG. 2

FIG.1   RESULT   FIG.3

Paper tearing is quite easy. The paper is folded as indicated at A, B, C and D above. The white parts are then torn away. On unfolding, very artistic patterns result.

FIG.1   FIG. 2   FIG.3

TEAR

HELL

FIG.4   FIG.5

Fold letter paper along the dotted line, as in Fig. 1 at the left. Then fold as in Fig. 2, and follow with Fig. 3. Now either tear the folded paper along lines 1 and 2, as indicated in Fig. 4, or fold in half and tear one-third the way from the folded edge, so as to complete the operation in one tear. Upon unfolding, it will be found that a cross and the word above may be made from the pieces.

JACOBS LADDER

THE FIR TREE

A roll of newspaper about twelve inches wide and containing five or six double sheets is torn as shown at B, and then folded over as at C. Pulling the top rung forms a paper ladder. A similar roll torn as shown at D, when opened produces a fir tree. In this case, the performer inserts his finger into the center of the roll and pulls it outward. The bottoms of the rolls should preferably be fastened with rubber bands.

Take a small square sheet of paper about six inches on a side, and fold it as indicated at A. Turn the paper over again and turn each corner to the center, forming the figure shown at B, and now color those portions marked G with green crayon. Fold in half, as shown at C, and then insert the thumb and index finger of each hand into the cups formed. Open and close the fingers to produce a very pretty effect.

A   FOLD

B   C   D

Lifting Stunts for Your Parlor

— Try these "Physical Stunts" in your parlor —
ALL BASED ON PARADOXES IN APPLIED PHYSICS

A Number of Scientific Parlor Stunts Are Illustrated Above. First We Have a Few Simple Hand and Finger Tricks, Winding Up, With the "Georgia Magnet" and "Johnny Coulon" Lifting Stunts, Which Will Surprise You, Once You Have Tried Them.

FOR several months a young American athlete and pugilist, one Johnny Coulon, has been interesting the French public with his remarkable demonstrations of a seemingly mysterious magnetic or other power, which, call it whatever you like, has effectually prevented the strongest men in Europe from lifting his 110-pound body from the floor.

There are a number of interesting and striking preliminary experiments in physics, which, if you have not already tried them out, will provide suitable entertainment for your friends. With the aid of the accompanying illustration, we will attempt to elucidate some interesting preliminary "stunts," before taking up the methods whereby Miss Annie Abbott, the "Georgia Magnet," Johnny Coulon, and others have defied a single man or a group of them, to lift the performer from the ground.

Fig. 1 in the illustration herewith, shows a simple experiment which will prove quite surprising even when performed with a child. It is usually more effective when performed with the aid of a young woman; the lady placing either one or both of her hands firmly on top of her head as shown. You will find that it is practically impossible in most cases to lift a single hand from the head, or if both hands are clasped together with the fingers closely locked and held firmly down on the head, the entire body can be lifted by pushing upward under the arms at the wrists, but rarely is it possible to push the hands upward from the head.

Some Interesting Paradoxes in Everyday Physics Including the "Johnny Coulon Lift" and Why Miss Annie Abbott, the "Georgia Magnet," Cannot be Lifted.

The second experiment is illustrated at Fig. 2. A woman is best selected as the subject, and it doesn't matter whether she is particularly athletic and strong or not. The results will usually prove sufficiently surprising, regardless of this factor. If the subject places her hands firmly against her chest with the finger tips just touching, it will require a strong man to pull the hands apart; if the lady's wrists are grasped firmly an attempt to pull the hands apart is futile. One attempting to separate the lady's hands must not stand sidewise or attempt to jerk the hands, but he must exert a steady pull, at arm's length or with the arms bent so as to improve the leverage, which will give a greater resultant pull.

A simple little experiment to demonstrate the great power of the female of the species over the male, and one which will nonplus any athlete is illustrated at Fig. 3. If the man (it doesn't matter how big or muscular he may be) doubles up his fists and places one over the other, you will be surprised to find that even a young boy or girl can, by simply snapping one finger of either hand against each of the two fists, separate them every time. And more paradoxical still, the harder the "strong man" attempts to hold his fists together, the more easily are they separated.

LIFTING THE HUMAN BODY WITH FIVE FINGERS

What is known as the *five finger lift* is illustrated at Fig. 4, and this provides considerable fun and scientific entertainment for parlor and club gatherings. If it is desired to put the experiment on with sure-fire success, the manager of this little act should take precautions to have his committee of four men lift the subject, picking out preferably a lady weighing about 130 to 140 pounds. If good muscular men are selected for the committee, which can usually be arranged, a woman weighing 150 to 200 pounds can be lifted with ease. The editors have tried this experiment successfully many times and with four men of the average muscular development, succeeded in thus lifting easily a 140-pound woman.

Fig. 4 shows how the lift is made. One of the committee stands behind the subject and places the index finger of each hand under her arms. One man is placed on either side of her in a stooping position and each places one finger under either foot, while the fourth man stands directly in front of the subject and places one finger sidewise under her chin. All lift simultaneously.

MISS ANNIE ABBOTT, THE "GEORGIA MAGNET," DEFIES FIVE MEN TO LIFT HER

A surprising fact is that by careful observation and experiments, first instituted by Dr. Leon Lansberg, and published in a recent article by Miss Grace Nicholas of the New York *Evening World*—Miss Nicholas was able to duplicate the lifting stunts performed by Miss Abbott—such as defying five men to lift her.

At Figure 5 is shown the best and in fact the only way in which a woman, or man, can be lifted; that is, they must—as Dr. Lansberg pointed out—lock their arms or rather their elbows tight to the body. Try this on your wife, sister, sweetheart or mother, and even if she weighs 140 pounds or more you will be surprised how easily two men, with one hand under either of her elbows and the other hand grasping her hand on either side, can lift her 10 to 12 inches above the floor.

At the offices of the New York *Evening World* where the writer was present and assisted in the demonstrations given by Miss Annie Abbott, Miss Grace Nicholas, an athletic young lady, weight about 130 pounds, successfully resisted the efforts of five muscular men to lift her from the floor.

Now for the secret, as it was pointed out by Dr. Lansberg: The subject who is to be lifted, first permits her arms to be held in (or holds them in tightly against the body) and the lift is at first "allowed" with two or perhaps five men, to show that she *can be lifted* up while the "magnetic power" is switched off.

After a little coaching of your lady subject, and after a few experiments, you will find that the secret of *resisting the efforts* of five husky men to lift her from the floor is accomplished by allowing her arms to remain flexible and loose from the shoulders, so to speak, and not to tense the muscles.

Another one of Miss Abbott's tricks is to have a number of men stand in a row back of her, while she places her hands against a wall and braces her body and arms.

HOW JOHNNY COULON WORKS HIS MARVELS.

Much mystery and secretiveness has surrounded the performances of Johnny Coulon, who has successfully demonstrated to the French public that he cannot be lifted when he "so wills it," by even the most powerful man, including the champion weight lifters of France: Johnny Coulon weighs 110 pounds.

When ready for the lift, Johnny Coulon allows the lifter to raise him by the waist. Of course the hands must come in contact with the bare body. This, according to the investigators, is quite a hindrance, the hands slipping away rapidly due to the velvety skin effect. Coulon now places his right hand upon the wrist of the lifter and the index finger of his left hand upon the jugular vein region in the neck and by pressing upon both points defies the strongest man to lift him.

Optical Illusion

Take a piece of tracing paper and trace on same parallel lines, spaced about one-eighth of an inch apart. After this trace a second series of lines crossing the first lines at a right angle, and after this trace two other series of lines at an angle of 45 degrees from the first ones.

You will obtain in this manner a lattice of such fineness that in placing it on printed or written matter it is impossible to distinguish the characters thru the lattice.

Let anybody try to read thru this tracing paper and they will find it impossible.

Place the tracing paper again on the written or printed matter which nobody could read before and give the tracing paper little rapid jerks. The characters will at once appear very distinctly and you can read them very easily.

This is the same phenomena of Optics which occurs when you ride on a railroad a few yards from a fence having small openings between each board; you can look right through the fence as if the boards did not exist.

A Clever and Puzzling Optical Illusion Made By Anyone With a Ruling Pen and a Piece of Tracing Paper.

Hero's Fountain

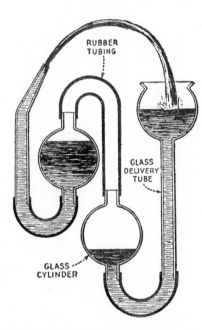

A simple model of that most interesting demonstration apparatus known as Hero's Fountain may be made as shown above. A glass delivery tube, 3 pieces of rubber tubing, 2 glass bulbs and a nozzle are all the apparatus required. Assemble them as shown, placing the parts at the various relative heights indicated. Pour water into the delivery tube until the entire system is full. The water will then flow from the nozzle and if the latter is properly directed, will fall into the delivery tube as shown. The length of flow depends upon the constriction at the nozzle. Some of these fountains have been known to flow for 12 hours without stopping.

Fire Under Water Stunt

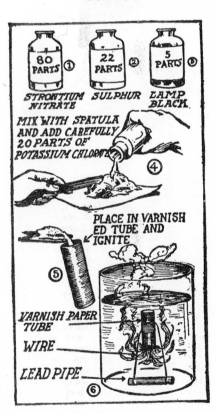

By mixing the chemicals in the ratios shown in the above sketch very carefully, adding the potassium chlorate last, and placing them in a varnished tube supported by wires, attached to a lead pipe, igniting the chemicals and placing the whole in a jar of water, the fire can be made to burn and the flames pass up through water. The lead pipe is used to hold the tube and chemicals under the water.

PARLOR SORCERY

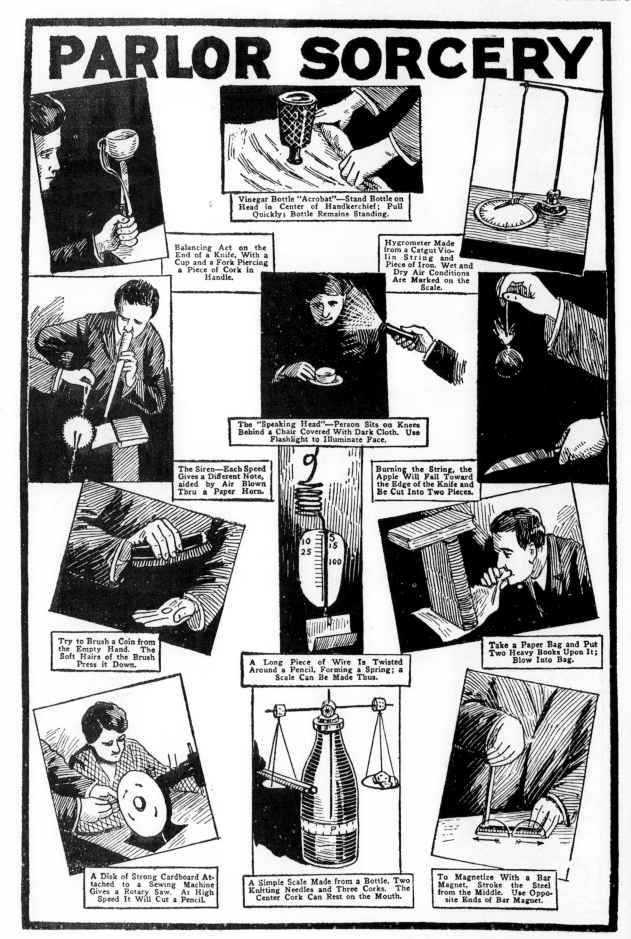

Vinegar Bottle "Acrobat"—Stand Bottle on Head in Center of Handkerchief; Pull Quickly; Bottle Remains Standing.

Balancing Act on the End of a Knife, With a Cup and a Fork Piercing a Piece of Cork in Handle.

Hygrometer Made from a Catgut Violin String and Piece of Iron. Wet and Dry Air Conditions Are Marked on the Scale.

The "Speaking Head"—Person Sits on Knees Behind a Chair Covered With Dark Cloth. Use Flashlight to Illuminate Face.

The Siren—Each Speed Gives a Different Note, aided by Air Blown Thru a Paper Horn.

Burning the String, the Apple Will Fall Toward the Edge of the Knife and Be Cut Into Two Pieces.

Try to Brush a Coin from the Empty Hand. The Soft Hairs of the Brush Press it Down.

A Long Piece of Wire Is Twisted Around a Pencil, Forming a Spring; a Scale Can Be Made Thus.

Take a Paper Bag and Put Two Heavy Books Upon It; Blow Into Bag.

A Disk of Strong Cardboard Attached to a Sewing Machine Gives a Rotary Saw. At High Speed It Will Cut a Pencil.

A Simple Scale Made from a Bottle, Two Knitting Needles and Three Corks. The Center Cork Can Rest on the Mouth.

To Magnetize With a Bar Magnet, Stroke the Steel from the Middle. Use Opposite Ends of Bar Magnet.

Popular Home Magic

Stunts That Mystify and Can Be Performed with Simple Apparatus

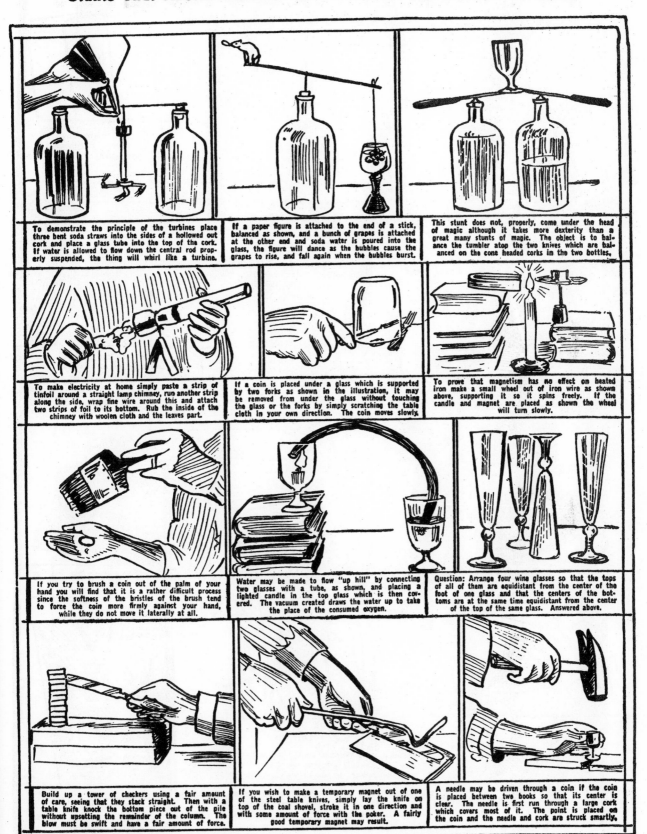

To demonstrate the principle of the turbines place three bent soda straws into the sides of a hollowed out cork and place a glass tube into the top of tha cork. If water is allowed to flow down the central rod properly suspended, the thing will whirl like a turbine.

If a paper figure is attached to the end of a stick, balanced as shown, and a bunch of grapes is attached at the other end and soda water is poured into the glass, the figure will dance as the bubbles cause the grapes to rise, and fall again when the bubbles burst.

This stunt does not, properly, come under the head of magic although it takes more dexterity than a great many stunts of magic. The object is to balance the tumbler atop the two knives which are balanced on the cone headed corks in the two bottles.

To make electricity at home simply paste a strip of tinfoil around a straight lamp chimney, run another strip along the side, wrap fine wire around this and attach two strips of foil to its bottom. Rub the inside of the chimney with woolen cloth and the leaves part.

If a coin is placed under a glass which is supported by two forks as shown in the illustration, it may be removed from under the glass without touching the glass or the forks by simply scratching the table cloth in your own direction. The coin moves slowly.

To prove that magnetism has no effect on heated iron make a small wheel out of iron wire as shown above, supporting it so it spins freely. If the candle and magnet are placed as shown the wheel will turn slowly.

If you try to brush a coin out of the palm of your hand you will find that it is a rather difficult process since the softness of the bristles of the brush tend to force the coin more firmly against your hand, while they do not move it laterally at all.

Water may be made to flow "up hill" by connecting two glasses with a tube, as shown, and placing a lighted candle in the top glass which is then covered. The vacuum created draws the water up to take the place of the consumed oxygen.

Question: Arrange four wine glasses so that the tops of all of them are equidistant from the center of the foot of one glass and that the centers of the bottoms are at the same time equidistant from the center of the top of the same glass. Answered above.

Build up a tower of checkers using a fair amount of care, seeing that they stack straight. Then with a table knife knock the bottom piece out of the pile without upsetting the remainder of the column. The blow must be swift and have a fair amount of force.

If you wish to make a temporary magnet out of one of the steel table knives, simply lay the knife on top of the coal shovel, stroke it in one direction with some amount of force with the poker. A fairly good temporary magnet may result.

A needle may be driven through a coin if the coin is placed between two books so that its center is clear. The needle is first run through a large cork which covers most of it. The point is placed on the coin and the needle and cork are struck smartly.

Parlor Juggling

Tricks That All Can Do

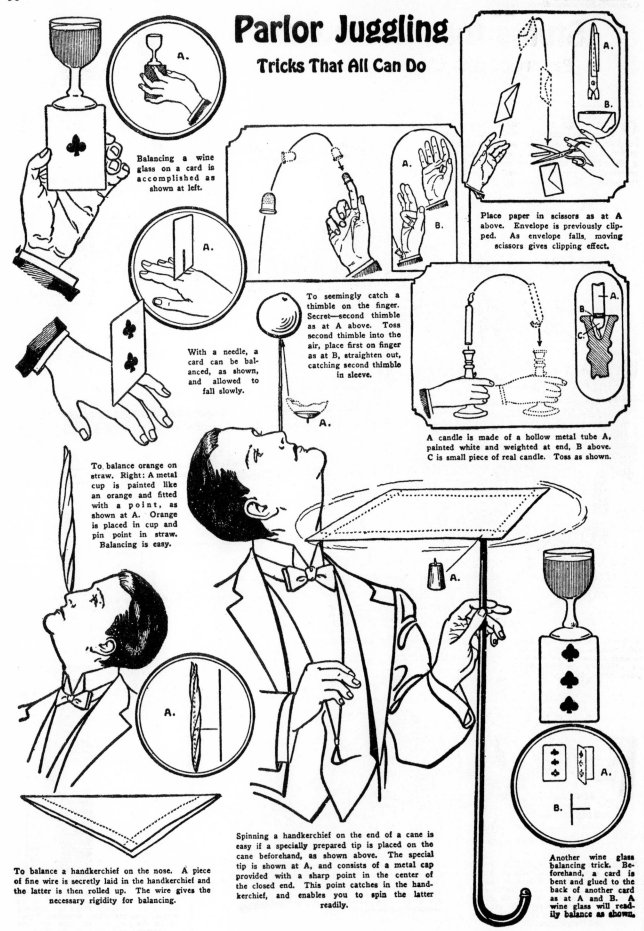

Balancing a wine glass on a card is accomplished as shown at left.

Place paper in scissors as at A above. Envelope is previously clipped. As envelope falls, moving scissors gives clipping effect.

With a needle, a card can be balanced, as shown, and allowed to fall slowly.

To seemingly catch a thimble on the finger. Secret—second thimble as at A above. Toss second thimble into the air, place first on finger as at B, straighten out, catching second thimble in sleeve.

A candle is made of a hollow metal tube A, painted white and weighted at end, B above. C is small piece of real candle. Toss as shown.

To balance orange on straw. Right: A metal cup is painted like an orange and fitted with a point, as shown at A. Orange is placed in cup and pin point in straw. Balancing is easy.

To balance a handkerchief on the nose. A piece of fine wire is secretly laid in the handkerchief and the latter is then rolled up. The wire gives the necessary rigidity for balancing.

Spinning a handkerchief on the end of a cane is easy if a specially prepared tip is placed on the cane beforehand, as shown above. The special tip is shown at A, and consists of a metal cap provided with a sharp point in the center of the closed end. This point catches in the handkerchief, and enables you to spin the latter readily.

Another wine glass balancing trick. Beforehand, a card is bent and glued to the back of another card as at A and B. A wine glass will readily balance as shown.

Stunts for the Smoker
Performed with Cigars and Cigarettes

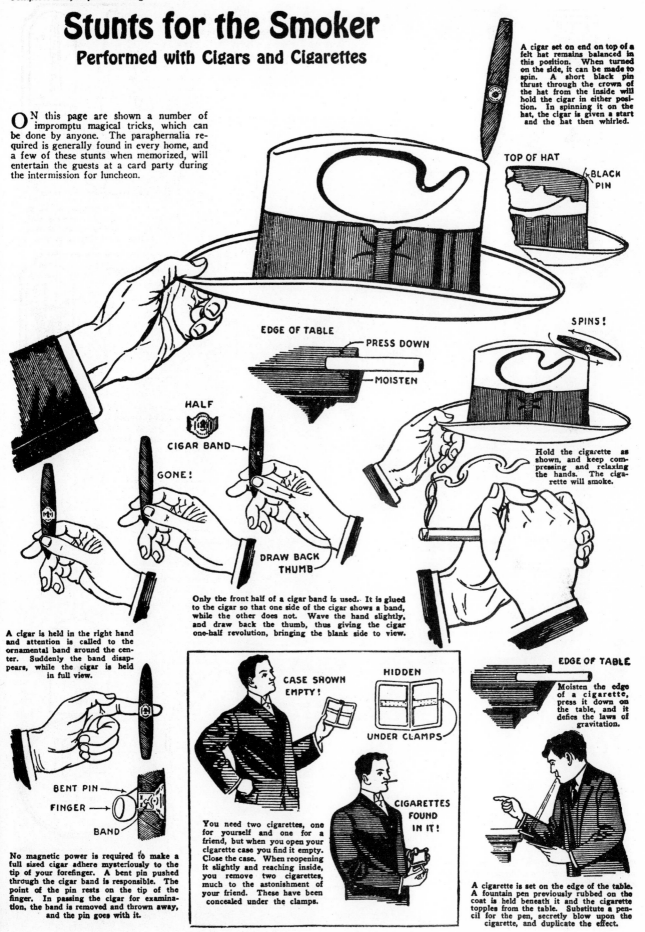

ON this page are shown a number of impromptu magical tricks, which can be done by anyone. The paraphernalia required is generally found in every home, and a few of these stunts when memorized, will entertain the guests at a card party during the intermission for luncheon.

A cigar set on end on top of a felt hat remains balanced in this position. When turned on the side, it can be made to spin. A short black pin thrust through the crown of the hat from the inside will hold the cigar in either position. In spinning it on the hat, the cigar is given a start and the hat then whirled.

TOP OF HAT

BLACK PIN

EDGE OF TABLE

PRESS DOWN

MOISTEN

SPINS!

Hold the cigarette as shown, and keep compressing and relaxing the hands. The cigarette will smoke.

HALF

CIGAR BAND

GONE!

DRAW BACK THUMB

Only the front half of a cigar band is used. It is glued to the cigar so that one side of the cigar shows a band, while the other does not. Wave the hand slightly, and draw back the thumb, thus giving the cigar one-half revolution, bringing the blank side to view.

A cigar is held in the right hand and attention is called to the ornamental band around the center. Suddenly the band disappears, while the cigar is held in full view.

BENT PIN

FINGER

BAND

No magnetic power is required to make a full sized cigar adhere mysteriously to the tip of your forefinger. A bent pin pushed through the cigar band is responsible. The point of the pin rests on the tip of the finger. In passing the cigar for examination, the band is removed and thrown away, and the pin goes with it.

CASE SHOWN EMPTY!

HIDDEN

UNDER CLAMPS

CIGARETTES FOUND IN IT!

You need two cigarettes, one for yourself and one for a friend, but when you open your cigarette case you find it empty. Close the case. When reopening it slightly and reaching inside, you remove two cigarettes, much to the astonishment of your friend. These have been concealed under the clamps.

EDGE OF TABLE

Moisten the edge of a cigarette, press it down on the table, and it defies the laws of gravitation.

A cigarette is set on the edge of the table. A fountain pen previously rubbed on the coat is held beneath it and the cigarette topples from the table. Substitute a pencil for the pen, secretly blow upon the cigarette, and duplicate the effect.

Handkerchief Tricks

Can you make a handkerchief stretch? Can you tie a knot in a handkerchief without letting go of the ends? Can you demonstrate that a handkerchief is fire-proof, and can you prove that one from four equals five? All of these effects may be produced by duplicating the systems illustrated on this page.

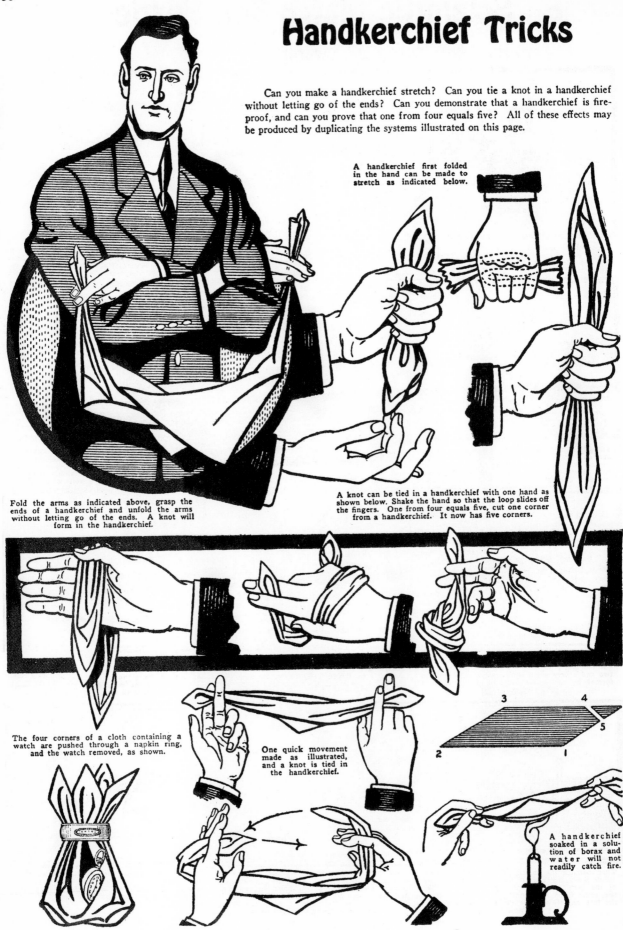

A handkerchief first folded in the hand can be made to stretch as indicated below.

Fold the arms as indicated above, grasp the ends of a handkerchief and unfold the arms without letting go of the ends. A knot will form in the handkerchief.

A knot can be tied in a handkerchief with one hand as shown below. Shake the hand so that the loop slides off the fingers. One from four equals five, cut one corner from a handkerchief. It now has five corners.

The four corners of a cloth containing a watch are pushed through a napkin ring, and the watch removed, as shown.

One quick movement made as illustrated, and a knot is tied in the handkerchief.

A handkerchief soaked in a solution of borax and water will not readily catch fire.

Scientific Match-Box Puzzles
Simple Entertainments with Safety Matches

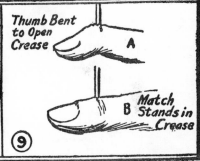

Place three matches as shown in the sketch above, two of them thrust in between the drawer and the sides of the box. Light the cross match in the middle and ask which end will ignite first.

After all the opinions and bets are in light the central match and watch the fun. The pressure of the other two matches will throw the burning stick in the air. The others do not light.

A simple variation of this stunt is to pin two matches in the form of a cross as shown above and lay two other matches across the ends of the cross. Light the center. The matches fall off.

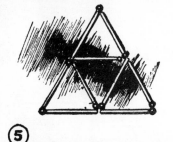

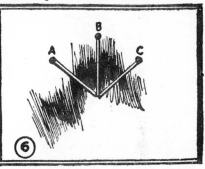

This is a third variation of the same stunt, shown above. Instead of the cross use only one match as the support and stand the other two at its end. They, as before, fall to safety and are not ignited. The supporting pin will become warm.

Ask your audience to form five triangles with nine matches. Give them the matches and let them try it. All the triangles are equilateral and none of the sticks must be broken. The solution of the puzzle is shown in the sketch.

Place three matches in the sketch as shown above and ask someone in the crowd to form an equilateral triangle with them by moving only the match marked "B." The other two must not be moved. Be sure that the ends are square.

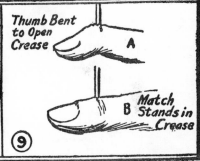

The solution to the problem is simple. Simply put the match "B" at the bottom of the other two and a very small equilateral triangle will be formed by the square bases of the matches as shown in the sketch.

This is a great feat of equilibrim. Place the small match stick on the thumb and make stage play of great difficulty to keep it balanced. Unless some one knows the trick they will say you should be on the Keith Circuit.

They will change their mind, however, when the explanation is given them. The thumb is bent down as shown in the above sketch and the match is inserted in the wrinkle of flesh where it is firmly held in the upright position.

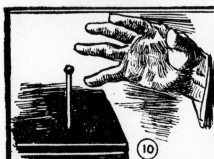

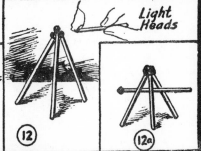

Then balance the match on the table surface. While the audience isn't looking moisten the end of the match. When placing it on the table use some force in standing it upright. After the feat secretly remove the moisture with the finger.

Split the ends of two matches and wedge them together. Then place a third one against them forming the tripod as shown above. Ask someone to lift the three with one match. The solution is to let the loose match fall between the lifting stick and the two wedged ones.

To lift three matches with their heads together, light them and extinguish the flame with a breath. The heads will be found to be welded together so that they may be easily lifted from the table.

Balloon Tricks

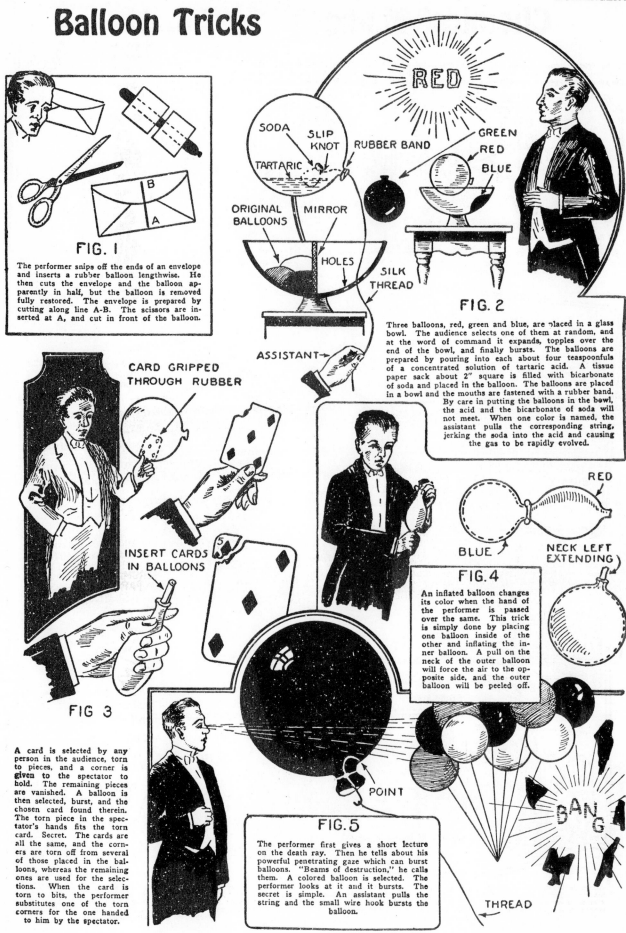

FIG. 1

The performer snips off the ends of an envelope and inserts a rubber balloon lengthwise. He then cuts the envelope and the balloon apparently in half, but the balloon is removed fully restored. The envelope is prepared by cutting along line A-B. The scissors are inserted at A, and cut in front of the balloon.

RED

SODA
SLIP KNOT
RUBBER BAND
GREEN
RED
BLUE
TARTARIC

ORIGINAL BALLOONS
MIRROR

HOLES

SILK THREAD

FIG. 2

ASSISTANT→

Three balloons, red, green and blue, are placed in a glass bowl. The audience selects one of them at random, and at the word of command it expands, topples over the end of the bowl, and finally bursts. The balloons are prepared by pouring into each about four teaspoonfuls of a concentrated solution of tartaric acid. A tissue paper sack about 2" square is filled with bicarbonate of soda and placed in the balloon. The balloons are placed in a bowl and the mouths are fastened with a rubber band. By care in putting the balloons in the bowl, the acid and the bicarbonate of soda will not meet. When one color is named, the assistant pulls the corresponding string, jerking the soda into the acid and causing the gas to be rapidly evolved.

CARD GRIPPED THROUGH RUBBER

INSERT CARDS IN BALLOONS

FIG 3

A card is selected by any person in the audience, torn to pieces, and a corner is **given** to the spectator to hold. The remaining pieces are vanished. A balloon is then selected, burst, and the chosen card found therein. The torn piece in the spectator's hands fits the torn card. Secret. The cards are all the same, and the corners are torn off from several of those placed in the balloons, whereas the remaining ones are used for the selections. When the card is torn to bits, the performer substitutes one of the torn corners for the one handed to him by the spectator.

RED

BLUE
NECK LEFT EXTENDING

FIG. 4

An inflated balloon changes its color when the hand of the performer is passed over the same. This trick is simply done by placing one balloon inside of the other and inflating the inner balloon. A pull on the neck of the outer balloon will force the air to the opposite side, and the outer balloon will be peeled off.

POINT

BANG

THREAD

FIG. 5

The performer first gives a short lecture on the death ray. Then he tells about his powerful penetrating gaze which can burst balloons. "Beams of destruction," he calls them. A colored balloon is selected. The performer looks at it and it bursts. The secret is simple. An assistant pulls the string and the small wire hook bursts the balloon.

Chemical Magic

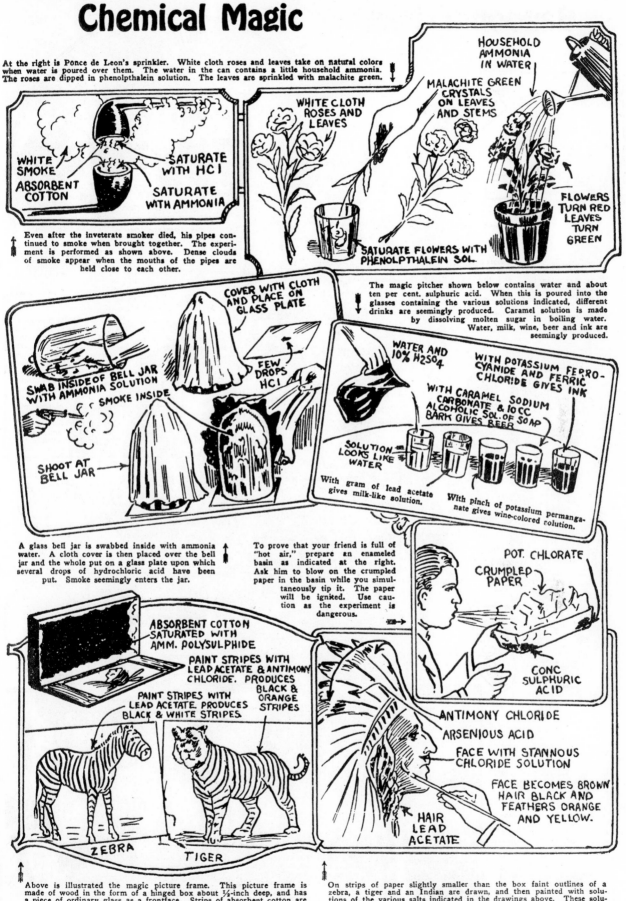

At the right is Ponce de Leon's sprinkler. White cloth roses and leaves take on natural colors when water is poured over them. The water in the can contains a little household ammonia. The roses are dipped in phenolphthalein solution. The leaves are sprinkled with malachite green.

HOUSEHOLD AMMONIA IN WATER

MALACHITE GREEN CRYSTALS ON LEAVES AND STEMS

WHITE CLOTH ROSES AND LEAVES

FLOWERS TURN RED LEAVES TURN GREEN

SATURATE FLOWERS WITH PHENOLPTHALEIN SOL.

WHITE SMOKE
ABSORBENT COTTON
SATURATE WITH HCl
SATURATE WITH AMMONIA

Even after the inveterate smoker died, his pipes continued to smoke when brought together. The experiment is performed as shown above. Dense clouds of smoke appear when the mouths of the pipes are held close to each other.

COVER WITH CLOTH AND PLACE ON GLASS PLATE

FEW DROPS HCl

SWAB INSIDE OF BELL JAR WITH AMMONIA SOLUTION

SMOKE INSIDE

SHOOT AT BELL JAR

The magic pitcher shown below contains water and about ten per cent. sulphuric acid. When this is poured into the glasses containing the various solutions indicated, different drinks are seemingly produced. Caramel solution is made by dissolving molten sugar in boiling water. Water, milk, wine, beer and ink are seemingly produced.

WATER AND 10% H2SO4

WITH POTASSIUM FERRO-CYANIDE AND FERRIC CHLORIDE GIVES INK

WITH CARAMEL SODIUM CARBONATE & 10 CC ALCOHOLIC SOL. OF SOAP BARK GIVES BEER

SOLUTION LOOKS LIKE WATER

With gram of lead acetate gives milk-like solution.

With pinch of potassium permanganate gives wine-colored solution.

A glass bell jar is swabbed inside with ammonia water. A cloth cover is then placed over the bell jar and the whole put on a glass plate upon which several drops of hydrochloric acid have been put. Smoke seemingly enters the jar.

To prove that your friend is full of "hot air," prepare an enameled basin as indicated at the right. Ask him to blow on the crumpled paper in the basin while you simultaneously tip it. The paper will be ignited. Use caution as the experiment is dangerous.

POT. CHLORATE
CRUMPLED PAPER
CONC SULPHURIC ACID

ABSORBENT COTTON SATURATED WITH AMM. POLYSULPHIDE

PAINT STRIPES WITH LEAD ACETATE & ANTIMONY CHLORIDE. PRODUCES BLACK & ORANGE STRIPES

PAINT STRIPES WITH LEAD ACETATE. PRODUCES BLACK & WHITE STRIPES

ANTIMONY CHLORIDE
ARSENIOUS ACID
FACE WITH STANNOUS CHLORIDE SOLUTION

FACE BECOMES BROWN HAIR BLACK AND FEATHERS ORANGE AND YELLOW.

HAIR LEAD ACETATE

ZEBRA

TIGER

Above is illustrated the magic picture frame. This picture frame is made of wood in the form of a hinged box about ½-inch deep, and has a piece of ordinary glass as a frontface. Strips of absorbent cotton are tacked inside of the wooden frame and saturated with ammonium polysulphide.

On strips of paper slightly smaller than the box faint outlines of a zebra, a tiger and an Indian are drawn, and then painted with solutions of the various salts indicated in the drawings above. These solutions are invisible until developed by putting them in the frame in which they gradually color.

Scientific Tumbler Tricks

The problem in the trick shown at the left is to remove the top glass and drink the water in the bottom one without touching them with the hands. The top glass is removed with the chin as shown and the bottom one is tipped on the edge of the table with the teeth so that the water may be imbibed.

Blow through a glass of water? Impossible! Well, try it anyway. Set a lighted candle immediately behind a glass as shown and blow from the opposite side. The flame will be extinguished. The air currents join on the opposite side of the tumbler.

Ordinarily a sheet of writing paper supported at its ends would never support the weight of a tumbler. Corrugate it as shown above and no trouble will be experienced in making it support a glass.

MATCH STICK

Some little bit of dexterity is needed in the performance of this stunt. A full glass of water is balanced on edge on the tablecloth. The stunt is quite impossible to any but the experienced juggler unless the aid of the match stick beneath the table cloth is sought as shown in the above illustration. If this is used, however, a little practice and a steady nerve will enable anyone to perform it. The match may be placed and removed without the observers noting it.

With the glasses placed as seen below, the bottom one filled with water, the question is to pour the water from B to A without handling the latter. Performance is accomplished by gripping A with the teeth and raising it to an upright position as shown and then pouring the liquid into it. Be careful of the added weight of the water, it may bring about disaster.

If pushed off the edge of a table as shown above, a tumbler will fall on its rim and the shock will not break it. This stunt should be practiced before public performance is attempted — and practiced over a pillow.

TAKE HOLD WITH TEETH HERE

PULL HERE

In the above illustrated stunt the napkin may be pulled out from under the tumbler of water by giving it a sharp jerk. At the left below is shown the method of picking up six glasses at once. Each of the fingers holds an outside one while the inward pressure holds the center one.

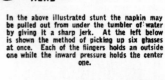

PALM
HOLLOW

Magnetize the bottom of a tumbler? It can be done if a glass with a hollow bottom is selected and the rim of the bottom is slightly dampened before the performance of the stunt. The palm of the hand is pressed down firmly upon the bottom and the slight vacuum formed will be sufficiently strong to support the weight of the glass.

Easily Performed Match Tricks
Mystifying Stunts Which Entertain

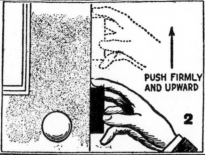

One of the most mystifying stunts which can be performed with a box of safety matches is sticking it to a flat surface seemingly without any support. This stunt is performed with apparatus found around any home. Above, the match box is shown sticking to the end of an open door. The surface must be smooth.

The match box may be stuck to the door simply by pressing it firmly against the wood, and at the same time moving it upward. Several trials may be necessary before you can perform the trick. Either an empty or full box may be used. Press the box from sides and corners, as pressure from the top will not work.

This stunt, shown above, is a simple variation of the one shown in the first two illustrations, except that the sanded edge of the box is used instead of its back, and the box is supported from the coat sleeve instead of the door. A box of non-safety matches with a sanded side is required in this stunt.

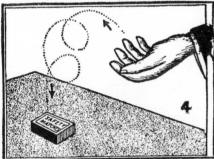

Hurl a box of safety matches in the air. It lands on the table with the label side up. Repeat the whirl two or three times. The box always falls flat, label side up. The box may be whirled by someone else, and in spite of anything they do, if they actually throw the box into the air, the results will be the same.

The secret of the trick just described lies in an old, old law. It is performed by virtue of a heavy coin placed in the bottom of the box between the drawer and the case. Preferably a heavy coin should be used. The weight of the coin causes the bottom of the box to fall downward.

Borrow a box of safety matches from a friend, shuffle it in the hand, be very mysterious, and then tell which way the heads of the matches are pointing. Your results will be much more certain if the box of matches is a full one, since the difference in the weight of head end and tail end performs the trick.

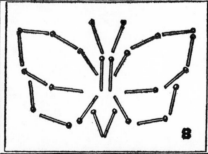

The mystery helps the effect, but the trick itself depends entirely upon the good old law of gravitation. By grasping the box in the center very lightly the added weight of the heads of the matches will force one end of the box lower than the other, thus giving an indication of the direction of the heads.

This stunt is not at all mystifying, but it will add greatly to any impromptu entertainment. Simply take a handful of small safety matches and lay them out on the table in some preconceived design. If the design is viewed through half closed eyes from some distance, its effect will be surprising.

A thumb tack is necessary for the performance of this stunt. It is thrust part way through the cover of a match box as illustrated and a match is made to stand upright after the performer has made a lot of stage business seeking to lead his audience to believe that he is having trouble balancing the match on the box.

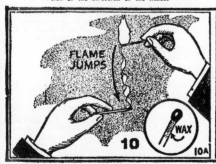

Introducing the acrobatic flame. Light two matches, blow one out and as the smoke curls up, hold the flame of the other match above it. Suddenly the flame slides down the curl of smoke and relights the lower match. The lower match must be previously coated with paraffine as an ordinary match will not work.

Here is a real puzzle. Break open the cover of a match box and set it so that it forms a sort of tunnel. Place the empty drawer of the box on the opposite side of the cover and then ask one of the audience to bring the drawer through the tunnel without touching it. The tunnel stands between him and the drawer.

The solution of this trick is indeed clever. It is only necessary for the performer to cup his hand in such fashion that it will reflect a stiff breath of air onto the drawer. By this means the wind will act against the drawer forcing it through the tunnel. With a slight amount of practice this may be done with ease.

Dice Tricks Simplified

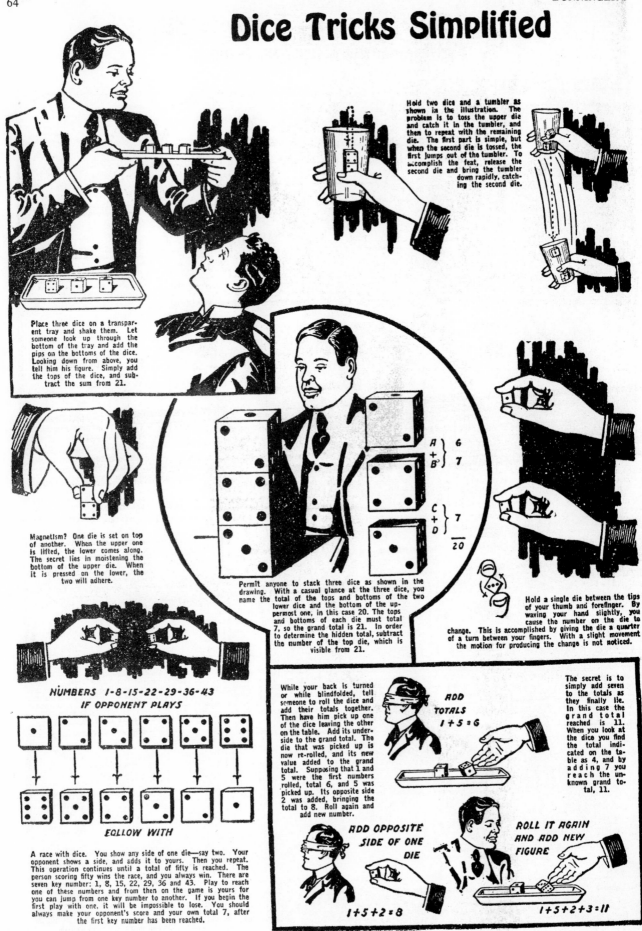

Place three dice on a transparent tray and shake them. Let someone look up through the bottom of the tray and add the pips on the bottoms of the dice. Looking down from above, you tell him his figure. Simply add the tops of the dice, and subtract the sum from 21.

Hold two dice and a tumbler as shown in the illustration. The problem is to toss the upper die and catch it in the tumbler, and then to repeat with the remaining die. The first part is simple, but when the second die is tossed, the first jumps out of the tumbler. To accomplish the feat, release the second die and bring the tumbler down rapidly, catching the second die.

Magnetism? One die is set on top of another. When the upper one is lifted, the lower comes along. The secret lies in moistening the bottom of the upper die. When it is pressed on the lower, the two will adhere.

$A + B \Big\} \begin{matrix} 6 \\ 7 \end{matrix}$

$C + D \Big\} \dfrac{7}{20}$

Permit anyone to stack three dice as shown in the drawing. With a casual glance at the three dice, you name the total of the tops and bottoms of the two lower dice and the bottom of the uppermost one, in this case 20. The tops and bottoms of each die must total 7, so the grand total is 21. In order to determine the hidden total, subtract the number of the top die, which is visible from 21.

Hold a single die between the tips of your thumb and forefinger. By waving your hand slightly, you cause the number on the die to change. This is accomplished by giving the die a quarter of a turn between your fingers. With a slight movement the motion for producing the change is not noticed.

NUMBERS 1-8-15-22-29-36-43
IF OPPONENT PLAYS

FOLLOW WITH

A race with dice. You show any side of one die—say two. Your opponent shows a side, and adds it to yours. Then you repeat. This operation continues until a total of fifty is reached. The person scoring fifty wins the race, and you always win. There are seven key number: 1, 8, 15, 22, 29, 36 and 43. Play to reach one of these numbers and from then on the game is yours for you can jump from one key number to another. If you begin the first play with one, it will be impossible to lose. You should always make your opponent's score and your own total 7, after the first key number has been reached.

While your back is turned or while blindfolded, tell someone to roll the dice and add their totals together. Then have him pick up one of the dice leaving the other on the table. Add its underside to the grand total. The die that was picked up is now re-rolled, and its new value added to the grand total. Supposing that 1 and 5 were the first numbers rolled, total 6, and 5 was picked up. Its opposite side 2 was added, bringing the total to 8. Roll again and add new number.

The secret is to simply add seven to the totals as they finally lie. In this case the grand total reached is 11. When you look at the dice you find the total indicated on the table as 4, and by adding 7 you reach the unknown grand total, 11.

ADD TOTALS
1 + 5 = 6

ADD OPPOSITE SIDE OF ONE DIE
1 + 5 + 2 = 8

ROLL IT AGAIN AND ADD NEW FIGURE
1 + 5 + 2 + 3 = 11

Scientific Coin Puzzles
Simple Stunts with Ordinary Articles

This surprising little novelty is easily performed. The one cent piece sticks against the forehead as though it were glued there. The trick is performed simply by pressing the coin to the forehead and moving it upward. Dampening may help.

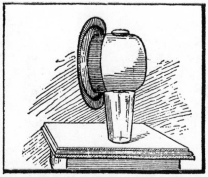

Set the coin on top of the hat as shown, so that the coin is directly above the tumbler. Give the hat a sharp jerking blow and it comes out from under the coin which drops into the glass. Ask a bystander to attempt the same stunt. He will probably fail unless he knows how.

The success of the preceding stunt depends entirely upon the fashion of the blow and the point at which the hat is struck. To make the stunt successful, the operator must hit the inside of the brim of the hat, as illustrated above, a very sharp fast blow, so that the coin falls perpendicularly.

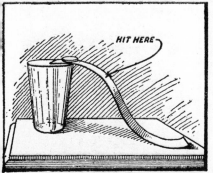

If a heavy strip of paper is laid on the edge of the tumbler and a coin balanced across the edge of the tumbler and paper as shown, and the paper is struck a sharp downward blow in the proper place, the coin will fall into the glass.

Another stunt which requires a bit of practice before the performer may work it successfully is illustrated above. A quarter or half dollar is balanced between two needles and caused to spin by blowing on it.

Lay a coin on the bottom of an inverted tumbler and tell the audience that it is impossible for anyone to lift the coin "from the top of the glass" with two matches. You may lift it—but not "from the top of the glass."

Balance two coins on the edge of a tumbler as shown above and challenge someone to remove them at the same time, and hold them between finger and thumb, touching one coin with the thumb only and the second with one finger only of the same hand.

The method of performing the previous trick is simple. With a great deal of care, grip the coins as shown, causing them to slide down the side of the tumbler. Then draw them around the side of the glass and snap them together.

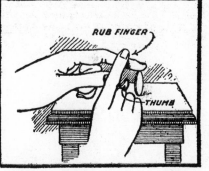

Seemingly when the operator rubs the top of his forefinger which balances the coin, the coin rotates as a result of the massaging movement. However, note the thumb and the ease with which it can strike coin and make it spin.

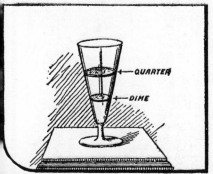

Set a dime and a quarter in a tapering goblet as above. The dime being smaller sits below the larger coin in the glass. The problem is to remove the dime from beneath the quarter without touching or removing the quarter.

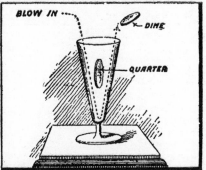

The illustration above shows how the preceding trick is performed. The operator simply blows down one side of the tumbler, causing the larger coin to tilt over edgewise and the small coin to slide out past the large coin.

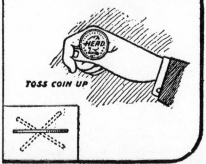

By placing the coin over the fingers as shown, and tossing it—not spinning it—into the air, the coin can be made to fall with the same face up as the coin lay on the fingers. The coin wiggles and seems to spin.

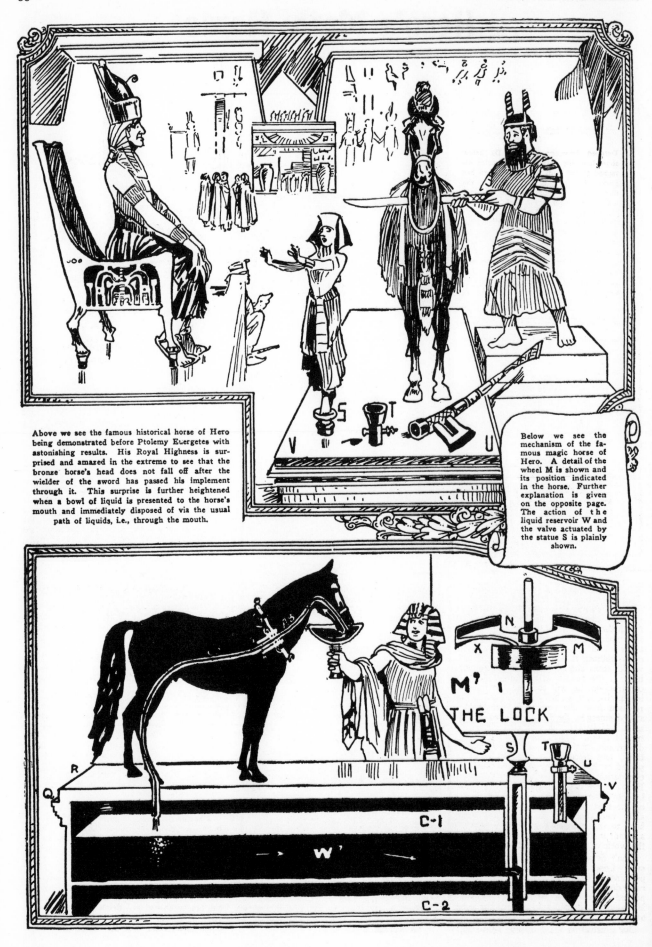

Above we see the famous historical horse of Hero being demonstrated before Ptolemy Euergetes with astonishing results. His Royal Highness is surprised and amazed in the extreme to see that the bronze horse's head does not fall off after the wielder of the sword has passed his implement through it. This surprise is further heightened when a bowl of liquid is presented to the horse's mouth and immediately disposed of via the usual path of liquids, i.e., through the mouth.

Below we see the mechanism of the famous magic horse of Hero. A detail of the wheel M is shown and its position indicated in the horse. Further explanation is given on the opposite page. The action of the liquid reservoir W and the valve actuated by the statue S is plainly shown.

THE LOCK

Hero's Magic Horse

Detailed drawings D1 and D2 below show how the horse's head remains attached to the body after the sword has passed through and also shows how the drinking tube opens and closes, first making way for the sword and then closing so as to allow the horse to "drink" by means of the partial vacuum formed in the chamber shown on the opposite page. The sword first revolves a wheel, M, which allows the sword to pass but still holds the horse's neck and body by locking in the grooves. The sword then proceeds to first open and close the drinking tubes by means of segments, K and L.

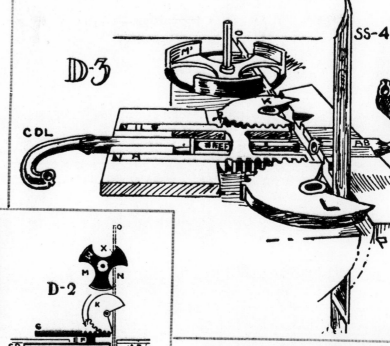

Above is shown a cross-section perspective illustration of Hero's magic horse's neck. The sword has nearly finished its passage through the neck and is about to actuate segment L, which, when rotated slightly, will close the drinking tube, telescoping section EF into section AB. The upper point of segment K will at the same time recede from its notch and that of L will lock into a similar notch.

HERO'S horse is an animal which submits to having a sword passed through its neck from top to bottom, yet the head never falls. After the sword is passed through the neck and emerges therefrom, a cup of beer or other liquid is presented to the animal who cooly imbibes it, although the sword cut, it would seem should prevent it from drinking. If the reader will follow through the construction, he will see that the interlocking mechanism is such that the head is never released from the body, and that when the sword emerges, the head is locked fast just as it was before; he will also see that the tube through which the animal drinks is drawn out of the way of the sword by the cams, and reinstated after the sword has passed by it. And now we leave the further elucidation to the drawings and description. Hero's horse is absolutely authentic. It will be remembered that Hero was the inventor of the first reaction steam engine, and now after two thousand years, we are coming back to the reaction engine in the shape of a steam turbine and in a fair way to forget the work of Newcomen and Watt.

Don't decapitate, Mahh-Mood would have said. Long ago at the Gate of Mecca, the prominence of two bow-string executioners, reminded one that life there entirely depended upon one's ability to pronounce Mohammed's name, according to the school of Islam.

Our illustration shows Hero's 78th Proposition before Ptolemy Euergetes. The chief Executioner has put his sword through the horse's neck several times—so he is now trying to saw his way down through it—without result. Then he silently wishes his own head was fastened as securely upon his own shoulders—for the Pharoah might say something, you know. But he didn't. The ordinary Egyptians were apt to believe the horse was a son of Isis—for superstition was the rule of Egypt—as in no other way could the common people be held in control by the ruling classes. Still Ptolemy himself was surprised to see that *decapitation didn't decapitate.*

"THE REVOLVING LOCK"

"D-1" shows the sword in its operation as follows: A cross section of the sword blade, shown in cross-section at "SS-1," has entered the slot at "O" and striking in the cleft "N" of the wheel "M" turns it exactly 120 degrees; this leaves it in the same relative position shown in "D-2"; thence the sword strikes the cam gear wheel "K" at "SS-2" in "D-1" which pushes the frame "GH" which holds the male cylinder "EF" to the left and out of the female cylinder "AB," whence the sword blade goes to "SS-3" in "D-2" where it strikes the cam gear wheel "L" which reverses the whole motion and reinserts the male cylinder "EF" into the female cylinder "AB," making an airtight joint; then the sword blade passes out of the slot at "P"—which completes the sword operation.

The third figure, "D-3," shows the sword "SS-4" striking the last geared cam "L"—and also the wheels "K" and "L" each in the notch lock—which could not be moved under pressure. Figures "CDL" and "ABL" are lead pipes soldered to the cylinders "CD" and "AB" to merely show how lead piping was made. The turning and boring of cylinders is described in Hero's *Pneumatika* in detail, and it may be found in all the manuscripts in Arabic, Greek and Latin. The casing which covers this mechanism fits like a mould, and if all the pivots were removed the wheels would perform accurately. Note that the rim on wheel "M'" is not centered upon its spokes—but ¼ of the rim is on one side and ¾ on the other—so that while it is in its circular slot the exact center of the rim rests upon a slight ridge in its groove. Mechanically this quadruple lock of Hero's is equal to any modern gun lock so far devised.

THE HORSE DRINKS

The bronze horse shown drinking his beer—operates as follows: "AB" and "CD" now being a siphon, its operation is started by the turning of the valve "S," whose handle is a soothsayer. That lets the water out of the airtight chamber "C-1"; this creates a vacuum whose suction starts the siphon "AB" and "CD" that runs through the horse's leg to its mouth—consequently the brassy animal can drink as long as supplied with any kind of liquid; in fact, he could drink more beer than an entire army.

Sawing a Woman in Half

A Mystifying Trick That Is Not So Magical As It Appears

One of the Most Mysterious Acts Which Can be Produced Either for Semi-Professional or Amateur Theatricals, Is the Trick Here Illustrated—of Sawing a Person in Half. As the Illustrations Indicate, Two Young Women are Necessary in Producing this Illusion and the Large Table Used Must Have a Hollow Top of Sufficient Depth to Accommodate One of Them. The Illustrations, Together with the Detailed Description Given in the Article Below, Will Render Perfectly Clear the Successive Phases of this Magic Act.

THE cold-blooded dismembering of a young and otherwise very attractive young woman for no other purpose than the delectation of an audience of amusement seekers can be easily imagined as occurring in the arenas of ancient Rome, but it is well nigh impossible to describe one's impressions upon witnessing such a feat on the modern vaudeville stage.

The surgeon extraordinaire appears before the curtain is raised, explaining that he is about to saw his lady assistant completely in two and that the operation, while a very delicate one, is performed absolutely without pain. Then, as tho to put his audience at ease, he adds that she will be promptly restored to her normal condition, after the operation, and that she has consented to the experiment without coercion.

After thus enlightening his audience, the arch-vivisectionist turns to the rising curtain and greets the victim, a charming little miss, who instantly makes you resent the perpetration of any such villainous assault upon her anatomy as is contemplated.

The performer calls for assistants from the audience and after selecting two and seating them upon the stage he turns to the victim, suddenly holding before her eyes a small crystal ball. And now a secret—gentle and unsophisticated reader—the effect

of this act is much greater on the audience than upon the subject. No, I do not mean, as I have sometimes heard it said, that the entire audience is hypnotized and consequently sees things that it does not see, but for some unknown reason hypnotism and magic seem to have linked themselves inseparably, and it is, therefore, entirely befitting that she should be placed in a comatose condition before proceeding further. Having been thoroughly satisfied that the subject is under the hypnotic spell, the audience is willing to believe almost anything possible. In other words, a *mystic atmosphere is created.*

The victim is then laid upon a table; two straps are lowered from the flies or above-stage, and after being securely fastened, she is raised a few feet in the air to make room for the cabinet into which she is to be placed.

"Aha!" says my reader, "the Hindu sword and basket trick again!" but wait. The victim is lowered into the cabinet, which is a bit short, her head and arms protruding from one end and her feet from the other. The two ends of the cabinet are placed in position, these latter having semi-circular openings for the neck, hands and feet. The cabinet and table are then swung around a quarter turn so that the cover may be closed and locked in full view of the audience and its committee of two. This accomplished, the cabinet and table are swung

back into their original position. One of the committee is assigned to the holding of a dainty pair of ankles at the foot of the cabinet and the less fortunate one vice versa.

The saw, about the capabilities of which there can be no doubt, is brought upon the stage and examined, and then, amidst goose flesh music by the orchestra, the cabinet, and incidentally its occupant, are cleanly severed while the audience holds its breath and shudders.

A slide is then placed in each section of the cabinet, thus mercifully sparing the audience from an inspection of the debris, and the two sections are pulled apart in order that the performer may walk between them and show that there is no deception. Two window curtains of the proper size may be used to close the cabinet compartment, operating them by strings, etc. Upon placing the sections of the cabinet together again and unlocking the cover, the young lady, much to the relief of the audience, arises none the worse for her experience.

The inventor of this illusion, as are all followers of magic, is a true disciple of Barnum, and of his doctrine that the public likes to be fooled, and in this he has certainly succeeded.

It is not the author's purpose to write an exposé of the act as presented but merely to point out how such an effect could be accomplished.

First, it may be stated that two female assistants, instead of one as supposed, would be required, and while they need not look alike it would be highly essential that the limbs of each be carefully selected for similarity. An examination of the accompanying sketches should make the reason clear.

Victim number one comes upon the stage and is placed in the cabinet, hands, head and feet remaining in full view of the audience. The ends are placed in position and the cabinet given a quarter turn so that the feet face the rear of the stage. Ostensibly this is for the purpose of lowering the cover and locking it, but as soon as the cover is lowered victim number one withdraws her feet and doubles her body into as small a compass as possible, while victim number two, the silent partner, who has been reclining comfortably within the table all this time, substitutes her ankles for those of victim number one. It will thus be seen that the cabinet, which by the way may be made of heavy cardboard and decorated with an appropriate design, is free to be cut into two equal sections with no danger to its occupant or rather occupants.

After the cabinet is sawed in two the sections, and apparently the victim as well, may be separated by sliding the part which contains the *trunk* and head. It is well to remind the prospective magician, however, that the slides referred to above must be first placed in position and also that any attempt to slide the lower section on the table would result in the more or less sudden disappearance of milady's ankles within the cabinet.

The victim can be "reassembled" by a reversal of the moves already described. Do not, however, forget to first remove the slides or serious complications may arise.

The illusion is an innovation in the realms of magic and the effect upon the audience is all that could be desired by the most fastidious wizard of the wand.

Trick Stage Makes Dwarfs

DURING the summer months of 1922 there was exhibited at Coney Island, New York, a most remarkable performance in the apparent reduction in size of human beings. When we say reduction of human beings we refer to the apparent reduction in the size of humans, without their undergoing any physical discomfort whatever. For that was actually what took place on a stage before the very eyes of the audience.

In a spacious lobby of the Tanagra Theatre, a "barker" called the attention of pleasure-seeking people to an exhibition, or rather performance, to be given on a stage 12 inches high and 24 inches wide, with as many normal-sized human beings on it as it could comfortably accommodate. Such a remark as this would naturally bring forth various comments from most any one; among them we heard "fake," and what not. Others said that the audience was hypnotized into believing that such a thing took place, etc.

The writer, like others, wanted to be "shown," and he as well as a number of others paid the entrance fee of ten cents. In due time, we witnessed a really interesting and entertaining performance of high-class vaudeville on this miniature stage. It was startling to see real human beings on such a small stage. These performers were going through their regular entertaining act.

After the performance, the manager of the theatre requested those of the audience who cared to be "reduced" to come in back of the stage so that their friends might see them in the guise of dwarfs. The writer was one of those that volunteered with over a dozen others. We, of course, experienced no ill effects, nor were any magic passes made before our eyes, nor were we told anything by the manager. The curtain was hoisted and there our friends beheld us reduced to a stature of about 8 inches. Immediately there arose a great applause and calls to wave the hands or other members of our anatomy, which we obligingly did.

The writer having at one time studied physics, made it his business to find what the real "trick" was that caused this reduction. In the course of a few minutes a lens and a pair of plain glass mirrors were noted. A second performance showed the entire *modus operandi*, and it is for the first time since this interesting device was imported from Germany that it was disclosed for the curiosity seekers.

As the diagram shows, the subject is placed before a dark background; he is then focused upon a plain glass mirror by means of a large lens, and the angle of reflection corrected by a second mirror. From this second mirror the image is reflected upon an ordinary glass plate fitted into a picture frame, and appearing as a miniature stage, with the conventional drop curtain on which was painted ASBESTOS. The subjects wore colored clothes of high contrast, in order that the effect might be more striking. The lens was a fixed focus one.

Recently this clever optical system was employed at an exhibition of manikins at a ladies' fashionable clothing establishment, and motion pictures were even made of the characters on this unique reduction stage.

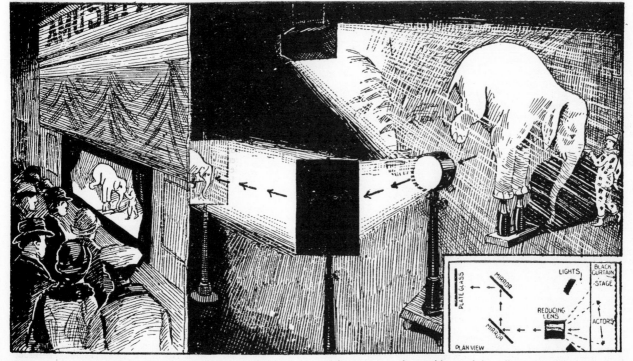

Miniature actors and animals go through their respective performances on a miniature stage to the astonishment of the audience, who cannot believe that beings could be so small and still live, but the method of arranging the reducing lens and the mirrors as shown in the view above explains the effect. The plan view inserted in the lower right hand corner makes the arrangement of the apparatus still clearer.

How Electricity Makes Possible Modern Stage Wonders

IT is a far cry from the present-day theater, with its thousands of electric lamps which can be flashed on and off in the twinkling of an eye, back to the gas-lighted theater of our grandfather's time. The stage electrician of the present generation is king of all he surveys, and a king he truly is, for he can mar or make any theater production. Some of the interesting things which are actually being done on the stage today are described in the following article—electrical and mechanical and stagecraft tricks which the audience never sees.

REVOLVING AND ELEVATING STAGE FLOORS

In order to expedite the change of scenes in the more elaborate theatrical productions, especially those having several different

the rear, where they will not show in the setting. Under the lower platform, which normally is level with the basement floor, there is placed a battery of *hydraulic elevators*, which operate by water under pressure. For the second scene shift, scene No. 1 may be set on either the upper or lower platform, and the second scene brought to the stage level in a few seconds by the hydraulic elevators. That is, considering that a two-act show is being put on. With a three-act show or a production having several acts with many changes of scenes, then at the start, scene No. 1 would be set on the lower platform, while scene No. 2 would be set on the upper platform. When the curtain goes up, scene one appears before the audience, the setting of scene two being 20 feet above the stage. The

use at figure 2. Two, three, or even four scenes can be set up at one time on this revolving stage. Where an elaborate musical comedy or extravaganza is to be produced with anywhere from 10 to 15 changes of scenery, the convenience and speed with which the different scenes may be changed and the show run off, will be appreciated. The revolving stage is rotated when desired by a throw of a switch, controlling an electric motor which rotates the platform thru a powerful worm gear underneath the floor. The platform rotates on roller bearings.

At figure 3, there is shown the checkerboard scheme of quickly changing the scenes in a show. In one scheme now in actual use, the scenes for the three acts are set up on the right, left and rear scene

Scene from "The Storm" by Langdon McCormick, a Most Realistic New York Theatrical Production. In the First Act, There is a Very Good Snow Storm Effect; the Bushes and Trees Swaying in the Moaning Wind. At the End of the Third Act, the Audience is Treated to One of the Greatest Masterpieces Ever Produced in Stage Settings,—a Sure-enough "Forest Fire" with Crashing Trees and Howling Wind,—and Not One Speck of Real Fire on the Whole Stage. In This Sensational Scene, the Fire May Be Seen to Creep Slowly Thru the Trees in the Distance. As It Gains Headway the Flames Leap Higher and Higher Until the Whole Stage Is Enveloped in Flames. Trees Fall, the Bushes and Underbrush Sway in the High Wind, the Largest Tree on the Stage, as Shown Above, Crashes Thru the Cabin Occupied by Burr Winton and David Stewart. The incandescent or Burning Wood Effect on the Trunk of the Trees, Is Created by Electric Lights, Suitably Camouflaged Behind Colored Silk, Etc. Those Lights, Blinking on and Off, Enhance the Effect. Powerful Electric Sirens Produce the Wind Noise and the Creeping Fire Thru the Trees in the Distance Is Projected From Back Stage on to the Back Drop by Special Lanterns Provided With Moving Colored Discs.

scenes to each act, many novel ideas have been developed and installed in several New York theaters, including revolving, as well as rising and falling stage floors. Three different forms of these movable stage floors, which enable several different scenes to be set up at one time, are illustrated at figures one, two, and three. Each of these three ideas, for providing multiple stage floors, have been actually tried out and proven successful.

Figure 1 illustrates a rising and falling stage in use at one theater. Two platforms, each large enough to carry the stage setting as shown, are built in the form of a gigantic elevator, the top platform being separated about 20 feet above the lower platform, with steel girders at the ends and at

lights are then winked off for a few seconds, or the front curtain is dropped for a moment and raised again, when, Lo! and behold! the scene has changed! How is it done? Simply by operating the hydraulic elevator cylinders and plungers to lower the platform structure, so that scene No. 2 which was above the stage is now level with it, and the lower platform containing scene No. 1 is level with the basement floor, where the scene shifters immediately get busy and remove the scenery of set No. 1, and dress it with the scenery for scene No. 3.

The revolving stage which is in use in one of the largest New York play-houses, which is necessary as this circular floor is of quite a large diameter, is illustrated in

platforms, as shown. These platforms are mounted on substantial rubber-tired wheels, so as to make a minimum amount of noise when the scenes are changed. When act No. 1 has been placed, the curtain is dropped and the platform carrying scenery for this act is rolled to the right, and the platform carrying the scenery for act No. 2, is pulled into place. One of these sets, including the platform, is quite heavy, and while it can be shifted by a number of men, recourse is had to a series of ropes fastened to the platforms and also to a powerful electric motor winch in the basement, whereby any one of the three platforms can be moved either into or out of its position before the foot-lights.

Mysteries of Stage-Craft

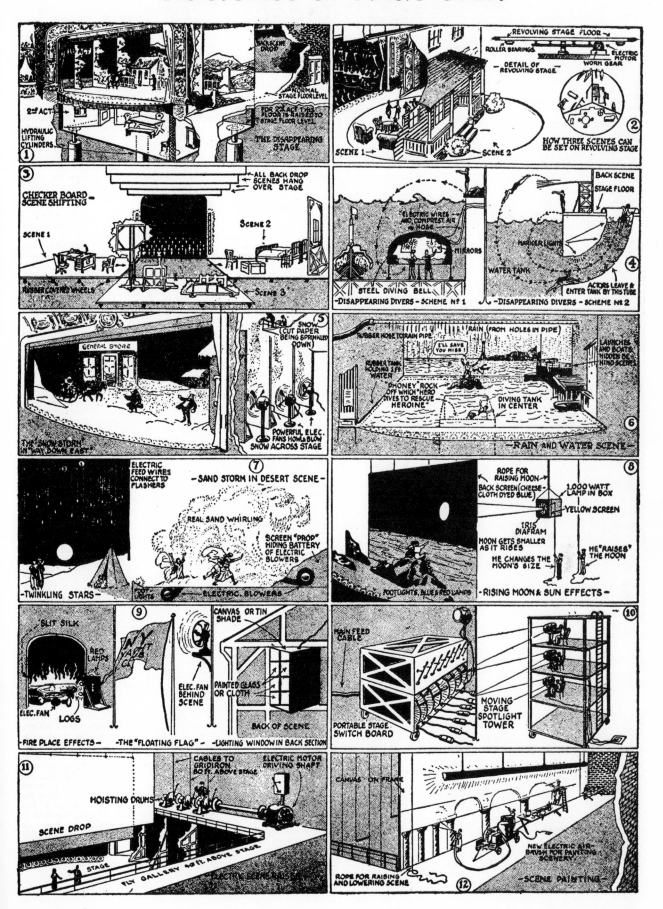

WATER, SNOW AND RAIN EFFECTS

The "Disappearing Divers" have long proven a complete mystery to most patrons of theaters such as the New York Hippodrome. In such productions, as the reader probably is aware, a considerable mystery is evolved by having several people (sometimes as many as 20 or 30) dive into a large water-filled tank and they disappear completely, not coming up again for a space of twenty minutes or more. There are several ways of accomplishing this trick, and two of them which have been successfully adopted are illustrated herewith at figure 4. The first is that utilizing *diving bells*. These diving bells, one or more of which may be used as required, according to the size of the tank, are made of steel and must be air-tight. They act on the same principle that when you place a drinking glass or cup into a basin of water, the water will not rise all the way up in the glass, due to the compression of air within the glass. Thus, when the divers plunge into the water, they are enabled to see the position of the bell, owing to the fact that it has electric lights inside of it, which lights up the water at the bottom of the tank, and indicates the hulk of the diving bell very plainly. When they reach the bottom of the tank, they swim towards the bell and pull themselves up inside of it, under the rim. Compressed air is forced into the bell thru a pipe in order to keep the water at as low a level as possible within it, and where a number of swimmers have to remain in the bell for any appreciable time, proper air outlet and inlet pipes have to be provided, so that an exchange of air is made possible within the bell chamber. For a shorter period, and when not many people breathe the air within the bell, they can get along without fresh air being supplied. With fresh air under pressure being pumped into the bell, some of the air and its products, such as carbon dioxide gas, will bubble out thru the water and thus help to refresh the atmosphere within it. Mirrors are arranged inside the bell so that the fair swimmers may adjust their hair and clothes.

Another stunt for accomplishing the "Disappearing Diver" trick is that employing one or more tubes leading out from the tank to a place on the rear of the stage. The position of the tube running into the tank is either known to the swimmers, or in large tanks they are lighted up by blind bullseyes or lamps, which only the divers can see, and by holding their breath for a few seconds, they manage to swim for the tube-opening as soon' as they dive into the water, up thru which they crawl by means of ribs on the wall of the tube, to the stage floor level. As is well known, the water in the tube will not rise higher than it is in the tank. When it is time for the divers to appear, they pass down thru the tube and, Wonder of Wonders! they come popping right out of the water as fresh as a daisy. In the case of the diving bell, they simply hold their breath, slip out from under the bell, and swim to the surface of the tank. In one of these productions a Viking ship slowly rose to the surface of the water on which the swimmers, about 20 in number, stood, as the deck eventually cleared the water. Truly a wonderful spectacle! To produce this astonishing display, the ship has wheels running on an inclined track up to the surface of the water. A gripping tackle is provided at the bottom of the tank to pull the ship up at the desired moment. The masts which are quite high are made telescopic and these are raised under the control of one of the men in the diving bells. Then, when the masts have been raised about half-way out of the water, all of the swimmers pop out from under the diving bells, holding their breath and stand on the deck of the good ship "Viking." The captain of this mysterious craft pulls the lever releasing the clutches, and the ship rapidly rises to the surface,

the heads of those standing on the deck appearing thru the water first, the water running from their clothes and shoulders as they emerge from the watery depths.

At figure 5 is shown an interesting snow scene in the production of "Way Down East," the play that has successfully "held the boards" for many years. The snow in practically every show is produced in the form of small bits of cut up white paper. The "snow" is spilled down from the fly gallery 40 feet above the stage, or in some cases, it is simply thrown from the stage floor level by some other means. At figure 5 it is shown being dumped from trays along the fly galleries and as it reached a point several feet above the stage floor, it was caught by the breeze from powerful electric fans placed between the wings on either side of the stage, which caused it to be blown out on the stage in a very realistic manner. At the same time the "wind" noise is caused by the whirring of the fans.

A very realistic rain and river scene with real water was produced several years ago in a traveling or road production, with which the writer had some experience—in fact he had the pleasure of "controlling the rain," and that is some pleasure, "Believe me, Xantippe!" Well, to cut short the suspense, the rain was made by simply having a pipe extend across the front of the stage, and which pipe was perforated with several dozen small holes. This rain-making pipe was then connected with a hose to a water pipe at one of the fly galleries, where the person controlling the rain is standing. When he gets the cue from the stage manager, to "let 'er go," he immediately opens the valve and the water descends from the openings, dropping to the tank or rubber apron below, in the form of "sure enough, honest-to-goodness" rain! This forms a sheet of rain and for most purposes gives a very satisfactory effect.

This show had a most exciting water scene, and the method for staging it was one of the most wonderful that the writer has ever come in contact with. The production carried a large flexible rubber tank, the full length of the stage and about one foot deep, which would thus hold enough water to float row-boats or a small launch. In the center of the tank there was a deeper pocket, measuring about 10x7 feet which projected down into a wooden frame under the stage, and into which the hero proceeded to dive in the second act in order to save the beautiful blonde heroine. If the "villiun" had felt real interest in, or had been jealous of the affection of the hero for the heroine "off stage," he could move the "phoney" canvas-covered "rock," and if our hero dived he would then make a miscalculation and end by dropping into one foot of water, instead of ten. With this improvised and somewhat shallow tank of water, a very exciting melodrama was "put-on"; the scenery was hung over the sides of the tank so that just the water line appeared to the audience, and in fact no part of the tank whatever. A band of counterfeiters floated up the river in a launch, while the police boat, chasing them, fired several dozen revolver shots thru a phoney machine gun. It was some exciting plot and very realistic.

SUN, MOON AND STAR EFFECTS ON THE STAGE

In the "Garden of Allah," one of the most pretentious scenic productions put on in New York in several years, there was a very realistic *desert sand storm*. Real sand was used in producing this storm scene and as shown in figure 7, the sand was caused to be blown upward, and then caused in turn to whirl in eddies by means of electric blowers placed at the proper points about the stage. These electric blowers were camouflaged under small stage props, which were colored and arranged to fade in with the sand of the desert. The twinkling stars

were created by a large number of tiny electric lights being hung against a dark blue background, the various circuits of lamps being rapidly switched on and off by an automatic flasher. As the lights were staggered and placed in an irregular formation, and as the lights in different levels were alternately illuminated and extinguished, no regular coherence of effect could be gathered and the audience was thus charmed with the display.

At figure 8 is shown an arrangement in use for producing the best type of moon or sun-rise, or also the setting of the moon or sun. In the ordinary production attention is paid to the well known fact that the moon or sun is always larger when down near the horizon, growing smaller in diameter as it mounts to the heavens. The moon effect, for instance, is produced in the following manner:—a powerful lamp, such as 1,000-watt incandescent gas-filled bulb, is placed in a light-tight box. In the front of this box there is arranged a slide in which colored screens can be placed to give a yellow or other tint to the light, and across this opening there is mounted an iris diafram, similar to that used in camera shutters. This diafram is fitted with a lever extended from the side of the box, and from which a cord depends downward. The box is now carefully elevated by means of a rope, or two ropes, such as will allow it to be pulled upward in a slow manner. At the same time the operator controlling the moon-rise slowly closes the iris diafram, causing the "moon" to gradually grow small as it mounts up from the horizon painted on the scene.

Figure 9 shows how *open fire place* effects have been produced as well as *blazing fire* from other stage mountings. It is seldom that a real fire is used on the stage, both because it is not necessary and also because it is somewhat dangerous where there is so much canvas scenery about, altho these are fire-proofed as best they can be. The *flame* of such fires is produced by thin red silk ribbon or else by pieces of red silk. An electric blower or fan is so placed as to blow these silk strands and cause them to resemble a flame, especially when lighted from behind or beneath by means of red lamps. Figure 9 shows also how windows in small houses, appearing in the back of the settings in certain scenes, are lighted up. In a recent Belasco production, "Dark Rosaleen," all such stage effects as this are very carefully worked out so as to produce an exact and true scenic setting. The electric lamps for lighting up the windows are shielded by a canvas flap in the manner shown, so that no light flashes up above the frame of the house or reflects back onto the scenery, which would, of course, spoil the scene. The windows are made of celluloid or similar material, either colored or painted. Where scenery glass is required, and unless some desperado is to do the "business" of jumping thru a window to the accompaniment of crashing glass, then ordinary window screening is used. In one of these large windows containing about 20 openings, it was surprising to note how well this screen resembled glass, and moreover it had been painted around the edges so as to give the effect of a long accumulation of dust and dirt. Flags are often used in spectacular productions, dramas, etc., and of course the best effect is created by having the flag wave. This is usually done by placing an electric fan near the flag and just behind a piece of scenery so that the fan is out of sight with respect to the audience.

MISCELLANEOUS STAGE TRICKS

Some of the more elaborate stage productions carry with them a portable electric switch-board of their own, as shown at Fig. 10. One of these switch-boards which the writer recently saw, contained a whole battery of dimmers (rheostats) for controlling the lamps of various border and spot lights—this portable switch-board rolling about on wheels, and being connected to the electric supply mains by means of a flexible rubber covered cable. At Fig. 10, there is also shown the three stage revolving spot-light platform which is used in some of the spectacular productions produced on large stages. The spot-light operators are located on the different stages of the platform which has a total height of thirty feet or more. Flexible rubber covered cables supply current to the spot-lights from the stage floor pocket. Arc lamps for stage spot-lights are rapidly going into disfavor and the new 500- and 1,000-watt gas-filled tungsten lamps are taking their place. At Fig. 11, there is shown a motor-driven scene raising and lowering mechanism installed in one of the New York theaters. All large theaters today have what is known as a grid-iron, and fly gallery above the stage, the height of the grid-iron being about 80 feet above the stage floor. Large drops, ceilings of rooms, house roofs, and all such scenic effects are hoisted by means of ropes and suspended from the grid-iron, so that they hang about 40 feet above the stage, and just over the particular setting which happens to be in use. Sometimes 40 or 50 scenes may be seen hanging from the grid-iron and above the actors' heads. In the usual theater, these scenes are correctly balanced by heavy iron weights, so that they can be raised and lowered by one man, without undue exertion. At this particular theater, however, an electric motor drives the shaft which runs along one side of the fly gallery. The ropes coming down from the various pulleys up on the grid-iron, and by means of which the scenes are raised, pass down to this motor driven shaft, each rope being secured to a suitable winding drum. By means of a clutch attached to each rope hoisting drum, it is possible to quickly raise or lower any scene desired, the electric motor doing all the work. By throwing in several clutches at once, as many as four or five scenes can be raised simultaneously. When the scene is raised to its proper height and in order to prevent breaking the ropes and dropping the scene, an automatic electric cut-off is fitted to the hoisting ropes which stops the motor if the scene is raised too far up.

SCENE PAINTING

Little is known regarding the life of the *Scene Painter*. Painting scenery is a profession by itself, and naturally the first requisite is that the scene painter shall be an artist. Also, to be successful, he should be an engineer, an architect, and a thoro student of electric lighting effects, especially with respect to colors. The brilliant colors which are sometimes seen in stage productions are very flat and commonplace-looking when seen in daylight. All of these things the scene painter must take into consideration constantly, while he is painting the scene.

Figure 12 shows a scene painting bridge at a large New York playhouse. The colors are made up in large quantities in dishes and bowls placed on long tables along the bridge,—this bridge being 40 feet above the stage floor and having no rails on it. The canvas on which the scene is to be painted is mounted on a large and fairly heavy wooden frame, which is swung on ropes from the grid-iron 40 feet above the bridge. By means of ropes on either end of the bridge, the scene painters can raise or lower the canvas as desired. Large scenes measure about 85 feet long by 40 feet high. All of the scenes, no matter of what building or other view they may represent, are invariably laid out on the canvas with chalk lines and scaled off from a miniature scene, in much the same manner as a house builder constructs a house from the architect's plans. Room scenes where elaborate sets are used, are sometimes provided with heavy wooden doors and framed windows; these are also constructed at first in miniature, even down to the tables and chairs and the vases and clock on the mantle. These parts are scaled off and constructed to exact detail and size by the stage carpenters from the scenic artist's master model. These models are generally but a few feet in length and some of the miniature views, from which back drop scenes like the one shown at Fig. 12, are painted, are no larger than an 8x10 inch photo. Photos are often used to paint scenes from or to help the artist in depicting correctly certain foreign views, such as Chinese buildings, et cetera.

Stage scenes are painted in strips, i.e., when several painters are working upon the bridge, they all work across the canvas at an average height of say 6 feet. After this 6 foot strip across the canvas has been painted, the frame is lowered this amount, and a new six foot strip across the scene is painted, and so on, until the whole canvas is finished.

A new departure in scene painting is that involving the use of a large *air brush* which is shown at Fig. 12. One of the most successful scenic artists who was the first to make use of the air-brush in painting scenes on such a large scale as this, is Mr. D. M. Aiken of New York. The beautiful and truly magnificent color effects known only to the air-brush artist, have been available for a number of years in connection with small photograph retouching; and now that these wondrously beautiful color creations are available to the stage scene painter, we can expect to see some extraordinarily entrancing stage settings.

Plaster Masks Simply Made

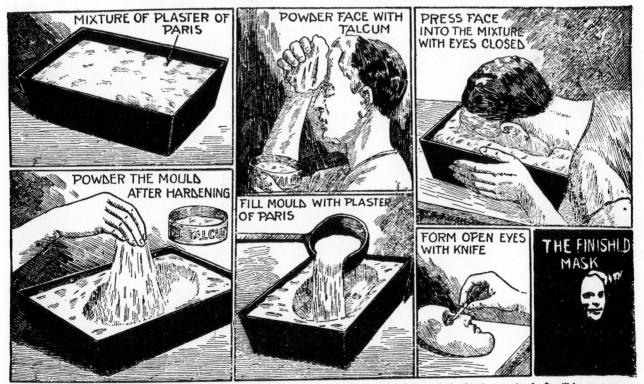

Masks may be easily made at home, and if a little care is taken, there is no reason why they should not be fully as artistic as the professionally made articles. First make a mixture of plaster of Paris and water of the consistency of thin dough; then powder the face thickly with talcum. Press the face into the plaster of Paris with the eyes closed. It will be necessary that the consistency of the plaster be proper, so that the features of the face will be retained. Then powder the mould and pour in the plaster for the cast. Form open eyes with a knife or pointed tool.

All Travelers Who Have Visited the Orient Have Seen the Famous Basket Trick, in Which a Hindu Boy is Placed in a Basket and a Sword Plunged into it Repeatedly. On Opening the Basket, the Boy is Found Alive, or Perhaps Has Disappeared to Come Running into the Scene from a Distance of a Hundred Feet or More. He Escaped Through a Slit in the Basket Under the Robes of the Magician and His Assistants (Upper Left). The Upper Right Hand Diagram Shows the Way a Similar Trick is Performed on the Stage. Two Mirrors Conceal the Victim from View. These Mirrors are Attached to the Rear Table Legs and Slant Forwardly, Joining at the Center. The Lower Diagrams Illustrate: To the Extreme Left—Person Escaping from a Trunk and Later Found in a Cabinet, the Cabinet Itself Being Mounted on Legs. In the Center Illustration is the Orange Trick: The Assistant in Back of a Mirrored Table Conceals the Orange in a Black Gloved Hand Blending with the Draperies. At the Extreme Right, the Trick Performed by Fakirs, Known as "Buried Alive." The Tunnel Communicates with a Hollow Tree from Which the Fakir Escapes

SIR ARTHUR CONAN DOYLE in his self-appointed mission to this country has rearoused widespread and intense interest in all phases of occultism, including ghosts, fairies, departed spirits, and even the long-familiar performances of Hindus, who make a pretense of being Yogis, but who are mere fakirs; with which last-named some skeptical people are inclined to identify the extraordinary spiritualistic manifestations reported by the eminent British lecturer, author and scientist. Such identification would be, however, equivalent to utter condemnation of all the phenomena related and described by Sir Arthur, for there can be no question that the performances of Hindu fakirs are nothing in the world but clever trickery, such as is practised by every sleight-of-hand entertainer since the days of the famous Signor Blitz. It is true that the exaggerated accounts given by many travelers are calculated to produce the belief that innumerable vagabonds and mendicants in India are endowed

with supernatural powers and are able to perform feats inexplicable by any known law of nature. But the fact is that the so-called Indian fakir is indeed a faker in our common approbrious sense of the word. He is a juggler, a trickster, and his apparently magical performances are sheer deception. True Yogis do appear to possess powers transcending ordinary conceptions of nature, but they never make public exploitation of them.

One of the best known of the performances of Hindu fakirs is what is known as the Basket Trick. A small boy is placed within a large oblong basket, the lid of which is strongly tied down. The fakir then thrusts a sharp sword into the basket; a scream of mortal agony is heard; and the sword is withdrawn dripping with blood. The basket is then opened and, to the relief of the horror-stricken observers, is found to be empty, while the child, safe and sound, appears at a distance among the bystanders.

In some cases the child is found in the basket, but quite unharmed.

The explanation of this is quite simple. The fakir has a number of assistants around him, all dressed and looking alike. In one side of the basket there is a slit, imperceptible when it is closed, but which can easily be opened by springing the osiers apart. When the fakir leans over the basket and places his knee upon it, to draw as tight as possible the straps which secure the lid, the child crawls out through the slit underneath the fakir's ample flowing robes, and thence under the robes of his assistants who stand close by, and so makes his way unperceived to the outskirts of the crowd, whence he returns after the basket has been opened. The screams apparently uttered by the child within the basket are the result of ventriloquism, and the blood on the sword is the blood of a bullock or some other red fluid, contained in a bladder hung within the basket. In those cases in which the child is found within the basket, the performance is simpler still.

Hindu Fakirs

The child simply squirms into such a position as will avoid the thrust of the sword.

A variation of this basket trick was performed about fifty years ago in a London theatre by the celebrated Hungarian magician, Kratki Baschik, to the bewilderment of numerous crowded audiences. The trick was introduced by the relation of a romantic story. The magician, he said, had been deeply enamored of a beautiful dancer in the ballet, but she had deceived him in favor of another man, and he was consequently resolved to wreak his vengeance upon her. She will come to a rendezvous which he has appointed, and then he will kill her. Presently she comes upon the stage, and he pretends to be reconciled to her. Then he invites her, just for fun, to see if she can stow herself within a big basket which stands on a small table in the centre of the stage. She at first objects, but presently is persuaded to get into the basket. Instantly he clasps down the lid and fastens it, and then plunges his sword through the side of the basket. Her shrieks of agony are heard, growing fainter and fainter, and at last dying away to silence. Then he opens the basket, and finds nothing but the woman's skirt. She herself has vanished. He closes the basket-lid again and indulges in a long monologue, repenting of his deed and wishing that his beautiful mistress were alive again. If she were, how he would love her! Then he again opens the basket, and lo! she is there, alive and unharmed.

The explanation of this trick differs materially from that given for the trick of the Hindu fakirs, and it depends upon the construction of the table upon which the basket is placed. This is apparently a simple table, supported by four legs, and open underneath, so that the spectators can freely see under it. But in fact there are attached to the two hind legs two mirrors, extending forward diagonally, meeting each other in the centre. Looking into these the spectators behold the reflection of the draperies at the sides of the stage, looking exactly like those at the rear, and of course suppose that they are looking straight through under the table, while the mirrors in fact serve as a screen behind which the woman makes her escape through a trap-door in the bottom of the basket behind the table. Her cries and shrieks of pain are uttered after she has left the basket and is underneath the table.

A similar device is employed in the familiar trick in which a man is bound hand and foot, placed in a trunk which is securely locked and strapped. In a few moments the trunk is opened and is found to be empty. The performer then goes to a wardrobe or cabinet, standing on legs at the other side of the stage, unlocks and opens it, and there discloses the man who had been placed in the trunk. The secret is quite simple. There is a trap-door in the bottom of the trunk, which is placed directly above a corresponding trap in the floor of the stage. Through these the man escapes from the trunk. He walks under the stage to a similar trap at the other side, through which he ascends into the wardrobe, the floor of which is provided with a trap directly over that in the stage. His passage through the space between the stage floor and the floor of the wardrobe is not seen, because he is behind a screen of mirrors attached to the wardrobe legs, just as in the basket and table trick.

Much mystification has been caused to innumerable audiences by the performance of a "magician" who from a vase draws any number of oranges. The vase is freely passed about for examination, and is seen to be quite empty. It is placed on a small table supported by four slender legs and apparently entirely open underneath. The magician bares his arm to the shoulder, so as to avert all suspicion of concealing the oranges in his sleeve. He once more exhibits the vase, to show that it is empty. Then he places it upon the table, and immediately picks an orange out of it. Again he turns the vase upside down and displays the interior, to show that it is empty, and again picks an orange out of it. These actions are repeated, in rapid succession, *ad libitum*. The explanation is that the table is provided with mirrors, as in the tricks already described, behind which crouches a confederate, whose hand and arm are completely covered with a black glove, so as to be quite invisible against the black background of the stage. He holds an orange perfectly concealed within his black-gloved hand, reaches up and places it within the vase, which, by the way, is also lined with black. This action is thus entirely invisible to the spectators. Then the magician readily picks out of the vase the orange which his confederate has placed within it.

Another orange trick, equally mystifying, is performed without the aid of mirrors. Standing on a black-draped stage, the magician extends his hand and apparently plucks orange after orange out of the empty air, the orange not being visible until it is in his hand. The simple explanation is that a black-gloved confederate stands behind the curtain and hands up orange after orange, concealed within his black-gloved hand, to become visible only the instant the performer picks it from within the black glove. The hand of the confederate is invisible against the black draperies, and the illusion of the oranges being picked out of the air is perfect.

Most formidable of all the performances of the fakirs of India is that of burying alive. In some cases there is reason to believe that there is actually suspended animation, due to the practice of what is called Pranayana, or regulation of the breath. Through this adepts are said to acquire the power of abstaining from eating and drinking and even from breathing for a long time, perhaps for months, and of becoming quite insensible to external impressions. A most competent and trustworthy observer, Dr. McGregor, has described such a performance which he witnessed at Lahore. A fakir was placed in a wooden box, the lid of which was locked, and was placed in an underground tomb. Above the tomb was a small garden house, which was also carefully locked, and around the garden was a high wall, which was constantly patrolled by armed sentries, and the only gateway through this was walled up. For forty days and nights the fakir was thus immured. Then, in the presence of the Maharajah, several of the Sirdars, and a number of British officers, the tomb was opened. First the gateway in the wall was reopened; then the garden house was unlocked; the subterranean tomb was opened, and the box was unlocked. Nowhere was there perceived the slightest trace of meddling. The fakir was found in the box, in a sitting posture, covered with a white linen sheet, and quite unconscious. Water was poured upon his head, followed with a cake of hot attar, and a plug of wax was removed from one nostril. In a short time he began to breathe again, then to speak in a low tone, and finally regained his normal vitality.

The majority of cases of burying alive are, however, sheer trickery. The man is placed, it is true, in a coffin or box, and is buried in the ground, in an open field, remote from any building or other object, and the spot is carefully watched day and night. At the time agreed upon the grave is reopened. There are no perceptible traces of any meddling with it, and the man is found within the coffin, alive and well after weeks or months of burial. The explanation is simple. A tunnel runs from the grave under the field to the edge of an adjacent grove, and there emerges within the trunk of a large hollow tree. As soon as the fakir is buried he opens the end of his coffin and crawls like a mole through the tunnel to the hollow tree. Thence he escapes and goes, perhaps, to his home, to remain in hiding until the time set for his resurrection. It is to be noted that the precise day and hour for the reopening of the grave are always agreed upon in advance, in order that he may know precisely when to return through the tunnel to his coffin. It is, of course, easy for him to feign unconsciousness, emaciation, or any other conditions which might naturally be supposed to have come upon him as a result of such a period of interment.

Another very common trick, which has been seen by almost every traveler in India and in which probably a large majority have faith as an actually supernatural achievement, or at least as one quite inexplicable to them on natural grounds, is the so-called mango trick. The mango is chosen partly because it is so familiar a fruit, as an apple might be chosen here, and partly because the exceptional readiness with which a small mango tree, when wilted and withered, responds to the application of water. The fakir exhibits to the crowd a mango seed, an empty flower-pot, and a napkin, or a shawl. He fills the pot with earth and buries the seed in it, in plain view of the spectators, then spreads the napkin or shawl over it and makes a few mysterious passes with his hands, beneath the cloth. Then he raises the cloth, and shows the onlookers a little mango tree, just bursting through the surface of the soil. He pours water upon it, with certain incantations, replaces the shawl, and makes further passes with his hands. After waiting a few minutes, he again raises the covering, and displays a little mango tree several inches high, with green leaves, apparently in healthy and robust growth.

The explanation is perfectly simple. When the fakir first makes the passes with his hands beneath the shawl, he buries in the soil in the pot the little mango tree which, wilted and shrivelled, he had concealed in the palm of his hand, leaving just the tip of it protruding from the surface. The water which he then pours upon it causes it in a few minutes to revive and straighten up, fresh and vigorous, as though it had just grown from the seed.

A number of supposed performances by fakirs, of most wonderful character, in fact never occur at all save in imagination. Many of the fakirs are adepts in the art of hypnotism, and this they apply to the spectators. When all are thoroughly hypnotized, the fakir suggests to their minds the trick he is supposed to perform, and when they are again brought out of the hypnotic spell, they firmly believe that they hav ewitnessed some astounding deeds which really did not happen at all.

"Modern Magic" and How They Do It

Scientific Stage Illusions

TO say that so-called stage illusions or tricks of magic are founded on certain peculiarities in the field of science may sound, perhaps, somewhat far-fetched, but such, however, is a fact in many instances. To begin with how many of us ever thought for a moment that the sword swallower we saw at the circus or dime museum, ever actually swallowed the swords, even tho he handed them to us for close scrutiny? Of course he was using trick swords which *folded* up or *telescoped* by pushing a secret button, as he apparently past them down his throat—but it seems that we were or are all wrong, for we learn on the pledged word of Harry Houdini in his recent book—"Miracle Mongers and Their Methods," that practically no first-class sword swallower ever has used a telescopic or collapsible sword, but due to the scientific fact that when the head is thrown back the œsophagus and mouth are placed in a practically straight line, the performer, after sufficient practise to accustom the lining of the œsophagus to this unusual effect, can actually swallow not one sword, but in some cases as many as seventeen swords simultaneously. Madame Edith Clifford, Champion Sword Swallower of the world, has succeeded in swallowing a 26-inch sword blade or in other demonstrations ten thin blades, which are removed one at a time, states Houdini. To be sure these swords are not sharp, i.e., they do not cut the tissue.

MAN IN HOT OVEN TRICK

For many years, altho not in favor at the present time, there were performers, who amused the people of both this country and Europe, with many hair-raising varieties of *fire-eating* and *heat resisting* tricks of the Black Art. Possibly one of the most popular tricks at one time was that in which a man enters a large hot oven, in which the flames can be seen thru a mica or grill-work door, the performer afterward emerging with a steak or piece of other meat cooked by the intense heat during his stay in the oven. Altho, as Houdini—the great miracle worker of the present day, points out in his book, there were, undoubtedly, several of these human salamanders, who could withstand remarkably high temperatures, even up to 300 degrees Fahr. and more, there is a certain trick method which was used by some of the magicians and which we show in the illustration at Fig. 1.

The oven might be constructed, for example, of sheet iron with a large window in the upper part of the door covered with plate glass or mica, with pieces of cotton waste soaked in alcohol, placed inside the oven and which could be ignited either by the performer after he entered the oven and locked the door, or else by an attendant passing a lighted taper thru a small hole in the oven wall. Other pieces of cloth soaked in alcohol are placed on top of the oven and when ignited, present a very spectacular effect, especially if the oven is arranged sufficiently high above the stage so that the audience can assure themselves that no mirrors or other artifices of the stage magician have been used to trick them, such as traps to permit the performer escaping thru the bottom of the oven while the fire is burning. Salt may be added to the alcohol to make a more spectacular flame.

The fire-eater?—Oh, yes! we almost forgot to mention that he invariably wore an asbestos suit, and further—as we all know, heat rises very rapidly. A strong draft of cool air is sucked in thru holes in the bottom of the oven, by the action of the blazing waste, and moreover the performer usually laid on the bottom of the oven, with his mouth directly over either an opening in the floor or else over a small pipe thru

---

How red hot swords are swallowed, steel boiler "escapes" made, and how Houdini gets out of the milk can full of water just in time to save himself from being asphyxiated—these and many other scientific stage mysteries are explained in the accompanying story. P. T. Barnum was right it seems, when he said, "the American public likes to be fooled." He did not mean this in a sarcastic way, but simply stated the fact that Americans like to be entertained by magicians and others. If you do not think that Barnum was right, just study a few of these tricks and propound them to your best friends or to the folks at home. You will be surprised indeed at the simplicity with which the keenest minds are often misled and shall we say "double-crossed" or entertained?

---

which he breathed fresh air. The piece of meat to be cooked was of course placed near the top of the oven so that some of the blaze and heat would reach it. When the blaze died down after a few minutes, the performer arose, opened the door and walked out with the *cooked meat.*

Those interested in Black Art performers of a generation or more ago, who swallowed not only tacks, nails and poisons, such as arsenic, but also boiling oil and a hundred other kinds of miscellaneous hardware and junk, and "got away with it," will find it extremely interesting to read all about them in Houdini's "Miracle Mongers and Their Methods."

THE DISAPPEARING ELEPHANT

Perhaps you were fortunate enough to have visited one of the New York theaters a season or so ago, when the art of magic was called upon not only to make a rabbit appear from a magician's high silk hat, or from a hat borrowed from a spectator, but to actually cause a full grown elephant to disappear right before your very eyes and surrounded by a solid brick wall at that! This disappearing elephant trick is illustrated in Fig. 2. When the curtain goes up, the rear and two side brick walls are exhibited already built. The elephant is then, with all due ceremony, paraded across the stage and led up an incline onto the platform supporting the walled inclosure. Masons then start in building up the front brick wall, and at the crucial moment when the elephant is all locked nicely inside his little brick jail, lo and behold—the same elephant comes ambling across the stage; and after some of the bricks have been knocked away you are convinced indeed that there is no trace of the elephant or even of his ghost left in the brick wall inclosure. The diagram in Fig. 2 shows how this trick was accomplished; after the front wall was about completed the elephant was led down the inclined floor, which was hinged, and was then led along underneath the stage, thence upstairs upon the stage once more, while the hinged floor was pushed up in place again. The action of the hinged floor was rendered invisible to the audience—thanks to a mirror placed at the proper angle under the front of the platform as indicated.

THE MAIL-BAG ESCAPE

The *mail-bag escape* is perhaps one of the best tricks of this nature performed, even at the present day, the audience being completely mystified as to how the performer gets out of the mail-bag once he has been locked in, especially if locked in the bag by men from the local Post Office Department, and using a standard mail sack fitted with the lock used officially. Fig. 3 illustrates how the escape from the mail-bag is made. To begin with the performer in some cases uses his own mail-bag, made exactly like a government bag in every particular and provided with a standard Yale or Corbin lock; or else he may challenge the Post Office officials to lock him in their own bag, provided with their own lock. In the latter case the performer does not see the bag or the lock until he is going to be placed in it. By his expert knowledge of all such locks therefore, he has to provide himself with a suitable skeleton key or else a standard key to fit the lock on the P. O. mail-bag. If he uses his own mail-bag and lock, he of course knows just what key to use. This key is secured to a piece of strong cord and this he secretes on his person before coming on the stage. The committee from the audience pull the straps tightly thru the loops on the bag and finally snap the padlock in place. The curtain of the cabinet is pulled down and in a few minutes the performer appears—free from the sack and also free of any handcuffs or leg-irons, with which he may have provided the committee, in order to make the trick seem more difficult. This trick is beautiful in its simplicity, the only thing being that you *must* know ahead of time what kind of lock is going to be used on the bag, or else take a long chance of guessing which type of simple skeleton key will unlock the Post Office padlock. As soon as the curtain is dropped on the cabinet, the performer, gets hold of his skeleton key secreted on his person (attached to the sole of his foot with adhesive tape if in swimming tights and bare legs, or carried in the pockets of his suit, if in evening dress), which key is fastened to the end of the string as you will remember. He thrusts his key out thru the small slit-like space in one corner of the bag, which may have to be forced open a little to make room for the key to be pushed out. The key is allowed to dangle down eight or ten inches. The string is tied fast to a vest button so that the key will *not* be lost; the performer then *feels* thru the canvas of the bag until he gets hold of the key —and noting the position of the lock he fumbles around with the key until he enters the key into the lock and opens it! He makes his escape, feeds the strap back in place and snaps the lock in place. The rest of the story is simple. He then appears before the curtain of his "Magic Booth," **a** free man once more. Aha!

THE ELECTRIFIED GLASS TRUNK

The glass trunk mystery illustrated at Fig. 4, has been performed for many years, but an improvement suggested by the author would be to cause high frequency currents to flash over the trunk all the while the performer is locked inside of it and endeavoring to make his escape. This trick does not lend itself to the needs of the amateur magician usually, as it is quite expensive to stage, owing to the trunk being built of ¼-inch thick plate glass. This glass trunk is built in the manner illustrated, the corners being firmly locked by right angle steel or brass bars, held in position by bolts passing thru the glass, while padlocks link thru holes in the bolts on their outer ends. The whole trick of escaping from this and other similar varieties of cabinets, lies in the fact that the bolts holding the hinges in place are *phoney* ones, but this fact is never noticed by the committee from the audience who come on the stage and inspect the glass trunk. The bolts holding the hinges are made with a threaded cap, so as to permit them to be taken apart from the inside. Two small holes in the cap for which a steel key is made of the form shown, explain the mystery.

The performer, once the curtain is drawn on his cabinet, takes his key and unscrews the phoney hinge bolts and pushes them outward, and then raises the glass cover sufficiently to allow him to escape from the trunk. He then proceeds first to pick the locks so as to release the bolts from the hinges, fastens the bolts to the glass side once more, then places the hinges over them and finally resnaps the locks in place. Added theatrical effects can be carried out in several different ways. A good scheme would be to keep the high frequency discharge going continuously all the while the *escape* is being made. Of course it is not safe to keep the discharge passing thru salt water (which may be sponged over the glass just prior to presenting the act) all the while the escape is being made by the performer, so a subterfuge is arranged for, so that no change in the spark effect will be noticed by the audience. By means of a by-pass spark-gap connected to the wires just behind the glass trunk as indicated in the diagram.

THE MIRROR AND WATCH TRICK

"Will some lady or gentleman in the audience kindly loan me a perfectly good gold watch for five minutes? I will guarantee to return it in perfect condition within the allotted time. Thank you, sir!" (Saying which he steps back on the stage with the gentleman's gold watch.) On his velvet covered magician's table in the center of the stage, the performer has a mortar and pestle in which he shortly proceeds to apparently smash up the borrowed watch—but does he?

He then takes the dismembered parts of the gentleman's gold watch and packs them down into the commodious barrel of an old horse pistol.

He fires—you think the various wheels and springs fly thru the air—and presto!— he had spoken the truth—for behold! before the shattered mirror. is the very gold watch which he borrowed only five minutes before from the gentleman in the audience.

This watch trick has been staged in several different ways, such as by breaking a cheap duplicate up and either placing the parts in a pistol, or else dropping the parts for an alleged *cleaning* into a glass pitcher of milk. Of course we may as well explain right here that your watch was never harmed or taken apart or anything like that. By a so-called *magician's pass* palming, or other subterfuge, the borrowed watch was either dropped into a pocket in the back of

the table or perhaps of a chair, as shown in the diagram, from which pocket either the magician or his assistant later picks it up— while the wheels and other parts are taken out from another blind pocket on the back of the table or chair, and placed in the mortar and pounded up. The substitute watch parts are loaded into a false barrel under the main barrel of the pistol. A blank cartridge is used, about .22 calibre, which is fired thru the usual barrel on the top of the pistol. If this trick is performed with a mirror held by the attendant it can be arranged with a double-faced mirror mounted on a vertical shaft, the bottom of the shaft being fitted with a powerful spring, released at will by a push button. In one way or another, such as by having the mirror lie on the magician's table or otherwise, the borrowed watch is placed on the cracked mirror face, or else the watch is placed in between the false back and the perfect mirror of the second arrangement shown in the illustration, where a spring operated hammer is released by the attendant holding the mirror so as to smash the glass when the gun is fired by the magician.

One of the best methods of presenting this act is by means of a trick picture or mirror frame shown in detail at Fig. 6-B. This frame is easily arranged with a half-flap which can be released by a string by an assistant behind the back scene drop. The frame is mounted on the scene drop and the diagram shows by means of the dotted lines, how the magician walks over to the chair, drops the borrowed watch into a (*servante*) pocket on the back of the chair, and how a moment later, his clown assistant may amble in and lean against the chair, making funny faces at him, *et cetera,* and most important of all *securing the watch from the servante or pocket.* Shortly the clown wanders out thru the door and then walks up behind the screen to the spot where the frame is located, places the good watch within the frame by means of the hinged door and all that remains is for the magician to fire his pistol at the frame; the attendant pulls the thread releasing the hinged half-mirror in the front, disclosing some broken mirror pieces in the top part of the frame, with the watch hanging among them.

THE FAMOUS MILK-CAN TRICK AND STEEL BOILER ESCAPE

The top is made very massive looking with several rows of rivets and a series of heavy hinged hasps which are locked securely with heavy padlocks. This is one of the best tricks ever performed on the American stage. As the can is brimming full of water just before the cover is placed on it, and as the performer rightly states before hand, if he does not get out of the can before his breath holding capacity is up, he will be a dead one. But never fear he will not die so young—thanks to two or more wing nuts or else phoney rivet heads, nicely provided with holes to fit a key, like that used in the glass trunk mystery.

The *steel boiler escape* is a clever trick due to Oudini (not Houdini) a master performer with the handcuffs and other mys-

terious tricks which he has performed successfully on the American stage for several years. The steel boiler as shown in Fig. 8, is usually made by some boiler concern located in the town where the performance is to be held.

Sometimes he provides his own boiler and of course this is an easier and less nerve-racking way to stage the escape. The boiler is ordered made in a perfectly substantial manner with two iron bars crossed at right angles, the ends of the bars being drilled to receive padlocks.

But in many cases the performer actually does saw his way out, if the bars are not light enough for him to bend or break with his hands, or else with a bar of iron secreted on his person when he enters the boiler. Of course if he saws or bends the bars in half and pushes the pieces out thru the holes, which gives him his freedom, it is almost impossible for him to rejoin the pieces of iron bars by cement or otherwise in the short time allotted him for the escape, for the committee would undoubtedly, in examining the boiler and bars, find the points where they had been joined together. To get around this difficulty, the performer carefully examines and measures ahead of time the bars used in sealing the boiler and top and provides himself with two exactly similar bars. These additional bars, drilled of course for the padlocks, he secretes between the two cloth walls of his cabinet and after making his escape from the boiler, which may take from twenty to thirty minutes, he picks the padlocks off of the old bar pieces, and puts his own new bars into place in the holes and then snaps the padlocks in place on them. The pieces of old bars are hidden of course in the walls of the cabinet and at the signal given, the attendant pulls up the curtain and—Presto! there stands our hero, outside and not inside of the boiler.

MAN AND GIRL TRANSFORMATION

Changing a man to a girl or a girl to a man as the occupant of a magic box or coffin, has always amused and entertained theatre audiences. As P. T. Barnum, the famous showman said—"the public likes to be fooled." The illustration, Fig. 9, shows the method invariably employed in performing this trick, altho several variations of the apparatus here used have been ingeniously worked out by various stage performers. In the present case, the box is fitted with a right angle shelf, pivoted in the lower corner as shown. It is surprising how far this box can be placed from the back drop or curtain, and the escape or exchange with another actor made, by passing a plank thru a slit in the curtain directly back of the box.

In some disappearing tricks where a person steps into a suspended basket and after entering the basket he makes his escape by passing thru the bottom thru a trap door, is camouflaged or hidden from the view of the audience by the stairs up which the actor or actress walks. Mirrors are also used in many of these acts which reflect things in a most mysterious way, so that what seem to be tricks of *Hindu magic,* are tricks conceived in the mind of an enterprising stage performer or showman.

Electric Snow Storm

WE take a table glass, one of rather large size, and of good quality, and place it upside down upon the table. Then we tear up some dry blotting-paper or tissue paper, so that we have a quantity of little scraps at our disposal. When we make these scraps of paper fall down upon the glass, nothing particular or surprising will happen. Now we remove the scraps and rub the glass with a silk handkerchief.

The rubbing must be continued some time —that is, three or four minutes. Care must be observed to rub all parts of the glass, excepting the foot, by which we hold it.

Violent rubbing is not essential. Now we repeat our experiment with the scraps of paper.

We drop them from above upon the glass. While formerly the scraps did not adhere to the glass, they now do so. Our artificial snowflakes act like the natural ones, sticking where they fall.

Suddenly one of the scraps disengages itself. It does not simply fall down, but jumps away from the glass. Soon a second follows, a third and thus one after the other, till at last no scrap at all clings to the glass. None of them fell down; they jumped down, or

better, were repelled. Thus this experiment shows us that there is electric repulsion as well as electric attraction. The glass, although a non-conductor, did not exercise any influence upon the scraps of paper until it was electrified. But after being rubbed, it became charged; it attracted the paper scraps and kept them fast. After having held them for a little while, it repelled them again.

The success of this experiment will depend on two factors—the quality of the glass and the absence of moisture. The silk handkerchief may be warmed before use.

The Cause of Illusions

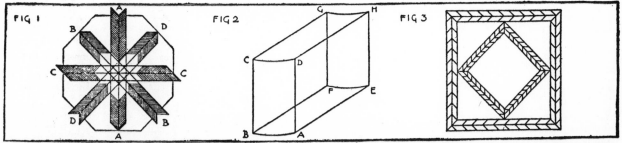

In the optical illusions shown on this page, we find that angle-illusion-figures reverse convexly or concavely near 150 or 170 in either direction. In Figs. 1 and 3 shown above composed by the artist G. Horowitz, the frames will be seen to alternate as convex and concave and remain so steadily, but when rotated around the center as a pivot, what was convex before becomes concave and vice versa, and they appear different to each eye. In Fig. 2 along the line G-H and A-B, the illusion changes from that of book lying book fashion, into that of a box with the top cover cut off. If viewed along the line B-H in Fig. 7 fashion, it will assume various positions as a square box with the top removed, or with its left hand wall removed, etc. These illusions may vary every five or six seconds with the fluctuation in blood pressure, which in this manner may affect the function of the neurons of the brain, thus affecting the understanding of the image. At least that is one theory.

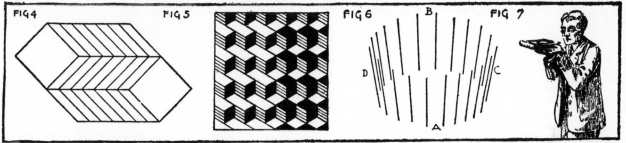

In Fig. 4 one angle seems convex and another concave. As one looks at the top or the bottom of the concave angle, it seems to waver between the two qualities. This is called an illusion, or in other words a "trick." The opinion held is that this is done by the brain which does not correctly represent the true image of the retina. Fig. 5 is very restless; truly shifting and "mocking"; the blocks now pointed in one direction will suddenly reverse. Fig. 6 viewed with one eye closed, as indicated at 7, shows the lines standing up (see "Psychology," by Professor R. S. Woodworth; and "Principles of Psychology," by Professor W. James). Horizontal lines can only be viewed in small parts at one time, while the vertical lines can be viewed entirely at one time. Hence the vertical lines as angles are seen as having the inner ends below and the far ends above the surface. Convexities and concavities remain so and change when the figures are rotated. All lines of black, white and spectrum colors singly or overlapping are clean cut. When horizontal and shaded they lose their identity. There is no "mocking" if one pupil is fixed upon any end of Fig. 4. If the other angles are uncovered and indirectly seen, they force the eye, reflexly, to view them by a "jump" of the orbit. Persistence of vision of the former image is still prevailing, while a new one is thrown upon the retina. A pupil focussed upon any structure and protected from irritation by indirect rays from other incompatible structures, gives no illusion.

The "Talking Table"

If the apparatus here described is fastened to the under-side of a dinner table it will set the table in vibration so that any number of persons putting their ears flat upon the table, will hear a person talking over the 'phone, if it is connected up as shown in the accompanying sketch.

A small piece of sheet brass is cut as shown in Fig. 1. A piece of soft iron wire, such as that used for cores of induction coils and about 6 inches long, is bent at one end as indicated at (A) Fig. 1 and put thru a hole in the center of the brass plate; the other end is bent into the form of a small hook. Next cut off about 2 inches of a cheap lead pencil and soak it in water till the lead will come out easily, then glue the pieces of pencil to the wire just above the hook. Take a piece of cigar-box wood and cut a piece about 1⅜ inches in the center so it will fit over the leadless pencil on the wire, and 2 holes to receive the two binding posts, Fig. 2. Glue the disc over the pencil on the wire near the upper end. The binding posts are then placed thru the other two holes. The pencil is now wound with No. 24 B. & S. silk or cotton covered wire, the ends of the wire being fastened to the two posts. A small weight, weighing about two or three ounces, is hung on the hook. The apparatus is then screwed to the under-side of the table and connected up to a microphone and battery.

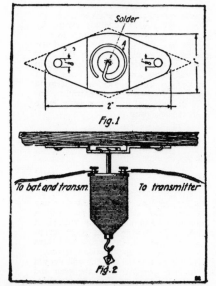

An Entertaining Wrinkle for the Electrical "Bug" to Try Out—the Talking Table. The Magnet Connects Up with a Microphone and Battery.

Balancing Egg

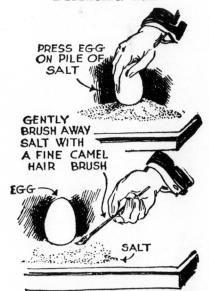

A very entertaining stunt for the dinner table is shown above. An egg is balanced in the center of a plate and stands perfectly. The method of performing the stunt is simple. Place a half teaspoon of salt in the center of the plate and press the egg lightly in the center of the salt. Then with the aid of a fine camel's hair brush slowly remove the salt from around the egg. At the completion of this operation the egg will seem to stand by itself.

The Magic Spirit Bell

PROFESSOR HARGRAVE was known to all magicians as the originator of many ingenious tricks and sleight-of-hand passes and consequently aroused a feeling of considerable jealousy among others in the same field of work which he himself was engaged in. When, however, he made arrangements to publish broadcast those of his more spectacular tricks, the Magicians' Council, an order of the "Black Art," as that science is known, attempted to stop him, but their efforts were fruitless.

By special courtesy this publication has secured his consent for placing some of his works before the public in such a way that the lay readers who are the least handy with tools can construct apparatus to duplicate his marvelous feats. With this end in view not only the "gift of gab," or magicians' "patter," as it is sometimes called, is given, but also the constructional data are given. Let us attend one of Prof. Hargrave's performances.

"Good-morning, ladies and gentlemen," ventured Professor Hargrave, as he stepped onto the stage in a recent performance at one of our largest theatres, "Evening, did you say?" he continued, "Oh, yes, to be sure it is, how absentminded I am. Well, what shall be your pleasure? This?" as he pointed to a beautiful bell hanging on a highly polished stand. "Very well."

Suiting his action to the words he reached for a pack of cards on one of the small tables and proceeded off the stage. Having

The "Mystery Bell"—The Magician Shows That the Bell as Well as the Hook Upon Which It Normally Hangs, Including the Stand Separating the Bell, Are All Separate and Independent Pieces, Having No Strings or Electric Wires Attached to Them; Yet When the Bell Is Replaced on the Stand and Combined With the Stand Support, It Taps Out the Answers to Various Questions Asked by the Audience. It's Easy When You Know How!!!

View of the Glass Bell, Which Can be Made From an Ordinary Chandelier Shade.

had the audience select three cards, he stepped back to the stage again. Carrying the bell forward in full view of the audience and placing the stand right down front, he exclaimed:

"Now, friends, I don't want to deceive you." He removed the hook from the rest of the stand; passing the hook to the public on one side of the stage and the bell down the other.

"Now examine those two articles carefully and note that there are no strings to deceive you; that hook is genuine silver. I bought it myself at Woolworth's jewelry counter, an emblem of the first thing I got when I appeared upon the stage some years ago from the enthusiastic manager." (To wit—the hook!)

By this time the bell had come back and Professor Hargrave continued: "The bell answers by ringing twice for *yes* and once for *no*." Then placing the hook into its position in the remainder of the stand, and resting the bell on its hook, he added: "Don't you, bell?" to the beautiful object of glass and metal.

The bell pealed forth two melodious sounds.

"Well, bell, suppose you tell me the number of spots which were on the first card I gave out? Seven? Very well. Did the lady choose hearts?"

The hammer rose and descended twice in succession.

"Seven of hearts. Was that correct, speak out, please?"

The victim answered in the affirmative.

"Thank you."

"Now, bell, will you please tell me the name of the next card? (You know I have to talk kindly to the Little Miss.) How many spots were on that card?"

One ring was the answer.

"Only one? Well, was it a spade?" The response was *yes* again.

"Ace of spades, was that right, sir?

Don't shake your head, because I'm too far away to hear it rattle."

"Now for the next card. Tell me the number of spots on that." Hargrave awaited an answer but no response from the bell. "What— don't you know?" The bell answered in the affirmative by ringing twice. "Well, tell me then." Again no

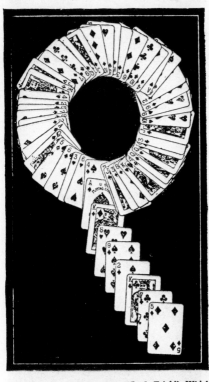

A Clever and Interesting "Card Trick" Which Anyone Can Perform at Parties and Evening Gatherings Without Lengthy Practise. The Performer Telling the Name of the Card Without Being Present. All That is Necessary Is to Know the Number of Cards in the Tail of the "Q" Formation.

response, whereupon the performer became excited, exclaiming: "I hope you will all excuse the bell, but I don't think she knows so we will have to go on with the rest of the performance." The patter then continues as long as desired.

THE CONSTRUCTION OF THE BELL AND STAND.

The stand consists of a long nickel-plated tube mounted on a tripod of the same material, with one wire running up each of two of the three legs, said wire connected to a large magnet made by winding eight layers of number eighteen double cotton covered magnet wire, on an iron core which does not extend all the way up the coil; but terminates within one inch of the end, a sleeve continuing the rest of the way. The coil is eight inches long and actuated by an assistant behind the scenes, a six volt current being used as the exciting force.

The hook is made of iron, nickel-plated, like the balance of the stand. When placed in position it acts as a core to the magnet concealed in the stand.

The bell is made of an ordinary electric light globe, which is fastened into a turned piece of wood (as shown in the illustration) with plaster of Paris. Through a small opening in the ring on top is passed a piece of soft iron bar, one end of which is connected to a lever-like piece of aluminum; the far end of this lever has a decorative piece of bone attached to its free end to act as a hammer.

Two wires lead thru the stand and down each of two of the legs, making contact with two plates concealed by the heavy rug.

When the stand is brought forward, it is carefully placed in position so as to make contact with the two plates, the bell then being tried before proceeding with the balance of the performance. The trial is made under cover of a little phrase, asking the bell to show how it answers. A typical magicians' forcing deck of cards being used, the assistant knows exactly what cards will be given out and goes thru the procedure as a regular matter of routine; pressing the key for each sound of the bell and the gong ringing at each break of the circuit.

It will be noted that when the soft iron core is attracted to the magnet, the hammer is pulled away from the bell, but on its sudden release the weight of the hammer allows it to swing downward, striking the bell just once.

TRICKS WITH THE "FIXED PACK"

This trick originated many years ago. It never fails to produce results. The cards are fixed in an orderly manner, and this order preserved—*the deck never being shuffled.* This order is very easily learned, and it is only necessary to see one card in the deck, either the top or the bottom card, to be able—in this manner, to tell the name or the position of any card in the deck.

First—the suits are learned in the following manner: Hearts, clubs, diamonds, spades, and then the following arrangement will be found very satisfactory: The cards are separated by three numbers; that is, one, four, seven, ten, thirteen, three, six, nine, etc., in which the King is thirteen, Queen twelve, Jack eleven and the Ace is one. In arranging the cards, they will fol-

low this manner: Ace of hearts, four of clubs, seven of diamonds, ten of spades, king of hearts, etc. In this way you can easily tell what the twelfth card in the deck will be and read the cards off without looking at them; also by giving a person a choice of any card in the deck, you will be able to discover just what that card was. For the "Q" trick, the cards are arranged in a definite manner. Any number in the circle and the number of cards in the tail changed after each performance. A person is instructed to count a certain number of cards up the tail and around the left side of the circular portion of the "Q" to suit himself. Then taking that card at which he stopped as number one, counting just as many cards but retracing his course, (except that this time he does not proceed down the tail), he continues around the circular position of the "Q," stopping in a similar position. There are eight cards in the tail—the person will proceed up the tail, around the left side of the "Q," stopping at, say, the 17th card. Taking this card as number one, he proceeds backward again, stopping at the seventeenth card again. The performer instantly tells him the card before he enters the room.

So much for the effect. Its mode of operation is simpler than the description of the trick and all that is necessary, is that the performer know the number of cards in the tail. Using the card from where the tail starts, as his starting point, he stops at the same card as the number of cards in the tail. In the example mentioned above, it would be the eighth card (inasmuch as there are eight cards in the tail) from the center position, that is, where the tail joins the "Q." A simple trial will readily convince.

The Steam Carousel

The little trick we will describe herewith is very interesting and if done right will give much enjoyment.

We need for this little experiment a bottle, two forks, two eggs, two thimbles, some wire and a pin.

Take the two eggs and empty the contents of same by drilling a small hole at one extremity of the egg and sucking out the contents. With a pair of pliers, make a harness with some wire around the eggs.

Take the thimbles and suspend them by means of the wire underneath the eggs as shown in our picture.

After having transformed these two eggshells into dirigible balloons, it becomes necessary to fill them half full with water. To do this, heat the eggshells gently and plunge them quickly in a pail of cold water. A certain quantity of water will enter into the eggs.

Now take the two forks and a cork and stick the two forks into the cork in which you have stuck a pin.

Next take a piece of money, place it on top of the bottle and place the cork with the two forks on top of the bottle so that

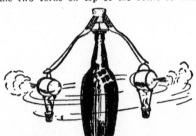

This Miniature Steam Carousel is Made From Two Egg Shells, Two Thimbles, Two Forks, a Pin and a Bottle, With Some Thin Wire or String to Tie the Parts Together. The Eggs Are Filled With Water, as Explained in the Article, While Some Cotton Soaked in Wood Alcohol is Placed Beneath Them and Ignited. The Steam Generated in the Egg Boilers Shooting Out From the Small Openings, Causes a Reaction on the Air and the Contraption Whirls Around Merrily.

it can rotate easily, being careful to balance the two forks exactly.

Attach to each fork a piece of wire and suspend from this piece of wire, the two eggshells. Put a little cotton into both of the thimbles and pour some wood alcohol on the cotton. If the two forks should not be absolutely balanced you can put little pieces of metal or glass in one of the thimbles, so as to have them absolutely in a free-balancing state. Now our apparatus is ready to function.

With a match, light the alcohol contained in the thimble and in a few seconds the water contained in the eggshells will begin to boil and you will see a little stream of steam escaping from each one of the holes.

On account of the reaction of the steam against the air, the carousel will begin to turn slowly first, gaining in momentum all the time until it turns quite quickly, not stopping until the alcohol is absolutely consumed or the water evaporated.

Optical Illusion

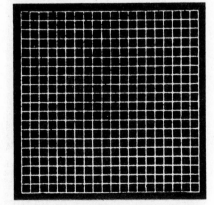

Look at the Grating at the left in the Regular Way. Then Hold it About One and One-half Inches Away. The White Lines Will Appear Dark. Look at it Through Small Hole in a Card. The Horizontal Lines Will Disappear. Looking Through the Hole at the Regular Focal Distance the Vertical Lines Disappear.

←

This Trick is Easily Performed by Pinching a Small Bit of Skin Between the Box and the Container of a Safety Match Box. If the Hand is Now Bent, the Box Will Immediately Fly Upright.

➡

Match Box Trick

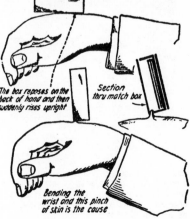

The box reposes on the back of hand and then suddenly rises upright

Section thru match box

Bending the wrist and this pinch of skin is the cause

The Magic "Fire-Bowl"

A SHORT time after I stepped off the train, I arrived at the pretty Long Island home of Professor Henri Hargrave, the noted magician. The servant admitted me a few moments later, and ushered me into the professor's study, requesting that I make myself at home. Somehow or other I never was able to do this when there are surroundings of the same nature as those at the Hargrave estate, consequently the servant's invitation was, I am afraid, superfluous.

The spacious study filled with weird, mysterious objects was now under scrutiny, each piece of workmanship was critically examined. While thus engaged the Professor entered, just as I turned to meet him.

"Well, well, how are you?" he exclaimed, presenting his hand in a hearty shake. "Have a chair, have a cigar, have a—— What can I do for you?"

These questions were fired at me so quickly, I stood there wondering which one to answer, and while still pondering, altho for only a short time, Professor Hargrave thrust one of the cigars between my teeth, eliminating the necessity of answering his inquiries.

After a few puffs on his cigar, he rose to his feet and said, "Well, 'Old Timer'—what shall we give them this time? Will the 'fire-bowl' do?"

I nodded in the affirmative.

"Don't shake your head, because I can't hear it rattle," he added jocularly, repairing to the back of the study.

A few moments later he stepped forward

Making Fire While You Wait and So Simple That Anyone Can Do It. Read on MacDuff, Read On.

While thus engaged with his little epigram, he lifted a cover from the table nearby and placing it on the bowl, extinguished the mass of flaming gases. Removing the cover again with the same speed which characterized all his motions I beheld the same bowl, which only a moment before was belching forth streams of fire, full of flowers of all hues and shapes!

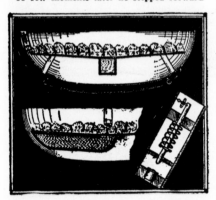

The Above Drawing Depicts the Construction of the "Fire-Bowl." The Tube Containing Alcohol Is Seen Slightly Inclined, Likewise, the Position of the Pistol-Like Device for Setting Off the Inflammable Mass. Slight Pressure on the String Is Sufficient to Cause the Mass to Burn, Its Flames Reaching to a Height of Four Feet.

waving a large red cloth in his hands. Showing both sides of this repeatedly, he suddenly produced from its folds a nickel plated bowl, from which streamers of fire poured forth to lick the ceiling.

"You will note that there is very little 'gift of gab' necessary for this trick. It depends more on the result than on the ability to talk. I've performed this same stunt before all the crowned heads of India, the big heads of America and the boneheads of Germany, and it never fails to produce an effect short of miraculous."

Note How the "Fire-Bowl" Is Suspended from the Belt. It's Great to Have a Little Heat Under the Belt in These Days of "Prohib.," and Just Imagine!—"Real Alcohol" Is Used as Fuel."

Placing the bowl upon the table and drawing his chair alongside of mine, he said, "Do you think that will do?" and seeing that no reply was forthcoming, he added, "I think so. But what's the matter with your 'weed,' is it out again?"

This, in reference to my cigar, which I had forgotten about during the performance. Lighting up both our cigars, he continued with his discourse.

"I think that the best way that I can explain the trick is to show you how it is done, and then you will be more able to grasp the meaning of the various parts and their relation to each other, together with their proper functioning."

Reaching for the bowl on the table he hung it from his vest under his coat in such a position that it covered the lower left vest pocket—then secured the cloth. Waving it in such a manner that one is convinced that there is nothing on either side, he slung it over one arm, covering, in this way the movement of the other hand in its journey to the bowl. This time it was quite apparent that the bowl did not come from mid-air as it seemed to do originally; but the clever manipulations which the performer executed could only have been gained thru practice.

"You see," he exclaimed, removing the bowl from the table, upon which he had replaced it, and handing it to me, "The bowl is suspended from this little hook on the edge, from the performer's belt, and held in a vertical position, being covered by his coat. In its center you will note a small hollow, saucer-like affair, which communicates directly with a long tube. This tube slopes a trifle so as to allow its contents to

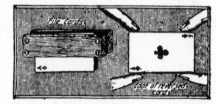

Method of Making a Deck of Cards Which You Should Never Use in a Poker Game Unless You Care Nothing for Your Life. The Cards Clamped in a Wooden Vise Are Shaved Down at One End, Whence by Simply Reversing Any Card It May Instantly Be Withdrawn from the Deck, the Fingers Being Placed as Shown.

leak out when the bowl is placed on a level keel. The tube is of course filled with alcohol or some other inflammable material, in an upright position, whence it acts much the same as a bottle with its cork removed.

"Gently sloping toward the central tube receptacle is a round sheet of asbestos, covered with a layer of absorbent cotton fastened in place by wire, and sewed onto the asbestos. The asbestos sheet holds its position by virtue of several sheet iron legs, which are fastened to the bowl with ordinary solder.

"So much for the bowl and its reservoir. Now we come to the method of igniting the inflammable mass. This consists of a simple holder which will take an ordinary blank cartridge, mounted on the base, at one end. A steel plunger, which is free to slide between two bearings; has been sharpened at one end (the end which sets off the cartridge), and has a notch filed in the other end. This notch is filed in the rod in such a way that a small, flat piece of brass (also placed in a bearing of its own) will hold the rod back until it is ready to be discharged. In other words it acts as a trigger. Around the rod is coiled a stiff piece of steel or better still, a steel spring. A flat piece of metal is then adjusted to the rod to hold the spring in place; it being held at the other extremity by the bearing. A glance at the accompanying sketches will fix things clearly in your mind.

"To the trigger is attached a piece of strong silk. This is led out thru a tiny hole in the side of the bowl made for that purpose, passing thru two holes in the small one-quarter inch legs. It is then fastened to a button on the other side of the bowl.

Detail of the "Fire-Bowl" Trick, Showing How the Flowers Are Concealed in a False Compartment.

"Before commencing the trick, a blank cartridge is prepared by first removing the hard cardboard in the end of the shell.

This is replaced with tissue paper after the powder has been loosened. It is then inserted into the holder, the spring pulled back, and the trigger set. The cotton in the bowl is now saturated with alcohol and sprinkled with ordinary salt (sodium chlorid). This gives a pretty yellowish tint to the flames, after the production of the fire bowl. The bowl is now placed in a vertical position, and the well in the center filled with alcohol so that there will be enough alcohol left to burn for quite some time.

"When the bowl is presented, it is then only necessary to pull on the string which releases the firing pin; this in turn explodes the cartridge, the latter not going off with a report—but burning like a slow flashlight powder. When this occurs, the cotton impregnated with alcohol and salt is set on fire and burns as you have just seen."

"Yes, but how about the flowers?" I intervened.

"We are just coming to that. The top as you will note is made up seemingly of one piece but in reality two. Inside the false top are arranged large quantities of silk flowers, each of which has a spring inside of it so as to insure perfect opening the moment they are released. This effect is obtained by placing the two tops on the bowl together. (They being held so by a hook-like affair which passes thru the bottom plate in a slot made for it, and held there by giving it a slight turn. On removing it again only one top is taken away, thus giving rise to the rush of flowers.

"Here are a few sketches which will help make it clear; you may take them if they will help any."

Thus concluded the magician's discourse on his Fire-Bowl mystery.

AN INTERESTING CARD TRICK

The Universal Pack: A pack of cards similar to that made by any leading magic supply house, which is universal in its use

and the fake not easily detected, is made very simply. Take a deck of cards (a straight deck), which has a plain back, in other words, a back which lacks a margin. These are clamped rigidly between two blocks of wood, the latter having been shaved down so as to be quite smooth and the cards and wood all flushed together at one edge. A file is now passed over the edge, shaving in this way the cards and wood at the same time, thus preventing any marring or turned edges. Some very fine sand paper is now applied to the edge, finishing the job smoothly. The cards may project at one end and be filed off.

It will be noted that all the cards are narrower at one end than at the other, but only *slightly* so, thus making detection almost impossible. The cards are then shuffled and presented to the victim, who draws one, looks at it and replaces it in the pack, whence they are shuffled again. During the operation, however, the performer reverses the deck in his hand and when the card is replaced, it is only necessary to pass the fingers along the edges of the cards, when one card, the card chosen, will be withdrawn, due to the fact that it is wider than the rest of the deck, it having been replaced in the reversed position. It is then brought to the top and may be presented in any way thought desirable.

Likewise, all four aces may be inserted into the pack, reversed, of course, and completely shuffled, and with one cut may be brought to the top and dealt off. The pack can also be divided into red cards and black cards, with one cut in this case; all the red cards should be reversed before commencing the trick. After shuffling thoroughly the performer runs his fingers along the edge of the cards several times to insure perfect separation, and then with one cut he is able to divide the "reds" from the "blacks."

Countless other stunts may be performed in a similar manner, taking advantage of this prepared deck.

Thimble Ice Factory

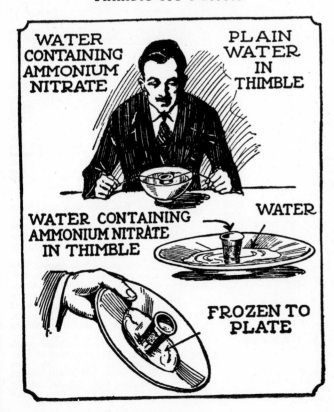

WATER CONTAINING AMMONIUM NITRATE

PLAIN WATER IN THIMBLE

WATER CONTAINING AMMONIUM NITRATE IN THIMBLE

WATER

FROZEN TO PLATE

It is a Simple Matter to Make Ice at Home, Using a Solution of Freshly Prepared Ammonium Nitrate. The Solution may be put in a Bowl and Water may be put in a Thimble or the Solution may be put in a Thimble and a Few Drops of Water put on the Plate as illustrated.

Parlor Trick

PLACE MATCH IN CRACK IN TABLE AND BALANCE COIN ON IT WITH CIGARETTE PAPER BENEATH

MOISTEN FINGERS AND STRIKE PAPER WITH MOVEMENT AS INDICATED BY ARROW. COIN REMAINS BALANCED ON MATCH STICK.

It is Comparatively Easy to Balance a Coin on the End of a Match if the Principle Shown Above is Followed. The Stunt is Quite Mystifying.

The "Talking Skull"

ON one of these fine mornings when the snow and slush prevents traffic in the city streets, an ideal way for killing time (which I never have) occurred to me, namely, to see about another—er—bit of news from Professor Hargrave. Scurrying to his room

well forward and the back of the head in the region of the great foramen on a sort of a block. You could look all around it. After this cursory examination, I turned to the professor and said, "It looks mighty fine but kind of scarecrow like. What does it do?" "N-O-T-H-I-N-G." This in a

ment and then exclaimed, "What was that?" Again the sound and a pleased twinkle in the eyes of the professor. Ah! Now I knew what it was! Tip-toeing up to the skull, I lifted it easily in order to disconnect the wires which I thought were leading to it. To my amazement, it emitted

What the ——? ——? Exclamations of This Nature and Then Some, Emanate from "Friend Hubby" When Wifey Tries the "Talking Skull" Trick On Him.
This Is One of the Finest Tricks (Undetectable) for Parlor Magic.

in a New York hotel, where he lives during the winter season, as the railroad traffic is abominable, I found him busy over the remains of some departed friend.

There on the table with tools lying all around it, rested a "skull"—of what he claimed to be that of his Mother-in-law (sob stuff). After the casual greeting, he begged me to be seated while he proceeded to dismember the cranial vault and then tinkered around it some more. All the while he did not say a word. Finally, he exclaimed, "There now, I've got it," and then looking toward me, he remarked—"I didn't expect you this early, but I finally got it all set up for you. How do you like it?" I must say that the skull seemed very impressive. There it stood with its teeth grinning at me and the most villainous look upon its face. It was reposing quietly on a glass shelf suspended about six inches above a polished table by means of four wires coming down from a bracket-like arrangement.

The point of its chin rested

loud weird voice which I knew never came from the professor. The voice was in that very room—in front of me—on the sides—all around me! I trembled a mo-

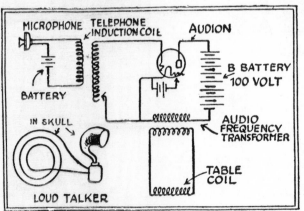

A Detectaphone Tells the Operator What Is Going on in the Room. The Operator Then Transmits His Answer Which is Amplified In the Audion Cabinet. By Induction the Loud Talker in the Skull Answers. No Connections Lead to the Skull.

a fearful howl which came from right within the inside. Did I drop it? Well I should say so. To go into a dimly lighted room and see a skull and in lifting it up hear it talk is enough to make anybody depart, rather in peace than in pieces.

In my haste to get away, I was caught by the professor, just as I stumbled over a little footstool. Turning me around quickly, he stated, "That is my new trick and it's extremely simple, too. You see, you can use this in conjunction with any card trick, clairvoyant act, or in fact any fortune telling or other scheme."

"The skull has absolutely no electrical connections to it of any sort," he continued as he lifted it from the table, passing his hands all around it, back and in front, and allowing me to examine it. Then continuing, he stated—"Still, when I talk to it, it will answer back," and addressing the skull, said, "How do you do, Mother-in-law?" "How do I do what?" came back the gruff reply. Then, addressing me, "Here, you hold her, while I talk to her, or place her on the table if you desire, she's too desperate for me." Continuing his conversation with the skull, he added, "Do anything?"—"I would like to do you," came back the snappy retort.

Well, that was enough. I wanted to see how it was done. So going over to the side and examining the wires which held up the plate, I was surprised to see the professor remove the glass shelf and proceed to question the skull and receive just as many answers to his queries as he had received before.

"Come, don't keep me in suspense!" I exclaimed. "How is it done, that is just what I want."

"Well," he said, "very simple, nothing to it, and I am really surprised that more magicians do not carry a device of this nature around with their usual outfit."

Removing the top portion of the skull, he showed me simply a coil of wire arranged so as to fit snugly inside the vault and consisting of 300 turns of No. 38 enameled magnet wire connected to a telephone receiver having a horn attached to the hard rubber cap. Looking at it I could see no wire coming from it and finally an idea beamed!!! "INDUCTION?" I asked.

"Exactly," he exclaimed, "and very simple at that. You were examining the glass shelf and the wires leading to it and like everyone else discovered nothing, because there is nothing there to discover. The en-

tire trick rests not in the glass shelf but in the table under it." Lifting this up and turning it over, he showed me a microphone attached to a large diaphragm. "That is the communicating phone by means of which my assistant in the other room knows of the skull's affairs."

This microphone was connected to two wires which ran down to two metallic floor connectors and in series with a battery and a pair of phones to his assistant in another room. Two other wires running up the leg of the table terminated in a coil, about 1½ feet in diameter, consisting of 300 turns of No. 22 D. C. C. magnet wire. To all appearances this was all there was to the apparatus, but following the professor from the room, I came upon the *operator-in-chief* of the device. There he sat, with a pair of phones clamped over his ears enjoying a hearty laugh.

A telephone transmitter was fastened to the table and this in series with the typical audion amplifier. This is how he managed to get such a powerful voice, the professor explained. You see, even the finest telephone transmitter is capable of delivering but a very small amount of current. In order, therefore, to get sufficient induction in the coil inside the skull, at least enough to make the sound emitted by the 75 ohm loud-talker sonorous enough to be heard, we must employ an amplifying circuit. The ordinary vacuum tube is used and connected directly with the small induction coil to the transmitter. This will magnify any voice modulations about 400 times with a two-

stage amplifier, i.e., an amplifier using two bulbs. This current then passes into the large table coil. The operator in this room can hear everything you say because of the dictagraph device under the table made possible by use of the *Skinderviken* transmitter button, a minute transmitter answering the purpose very nicely. Upon hearing your question and giving sufficient thought to the matter (if any thought is necessary), he formulates an answer. This then is transmitted into the table coil and by *induction* is heard from the loud-talker within the skull.

"It is, I believe, the simplest trick that has ever been used," said Professor Hargrave," and is original in the present adoption, inasmuch as the voice is amplified, which is contrary to other devices of similar nature. The transformer used in the diagram which I am about to draw is the ordinary audio-frequency iron-core transformer used in radio circuits. For a one-stage amplifier, employing only one bulb, this is entirely unnecessary. An ordinary telephone transformer answers the purpose very well. A heavy duty transmitter is used at this end of the line, and a *Skinderviken* microphone button at the other end (the skull end). A good 75 ohm telephone receiver, such as that built by the leading telephone companies, answers for the loud-talker, as a horn is added to it. Carefully checking over of the diagram will show exactly the set-up and arrangement of the apparatus, together with dimensions necessary for duplicating this stunt."

Mysterious Shadow Illusion

Novel Stage Effect Gained with the Aid of Lighting Plan

In the illustration above a large silhouette is seen on a screen. The lights are dimmed and the actress steps out from behind the screen while the shadow still remains. The screen is removed from the stage with the shadow still in place. The illusion is gained by using a projector in connection with the concentrated silhouetting lights in front of the screen. The method is illustrated in the sketch. The actress poses in the predetermined position. The audience sees her shadow. The lights fade but the silhouette remains, thanks to the projector which casts the same silhouette of the actress which is on the slide upon the screen. In the last act the man and girl carry the screen with their shadows still in place off the stage. Two life-sized silhouettes are back of the screen, illuminated by small lights, as shown.

The Rapping Hand

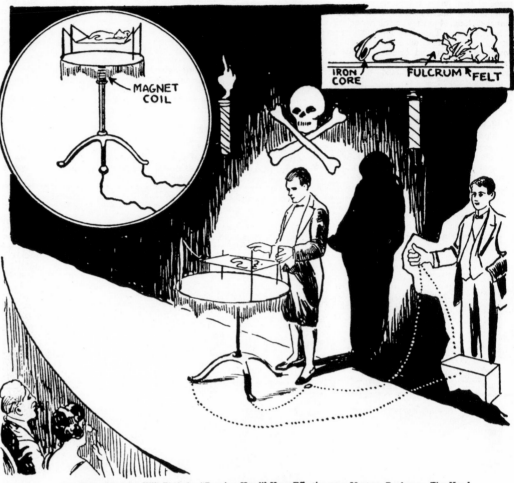

The Home Magician Will Find the "Rapping Hand" Very Effective as a Mystery Producer. The Hand is "Worked" by an Electro-magnet, the Circuit Being Closed by a Confederate, Usually.

PROFESSOR HARGRAVE had been very busy on some new research for quite a while and I couldn't find opportunity to see him as often as I desired, but as fate would have it we finally ran into each other, so to speak, at a New York playhouse where he had gone to meet an old friend of his, now entertaining the public with a "Magic Act."

A short time after this we were en route to his Long Island home again where he had "something new." "Now, old timer," he exclaimed, after we had made ourselves comfortable, "I have a little device here which has been *killed*, or practically so, by the magical profession. It is very clever and quite undetectable and will come in very handy, particularly now when the *Ouija Board, Spiritual Seances, Rappings*, etc., are being held so reverently. Wealth, sport and fun can be obtained from the same. Just to demonstrate," he continued, "you see here we have an ordinary hand made of wax or molded wax composition. Look it over and examine it carefully. You will note that there are no springs, wires, threads or in fact anything connected to it now or at any time.

"I take this hand and place it upon this glass plate, I allow you to select any card from the deck, you return it. There, that's fine! By placing the deck into this little black bag I can know the name of your card by only asking the rapping hand what it was, using the same code that was used in the *Bell Trick* described some time ago. You will remember that two rings signified YES and one NO. You don't believe it? Well, just to demonstrate."

Professor Hargrave had now placed the molded wax hand upon the glass plate which he held about four inches above the table. He next proceeded to adjust four little wires at the ends of which were small hook-like formations passing thru holes in the corner of the plate so that it was suspended horizontally. At the other end the wires were attached to four posts screwed into the table. Then continuing to address the hand he said, "Will you tell this gentleman by raps the number of spots which appeared on the card he had just chosen?" Immediately at the word of command the hand tapped out the answer, seven clear distinct raps, on the glass table.

I grasped for the hand, lifted it from the plate. There were no strings, no wires, or anything else connected to it. The Pro-

fessor laughed at my chagrin in not finding something I had expected and again reached for the hand. Replacing this he readdressed the hand.

"Was that card a diamond?" The answer in the affirmative convinced me that it *was a* pretty good stunt.

I had seen too many of the Professor's tricks, however, to become extremely excited or marvel at the results, although they couldn't be described with the same effect that they have when presented. To see a hand and wrist lying on the table rap out an answer to any question you may ask of it, provided the answer can be given as either "yes" or "no," is an extremely wonderful bit of entertainment. The mystery then continued in the shape of a fortune telling stunt until my strained eyes refused to watch any longer. The Professor then took the hand off the glass plate, disconnected the latter from the suspending wires and placed it on the regular magician's table, where he was demonstrating his trick.

We then stepped over to an adjoining library table, sat down and the Prince of Magicians busied himself with a fresh cigar. This tedious operation completed, he opened a drawer and leisurely extracted several sheets of paper and a pencil. Then laying these in front of him he proceeded to sharpen a pencil, another tedious operation, successfully completed after several *bad breaks*. "Well, now," Hargrave ejacu-

lated suddenly, "I suppose you would like to know all about this, wouldn't you?"

Tap—tap—tap. Wheeling around quickly I noticed the hand on the table rapping out a regular rat—tat—tat in time with music with which a phonograph in a distant part of the house was permeating the atmosphere. "Well, I'll be ——." The hand stopped short. "Here, here," the Professor interrupted, before I had gone much further, "you will scare it." It started again; slowly at first, however, then with increasing rapidity until the sound was more like machine gun discharges than anything I have ever heard. "All right, that will do," Hargrave shouted in a commanding voice, and the hand, mysteriously affected, now quieted down.

"Now to proceed with the work in hand. You wanted to know how this was done. Well, here it is. You see it is very simple. That hand is simply an ordinary wax model procured from many a store in the larger cities. It is sometimes used for demonstrating the quality of gloves and—sometimes—various other things, and is comparatively cheap, financially speaking. The model hand of wax is carefully balanced so that it is just a little heavier at the wrist than at the finger tips. The finger tips have been drilled open and iron cores inserted into two of them, the wax, of course, being carefully smoothed over the holes made for these cores. Iron wire answers the purpose very well. Of course, a hand must be obtained which will have a peculiar position such as shown in the photograph which you have there. This allows for a reasonable rocking motion and results in the subsequent raps.

"The table is arranged practically the same as in various other stunts of mine, namely, two wires travel up the legs and terminate at the top in an electromagnet 6 inches long, 4 inches in diameter, having a 1-inch core. This is wound with No. 18 D. C. C. magnet wire, making quite a powerful magnet and inserted in the table as shown in the diagram. When an electrical contact is completed thru a conveniently located storage battery by means of switches or buttons well within reach, sufficient magnetism is created to tip the hand over on to its finger tips and cause it to tap out the desired answer, the glass

table not affecting or disturbing the magnetic effect. The buttons as you see are connected in parallel to the same wires and so placed that I can move around and yet control the hand without it being noticed. There is no skill required in the making of the table and its wiring is simpler yet. The contacts in the legs are arranged so that the table may at all times be moved without creating suspicion and yet when placed over the floor plates immediately becomes operative.

"Four posts are placed in the table top and thin flexible wires of the same size are fastened to them. These posts may be of wood or may be nickel-plated as desired. The wires fasten into the four glass corners of the glass table, thru which tiny holes have been drilled or other suitable fastening means substituted which fastening means do not have to be very elaborate,

as the weight of the arm and hand is quite negligible."

"That is all very fine, Professor," I said, "but how did you know what card I had chosen from the deck?" "My dear man," he continued, "you are a worse magician than I thought you were. Only a short time ago I told you of the universal pack and here you turn right around and forget it. In addition, you will find that the hand will rap better upon the table, causing a louder sound than on the glass, and sometimes the effect is clearly enhanced if this is done." "Yes, but what made it tap in time with the music when you were sitting at the table?" "Look under the table," he said, "and you will see." A telegraph key in a convenient position revealed the answer. This accounted for the speed of the taps transmitted.

Ghost Spectacle for Amateur Stage

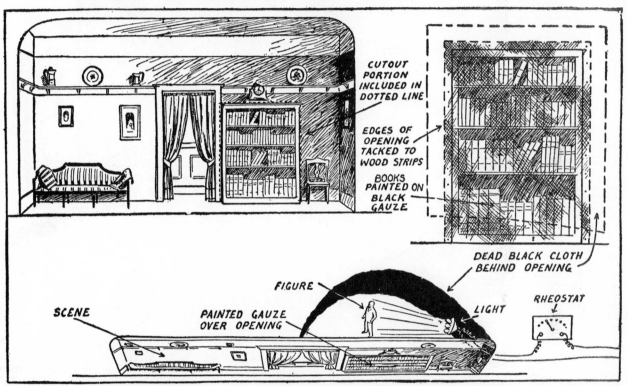

Many times amateur productions on the stage are put to it to show a ghost or apparition. A simple method of creating the illusion is to take a spot in the back drop, say a book case, cut out the regular canvas upon which it is painted and substitute theatrical gauze. Paint the same piece of furniture on the gauze and drop a solid black drop behind it. When the apparition is supposed to appear it is only necessary to place the figure behind the gauze, darken the stage lights and throw light on the figure. Thus the figure is seen through the piece of furniture. He disappears when the lights are turned up, and the light is taken off the figure.

"Spirit" Slate-Writing

Two thin slates are brought forth and offered for examination by the audience. The operator then places in between the two plates a small piece of chalk and hands the two slates to someone (it does not matter whom) to tie with a string or seal all around with sealing-wax. After a few minutes or so, the slates are taken apart and Presto! there is found a message from the "spirit world" written with the chalk, which was placed in there by the "Medium."

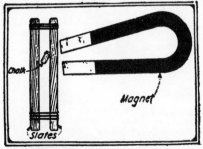

"Spirit" Slate Writing May Be Performed With This Simple Apparatus. The Chalk-Container Could Very Well Be a Small Perforated Ball Filled With Powdered Chalk. The Slates Should Be Held Horizontally.

The way it is done follows:

The chalk is of special formation; it is made of chalk dust mixed with iron-filings and a little glue. A strong (need not be very big) magnet is used to make the chalk move and write the message. The "Medium" located the chalk by tipping the slates to one corner and placing the magnet under it.

This works better in the dark for the simple reason that the people will not notice the magnet and its use. The darker the better.

The Mystic Roulette Wheel

SPRING had come, but very late, it being toward the latter part of May when I decided to take an unannounced trip to Professor Hargrave's home. Generally he was not to be found

there, except by appointment, but this time I was willing to risk it.

The butler at Prof. Hargrave's home knew me by this time, so it was unnecessary for him to announce me when I event-

ually arrived at the Professor's estate. I was ushered into a room which had been changed somewhat since my last visit, and immediately my attention was centered upon a group at a pretty checkerboard-like

The Mysterious Roulette Wheel Kept Professor Hargrave's Guests On the Alert for Many Hours, After they Had All Lost Their Piles of Gold He Explained How He Could Stop the Wheel At Any Point Desired and Then . . . Returned Their Money.

REVOLVING TOP

BRASS

MAGNET

table. Their attention was riveted to the center of the table where a roulette wheel was merrily spinning. Little had I ever thought or even dreamed that Professor Hargrave's home was used as a decoy to harbor roulette fiends.

Looking around the room in an attempt to find the Professor with his hypnotic smile, I could notice him nowhere, neither was my entrance observed by those at the game. A few minutes later I found myself just as interested in the merry spinning of Dame Fortune's wheel, perhaps even more so than my companions around me; so wishing to be in style, I placed my money on various numbers and took a chance with the rest, sometimes winning, but more often losing!

A few minutes at this and the Professor entered, altho I was not aware of his presence. Patting me on the back, he exclaimed, "So, there you are, old timer, why didn't you announce your coming? You see, now I have nothing ready for you. I cannot show you a thing while attempting to entertain my guests, so I think you had better stop in tomorrow or perhaps the day following at this hour."

Wondering if this was a polite way of getting rid of me or whether he didn't want to see me lose my money, I answered, "All right, Professor, I will be very glad to see you on the morrow; I guess I will be going now." "Oh, no," he added, "you might just as well stay, now that you are here, and enjoy yourself for the rest of the evening. I did not mean that as a polite retreat." Then leaning over to the roulette wheel, he placed his money on number nine as winner, but much to his apparent dismay, he lost, and continued to do so until he became a very heavy loser. Meanwhile, I had begun to reap the benefits of his and the other guests' losses.

Later as the game progressed, the Professor won one round and then lost two again in succession. After that fate seemed to travel in his direction; every time he played, it seemed as tho the numbers would come out expressly for his benefit; until even I. O. U's were being passed around the table.

All the good luck which had beset me until this time, suddenly melted and I was only contributing to the popularity of the Professor's coin, heaped high at his corner of the table. At last to break the monotony of the silence which had ensued, the Professor said: "Come, we've had enough of this," and alloted to each one the same sum of money they had at the beginning of the game. We wondered what had happened, open mouthed with amazement, all refusing the money, claiming that he had won it and therefore had a perfect right to keep it, but our requests only fell upon deaf ears.

"You have all been a bunch of fools, dupes, easy victims to a clever contrivance," the Professor began. "Why, that table is faked, and I can make it stop at any number I desire. In order to prove it to you—you see that the disc now is absolutely stationary, yet by wafting a little air, like this, across its surface (an appropriate movement of his hand reinforced his statement), I can make it move just as I desire."

We were awed by the disc moving, seemingly of its own accord. Immediately, I thought of strings, springs, or electricity, and lifting up the wheel, I examined it carefully, but there were no *two electrical contacts* anywhere similar to those in his other features. Replacing the wheel and spinning it, I requested that he stop it at figure "1." A short time later, when its momentum had died down sufficiently, it came to a stop at the number "1" desired.

On hands and knees, I crept under the fancy table to look for push buttons or other things which might give me a clue as to the operation of the mystic roulette wheel. Not a sign! A rapid scout thru the rooms skirting the one we were in convinced me that there was no external operator. How then could it work? I surely should have known enough of the Professor's apparatus by this time to attempt to see thru the thin veil of disguise which he used to conceal his instruments, but no such luck this time.

Our puzzled faces grew even more perplexed when the Professor burst out in an uproarious laugh, "Simple; why, it's so simple," he ejaculated. Taking the wheel itself from its suspended pin, he stated: "Now this wheel is 12 inches in diameter, perfectly balanced, having a jewel bearing or a cup shape bearing in one end which rests upon this pointed steel rod. There are no wires leading to the wheel itself, but under the arrow at this end is a curved flat piece of soft iron. This is balanced by a piece of copper at the opposite end similarly placed. The entire bottom is then covered over with a thin piece of black paper and varnished so that the iron and copper embodied in the wood base will not be seen in the event that the wheel be removed.

"The disc upon which it rotates is numbered as you see from 1 to 10, and in the false bottom of the table is the mechanism which controls the wheel. This mechanism chiefly consists of ten electric bell magnets taken from ordinary electric bells, and so mounted that they will act directly upon the iron base inserted into the wheel. Thus when an electric circuit is made thru any of the magnets, the wheel naturally stops at that point, being first slowly retarded and then held in place (due to the relatively long iron armature). In order, however, that the action be invisible to the spectators, the wheel is allowed to slow down considerably so that it barely moves along.

In the false bottom of the table likewise, is the required battery. Here, three ordinary dry cells are employed, altho more compact units could be used. As to the wiring, I shall show you this presently."

Releasing the catch on the side of the table, he lifted the cover off, much the same as one opens a phonograph box. The wiring there was clearly apparent. "You have noted by this time," he added, "that the table is made up of small brass squares, fastened to the wood seemingly for an artistic effect, but mainly for concealing the method of making contact to the magnets. *This consists in shorting two adjacent brass squares.* These are all placed on the diagonal, as shown in this little sketch. It is very simple now for me to place my hand over the required square and when the wheel slows down sufficiently to allow the ring on my finger to make contact between the two squares, which excites the respective magnet. This accounts for the wheel stopping at the place I desire. Incidentally, if I should energize the magnet following the one where the wheel has stopped by placing my finger across those contacts, the wheel will move forward due to the action of the magnets making a sort of an electric motor from the device."

Closing the cabinet he showed how, by placing his ring between two adjacent points, and running his hand across the table in a careless sort of manner, he could cause the roulette wheel to rotate with increasing speed every time he repeated this procedure. "It can readily be stopped instantly by just going backward, like this," and demonstrated that by passing his hand along adjacent squares in an opposite direction, brought the wheel to practically an immediate stop. "Neither of these systems are generally used because of their very perceptible fraudulent trait. For that reason, the wheel is always allowed to slow down sufficiently before the current is permitted to flow thru the magnets."

The visitors eventually left, and before I went I said: "Can you give me a diagram of the hook-up of that outfit, Professor?" "With the utmost of pleasure," he answered, and scribbled down the diagrams which we are able to reproduce here.

"By the way, Old Timer, I've received quite a number of letters from individuals who think that I am revealing the secrets of the magic profession, but I would like to state here that all my experiments have been *original with me*, and in all my years in the magic field I have never come across any similar ones. It may be that since I have retired some devices apparently similar to mine have come out, but I wish to state here that I will attempt to keep my devices strictly within new and unknown fields, and in no way will I attempt to present to the public sleights of hand or 'Black Art' tricks, which are so old that they have whiskers sprouting out all over them. Some of them would do good to get shaved at least once every hundred years." "I've noticed that also," I added, "but every knock is a boost, you know." Then thanking him for the pleasant evening I had enjoyed, I departed. More anon.

"Silvered Egg"

If an egg is thoroughly blackened in a flame and dropped in water it takes an iridescence like silver.

Inertia Experiment

If a dime is placed on top of a stiff hoop of paper which rests on a bottle top as shown, and the hoop removed by a quick sidewise blow the dime falls in the bottle.

Orange Fireworks

If the juice from an orange peel is thrown into a candle flame, fireworks result.

The Coin Wand

PROFESSOR HARGRAVE had not yet recovered from the effects of his long vacation, when I pounced in on him just prior to a terrific thunderstorm which a short time later enshrouded the entire villa in a veil of darkness, except at the frequent intervals in which livid lightning flashes illuminated the scene, each flash being accompanied by an incessant roar a second or so later, proving that the storm was very close. After answering each other's questions for half an hour or so, the storm abated sufficiently to allow us to proceed with the main mission of my errand.

Hargrave answered my question with, "Do you know, old timer, when I go away on a vacation I take a complete rest and do not attempt to ferret out any further mys-

millions of particles of this silver substance in a pure state, exactly identical with the coin content! If all of this silver which is annually rubbed off coins could be collected, we would be quite wealthy, but meanwhile we can collect all that is floating around us."

So saying he swept his wand thru the air and there—lo and behold—was a coin right at the end of that instrument! With a quick shake the coin could be heard clattering into the hat, to meet its mate, and before I knew it he had collected 12 to 14 coins.

"You see if it weren't for the noise made by the coins falling into the hat you could scarcely hear them." After assuring me that the coins were not counterfeit, I requested to examine the wand which he did not hesitate to let me do. There was noth-

possible and over-lap each other. The little spring holds them in a closed position so that they cannot be seen unless the wand is in operating condition. The springs are mounted as you can readily see by this rough sketch enabling this position to be maintained. The wand itself is ½ inch in diameter, which is amply sufficient to conceal the half dollar. At the same time when the coin opens, it projects on both sides, giving rise to the illusion that the coin is being held at the end of the wand in some manner not readily ascertained, which in itself constitutes quite a puzzle. In order to enable the opening of the coin we have a solenoid (electro-magnet) embodied in the wand. This solenoid has a soft iron core three inches long, the core coming to a flat point at one end. This

Above We See the Paper Cutting Trick Wherein, Try as Hard as You Will, by Cutting a Band of Paper in Half, Longitudinally, You Cannot Help But Make Two Bands. Yet When You Know the Art of the Trick, by Cutting the Band in the Same Manner, You Can Make One Continuous Band or a Linked Band, or Even One With Several Knots.

Here is a Diagram of a Magic Coin Wand Which Foils Detection, It is Electrically Controlled. Note How the Ring Makes Contact Between the Two Metallic Bands on the Handle Closing the Circuit, and in This Way Causes the Current to Flow Thru the Solenoid, the Core of Which Separates Two Split Coins, Making it Appear as Tho the Coin Was Caught in Mid Air.

teries. I have a little stunt here, however, which will please your readers, particularly in view of the fact that it is simply made and employs, as do my other tricks, electricity in the very simplest manner. Let me have your hat—no, this will never do: I thought perhaps that you might have secreted about you one of those stove-pipe affairs. Wait a second until I procure one of mine."

A few moments later he was back in the room with a high silk hat in one hand and a little black stick about 15 inches long in the other, which he called his *Coin Wand*. Proceeding to demonstrate the effectiveness of his little instrument he said, "A very simple method of making counterfeit, as you undoubtedly know, is to pass a stick of this nature thru the air and collect the particles of silver floating in the atmosphere into one unit mass, forming them into a coin at the same time. You see each time that we handle a silver coin we rub off some of the silver. That accounts for some coins becoming thin from wear. This silver of course does not remain on our fingers but is brushed off, and due to the air circulation we soon have floating about

ing unusual in its construction. A black metal band fitted on one end, and two parallel nickel-plated bands on the other. Aside from that it was quite a solid construction with nothing to indicate the way in which the coins came or were even suspended at the end of the wand.

After toying with me a little longer he gave me the secret of one of the cleverest little devices which he had ever originated. Stepping forward he took the wand from my hands with: "You're not as green about magic as I thought you were,—you're worse." Pulling at the metal cap at one end he removed it, and then the trick could be readily seen, for a slot in each side of the wand concealed half of a coin. Of course I desired more details of constructions which with Professor Hargrave's frank and willing manner to help, were not difficult to obtain.

Taking the wand apart he showed me its construction, explaining it in the following manner: "The original magicians' coins, as you know, resemble half dollars which are cut in the manner shown, so that an obtuse angle on the cut side is formed. These are hinged as near to the end of the wand as

core moves within the solenoid coil which is 2½ inches long and wound very compactly with No. 28 wire, or wire which can be taken from an old bell, until a total thickness of 7/16ths of an inch is eventually realized. This makes a very snug fit into the metal wand. A spring is attached to the core of the solenoid to draw it back so that it will not interfere in any way with the proper closing of the coin whenever the current is shut off. In the other part of the wand is the battery, simply removed by this end cap which must be pulled quite hard in order to remove the same. As you will note, two springs hold the cap in place. No one on examining a wand attempts to pull it apart or handle it roughly, particularly if cautioned beforehand. Therefore, the closure of this end is quite effective, and as it can be turned all around if one tries to unscrew the end, it is never thought to be 'part of the game.' The positive pole of the battery goes directly to the solenoid and the negative is passed out thru the wand to one of these metal bands. The other band connects with a lead from the solenoid. The method of closing the circuit is identical with the roulette wheel described, elsewhere in this magazine, and consists in making and breaking the circuit with a ring upon any finger. This arrangement is never noticed and does not generally allow meddlesome people to discover this secret.

"Is that clear?" I assured him that it was, and then asked, "But how about the wand when you gave it to me and how about the coins falling into the hat; surely there is some palmistry or some slight-of-hand work?"

"Not at all," was his answer. "You see I simply held the cap or cover of the end in my hand and when I presented you with the wand, I transferred the wand from one hand into the other, slipping the cap in place. On the inside of this cap is soldered half of a snap cuff-link or similar snap fastener, in the wand proper is inserted the female part, and when the wand is given to any person, this simple snap holds the end in place quite securely, as you can readily see from the diagram."

"But the coins in the hat," I interrupted, "I am sure I heard them fall."

"I wouldn't swear to that if I were you," he added, "as the reason I asked for a high hat is because it makes plenty of noise and the effect of dropping a coin into the hat was obtained by merely snapping my finger against the brim."

"Oh!"—was all I could say.

After having recovered from the effects of this, I said "These tricks are wonderful, Professor, but haven't you anything in your encyclopedia which doesn't need the preparation or the instruments which you have employed thus far? Some simple trick for every reader to perform." "Well, let me see —I believe I have. Wait a few moments."

I busied myself with a magazine which he had lying on the table, when, a short time later he returned with colored bits of paper, the ends of each strip were glued together making a loop about 4 ft. long and ½ inch wide. Throwing these upon the table he drew out a pair of shears and said to me, "Are you a good tailor? Insert these scissors here and cut all around the loop." It was a tedious operation but soon finished, and as a result I gave him *two* loops. Immediately he flared up. "What did you do that for. I told you to cut all around the band but did not say to make two loops out of it. One was sufficient, and then you even separate the loops, you should be taught how to cut." I was quite amazed at this sudden turn of affairs and then gradually becoming more bold, I demanded that he do better. Picking another of the strips he commenced cutting it the same way I had done. "Now if you had coaxed it along, you might have done better or perhaps if you had spoken some magic word over it and made a pass,—thus a word like "consologicaletcopitulationanthropohagenarianism," would have benefited your trick immensely." He had completed the cut and there were the two loops interlinked. Picking up another sheet of paper he said

"Maybe I can do better this time," and when he had finished cutting this, he had one loop left. Yes, to be sure I was not under the effects of "half of no per cent liquor." He had actually cut a loop in half, and after cutting it showed me one loop *twice the size of the original one!*

"Now I'll try once more," he said, and picking up the last loop of paper started to cut this. This was completed in a few moments and there he was with a loop of paper which had a knot in it. Which of these two stunts were the more remarkable is more than I could tell, but there to be sure was the mute evidence lying in front of me.

Hargrave laughed merrily at my chagrin, then gave me this secret. "You see old topper, the loop I gave you was unprepared. Those *I* had, I prepared and the preparation needed is very simple. The first loop is made so that it doesn't contain any twist in the paper. This you cut in half and try as hard as you will you cannot obtain anything but two separate loops from the paper. The second loop is made by gluing the two strips together but prior to gluing, the paper band is given a half twist, the third, two half twists and the fourth loop three half twists. These twists are never noticed in a narrow long band of paper, and the surprise of the cutting doesn't abate sufficiently to allow the onlooker to notice the double twist or the triple twist described. Try it when you get home."

With that he ushered me from the room.

"Perpetual Motion" Advertising Device

A Unique Easily Constructed Illusion

PROBABLY there is no other single idea which occupies the minds of more people, particularly inventors, the world over today, than perpetual motion. It is the "everlasting will-o'-the-wisp" which the crank inventors, for many centuries, including the present one, are forever chasing. We hope that those who are particularly interested in perpetual motion will soon experience the joy of standing in front of a local store window and witness the operation of this latest marvel, a perpetually (?) rotating machine devised by one Leander Davis Wheatley,

"Perpetual Motion" Would Seem to be Solved at Last, if You Perchance Happened to See One of the Machines, Like That Shown in the Illustration, Rotating at High Speed in a Show Window. It is not as "Perpetual" as It Looks However, for on Close Inspection We See That a Small Electric Motor Supplies the Mechanical Driving Power to the Disc, by Means of a "Live" Shaft Center.

of Pendleton, Oregon.

The editors must confess that it is one of the "slickest" schemes for advertising, and one of the finest devices for producing mysticism, even in the mind of educated people, that they have ever seen. Like many other real good things, Mr. Wheatley's invention is quite simple indeed, once you come to analyze it. On the periphery of the revolving wheel may be placed small advertising miniatures of the goods being demonstrated, but the inventor shows in his patent several glass tubes containing mercury, causing the onlookers to believe, that quite possibly this constant motion of the mercury, circulating thru the tubes, causes the wheel to rotate. The revolving wheel is mounted between two pointed bearings or pivots, which project into the conical bearings provided on the shaft at either end, as shown. One of these conical pivots is made so that only the point of it revolves, and this point is fastened to a small flexible shaft, the lower end of which is connected with a clock-work motor, this being wound when run down by an electric motor connected to an electric light circuit or other current.

The large revolving display wheel can be stopped by simply turning the screw at the side of the left-hand column, which causes the clutch in the base of the machine to be disengaged, thus stopping the flexible shaft which drives the "live" bearing cone. The display wheel can be removed and handed out for demonstration to anyone by simply turning the screw formation which throws out the clutch and at the same time increases the distance between the bearings so that the wheel can be removed. When the wheel is replaced this screw is tightened up, and automatically the clutch throws the machine into operation and away it goes again, to the great amusement of the onlookers. Of course, in building this machine, the uprights are kept very small.

The Wonder Fountains

I WAS virtually a stranger as I wended my way to the Long Island home of Professor Hargrave. Everything seemed so different, the grounds had been changed, the building had received its annual wash, and mosquito netting enclosed the porches. There at least is one invention which the famous magician has

in the room; one, however, took my particular fancy. This was a fountain composed of a group of mermaids, surrounded by sea horses, holding a bowl which resembled a gigantic lily, from the center of which sparkled the clear waters of a bubbling fountain. Shafts of vari-colored lights illuminated the spray. Suddenly, I heard

experiment, I will try and show it to you." With that he left the room.

His departure gave me the opportunity I had been looking for. Ah, thought I to myself, so it is the fountain; well, he won't fool me this time. I examined this sculptural masterpiece with the closest scrutiny. There was nothing unusual about it; it was

One of the Most Spectacular Magic Stunts Imaginable is the One Illustrated Above, in Which Professor Hargrave Becomes a Veritable Walking Fountain. The Effect is greatly Enhanced by Colored Lights Which Play Upon Him While the Feathery Streams of Water Shift From the Hand to the Head, Thence to the Foot, and Suddenly All Five Columns Sparkle Forth in the Artificial Light. The Wand Which the Performer Holds in One Hand May be Given to the Spectator. Water Flows From the Wand and at a Given Command it Stops. The Details of the Wand are Shown in the Lower Right Hand Corner of the Picture.

evidently not worked upon, namely, a method of exterminating mosquitos or making the female of the species less deadly than the male. Letting the knocker on the door fall gently, I was even surprised to see a different maid answer my call. On inquiring whether the Professor was in, I received an affirmative answer, and while the maid went to announce my arrival, I made myself comfortable in the parlor which had been converted into a den.

Here I was not left alone long enough to even acquaint myself with the new objects

the familiar call, "Well, well, old topper, I haven't seen you for quite a few months, where have you been keeping yourself?" The earnestness of this exclamation was intensified by a pat on the back, which shook me as tho I had been hit with a sledge hammer. Before I had a chance to reply, he continued, saying, "I am sorry, old chap, I am very busy today, but I have a little stunt here which I know you would like to see. It has something to do with that fountain over there. If you will excuse me while I don my costume for presenting the

simply a very decorative, self-contained fountain, a motor operating a small pump which forced the water up thru a tiny aperture and vari-colored lights under the basin, which was quite transparent, helped to illuminate the bubbling stream. Satisfied with my examination, I seated myself just a moment before Professor Hargrave entered the room. He was dressed in a Turkish costume, a turban covered his practically bald head. In either hand he held a wand.

"Before I show you this performance,"

he said on entering the room, "I think I will have a drink." Walking to the fountain he stooped over it, and seemingly drank quite a quantity of water, in fact so much, that without any sign of warning a stream of water, about seven or eight feet high, and very thin, wended its way almost to the ceiling, apparently originating at the top of his head. Here it broke and fell down upon him and upon the carpeted floor. He turned around and approached me, the stream never diminishing in height or in volume, but continued to flow from his head, until passing one of the wands over his head the water left the spot and spouted from the wand. Here it started to shoot upward from the very tip as high as before.

Meanwhile the fountain in the center of the room had ceased its mirthful splashing. Hargrave continued to approach me until I told him that I was not quite ready for a shower bath. Then moving the first wand toward the second one in his other hand, the fountain jet was immediately transferred. During the entire process he continued with a rather merry patter, which I could not duplicate, were I even to try. Purposely or accidentally dropping one wand, the stream of water suddenly shifted to his right foot and then placing the left foot over the right, he sort of quenched the tiny fountain, which then transferred itself automatically to the left foot. Then, as tho he were touching off a series of fireworks, the water sprouted from his head, both wands and both feet. At his command the streams all ceased with the exception of one, which continued to sprout from the wand held in his right hand, and then with the words, "To show you that there is no trick attached to this feat, I will let you have the wand, but be careful and direct the stream away from you, as otherwise you will get a shower which you do not desire." He then added, "Should I now tell the jet from the wand to stop, it will do so." My response was immediate, "I don't believe it." "Very well, then." Turning around and walking toward the fountain in the center of the room, he commanded the one in my hand to stop. It did so almost immediately, while the sculptural bowl in the center of the room again started to play and sparkle.

So pretty was the effect and so strange and uncanny were the results, that I even failed to ask him how it was done. He grinned at my expression of astonishment, then added, "Come, come, old timer, you don't mean to tell me you don't know the trick?" I had to admit that I was "green." He then continued as was his usual wont, to explain in detail the entire contrivance. "You see it is very simple. Suspended from a shoulder strap is this tank." Here he removed it. "The tank is made of brass 3½" in diameter and a little more than 10" long. To the bottom end is soldered——" Here I interrupted him with the exclamation, "now I see how it is done." "Well, well, the boy is coming to his senses," was his reply, "but to continue. To the bottom of the tank is soldered a piece of ordinary brass tubing, large enough to receive a rubber hose of about ¼" diameter. This rubber hose connects at the waist line to a five branched valve, the openings of which in turn connect to openings of considerably smaller diameter, as I have illustrated here. The distal extremeties of the valves or the outlets then communicate with rubber tubing, the hole of which is ⅛" in diameter. These tiny rubber tubes then connect to pointed nozzles located in the toes of both shoes and in the turban. On either hand a different type nozzle is fixed which takes the shape of an ordinary piece of brass tubing tapered slightly. This brass tubing connects with a hole in the wand thru which the water flows."

Here I interrupted him the second time. "I didn't see any hole in the end of the wand." "I know you didn't, foolish," was his retort. "Do you suppose for one moment that I would have handed it to you if I thought you were going to see anything? You saw nothing but the hole from which the stream of water flowed." I reached for the wand in order to give it a more thoro inspection, but he got there before I did, and the result was that I had to await his explanation. "You see one of those wands is not prepared at all. The water enters at the handle and makes its exit at the other end. The other wand *is* prepared. With regard to the tank again, I filled this tank about three-quarters full of water and then pumped about sixty pounds of air into the remaining space. Of course the tank must be thoroly tested first. This air pressure gives me sufficient energy to force the streams of water to a considerable height and the location of the streams is automatically controlled by the valve strapped to the belt. The valve is simple in construction, the details of which I can give you in a diagram more readily than in words. You will note that pressure upon the button either turns the stream of water on or off, but the pressure does not necessarily have to be maintained as the valve locks in either position. When I started the exhibit, you perhaps noticed that the fountain in the center of the room died down. The reason for that was the fact that a duplicate switch may be found at the base if you examine the floor closely. This switch turns off the electric motor operating the pump for the fountain. My first device constructed along this idea was an ordinary hot water bag, which was likewise strapped in such a position, that pressure with the arm upon the bag would force the water thru the pipes or tubes. This device was not as efficient as the one I am applying at the present time, and prevented freedom of motion to a very great extent, even tho the uninitiated would never notice this lack of freedom. With the hot water bag appliance, I simply added a stopper coupled to which was a small piece of tubing, but altho this idea may do for the amateur entertainer, it is advisable to use the better form of apparatus; that is all there is to the stunt."

I had taken the drawings he had made and already started to depart when I remembered that he had not described the wand and I called his attention to the fact. "Oh, that is the simplest of all," he continued. "It consists of an ordinary hollow wand fitted at both ends with a cap, the springs holding the caps in place similar to the coin wand, which I described sometime ago. At one end there is an opening into which the tapered brass connection in the performer's right hand fits. This brass tube is 3" long, the wand itself being 10" long and made of brass tubing. Here," and he illustrated it with a diagram, "is a washer about ½" long and fitted with a rubber end. The washer has a hole drilled thru it just a little larger than the tube over which it slides. A valve such as is used in some toy balloons closes this opening when this trigger is released. The spring inside will then cause the water to continue to flow, even when the wand is not connected with the water reservoir." "You commanded the wand to stop flowing, how did you do that?" "It is a simple matter, old top, to time the length of flow from the moment the wand leaves my hand until it stops, and it is only necessary for me to parry for that time, when I know that the wand will cease its flow, with remarkable accuracy at the predetermined instant." Changing the conversation for a few moments to other subjects, I departed, thanking him heartily.

Three Magic Pencils—A Magnetic Hoax

EFFECT: Three colored lead pencils are given out for examination, red, white and blue, for example. The performer leaving the room, tells anyone to choose any color pencil they wish, while he is out of the room, and to wrap it up in any color piece of paper or cloth, and to hand it to him securely wrapt when he returns to the room. Upon receipt of same the performer passes hand over pencil and tells exact color.

SECRET: Two of the pencils are "faked" in this manner. One of them is drilled with a 1/16 inch drill in the rubber end about 1 inch, and the other one is drilled half-way down or in the middle. Two pieces of Stubb's drill rod, ½ inch long by 1/16 inch diameter, are hardened, magnetized and inserted in the drilled holes and a piece of lead is inserted on top of the magnetized pieces and made flush with wood in rubber end of pencil, the rubber is placed on top and the trick is ready; the third pencil contains no fake whatever. In leaving the room the performer attaches a small compass inside

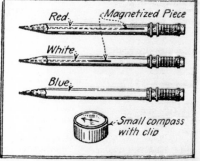

Want to Mystify Your Friends With Some Hindu Pencils? Here's How: With a Magnet Placed at Different Positions in Two or More Pencils, Conceal a Small Compass in Your Cuff. The Rest is Easy—You Can Tell at Once Which Colored Pencil Is Inside an Envelope, Even Tho it Was Wrapt up While You Were Absent from the Room.

his shirt cuff, (some of these compasses can be obtained as small as a dime, or even of less diameter), which aids him in detecting what pencil is wrapped up or concealed in the cloth or paper in this way: He slowly passes pencil in front of compass and watches needle until it quivers, which it will do when that part of pencil containing the magnetized steel passes needle. If the needle moves when the *end* of pencil is near it, the performer knows it is the *red* one. If it moves when near the *middle* of pencil, he knows it is the *white* one; if needle does not move, it must of course be the blue one. As the back of hand faces audience, the compass is invisible.

Many variations of this magnetic trick will suggest themselves to the wide-awake experimenter. Such as the magnetic "brass" ball—the inside of the ball is filled with iron filings and the small filling hole stopt up with brass.

Parlor Tricks Easily Performed

HARGRAVE himself came to the door in answer to my ring. He seemed to have dropped his serious attitude and acted very gleeful as tho he were tickled over something else which he had concealed up his sleeve. "Your are just in time," he ventured to say, as I entered, "as I want to show you a new production which I have just completed." "May I make a suggestion?" was my question. "Go right ahead," he answered. "Well, you see, Professor, this series of articles I am writing is being run for the *Amateur Magician* and up to the present time we have had very little amateurish about it. Almost all the tricks described were spectacular stage tricks or those intended for the more professional performer. Now, can't we——"

Hargrave interrupted me here and said, "Tut, tut, old timer, anybody can do those things and make them work and they are just as good for the amateur as for the professional." "Of course," was my rejoinder, "that is understood, but you must realize that many of the readers, altho they do like magic, would not consider entering the field to the extent of building the heavier apparatus, as you call it. Now just for a change, suppose you give us a little parlor magic with which anyone can entertain their folks at home. For instance, tricks with cards or coins." "All right, old top," he replied, "you might get your camera out and snap some of these stunts."

THE THREE COLORED CANDLES

"Now here is a trick," he said, "which any of your amateur readers can construct within ten minutes. Here are three candles, a red, a white, and a blue, and three sheets of opaque paper. I want you to take these candles and wrap them up in the paper, and I will enter blindfolded and will tell you which papers contain the red, which the blue, and which the white."

So saying, he left the room. A moment or so later I beckoned him back and told him that I was ready. Placing a handkerchief across his eyes, I gave him one of the paper wrapped candles. He passed his hand up and down along the side rapidly and then said, "That is a blue candle." I marked blue upon the paper and gave him another one. He repeated the operation and said, "That is a red one." I picked up the blue candle again and I gave it to him. Again he said, "This is the same one you gave me a moment ago, the blue candle." He removed the blind from his eyes and we opened the parcels, and sure enough he had named the candles correctly.

"Ah, that's the stuff," I said, not caring whether or not the term "stuff" brought to his mind the meaning behind the phrase. "Now, how does it work?"

"Very simple," he replied, not even forming a complete sentence. "You see each one of those candles contains a small piece of steel which has been magnetized. The blue one contains a piece of steel at the top, the white in the center, and the red at the bottom. Between the index and middle finger of my right hand I hold this small piece of iron and on passing my hand up and down along the candle I feel a slight tug, either at the top, middle or bottom of the candle. This gives me an inkling as to the color within the wrapper. Of course I know which is the top and which is the bottom by simply pressing upon the candle and if I feel a sharp edge I know that the bottom is present and if the top is present, the edge will taper toward a point. Now anyone can make this in a few moments."

THE DISAPPEARING COIN

"Now, have you a spare half dollar?" was Prof. Hargrave's next question. "I'd rather you would use one of your own," was my prompt reply. You see Hargrave once borrowed a $5 bill and made it disappear completely.

He produced a half dollar coin and requested that I mark the same, so that I

1—How the Coin Is Rubbed Into the Sleeve and Subsequently Found in the Collar. 2—By the Aid of a Blonde Woman's Hair, It Is Easy to Cause a Ring to Slide Up and Down on Command Upon the Pencil. 3—The Hair Again Comes to Our Rescue and Permits Us to Balance a Card on a Hat. 4—Could You Tell the Color of Three Candles Wrapped in Thick Brown Paper and You to Be Blindfolded While Doing This? 5—The First Stage in Changing the Face of a Card. The Forefinger of the Left Hand Pushes a Few Cards Downward. 6—In the Last Stage the Palmed Cards Are Placed on Top of the Deck and the Movement Followed by a Closing of the Fingers to Make It Appear That the Top Card Is Removed. 7—Second Stage. The Cards Are Pushed Down Far Enough Under Cover of the Hand and Palmed in the Right Hand.

would be able to identify it again. "Did you ever see a coin rubbed into the elbow?" he continued. "No? Well, watch closely." So saying he proceeded to rub the coin seemingly into his elbow. The first time it did not succeed, for he clumsily dropped the coin on the floor. He tried again and rubbed vigorously and then showed both hands empty. He then requested that I extract the half dollar which was protruding from his collar. I did so.

"Did that fool you?" he added. I had to admit it did. "Well," he explained, "the stunt is very simple. I rubbed the coin into my right elbow or so it seemed, and dropped it the first time, not accidentally but purposely. I then pick the coin up with my right hand and seemingly transfer it to my left hand, but in reality retain it in my right hand. I rub again and while the left hand is doing the rubbing, the right hand is inserting the coin into the collar. Simple?" "Yes, it certainly was simple," I admitted.

THE DANCING PLAYING CARD

"Now, let me have one of those cards if you please and your straw hat." He took the card I handed him and placing it upon my hat balanced it in an upright posi-

tion. I was speechless. "It does look hard, doesn't it, but it's not. You see I have a blonde hair about 17" or 18" long attached to the button of my vest. At the other end of this blonde hair is a tiny pellet of wax. When you gave me the card I secretly fastened this pellet of wax to the back of it and then standing the card upon your hat so that it tilted toward you slightly, I was able to hold the card in this position and even tho you were but a few feet away, you couldn't see the hair.

THE MOVING RING TRICK

"Your ring, please." I again complied with his request. He took a pencil from the drawer in the table and then passing the ring over the top of the pencil, said, "Now watch it."

"Up," and the ring rose upward on the pencil. "Down," was his command, and it fell down. "Now, you tell it to do something." I commanded the ring to go up; instead it went down. I commanded it to go down, and it went up. "You see it is operating exactly opposite to your commands, but it obeys me implicitly," and the ring again rose upon the upright pencil held in his hand. He awaited an answer from me and not

finding it forthcoming explained. "Again, old timer, the blonde woman leaves a hair there." I didn't see it but I said I did. At any rate the illustration shows how it works. The hair is fastened to the top of the pencil and the ring slipped over both.

A POKER GAME TRICK

"And suppose I were playing poker with you and you were supposed to get the seven of diamonds, which card is upon the top now. I would simply pass my hand over the face of the card, thus, and you would get the two of spades, whereas if I passed it over the cards again, thusly, I would get the ace of hearts."

And right there before me just as quick as a flash, the cards changed their faces and were not removed from the deck.

"Oh, so simple, so simple," he said, "you know I hate to give these tricks away, because there is really nothing to them, but inasmuch as you want them, why here they are. In this stunt the forefinger of the left hand pushes some cards downward from the back of the pack. They are palmed in the right hand and then placed upon the deck. The fingers of the right hand are then closed over the deck so as to make it seem that some cards are being removed."

This Clock Tells "Bug" Time

WE recently noted in a jeweller's show window an interesting clock which was labelled with the startling sign, "This Clock Tells 'Bug' Time!" and while the idea involved is almost as old as Methuselah, the action of the device is very novel and pleasing.

No doubt some of our readers have seen similar clocks in their home towns and cities. The clock in question comprises a regular clock-work movement mounted in a wooden cabinet, about 12 inches square by 8 inches high. The top of the cabinet was closed by an aluminum dial plate, or this might be brass, or any other non-magnetic metal or material. The clock may be mounted on a sheet of glass suspended on cords or wires well in the foreground, so as to show that no electrical or other form of energy is connected with the clock. Under the aluminum dial plate on the top of the clock the hands of the movement revolve in their usual procession. The hands in this case may have to be made a little stronger than usual, as on the outer end of each there is mounted a small steel magnet. These magnets act on the two iron "bugs" which tell the time. As will be seen from the illustration, the "minute bug" moves around on the outer circle of the dial, while the "hour bug" moves around on the inner circle of the dial. The aluminum of the dial can be as thin as 1/64 of an inch if necessary, but in any case, the thickness of this material will have no more effect on

weakening the magnetism than the same thickness of air.

This clock has proven a great attraction in store windows, and can be used in prac-

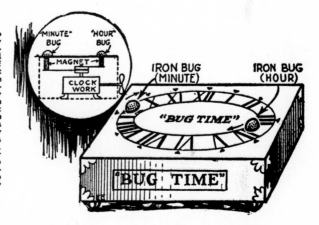

Thomas Reed Used to Tell Us Long and Lustily About His Clocks.—Electrical, Mechanical and Otherwise. But One of the Simplest and Most Novel Clocks Which the Average Electro-Mechanical "Bug" Will Probably Like to Build, Is This Real "Bug Clock" That Tells "Bug Time." As the Detailed Diagram Shows, an Ordinary Clock-Work, One From an Alarm Clock Will Do, Is Used, on the Outer Hands of which Two Fairly Strong Steel Magnets are Placed. The Two Iron Bugs Can Be Easily Made and Colored.

tically every business, such as drug stores, jeweller's stores, etc. The people like to watch the little "minute bug" as he slides along from minute to minute, and besides they—the people, not the bugs—almost forget to eat their lunch in arguing as to how

the bugs move over the dial. In five minutes you can hear about 14,000½ explanations of how the bugs tell the time,—including "psychical force"!*?!!

Well, here is your chance to do a little fooling of your own. Undoubtedly you can find many improvements which will make the action of the "Bug Time" clock more smooth, such as placing little rollers in the miniature iron bugs, etc.

The "Magic Wand"

Herewith is a sketch and description of a "Magic Wand" that will lift light objects and drop them at the command of the performer. But, mind you, this cannot change pictures into real stuff.

A cardboard tube, electro-magnet, two fountain pen flashlight batteries, and a small push button are all that is required. The sketch is so simple that no explanation is necessary for its construction. If you have no electro-magnet a suitable one can be made as detailed in the sketch.

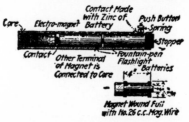

The Magic Wand Here Shown Can Be Built from an Old Electro-Magnet and a Fountain Pen Flashlight Battery.

The objects to be lifted must not be heavy, and for cardboard boxes, etc., a small piece of thin tin must be glued on them so as to be attracted by the magnet. A small piece of watch-spring steel may be sewed into handkerchiefs or pasted to playing cards to make them "magnetic" and permit of their being attracted by this wand.

A Few Good Parlor Tricks Without Apparatus

Five Card Monte. From the Last Pile, One Card is Taken Off Each Time and Placed on Each of the Other Four Piles.

The Vanishing Coin. Note the Substitute Ring on the Knee of the Performer, Upon the Bottom of Which is Attached a Piece of Paper Identical With the Sheet on Which the Trick is to be Conducted.

The Card Jumps Out of the Deck and Turns Over, Face Upward, when the Deck is Dropped Upon the Table, by the Simple Process Here Depicted.

THE Japanese servant at Professor Hargrave's New York residence admitted me without question. I had just walked briskly thru Central Park. The air altho very invigorating had enough of that cold tang to it to create a numbness of the fingers and a tickling sensation in the vicinity of the auricular members exposed to the elements. I entered Hargrave's studio without the usual announcement, and found him reclining in an easy chair, a circle of smoke wafting upward above his head, while he himself was yawning. Hargrave has a peculiar trait of constantly reminding a person of what he already knew—as many barbers do—and greeted me with, "Well, well, old timer, rather cold out." I informed him that I was very well aware of the fact, to which he replied, "Well, I'll soon make it hot for you." And rising he repaired to another part of the room returning with a large figure of a devil. "If that's another of your tricks," I interrupted, "just lay low for a while."

"So this is to be merely a friendly visit? Quite a pleasure indeed, but rather unusual. What's the matter, old man, out of a job?"

"This is not to be a friendly visit," I retaliated, "and I am not out of a job either, but I might be soon, unless you make this a real good snappy entertainment. The class of tricks particularly desirable should come under the category of 'parlor magic.'" "I can't say that I appreciate your telling me what tricks I should show you," he laconically replied, "but—" here he hesitated, opened the drawer of his desk and produced a deck of cards.

FIVE CARD MONTE

These he fingered for a while and then deftly making five piles by allowing some of the cards to drop off the bottom and remain on the table, he removed a card from the top of the fifth pile and placed it on the first; then another and placed it on the second, a third and fourth from the same pile and placed it on the third and fourth piles respectively. Touching the fifth pile, he said, "Take a look at the top card." I did as I was bid. "Put it back." I followed instructions. "Shuffle up the pack." I knew I had fooled him this time as he hadn't even seen the card, nor did he know where it was. He picked up the deck and turning it face upward, rapidly

ran thru the cards. Evidently he could not locate it. He asked me whether I was sure it was in the deck, and I told him I was positive of that fact, tho I do now recall that I used the word positive rather meekly, in that I had been positive of so many things in the past much to my discomfiture. Raising the deck about fifteen inches above the table, he dropped it, and seemingly from the center of the deck, a card flew out, turning itself face upward on top of the fallen pack. Before I could get over my astonishment, he had picked up all the cards and started to shuffle them.

He requested that I choose a card when I interrupted him, "Hold on a minute, haven't you forgotten something?" Hargrave was in the habit of jumping from one trick into another, not even giving his audience a chance to recover fully from one shock before the second one presented itself, and such simple tricks too. He assured me I would get the explanation later, but I informed him that I would rather have it now while the memory of the trick was still fresh in my mind. "Very well," he answered. "First we will count off from the face, one, two, three, four, five cards." His action suited his words, as he transferred five cards from the deck turned face upward to his right hand. Then he placed these on the bottom. "Lifting the entire deck we make five neat piles thus." Here his hand moved from left to right with the deck of cards. He stopped at intervals to drop a few from the bottom. The cards were now of course turned face downward.

"From the top of the fifth pile (back), I removed one and placed it on the first thus. I removed another and placed it on the second pile, always of course taking the cards from the fifth pile, or the very last one placed on the table. I repeated for the third and fourth piles and then asked you to look at the top card in the fifth pile, or what is now the top card."

"But how did you know the name of that card?" I had again interrupted him which I must admit was a rather rude thing to do. I knew that Hargrave did not like it very much because he snapped right back at me saying, "Now, what in the world do you suppose I took five cards off the top (face) for at the beginning of the trick." I hadn't the slightest idea. "When I reached the fifth card, I remem-

bered what that card was and in laying out the piles, I removed four and then the fifth card became the top card of the last deck, n'est ce pas?"

"Of course, of course, but you shuffled those cards."

"To be quite sure I did, but you have noticed that in doing so I used the riffle method of shuffling cards. In other words, I placed the two halves down on the table, lifted the corners and let them run together, but I took particular care that at least five cards which were originally on the top of the deck retained their original positions, by keeping the top half in my right hand, and making sure that five or more cards from the right hand were seemingly accidentally but purposely riffled to the top again. This thus preserved the original order of the top five. Is that clear?"

"Yes, but——"

"Now what?"

"How did that card turn over?"

"Oh, yes, how stupid of me. You see that is the extremely simple part of the trick. I, knowing your card, brought that card to the bottom of the deck. Then under cover of the hand, I pushed the card out so that it extended from the side of the deck. Still under cover of the hand, I dropped the entire deck, but due to the weight of the cards themselves the cards fall solidly or en masse. They are preferably dropped from a height of twelve to fourteen inches, and in order to give a better effect, the downward travel of the deck may be speeded up by a slight throw. The air affecting the thin card as it impinges upon that extended portion, causes that card to turn around and of course face upward."

THE DISAPPEARING CARD

Picking up the pack again, Hargrave shuffled it. "You fooled me like that once before. You had better let me shuffle them this time," I exclaimed. To this he assented. Turning the entire deck face down upon the table, he said, "Think of any number, then counting from the back down, turn over the card at the number thought of, thus." He picked up the cards preserving their same order, saying, "I have thought of the number fifteen—thirteen, fourteen, fifteen. I turn them over and note that the deuce of diamonds is the fifteenth card."

"Do you follow me?" I nodded in assent. "You do likewise," he continued. "Choose any card and remember its name and position in the deck." I did so. He picked up the deck, turned it face upward, and started to examine the cards, transferring them rather rapidly from his left hand to his right. He hesitated now and then and came dangerously near the card I had chosen, but past it by. "No, I think you fooled me this time." With the cards face upward on the table, he requested that I remove just as many cards from the top as the position of my card in the pack indicated. I did so. Then picking up the cards, he removed three more from the face end, and placed them face downward upon the table, stating as he did so, "One of those three cards is yours." I doubted him, and he asked me to turn up the cards and look at them. Again I carried out instructions. And then added, "Well, I fooled you that time, it's not there," but the smile on my face quickly changed. He seemed surprised at first, "Fooled me, that's impossible, it must be there! What was the name of your card?" I told him. "Tray of hearts?" he continued. "Impossible, why that card has been reposing in my pocket for quite a while. Here, put your hand in and take it out for yourself." Placing my hand in the side pocket of his smoking jacket, I extracted my card. Thinking perhaps that he had a duplicate, I checked thru the pack, but the tray of hearts was gone. Yet I was positive that that was the card I had originally chosen, which fact I tried to impress upon his mind. He saw that I was astounded, so before I could ask for an explanation he started.

"You're so easily fooled I think I'll sell you the Public Library to-morrow. The trick is simple in the extreme, and is undoubtedly one of the most easily mastered of all card tricks, nearly impossible of detection, and requires no practise at all. The cards are, as you undoubtedly know, shuffled by yourself or any other interested spectator. They are placed face downward on the table, and you select a card, counting of course from the back, to a certain position in the pack. You remember the position and also the name of the card. I then pick up the cards from the table, turn them face upward, and altho I seemingly hesitate and appear to be looking for the card, in reality I merely transfer the cards from the left to the right hand, reversing them in order, one at a time. I then take four other cards from what is now the bottom of the deck, and place them on top. Immediately thereafter I request you to remove the same number of cards from the face of the deck as the position of the card thought of indicated. Thus, assume that you chose the ace of spades, which occupied the tenth position from the bottom of the deck. In reversing these cards, the ace of spades again occupies the tenth position, but this time from the *face* end of the deck, but after the entire order of the cards has been reversed. Removing four of the cards from the bottom I place them on top. The ace of spades now occupies the fourteenth position from the top of the cards. I request that you remove the same number of cards thought of originally—ten—which brings the ace of spades to the fourth position in the deck. Removing the top three and placing them face downward upon the table, I make the assertion that your card is one of the three, knowing full well that it is not. This brings to the top the ace of spades which I place into my pocket. Savez?" Altho I didn't see him remove the four from the bottom and place them on the top, I could well understand how the trick worked, and on trying it subsequently, found that it was indeed very effective, and quite impossible of detection.

THE RINGS OF HINDUSTAN

As usual Hargrave never gave me a chance to discuss one trick before he started off with another one. Opening the drawer in the antique "trick" table he removed two rings which seemed to be of wood, altho he later informed me that they could be made out of metal, glass, rubber, or in fact anything. These rings were about 2 inches in diameter. He then procured a piece of plain white paper and placed this on top of the desk, gave me the rings to examine and also a card 2⅛ inches square, and then asked me for a coin. Past experience had taught me that a Chinese yen is the best coin to give Hargrave when he asks for one, but not having this currency in my pocket, I produced a genuine American cent. This may seem sort of cheap to the reader, but after he has seen quite a few coins disappear from his regular income, he can well appreciate my position. Magic and black art costs money.

Placing this cent on the paper, he picked up the card and covered one of the rings with it. He then picked up the second ring and placed it on top of the card and the first ring. Lifting the entire group he placed them over the coin. He now removed the top ring then the cardboard disk, and the coin had disappeared. On replacing the cardboard then the ring and, removing the entire group (two rings and card), the coin again made its appearance. "You can only do that trick by making this mysterious pass," he exclaimed, on duplicating this stunt, "and saying *oxyben zylmethylenglycolanhydride*, which of course means bakelite." In view of the fact that I could not pronounce the word, I assured him, in a jocular manner, that I could not reproduce the trick, but when I saw how it was done——.

Originally he had two rings which were absolutely unfaked. I examined them of course and returned them, and while I was looking for a coin he had substituted another ring for one of the two I had examined, to the bottom of which was glued a sheet of paper, exactly similar to the white paper upon which the trick was being conducted. The edge of the paper was carefully trimmed, so that to all appearances I was looking right thru the ring at the white paper sheet on the table. The order of the trick then followed thusly: Cardboard piece was placed upon the paper ring, another ring on top of this and the three placed over the coin. Top ring removed, cardboard sheet removed. The paper on the bottom ring was covering the coin, which seemingly had disappeared. Cardboard replaced, ring replaced, the three removed at once, the ring then taken from the top and the cardboard pushed aside. Care is taken that at no time shall the bottom ring be moved without having first been covered with the cardboard and top ring. Changing the rings is so simple that I never noticed it, my attention being distracted for the moment while fishing for the coin.

Electrical Spirit Writing

This is an interesting electrical trick which will mystify most people. Procure a picture frame, one about 4" x 6" will do, and let the cardboard in the back remain. Coil, as in Fig. 1, No. 28 German silver wire against the cardboard, leaving the two ends protruding from the back. Now paste over this a sheet of paper, completely covering the wire, and tack a piece of black cloth on the top sufficiently large to cover the frame. When this is finished, cut several sheets of paper to easily fit within your picture frame. Now dissolve one-half teaspoonfull of cobalt chloride in one-quarter of a glass of water. With this solution, write or draw any pictures you may think appropriate on the papers that were cut out. Writing is done with a clean gold pen, or a brush with quill (not metal) mounting may be used. The writing is invisible, but under the influence of a gentle heat it will appear in colored blue lines and surfaces. A few batteries and a switch is all that is necessary to complete the apparatus.

At the magician's command, a picture gradually appears on what was previously a plain white sheet, and disappears again when desired. The resistance wire in back of the frame causes the cobalt chloride with which the picture is drawn, to take on a blue tint due to the effect which heat produces upon that salt. Of course, in the presentation of this trick, the wires leading to the switch or push button and the source of current supply are concealed.

The performer should now hang the picture frame against the wall, and draw the curtain back. After announcing that he has command over a spirit who will write or draw for him, he places a prepared paper (drawing face inward) against the sheet which covers the wire. He then lets the curtain drop and turns on the hidden switch, which may be under the carpet or on the back of a chair. A minute later the switch is turned off, the curtain is rolled up, and the picture is removed. A picture where none was before will appear, completely mystifying the audience.

The German silver wire having been gently heated by the current from the batteries, causes the image on the treated paper to appear. Care should be taken in proportioning the current, so that the heat developed is not great enough to set fire to the whole outfit, surprising your friends more than ever. However, with a little care, the trick will terminate effectively.

Japanese Lanterns and Parlor Tricks

PROFESSOR HARGRAVE had been on the road for quite a while, and I must frankly admit that I missed his congeniality, his keen sense of humor, and his ability to puzzle and trick me, which ability I greatly admire. He was playing before a small audience in Washington, when I seized the opportunity to impose upon him for another article, which imposition he would never admit.

After what seemed to be an age, I managed

ceeded to get his apparatus in readiness preparatory to the rising of the curtain due in ten minutes.

I hustled out to occupy the seat he had assigned me, so that I would not have to request a change.

THE DISAPPEARING GOBLET

The curtain rose promptly at 10:00 o'clock, while members of the club were still drifting in, in groups of twos and threes. After a

to one of the members to come up on the platform. Hargrave then proceeded. Waving a heavy silk flag, he placed the glass of water upon the table and covered it with the flag. He then requested the President to lightly grasp the edge of the glass of water, yet with sufficient grasp to lift the glass up from the table, the flag of course covering it. Directly after the President had walked to the front of the platform, he said, "Now when I say *three* I want you to drop the glass of

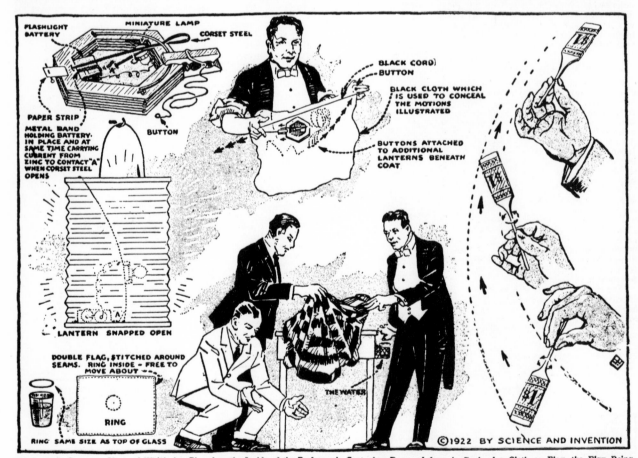

The Japanese Lanterns, Many of Which Are Pinned to the Inside of the Performer's Coat, Are Removed from in Back of a Cloth or Flag, the Flag Being Waved Each Time to Show that Nothing Is Concealed Behind it. Removing the Clamp Permits the Lantern to Snap Open, Simultaneously Closing the Circuit to the Light. The Disappearing Glass of Water and the Method of Making It Vanish are Clearly Demonstrated in the Lower Center Portion of the Above Illustration. By Rotating the Paddle and Swinging It at the Same Time, the Same Side of the Paddle Is Kept Uppermost, and the Rotating Movement Being Unobserved Makes It Possible to Change an Object Mounted on One Side of the Paddle to Another on the Opposite Side. This Clever Deception Is Shown at the Right of the Above Illustration.

to enter upon the precincts of the Carleton Club, whose limited members made me feel distinctly out of place. Of course, I had no right to be there, being neither a guest nor a member, but then there are a lot of places to which one goes, knowing full well that he should not have been there.

Hargrave greeted me more cordially, saying, "I am going to introduce a new trick this evening for the first time, and altho I have no doubt it will go thru without a hitch, I would like you to scrutinize the presentation intensely. If you will, I would prefer that you take a seat at the extreme left of the small platform here, so that you will be able to see how the trick is performed to better advantage than the others in the audience. I would like you to assist me further, and when in the disappearing glass stunt I say 'Gone,' I wish you would call out 'Up your sleeve.' Don't forget 'Gone' will be your cue."

So saying, he excused himself and pro-

rather brief talk, Hargrave introduced several of his older tricks, some of which have been described in previous articles in this issue. Securing a glass of water from an assistant, he proceeded with the trick here described, saying, "There is no doubt but that some of you think that I have trained assistants helping me in many of these tricks. I will ask your President or Secretary or any skeptic in the audience to step upon the platform to assist me for the next presentation. I also want the services of a good ball-player. Is there anyone in the audience who can catch a ball?—What, no volunteers? Surely, there is some one amongst you who— that's it—step right forward, sir! You are the President, I presume?"

The gentleman referred to had arrived upon the platform and nodded his head in affirmation to Hargrave's inquiry.

"Who is a good ball-player?" Hargrave asked of the President, who in turn beckoned

water. This gentleman here is to catch it without spilling a drop. I would suggest that in dropping the glass, you release your hold suddenly, opening your hand rapidly, so that the glass will fall straight downward. I shall hold on to the flag." With these instructions, he extended the President's arm so that the glass which he was clutching under the flag was far away from his body. The catcher crouched down and extended his hands to receive the glass while Hargrave grasped the end of the banner. "One—two— three," the signal was given. The President opened his hand suddenly. Hargrave snapped the flag away, and the catcher stood there, his mouth open, his hands open, and the glass nowhere to be seen.

"Gone!" I was not quick enough to grasp my cue, so Hargrave repeated it for my benefit. The truth of the matter was that the trick mystified me and I was watching it intently, not paying any attention to what was being said, for Hargrave once taught me not to listen to what the performer has to say. Chatter is very distracting, sometimes completely masking the method of performing a trick, and I did want to see how the trick was executed.

"Up your sleeve," I shouted. The audience first glared at me and then looked at Hargrave. A pleasant grin illuminated his suave countenance. "Anyone else imagine that the glass of water went up my sleeve?" he asked. No one else did. Then Hargrave added. "Of course it went up my sleeve. Look!" He extended his arm upwardly and a water spout burst out from the arm pit. Then water spouted from his waistline and from his shoe. The water continued to spout for some moments, then stopped suddenly. Hargrave then introduced his water fountain, described on page 88. Thanking the President and the baseball-player, who by the way was not attired as one, Hargrave led them to the stairs connecting the stage with the auditorium floor.

Lanterns from Nowhere

Hargrave now picked up a black velvet cloth. He waved this about and then produced from behind it a Japanese lantern fully extended and lit. He hung this upon a wire, waved the cloth again and produced another lantern. Again and again he repeated the action until the entire room was full of Japanese lanterns, and finally from beneath the folds of the small cloth, no larger than a couple of feet square, a lantern, six feet long and about four feet wide, was produced. This was the trick which he wanted me to watch, but I told him when I saw him later in the evening, that I'd be hanged if I saw how he could fold all those lanterns into such a tiny square. Many other tricks were comprised in his repertoire, but the two just mentioned are so easily performed that I thought it best to describe them more fully. Referring to the disappearing glass, Hargrave described it as follows:

"The patter in that trick makes it more effective than does the trick. In the silk flag which I use, and which by the way is made up of two identical pieces sewed to-gether at the seams, is a wire frame, the wire being soldered end on end. This frame is of the same size as the top of the glass. In covering the glass with the flag, I lift the wire frame so as to indicate how the glass is to be raised. At the same time, the other hand passes beneath the folds of the flag and extracts the glass full of water, placing it under cover of the table top, the flag, or the table decoration, in a compartment under the table, or if desired, upon a chair. With my hand still on the wire frame, but shifting it slightly, so that my rather unfortunate assistant may grasp the frame, I immediately direct him to walk toward the front of the platform, so that he cannot press down upon the table, discovering thereby that he is being deceived from that moment on.

Of course, when he releases his hold and I jerk the flag away, the ring sewed inside is pulled away with the silk banner. It slides to one end and is not noticed by either the victim or the audience. Of course, the rest of the trick is simple, and you described it in the article which I believe you called "The Wonder Fountains." I nodded in the affirmative. Hargrave then continued: "The second exhibition which you are so interested in, and, which I have called, 'The Japanese Lantern,' is a little more difficult to perform without preparation. The Japanese lanterns are purchased at any novelty store. In each a flashlight battery, bulb and socket are mounted. An automatic switch, which I am showing in this illustration, turns on the light at the proper moment. Each lantern is further equipped with a corset steel spring, so that it will snap open. These lanterns are then folded together and held in the position by a spring test tube clamp. Each test tube clamp is attached to a stout black thread at one end, and a little black button at the other end. The buttons hang loosely, just beneath the waistcoat, while half a dozen or more of the lanterns are suspended by pins from a little paper stub beneath the coat. Picking up the black cloth with one hand, and passing the other hand beneath the waistcoat with the fingers open, one of the buttons may be grasped between the fingers, that is, the hand is passed along the thread so that the thread passes between the fingers, and when the performer reaches the button, he has secured a grip on one or more of the threads. The black cloth which has been lifted in the left hand is then passed over to the right hand. Here care has been taken to bring the button forward, holding it under the fingers. The right hand with one corner of the black cloth is then passed over in proximity to the left hand, which grasps a corner of the cloth previously held by the left hand, and also the button. Showing both sides of the cloth, the performer moves his right hand to another corner of the cloth, permitting the black thread to slide between his fingers. By extending the arm slightly, one of the lanterns is pulled free of its attachment, and slides from beneath the waistcoat. It is a simple matter to detach the spring test tube clamp, permitting the lantern to open suddenly and lighting it at the same time. As one hand goes up to hang the lantern upon the stretched wire, the other hand reaches for another button, disposing of the test tube clamp, by dropping it into a chair *servante*. Not only can the lanterns be suspended from the waistcoat, but also from tables, chairs, drapery, etc. The large lantern which I produced is made like the smaller ones, but elaborately folded.

"By way of divertisement, there is an interesting little paddle trick which is being sold by street corner magicians. This is an ordinary wooden paddle made in the form of a tennis racket. Attached to it by a rubber band is a five dollar bill on one side and a one dollar bill on the other; both sides of the paddle are shown to the audience by a simple wafting movement, but during the course of seemingly exhibiting the other side, the paddle is given a half turn, so that in reality the same side is exhibited. This turning action taking place between the fingers is so slight that it is scarcely noticeable. Under cover of the palm of the left hand, the paddle is turned so as to bring the five dollar bill uppermost. Then the wafting movement is continued seemingly again exhibiting both sides of the paddle, but due to the slight turning action produced by the fingers, the dollar bill remains uppermost. In this way a five dollar bill can be changed to a one dollar bill and vice versa. The method of performing the trick is illustrated in the diagram herewith."

Chemical Stunt

To a solution of 1 teaspoon of cornstarch in a pint of boiling water add one drop of iodine tincture. Bottle the blue liquid and heat the bottle in water until the solution clears. Cork and seal with wax. When the bottle is brought to room temperature, the color returns.

Water and Oil Experiments

No capillary action in greased tube. Oiled and clean balls repel each other. Sawdust on water repelled by oil. Oil drop will stay suspended in solution as shown. Oil unaffected by centrifugal force.

Coin Trick

Place a coin in a dish of water and challenge anyone to remove it without wetting the fingers. This can be done by inserting two matches in a cork as shown above, floating the cork on the surface of the water and then lighting the matches. If a glass is now placed over the burning matches, and held in position for a few seconds, it will be found that all the water in the dish will be forced up into the glass. The coin will be left dry and can easily be removed.

The Black and White Slates

PROFESSOR Henri Hargrave had returned from a vacation at his summer retreat at Miami, Florida, and a week or so after his arrival, I was ushered into his presence in his palatial Long Island home. After we had exchanged confidences, and he had thanked me for letters from various magicians which I had turned over to him, he beckoned me to a chair, and excusing himself for a few moments, he retired to his laboratory. With the exception of a large black slate some distance to the left of me, there was little change in the room. That feminine touch, however, seemed no longer present and although Hargrave was not married, there was that indefinite something about the way his home was decorated, which usually made it so comfortable to the visitor. Hargrave had been gone but five or six minutes when he returned. Seating himself beside me, he said. "I haven't had much time to set things right, as yet, because I have been very busy with two spirit-writing slates which I can assure you are going to interest not only the amateurs, but also the professional magicians. Strange to say, Old Top, even though many of the magical societies are thoroughly in

favor of my continuing these contributions, there are a few individuals who can see no good in my disclosing my own original material. Nevertheless, the pleasant compliments which I have received from many associates, and the requests from magicians for apparatus similar to those I describe, make me believe that these original disclosures are of great value. As I have often stated, much of the mystery in magic is due to the presentation of the trick. I have found that some magicians employing apparatus of my own design would have thoroughly mystified yours truly, if I didn't remember having placed this apparatus within their hands. For instance, the Talking Skull apparatus was placed in a manikin on one occasion in England, where this manikin answered questions when placed in the lobby of a theater, and also when carried out among the audience, during a performance.

"The two tricks which I am about to show you today are simply constructed, and present no difficulty whatever in their presentation. The line of patter talk which the magician employs is extremely important, and I always lay stress upon this point when building special apparatus for amateur or

professional theatricals. A small trick is much more effective when properly presented, than a big spectacular stunt devoid of speech."

His Japanese valet had entered the room in response to Hargrave's ring. "Sing," commanded the inventor, "I am going to show Old Timer the slate. Will you bring forth the easel—Right there will do." Then turning to me he continued, "You see it is an ordinary slate but gifted with marvelous powers. For example——." He picked up a copy of a magazine, and pointing toward it said, "See that title, now watch the slate." I glanced in the direction indicated.

Slowly and for no reason whatever, bold white letters similar to those on the magazine cover progressively formed themselves on the black slate, just as though a heavy white brush was being swept across the slate by invisible hands, the brush itself being likewise invisible. At first I thought that instead of a black slate, the Professor was using a sheet of glass. I mentioned this fact to him, stating that someone was probably in back of a black glass sheet, painting upon its surface. He explained that such a method could of course be employed, but in this instance it

The Spirit Slate Upon Which the Writing Automatically Appears Is Really Made in Two Parts, the Letters Being Cut Out and Backed With a Black Tape Band, Which Band is Progressively Removed, Showing the White Background. The Writing Tennis Ball and Slate Trick Is a Cleverly Veiled Magnetic Appliance Almost Impossible of Detection. It Gives the Answer to Any Question by Writing Upon the White Paper in Bold Letters.

was not being done for obvious reasons.

"You would like to know how that's done, eh?" queried Hargrave. 'Well, it's simpler than you think. The slates which are placed upon the easel are made of black cardboard, in which the answers as well as the words which I desire to transmit to the audience, are cut. In other words, these letters are cut out in that black cardboard slate. Then in back of this black board and separated from it a distance of but one-half an inch, is another plate which has been painted white. This second plate may be removed in preparing the trick for its next exhibition. The letters which have been cut out of the black sheet are one-half inch wide, and as nearly continuous as it is possible to make them. Of course, small pieces of black material must be left to hold the center portions of the looped letters in place, but in words where these loop letters occur, such as the letter O or the letter D, I try to conceal these attachments by not closing the letters at the top. In back of these cut-out letters I then secure black electrician's adhesive tape, beginning to secure it at the end of the last letter and continuing until I have completely obscured the opening of the very first letter. The tape must be continuous. The end is then passed out through an opening in the center of the white sheet where it dangles from the rear of the slate. When I give the signal, Sing merely grasps this tape and pulls upon it, and in doing so the letters of the words are slowly and progressively unveiled, as the tape is removed."

I interrupted Hargrave with, "But I went over there to examine that slate, and I didn't see any cut-out. It seems to me to be perfectly solid."

The magician chuckled, "And what did you think my trusty servant was doing while you were walking toward the easel? You saw him changing the slates, did you not,

during which change he placed a dummy slate upon the easel for your most scrutinous inspection." Turning he continued, "Sing, bring out one of those white paper blocks, and get me a tennis ball and a large well of ink.—You had better put the ink in an evaporating dish instead of a well."

A moment later Sing returned with the ink and a tennis ball. He retreated almost immediately and coming into the room for the second time, placed a large paper pad,—such as artists are wont to draw upon when giving a stage exhibition—upon the easel. He then disappeared. Asking me to examine the tennis ball, Hargrave dipped it into the ink, unmindful of soiling his fingers. With the ink-soaked ball he walked toward the easel, and then with a word of command placed the ball in the center of the paper sheet, where much to my consternation it remained.

"You desire to ask any questions?" Hargrave queried.

For a moment I thought of a real tricky question, one which could not be answered by the words "yes" or "no." This was the question I placed. "What are the colors of the American flag?" The ball swung over to the left of the sheet, leaving a black ink mark as it rolled. Then it started to spell out the words, *red, white and blue,* all in one stroke.

"How does it work?" I continued. "Magnetism?"

"Correct," Hargrave replied. "You see immediately in back of the paper pad is a strong iron magnet capable of operating on 110 volt D. C. supply. This magnet has a wrought iron or annealed mild steel round core, measuring 7 inches long by ½ inch in diameter. At either end of the core a fibre or other insulating disc is placed, each disc measuring about ¼ inch thick, and 2½ inches in diameter. The winding space

between the discs should measure about 6 inches, and for 110 volts, D. C., with a current consumption of .1 ampere, the winding should comprise 3¼ pounds of No. 30 B. & S. gauge, single cotton covered magnet wire.

"If a battery electro-magnet is desired for the purpose, particularly where 100 volts direct current is not available, you will find the following magnet data very effective: The soft wrought iron or mild steel core should measure in this case 9 inches long by ⅝ inch in diameter and have two fibre or other insulating bobbin-discs placed at either end, and fitting tightly on the core. These discs may be ¼ to ⅜ inch thick, and measure about 1⅜ inches in diameter. The space between the two bobbin cheeks should be about 8 inches. In building either of these magnets, the iron core should be insulated with several layers of waxed paper, or better still, oiled linen, commonly called Empire cloth. After insulating the core, proceed to wind on 14 even layers of No. 22 B. & S. gauge single cotton covered magnet wire. This winding is designed for use on 8 to 10 dry cells, and when 15 volts from 10 such cells is applied, the current consumed is about 1 ampere, and a very powerful magnetic action results. In either case, one end of the iron core should be turned, filed or otherwise machined off, so as to resemble a small cone with a rounded nose. The iron ball which is dipped in ink may be a light hollow one, or even a pressed steel or a tin ball. If the ball is not too heavy, it may receive a thin felt covering which will hold the ink better for performing the trick. This magnet is suspended in back of the easel on a lazy tong bracket. An extension in the form of a wooden rod is attached to the magnet, which permits the operator to manipulate the magnet, forming words or phrases. A switch, at his control, turns off the current when desired.

Mystification in Candle Tricks

Chemistry Turns Magician for Entertainment

Connect several candle wicks with a piece of thread which has been soaked in a solution of potassium chlorate and sugar. Light one end of the thread and the flame jumps from candle to candle.

The faces on sheet metal perform this trick. The lighted candle is held to the gun powder, where the small explosion extinguishes it. The phosphorus in the pipe bowl relights the flame.

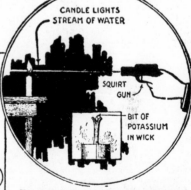

You may light a candle with a stream of water from a squirt gun if a bit of potassium is placed in the wick first. Be extremely careful in handling sodium or potassium. ALWAYS use tweezers.

An edible candle which will at once taste well and mystify onlookers, is made by constructing a cylinder from the fleshy part of an apple, and using the meat of a walnut as the wick. The walnut burns.

The performer touches the wick of a candle which has just been blown out with a wand, and it immediately relights. The wand is a glass rod dipped in sulphuric acid and potassium permanganate.

An ice candle which will burn is made by shaking together equal parts of water and ether in a test tube, and immersing it in a freezing mixture of ice and salt.

Shooting Through A Woman

A Loud Report Was Followed Almost Immediately by the Crashing of Glass, and the Hollow Thud of the Bullet as it Flattened Itself Against the Steel Plate. Water Trickled From the Edge of the Table. The Magician Had Obviously Sent a Bullet Through the Body of His Assistant Without Causing Her to Even Wince with Pain.

IT was a rather glum day, the sun after repeated efforts to penetrate the veil of mist and fog which overhung the city, had given up its attempt. I had just been settling myself down to the work on hand when the wailing peal of the telephone bell aroused me from a semi-stuporous condition.

"Hello." It was Hargrave's voice. I recognized it immediately. Professor Henri Hargrave is a well-known magician whose original magical creations are being here presented.

"Hello," he repeated, and when he learned I was at the opposite end of the line, continued, "I'm going to be quite busy toward the latter end of the week, so if you want some new stunts for another article, you had better run right out here. You will find me at my home. The next train leaves the depot at 10.10, so you had better speed it up." Without even awaiting my reply, he hung up the receiver.

I, of course, was only too glad to get away for a few hours, and in eighteen minutes I was speeding outward on the tracks of the Long Island Railroad.

Having reached the now familiar residence, I was ushered into Hargrave's presence. On the library table were a number of rifles which the master magician was evidently cleaning. Pointing toward a chair, which I accepted, Hargrave said:

"I am about to show you one of the most spectacular stage tricks which has ever been produced. As a matter of fact, I believe it compares favorably with the well-known 'Sawing a Woman in Half' stunt, which took the country by storm a little over a year ago. You are without a doubt, acquainted with rifles, and you also understand bullets, I presume?" I acquiesced.

He lifted an automatic pump rifle from the table and placed it in my hands, a box of .22 caliber bullets was now opened and pushed toward me. Just then his secretary tripped lightly into the room. "Did you ring, sir?" she inquired.

"Yes, I want to show this gentleman that new stunt of mine. Just come this way, please." So saying, he placed her in front of a steel plate, covered on the outside with asbestos, upon which a target was painted. Between the target and the girl's back a small table was pushed, and upon this was mounted a glass full of water. While he was doing this, I was filling the automatic rifle with .22 long bullets.

"Have you the gun ready?" he inquired. I ejected one of the cartridges, which I retained, and handed the fully loaded gun to him. He lifted it to his shoulder, aimed and then lowered it again, placing it upon the table with the other rifles. He then walked over and shifted the girl's position slightly. Coming back to his original position, he picked up the rifle again and carefully levelled it. A minute target below the girl's chest was the point toward which the rifle was being sighted. I was visibly nervous, in fact I jumped up, grasped the gun, and turned it away.

"Man alive, what are you trying to do, kill the young lady?"

"Tut, tut, Old Timer, you don't see her raising such a fuss at being shot, do you? Now you let me alone for a moment." He raised the rifle for a third time. There was a deafening roar followed immediately thereafter by the shattering of glass. Slowly the girl stepped aside, the water from the broken tumbler poured down upon the carpeted floor. Hargrave stepped forward and pried the bullet out of the asbestos sheet, and handed it to me. I was too

dumbfounded to speak. "That's the X-ray bullet," the magician explained. "Goes right through your body and you never feel it." It took me a few moments to recover my sangfroid, and obtain the explanation which follows herewith in Hargrave's own words.

"Didn't it strike you as being rather strange that a girl with a lace dress on should have a leather belt strapped around her waist? Well that leather belt secured the outfit necessary for the successful duplication of this stunt, but of course, in regular performances it would not be in evidence. In the small of her back is a rectangular steel block, which has been attached to this belt by means of two long projecting lugs; the block and belt recall the manner in which a wrist watch is strapped to the wrist. Drilled through this steel block is a hole which houses a twenty-two calibre short cartridge. The trigger is fastened over a vertical hole, which hole penetrates the steel block at right angles to the bore. This trigger is shaped as shown in the illustration, so as to line up with the vertical hole at its driven end, and its point centers over the cartridge. In this longer opening is placed a circular steel block, having a wire securely embedded in one end. The wire passes downward to the bottom of the block where it is looped. The looped wire serves the purpose of resetting the trigger. At right angles to this trigger hole another hole is drilled which provides for the insertion of a pin to hold the striking hammer. Two electro-magnets are taken from a bell and fitted with short curved extensions, made of soft iron. The armature of the bell from which the contact spring has been removed, has had a small steel pin inserted into its center. This pin penetrates the aforementioned hole, where it holds the striking hammer under tension. When current is permitted to flow into the coils, the armature is pulled toward the magnet and this action releases the hammer which in turn is driven upward by the action of the spring where it strikes the trigger, the blow being transmitted to the cartridge which explodes its charge. The circuit is completed by wires passing down the legs to metal pins protruding from the heels of the shoes, making contact with segments in a wired carpet leading to a battery and switch, which in this case was the rifle which I held in my hand."

"Very clever, indeed," I expostulated, "but what became of the bullets I placed in that rifle? You deliberately fired at the lady."

"Granted, but I fired a blank cartridge. If you will pick up the rifle you will find that there are just as many bullets in it now as when you loaded it. You will also see that there are several rifles on the table which are identical. One of thse contains blank cartridges only. This rifle is likewise fitted with a contact or circuit closing arrangement, passing from the trigger through rings on my hand (my usual procedure), thence down the legs to pins in the heels, as you will note." He lifted his foot to show the pins mentioned, which protruded about a half inch. "When I put the rifle aside for a moment seemingly changing the position of my fair accomplice, I

managed, in coming back to the scene of activity, to exchange my rifle for the one loaded with blank cartridges, and fitted with the contact making arrangement. It is obviously impossible to make a mistake in this manner, because the first thing I look for is the electrical device and also for the metallic lugs which I securely put in contact with the rings on each hand, so as to make sure that the device will not fail. Wires from the rings lead up the arm and thence to the carpet via the shoe pins. The rifle being filled with blanks permits me to eject the cartridge when I so desire, or fire repeatedly, if the electrical device does not operate properly the first time."

Hindu Rope Trick Exposed

There are several explanations concerning the method in which the Hindus do their famous rope trick in which a rope is thrown into the air, by a fakir and remains suspended there. A boy climbs up the rope and then disappears from sight, only to reappear again at some other place. Most investigators adhere to the theory that the trick was never done at all. The most plausible explanations, if we ignore this first mentioned belief are: 1—Clouds of incense are burned by the fakir. A coil of rope to one end of which two thin wires are attached is then thrown into the air, while assistants pull on the ends of the wire, suspending the rope beween trees. The boy climbs up the rope walks across the wire and climbs down the tree. 2—The same effect accomplished in a courtyard where some claim to have heard of its being performed. 3—Many believe that the East Indian possesses hypnotic powers and that the mobs "imagine" they see the trick.

How to Make an Ammonia Fountain

Obtain a wooden packing box about a foot square, turn it on its side and cut a slot large enough to insert the neck of the inverted colorless bottle B. A piece of glass tubing T, fifteen inches long is drawn to a fine point and past thru a perforated rubber stopper which fits B tightly. A stout wire W, is also past thru a fine hole in the stopper and bent at both ends as shown. By turning it at H, the capillary end of the glass tube may be broken off later.

When ready to fill with gas, have the stopper with its fittings removed from the bottle and see that the latter is perfectly dry. Next mix two parts of ammonium chlorid (sal ammoniac) with one part of fresh dry lime and place in a test tube supplied with a stopper and delivery tube. Pass this tube well up into the inverted bottle B, and then gently heat the test tube. The bottle will soon fill with ammonia gas, and when the delivery tube is withdrawn, the prepared stopper with its capillary tube and wire is quickly inserted in place and made tight.

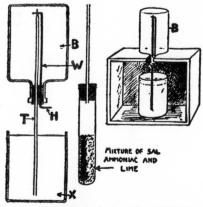

This Interesting Fountain Stunt Can be Tried by Even the Most Juvenile Chemical Experimenter. If Properly Executed the Change in Color of the Water from a Transparent to a Beautiful Red Tint Becomes Startling.

If the free end of the tube T, is now lowered into a vessel X, filled with water, the fountain is ready to operate. . First cool B with a fan or wet cloth and cause its gaseous contents to shrink. Then slowly turn H to break off the end of T. Instantly the water rises in T from X, and appears as a drop at the end of the capillary. The ammonia dissolves at once in it—causing a vacuum which lowers the pressure to such an extent that the water rushes in and can be heard as well as seen hitting the top of the bottle. This will continue until B is nearly full.

If some phenolphthalein is added to the contents of X, the water will turn red as it discharges into B. If any copper salt be dissolved in X, then the contents of B will be a fine blue color.

A little ingenuity will suggest other modifications of this rather striking experiment. A valve may be inserted between B and X and an open tube T may be used.

The Mysterious Candles

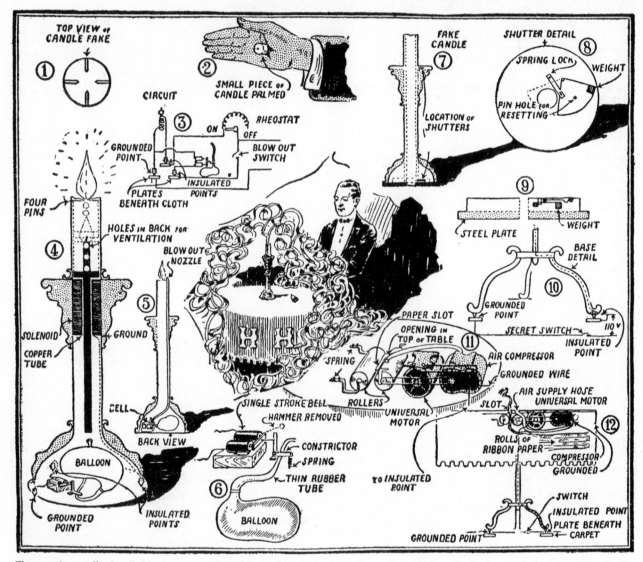

The mysterious candles described in the accompanying article are shown in the detail above. At 1, the four pins in the top of the fake candle also illustrated at 4, are seen. These pins prevent the lit candle concealed within the fake (4), from projecting too far when current to the solenoid is turned on. Note the balloon in the base of the candle-stick, which blows out the light on command. The arrangement of the blow-out pipe is seen at 5; 3 is a circuit diagram, and at 6 we find the construction of the blow-out valve. In the paper-presentation candle, 8 and 9 demonstrate the shutter arrangement for disguising the hollow candle-stick, and 11 and 12 the perspective and side elevation of the table. When the candle-stick is placed on the table, the opening in the base covers both the slot for the delivery of paper, and the air supply opening.

THE snow lay in drifts and, here and there, where the wind had blown it from the paved walks, blotches of ice, rough but slippery, lay before me as I wound my way to Hargrave's home. Upon entering into the library, it was some time before I was warm enough to talk coherently. Henry Hargrave, the master magician, with a cheery, "Hello, rather cold out this morning. Won't you have a chair," proceeded to demonstrate and explain two of his new novelties, which, in order to cover them fully in this article, will have to have most of the accompanying patter omitted.

Securing a candle-stick from the mantel over the open hearth fireplace and placing a lit candle in it, Hargrave blew out the light. Then walking toward where I was sitting, he proffered a box of Perfectos. Lighting mine and then his, he directed my attention to the candle-stick on the table by saying, "I guess we will have a little more light here." Tossing the lit match toward the table upon which the candle rested, I

was astonished to see it light up slowly. In a moment I was upon my feet making toward the candle-stick, but was interrupted by Hargrave's, "Not so fast, Old Man. See if you can blow it out from where you are." I blew, but the flame did not even flicker. I was fully twenty-two feet away from it. I tried it again with the same result.

"Don't blow so hard," was his exclamation.

"Well, let's see you do it," I challenged. Puckering his lips, he blew a scarcely perceptible amount of air in the direction of the lit candle. It wavered, flickered, and almost went out. "See that," he exclaimed, "Now you try it." I did, but could not improve upon my previous attempts. He again told me to blow more easily, to which I exclaimed, "Why, it is against all the laws of physics . . ." "Now don't let us enter into any scientific discourses or explanations," he interrupted, "Just watch me. I blew too hard the last time, consequently the air passed the candle too swiftly,

but if I blow very lightly—ever so lightly— we will see what we shall see."

He suited his action to his words and blew ever so lightly; in fact, I do not believe that a feather held three inches away from his lips would have quivered, because of the energy expended in that blow; yet the flame of the candle bent itself sharply and went out. "Well, I'll be——." "Now just a minute," he again interrupted. I've got something else here that I want to show you. The explanations will follow."

So saying, he removed another candle-stick from the mantel and placed it upon an adjoining table, such as magicians use. Breaking the top of it off, he drew out several hundred yards of paper ribbon. He then lifted the candle-stick, holding it at all times away from his body or the table, and placed it upon the table again, assuring me that he was at no time loading the candle-stick, which I was careful to observe he did not do. After he had thus replaced it he walked over toward me, saying as he did so, "I shall need a little more paper in order to start a fire," but before he had finished talking that candle was pouring forth an immense amount of paper. It actually tossed the paper ribbon free of the table over the floor, figuratively speaking, not literally so. "That is almost enough now, I believe," he stated when the paper had been heaped all around the table to a height of almost two feet. He removed the candle-stick from the table, again showing that there was no connection between it and the table. Replacing it he demanded more paper, and it poured forth another volume of the colored ribbon. The paper would stop at his command; it would start again when he so ordered, it continued to flow intermittently until the whole side of the library was massed high with it—until Hargrave himself could no longer wade through it toward the table, yet so rapidly did it issue, that no human hand could possibly have fed it.

Hargrave was a funny sight as he waded through the tangled mass, which, like so many snakes, was gripping his feet. He reached forward, picked up the candle-stick, and then walking toward me, handed it to me. I examined it. It was a neat, simple affair, only differing from the regular candle-stick by the fact that it was extremely slender. There was no opening in the top or the bottom, through which the paper could be made to exude. The bottom was perfectly flat, and the effect produced was without a doubt very spectacular.

Hargrave proceeded to explain the apparatus used. Extricating the table from the jumble of paper, he removed its lid, and there was the entire secret. A minute slot in the top of the table was all that could be seen from the outside, but beneath this slot, underneath the table top, was a relatively spacious compartment. Close up against the top of the table were a pair of rollers made of rather soft rubber, one of which was pressed by a small spring against its neighbor. The other was equipped with a two-inch pulley wheel, connected to a small motor in the table top. Wires led downward through the legs to points projecting from the bottom of two of the legs, which points made contact with metallic plates under the carpet. In addition to that a small rotary blower was directly connected to the electric motor for, as Hargrave explained, the paper ribbon had been in the habit of becoming clogged in the candle-stick and compressed air was found

necessary to force it out of the candle-stick, while at the same time it gave the ribbon the effect of flying out of the broken candle. The paper was placed in a compartment beneath this table in the usual coils, such as employed by magicians, except that the outer band of one piece of paper was securely fastened by means of glue to the inner edge of the roll immediately beneath it. In this way the eight or ten, fourteen-inch rolls of paper could be disposed of completely. It was easy to see that the moment the motor was started, the ribbon was forced up through the table due to the friction rollers which gripped and fed it. At the same time the blower operated, causing the ribbon to be waved about, the nozzle of the blower being adjacent to the slotted opening in the table top, but covered if desired by a small trap. Hargrave then grasped the candle-stick, introducing a long hat pin into the top and bottom, and pushed aside two shutters which exposed a long tubular opening extending through its center. I now saw the trick, or at least thought I did, but there were several things yet to be explained, namely, his ability to remove the candle holder from the table at any moment desired. This, I found, was very simple.

Hargrave merely turned off the current supply to the electric motor, and by pulling the holder across the table top severed the paper band, much the same as if he had used a pair of shears. The thinness of the candle-stick makes one suspect the table, at least it so affects one who is versed in magic technic, but when the candle-stick is finally passed out for examination, the effect becomes more mystifying and puzzling. The shutters in the candle-stick operate on pivots and when it is tipped over to one side the shutters swing closed, and practically lock in that position; to replace them an effort is required. There are several different types of traps made for these closures, Hargrave showed me several styles, but in view of the fact that the reader undoubtedly has his own opinion with regard to how these should be designed, only one is given here.

This explained the operation of one of the candle holders quite thoroughly, but not the other, which I found to be far simpler than the one previously described, and which could be built by the average amateur at a lower cost than the first.

Essentially this consists of a fake candle, which is a hollow tube representing a candle and perforated in the back with several

holes. A candle-stick is procured and drilled out, so as to house a solenoid $2\frac{1}{2}$ inches long, and $1\frac{1}{4}$ inches external diameter. A copper tube is now procured, $\frac{1}{2}$-inch internal diameter, and upon this No. 18 bell wire is wound, until the entire coil fits the hollowed-out portion of the candle-stick tightly. In this a long iron rod is placed, which will slide freely in the copper tube, upon the top of which rod a small plate is mounted holding a lit candle. When this device is shown, a small piece of candle is attached in the top of the fake, which is removed in the act of extinguishing the light, with the fingers; so small can this piece be that no difficulty will be found in palming it off. Wires connect to points in the base of the candle holder, thence to plates beneath the plush covering of the table, and down through the legs in the usual manner. Current to the solenoid will now cause the small piece of candle within the hollow fake to be propelled upward, due to the action of the solenoid on the iron core, which is attracted into the coil. The fake at the top of the table is so arranged that four points project around this top to prevent the candle from being propelled too high, as otherwise the increased size of the candle would immediately indicate to the audience that the device is merely a clever mechanical contrivance. For the extinguishing system, an ordinary single stroke electric bell in the base of the candle holder is attached to the spring held constrictor of a rubber tube. To the end of this rubber tube an inflated balloon is fixed with rubber bands.

A separate circuit to the bell from the twelve-volt storage battery, which is employed to operate this device, causes the constrictor of the rubber tube to open, permitting some of the air to escape out of the toy gas balloon. A copper tube bent at the top of the fake candle holder is lined up, so that a blast of air from it will cause the candle to be extinguished. In operating this feature, the control switch for the air is given a short sharp touch, closing the circuit momentarily. This is insufficient to cause the candle to go out, yet it will cause the flame of the same to flicker. This effect can be produced several times, after which the candle may be blown out. The toy balloon houses an amount of air great enough to blow out the candle even if it were lit several times.

Mystic-Colored Shadow Star

By means of an interesting experiment it is possible to show that, in certain circumstances, *a colored shadow* can be obtained from an opaque object. In the first place prepare a box formed of two sheets of glass

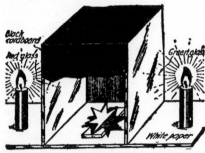

Arrangement of the Apparatus for Producing the Mystic-Colored Shadow Star—an Unusual Experiment.

(one red and the other green) and two pieces of black pasteboard. The sides of the box should be rather taller than they are wide and neither a top nor a bottom is required. Where there is any difficulty in getting colored glass plain sheets can be painted with the varnish dyes so widely sold for treating hats, etc. In this way very good colored glass can be prepared in any shade. The box might be of any convenient size; a good measurement for the sides would be about twelve inches wide by fifteen inches high. Now, from another piece of black pasteboard, cut out a shape similar to that shown in the diagram. This, as will be seen, is exactly half of an eight pointed star. The shape is fixed with an adhesive to a small flat piece of pasteboard so that it is held in a vertical position.

Place the box on a sheet of white paper. Then put a lighted candle on either side near to the glass. Extinguish all other lights in the room. Altho the rays of the candles pass thru the colored glass the light

on the paper floor of the box is white. This is owing to the fact that red and green are complementary colors.

Put the shape into the box so that its flat sides face the glass in the manner shown in the diagram. At once a most beautifully colored star shadow appears on the floor of the box. One half of this is green and the other half red.

Star Cut from Cardboard, to Be Mounted in the Center of the Box Shown at the Left.

The Obedient Candles

The effects produced by the flames of the candles in which their light flares up at the command of the operator, are developed by a tambour device placed in the gas line of the individual candles. Illuminating gas supplies each candle, the single stroke bells striking against the rubber diaphragm cause the flame to spurt up. The detail in the upper right hand corner shows the apparatus required, which is controlled by an assistant behind the scenes.

HENRI HARGRAVE, the famous magician, had promised to give me information regarding the *Obedient Candles,* a new electrical novelty, which he had just invented, so, inasmuch as I already had an appointment with him, which I did not hesitate to keep, I soon found myself in the throes of mysticism.

On a table in Hargrave's laboratory were ten candles in their respective candlesticks. "It won't do you much good to examine them," Hargrave commenced in explaining the trick, "because, as you have heretofore found, nearly all of the apparatus which I build, may be examined by skeptical individuals. So I will show you what the effect is at first and follow this up with the explanation. Suppose you take a sheet of paper and a pencil, and jot down a series of numbers, commencing at the figure 1, if you like, and culminating at the figure 9,999,999. You may choose as many figures as you desire, in any arrangement, and then total them up. Call them out as you write them." While I was calling out the figures, he was busy lighting the candles. Needless to say, I called out a group (jotting them down as I did so) which would stagger a skillful public accountant, if he attempted to total the amount.

Hargrave turned to me just as I had exclaimed "That's enough!" and said, "Before

totalling the figures you have given, I wish you would look at the candles. A flicker denotes a numeral. Three flickers in succession signify 'yes,' and two signify 'no' when numerals are not being considered. In this way, the candles will not only answer your questions, but will also add, subtract, multiply or divide for you. Just write down the number of flicks which emanate from the individual candles for your result."

Immediately my answer came. The first candle at the extreme left did not waver, the next one flared up and down five times in succession, the third one four times, the fourth one seven, and so on. According to Hargrave, my answer was correct. It took me some time to figure up the amount, but when I finally succeeded I found that the candles had told the truth. I asked them to subtract one number from the other, and before I could draw a line beneath the second group of figures I had jotted upon the paper, the candles were responding. I then commenced to ask them several questions. The entire group replied in unison. I then changed my tactics and asked the reply of candle No. 1, which was forthcoming. The flame in the others did not move, except for a slight draught of air, caused by an open window some distance away. When I asked of candle No. 3 whether candle No. 1 replied to my question, two flicks indicated "no," and

I was promptly informed which candle had replied by the number of flicks delivered by candle No. 6, to which the next question was put.

My age was given by candle No. 10, and many other replies which were received were extremely humorous.

Hargrave did not manipulate any controls. Finally he reached over, grasped one of the candlesticks, and blowing the flame out, came toward me. I examined it and found it to be an imitation candle, having a metal top with a small hole therein. Aside from that, it did not seem at all suspicious. It was up to Hargrave to give me the details. The base seemed so thin, it would have been almost impossible, in my opinion, to house any electrical apparatus therein. The usual method of making contact by means of points, was not in evidence, although I did notice two small wire brushes projecting from the base of the candlestick-holder.

Hargrave opened up one of the candlesticks, and the entire system was revealed. Essentially it was a gas appliance. A thin copper tube led to the top of a fake candle painted to resemble the real object, but for which a real one could be substituted if desired, the essential fact being that a hole must be drilled through the candle itself, to permit the introduction of the copper tube. Near the base of the candle-stick holder, a tin pill-box was located, the cover of which had been cut open leaving only the rim and the same was used to clamp a rubber diaphragm to the rest of the box. Another pipe leading from the bottom of this pill-box, led to a small funnel, having a diameter of approximately 1½ inches at its mouth. Close up against the base was a single stroke bell, the gong of which had been removed, and its hammer bent upwardly so that when the bell was operated the hammer would strike the rubber diaphragm. The circuit to the bell was completed by means of two wire brushes resembling pieces of wire hair brush. These were secured to a base of fibre, and the latter screwed to the candle-stick base. The table-top itself did not disclose any openings, being covered with cloth, but Hargrave took particular care in placing his candlestick down upon the table. When he removed it again, he showed me that the table also contained two wire brushes, which projected upward, and when the candlestick was placed down upon the table, the brushes interlocked, making, as he said, a more perfect contact than the plate and point method he had heretofore used.

Near the center of the candlestick-holder, directly under the funnel end of the small copper tube, a hole was drilled through the table-top which admitted a ⅛ inch tube. This tube did not pass through the table-cloth or cover, consequently, the opening remained concealed. The tube was connected to the illuminating gas supply line, which furnished the gas for the light, seen emanating from the candles. The gas itself burned with a yellow flame much like that of a tallow candle.

"It is evident," Hargrave continued, "that whenever the single stroke bell is energized, it strikes the rubber tambour. This causes the gas contained within the metallic box, to be compressed, which, finding its path of least resistance is in an upwardly direction, causes the flame to rise considerably above normal. The flame then drops down, and at a word of command, it can be made to fall below normal.

"But why did I not smell any gas when you extinguished the light?" I interrogated.

"For the simple reason," was Hargrave's reply, "that I took the precaution to open one of the windows slightly. The amount of gas passing from one of the candlesticks is very small indeed, and it would take quite some time before the odor would have made you aware of the fact that the candles operated on illuminating gas. By insuring a proper circulation, you would probably never realize that fact. Naturally I get a sort of Bunsen burner effect, except that the air is not forced upward with the gas. The lack of air supply produces the yellow flame. When my assistant, who operates the keys controlling the relative lights, presses any of the switches, the hammer of the bell contained within the base, strikes the rubber diaphragm of the tambour. This causes the flame to lengthen. When the key is released, and the circuit opened, the hammer flies backward and the flame drops below the normal point.

"As to the rapid calculation of figures, that is very simply accomplished. My Japanese valet, who listens to your questions by means of a telephone receiver which connects to a microphone placed in this room, takes down the numbers on a comptometer. By the time you have figured up the result, he has already completed the operation, and the answer is being transmitted by means of the light flashes."

Paper Butterflies that Fly

Here is a charming little experiment that can be carried out by means of a Seidlitz powder, one of the last things in the world from which one would expect any amusement. Secure an empty jam jar and get a good-sized cork to act as a stopper to this. In the centre of the cork bore a hole thru which opening a funnel is pushed. The way in which this is done can be seen from the sketch. Next, from brightly colored tissue paper, cut the shapes of three or four butterflies. In the middle of each of these, just between the wings, fasten a thin strip of cork with glue. This serves to act as a body for the paper insect and also helps in the balance of the butterflies when they are in the air.

Fill the jar about half full with water. Then, into it, tip the contents of the packets forming the Seidlitz powder. Quickly replace the cork in the jar and put the paper butterflies into the funnel. Soon the gas generated by the effervescence rises and this causes the butterflies to fly up and down

The Paper Butterflies Seen in the Accompanying Illustration Are Caused to Flit About by the Action of a Seidlitz Powder Dissolving in Water.

in a most life-like manner. The effect continues for quite a good while seeing that the comparative smallness of the opening of the funnel only allows a little of the gas to pass out at a time. This is all sufficient to keep the butterflies flitting up and down in a most fascinating manner.

CEMENT FOR GLASS

Many amateurs have often desired to join pieces of glass or glass tubing together, but as they are not skillful enough at glass blowing and in handling glass, they have hesitated to try various experiments.

A solder for glass can be made by first melting 95 parts of tin and then adding to it, 5 parts of copper. Zinc in the proportion of ½ to 1 per cent. makes this solder harder, whereas lead in the same proportion, makes it softer.

Glass tubing, united by this means, will separate at any other point sooner than at the point of junction.

Musical Glasses

Set two glasses side by side. Across one of them place a thin iron or steel wire bent as illustrated. Then add a little water to the glass. Take another glass of the same size and construction and fill with the same

amount of water so that when struck it produces a musical note identical with that produced by the first glass.

Now experiment upon the second glass and if you produce a musical note by rubbing its top with resined fingers the wire on the first glass will be found to dance. This is due to the fact that both glasses vibrate in unison to the musical note sounded. If a violin is handy and the same note is struck on the violin and wires are placed on top of both glasses they will both vibrate.

If a lighted candle is placed in a bottle containing solution as shown at the right, a flame will burn on top of the bottle as long as the candle remains hot.

Will-o'-the-Wisp

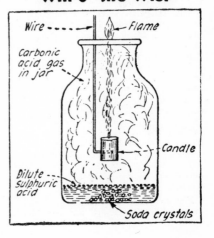

Chemical Entertainments

LIGHTING AN ALCOHOL LAMP WITH AN ICICLE

To light an alcohol lamp with an icicle place a small piece of metallic potassium on the wick. Touch the potassium with an icicle. The reaction will ignite the wick.

BLOWING VOLUMES OF SMOKE FROM TWO CLAY PIPES

Clouds of dense, white smoke will be produced if a piece of absorbent cotton soaked with strong ammonia is placed in the bottom of one pipe and another piece treated with hydrochloric acid is put in another pipe and blown through.

FIRE PRODUCED BY CHEMICAL REACTION

A few drops of suluhuric acid will start a reaction which will result in great fire between a mixture of granulated sugar and potassium chlorate. Keep the flames away from inflammable substances.

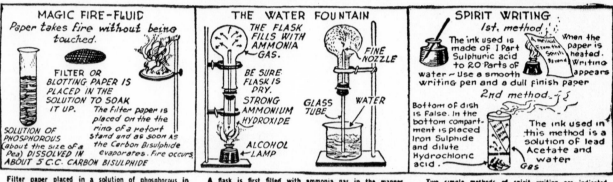

MAGIC FIRE-FLUID

Filter paper placed in a solution of phosphorous in carbon bisulphide takes fire spontaneously when the solvent evaporates. Do not handle phosphorous with the fingers.

THE WATER FOUNTAIN

A flask is first filled with ammonia gas in the manner shown. When fitted with a stopper and glass tube, and when the tube is placed under water, a pretty fountain develops.

SPIRIT WRITING

Two simple methods of spirit writing are indicated above. These methods are often used in circus side shows and street fairs.

Pocket Shocking Coil

A screw-cap shaving stick tin is cut thru the middle, the halves separated ½" as shown at A, Fig. 1, and the gap is bridged by a 1" length of fibre tube that fits tightly over the two halves of the tin. These two portions, insulated from each other, form the *handles* for taking the shock.

The coil heads are ¼" thick hard wood, paraffin waxed, and make a snug fit inside the tin. A ⅜" hole is bored thru the center of each for the core and the front head has holes made and the vibrator fixed on as shown in Fig. 3. The other coil head requires a small hole for the start of the secondary to pass out thru.

The vibrator is a 1¼" length of spring from an alarm clock with a silver contact soldered or riveted on as shown. Bend a ⅜" x ⅝" piece of sheet iron over the vibrator for the core to pull on. Hammer it tight so it does not shift.

The core is formed of a bundle of soft iron wires 3" long and ⅜" in diameter. The space between the coil heads is 2 7/16".

After fitting the heads tightly on the core, wrap three or four layers of shellacked brown paper around it and wind on the two layers of No. 24 S. C. C. wire for the primary coil. The start of the primary winding is brought thru hole F, Fig. 2, and fixt to the vibrator; the end of the winding is taken thru hole H and then back thru K.

Over the primary wind three layers of shellacked paper and then put on the secondary which consists of eleven layers of No.

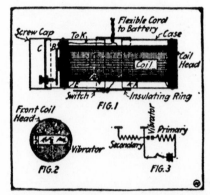

This Shocking Coil, Built Into a Metal Shaving Stick Container, Will Afford Lots of Fun for You and Your Friends. You Will See the Point More Quickly Than They, However! The Two Handles Are Formed by Dividing the Metal Case Into Two Pieces, by Means of a Fiber Ring or Sleeve.

36 enameled wire, covering this again with a further wrapping of shellacked paper.

Next bore a hole thru the fibre ring for the flexible cord from the battery and rivet a piece of springy brass strip about ¼" wide and 1¼" long diametrically opposite this hole, fixing one wire of the flexible cord thereto. This strip acts as a push button and controls the battery current.

Twist the bared ends of the secondary winding over the coil head at each end so that they will make contact with each half of the container when in position. Smear some cement (a kind that will stick glass or iron) on the inside surface of the fibre ring and push in the ends of the container leaving about half an inch space between them.

Finally solder inside the tin the stiff brass strip, C, which acts as a contact pillar, having previously attached a nut for the screw to work in as shown. A fairly stiff spiral spring made of brass wire and placed under the screw head will prevent it slacking back when in use and is more convenient than a lock nut.

To make it real "hot" wind on more layers of finer wire or use more battery voltage. This gives quite a shock.

Tricks of Mediums

A table in the dark room jumps, rocks and dances, although the medium's hands and feet are held by others in the circle. At any moment the lights may be turned on and the table examined for ropes or wires.

Two accomplices, one on either side of the center of the table, can tip it with uncanny effect by use of the harness here shown which is concealed by the vest.

The medium's hands and feet are held, yet strange raps are distinctly heard emanating from the table. The medium may be examined at any moment.

Attached to the garter of the medium's leg is a tube in which a needle slides. To the bottom of this needle a thread is secured terminating at a hook fastened to the other trouser leg. Spreading the legs raises the lead hammer causing a rap.

The medium stands on a chair with his toes lightly resting on the hands of two of the sitters in the circle. Under cover of darkness he is believed to be floating around the room.

Under cover of darkness the shoes are slipped off, grasped by the hands and made to move about the room. The spectator is requested to hold on tightly but not to restrain the movement.

A blank slate is signed on both sides by a spectator to prevent substitution. A message mysteriously appears on the slate a short time later. The slate need never leave the spectator's hands.

A message previously written on the slate is covered by a silk flap. This side is presented for signature first. When the slate is turned over, the assistant pulls the silk flap away. The effect is quite astounding.

Questions written by audience on folded slips of paper are answered by clairvoyant.

The folded billet is held to the forehead and the contents are revealed. Any slip is lifted and a fake message is given. The billet is then unfolded as if for confirmation, but actually to read the next message. Thus the medium reads one ahead all the time. The last slip of paper is a blank.

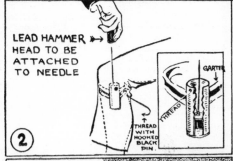

Tricks of Mediums

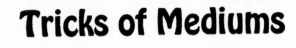

O N this page we show a series of pictures illustrating another group of effects that are found in the repertoire of most spiritualists. All of these effects have actually been worked in dark room seances by the author of the article, and are being used by a great many would-be mediums throughout the country, even at the present time. Even though the effects are surprisingly simple, they produce very uncanny results in the dark.

The above illustration shows a medium tied in a sack. On her lap is placed a slate which is held by two sitters. The medium writes with a thin pencil through the meshes of the sack.

The two photographs at the right illustrate a typical effect often performed in a seance room. A heavy cord or wire is passed through the cuff button holes in the sleeves of the medium's shirt. The cord is held by the sitters. The medium slips off the cuffs and does his work without interference, while the sitters believe that his hands are in absolute control.

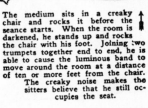

The luminous band on the end of the trumpet seemingly floats with the trumpet around the room. As it passes the medium's lap, he covers the trumpet band with a black cloth and exposes a round circular band previously hidden in the cloth. This he moves with great dexterity, and at high velocity in front of the sitters' faces, demonstrating in this way remarkable "spirit control."

The medium sits in a creaky chair and rocks it before the seance starts. When the room is darkened, he stands up and rocks the chair with his foot. Joining two trumpets together end to end, he is able to cause the luminous band to move around the room at a distance of ten or more feet from the chair. The creaky noise makes the sitters believe that he still occupies the seat.

The medium knows that spirit manifestations are taking place. He asks Miss Steinmetz to hold his left hand, meanwhile operating the trumpet with his right. He then says, "Hold my right hand, Miss Foote," and he operates the trumpet with his left. After repeating the phrases for a while, he insists that both hands be held tightly. With his hands under control he lifts the trumpet to his mouth with his feet, as the three accompanying illustrations show.

Tricks of Mediums

When the seance begins, the spiritualist's right hand and left wrist are held by those closest to him in the circle of sitters.

The medium, going into a trance, jerks his right hand loose, but immediately calls attention to the fact that his hand is not being held. Seemingly both hands are again under control. Actually they are not.

A spirit hand pinches a sitter. Note the lazy tong grip.

A remarkable similarity to the sound produced by a hand pump may be effected by collapsing and extending a spirit horn.

Sliding the horn across a carpeted floor produces a sound of wood being sawed.

A luminous button on the end of the collapsible rod produces "spirit lights."

The sound of a person drowning is produced by blowing into horn, as shown.

Daylight trumpet mediumship is effected as illustrated. Even those standing eight inches away cannot hear him whisper.

BUTTON COVERED WITH RADIUM LUMINOUS PAINT

LUMINOUS PENDANT

SMALL MUSIC BOX IN MANDOLIN — HOLE FOR ROD

RUBBER COVERED CURVED ENDS FOR LEVITATION OF GLASS OF WATER AND "BABY" TOUCH, ETC.

The luminous objects and the mandolin are moved about the room by a collapsible rod which the medium uses. Diagram of lazy tong also shown.

Science Odds and Ends

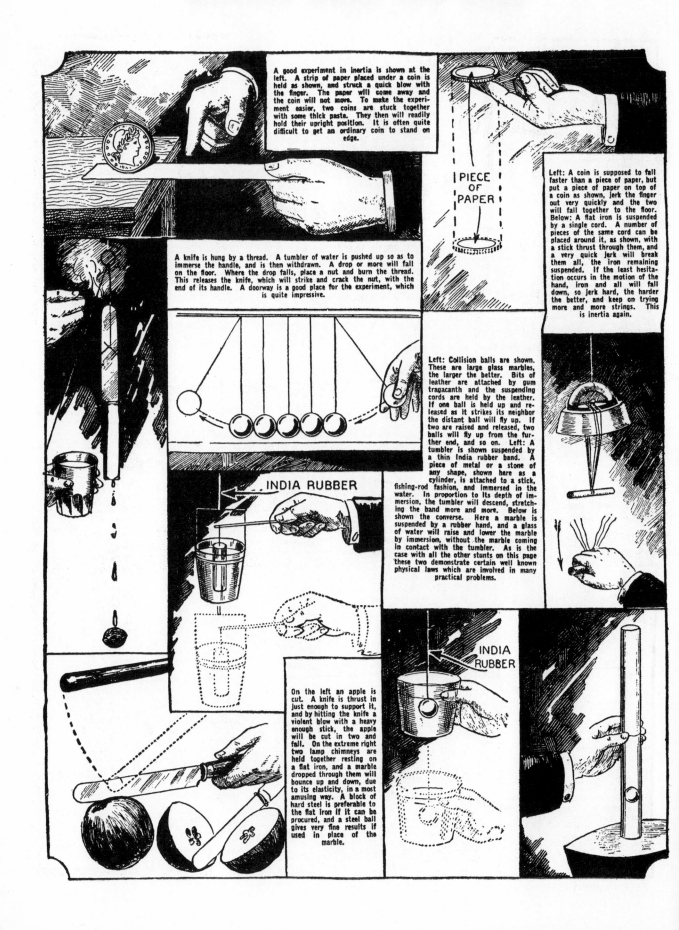

A good experiment in inertia is shown at the left. A strip of paper placed under a coin is held as shown, and struck a quick blow with the finger. The paper will come away and the coin will not move. To make the experiment easier, two coins are stuck together with some thick paste. They then will readily hold their upright position. It is often quite difficult to get an ordinary coin to stand on edge.

PIECE OF PAPER

Left: A coin is supposed to fall faster than a piece of paper, but put a piece of paper on top of a coin as shown, jerk the finger out very quickly and the two will fall together to the floor. Below: A flat iron is suspended by a single cord. A number of pieces of the same cord can be placed around it, as shown, with a stick thrust through them, and a very quick jerk will break them all, the iron remaining suspended. If the least hesitation occurs in the motion of the hand, iron and all will fall down, so jerk hard, the harder the better, and keep on trying more and more strings. This is inertia again.

A knife is hung by a thread. A tumbler of water is pushed up so as to immerse the handle, and is then withdrawn. A drop or more will fall on the floor. Where the drop falls, place a nut and burn the thread. This releases the knife, which will strike and crack the nut, with the end of its handle. A doorway is a good place for the experiment, which is quite impressive.

Left: Collision balls are shown. These are large glass marbles, the larger the better. Bits of leather are attached by gum tragacanth and the suspending cords are held by the leather. If one ball is held up and released as it strikes its neighbor the distant ball will fly up. If two are raised and released, two balls will fly up from the further end, and so on. Left: A tumbler is shown suspended by a thin India rubber band. A piece of metal or a stone of any shape, shown here as a cylinder, is attached to a stick, fishing-rod fashion, and immersed in the water. In proportion to its depth of immersion, the tumbler will descend, stretching the band more and more. Below is shown the converse. Here a marble is suspended by a rubber band, and a glass of water will raise and lower the marble by immersion, without the marble coming in contact with the tumbler. As is the case with all the other stunts on this page these two demonstrate certain well known physical laws which are involved in many practical problems.

INDIA RUBBER

INDIA RUBBER

On the left an apple is cut. A knife is thrust in just enough to support it, and by hitting the knife a violent blow with a heavy enough stick, the apple will be cut in two and fall. On the extreme right two lamp chimneys are held together resting on a flat iron, and a marble dropped through them will bounce up and down, due to its elasticity, in a most amusing way. A block of hard steel is preferable to the flat iron if it can be procured, and a steel ball gives very fine results if used in place of the marble.

Science Odds and Ends

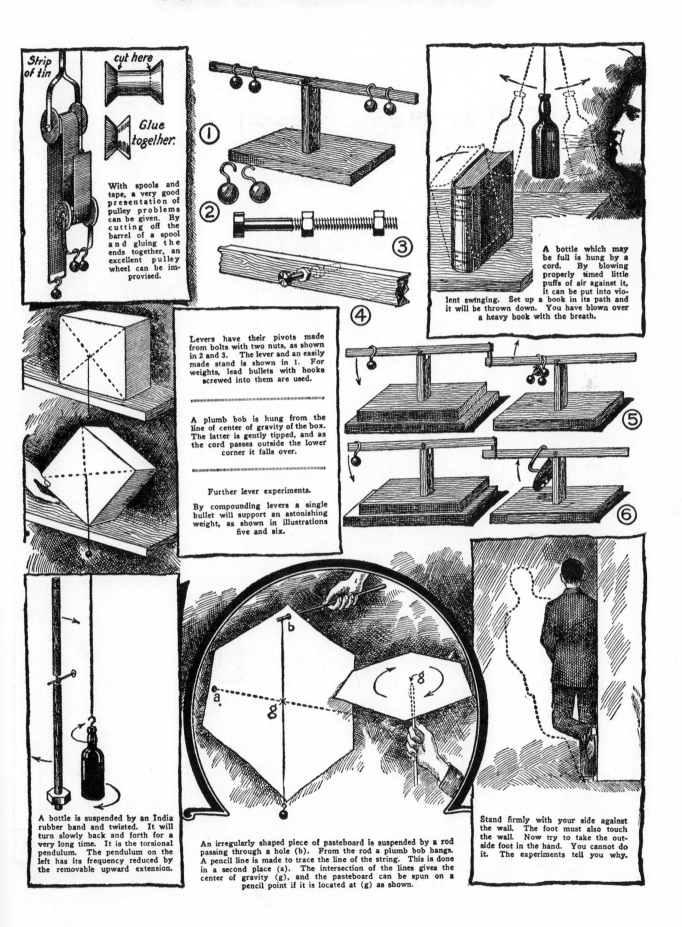

Strip of tin

cut here

Glue together.

With spools and tape, a very good presentation of pulley problems can be given. By cutting off the barrel of a spool and gluing the ends together, an excellent pulley wheel can be improvised.

① ② ③ ④

A bottle which may be full is hung by a cord. By blowing properly timed little puffs of air against it, it can be put into violent swinging. Set up a book in its path and it will be thrown down. You have blown over a heavy book with the breath.

Levers have their pivots made from bolts with two nuts, as shown in 2 and 3. The lever and an easily made stand is shown in 1. For weights, lead bullets with hooks screwed into them are used.

A plumb bob is hung from the line of center of gravity of the box. The latter is gently tipped, and as the cord passes outside the lower corner it falls over.

Further lever experiments.

By compounding levers a single bullet will support an astonishing weight, as shown in illustrations five and six.

⑤ ⑥

A bottle is suspended by an India rubber band and twisted. It will turn slowly back and forth for a very long time. It is the torsional pendulum. The pendulum on the left has its frequency reduced by the removable upward extension.

An irregularly shaped piece of pasteboard is suspended by a rod passing through a hole (b). From the rod a plumb bob hangs. A pencil line is made to trace the line of the string. This is done in a second place (a). The intersection of the lines gives the center of gravity (g), and the pasteboard can be spun on a pencil point if it is located at (g) as shown.

Stand firmly with your side against the wall. The foot must also touch the wall. Now try to take the outside foot in the hand. You cannot do it. The experiments tell you why.

The Magic in Physics

Illusions

PRACTICALLY all of the so-called "illusions" that are brought before the public, whether on the stage, at private entertainments, or sometimes in swindles, are based on fundamentals of physics. Hence it is fitting in a subject for any article on "Experiments in

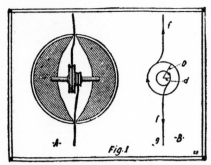

The "Obedient Ball" and How It Is Made from a Wooden Croquet Ball Hollowed Out as Shown. In This Space Are Placed Two Small Silk Spools with Strings Attached. The Ball Rises or Falls on the String at Command.

Physics" to deal with this topic. Illusions may be divided into four classes: (1) Optical, (2) mechanical, (3) chemical, and (4) sleight-of-hand. The first two types are of especial interest to us from the standpoint of pure physics.

Perhaps the most mysterious of the magician's tricks, and one which appeals to all boys, is the *obedient ball*. All ball players appreciate the value of an obedient ball, especially the kind of ball that will "come to papa." As usually presented to the public from the stage the magician passes a piece of string thru the center of a good sized wood ball and then holds the string vertical. At his command the ball slides up the string, down the string, or else remains stationary. The *obedient ball* can be easily made at practically no cost. Divide a croquet ball in half by the use of a very fine saw. Carve out enough of the insides so as to have enough room for two small silk spools to revolve freely, see figure (1) A. The spools are glued together and fastened to the inside of the croquet ball by a dowel rod used as an axle. String is wound around each of the spools and the ends led out thru holes at the end of a diameter of the ball, perpendicular to the axle. The ball is glued together, sandpapered, stained and shellacked,

Altho Not Filled with Spirits, This Obedient Bottle Will Lie Down and Stay Down Only for Its Master—the Magician. How Does It Work? Read on!

and if a good job is made of it no one will suspect that the ball has been cut open.

Figure (1) B explains why the ball will rise, fall or stand perfectly still. If the string is held loosely, the ball will fall, due to the pull of *gravity* on it. As force is applied to the ends of the string, gradually a point will be reached where the force of gravity is just overcome by the advantage gained by pulling the upper string (since the diameter of the spool to which the upper string is attached is larger than the diameter of the spool to which the lower string is attached). Greater force will cause the ball to move upward. It should be noticed that as one spool winds the other unwinds in each of the cases where the ball rises or falls. Hence the total length of the string in view changes according to the difference in the diameters of the spools. It remains for the performer to detract the attention of his audience away from this fact. The illusion is one of pure physics, more particularly mechanics. The equation for the motion may be written as follows:

Let g represent the force of gravity, f the force applied to the string by the performer, and D and d, respectively, the diameters of the spools. $Df - d(g + f)$ causes the motion. When f is zero (when the performer holds the string loosely) the tendency to move upward (Df) is zero and tendency to move downward is dg, and the ball moves downward. When f is such that $Df = d(g + f)$, the tendency to move upward equals that to move downward,

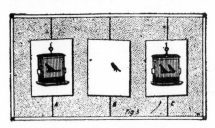

If Two Cards Are Drawn to Resemble Figures A and B, Placed Back to Back on a Cord and Then Spun Rapidly, Two Birds Will Appear in the Cage, as at C.

and the ball remains stationary. When f is large enough so that Df is greater than $d(g + f)$, the tendency to move upward is greater than that to move downward, and the ball moves upward.

Speaking of the *obedient ball*, the event of July 1, 1919, leads us naturally to the *obedient bottle*. A small wood bottle (empty since July 1st) of the shape indicated in figure (2) A, is placed on the table and told to "lie down—and stay down," and the bottle does so. (Nothing remarkable.) The performer then picks up the bottle and passes it around, defying anyone else to cause it to "lie down—and stay down!" No one is able to do so. The performer then takes the bottle again, coaxes it and causes it to lie down as before. This is another case of pure physics, more particularly mechanics. The bottle is weighted with lead as shown in figure (2) A, so that its center of gravity C is very low. It is seen from figure B, that placing the bottle on its side causes the center of gravity to be raised to the position c'. It is well known in mechanics that a body is in stable equilibrium (will return to the

same position when displaced) when its center of gravity is at its lowest. Hence it follows that the bottle will always return to its stable equilibrium position (standing up). How, then, does the performer cause it to lie down. He keeps concealed up his sleeve or "palmed" a long narrow weight

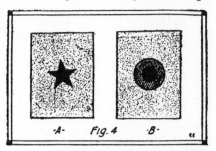

An Interesting Illusion Experiment Based on the Persistence of Vision. A Black Star Drawn on a Blank Card, When Spun Rapidly, Will Change Into Two Circles—One Gray and One Black.

which he slips into the neck of the bottle whenever he wishes it to lie down. The addition of this long narrow weight causes the center of gravity for the upright position of the bottle to be high, so that placing the bottle on its side causes the center of gravity to be lowered; hence this will now be the position of stable equilibrium. In picking up the bottle before passing it to the audience for examination, the performer allows the weight to drop back into his hand again.

In order not to disappoint those accustomed to "seeing double," the following is inserted for trial any time after July 1st. Draw a bird in a cage on one side of a blank card. On the *reverse* side draw another bird. Attach a piece of thread to the top and bottom of the card and twirl the card about this thread as an axis. TWO *birds will be seen in the cage.* Many variations of this illusion can be tried. The cage alone on one side and the bird on the other; a glass of "Bevo" on one side and an open mouth on the other, etc., etc. The result obtained is due to physiological rather than physical reasons. The phenomenon is known as *persistence of vision.* The retina of the eye retains any image thrown upon it for a moment after the object has been removed. Hence when the card is turning thru 180 degrees the imagine remains if the speed of the card is sufficiently high. The image of the reverse

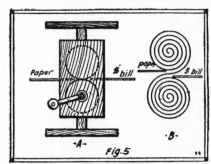

Making Money by Magic. A One-Dollar Bill Run in One Side of the Machine Comes Out a Ten-Dollar Bill, or a Piece of Paper Changes Into "Real Money." Ain't It Wonderful? Yes, It Is —NOT!

side strikes the retina while the image of first side is still on it, and hence BOTH objects appear to be in view. This is the fundamental principle of the *motion picture*.

Figure (4) is another example of an illusion due to persistence of vision. A black star is drawn on a blank card. If the card is placed on the forefinger and spun around, the star will disappear and TWO circles will appear as in B, the inner one *black* and the outer one *gray*. As the card is spun around the image of the points of the star and the image of the white card between the points strike the eye in rapid succession, so that due to persistence of vision, both black and white are seen and the result is the gray circle or mixed shade. Since the center of the star is all black, the center circle is black.

Even tho money is not of much use to many of us now, the following interesting device for "Making Money" provides a fitting conclusion to any performance. A small miniature clothes wringer is brought forth. A piece of paper is cut to the size of a dollar bill. The paper is inserted in the wringer, *the handle is turned and a brand new, crisp dollar bill comes out from the other side!* This may be repeated indefinitely

(provided the performer is a multi-millionaire). Figure (5) tells the secret. The two rollers are not two distinct rollers, but are made of a continuous piece of goods wound as in B. Beforehand the performer has wound some dollar bills into one of the rollers and then on performing the "stunt" places the paper in the other roller. *As he winds the paper into one roller, the dollar bill is unwound from the other roller.* If the apparatus is well made and carefully put together, a great deal of fun can be gotten from it without the *modus operandi* of the illusion being discovered.

Mysterious Japanese Mirror

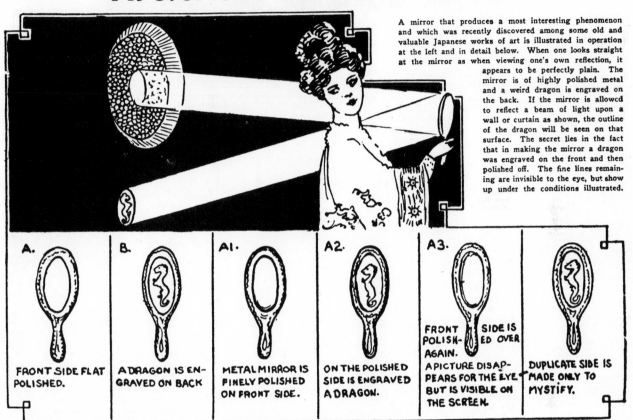

A mirror that produces a most interesting phenomenon and which was recently discovered among some old and valuable Japanese works of art is illustrated in operation at the left and in detail below. When one looks straight at the mirror as when viewing one's own reflection, it appears to be perfectly plain. The mirror is of highly polished metal and a weird dragon is engraved on the back. If the mirror is allowed to reflect a beam of light upon a wall or curtain as shown, the outline of the dragon will be seen on that surface. The secret lies in the fact that in making the mirror a dragon was engraved on the front and then polished off. The fine lines remaining are invisible to the eye, but show up under the conditions illustrated.

A. FRONT SIDE FLAT POLISHED.

B. A DRAGON IS ENGRAVED ON BACK.

A1. METAL MIRROR IS FINELY POLISHED ON FRONT SIDE.

A2. ON THE POLISHED SIDE IS ENGRAVED A DRAGON.

A3. FRONT SIDE IS POLISHED OVER AGAIN. A PICTURE DISAPPEARS FOR THE EYE BUT IS VISIBLE ON THE SCREEN.

DUPLICATE SIDE IS MADE ONLY TO MYSTIFY.

Magic "Setting Sun" Picture

There is no magic so mysterious as the magic of chemistry. In the laboratory, we constantly obtain effects which, on the stage, would be regarded as little short of marvelous. This is amply demonstrated by the trick which we shall call "The Setting Sun Picture."

Effect: The magician, using a clean sheet of white paper and an improvised brush as the utensils of an artist, together with a vial of water as the paint, produces a beautiful landscape in colors. The scene is a cerulean lake, set between rocky shores. An intensely red sun illuminates the sky, reflecting itself in the water; then, before the eyes of the audience, the sun slowly fades from the sky, leaving only the unbroken calm of the placid lake.

Explanation: On a clean sheet of white paper, outline a picture similar to the one shown in the figure with a light pencil. Paint the sections marked 1, 2, 3 and 4 with a saturated solution of copper sulphate, using a soft camel's hair brush. Paint sections 5

and 6 with a 1:10 solution of mercurous nitrate in water, being careful not to over-

The picture of a setting sun as illustrated above, is made in but a few seconds, by washing a clean sheet of paper with what the audience believes to be pure water.

lap the already painted sections. Let each solution dry before proceeding to the next and keep your brush clean. Then paint sections 2 and 3 again, this time with a 1:100 solution of phenolphthalein in 50 per cent. alcohol. If the paper is not free from color when dry, warm it gently, taking the proper precautions against charring. Erase the pencil lines.

The *water* used is ammonium hydroxide, Tie a pocket handkerchief to the end of your wand (which is merely a length of glass tubing) and smear the ammonia over the surface of the picture with this. By thus proceeding, the sky and water will come out blue, the rocks and bushes a peculiar drab color and the sun, of course, red. The first two colors are permanent, but the red of the sun soon fades, owing to the escape of ammonia gas. Hence the appellation, "Setting Sun."

Other combinations can be worked out by the reader.

WIRE HOOK

CELLULOID CONE

PAPER CONE

WATER IN CONE HOOKED TO BACK OF CHAIR

How the "Enchanted Cornucopia" trick is performed.

WATER

MAGIC

MATCH

Allah's Candle

THIS magical device can easily be constructed by the reader. Effect: The magician exhibits what seems to be an unprepared tallow candle. He lights this—then with some patter (talk) about an Indian high priest who could light candles by power of will, he blows upon the candle and extinguishes it. A few passes and the candle relights—another pass and it goes out again. Secret: A wick saturated with benzine and operated by the slide pulls the flame in and out of the metal candle.

The Enchanted Cornucopia

THIS effect trick is illustrated at the top of the page. The magician first makes a cornucopia of paper. He then fills this paper cone with water from a pitcher. Putting the pitcher aside on the seat of a chair, he asks his assistant to light a match and set fire to the cone. This slowly burns until entirely transformed into ashes, which drop to the floor. The water has vanished. Explanation: The cornucopia, which can be rolled out of flash paper to produce a more spectacular effect or out of newspaper, is rolled up and then, while reaching for the pitcher of water, is passed behind the chair to pick up a celluloid cone hanging there. The water is now ostensibly poured into the paper, but actually into the celluloid cone. Another pass and the cone containing the water remains suspended on the back of the chair after which the paper is burned. With a little practice and misdirection, this trick can be presented so as to leave the audience quite bewildered. This and the Allah's candle trick are good foils for each other.

Ultra-Coin Trick

ONE of the greatest difficulties in the manipulation of coins is to handle them with that dexterity only possible by experts at sleight of hand. The novice or student often prefers short-cut methods because they have not the time to devote to hours of practice. A thimble, soldered to the center of the coin will prove of great advantage. With the coin palmed, the wizard has but to close his fingers, insert the middle finger into the mouth of the thimble and open his hand. The coin will be carried to the finger-tips in an expert-like move.

WICK

CANDLE RELIGHTS

CHEMICALLY SOAKED COTTON.

THIMBLE

COIN

The Headless Wizard

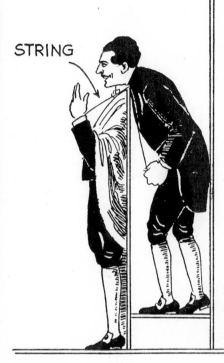

After the magician has gone through a series of tricks, he steps before a black curtain to accept the applause of the audience, and just before the curtain goes down, he removes his head from his body and places it on a side table. This affect is accomplished by the aid of a slit in the back drop behind which the magician stands and in front of which a dummy is affixed. A string operates the hand of the dummy to produce a life-like movement. The slit is cut on an arc from a point behind the collar and the position of the head indicated in the diagram. The performer, by swaying his body, will produce this remarkable illusion.

THIS is a very sensational illusion, of amazingly striking effect. It is one those few truly big tricks, that can be easily be constructed with a very slight expense. We will say that the magician has concluded his program, during which he has presented an array of many startling mysteries, that have produced in the audience high-spirited admiration. In accordance with their applause, the curtain is repeatedly lifted, during which appearance the magician accepts applause accorded him. During one of these bows, as the curtain has been several times lifted, the magician takes his own head off from his shoulders, and places it upon a near-by stand. The eyes of this decapitated head are sparkling, and a broad smile overspreads its countenance; and this bodyless head speaks words of thanks and appreciation, as the curtain once more lowers upon this final scene. To accomplish this effect, the magician prepares himself with a screen, through which has been cut a semi-circular sliding panel, as illustrated. Behind this screen is concealed a headless dummy body, of exact size and dress, to resemble that of the wizard. The hands of the dummy are attached to strings, working over pulleys. The sections of these mechanical hands and arms are hinged together, so that when the strings are pulled, the hands will raise themselves, and lift upward, to the performer's head.

When the curtain is lowered, during the bows, the magician takes advantage of this moment. He attaches the dummy body to the front of the screen, in position directly below the sliding panel. A hook, attached to the dummy, helps to adjust it into position quickly. He now pushes his own head through an opening in the panel, so as to have it rest on the edge of the collar of the figure. When the curtain is thus raised, the audience is of the impression that the magician still stands before them.

The entertainer now secretly pulls the strings, behind the screen, which have been attached to the arms of the figure. This seems to be a natural action. By lowering his head as far as the panel will permit, it will, to all appearances, be carried from off the body, and placed upon the side-stand.

The curtain is slowly lowered, while this effect is taking place, so as not to allow too much time for the audience to discover the details of the illusion. The rapidity of this action makes it quite impossible for any one to study the setting. The writer, some years back, presented this effect, and has found it exceptionally practical and mystifying. The screen, before which this trick is presented, should be of deep color and confusing design. This will help greatly in disguising the presence of the sliding panel. It is best not to have a spot-light or otherwise brilliant light focused upon this illusion. A semi-dim effect, or colored foot-lights, if obtainable, will be found the best form of illumination for the trick.

Candle-Eating

The performer suddenly craves food and takes a bite of a lighted candle, which portion he eats. He relights the candle and passes it

for examination. A portion of a real candle is fitted with an apple top and brazil nut wick. The nut itself will burn if ignited.

THE necromancer, during the presentation of his magical performance, notices that a young lady, among his spectators, has been making a Roman feast of a box of chocolates, resting comfortably balanced in her lap; and he explains to the audience, that by power of suggestion, the lady has caused quite a hungry feeling to come upon him, unaware. Without further hesitancy, he reaches to a lighted candle which has for some time been brightly burning in a candlestick, upon his table, and bites off the lighted portion; which he at once proceeds to chew, and swallow, much to the amazement and laughter of the audience.

The upper part of the candle is, in reality, a piece of apple, cut to the proper shape, which has been held in place by a needle point, as is herewith illustrated. The wick has been made of a piece of a Brazil nut. My readers, both amateur and professional, will find that magical tid-bits of this nature, unexpected additions of mystic fun, have an uplifting influence over an audience, and help to make a magician's act impressive.

The Spirited Match

While it is possible to make a match move, due to static electricity produced by a fountain pen rubbed with wool, the same movement can be reproduced by the aid of a pen-knife or the finger if the performer will blow the match as the diagram indicates.

TWO matches removed from an ordinary case, are passed for thorough inspection. These are now placed on the table, in the shape of a cross. The wizard now requests the loan of a pen-knife, which is likewise inspected, and found intact. A blade of the knife is opened. The wizard, by directing the point of this implement toward the matches, apparently causes the top match to move about in any direction he chooses. The effect is amazing, inasmuch as there seems no apparent explanation.

The knife has nothing whatsoever to do with the trick. It merely acts as an item of "mis-direction." To move the match, the magician passes the knife in the direction in which he wished it to move. The secret rests in the fact that the magician quietly blows the top match, to move it. Explaining as he does that the power is actually in the point of the pen-knife, all eyes are centered in the direction of the blade, and it is not likely that anyone will notice that the blowing governs the movement of the match.

Anti-Gravitational Chair

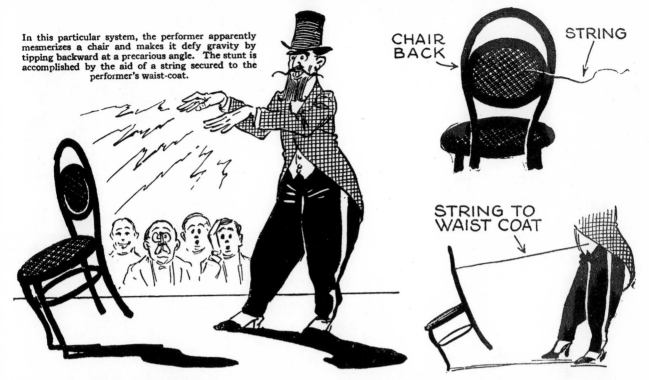

In this particular system, the performer apparently mesmerizes a chair and makes it defy gravity by tipping backward at a precarious angle. The stunt is accomplished by the aid of a string secured to the performer's waist-coat.

CHAIR BACK

STRING

STRING TO WAIST COAT

A SPLENDID spiritualistic effect—in which the conjurer defies the natural laws of gravitation, and introduces an impressive demonstration, bordering upon the seemingly impossible.

The magician invites a committee upon the stage, and asks them to inspect a number of cane chairs, which are there displayed. One of these is chosen, and rigidly inspected. After it is found to be genuine, the magician requests the committee to be seated upon the remaining chairs, and form two groups at opposite sides of the stage, so that they can plainly see all that transpires. The wizard now carries the one selected chair to the center of the stage, and attempts to balance the chair upon its front two legs. Suddenly, he removes his hands, and the chair is seen to remain in this impossible position. Motionless, it remains so held, without any visible means of support. Mystic passes are made by the magician, as if supplying the necessary magnetism to hold the

chair, so suspended, at this angle. At any time, the committee may be called upon, to re-inspect the chair. They may offer one of their own chairs, upon which they are seated, in substitution for the one the wizard has been using. He will find no difficulty in duplicating this feat, with any of the chairs so submitted.

Once more, the black silk thread comes to the entertainer's rescue. To present this problem, a short length of this thread has been attached to his waist coat button. The free end of this thread has been knotted several times, in order to easily enable him to gain possession of its end. The back molding of the chairs is such as to grip the thread tightly, when it is so placed by the magician. (See illustration.) This enables him to balance the chair, at an apparently impossible angle. When the thread is released, it is quite invisible at a short distance, blending in nicely with the color of the magician's evening dress.

A Matchless Problem

THE magician places a match between two goblets, which have been placed, mouth down, upon the table, as illustrated. He now challenges any member of the audience to remove either tumbler, without the match falling to the table. A moment's glance is enough to convince the spectators that this is quite impossible. It being the magician's business, however, to do the unusual, and he proceeds to demonstrate.

He simply lights the head of the match with another, permits it to burn for a moment, and blows it out again. The match will now adhere to the tumbler, making the removal of the other goblet possible. A wax match seems to give the best results.

A match can be made to sustain itself in the air, jutting out from the side of a glass, if the match is ignited while held in direct contact with the glass.

MAGIC

PENCIL IN TUBE

BALL END

STRING OFF STAGE

HOOP

HOLES IN GLASS

PENCIL FLIES INTO TUBE

Mesmerized Pencil

TO present this startling little pocket trick, the only essential paraphernalia is the attachment made for regular pencils to be used for turning the dials on a dial telephone, and a metal tube into which the pencil will loosely fit. Both of these pieces can be obtained in the average five and ten cent store or in a stationery store. Close inspection of the pencil, the metal dialing end and the tube, reveals no preparation. Holding the case in the left hand, the magician draws the pencil out of its holder with the right hand, the pencil and tube being supported horizontally. Suddenly releasing the pencil, it is found to quickly snap back into its holder as if drawn in by a powerful suction apparatus or by a rubber band. The pencil is again passed for examination, as is the holder, but the closest of inspection proves it to be devoid of any mechanism or arrangement. The secret: This trick is an exception inasmuch as the apparatus is exactly what it seems to be; namely, quite unprepared. The round ball, attached to the end of a pencil (commonly used for dialing a telephone) is held between the thumb and index finger. By squeezing these fingers together and sliding them slightly, enough force is produced to cause the pencil to snap back into the holder with such speed that the spectators actually believe a rubber band or a spring accomplishes the effect.

The Floating Glass

A GLASS and a pitcher of milk is carried forward by the magician. The glass is filled with milk and a few mystic passes are made over it with one hand. The other hand then lets go off the glass which remains suspended in the air. The glass is now caused to float away from the performer's hands and again when he beckons it, it glides back to his fingers. During this mystic levitation, the magician removes a hoop which has been hanging around his neck and passes it around the glass. Secret: This is a variation of a trick originated by the author many years ago. As will be observed, the black silk thread passes through two holes in the glass, loops around the ear at one end and is held by an assistant at the other. By manipulating the thumbs of the hands over the thread, and by the concealed assistant raising and lowering the thread, the glass is caused to float in various directions. The hoop is handled as illustrated.

Powerful Spirits

THIS demonstration is excellent for an anti-spiritualist act. The magician directs attention to a strongly built large size kitchen table and invites a committee of five or ten to step up on the platform and examine the table. After it has been declared unprepared, one of the spectators is asked to sit on the tabletop and the rest are then requested to put their palms on the table and press down upon the same. A few mystic passes and the table floats into the air, even though every effort is made to hold it down. The secret: The magician has a confederate in the audience who is called upon the stage as a spectator. Both magician and confederate are equipped with a special harness (if the magician partakes in the lifting stunt), or if he moves away from the table, two confederates are supplied with the harnesses. The illustration makes

HARNESS ON CONFEDERATE

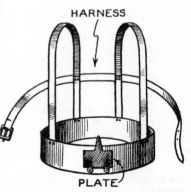

HARNESS

PLATE

TABLE OFF FLOOR

the type of harness clear. Note the plate which is pulled down in such a way that it comes under the table top and this serves as the means for lifting the table clear off the floor. The assistants need merely stoop a little, pull down the plate, and then lift.

Pharaoh's Finger

NOVELTIES as good as this one I am about to describe, are very few and far between. The simplicity of construction, plus the amount of amusement the trick creates, should be an inducing element; so that my reader should find no hesitance in adding this effect to his box of tricks.

The magician explains that years ago, while in the mystic land of Egypt, a caravan trailing its way through the burning sands of the deserts rested for a few brief moments in the shadow of the pyramids. The magician, who had been traveling through the Holy Land, in search for things mystic, met the chief of this tribe, and befriended him. Months later, the chief found himself in a position which threatened his life, and guided by an impulsive streak of heroism, the conjurer saved his life. In payment therefor, the chief presented him with a finger which was said to have been at one time affixed to the hand of the Pharaoh dead these hundreds and thousands of years. The finger, he explains, much to his amazement, although mummified, possesses a striking, lifelike appearance, as if its owner had never died. In fact, the warmth of natural life is still to be felt in its fleshy substance. All this time, the magician has held in his hands, a small Oriental figured box of odd dead-wood color, bearing high-light hieroglyphics–written, as he explains, in the language of the ancient kings. The spectators are requested to gather about the performer. Slowly, and with much ceremony, he now lifts the lid of the box. There, resting upon a small pillow of white cotton, the audience sees a severed finger. So natural, so lifelike, that is is startling and uncanny. They are permitted to feel this finger, and to their absolute amazement, find it to possess the natural human warmth, in accordance with the wizard's previous description. Carefully the box is closed, and carried away to a chest, where, with much precaution, the wonder-worker locks it away.

It is amusing to listen to the many comments, which establish themselves, after this exhibit. Some say it can't be real, but they must agree that it is the most lifelike thing they have ever seen. Others are assured it is a genuine part of a human being, but cannot conceive that this long petrified finger has not changed in form. You, my dear reader, do know that it is a human finger, as the tell-tale illustration has shown clearly the small hole in the bottom of the little treasure-chest. The diagram further clear the fact that the finger is none other than that of the performer, who sticks it through the hole, in the fashion likewise illustrated. Holding it in his outstretched hand, this deception is quite unnoticed. The bedding of cotton helps considerably to perfect the illusion, and likewise conceals the edges of the finger hole.

Those who do not choose to construct a box with ancient markings, will find a jeweler's plush box easily securable, and likewise as effective. The writer has a set of three nested boxes of Egyptian type in his treasure chest, holding Pharaoh's finger. The smallest of this set, is, of course, the only one prepared.

COVER

HOLE IN BOTTOM
OF BOX

If a hole is cut in the bottom of a box and the box itself is filled with cotton and a performer's finger is then inserted and dusted over with powder a very gruesome effect is produced. The finger can be animated to enhance the effect, but this exposes the trick.

The Magical Dummy

(A Ventriloquial Novelty)

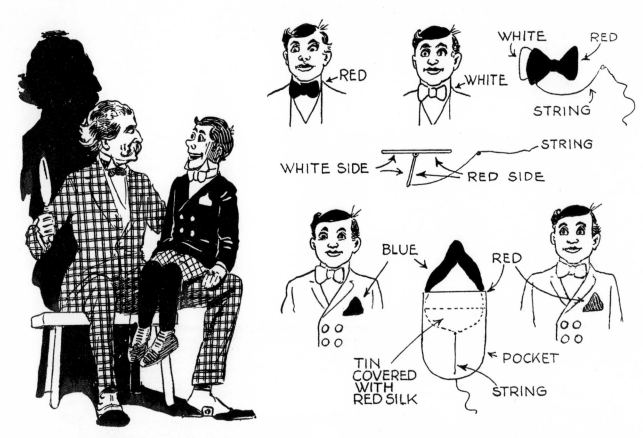

A very impressive dummy for a ventriloquial act can be produced by the aid of these two artifices. The ventriloquist asks the dummy why he is wearing a red tie. The dummy responds that the tie is white. The tie instantly changes its color. The same effect is true of the handkerchief tucked in the dummy's pocket. In the former case the tie is made of metal and is hinged at the center. In the latter a piece of tin slides down revealing the red kerchief. The red handkerchief may be real or imitation.

STRANGE, but true, it seems that a great percentage of our present day wonder-workers (I mean, thereby, entertainers in the mystic art of conjuring) possess the abilities of voice-throwing, commonly known as ventriloquism. In fact, as I look over my scrap books of magical history, I glance over the advertising of many fellow magicians, who likewise advertise their ventriloquial ability. It seems surprising that, to the best of my knowledge, none of these manipulators of fingers and voice have ever tried to combine the two forms of entertainment. I therefore offer this article as a suggestion or foundation, upon which I am assured my many fellow followers of the mystic art will eventually elaborate. Why not make the dummy do a few magic tricks? The block-headed entertainer whom I am here describing is so constructed as to present two rather startling magical effects, which I feel assured my readers will agree, are not only mystifying, but are laugh-creating as well.

The ventriloquist, during considerable coversation with the dummy, seems to discover a brilliant-red bow neck-tie, affixed to the young man's collar. The wizard criticizes this apparel, and explains to the audience, the bad judgment displayed in the selection of a color so brilliant.

Johnny (the dummy) with a broad smile, looks up into the face of his master, and says: "You're a magician, why not change it." Some conversation of a humorous nature follows, and the magician finally astonishes Johnny (likewise the audience) by transforming the color of the tie to white.

The dummy, who is overcome with bewilderment, suddenly looks down upon his own handkerchief, which is projecting in a fashionable way out from his upper coat pocket; and enters into conversation with the wizard as to changing its color, which is likewise a brilliant red. More conversation follows. The magician finally commands a change to take place, and the handkerchief is instantly transformed to one of light blue. The dummy, after a moment of apparent thought, remarks "You failed. It's the same color, only the wind *blew* it." My readers, I am sure, will grasp the possibilities and will find a series of similar transformations which can be easily effected upon poor, helpless Johnny.

The illustrations in this trick are quite descriptive, showing clearly that the neck-tie, which is made of metal, can easily be changed from one color to the other by the mere pull of a string, operated from behind the dummy's back. The red silk handkerchief consists of a piece of tin, cut to shape, which has been covered with the proper colored silk. This conceals a piece of blue silk which is permanently attached to the dummy's coat pocket. When this string attached to the metal is pulled (likewise from Johnny's back) the red disk is drawn into the figure's pocket, where it remains concealed. The blue silk (handkerchief) is exposed to view.

Rainbow Water

THIS trick, of highly magical nature, will be found to be just the proper one for magicians seeking something out of the ordinary. A decanter, and four empty drinking glasses, are brought forth upon a tray, by an assistant. This array is placed upon a small undraped table, which is moved to the center stage. The wizard explains that there is magic in the very atmosphere, and relates stories of how Benjamin Franklin first drew electricity out of the air, assisted by a key, tied to a kite-tail. He says that this has offered to him a rather odd suggestion; and he has, by a process, the secret of which he will not divulge, succeeded in drawing a good deal of coloring from the rainbow, which he has bottled in the container.

He now holds up the decanter, which, being made of clear, transparent glass, seems to be full of water, or a liquid, similar in appearance. Nothing of a colored nature can be found. The magician invites the spectators to step forth, permitting them to examine the glasses, to their hearts' content. These tumblers are found to be entirely free from chemical preparation whatsoever. The wizard now proceeds to offer his rainbow experiment. He pours some of the contents of the decanter into the glass, which is seen to turn a deep blue, in color. The second glass is likewise filled. This changes to milk-white. Liquid is poured into the third glass, and this is found to be red, and the contents in the last glass transformed to Nile-green. The decanter may be passed for inspection, and it will be found to be in no way prepared, being actually transparent, and free from compartments, or divisions, usually employed in more ancient forms of tricks of this nature.

In order to bring about this effect, the performer must provide himself with the following: Purchase four small packages of aniline dyes, in colors to correspond with those used in the trick. Red, milk-white, blue and green. Secure also a small quantity of glycerine. Now mix a little water and glycerine, in equal proportions. Secure four small pots, such as are commonly used by chemists or druggists, for holding salves, etc., and mix each of the dye powders with the glycerine and water, until it reaches a pasty substance. Place each of these dyes in a separate pot, and label them. The decanter is beforehand prepared in the following manner. Take a small dab of each of the four colors, and arrange them, as in the diagram, along the upper mouth-edge of the glass container. Clear water must previously have been placed in the decanter. As the water is poured from out the jar, into the glasses, it is permitted to pass over each respective dye daub. The water naturally is colored when it reaches the glasses. Care, of course, must be exercised, that the decanter is not tipped to too great an angle, so that the water will not pass over more than one color, at a time. After the trick has been performed, and the contents of the decanter has been emptied, the dye substance has entirely been washed from off the mouth of the glass container, which can, therefore, now be freely passed for examination. A quantity, sufficiently large to last for a great number of performances, can be prepared and preserved with ease.

Rainbow water is produced by the addition of a slight quantity of aniline to the water. The aniline itself is mounted on the lips of the flask as the diagram indicates. Glycerine may be used to form the colored paste. The water changes as it is being poured from the mouth of the flask. The audience, therefore, cannot suspect that the color is in the glasses.

The Haunted Eye-Glasses

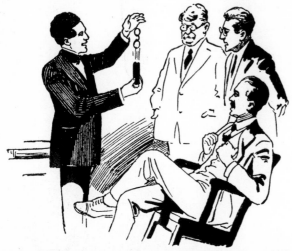 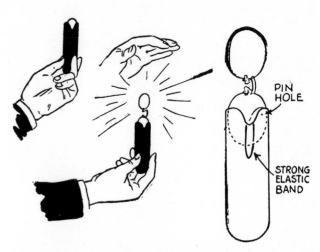

Provided an eye glass case with a rubber band as the diagram indicates. The glasses are held in place by means of a pin. The pin is removed and at the same time the sides of the case are pressed

together holding the glasses in place. On releasing the pressure the glasses leap up into the air. The effect should be practised with a cheap or discarded pair of glasses.

IMPROMPTU tricks are always fascinating. As this volume is written with the intention of pleasing all, I have herewith devised a trick, particularly suitable to those of my readers who might be wearing eye-glasses. Some friend, we will say, for description's sake or example, gives the magician a book, pamphlet, or letter, to read. The conjurer removes his eye-glass case, proceeding in the usual manner, to obtain possession of the glasses therein, but suddenly remembers his magical powers. Holding the case, which must be of the open-end variety, in his left hand, he proceeds to make a few magnetic passes over it, with the right. Slowly the glasses are seen to rise out from the case. This procedure continues, until they are well out, when the performer takes them, and adjusts them to his nose, prepared to read the presented literature.

The eye-glass case has been prepared beforehand. A strong elastic band is attached upon the inside of the case. When the glasses are pushed firmly down, they are so placed as to allow the loop of elastic to form about them. By releasing the finger pressure from the case, the band will naturally force the glasses up, and out. The glasses are prevented from making their appearance beforehand, by merely running a small pin, through a pin-hole in the top of the case. This pin is secretly withdrawn, and sufficient resistance applied by finger pressure to hold the glasses down when removing the case from out of the pocket. Experiments of this kind are good advertising mediums for any magician. An effect of this nature is not easily forgotten by a spectator, who often repeats the story of such a spectacle, to his numerous friends. In magic, as in business—advertising pays.

A Voice in the Dark

DURING the mentalist's absence from the room, spectators are requested to conceal a collar button, stick pin, ring, or similar object, secretly, somewhere about the place. The wizard has previously explained that he is guided by a tell-tale voice in the dark, that by some uncanny force, will direct him to its hiding place.

Therefore, in accordance with his request, all lights are

put out before he re-enters the room. As he makes his re-appearance, he is told what sort of an object has been selected and hidden. It is up to him to find its whereabouts. This he accomplishes in a remarkably short space of time.

Here is the modus operandi. He has a confederate in the audience. This man has in his possession, a watch, with a rather unusual loud tick. He, being unsuspected, is a silent observer, as the object is concealed. He manages to extinguish the lights, before the magician enters the room, and secretly leaves the loud-ticking watch as near the hidden object as its hiding place will permit. The magician, when entering the room, dictates that the lights are to remain out, until the article has been found, as the silent voice that guides him, works only in the darkness. The wizard now listens for the ticking of the watch, locates it, and walking toward the place where the ticking comes from, picks up the watch and pockets it. He now seeks the hidden object, already having been told what it is, and requests that the lights be turned up. This must all be accomplished quickly, and in a mysterious manner. This secret is very little known, even among professional wonder-workers. It is not advisable to repeat this trick too often. Repetition may furnish a clue.

A loud-ticking watch will enable the performer to locate any object in the dark.

Fire-Water

IN THIS unique problem, the magician claims that he will demonstrate a trick which is quite contrary to natural principles. Although water has, for centuries, been used to extinguish fire, he states that a magician has the power of reversing its chemical qualities; and in accordance with this comment, he will prove that, in the hands of a wizard, water can be made to produce a flame.

To prepare for this trick, the magician shows a candle, of the ordinary tallow kind, standing in the usual upright position, in an unprepared candle-stick. A transparent tumbler, containing water, stands close by, upon the table. Previous to this presentation, the magician must prepare as follows: procure a small piece of phosphorus, about the size of a pin's head. With a small piece of tallow, stick it on the edge of the drinking glass. Now proceed, by lighting the candle, which is permitted to burn for a minute or two, while you utter further descriptive patter, of suitable nature to this problem. Blow out the candle, and apply the edge of the glass to it, so that the hot wick will touch the phosphorus. One will find that the candle will be at once relighted, as the hot wick will ignite the phosphorus. As this is done, it is of course necessary that the glass be tipped, at the same time, so that the water nearly, but not quite, reaches the phosphorus. If this is cleverly done, it looks as if it were the water which relights the candle. There is nothing to prevent the magician from passing the candle, candle-stick, and glass for inspection, after the trick.

Care must be taken in handling phosphorus; it should be cut only under water, and should not be allowed to remain exposed to the warmth of the fingers in the open air, as it ignites with extraordinary quickness at a comparatively low temperature.

The performer can extinguish the flame of a candle and then relight it by the aid of water if the small portion of phosphorus has been affixed to the mouth of the glass.

A Rapid-Fire Magician

A SPECTATOR is requested to hold his left hand outstretched, and a twenty-five-cent piece is placed in his palm. The magician explains that speed is the secret of a successful magician; and in order to prove his digital dexterity over that of the average person, he announces that, disregarding the fact that possession is nine points of the law, and that the coin is held in the spectator's possession, he (the magician) will take the coin out of the subject's hand, before the spectator is able to close his fingers in fist form, thereupon. It is agreed that the test is to be demonstrated at a given moment, and at the count of three, the spectator is asked to close his fingers, in the fastest manner possible,

in an attempt to outwit the mystic. One, two, three The fist is closed, and when the fingers of the spectator's hand are opened, the coin is gone, much to the amazement and amusement of the onlookers.

This effect, if instructions, per illustration, are followed, will be found to be extremely simple. At the count of three, the performer must strike the spectator's palm, with a quick, sharp blow, which will leave the coin resting in the magician's hand. This principle is, to some respect, similar to the well-known principle of pulling a table-cloth from beneath a table full of china, without disturbing, or breaking any of the china. A similar quick, sharp stroke of the palm, is essential.

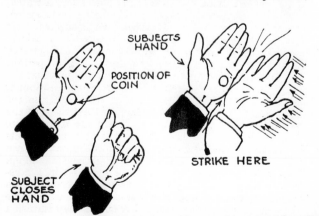

A coin can be removed from a subject's hand by striking a sharp sideways blow as indicated in the diagram.

Buried Alive—India's

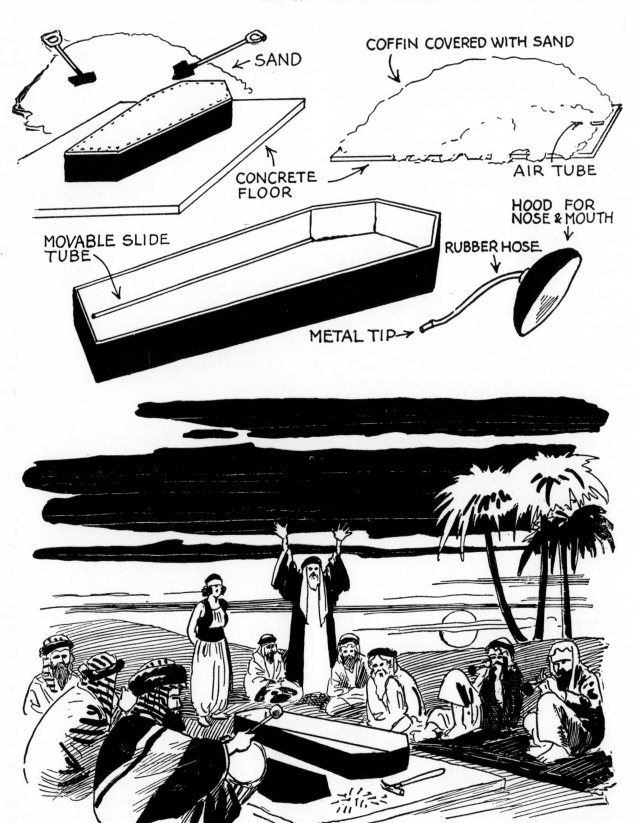

SAND

COFFIN COVERED WITH SAND

CONCRETE FLOOR

AIR TUBE

MOVABLE SLIDE TUBE

HOOD FOR NOSE & MOUTH

RUBBER HOSE

METAL TIP→

While a person may live in a coffin for an hour and a half or more if the same is placed in water to cool the interior, if buried in sand the heat becomes rather oppressive unless fresh air is constantly supplied. This can be accomplished by the aid of a tube as indicated.

Greatest Mystery

IN THE ancient land of far-off India, mystery seems to prevail in the very air that one breathes. One cannot speak of this enchanted sphere, without visualizing the uncanny, white-clad subjects, assembled in their temples, paying homage in worship of their gods, with their practice of things uncanny.

China, although an Oriental nation, has presented little of magical value to our Western civilization. The one and only name in the minds of authorities upon this subject, is that of Ching Ling Foo. He seems to have been the exception to the rule, a clever master of the mystic art. To the knowledge of the writer, Japan can boast of no leader in this chosen profession. England, often referred to as the home of mystery, seems to be on a par with the United States; inasmuch as from these two nations have come forth the entertainers that have made the name of magic most revered.

But yet, for some historical reason, it seems that India is looked upon as the melting-pot of mystics. Travelers through the cities of this mystic people refer to weird experiences they have witnessed, for which there seems no apparent explanation. Aside from the usual routine of items in conjuring with which they are most adept, clever men testify to having seen things that scientists are at a loss to analyze. It is a common belief among Europeans that the piercing, enchanting black eyes, that glare forth from beneath the turban of white, are hypnotic. Yes, hypnotising indeed; as scientists have often said, they can hypnotize an audience of hundreds at a time, actually causing them to *see* things, that in reality never existed. It is the writer's belief, however, that notwithstanding the fact that Hindoos make clever hypnotists, they cannot mesmerize so large a number of human beings; although in all probability, they are capable of presenting marvelous demonstrations of their Oriental wisdom, as to mind over mind.

Many of our learned investigators, not familiar with the inner workings of Hindoo magic, who have been mystified completely by the strange creations of the Hindoo, prefer to call it all hypnotism, as their scientific education cannot offer any other explanation, near as acceptable or plausible, as this. I have seen Hindoo magicians, or so-called *fakirs*, throw themselves into a *cataleptic* state. In this form of artificial death, they were placed in coffins, and buried deep below the ground. In this condition, they would remain for days, after which they would be dug out again, and they resurrected themselves, to remain for a length of time further in this universe of the living.

In some instances, of course, trickery has been resorted to; and the method the writer herewith discloses is one that the Yogi fakir has undoubtedly found most practical. One cannot truly blame the Oriental for resorting to trickery, as in India this is his only form of livelihood. Being therefore obliged to present this uncanny burial feat, several times during the year, hypnotic methods would prove, to an extent, injurious to the operator. Repetition of applied catalepsy, for so great a length of

time, presented many times in succession, would wear down the Hindoo's physical endurance, to a great extent, and weaken his power of resistance to so low a degree, as to make it dangerous. Therefore, trickery is resorted to.

As to my effect.... A coffin, of plain black wood, and apparently crude construction, is exhibited. The dark-skinned wizard throws himself into an apparent state of catalepsy. In this rigid position, the poorly-clad assistants lift him from the ground, and place him in this box of death, the cover of which is rapidly nailed down upon him. A cemented floor base has been previously made by these conjurers of the Himalayas. Upon this platform of cement, the coffin is now placed. The natives lose no time in covering this box with sand, until a large pile, which has been collected near-by, has diminished considerably in size. A small mountain of the sand has been heaped upon this conjurer of the living death. Amid the sounds of tambors, and the weird, strange music of the Eastern pipes, played by the tamers of the Cobra, the attendants now begin to collect contributions from the spectators. You are asked to stand by, until the magician is again brought forth to view.

Hindoo jugglers now entertain, with varied problems, after which another collection is made. With an eye to further business, the religious master of the Eastern spirit dances upon a bed of nails. Snakes are now charmed, and the bony hands of the black artists smooth the slimy skin of these crawling reptiles. Much time has now elapsed, and once again the attendants proceed to remove the sand, and unearth the coffin. The cover is pried open, and there in deadly silence, lies the apparently lifeless figure of the black-bearded necromancer of India.

Slowly his eyes are seen to open. Some see a ghastly expression overcome his face. Assisted by his worthy attendants, and partners in fakiry, he is helped out of the box and another collection is made.

The coffin, dear reader, was not as ordinary and crude, as our Hindoo entertainer would have us believe. The lower, inner edge of the moulding, which seemed to act as re-enforcement for the box, was a sliding tube. As the coffin was being covered with sand, the man of mystery, upon the inside, was secretly sliding this tube, out from the coffin. Always further he would slide it, thereby obtaining the necessary air, which would keep him from passing into eternity. The coffin was so placed, at an angle, away from the spectators, that it completely concealed the sliding tube from view. It is simple to conceive, that our friend could remain comfortably alive, for hours, or days, if need be, in this condition.

A mouth-and-nose-piece, which had been concealed in his robe, was attached to an inner socket, in the tube, to further his comfort, in the black box of mystery.

After all is said and done, the entertainment provided by the fakirs, was a good one, and well worthy of the money they obtained, in payment therefor. Mysticism is a fascinating form of entertainment, and a trip to this land of many mysteries is quite incomplete, without attending a spectacle of this kind. Granting as I must, that the American conjurer is to a great degree the superior mystery man, it is with fairness to the Orientalist that I say, there has been much within the past century, that he has presented beneath the Indian skies, that our investigators have not yet fathomed.

Ice and Cigarette Trick

THE magician, whose doings are generally contrary to accepted laws of human nature, now presents a very startling trick, in which he clearly shows extraordinary powers of his so-called mystic control. It is common to see the average man light his cigar or cigarette, with an ordinary match, or mechanical lighting device, but it is safe to state that none would believe that a light could be secured with a piece of ice, however. This, strange to say, is exactly what transpires in this demonstration.

The wizard removes an ordinary-looking cigarette from his case, and places it to his lips, in usual fashion.

end, as the ice is quietly placed upon a nearby saucer. The magician comfortably reclines in his chair, and proceeds to enjoy his smoke. The look of amazement upon the faces of his friends, who are seated about the dining table with him, can easily be imagined.

The wizard has previously prepared for this test, by specially treating the cigarette. A small piece of the metal *potassium* has been placed and covered with the tobacco, very near the end of the cigarette. When the ice comes in contact with the potassium, it instantaneously ignites. A very small piece of potassium is used. This need only be about three times the size of an aver-

By the aid of a pellet of potassium or sodium a cigarette may be lighted by a piece of ice. The sodium does not impair the smoke.

He now takes a piece of ice, which has been used to cool the oysters on the half-shell that have just been served, or perhaps he takes a small piece of ice out of his glass of iced tea or coffee, as the case may be. On raising the ice to the tip of the cigarette, the latter immediately ignites. A bright flame is seen to kindle at the cigarette's

age pin head. (Care must be exercised in handling the potassium, as any kind of water, moisture, or even damp fingers, will produce a flame. The magician must further exercise great care not to place the wrong end of the cigarette in his mouth, as this would prove quite injurious. Potassium should be kept in a bottle of kerosene.)

The Spirit Table

THIS is one of the very few inexpensive stage effects that, in the hands of a clever showman, will leave a decided impression upon an audience. The magician announces he is about to present a spiritual effect, in which he will demonstrate that he will defy all laws of gravitation, and prove that the power of mind over matter is by far stronger than our accepted universal law, that everything that goes up, must come down. A committee of two spectators from the audience may be

chosen, if the performer chooses to make this problem more elaborate. These gentlemen are seated at opposite sides of the stage, until needed.

The magician's assistant now brings forth a table, which in size would compare favorably with the average card table. This piece of furniture is most innocent in appearance, being of the usual four-legged type, quaint in appearance, and made entirely of wood, free from the usual drapes or fringes, affixed to the average magician's

ASSISTANT
BACK STAGE
MOVES STOOL
BY MEANS
OF STRINGS

An assistant back stage operates the strings which permit of the table levitation illustrated in this stunt. By the aid of three or four strings very unique effects can be produced. If this trick is performed with the proper amount of showmanship it is bound ing attention.

paraphernalia. Amid the sounds of weird music and the possible beating of a tom-tom, the wizard assumes a mystic pose. Standing a few feet away from the table, he rubs his hands violently. Creating as much of a picture as possible, he begins making mystic passes over the table, two legs of which seem to slowly leave the floor, and rise upward into mid-air. Slowly, the tipping of the table continues, until the table stands, without apparent assistance, suspended in this position, at an angle of an angle of about forty-five degrees. With a wave of the wizard's satanic fingers, the table sinks downward, until its four legs are once more resting upon the floor of the stage. This impressive experiment is several times repeated. The magician, is now apparently much ex-hausted from the terrific amount of energy he has mentally employed to obtain the effect.

The diagram is sufficiently descriptive to explain at a glance exactly how this phenomenal effect has been accomplished. A concealed off-stage assistant, of natural ability, supplied this spiritual force. The thin, strong thread that did the table tipping, is of course withdrawn, prior to offering the table for inspection. The magician has but to pose, as the assistant does the work. Posing, however, is but a small percentage of the necessaries. Showmanship is, as ever, the greatest asset. A good flow of language, and appropriate patter, goes a great ways, as in the words of the tradesman, toward selling the trick to an audience.

Mystic Coin Trick

THE wizard borrows three pennies or nickels, from the audience. (Spectators rarely ever permit a conjurer to borrow twenty-dollar gold pieces.) The borrowed coins are placed in a row upon the table.

BLINDFOLDED

COIN
IN FIST

A blind-folded magician can tell which coin has been removed from the table and held for a few minutes by a spectator by merely judging the temperature of the various coins.

The magician requests that during his absence from the room, one of the spectators hold the coin in his closed palm, slowly count ten, and put it back again upon the table, in its original position. The magician re-enters the room, and successfully selects the one that has been chosen, during his absence. This may be repeated several times, with equal success. The experiment is doubly interesting, when my readers appreciate the fact that the trick is accomplished without the assistance of a confederate.

Talk, for a few moments, about the trick, after the coins have been arranged upon the table. Impress the value of the count, during your absence. Upon your re-entrance to the room, you pick up the coins, one after another, and with a studied expression upon your face, pretend to weigh them. The one that the spectator has secretly selected, will be found to be quite a bit warmer than the others, so caused by the spectator's handling and holding it. The coins again cool rapidly, when replaced upon the table. This makes repetition possible.

The Educated Coin

MYSTIC jugglery of a decidedly mystifying nature, plays the master part in this trick. The magician borrows a half-dollar coin, from any member of the audience. This may, if desired, be marked for future record. The wizard next presents a common silver table knife, which he passes for inspection. The knife, upon its return to the magician, is held in a horizontal position, as illustrated. The wizard now proceeds to balance the coin upon its edge, upon the edge of the table knife, which feat, after steady persuasion, he seems to accomplish. Impossible as it may appear, he further induces the coin to roll to and fro freely, upon the edge of the knife. This procedure is exercised several times. The knife is again passed for inspection, and the marked coin returned to its owner. To accomplish this feat, he

must provide himself with a piece of apparatus, as pictured in the diagram. This consists of a disk, slightly smaller than the half-dollar piece used. Upon this disk is affixed another disk, still smaller in size, as illustrated. Upon the free surface of this smaller disk, a small quantity of adhesive wax has been smeared.

This contrivance is palmed beforehand. The coin is borrowed, and the disk secretly affixed thereto. This forms a groove, through which the blade of the knife will fit conveniently, making the rolling of the coin a simple matter, requiring little practise. The disk is detached, and secretly retained in the magician's hand, when the money is returned to its owner. The knife requires no special preparation.

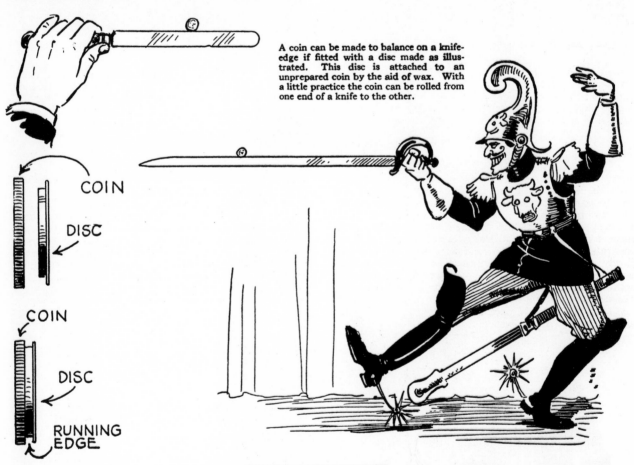

A coin can be made to balance on a knife-edge if fitted with a disc made as illustrated. This disc is attached to an unprepared coin by the aid of wax. With a little practice the coin can be rolled from one end of a knife to the other.

COIN

DISC

COIN

DISC

RUNNING EDGE

A Magnetic Pencil

THIS embodies an absolutely new and original principle, that has never previously been used in a trick of similar description. It is an exceptionally pleasing pocket trick, simple to construct, and highly effective.

The wizard passes a small cardboard tube for inspection. This is closed, at one end, and open at the other. A pencil of full length is now taken from the performer's vest-coat pocket, and placed, point downward, in the tube. The tube is just sufficiently large to conceal two-thirds of the pencil from view, therefore the upper end of the pencil is quite visible to the audience. The tube

is held in the magician's right hand. With his left, magnetic passes are made over the pencil, which is seen to rise slowly in an upward direction, from the tube. It is pushed back into the tube, more hypnotic passes are made, and again the pencil floats upward. This uncanny effect may be accomplished over and over again, without fear of its secret being detected.

The pencil is of mechanical construction. That which would ordinarily be the lead, is in reality a small steel rod, working freely in and out of the pencil, by a plunger arrangement, acting by the force of the spring, to which it is affixed. The diagram simplifies the arrangement.

A pencil may be made to rise up out of a paper tube—if the pencil has been previously provided with the spring arrangement here indicated.

A small screw prevents this plunger from working, when not required. As the pencil is placed point downward into the tube, the plunger is secretly released. Slight finger relaxation, or a lessening of the pressure upon the outer side of the cardboard holder, will cause the pencil to rise slowly upward. When the pencil is pushed back into place, a semi-turn will tighten the screw thread, allowing the pencil to be removed, as the paper tube is passed for inspection. It would be a simple matter to exchange th pencil, for one of duplicate appearance.

The Vanishing Cigar

THIS is an experiment in sleight-of-hand, and although very mystifying, it is not extremely difficult to present. The conjurer requests the loan of a cigar. As this is given him, he holds it by the point, between the thumb and index finger of his right hand, as illustrated. His left hand is now closed, fist fashion. Slowly, the cigar is pushed into the left hand, until it is hidden entirely from view. The hand is gradually opened, and the fingers held wide apart. The cigar has vanished.

No cumbersome paraphernalia or strings are necessary to accomplish this feat. While the magician is apparently pushing the cigar into the left hand, it is in reality, being pushed through the opening in the front of the vest. The hands must be fairly close to the body. At short distance, the illusion is perfect. The vest should be rather tight, to prevent the cigar from falling to the floor. An accident of this kind would, of course, prove fatal to the wizard's reputation.

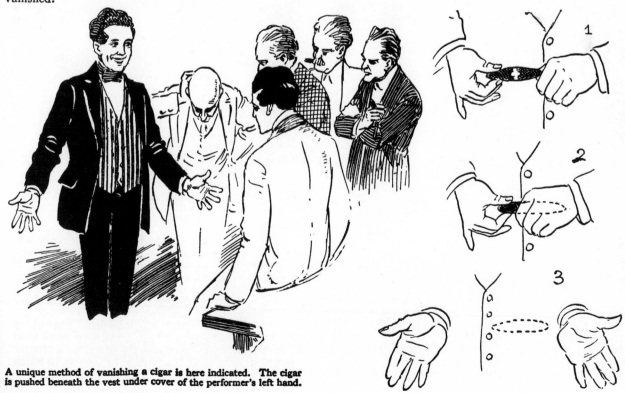

A unique method of vanishing a cigar is here indicated. The cigar is pushed beneath the vest under cover of the performer's left hand.

A Matchless Match Trick

DUPLICATE MATCH IN HAIR

After lighting a match on the box and demonstrating that it 'is burning, the magician extinguishes the same, rubs it through his hair and relights it. During the rubbing movement he has exchanged the first match for another concealed in his hair.

WHILE seated with friends at the dinner table, there is nothing of greater value at the threshold of popularity, than a good, impressive, mystifying, pocket trick. This is an original deception, with which the writer has produced much amazement, as well as a considerable amount of fun, when the other fellow tried "to do it."

The magician uses matches, of the old-fashioned, individual variety (stick matches, not the paper-packet kind). He explains that he will strike the match once, blow the light out, and relight the identical match, by securing some mystic form of phosphorus, contained in his hair. In order to illustrate, therefore, he passes it several times through his hair, re-strikes the match upon the box, and behold, the match relights. His friends try over and over again, to duplicate this feat, but their endeavors are quite in vain. It can't be done.

In fact, a magician could not do it, were it not for a duplicate match, concealed beforehand, in his hair. In running the burned article through the hair, it is secretly deposited there, and the duplicate brought to view. It is naturally necessary for the performer to strike the duplicate quickly, so that his friends will not observe the difference in color, between the two heads of the matches (the burned one, and the genuine). I would advise bald-headed magicians to eliminate this trick.

The Obedient Card

A SOMEWHAT unusual trick, appealing particularly to those who are desirous of obtaining results out of the ordinary array of card wizardry. A card is freely chosen from a deck, returned thereto, and the pack shuffled. The deck is now placed in the magician's lower waistcoat pocket. At command, the card mystically and slowly rises from out the deck, creeping slowly upward on the performer's coat, as illustrated.

Explanation: A card, constructed by gluing two cards to a piece of metal, is prepared before-hand, attached to a pellet of wax, and concealed in the pocket. From this pellet leads a fine silk thread, through a small eyelet

EYELET EYELET WAX METAL CARD AMONG THE OTHERS STRING

STRING WAX METAL CARD

By the aid of a string and a small pellet of wax the magician can make a previously selected card rise up from his lower vest pocket

to the top of his vest. The method employed is illustrated in the diagrams above, which make the explanation clear.

around the performer's coat, as illustrated. When presenting the trick, a duplicate of the metal card is forced upon the spectator. When this card is shuffled back into the deck, the pack is placed in the pocket containing the prepared card. The string is secretly pulled by

the performer's hand, and the card, in its ghost-like fashion, begins its travel and creeps up the performer's clothing. The pellet of wax makes the removal of the card afterward possible. The weight of the metal card bearing down upon the string, helps the illusion.

Ghostly Power

THE uncanny fellow once more displays an experiment, little short of miraculous. A large glass tube, or cylinder stand, as shown in the illustration, is freely inspected. Upon its return to the magician, with the indorsement of its genuineness, he proceeds to

If an egg is placed in a dilute solution of hydrochloric acid, the bubbles of gas forming on its surface will cause it to rise to the top of the liquid in the container.

fill it with water, contained in a transparent glass pitcher.

The magician next exhibits a tray, containing eggs, some nine or ten in number, from which one is freely chosen, inspected, and marked with someone's initials. This egg, without suspicious handling, and without substitution, is freely and visibly dropped into this jar. The egg rapidly sinks to the bottom. The conjurer proceeds to make a few hypnotic passes over this cylinder, when the egg is seen to rise slowly and mysteriously, upward. Higher and higher the egg floats, until it finally reaches the upper surface of the water. Further mystic passes are made, and the egg is seen to rotate slightly. Positively no strings or wires are used in this trick; and inasmuch as no cumbersome secret apparatus is depended upon, the experiment should be of unusually high value to the entertainer.

Explanation: The glass pitcher, which to all appearances, contains clear water, is in reality filled with dilute hydrochloric acid. It is in this chemical that the egg is placed. After sinking to the bottom, the egg, after a short time, will rise and slowly rotate. Small bubbles of carbonic acid gas form on the shell, which cause it to revolve. The magician must be extremely careful, in this, as in all other chemical tricks, not to leave the acid stand about carelessly; as it might easily be mistaken for water, which would have disagreeable consequences. Put chemicals in corked bottles, away from reach.

A New Ink Trick

THIS is one of the very best of present-day deceptions. It is a remarkably clever trick, and at its first showing, has mystified some of the best posted exponents of the mystic art. A large glass container, about fourteen inches high, is shown. All parts of this are made of clear transparent glass, with the exception of a wooden base, sufficiently wide to hold it erect. The magician exhibits a glass pitcher, full of ink to the brim. The liquid contents of this pitcher may be inspected, should anyone be skeptically inclined, and call for this examination.

The liquid is poured slowly into the container, and is sufficient in quantity to fill it, save for an inch or so, from the top. A large cloth, which has been freely inspected, is thrown over the container. It is now placed upon the performer's outstretched hand. The wizard explains that he is about to accomplish the seemingly impossible, an effect little short of miraculous. With a sharp action, the cloth is pulled from off the cylinder, and tossed aside. The container is found to be entirely empty. Not a trace of the large amount of liquid poured into it but a few moments before, remains. The secret of this startling experiment, is as follows:

The container is in reality a bottomless glass cylinder. This stands directly over an opening in the table, beneath which is affixed a small, water-proof tank. As the ink is poured into the cylinder, it actually passes clear through it, into the tank beneath it. The illusion of the ink entering the cylinder is accomplished as the diagram shows. A cylinder of water-proof silk, folded bellows-fashion (similar to the toy Japanese lanterns) has been concealed beneath the foot of the cylinder. As the ink enters the container, a string is secretly pulled, which

pulls out this silk bellows, and brings it gradually to view. The cover, when lifted off the container, secretly carries the lining with it. The lining, of course, is of dull black material, representing the color of the ink. At a short distance, this substitution cannot be detected. The ink used in this trick, should be greatly diluted. About half a tumbler full, to a quart of water, will do nicely. This will give the absolute black effect, and can be handled more easily. It will not stain as readily, as undiluted ink might. Should some of this ink, in the action of being poured into the cylinder, touch the cloth lining, no harm will be done. The water-proof quality of the cloth will prevent its spreading, and leaving its marks upon the surface of the glass. The writer has found that it is best to use a black cloth, with which to cover the tube. One is then doubly sure that even carelessness in handling will not expose the lining, hidden in the folds of the cloth, as it is removed. A small black bead, tied to the free end of the string which has been affixed to this lining is advisable. This enables the magician to find its end easily, when required, and eliminates unnecessary fumbling.

A small drape, or fringe, attached around the edges of the table, helps to beautify the apparatus, and likewise assists nicely, to conceal the metal well.

With some practice, a good clever showman can bring this trick to an extremely high degree of entertainment, and make it a master-piece of modern conjuring. This is truly a stage trick, and readers are therefore advised to use it only when entertaining an audience who are seated at a reasonable distance from the operator. Parlor entertainers should not attempt its use, as their spectators are seated entirely too close to be mystified.

Ink may be made to instantly disappear from a cylinder by having the cylinder open at the bottom, through which the ink flows and by pulling up a black lining at the same time that the ink is poured into the cylinder. The lining itself apparently fills the cylinder with the black fluid. It is removed with a cloth cover. Observe that the ink pours into a reservoir in the table top.

The Ghost Production

APPARENTLY EMPTY GLASS TUBE

AUDIENCE IS CONVINCED THAT GLASS TUBE IS EMPTY

GLASS TUBE

METAL STRIP

SILKS ARE CONCEALED IN THIS COMPARTMENT

BLACK STRIP OF TIN

The ghost production consists of a tube of glass in the center of which we find the long strip of black tin. This tin splits the glass tube into two compartments, behind one of which the handkerchiefs are concealed. When the tube is exhibited against the performer's full dress suit or tuxedo, the audience can apparently look right through the tube. A handkerchief may be placed into one side of the tube and exchanged for another of a different color or the apparently empty tube can be employed to produce silks or it can also be used to vanish silks. The metal from a ferrotype plate such as photographers use for putting the gloss on pictures, is ideal for the strip running down the center of the glass tube. This trick is unique and very easily constructed.

THIS trick is one which the writer has used for a number of years, and found to be highly practical, and exceptionally effective. A glass chimney or cylinder, open at both ends, is shown. (This is of the common type, used as a lighting fixture, securable in any lamp store.) The cylinder is found to be quite empty, and is in this manner held between the performer's hands. His palms close the opening upon either side of the tube. At command, and instantaneously, the tube is filled with with handkerchiefs, flags, and ribbons of various colors. These are removed, one after another, and the supply seems almost inexhaustible. As the last silk is removed, the tube is without hesitation passed down among the spectators, for minute examination. My readers, of course, understand that any time a magician passes an article for inspection, it is naturally free from preparation. This instance is no exception to the rule, and, therefore, the tube is found quite innocent.

A compartment, or division, of tin, in size as illustrated, has been made and placed in the tube. This should be covered on both sides with black velvet, and should slide easily in or out of the cylinder. The load of silks and ribbons is concealed behind this division. When held between the palms of the hands, as illustrated, at a low angle, and directly before the black clothing the magician is wearing, the effect is quite deceptive. The audience seem to think that they are looking clear through the glass, and see the performer's trousers, right through. With a half turn of the tube, the silks are brought to view. When removing from the cylinder, a black silk handkerchief which has been placed there, as part of the load, the metal division is secretly removed with it. It is placed upon the table, together with the rest of the silks, where it remains quite unnoticed. There remains nothing, therefore, inside the tube, that will not bear inspection, when the examination is afterward made. Amazing as it may seem, this trick may be worked with a lime- or spot-light, focussed upon the tube, without fear of the metal section being seen, at a reasonable distance.

It is advisable to stand this tube in back of other paraphernalia, before it is wanted for the trick. Otherwise the division, without the necessary background, would be visible to the naked eye.

Enchanted Candles

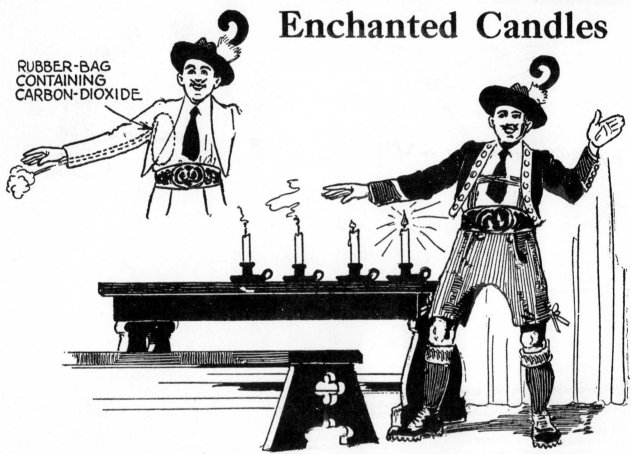

RUBBER-BAG
CONTAINING
CARBON-DIOXIDE

An exceedingly clever method of extinguishing the light of candles by merely manipulating the fingertips over the candle is here described and illustrated. Carbon dioxide gas in a bag is gradually expelled which snuffs out the light in an uncanny fashion.

FOUR or five candles are standing in a row, supported in upright position in an equal number of candlesticks of corresponding type. The conjurer requests a committee to step forward, and inspect this apparatus. After these gentlemen are convinced that the material used is quite intact, and unprepared, the magician requests that they kindly light all of the candles. The magician offers suitable patter, explaining that he possesses a magical touch, and will cause the flames of each and every one of the candles to extinguish at his command. Holding his fingers several inches over the flame, he passes his hand slowly over the lighted wicks. The flames quickly die, as if extinguished by magic. They may be relighted several times, as the performer is continuously successful in mysteriously putting the flames out.

To prepare for this trick, the performer must provide himself with a rubber bag, or lining, such as is commonly used in the interior of a football; a long rubber tube is affixed to this bag. This tube leads down along the performer's arm, so that its free end comes almost to his cuff. The bag is held, assisted by several straps, between the body and upper arm of the magician. It is naturally concealed below his clothing, and its presence is therefore unsuspected. The bag has been beforehand filled with *carbon-dioxide* gas. Pressure of the arm upon the bag, will force this substance through the tube, and extinguish the candle flames, as the hand is held above them. The hand should be passed slowly, so that the audience sees quite clearly how the flame is extinguished. With proper presentation, the effect will seem most unexplainable. It is always well to invite the audience to bring their own candles, if they choose to do so. In this instance, they are naturally unprepared, so the wizard is quite safe in his invitation to prefer their candles for his own.

Queer Arithmetic

MAGICAL mathematics would be quite a proper name for this trick. The magician asks any person what a half of twelve is, and the natural reply thereto will, of course, be six. The wizard, of course, is prepared to prove otherwise, and when he informs his listeners that the half of twelve is seven, he is invited to prove it.

With the assistance of eight matches arranged as illustrated, the conjurer forms a Roman twelve (XII). Now by taking half away, lengthwise (four matches), the

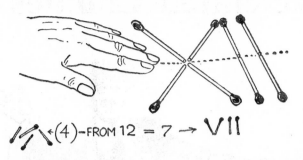

Four from twelve is equal to seven. If you don't believe it try the experiment here illustrated. You will find that the Roman numerals twelve are formed by the matches and when four of the matches are removed, the Roman numeral seven is left. Coincidentally one can add four to seven and make twelve. This is merely another version of the effect.

Roman figure seven (VII) remains. This unusual little trick is very little known, and is a fun-creating item, well worthy to remember. In a variation of the trick, one might ask what four from twelve would leave. The answer naturally would be eight. Still, by this procedure four from twelve leaves seven.

A Blotter Trick

FORTUNATELY the unexpected is expected from magicians, and for this reason the following effect, although presented entirely unaware to the victim or subject, proves little short of miraculous.

A guest quite often has occasion to jot down a note or two, or perhaps write a letter during a stay, as a guest of the conjurer, during a week-end visit, say. His mystic host directs him to his writing desk, and asks him to make himself quite at home. Pen and ink, paper, envelopes, a blotter or two, are all at his finger tips.

Unconcerned, the conjurer at once steps aside, as his guest uncorks the ink bottle, and at once begins to trace upon paper the necessary notes of his mental desire. After several sentences have been written, the victim blots his script in the usual way, and to his amazement, the writing disappears from the paper.

Yes, dear reader, the trick is in the blotter, which has been prepared beforehand in the following manner: the blotter has been dipped in a solution of oxalic acid, and permitted to dry, and several more applications of the acid are made. A blotter so treated will remove fresh ink completely, when applied.

BLOTTER

BLOTTER BLOTS PAPER

WRITING VANISHES

Fresh ink may be made to disappear from paper if it is blotted with a blotter which has been previously dipped in a solution of oxalic acid.

Watch Out

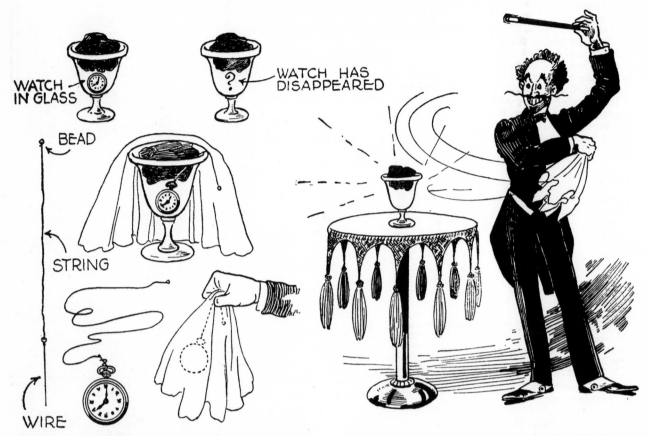

A watch is placed in a glass and covered with a kerchief. Another cloth covers the contents of the glass. On pulling the cloth away, the watch will have disappeared. The secret lies in the fact that the watch has been previously fastened to a string and both string and watch have been removed at the time the covering cloth is removed. Be sure to grip the watch string tightly.

THIS delightful addition to the conjurer's program, will be found indispensable to those presenting a trick wherein a watch is used.

The conjurer borrows a timepiece from some member of his audience. To prove that this cannot be tampered with or exchanged in any manner or fashion, it is placed in a transparent glass goblet. Further to secure the watch, a silk handkerchief is stuffed into the mouth of the goblet. A second handkerchief, borrowed from the audience, acts as a covering for the whole. Mystic words are uttered, or fantastic gestures made, and the handkerchief covering is removed. The watch has disappeared. It is afterward discovered elsewhere.

Explanation: A string, such as illustrated, has been previously concealed in the magician's pocket. To one end of the string, a short piece of wire has been tied; to the opposite one, a black bead has been attached. As the performer borrows the watch, and returns to the stage, he secretly winds the wire about the ring, attached to the watch stem. In this position, it is dropped into the goblet, and the handkerchief adjusted. At a short distance, it is impossible to observe the thread, the bead-end of which is left hanging outside of the glass. The apparatus is now covered with the second handkerchief. When this is removed, the bead is secretly drawn upward with it, drawing the watch out from the glass. The timepiece is thus hidden between the folds of the handkerchief. All eyes are now directed to the empty glass. The watch may be secretly palmed, and brought to view elsewhere, at a later point in the program. As the magician walks down the steps among the audience to return the watch, the wire may be easily detached, and the string pocketed.

The Topsy-Turvy Pencil

A SMALL tube is constructed of paper, sufficiently large to conveniently receive a full-length pencil, and project about an inch over the top of same. One end of this paper cylinder is closed, by turning the paper up several times, at its end. This innocent little cylinder, so constructed, is passed about for inspection.

The magician requests the loan of a pencil, but upon several being submitted, finds them to be too short for the trick he is about to present. He therefore begs leave to use his own, which he quickly draws from his pocket. This, to all appearances, is a wooden pencil of common type, with a metal slide fitting over the end. The pencil has been nicely sharpened, with a fine point projecting.

Holding the tube, closed end down, the magician now places the pencil, point down, into the tube. He now states that by magical power, he will cause the pencil to turn completely around in this narrow tube. His audience are not apt to believe this difficult feat possible. The wonder-worker, however, proceeds to draw the pencil from its hiding place. To the bewilderment of the onlookers, the blunt end of the pencil is discovered in the position where the point originally was placed. Upon lifting the metal cap, the pointed end is found beneath. Both pencil and cap are now passed for inspection.

Explanation: The pencil is pointed at both ends. The exposed end, however, is in reality a short piece, which has been held in position with beeswax. This is the end which is placed point first into the tube. A little finger pressure upon the outside of the paper, breaks this piece off the pencil proper. The piece is secretly left in the paper tube, which is crushed and carelessly tossed aside. The original pencil point, which has at all times, been below the metal cap, is now displayed. There is nothing to prevent the magician from passing what still remains of the pencil and its cap, for inspection.

The topsy-turvy pencil above illustrated is described in the accompanying article. Note the two pencil tips.

Eggs Extraordinary

This diagram illustrates how the card is contained in the egg cup to be pushed into the previously marked egg.

AN ORIGINAL trick, very different in effect from the usual routine of conjuring array, and one that is sure to leave a lasting impression upon the minds of even a most critical audience.

Effect: A deck of cards, which has been thoroughly examined and shuffled, is given to a spectator to hold. Someone is asked to call the name of any card, which is chosen, and the volunteer assistant is requested to remove the corresponding card from the pack. This card, which we will, for example's sake, say to be the three of hearts, is torn into small pieces, which are loaded into the muzzle of the magician's pistol, which may likewise be inspected. A tray of eggs is now brought forth by an assistant, and one chosen. The selected egg is marked for identification.

It is now placed in an egg cup, which remains in full view of the audience. A spectator breaks the shell, and discovers the card.

Explanation: When the card is selected, and the name mentioned aloud, an assistant off stage secures possession of a duplicate, which is tightly rolled and placed in the cavity of the egg cup, especially prepared for it. When an egg (unprepared) is chosen, it is thrust into the cup rather sharply, the hidden card breaking its way through the lower part of the shell of the egg. It is afterward brought to view from the upper end, by the spectator.

The Pellet Trick

PELLET IN EAR

Rubbing a pellet through the arm into the hand is accomplished by the use of three paper pellets. One is concealed in the air, one is held in the right hand, and the third is apparently rubbed into the sleeve. The spectators, however, believe that only two pellets are being employed. The one which apparently vanishes into the coat sleeve actually is palmed between the fingers. Under cover of this rubbing movement the second pellet is secured from the performer's ear.

A MOST excellent trick for amateur conjurers. It requires very little practice, and still less magical experience; yet, to all appearances, it resembles a most unique experiment in pure sleight-of-hand.

The wizard displays two small pellets of paper, each about the size of a large, green pea. He now bares his arms to the elbow, emphasizing that the use of sleeves, as an aid to this problem, is quite out of the question. One of the spectators places one of these pellets in the performer's palm. He immediately closes his fingers thereupon, so that the paper is held firmly in his fist. He now displays the other pellet, in his other hand, and

rubs same, apparently, in the elbow. The pellet is found to vanish from this hand, and to all appearances, has traveled up the performer's arm; inasmuch as the two are found in the hand, which, a moment previous, held but the one.

The secret of this trick is extremely simple. Three pellets of paper are used. One of these is concealed in the performer's ear, as illustrated. In the action of rubbing the elbow with the other, possession of this one is secretly secured, and the two exhibited. The one which apparently does the traveling, is secretly palmed between the performer's fingers, and is afterward disposed of.

The Spirit of the Sweets

THIS is an original problem, and one of the very best after-dinner tricks it has ever been my good fortune to create. After the conjurer and his friends have feasted the inner man, and have demonstrated their belief in spiritualism by the departure of some liquidated spirits, the magician requests one of his spectators to

pass him the usual bowl of lump sugar. One lump therefrom is removed, and held firmly between the magician's fingers, as illustrated. Striking a match, he holds it to the end of the sugar, which seems to take fire and burn merrily. He extinguishes the flame, and invites his friends to try to duplicate the trick. They see no mystery therein, until they try it. Needless to remark, they will exhaust the amount of sugar in their fruitless attempt to light it, inasmuch as no amount of coaxing between the sugar and the lighted match will aid them to success.

An exceedingly interesting parlor trick is described at the right. One will find it comparatively difficult to burn sugar, yet after the sugar has been dipped into ashes found in the bottom of a cigarette tray, it can be ignited very readily. The dipping movement should be made in such a fashion that the spectators will not know what is going on.

The magician, of course, did not tell them that the lump he lit, for a moment rested in the ash tray, near by him. A slight amount of ashes, forced by pressure upon the sugar surface, made this effect possible.

Mystic Jugglery

THE art of jugglery and that of conjuring, have for years been in close affiliation. Experts in both have been known to call them kindred. With this in mind, magicians have created bits of amusement by adding bits of mystic jugglery to their programs of entertainment. The writer here explains an effect which experience has proven to be impressive to an audience.

Concluding some handkerchief trick or other, the magician takes one of the silks, and his wand, to attempt some juggling. Holding the silk by one of its corners, as illustrated, he attempts to balance the other end on the tip of the stick of mystic widsom. As he slowly removes his grasp upon the handkerchief, it remains standing upon the one tip edge, as illustrated.

The diagram shows clearly how this is accomplished This trick of apparent skillful manipulation and years of practice, is likewise a deception. A thin rod of steel, attached to a pivot, is responsible for the trick. It can be stood erect, beneath cover of a handkerchief, to enable the magician to perform this feat, and again leveled to the surface of the wand, when not wanted. In this manner it is hidden completely from view. A handkerchief of rather heavy woven material should be used, as a flimsy substance might have a tendency toward exposing the rod concealed into its folds. Painting the rod and wand a dead-black or coach-black, will be found best. Should the performer choose to use a long rod, in preference to his wand, the feat will seem more difficult.

By the aid of the thin rod attached to a wand, a kerchief can be balanced on the end of the performer's wand.

The Disappearing Coin

A borrowed coin is placed into a handkerchief and the corners of the handkerchief are folded over the coin, then the entire is given to a spectator to hold. Grasping hold of one of the corners, the per-former vigorously shakes the handkerchief, proving that the coin is no longer there. The stunt is accomplished by secretly attaching a pellet of bees wax to the coin and to the corner of the kerchief.

A half-dollar piece is borrowed from a member of the audience, and is marked for further identification. A handkerchief is likewise borrowed and placed upon the performer's outstretched hand. The coin is placed in the center of the handkerchief, and slowly the handkerchief is folded and given to a spectator to hold. The magician now takes one of the corners of the silk by the tips of his fingers, and shakes it out; when, behold, the coin has vanished! The handkerchief is found empty, and returned to its owner. The coin is afterward reproduced elsewhere in any form or fashion the magician fancies.

Explanation: The conjuror has secretly fastened to one side of the coin a very small piece of beeswax, which is quite invisible at close quarters. He places a coin in the center of the handkerchief, the waxed side uppermost. The silver disk is first covered with the corner of the handkerchief, and a little pressure applied, so that the coin adheres to it. The other corners of the handkerchief are likewise drawn over the coin, and the affair given to a spectator to hold. The magician, on taking the hand-kerchief, gets possession of one of the free corners, and holding it, shakes the handkerchief thoroughly. To all appearances, the coin has disappeared. When the hand-kerchief is returned, the magician secures secret possess-ion of the coin, which is afterward produced elsewhere.

A Spiritual Apparition

WHO has not, at one time or other, attended a seance of a spiritual mystic medium? Those who haven't, should, whether believers or otherwise. It is well to know the things that are going on, if only from standard of scientific interest. It is not the writer's intention to ridicule spiritualism from a religious nor a scientific standpoint; nor is it his desire to state that all of the many phenomenal things that have been seen by learned men, have been produced by the aid of trickery. It is not probable, however, if there is an existence after death, that the "astral force," which leaves the natural lifeless substance behind it, has any power of communication with this natural sphere.

In simpler words, the writer does not think it possible for any medium to be capable of bringing to earth, the spirit of any of those in the tombs of the past, for an accepted fee. SCIENCE AND INVENTION MAGAZINE, through whose co-operation this book is created, is at this time offering a reward of $21,000, to any medium here, or abroad, who is capable of presenting any effect, in so-called "spirit-phenomena" of "ghost-production," that the staff of the magazine, through the direction of the writer, cannot reproduce, or explain, by natural or scientific means.

The effect herewith described is one employed by a present-day European medium. He has attained phenomenal reputation, both here and abroad, through his successful and seemingly seances, where *ectoplasm* is produced as frequently as dessert follows the average American meal. In a room with no light predominating, and atmosphere that makes one feel as if surrounded by the walls of a mausoleum, this clever so-called demonstrator of the occult exhibits his phenomenal power. Tightly bound to a chair, he quickly enters a trance, which, his lecturer at once explains, associates him with the spirit world. In this position, he is placed in his cabient, the curtains of which are closed, and hymns are sung in a low tone, to the harmony of an old-fashioned foot-power organ, for some moments.

Slowly, there seems to enter a glow of uncanny light, forming its materialization three or four feet away from the cabinet, and but a few feet in front of the sitters. Many of these attenders of the mystic cult begin to rub their eyes, not knowing whether this substance is a reality, or merely their imagination, prompted by the creepy atmosphere. The substance, however, slowly becomes larger, and the glow more prominent. In a short space of time, the vapor-like form assumes the likeness of a child; and there, in belief of the majority present, is the ghost of a baby, its slender, infant fingers, and outstretched arms, moving about slowly and mystically, as the figure floats about the room.

Little does one know, however, that the medium had beforehand prepared himself with a long telescope-fashioned tube, which had been hidden in his trouser leg. To the end of this collapsible contrivance, was attached a cup arrangement, which held a silk figure, of balloon fashion, air-tight structure. The miracle man, in the cabinet, had but to open the tube to its full extent, and by blowing into the end of it, slowly inflated the spirit baby. By moving this rod about, the ghost-child, to all appearances, floated over the heads of the believers. When the air was permitted to escape, the vision, apparently, de-materialized itself. The mystic withdrew this substance of apparent "ectoplasm," back into the

A silk figure attached to the end of a telescopic tube materially aids the spiritualist in producing an illusion in the dark.

cabinet, and re-concealed it in his trouser leg.

Slowly the lamps around the room were lit, and the cabinet was opened. There could be seen the medium, in a much exhausted condition. Slowly he came to, and was rewarded for his strenuous mental effort, in bringing to earth one who had passed to the great beyond. Liberal contributions, however, rewarded him for this tremendous mental strain. The medium, after depositing a stack of greenbacks in the bill compartment of his wallet, slowly walked into his library, where he gazed in admiration, upon a small motto, which hung *in passe partout* fashion over the head of his desk. There, in colored Roman type, could be read these words— "BARNUM WAS RIGHT."

The Spinning Half Dollar

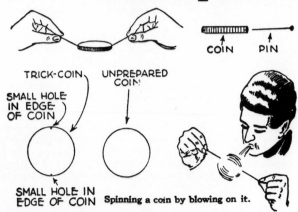

TRICK-COIN
SMALL HOLE IN EDGE OF COIN

UNPREPARED COIN

SMALL HOLE IN EDGE OF COIN

Spinning a coin by blowing on it.

IN THIS effect, a half-dollar piece is lifted off the table, by the points of two ordinary pins, and the coin made to spin, freely between these points. This seemingly difficult trick can be easily mastered, when one realizes that two very tiny pin-holes have been drilled, in the opposite ends of a diameter, in the edge of the coin. The pins are inserted into these holes, and the coin lifted, as illustrated, about four or five inches away from the mouth. The magician now blows fairly hard, toward the edge of the coin, causing it to spin merrily.

In order to obtain the usual magical effect, the silver piece and pins are offered to your friend, who tries this feat, but fails. This is due to the fact that the wizard has secretly exchanged the coin for a duplicate, which of course, is un prepared.

Mercury's Coin

COIN PAPER SLIDE

DISC SEWN IN HANDKERCHIEF

NEST OF 3 ENVELOPES

DISC

HAND REACHES INTO INSIDE COAT POCKET FOR COIN

The Mercury coin trick in which the coin is permitted to slide to the innermost of three nested envelopes by means of a paper slide tube communicating with the innermost of the envelopes.

TRICKS of a spectacular nature are numerous. Problems that will leave a lasting impression, however, are considered rather scarce. Often in my travels I have met people who, without hesitation would refer to some impressive trick they had witnessed some twenty or thirty odd years ago, by some past master of the mystic art.

Often I have heard descriptions, by laymen, of the once famous trick presented by the past dean of American magicians, the late Harry Kellar. Conversation would rapidly drift to a description of how his famous flower-growing trick impressed. Tales they would unfold, of how they actually saw (as they imagined) the buds of the rose-bush bloom forth in natural splendor, to full-grown roses. So impressive was the trick that some of Kellar's admirers would speak of how they saw hundreds of flowers bloom before their very eyes, out of an empty pot.

Then again, I have met gentlemen who spoke of happenings of an earlier date, when Alexander Herrmann, the wizard immortal, offered his famous rice, cone, and orange trick. With progression, and the change of time, a newer angle of mystic entertainment has arisen. So, as we find the old-time songs but a lingering memory, with present-day melodies, termed twentieth-century music, upon the lips of all; as we find the slap-stick comedian of days gone by gracefully making his bow, as the modern bright-witted monologist makes his entrance; so has magic likewise changed. It is not many moons ago

that the wizard who graced the stages of our theatres made his entrance in the long robe characteristic of the traditional astrologer, pictured often in association with the sign of the zodiac.

And so, dear reader, I herewith offer a problem which I know, if handled properly and presented in showmanlike manner, will leave its impression with the man of today, and remain a delightful story to be told by the grandfather of tomorrow. The trick, although by no means difficult, requires considerable practice, truly more in showmanship and presentation, than it does in manipulation or digital dexterity.

The wonder-worker borrows a coin from a member of the audience, which is marked with a pen-knife, by a volunteer spectator. The conjurer covers this coin with his handkerchief and in this position, offers it to a spectator to hold. He now reaches into his inside pocket (his own), and pulls forth an envelope, which he places upon a stand of slim construction (as illustrated). The magician now explains that he will cause the money to vanish from the hands of his assistant, and mystically travel into the envelope, comfortably resting in full view upon a slender side-table, situated in a distant corner of the stage or room, as the case may be.

Suiting the action to the word, he takes the handkerchief (still held by the spectator), and snatches it away from his fingers. The coin has vanished. The handkerchief is shown from both sides. The wizard now requests a spectator to take a pair of shears, which are openly displayed, from the table, and open the envelope, still resting on the stand. The wizard is sure to emphasize, and impress firmly upon the minds of the audience, that he, personally, does not handle or touch the envelope, in any manner whatsoever.

An end is thus cut from the envelope, and a second envelope produced therefrom. This one is also cut open, and still a third envelope is found to have been nested therein. This last one, upon being opened, is found to contain the original marked coin. The money is identified and returned to its owner. Yes, dear reader, the envelopes, shears, and stand may be examined. They will offer no clue as to the method employed. The illustration, however, I trust will help considerably in clearing up the mystery.

A small disk attached and hidden in the center of the handkerchief (to represent the borrowed coin, this must be of equal size and weight) is really what the spectator holds. The magician, in apparently covering the borrowed coin, permits it to slide into his sleeve, and the substitution is made, as illustrated. During his patter, the magician secretly allows the coin to slide back into the palm of his hand, where it is retained. The nesting of the three envelopes, and sealing thereof, has been so arranged as to permit a flat metal tube to remain projecting through the edge of this nest. As the magician reaches into his pocket, which is natural, in order to secure possession of the envelopes, the borrowed coin is permitted to slide into the tube, and naturally rests in a corner of the smallest envelope. As the envelopes are brought out from the pocket, the tube is left behind. The trick has been accomplished. All that remains to be done is to shake out the handkerchief, to effect the "vanish" of the supposed coin.

The envelopes are opened, and the marked piece of money is seen to have made its invisible flight. It may be best to use a rather large envelope, so that it might be seen with greater ease, in a large auditorium. The stand holding the envelopes, should be of the simplest possible kind. A mere paper clip, attached to a foot and base, will answer the purpose quite well.

Chameleon Wand

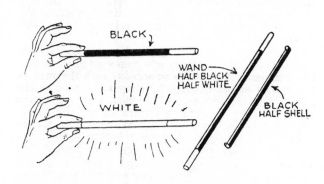

A half shell of black metal covering the magician's wand will enable the magician to automatically change the color of the wand from black to white. The entire wand is rotated between the fingers under cover of a wafting movement so that both sides are apparently shown and the wand is thus proven black.

A SNOW-WHITE wand is held in the hands of the magician, as he makes his entrance upon the stage. Realizing that a black one would be more in harmony with the color of his evening dress, he causes the wand to change instantaneously its color from milk-white to jet-black.

As illustrated, the wand is made of the usual dull-stick type, and is painted before-hand, one-half white, and one-half black. A long, thin metal shell, likewise, is affixed to the wand. This shell is free-working, so that it can be easily turned about the stick. A half turn of the hand, will, of course, transform the wand from white to black. A half turn of the shell will now cover the white part entirely, so that the wand may be freely handled, throughout the evening. This eliminates any probable thought of pre-arrangement.

The Devil's Key Ring

A key ring made as illustrated will provide many hours of amusement.

A LOOP of silk cord, such as illustrated, is passed for inspection. It is easy to see that, to all appearances, this loop is unprepared, as its ends, or knots, have been joined together with sealing wax, making it quite impossible for anyone to untie them.

The magician borrows a number of finger rings, or keys, from his spectators. These borrowed objects, together with the loop, are held in his hands, which are then covered with a borrowed handkerchief. Within a few moments the wizard holds forth the loop. The keys and finger rings have mysteriously interlinked themselves upon this loop. The affair is once more covered with the handkerchief, under cover of which, the borrowed articles are again mystically removed. The innocent apperance of the loop is quite convincing. Its appearance, however, is a clever deception.

The illustration clears the mystery. A small screw has been attached to the free end of the cord, which fits conveniently into a small receiving socket, secreted in the wax. The covering of the handkerchief, therefore, conceals the action of screwing the plug in and out of place, thereby enabling the magician to interlink, or unlink the keys, etc. With a little patience, any one with slight mechanical ability, can construct this very clever little pocket trick. It is well to conceal the screw end well in the body of the wax, so that its edges will not show upon examination. If the performer chooses, he may have a duplicate string or cord, which has been genuinely tied, and secured with sealing wax. The prepared one may then be exchanged, for this duplicate, which may be passed for rigid examination.

The Jumping Spoons

LUMP OF SUGAR

SPRING

WHEN SUGAR MELTS SPRING EJECTS SPOONS

A simple piece of spring brass dropped into the bottom of a coffee cup in which a lump of sugar serves as a trigger will cause spoons to jump out of the cup into the air. This stunt can be easily and quickly built by any reader of this work and will afford much amusement.

THE writer takes pleasure in explaining a simplified, and novel method of presenting the ever-famous "jumping-spoon" trick. The apparatus can be made in a few minutes, by almost anyone, and is as practical as the more complicated appliance now upon the market.

In effect, water is placed into a cup. This cup is of non-transparent china, and of usual type and design. Two teaspoons, which have been previously examined, and placed in the cup, as illustrated, are left in full view of the audience. The spectators may, if they desire, stand completely around the table upon which the apparatus is resting. The circle must be grouped, however, at a fair distance, away from the cup.

At the command of the wizard, both spoons leap high into the air, in most mystifying fashion. They have not been touched by anyone. The spoons and cup may be afterward examined, but no evidence of is found.

A piece of steel clock-spring has been bent into shape, as shown in the diagram. A piece of lump-sugar is forced between its two points. This piece of apparatus is, beforehand, secreted in the bowl of the cup. The spoons are set into place, with the mouths resting upon the spring. The water, within a short period of time, dissolves the sugar. There being no further resistance, the spring snaps upward, tossing the spoons into the air. While the spectators are busy inspecting the spoons, the wizard finds opportunity to secretly remove the apparatus from out the cup, and pocket it. All may now be examined. The spoons should not be of too heavy a material. The lighter the substance, the higher they will fly. You should experiment, to see how long it will take the sugar to dissolve, so as to time the command, properly. Always use the same brand of sugar.

Wonder Blocks

THIS is an absolutely new and original trick, never previously published elsewhere. It is the sole creation of the writer, who has personally worked the trick, and has found it absolutely practical, and extremely bewildering. The necessary equipment consists of the following items, a transparent glass tank, about twelve inches in diameter, and fifteen inches high; a fair-sized pitcher, containing water, a small screen, of the three-fold order, large enough to cover and conceal the tank from view, and several blocks, each about two inches square, individually numbered, from one to six, respectively (more or less may be used, if the performer chooses).

Presentation: All of the above-mentioned apparatus may be fully examined, before and after the trick. The blocks are so constructed and weighted, that they will sink to the bottom, if placed into water. The glass tank is filled with water from the pitcher, and all of the blocks placed therein. The small screen is opened, and placed in front of the tank, concealing same from view. The wizard now clears his arms to the elbows, and requests that anyone call for one of the numbered blocks. Let us say, for example sake, that number three is chosen. The magician, for a moment, places his hands behind the screen, and at once produces block number three. His hands, and arms, however, are perfectly dry, so the theory is accepted that he could not have placed them in the water. To eliminate any theory upon the part of a skeptic, that this is not the original block, the screen is removed, and block three is seen to be plainly missing. The screen is replaced, another block is called for, and the one corresponding in number, is likewise removed, under similar mysterious circumstances. The screen again is lifted to prove evidence of the genuineness of the problem. The second block is likewise plainly discovered to be missing. In similar fashion, the remaining blocks are mystically taken from the mysterious tank. The performer's hands, upon inspection at any priod of the trick, are found perfectly dry. In conclusion, the tank, pitcher, water, blocks, and screen, are again passed for inspection. The examining committee, likewise the audience, are at an absolute loss to discover the secret.

Explanation: The preparation for this remarkable problem is extremely simple. All of the paraphernalia is unprepared, and exactly as its appearance indicates. The wizard's hands and arms, however, have been beforehand, treated. They have been rubbed well with *lycopodium* powder. This powder forms around the fingers and hands, in a coating, similar to that of a glove, and the water has no more action upon the flesh, and rolls off as easily, as it would on a duck's back. The magician has, therefore, simply to remove the blocks, in the order in which they are called, from behind cover of the screen.

You can remove any one of a number of blocks from a bowlful of water without getting your hand wet if you either dust your hand withl ycopodium powder (obtainable at your drug store) or sprinkle this powder over the surface of the water in the container.

The audience does not know, however, that this condition exists. They have mental theories of trick blocks, wires and strings that pull them out, a probable trap or opening in the tank, chemicals, a trick about the screen, etc., etc.

As the audience are not generally not willing to accept the theory that the magician could place his hands inside the liquid, and yet remove the objects with his hands still dry, the trick becomes doubly mystifying. It is, therefore, well that a clever wizard use his ability of verbal, as well as active mis-direction, to cause them to think that the secret lies in the paraphernalia, to entirely misdirect them from the actual secret. Finding the articles unprepared, later on, leaves the audience quite bewildered.

The Mesmerized Tumbler

THIS is a very neat and exceptionally clever after-dinner trick, which may be performed without any special apparatus or prearrangement, after little practise. In effect, an examined glass tumbler is made to adhere securely to the performer's palm, after several apparent hypnotic passes have been made with the other hand. So firmly will the magician's power, or magnetism, hold the glass to the hand, that even a fairly firm straight, pull will not release it.

Secure a rather heavy glass tumbler, with a hollow bottom. Hold the palm of the hand open, with the fingers half closed, and twist the glass upon the palm slightly to the right or left, while forcible pressure is maintained. To dampen the hand, before commencing the trick, will improve the working thereof. When properly done, a slight suction will be felt. It is then safe to raise the hand, and the tumbler will follow. It is always best to secure a tumbler with a smooth bottom, to prevent a possible cutting of the palm. Such a tumbler will also remain in position longer.

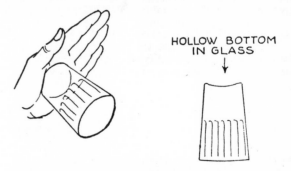

HOLLOW BOTTOM IN GLASS

A hollow bottomed glass can be made to adhere to the surface of the palm if the palm is slightly dampened and pressed into the bottom of the glass and then an attempt is made to straighten out the hand. The partial vacuum produced will cause the tumbler to remain suspended and attached to the palm in an uncanny fashion.

The "Sole" of the Wizard

A VERY good impromptu trick, with an amazingly impressive climax, one of those few problems that is simple to accomplish, and yet has the appearance of being the outcome of expert manipulation. The magician shows a playing card which, for example, we will suppose to be the jack of hearts. This is shown,

This card is then picked up, and presented for examination. Nothing of pre-arrangement, or of an unusual nature, can be found.

Two cards are used to do the trick. They are firmly held together, and shown as one. Taking care not to disturb the position, they are placed upon the floor, the

A card is placed on the floor and the performer steps upon it changing its face value. The effect is accomplished by placing two cards on the floor, one on top of the other and attaching a small piece of wax or gum to the shoe. The top card sticks to the sole of the shoe.

both back and front, and to all appearances, seems intact. The magician now places this card face upward, upon the floor, and puts his foot upon it, so that the sole of the shoe completely conceals the card from view. As the foot is lifted, an impressive transformation is observed. The card has mystically changed into the five of spades.

face of the upper card, uppermost. A bit of gum, or wax, has been previously attached to the sole of the show. When the foot is placed upon the card, the sticky substance compels the card to adhere thereto; and when the foot is lifted, the top card sticks tight to the performer's under sole, and cannot be seen.

The Enchanted Pellet

A SMALL pellet of paper, twice the size of a pea, is passed for inspection. A spectator is requested to place this pellet in the center of the performer's palm. The arm is bared to the elbow, and the hand held far away from any part of his body. The performer now closes his fingers for a moment, and when it is again opened for a moment, the pellet has mysteriously van-

ished. This action is repeated several times, the ball of paper vanishing and re-appearing most mystically, much to the amazement of the onlookers.

Before presenting the trick, the magician has secretly covered the third finger-nail of his hand with beeswax. This wax is adhesive. The pellet of paper is placed in the hand near the ball of the thumb. The instant the hand

is closed and the fingers brought to the performer's palm (fist fashion), the paper will adhere to the fingernail. Upon opening the hand, the magician must be careful to hold his hand at the proper angle, so that the paper will not be seen. A little practise will perfect the move. The trick may, of course, be repeated as often as desired.

By the aid of a piece of wax attached to the nail, a paper ball can be easily disappeared and made to reappear.

Novel Card Rising Effect

By glueing several cards together and attaching a small wheel indicated in the diagram, a very novel card rising effect can be produced.

IT SEEMS that for the past twenty odd years, no one individual effect in magic has been accepted with as much emphasis of choice, as the ever-popular rising-card trick, in which cards previously chosen, and shuffled back into the original deck, mysteriously rise, in called-for rotation, out from the deck, without any visible means of operation.

I therefore believe that this most unique and practical method for bringing about the above described illusion, will be accepted by my many amateur and professional friends; who, I trust, will appreciate the simplicity of this apparatus, together with its superiority over most mechanical contrivances, which have been offered to the wide-ranging field of mystics.

A number of cards, which have been glued together, act as a backing through which a small gear-wheel has been affixed. This inexpensive arrangement can be constructed within a few moments by anyone, with slight mechanical experience. Any number of cards, placed between this layer and the loose cards, as illustrated, can easily be caused to rise, by simply operating the gear with the index finger. Placing the cards in a case will help the handling considerably, as well as heighten the effect of presentation.

The Enchanted Chapeau

Under cover of lifting a number of silk handkerchiefs from the table, a collapsible hat is picked up. This is rapidly fanned open and the remaining silks are vanished into the interior of the hat.

THIS is a very sensational transformation trick, and one that I am assured my readers will accept as a rather smart magical novelty. The wizard, after showing his hands unquestionably empty, steps to his table, from which he removes seven or eight large, silk handkerchiefs of various colors. Waving them gracefully up and down, he rolls the silks into a small ball, when suddenly they are seen to transform into a beautiful silk hat of jester's type This hat is composed of the various colors, which correspond directly with the handkerchiefs employed. The hat is placed upon the head of an attendant, who walks proudly off the stage, displaying his newly-produced chapeau.

To prepare for this trick, the magician provides himself with a frame, consisting of eight wire sections, such as are herewith illustrated. This frame is held in proper shape, assisted by a number of strings, tied to these ribs, at the proper distance. A silk covering is sewn to this frame. This covering, of course, is composed of various colored silks. It will be seen that this hat may be folded perfectly flat, and when opened in fan-like fashion, assumes the appearance of a genuine chapeau. It may be held in place, with a small catch. This hat, in collapsed form, is picked up secretly behind the cover of the silks, from the conjurer's table. Waving his hands up and down, the magician rolls the handkerchiefs into a ball, and quickly opens up the hat. The handkerchiefs, tightly rolled, are concealed in the crown of the hat when the same is displayed. A rubber band, stretched tightly upon the inside of the hat, will help to hold the silks in place and prevent their falling, when the chapeau is placed upon the assistant's head.

The Colors of Diablo

A RATHER surprising trick. With slight practise, this can be made a rather striking and unexplainable mystery. A glass goblet with a metal foot is shown. The goblet is found to contain a red liquid. It is for a moment covered with a handkerchief. When the cover is removed, the liquid is seen to have mystically changed in color, to a deep green. This is again covered with the handkerchief, which in similar fashion, is once more removed. The color of the liquid this time, has been transformed to yellow. Once more this container is covered. Upon removal of the handkerchief, the liquid is now seen to be pure water. This is poured into a basin, and the goblet passed for immediate inspection.

Three celluloid shells are used. These, as described in the diagram, are so made, as to fit half way around the cylinder section of the goblet. They are all of different colors. These are nested, one on top of the other, in the goblet, before presenting the trick. Beneath the cover of the handkerchief, one shell after another is removed.

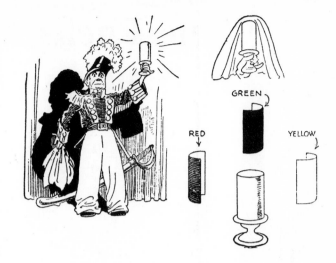

> A colorless liquid preferably water placed in a glass cylinder is made to appear yellow, green or red by colored semi-cylindrical sheets. These make the water take on a colored aspect. They are removed one at a time.

These are disposed with, in the action of placing the kerchief upon the table. They can easily be left in back of other pieces of paraphernalia, standing upon the table, or may be dropped into a trap, if the magician chooses. Clear water is actually placed in the goblet. This liquid may, of course, be poured out, and the container passed for inspection after the shells have been removed.

Hypnotized Cards

Instead of using the pin to produce the hypnotized card stunt, a thin hair is substituted for the pin. This encircles the palm and enables the performer to stack a great many cards under it. Pressure on the cards will break the hair, and permit the cards to fall.

THIS is a new, improved method of performing that ever-popular trick, without tearing up the skin of the hands with a needle, as in the old discarded method. In this offering, a number of cards are taken from an unprepared deck by the wizard, who arranges them upon the palm of his hand, in the shape of an eight-pointed star. The magician turns his palm downward, and not a card drops to the floor. At the performer's command, however, all the cards drop to the floor.

To accomplish this interesting little feat, the performer has provided himself with a fine hair loop, large enough to go over his hand, and hold several cards, as illustrated. There need be no fear of detection, inasmuch as the hair is quite invisible, even at close range. When the entertainer desires the cards to fall, after performing the trick, the breaking of the hair is easily accomplished by half closing the hand. The hair cannot be seen when the cards are picked up from the floor to examine them.

Improved Candle and Handkerchief Trick

CANDLE

THREE SECTIONS CONTAIN HANDKERCHIEFS ETC., ETC.,

CANDLE ROLLED INTO PAPER

PAPER COVER

BROKEN INTO PARTS SILKS EMERGE

A metal candle made up in three sections is rolled into a paper cover and used in the production of handkerchiefs.

THIS very unique and popular effect has in later years, been discarded from the program of some of our brilliant entertainers, due to the fact that the prior construction of the necessary apparatus became too troublesome an item to retain. Much time in preparation, plus the trouble of securing the proper necessary material, seemed to further a desire to substitute the trick. The method I am describing is a vast improvement over the original; and its simplicity in working, as well as in construction, I feel assured, will be appealing to lovers of the trick. The effect consists of wrapping a candle, which had been previously burning, in a sheet of paper, which is clearly left in view. A handkerchief is now disappeared, (by any of the popular methods). The parcel, apparently containing the candle, is now torn, and therein is discovered the missing handkerchief. The candle (a duplicate), is produced elsewhere, afterward.

Explanation: The candle, in this method, should be made of metal tubing, painted to resemble the original article. It should be made to divide in three parts, and well constructed so that this is not noticeable at fairly close quarters. A piece of tallow candle, which fits into the top, supplies the flame. A duplicate handkerchief is concealed in this piece of apparatus. When wrapped in paper, it will be seen the parcel can easily be broken, and the handkerchief discovered. The paper, containing the metal sections of the candle, can be crushed into small compass, and tossed carelessly upon the table. The fact that the paper may be torn into three parts, will satisfy the spectators that the candle (supposedly and acceptedly a genuine one), has completely vanished.

Lights Out

THIS trick, although known to quite a few professional magicians, has always been considered an excellent impromptu experiment. It requires very little practise, and should be an interesting addition to the amateur conjurer's program.

The conjurer takes a match and strikes it on the box, then holds the burning match in his right hand, at arm's length, away from his body. On blowing down the left sleeve, the light of the match will go out.

It is necessary to use a wooden match to perform this

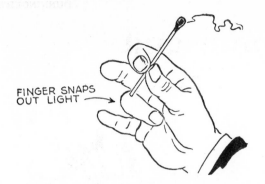

FINGER SNAPS
OUT LIGHT →

trick, as it cannot possibly be accomplished with any other kind. The match must be held at arm's length, in an upright position, while you blow down the other sleeve. As you blow, you simultaneously strike the other end of the match, with some force, with the third finger. The move will be quite unnoticed, and the flame will instantly be extinguished. Practise before demonstrating, so as to perfect the movement.

Another method of snapping out the light with the finger is to hold the match between the index and middle fingers and strike the end with the thumb. This is not shown.

A New Cigar Trick

PAPER CIGAR ←

HANDKERCHIEF

While our artist has shown one use of the paper cigar, this is not necessarily the way this trick is presented as the accompanying article shows.

THE wonder-worker clears his arms to the elbow. He now shows his hands unquestionably empty, displaying both the backs and palms thereof. Removing a cigar from his pocket, he holds it at fingers' tips, as illustrated. Bringing his hands together, he slowly begins to wave them up and down, rolling the cigar between his fingers. Mysteriously, a red silk handkerchief, of bright tint, is seen to make its appearance. This slowly materializes, until it becomes a handkerchief, some fourteen inches square. The hands are again shown empty. The cigar has entirely vanished. The hands may be freely examined, if the audience desire.

The cigar used in this trick, is made entirely of brown paper. It is hollow, and contains the handkerchief, afterward produced. A colored-paper band is pasted around the cigar, to give it its natural appearance. At short distance, it cannot be told from the genuine article. Under cover of the hands, the handkerchief is slowly worked into view. When it has been entirely liberated from out its paper tube, the paper cigar is rolled secretly into a small ball. This being very compact, is quietly disposed of, under cover of placing the silk upon the table. The hands may then, of course, be shown. This idea is entirely new, and has never previously been employed, in obtaining a similar effect.

Twentieth-Century

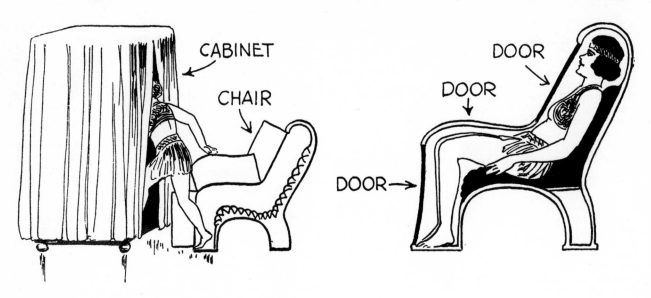

A cabinet is first examined by the audience. This is open on all four sides and after being shown freely, is covered with a cloth. The cabinet is again shown, mesmeric passes or perhaps a shot, and the cloth is suddenly jerked away revealing an oriental dancer in costume. There is no trickery about the stage, the platform, or the back drop.

However, a chair conveniently placed in back of the cabinet is not as innocent as it appears. This chair contains the dancer. Four silently operating doors permit her to escape from the chair and enter the cabinet through the back. Naturally, when the drape is removed the dancer will be found in the cabinet.

Cabinet Illusion

A VERY effective stage illusion, quite original, both in effect and "modus operandi," is here described. Upon a brilliantly lighted stage, the illusionist's assistants stretch a large carpet or cloth, to prove the absolute absence of stage traps. A small skeleton frame-work cabinet is now wheeled forth, directly into the center of this floor-cloth. This cabinet consists of nothing more than an elevated base, about two and one-half feet square. The elevation consists of four short legs, with ball-bearing rollers. The elevation makes it quite possible for the audience to see beneath, during the entire proceedings of the trick. The base is but an inch or so in thickness, all around. To each corner of this platform, are attached metal rods, two inches in diameter and about six feet tall. A small frame top, of innocent piping, completes the structure.

Amid the strains of mystic music, and the sounds of the Oriental tambor, the magician winds a large cloth around this cabinet, completely concealing the rods from view. A shot is fired, the cloth drops to the ground, and there, behold, stands a beautiful girl, in a striking costume of an ancient Egyptian princess! She steps out from the cabinet, the brilliant colored stones of her costume playing merrily in the limelight, as the magician gracefully escorts her to the wings. She bows pleasantly, in acceptance of the applause, and exits.

Furniture of a type ordinarily found in theatres, and used to heighten the display of a set, is responsible for the lady's hiding place. A chair of the usual type of stage upholstery has been standing a few feet to the rear of this cabinet. This chair which, in reality, is a special constructed box held the lady, until the proper moment. This moment arose when the illusionist was winding the cloth around the cabinet. It acted as a screen, in back of which the lady liberated herself, and walked quietly into the interior of the cabinet, through the curtain opening. The chair is so constructed, that the doors through which she made her appearance, will again immediately close. Spring hinges make this a matter of simplicity. It is well to have one or two more chairs, of similar type, displayed around the stage, so that the one that is actually used, is not suspected. The magician and his assistant should spend some time in adjusting the cloth upon the cabinet, as the young lady makes her secret entrance. Whatever vibration or shaking of the cloth, she might so produce, will seem natural, and therefore is credited to the magician and his assistant. This also gives the girl time to enter the cabinet.

A New Lemon Trick

AN absolutely new and original novelty, quite different, both as to method and effect, from anything heretofore offered. The wizard displays a small box, made entirely of wood, about four inches square. This has hinged to it a lid of simple type. The box is shown entirely empty, and the lid closed. Further to prove the innocence of this contrivance, and to assure the audience that nothing can possibly enter the box, a long hat-pin is thrust clear through it. There have been drilled through the sides of the box previously two small holes placed at corresponding points to enable the pin to pass through conveniently. The box, with the pin so penetrating it, is placed upon a small undraped sidestand. The magician now shows a lemon, which mystically disappears between his fingers. Upon opening the small wooden casket, the lemon is found to have made its way upon the inside. The pin is seen to be thrust clear through the fruit. The pin is withdrawn, and the lemon at once passed for inspection. It is found to be the genuine article.

The box is mechanically constructed. A false bottom-and-shelf arrangement operates upon a pivot. The principle is similar to the old inexhaustible box, with which my readers are undoubtedly quite familiar. The lemon rests secretly upon the shelf, behind the bottom of the box, when the lid is raised to prove it empty. As the lid is replaced, the bottom is secretly forced inward, causing the lemon to enter its interior. The pin is now thrust through the fruit, as it passes through the apparently empty box. A duplicate lemon is used. This must be identical, in appearance and size, with the one in the box. In the action of picking the lemon from the table, it is dropped into a trap, and the hand brought forth, as if holding the fruit. This accounts for the disappearance.

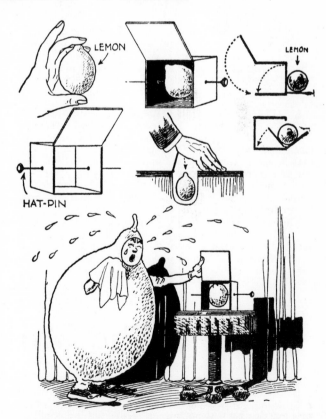

A hat pin is pierced through two sides of a box. A lemon is vanished and reappears within the box, pierced by the hat pin. This is accomplished by the aid of a cabinet provided with a hinged back as the illustration shows.

A Novel Transformation

LAYER OF MATCHES
CUT DOWN HALF SIZE

MATCH LAYER
ATTACHED TO
CENTER OF
HANDKERCHIEF

A layer of matches cut down to half size and attached to the center of a kerchief is put into a match box. When the box is first exhibited, it appears to contain nothing but matches. Opening the box from the other end the kerchief is produced and the matches disappear.

A POCKET match-box, full of matches, is displayed to the audience. The box is closed and given to a spectator to hold. A handkerchief is now vanished (by any method the performer desires). The match-box is now opened, and the handkerchief discovered therein. The matches have entirely vanished. The handkerchief is removed from the box, which is immediately passed for inspection. The matches may be produced elsewhere, if desired.

The secret is exceedingly simple. Construct a layer of matches, cut down half size, as illustrated. This should be mounted upon a small piece of metal, which is then fixed to the center of a large handkerchief. The handkerchief is then placed into the box, with this match layer showing. To all appearances, the box is full of matches. The box is closed, and given to someone to hold. A duplicate handkerchief is made to vanish, and is apparently found in the box. By pushing the drawer out of the box at its opposite end, the handkerchief is brought to view. When the silk is removed, the fake matches are secretly removed with it. The box may then be passed for inspection. Genuine matches are afterward produced elsewhere. These, supposedly, are the ones that originally occupied space in the box. A bit of mis-direction and good showmanship is essential, to present this trick properly.

The Musical Fork

THE magician, for this problem, requires an ordinary steel fork, and two drinking glasses, of the usual type. He explains that he is about to present a problem dealing with sound, music, and general scientific acoustics. He explains that sound usually travels at an incredible speed, and upon the strength of this scientific phenomenon, will demonstrate an extraordinary sound effect. Displaying the fork, he begins by plucking the prongs. This action, causing vibration, produces a musical note. The wonder-man asserts that, with the assistance of the two glasses, he will demonstrate his powers of driving sound into any channel he desires. He now again plucks the prongs of the fork, this time apparently transferring the sound into the glass.

To accomplish this experiment, the fork is held in the performer's hand, as shown in the diagram. The handle is held clear of an ordinary match box, which is palmed secretly, and held in the same hand with the fork. As the performer plucks the prongs, he forces a vibration; and if the handle of the fork is then secretly allowed to touch the matchbox, a distinct clear note may be heard.

A match box held in the hand and serving as a resonator will be the means of much merriment in this simple parlor stunt.

"MUSIC BOX CONCEALED IN HAND"

The match box, in this fashion, acts as a sort of sound box, through which the note, so caused, vibrates. When the prongs of the fork are plucked, the conjurer immediately holds his fingers over the drinking glass. He then lets the fork handle touch the box, and the note seemingly comes from out the glass. Sending the sound, from one tumbler into another, is produced in like fashion.

The High Priest of Baal

SOME years ago the later Harry Kellar created quite a sensation by offering to the American public a strange automaton. This was a small figure of a Turkish boy, who was seated, in Oriental fashion, upon a small platform. This contrivance was supported high above stage level, resting upon a large glass transparent tube, about twenty inches in diameter, and two and a half feet high. The figure, although apparently devoid of any connection with any outer force, would answer questions, pick up cards and numbered blocks, solving methematical problems in this fashion. Another automaton, some years back, which was produced with signal success in the larger vaudeville theatres, was known as Gonday Humanus. This was a large man-like figure, built of steel, the body of which was opened, displaying an array of machinery in action. This figure would ride a bicycle, walk about, and do other life-like things.

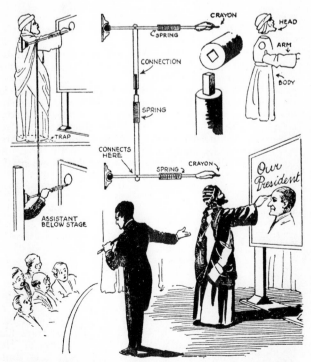

Details showing how the automaton is operated by an assistant.

Perhaps one of the best universally known automatons, was Ajeeb, the chess-playing automaton. This was a life-sized figure of a Turk, composed apparently of machinery, who would play chess with anyone, and generally be the winner. (It was operated by one of the best players in the world.) For many years this was one of the feature attractions of the old Eden Musee, located on Twenty-Third street, New York.

All of the above-mentioned figures were expensive contrivances, and for that reason, it seems there were no duplicates. Furthermore, they were built by master machinists, who had taken years to perfect them, and guarded the secret of their constructions carefully. I am herewith describing a mechanical figure, which should be appealing, for its simplicity of construction. It consists of the life-sized figure of an Oriental, clad in the regalia of a high-priest. The lecturer explains, that for centuries, this figure has been subjected to the worship of thousands, in the temple of Baal, and with the years, has become sensitive to their words. It can, as the show-man explains, actually understand, as he is are about to demonstrate. The hand, arm, head, and leg, of the figure are removed, proving that it is actually a dummy, of mechanical construction. The figure is now placed in position, in front of a large blackboard, and a crayon fixed to his fingers. Numbers and names are suggested by the spectators, which the figure clearly repeats, in writing, upon the blackboard. Totals are added, and other problems in arithmetic solved, by the High Priest of Baal.

The mechanism is clearly described in detail, in the illustration. The writing is done below the stage, by an assistant, upon a duplicate blackboard. The rod connection, leading upward through a trap in the stage, enables the figure to duplicate the script. The concealed assistant easily overhears the conversation, and answers the problems and questions, accordingly. Various socket connections make the dissection of the limbs and head of the automaton practical. The long silk robe, worn by this Oriental dummy, easily conceals the opening in the floor of the stage, as well as the connecting rod, leading up into it. The body of the figure is built upon a metal frame work, to enable it to stand erect. After the demonstration, the rod is withdrawn by the assistant below the stage, who closes the trap behind him. The figure may then be carried off. The bottom must be weighted considerably, so that it will not move out of place, during its demonstration.

The Magnetic Cigar

RING WITH PIN

CIGAR

FINGER-RING

NEEDLE POINT

Cigars, cigarettes and various other objects can be made to adhere to the palm of the magician's hand if he has previously provided himself with a ring to which a needle point has been soldered Remove the ring, shortly after demonstration, to preserve the secret.

A GOOD, thorough, practical magician, can ordinarily seat himself conveniently in a theatre, and find no difficulty in analysing the "modus operandi" of a complicated conjurer's problem, the very first time he views its presentation. Strange as it may seem, however, quite often, one of our best-posted magicians will be mystified by some small pocket effect, and will be at an absolute loss to offer a method anywhere near a practical one, in explanation thereto.

The original trick I am herewith about to describe is one of these few that holds its reputation of having puzzled many big men in magic. The magician's fingers and hands are examined. They are found intact. An examined and unprepared cigar is placed upon the table. The conjurer for a moment places his fingers upon the cigar, which clings to his fingers, when he again raises his hand. It remains sticking thereto, as if magnatized. The magnetic power is then released, and the cigar passed for inspection. The secret lies simply in a needle point, which has been soldered to a plain band finger-ring. When the palms are examined, the needle point is at the back of the hand. When the hand is reversed, the point end is carried to the palm. It is this needle point which penetrates the cigar, and makes this levitation possible.

Enchanted Mirror

A HAND-MIRROR, with a handle attachment, similar in construction to the one illustrated, is shown to the spectators. The magician explains that this mirror is thousands of years old, having been dug up from the tomb of Cleopatra. He further describes that a band of Egyptians endangered their lives in securing the looking-glass; and he has been extremely fortun- ate in his method of business persuasion, to make this antique relic his property. The mirror has been be- witched by an old wizard, who originally gave it to this Egyptian queen. Although unearthed so many thou- sands of years ago, it has not lost its powers of reflection nor enchantment, which he proceeds to demonstrate.

A pack of cards is offered to a spectator, with the

request that one be freely selected. One is thus removed from the pack; which, for example, we will say to be the three of diamonds. The spectator is requested to hold the card in an upright position, before the mirror surface of the hand-glass, which is held a foot or so away from the card. This action is further shown in the diagram. The reflection of the card is naturally seen in the mirror. A moment afterward, the card is withdrawn from its position, and placed upon the table. Much to the surprise of the spectators, upon looking in the glass, they find that the reflection of the card still remains, and a photograph of the three of diamonds has mysteriously affixed itself to the mirror surface.

The mirror is, of course, a specially prepared piece of apparatus, constructed so as to be as innocent in appearance, as possible. A "spirit photograph" of the card, consists of three spots, in resemblance to those on the playing card, which have been painted upon a strip of thin, clearly transparent celluloid. This is originally concealed between the backside of the frame, and the looking-glass proper.

To either corner of the upper edge of the celluloid, is affixed a rubber, or elastic band, which leads up over the glass, beneath the edges of the framework. A catch, operated from the front of the mirror frame, releases the celluloid shade, which flies up in front of the looking-glass, at the desired moment.

Owing to the clear transparency of the celluloid, its presence is practically invisible in front of the glass, which shows through, in the usual manner, and looks like its natural surface. Spots of the playing cards, therefore seem strangely apparent.

The magician has no difficulty in assuring himself, that the selected card will be the desired three of diamonds. He has beforehand, provided himself with a full deck of fifty-two cards, which are all alike. (Of the one denomination, the three of diamonds.) One card of a different suit may be placed upon the bottom of the deck, so as to disguise the pack. Little attention, if any, will be paid to the deck, as an audience is ordinarily willing to accept the fact automatically, that the cards are not pre-arranged, or prepared.

The showman presenting this trick, is given a splendid opportunity of demonstrating his ability in mis-direction. All attention must be drawn to the enchanted mirror, and its strange qualities of ghost reflection. With a

THE MAGIC MIRROR

REFLECTION OF CARD

ELASTIC

MIRROR

CATCH

REFLECTION REMAINS

CELLULOID WITH SPOTS OF CARD

By the aid of a strip of celluloid on which the spots of a card are printed and which comes into view when the performer desires, a very mysterious yet beautiful effect can be produced. The reflection of a card apparently remains on the magic mirror.

little practise, and good, suitable patter, an entertainer will find no trouble in making this trick one of the highlights of his program. If the magician has been presenting card tricks, with an unprepared deck, earlier in the evening, it is still less likely that an audience would suspect an exhange, to this pack of all-alike.

The Spooky Dollar Piece

Move back and the coin creeps away from you.

THE magician exhibits what to all appearances seems to be an unprepared silver dollar, of Uncle Sam's coinage, and passes same for inspection. It is found intact, and returned to the wizard. This coin, although ordinary in appearance, has been infested with a strange and uncanny power, explains the wizard. In India, some years ago, a Yogi made several passes over the pocket piece, and uttered words of enchantment which have left a marked and unusually creepy effect; so creepy, in fact, that the coin still creeps. The magician now demonstrates. The coin is placed upon a small velvet covered table, and begins slowly to creep away from the conjuror's body, and towards the opposite edge of the table top and is passed for reinspection.

The coin is quite unprepared, and is placed upon a small pellet of wax, attached to a string, drawn about the table top, in the manner illustrated. The free end of this fine silk thread, is affixed to a button of the performer's waist-coat. As he draws away from the table edge, the coin naturally travels in the opposite direction.

Improved Miser's Dream

In the improved miser's dream effect, the handles on both sides of the pail serve to conceal the actuating mechanism and also the coin holders. The coins are released one at a time and fall into the pail with a rather audible sound and seem to come out of the air.

SOME years ago, the professional coin manipulator, offered a very interesting problem, in pure sleight of hand, which was known as "the miser's dream." In this trick, a large number of silver dollars were produced at his finger tips. As these coins were magically created, one after another, they were dropped into a derby hat, which was held in the magician's hand. This very entertaining spectacle, however, was included in the program of only experienced wizards, inasmuch as it required years of constant practise, and a great amount of trained digital dexterity, to present this effect successfully.

In the version of the trick I am about to describe, very little pure sleight of hand is necessary. As illustrated, the apparatus substituted for the derby hat in this trick establishes by far the most effective method. This appears to be a small silver pail, into which the money is dropped as it is apparently caught in mid-air. Two coin holders, with springs attached, are affixed to opposite sides of the pail. Each of these containers is sufficiently large to hold half a dozen, or more, coins. These may be easily pushed out from the holders, with the fingers. One coin, after another, can in this way be dropped into the pail. Its clink, as it strikes the bottom, clearly establishes its presence. The magician holds this pail in the hand in a manner such as to conceal the dropper beneath his fingers. In this fashion, it is simple for him to govern the dropping of the coins. In the other hand,

he has one coin, which he shows, and apparently drops in the pail. In reality however, the coin is retained in the hand, and a duplicate slides from out the hole. This action is repeated, until the coins in the holders have been exhausted in their supply. The effect upon the audience is as if the magician was producing coins, one after another, in his other hand.

The silver tub can be thoroughly examined after presentation of the trick and it is doubtful whether anyone in the audience will suspect that the two handles of the pail even though they might be a trifle shaky, assist in the production. In the drawing, in order to make the matter clear, the circular ends of the coin holders is shown cut away. In the actual model these ends are solid and the slot through which the coin escapes is on the under surface of the holder. Several of these pails may be found on the stage so that while the coin production is taking place in one of them, another one can be examined or if the performer desires, he may produce a coin in each of the pails successfully and progressively. The entire heap can eventually be poured on the table-top, apparently demonstrating the magician's digital dexterity.

It must be remembered that every trick in magic requires the personality of the magician. Applying proper showmanship to the execution of any magical stunt will do much to arouse the spectator's interest and gain his applause.

The Obedient Time-Piece

THIS is an effective trick, of simple preparation, that never fails to mystify. The conjurer borrows a time-piece, from either lady or gentleman. The magician explains the power of mind over matter, and prepares to demonstrate the force of his individually gifted mind. The watch is placed in the center of the table. The magician commands the works therein, to stop. Immediately the tick ceases, and the hands of the watch stop. The conjurer re-commands the watch to go and once more hands it to its owner, who finds it ticking away merrily, as ever. In order to prove his theory, the magician offers to repeat the experiment. Explaining that the trick cannot be presented, unless the watch is insulated entirely from human touch, he places the watch upon the cover of a book, which the owner of the time-piece is permitted to hold. Repeating the command, the mechanism of the watch again stops.

A watch may be made to stop when placed in the center of a table or on a book if the table or book has been equipped with a magnet as indicated.

To do this trick, the magician must provide himself with two small magnets. These are usually referred to as toy magnets, and are purchasable in any toy shop. A cavity, sufficiently large to receive one of the magnets, is cut in the table top. The magnet is placed in this groove, and the table top is covered with a cloth, so that the magnet cannot be seen. The second magnet is secretly concealed beneath the cover of the book. It is held in place in a cavity prepared for it. If any watch be placed directly over the poles of either magnet, the magnetism will stop the watch.

Bewitched Oranges

TRICKS that one can do readily, without specially prepared apparatus, seem to be most popular with amature magicians. The one I am about to describe is an original trick, which in the hands of a clever student of the art should prove to be a masterpiece in modern mysticism.

Effect: A tray of oranges is passed about, and one is freely selected, and held by some member of the audience. The magician requests the loan of a twenty-five cent piece, which is marked for identification. The coin mystically disappears. The selected orange is cut into halves, and upon the inside thereof is discovered the marked coin

Explanation: The oranges are unprepared. The coin is disappeared by any one of the various methods, described elsewhere in this volume. It is secretly recovered afterwards, and affixed to the back of the blade of a table-knife, where it is held in place by a piece of wax. When the fruit is cut in halves, this prepared knife is used, the blank side of the knife upward, of course. The marked coin is thus deposited in the orange. A certain amount of practise is necessary to present this trick successfully. Misdirection must be practised. In cleaning the knife with a napkin, as if removing the orange juice after the trick, all marks of the wax are secretly removed.

A simple method of getting a coin into an orange is to attach the coin to the knife with which the orange is to be cut by means of a small piece of wax. Cut the orange with the heel of the knife and then when the cut has been practically completed, draw the knife through the divided halves of the fruit and as the coin approaches the center of the orange, wipe the coin off with the pulp.

The Reverso Match Trick

THIS is undoubtedly one of the very best and most mystifying pocket tricks that has ever been offered to this wide-ranging world of wonder-workers. A match box, of the usual type, is taken from the performer's pocket, and exhibited. The drawer section is

all completely turned around. The head ends of the matches are now seen, on the other end of the box, directly opposite to the one that had been marked.

Explanation: The magician has previously provided himself with a small strip of metal, painted to represent

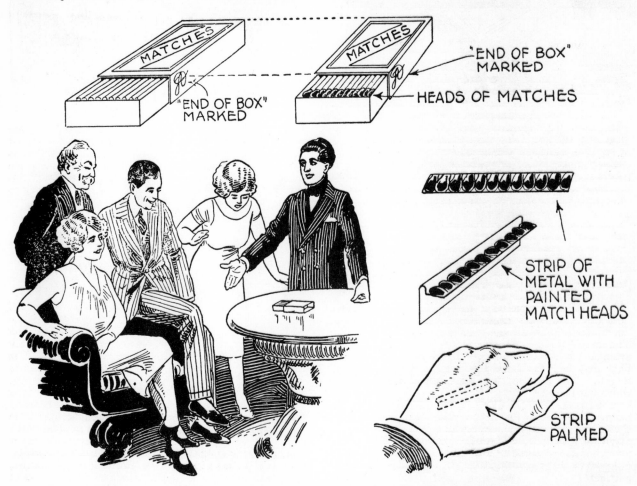

With the aid of a small strip of metal on which the painted heads of matches may be found, the contents of a match-box can be apparently reversed.

pushed open, enabling the spectators to see the heads of the matches. This end of the box is marked with some signature or other, so that the audience may distinguish the end afterward. Without any cumbersome moves whatsoever, the conjurer commands the matches to turn around in the box. Much to the surprise of his spectators, the matches seem to have become obedient, as, upon opening the drawer, the matches are seen to have

the sides of the box. The inner strip is painted to represent the heads of matches. This contrivance fits over the end of the box, and to all appearances represents the original match heads, when the box is opened. (The original matches are actually reversed, unknown to the audience.) After the end of the box has been marked, the performer secretly palms this small strip in the action of closing the drawer, and the trick is done.

The Crystal Casket

A SOMEWHAT new effect—a small casket, made entirely of glass—is balanced upon the wizard's open hand, as illustrated. A small metal framework, sufficiently wide to hold the glasses together, forms the skeleton of its construction. Upon the inside of this casket is found a large quantity of confetti, all white in color. The magician fans the casket, and without cover-

ing it in any way, the confetti mystically changes its shade to a brilliant red. The entire contents of the box is thus transformed.

The box is not quite as innocent as its outer appearance dictates. It is divided into two compartments, by a metal division, attached lengthwise, from one of its corners to the other. In the one side of this casket, the

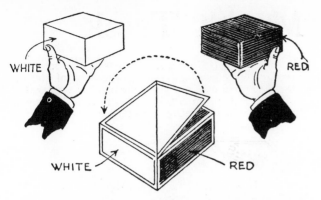

A red box may be changed to a white one if it is provided with a hinged top and painted as indicated.

white confetti is placed. The opposite side is entirely filled with the red. A triangular piece of metal, hinged to the center division, swings back freely, working upon a set of hinges. Upon the one side of this flap, a quantity of white confetti has been pasted. Upon the opposite side, a quantity of red confetti has been glued in similar fashion. By swinging this section about, the upper part of the box effects its entire transformation of color. To work the trick, the box must be turned around secretly, and the flap reversed. This action is easily accomplished, beneath cover of slowly fanning the casket. The thumb of the hand holding the box, controls the flap. The color of the confetti may thus be made to change back again, if the performer so desires.

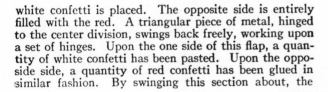

The Penetrating Handkerchief

A TRICK, simple to operate, which is so amazing in effect as to credit the performer with clever dexterity, and the powers of expert manipulation. The magician calls for a volunteer assistant. This attendant is turned around, several times, so that his back may be seen, without calling particular attention thereto. The conjurer takes one of his handkerchiefs, which has been laying close by upon a table. The handkerchief is made to disappear, by rolling it between the magician's thumbs. After the hands have been clearly shown, and no trace of the kerchief is evident, the magician asks his volunteer assistant to turn around. Stretched across his back, and hanging down to the edge of his coat, the elusive handkerchief is seen. How did it get there?

Quite simple, dear reader, as are many of our other tricks. Two handkerchiefs, exactly alike, have been used. One of these has a small hook, sewed to one of its corners. This handkerchief is tucked into a hollow wand, the hook end projecting, as illustrated. The duplicate to this silk is disappeared by any method the conjurer favors. The magician, who has been carelessly waving his wand in the air, while placing his subject in the proper position, has, at an opportune moment, secretly forced the hook into the back of the subject's coat. On drawing the wand downward, this action completely releases the duplicate handkerchief, and leaves same, clinging to the assistant's back. It is of course, needless to remark that this is secretly done while the assistant faces the audience. This effect will be amazing, not to the spectators alone, but likewise to the volunteer assistant, who will be at at an absolute loss to explain the mystic re-appearance.

Another version of the penetrating handkerchief is to fasten a third kerchief under the assistant's coat. After the first one is disappeared, the second kerchief is hooked to the assistant's coat as indicated in the diagram at the left. This is removed,

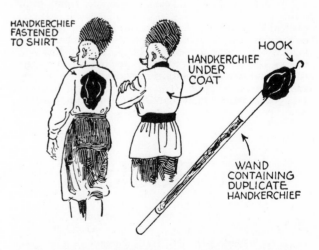

HANDKERCHIEF FASTENED TO SHIRT

HANDKERCHIEF UNDER COAT

HOOK

WAND CONTAINING DUPLICATE HANDKERCHIEF

again disappeared and the statement is made that it has penetrated under the assistant's garment. When he removes his coat, the kerchief is there. This latter effect is another variation which may be easily worked.

The Ghostly Key

While a key placed in a plate apparently produces spirit messages actually the sound comes from a small lead weight suspended on a string. The lead weight is operated by an assistant and the weight actually hits the plate, producing the noise.

THIS is a very new and unusual deception. The magician borrows a large handkerchief from a member of his audience. He also requests the loan of a key. An ordinary china plate, or saucer, is next passed for examination, and the borrowed key placed in the center thereof. The saucer and its contents is now placed in the center of a small side-stand. The wizard may, if he chooses, invite a spectator from the audience to step upon the stage, and examine the side-stand, prior to this procedure.

We will take it for granted that this has been done, and the wizard proceeds to illustrate what he claims to be an uncanny force, over the borrowed key. He explains that the key has a tendency to jump up and down in the saucer, and answer questions, by its various clinks, against the china plate. The examined kerchief is held by opposite corners in his hands, and is held in position in front of the plate, so as to conceal it entirely from view. The key is now heard to clink several times, and thus answer questions, in the manner the performer predicted. The stand, saucer and key, may be examined at any time.

The secret: A fine silk thread has been previously stretched across the stage. A very small lead shot slides about freely, upon the thread. The free end of this thread is held in the hand of an assistant off-stage. By pulling the thread up and down, the shot strikes the center of the plate, and thereby are the clicks produced. The key really never moves. This fact is not likely to be discovered, as the handkerchief conceals it from view. The thread is lifted out of sight, high above the level of the magician's head, when the articles are passed for examination. A finger ring may be used instead of the key, if the magician chooses to vary the trick.

The Book of Mystic Knowledge

SEVERAL cards are chosen from the pack. As there is no forcing of any kind used, and inasmuch as the deck is really unprepared, this selection is genuinely made. After the names of the cards have been memorized by the individuals who selected them, the cards are taken up by the magician, and individually inserted, between the pages of a large book. The titles of the cards are now called in their selected rotation, by the spectators. As the card is named, it mysteriously and slowly rises upward, from out the book. After the levitation has thus been accomplished, to about two-thirds the length of the card, it is taken out of the book, and immediately passed

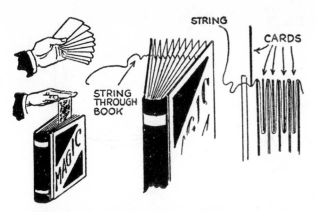

In the book of knowledge, a string is passed through small holes punctured in the pages. The pages themselves are made of

heavy paper, or preferably card-board. Cards are pushed down into the book, and as the string is pulled, the cards appear.

to the person having made the selection, for absolute inspection. If the performer chooses, the spectators may be requested to write their names or initials upon the cards, thereby proving that those that are originally selected, are ctually the ones that are used throughout the trick.

Explanation: The book used is an ordinary one, save for the fact that small holes have been punctured completely through all the pages. Through these holes a

fine silk thread is passed, which is firmly affixed at the one end to the book cover. The selected cards are placed into the pages of the book, in a manner such as to carry the thread down beneath each card's edge. The free end of this thread is secretly pulled, forcing the cards upward.

A good method, of pulling the string, is to attach its free end to a waistcoat. By moving the book away from the body, the cards are slowly brought to view.

The Obedient Eggs

THIS is a neat little experiment, the secret of which, unknown to the audience, consists of a common law in natural science. The clever wizard, however, employs his verbal ability to convince the audience of his absolute so-called magic power, in the matter, and therefore uses the principle to bring about a truly interesting experiment.

The wizard has, standing upon his table, two tall cylinders, such as are herewith illustrated, each filled, as he explains with clear water. He likewise shows a tray, containing a dozen eggs, which he passes for inspection. The magician takes pains to explain that it is absolutely impossible for any one to trick, or prepare an egg, in such a manner as to make its preparation invisible to the naked eye. He therefore challenges his audience to prove that the eggs are not entirely unprepared. (Knowing, as he does, that they are quite ordinary, there are no possibilities of his being embarrassed by their

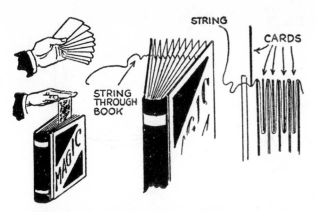

Eggs can be made to sink or swim if placed in salt solutions of different densities. Observe the instructions for filling cylinders.

challenge.) He requests that two of these eggs be selected from the rest. Some one in the audience is now asked to write on one of the eggs, the word, "sink," and write his initials upon the other egg. The magician now places one egg in one cylinder, and the other egg, in the second container. A rather puzzling spectacle is now witnessed. The egg, marked "sink," drops to the bottom of the cylinder; whereas the one marked with the spectator's initials, is mysteriously suspended, half-way down the other glass.

Explanation: All the eggs, likewise the cylinders, are entirely unprepared, and exactly as their appearance indicates. The little joker, this time, is in the water. This seems quite pure and clear, but is by no means free from deception. Take about a pint of water, and in it dissolve as much salt as it will absorb. With this solution, half fill one of the glass cylinders. Into the remaining part of the container, carefully pour some pure, plain water. It is important that this be very carefully done. Pour it down very slowly, along the side of the glass, or better still, into a spoon, so as to break its fall. The pure water will thus flow, (as it is considerably lighter) upon the prepared liquid, without mingling. The appearance and color of the two, are naturally identical, so the entire contents will give the absolute resemblance of clear water. The other container is actually filled with pure water. Into the prepared cylinder the initialed egg is dropped and it will remain suspended half way down, as described. The other egg, marked "sink," is dropped into the opposite container, and will sink to the bottom. Long-stemmed spoons should be used to remove the eggs from out the water, in order not to disturb the specially prepared liquid; especially if the performer chooses to repeat the trick, with other eggs.

At the conclusion, it is good policy to pour the contents of both cylinders into one large basin. This will enable the spectators to examine the cylinders. Should anyone suspect the liquid, and now drop an egg therein, he will find it quite impossible to duplicate the trick.

Which is Which?

The difference between a fresh egg and a boiled egg can be quickly determined by spinning the eggs. A fresh egg will not spin, whereas a boiled egg spins very easily. A plate should preferably be turned upside down, on which this effect is to be tried, and the magician should practice the spinning movement before attempting it in public so that he will not inadvertently permit the egg to fall.

IT SEEMS that audiences appreciate most the magician who has been gifted with the faculty of presenting various little tricks, with common small objects, in an impromptu manner. It is well for the average magician to remember this pretty little effect, as it requires simply knowledge, and no skill whatsoever, to present.

Let us say that the conjurer is visiting the home of friends, and while sitting about, awaiting the butler's invitation to the dining table, he has been requested to present some trick or other, to help make the minutes fly. He requests someone to go into the kitchen, and bring forth a tray, containing a dozen or more eggs. He requires these to be fresh, raw eggs, with the exception of one, which has been boiled. He asks that this one be mixed with the remaining eleven. After the plate has been brought forth, the conjurer asks the audience if they can detect the hard-boiled egg from the others, without breaking any of them. Other than the probability of a guess, this feat, from all appearances, is quite impossible.

There is, however, one way this can be done; and after the task has been given up by the spectators, the magician proceeds to show the method. To distinguish the hard-boiled egg, the magician must take them, and after placing them, tip down upon the table, swiftly spin the eggs. Those that are raw will spin with a sort of wobbling motion, swaying to and fro; while the hard-boiled egg, (there being no liquid substance in its shell) will spin like a top, in a firm, upright position. It is essential that these eggs be spun upon a clear-topped table. Should a cloth be beneath the eggs, it would be of great interference. Preventing the egg thus from being spun properly would result in confusing the magician as to the analysis of "which is which."

If the performer cares to practise a unique effect, he might try to spin the egg by rotating the plate upon which it rests. A fresh egg cannot be made to spin, a boiled egg spinning quite easily. The trick should be practised well to prevent accidental dropping of the egg on the floor and thus spoiling the magicians reputation because of his carelessness.

Enchanted Ashes

A SOMEWHAT different effect, worthy of a stellar position on the program of any modern miracle-man. The magician offers, for inspection, a deck of playing cards which are found unprepared, and returned. One of these cards is selected, and the name called out aloud. We will fancy this card to be the three of diamonds. The magician now requests a spectator to tear the card into small pieces. This is accomplished, and the pieces placed in a small previously-examined saucer. Spirits are poured over the contents of the dish, and a lighted match applied thereto. While the card is burning merrily, the magician explains that the master hand of nature, has, by strange development, produced a force of resurrection. Although the card is changing in form, and will in a moment be a heap of ashes, it can be brought back to its natural condition, he asserts. In him has been invested the power of restoring this substance. A sheet of newspaper is stretched upon the vacant surface of the table. In the center of the paper, the magician empties the ashes, which are immediately covered with a smaller sheet of paper. A dagger is next brought forth. The magician, with some ceremony, sinks the point of this knife through the center of the papers. The dagger now rips through the sheets, and upon its point is found the three of diamonds, completely restored to its original condition, as he predicted.

This trick requires an assistant. He has been listening off stage, when the selection of the card was made. Hearing that the three of diamonds was chosen, he at once proceeds to secure possession of a duplicate. A pocket of newspaper, made from a sheet duplicating the one used, has been glued to the paper proper, as illustrated. In this pocket, the three of diamonds is placed; and the paper is brought forth, and handed to the wizard. The ashes are now emptied upon the paper, and the second sheet is placed directly over the concealed pocket. All that now remains to be done, is to pierce the papers with the dagger, and bring the card to view.

It will be well to remember that almost any one can do a trick; but to present an item well, is ability given to but few. Experience in proper delivery of patter, grace in manipulation, proper stage presence, the psychology of selecting the proper assistants and spectator volunteers from an audience—all these things are essential to the makings of a master magician. Magic is an art that requires absolute study to perfect an artist; so remember, please, dear reader, that too much conscientious practise is impossible. Repeat a trick often, privately, before attempting it upon an audience. If a student finds an experiment too difficult for his handling, it is better to eliminate it entirely from his program, rather than to expose it accidentally.

BURNING CARD

ONE SHEET
OVER THE OTHER

POCKET IN
NEWSPAPER

DUPLICATE
CARD

An assistant back stage or in another room, hearing the name of a card announced, places this in a suitable pocket formed in a newspaper and brings the newspaper into the room. The selected duplicate of this card is burned, the ashes are poured upon the paper; another sheet covers the ashes and then the card is made to mystically appear via the agency of a sharp knife and the newspaper.

Cigarette-to-Handkerchief Transformation

In the illustration, the vanisher has been purposely shown; actually it is much smaller than indicated and is concealed in the palm of the performer's hand. When the performer grasps the vanisher, he can disappear a cigarette and cause the kerchief to appear.

PROBLEMS in which a lighted cigarette are employed are usually accepted as being extremely difficult; as an audience seems to realize the treacherous nature of a burning object, which makes difficult its being successfully manipulated by the artist. Knowing that, whether a "production" or "vanish" is effected with a lighted cigarette, there is always a question as to how it could have possibly been concealed without burning the performer's fingers, or doing injury to his clothing.

The conjurer, however, clever fellow that he is, again gives his audience absolute food for thought by taking a lighted cigarette between his finger tips, and instantly transforming the same, into a large silk handkerchief, which may be passed for inspection, and used in other handkerchief tricks, if he so desires.

The diagram shows the construction of a special piece of apparatus, sufficiently large to hold the handkerchief, with an inner-tube attachment, which receives the cigarette, and extinguishes the burning end. This arrangement travels up the sleeve, assisted by elastic.

A Chameleon Glove

THE wizard enters, dressed in Beau-Brummel attire, wearing a cape, persuasive of an air of Satanic influence. A liveried assistant makes his way toward the center of the stage, and stands erect, with an air of military obedience, prepared to receive the magician's cloak. The wizard at once casts aside this satin-lined mantle, which is rapidly followed by his opera hat, and walking stick. He is about to remove his gloves, when much to his dismay, he discovers that the ones he is wearing are of different colors—the one is white and the other black. This creates considerable laughter, as the spectators are led to believe that the performer has been obliged to hasten, and has, therefore, made this mistake, by oversight. He removes the white glove, which he hands to his attendant. On peeling the black glove from off his other hand, it instantaneously changes,

Two gloves sewed back to back will permit of this change. One of the gloves is black, and the other white. This trick can be suggested for a very good comedy effect.

in color, to one of snow-white likeness.

This novel transformation is brought about with a trick, or previously-prepared glove, as my readers have probably guessed. This consists of two gloves, the one white and the other black, that have been sewn together about the edge, as illustrated. The white one is stuffed inside the black, so as to completely conceal it from view.

The miracle man has merely turned the one inside out, to effect this chameleon transformation. A bit of practice is essential to perfect this move, with grace and cleverness, so as to completely disguise the action of turning the glove inside out. The glove must, of course, be made of thin, closely-woven material, so that its transparency will not expose the illusion.

A Strange Disappearance

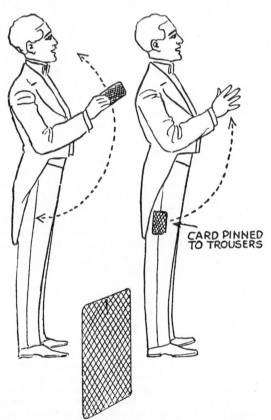

This effect will prove of great value to the amateur conjurer, who has not had sufficient experience or practice to warrant his using his hands to obtain a similar result. It is a most practical method of perfecting the disappearance of a single playing card.

With a quick movement, the hand is directed upward, and the fingers displayed apart. The card has made a strange disappearance. By repetition of this arm-and-hand action, the card reappears.

A needle point has been affixed to the card. In the up-and-down action of the hand, the card is secretly deposited at the side of the performer's trouser leg. The pin holds it in place.

The Traveling Table-Knife

The tip or heel of a table knife fastened to the end of a long pin is used to produce this traveling table-knife effect.

A VERY excellent after-dinner trick. Suitable only when the magician is seated in a company around the table. He picks up a table knife, and passes it for inspection. The knife being returned, he at once proceeds to roll it into the center of a napkin. To prove that no deception has been practised, he reaches down into the folds of the napkin, and pulls up the knife blade, into view. The wizard now invites his guests to watch him very closely, and center their eyes upon the knife. With a sharp jerk, the napkin is suddenly unrolled, and the table knife found to have suddenly vanished. The knife is afterward produced elsewhere.

Explanation: The magician sees that his napkin, for the evening, is slightly different from the rest. This napkin has a concealed pocket. Upon the inside of this pocket, one may find a short piece of knife-blade, which has been affixed to a short length of elastic. The genuine knife is loosely rolled into the napkin. Reaching down into its folds, the magician draws the trick blade to view, secretly permitting the real knife to fall into his lap. Finger pressure holds this blade in view. When pressure is released the blade is drawn back, into its pocket, by the force of the elastic. The napkin may thus be shown, and then be rolled into a small ball, and laid aside. The knife, under cover of the tablecloth, may be secretly placed in the conjurer's sleeve, and thus carried to some other place, for a later reappearance. This trick is exceptionally simple to operate.

Paper Levitation

THE magician delivers a brief array of "patter," dealing with hypnotism, magnetism, etc. He explains that he has developed a magnetic touch, and although many claim that is the way he secured possession of his watch, he begs to emphasize the contrary. A liveried assistant walks forth, holding a tray of the usual type. Upon this tray may be seen four or five sheets of tissue paper, of various colors. These are each about ten inches square. The magician requests that one of these be freely chosen.

After this has been done, the conjurer takes the selected paper into his hand, and rolls the tissue into the form of

THREAD

A small ball of paper can be made to rise vertically into the hand if care has been taken to twist a piece of thread into the paper, when making the ball. Notice that the thread is fastened to the back and passes over the ear of the performer. If the thread is of the proper length, the performer need but slowly extend his hand. This movement will cause the paper to slide up into the hand held apparently ready to receive the rising ball.

a small ball, between his palms. The ball is now placed back upon the tray, which is held by the assistant, as illustrated. The magician makes a few passes over the paper, when slowly, it is seen to leave the tray, and gradually float upward, until it settles in the performer's outstretched hand. The hand has been held at a distance of a foot and a half or more, away from the paper ball.

The illustration helps to explain the secret. A piece of fine silk thread has been attached to the performer's coat collar. This leads over his ear, and the free end of the thread is rolled together with the paper, when shaping it into a ball. Passing over the magician's thumb, as further illustrated, the thread causes the ball to descend into the wizard's hand. The ball may be tossed to the audience, after its levitation, for inspection. As there is no resistance, the thread is easily drawn out from the paper. The trick may be repeated, by using two or three more sheets, with similar effect. Care must be taken that no brilliant light is burning in back of the performer, as this might show up the thread. If the trick is presented at a fair distance, it will prove mystifying.

The Devil's Touch

SPRING

MATCHE   MATCHES

SPRING

SPRING

TOP-VIEW

MATCH

SAND PAPER

THE unexpected predominates again, in this instance. The entertainer, we will say, is about to present some problem wherein a lighted match is required. A candle trick, perhaps, or let us say he is about to perform a cigarette transformation, described elsewhere in this book. He takes an ordinary match box, of usual size and design, from his conjuring table, and pushes out the small drawer therein. Immediately, and much to the amazement of the spectators, a lighted match is seen standing upright, upon the side of the box. This the performer removes, lights the candle or cigarette, as the case may be, and proceeds with the trick.

The box is constructed as illustrated. The match is held in a small receptacle, operating freely up and down, upon a small arm, to which is affixed a rather strong free-working spring. At the opposite side, likewise working upon a spring, can be found a small piece of metal, to which has been glued a piece of sand-paper, of corresponding size. Before operating, a match is placed in the receptacle, which is lowered into the box. The sand-paper slide is pressed down on top of the head of the match, and the box closed. It will be seen that when the box is re-opened, the match being forced upward, into position, causes the sulphur head to light, as it passes and strikes the sand-paper. Easily constructed, and well worth the time involved. It might be advisable to construct the entire match drawer of tin, as it will be found more durable and lasting.

Make a small metal slide which will fit into a match-box and fasten a match to the arrangement indicated. The instant that the drawer of the match-box is pushed out, the match will light. It can be removed from its holder and passed to the guest if the performer decides that this is the better procedure.

Flying Goblets

SPRING HINGE

RIGHT WAY
TO PAINT
GLASSES

WIRE

WIRE IS PULLED—
GLASS APPEARS

BLACK DISC TOP

COLLAPSIBLE GLASS

TRAY

SPRING

DISC IN
HANDKERCHIEF

There are several ways of disappearing glasses from a tray.
The diagrams above show some of these methods and the
explanation of the diagrams is given in the accompanying text.
The glasses are apparently full of water or other fluids when
disappeared.

PRESENT day wonder workers are continually on the lookout for something new and surprising. Commonplace objects such as handkerchiefs, cards, coins and other familiar pieces of properties found in every household, are found in favor.

This experiment has to do with goblets. To make it more interesting, these goblets, so patters the magician, have the faculty of flying.

Effect: Three goblets stand on a tray held at arm's length, by one of the miracle man's assistants. At the opposite side of the stage or platform stands a second assistant holding an empty tray.

Covering one goblet at a time with a large colored handkerchief, the magician commands it to fly and appear on the empty tray.

This is repeated until the three goblets have vanished and re-appeared on the empty tray.

A seeming miracle from the Land of Mystery east of the sun and west of the moon—!

There are quite a few ways to accomplish this trick and for the benefit of the readers several of the methods are given in the following explanations. The reader himself can devise other systems.

How It Is Done: The two trays are of mechanica construction. I will first describe the one from which the goblets disappear. This is made of thin strips of wood, with three wells sunk into the top, as illustrated. Out from each well, respectively, comes a spring, to which is affixed the lower section of a goblet. These goblets are of a collapsible type, consisting of a series of rings fitting inside one another, and tapering downward, so that the goblets will collapse perfectly flat, with slight force of the hand. To the top, or mouth of the goblet, is attached a disk, slightly wider than the goblet itself.

It will be understood, therefore, that when the goblets are closed, the disk, projecting over the edge of the tray, will conceal all sections of the goblet completely from view. A handkerchief of the usual bandana type, preferably of dark and confusing design, must be likewise prepared. To the center of this kerchief, is sewed a disk in size to correspond in diameter with that of the mouth of the goblet proper. Beneath the cover of this handkerchief, as it is placed over the goblets, the magician secretly forces the goblet into its hiding place in the tray. The handkerchief is now brought forth, the fingers encircled about the rim, leading the audience to believe that the goblet is still beneath it. One after another, the goblets are made to vanish in this order; in each instance the handkerchief is shaken, by holding it at one of its corners, thereby effecting the illusion of the goblets' disappearance.

The tray held by the assistant standing at the opposite side of the stage, upon which the goblets apparently reappear, is quite different in construction. It corresponds, in size and appearance, identically with the other one. In this tray have been cut cavities, sufficiently large to receive three goblet shells. These shells are constructed so that they appear intact, and complete, at a very short distance. They are, in reality, however, but halves of goblets. The lower end, which rests flush with the tray top, is permanently affixed thereto, acting freely up and down by a spring-hinge arrangement; the spring being so placed as to force the goblet upward, and erect, upon the tray, when there is no resistance. Resistance, however, is essential, so that they cannot fly up, until required to make their mystic appearance. Three fine wires, working freely, as illustrated, are therefore attached to the tray. The magician's attendant can easily manipulate these, with very little practise, thereby causing the goblets to appear in their desired rotation. Best results, as to camouflaging this apparatus, will be obtained as follows. See that all parts of the goblets are hidden in their respective places, in the various cavities in both trays. Now cover the entire apparatus with fish glue. Secure some cloth of a small dazzling design, and of deep color, and cover both tray tops with it. After the glue is dried, the edge of the tray, as well as the working parts of the trick, can be easily cut free, with the use of a sharp razor blade.

I would suggest that the lower parts of both trays be covered with black velvet. Experience has proven that, if so covered, the trays will appear to be remarkably thin, at a short range; by its destroying, to all optic appearances, the depth of the trays. It will heighten the effect considerably, destroying all suspicion in the minds of an audience, as to any mechanical construction existing. Rehearse this trick several times, before presentation, as the two assistants play quite an important part in the trick. They must experiment in order to hold the trays at proper angles. The appearance of the goblets must be likewise practised, to be harmonious with their apparent vanishing from beneath the bandana handkerchief. A bit of music is always essential in a trick of this kind, as it helps considerably to conceal the slight clicks and sounds which are unavoidably made, by operating the mechanical parts of the apparatus. If the performer desires to disappear the glasses while walking among the audience, he may cover the sound of the clicks by a sharp command. Each and every magician knows how to mask the movement and sound. Rubber bands, placed on the pieces of metal which strike each other, may also dim the sounds produced.

Multiplying Cigar

FOR a number of years, magicians have exhibited their skillful powers of deception, together with their ability in digital dexterity, by demonstrating now things would mystically multiply, at the touch of their finger tips. Numerous are these effects; the writer can remember multiplying billiard balls, coins, cards, eggs, and even cigarettes, but to the best of his knowledge, the cigar has been neglected. Believing, therefore, that a multiplying cigar would actually be something new and different, I have here created a method by which this novel and striking little diversion can be presented.

The magician is seated comfortably in some gathering, or perhaps he finds himself reclining peacefully in an arm-chair, after a meal at the home of an associate. He takes a cigar from his pocket, when he suddenly discovers that some friend seated nearby, is without a smoke. Explaining that he has but one, he, in order to prove his unselfish spirit, attempts to persuade his friend to accept the smoke; and the other, it is safe to wager, will refuse it. Some nearby joker is sure to prevail himself of the opportune moment, and remark, "You're a magician. Why not produce another?" A comment of this kind will be found to have a contagious effect, as the wizard will shortly learn that quite a few of his friends will be joining in the chorus to this request. The wonder-worker is not embarrassed however, as he immediately proceeds to bare his arms, and roll his sleeves to the elbow. Holding the cigar at outstretched arms-length, and far away from his pockets or clothing, he proceeds to offer his apparently impromptu performance. Directing the attention of the audience to the lone smoke, held between his thumb and index finger, he waves his hand up and down once or twice, when, behold, a second cigar appears. This newly developed and mystically-produced cigar he offers to his friend. The gentleman at once proceeds to light the smoke, and much to his surprise, finds it to be of the average type, and of good tobacco. It is not as he anticipated, a trick or artificial cigar. The wizard, by this time, has explained that he prefers to take his smoke a little while later, and again places the number one cigar back into his pocket.

This sudden change, in attitude toward the smoke, is not altogether the choosing of the magician. He could not very well smoke the one he was holding, as it was but a shell, made as illustrated, which fitted over the genuine cigar. When the smoke, with shell attached, was originally shown, it naturally appeared as one. In manipulation, the cigar was permitted to slip out from the shell, which resulted in the mystic multiplication. Being of similar appearance, the audience could not tell one from

Similar to the billiard ball production is the multiplying cigar shown in the illustration above. It will be observed that one shell is used and three genuine cigars are employed in the production. There is a decided advantage to be gained in this system in that the cigars can be passed for examination and may be smoked. A standard brand of cigar should be employed.

the other, but the magician, knowing by the sense of touch, which one to pass out, was naturally obliged to place the shell into his pocket, in order to retain the secret of the trick. If he has provided himself beforehand with a supply of cigars, held elsewhere in his clothing, the trick could be repeated. In this instance, he would simply have to "nest" the shell upon another genuine cigar, when placing the shell in his pocket. This move could be quite easily made, without danger of detection.

The Balancing Ace

It is quite easy to balance a single card on the back of the hand if the card is supported by a pin, held as shown above. The pin may

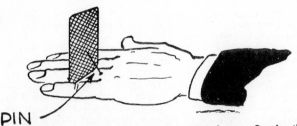

also be gripped between the index and middle fingers. Opening the fingers permits pin and card to fall.

Cagliostro's

1

5

9

2

6

3

7

0

LEGS CROSSED
— EMPTY

CONFEDERATE
IN AUDIENCE

4

8

In this unusual trick, any member of the audience is requested to place some object in a strong steel box. This is then locked and the magician is recalled to the room. This personage then seemingly telephones to a departic Mystic and announces the contents of the chest. The secret lies in the fact that the magician's assistant has a pair of educated feet which code the message to the performer. The telephone serves to pass away a few moments while the performer is getting the message.

THIS is a new and absolutely original test, the like of which has never been previously explained. The proper performer, an experienced show-man, is able to create a sensation with this trick. The effect is entirely foreign from anything that has been previously demonstrated, and the trick offers an inexhaustible array of possibilities.

The magician has been demonstrating a number of tricks in magic and mind-reading, and announces that the final number of his program is a positive master-

Telephone

piece of modern second-sight. He explains that for years, Hindu magicians have been credited with being expert mentalists, and able to send thought waves from the minds of one subject to another. This amazing test, he explains, has been presented, regardless of distance, and, in some cases, statistics prove that a message has been sent successfully, over an area of thirty some odd miles. "More remarkable than that," he continues, "I will this evening, ladies and gentlemen, present for the first time, before the American public, an instrument which is acknowledged by scientists, and investigators, to be an unexplainable phenomenon. Never, in the pages of history, has anything as remarkable, come to the notice of civilization." (Brings forth a telephone.) "This instrument requires no introduction, as far as appearance is concerned. Although it resembles, and really is, a telephone, in many respects similar to the one that you all have spoken into daily, it differs greatly in one remarkable respect. As you see, it has absolutely no wire connection; yet, with it I can speak to departed spirits. Of course, I do not mean that any of you ladies or gentlemen could use this as an instrument of conversation, with any of your dear ones that might have passed across the borderline. This phone you see, my friends, is a direct wire to Cagliostro. For the benefit of those who may not recognize this name, it may be well to state that Cagliostro was a learned scholar of black-art, and witchcraft, who died several centuries ago. The old fellow, however, has never been silenced, and still keeps in touch with the modern world, or astral sphere, upon which we mortals dwell. In fact, kind friends, I am daily in communication with my fellow wizard of the other land, and in my various chats with him, tell him all that transpires here. I tell him all about our greatest events, keep him posted upon all sports, tell him that the spirits are diminishing since Volstead invaded our gathering; in short, dear friends, he knows all about the doings on this earth. But he is by no means an ungrateful fellow, and in return for the information I give him, he often tells me things about you and your doings, that you would really be surprised to learn about. I see you smiling, dear friends, as if you were in doubt as to the truth of my assertion. Permit me to assure you that I would not deceive you for the world. If you will permit me to, I will demonstrate, that you can't do anything while my back was turned, that good old Cagliostro would not see, and tell me about for the asking. I have here a steel chest, also a key that fits the lock thereto, both of which I implore you to examine." (The entertainer here takes a box from the table, and passes it for inspection This is found to be made of sheet iron, firmly riveted, of massive construc-struction, and impressively secure. A strong Yale lock built into the box, secures the lid firmly, when the key is turned. It may be well to advise my readers that the box is exactly what its appearance conveys. It is in no way prepared, there are no secret panels or slides, in short, it is the genuine article.)

"Now, my friends, I will leave the room, and during my absence, some one in my audience will be good enough to take an object, and lock it in this chest. I respectfully request you next to lock the box, in which condition you are assured I cannot possibly tell its contents, and place the chest upon this table, along side of this telephone."

The conjurer leaves the room, and during his absence, some lady, we will say, takes a small hand mirror, out of her purse, and secretes it in the inside of the box, which is then locked, and placed upon the table.

Re-enter, the performer. "My friends, I believe you are completely assured that there is no one with an X-ray eye, sufficiently powerful to pierce the metal cover of the box, and see its contents. I will call up my old mystic friend, who has been watching you all this while, and who, I believe, will tell me all about it." (Lifting from the phone the receiver, which he places to his ear, he now begins.) "Hello! Hello! well, well, it is good to hear your voice again. How is my old friend, Cagliostro....Well, and happy as ever....That is surely pleasing to know ....I have a question I would like to ask you....What's that you say, professor.....you know all about it..... oh, you do know the question....and you also know where I am.....Well, it is amazing to see that you are wide awake, or I should say, as wide awake as ever.... Yes, indeed, I am interested in the contents of the box ....What's that you say....'A lady's small hand mirror.'....Oh, it is....Thank you, professor....I will hang up for the present, but call you back shortly.... I have a few skeptics present, who are doubtful of your ability....Thank you, ever so much....Good-bye for the moment."

The wizard hangs up the receiver, and opens the box, Removing the mirror therefrom, he returns it to the owner. After the applause has subsided, the magician offers to repeat the experiment. He again leaves the room, and during his absence, another article is locked into the box. The magician returns, and once more rings up Cagliostro, who without difficulty again analyzes the contents of the locked chest. Several times the experiment is repeated, but always with success. The effect of this trick cannot possibly be described to satisfaction, in cold type. It is little short of miraculous. Some well-posted entertainers, and exponents of the mystic art, have found themselves at an absolute loss for a practical solution.

The trick, rather difficult as it may appear, is comparatively simple. It requires considerable practice, however, before a demonstration should be attempted. The magician has a secret understanding with an assistant, who sits among the spectators. He has studied a silent code, by which he signals the necessary information to the wonder-worker. So clever, and natural, is this form of transmission, that it will deceive the cleverest observer. This confederate, quietly smoking a cigar, and apparently an inactive member of the audience, has a pair of restless tell-tale feet. By the way his feet are resting upon the floor, together with the manner in which his toes are pointed, the magician is at once able to tell the object secreted in the box. The language of the feet, conveys a number code as follows:

No. 1. Left foot and right foot, flat to the floor, toes pointing forward.
No. 2. Right foot, with toe pointing away from body, left foot still.
No. 3. Right foot, toes pointed inward, toward body, left foot still.
No. 4. Left foot, with toes turned inward toward body, right foot still.
No. 5. Left foot, toes turned away from body, right foot still.
No. 6. Soles and heels of feet close together, straight position.
No. 7. Heels together, toes of left foot turned outward.
No. 8. Heels together, toes of right foot turned outward.
No. 9. Toes of both feet touching, heels a distance apart.
No. 0. Feet a wider distance apart, flat and straight upon the floor.

My readers will conceive that the silent assistant can, therefore, transmit any number to the magician, by the language of the feet. A chart, which has been previously

Cagliostro's Telephone

memorized by both, is not only prepared in rotation, but must be arranged with a number arrangement as well. A sample chart is herewith submitted.

No. 1. A finger ring.
No. 2. A handkerchief.
No. 3. A lady's watch.
No. 4. A gentleman's watch.
No. 5. A cigarette.
No. 6. A cigarette case.
No. 7. A cigar.
No. 8. A cigar-case.
No. 9. A pencil.
No. 10. A pen.
No. 11. A visiting-card.
No. 12. A card-case.
No. 13. A playing-card.
No. 14. A playing-card case.
No. 15. A necklace.
No. 16. A bracelet.
No. 17. A stick-pin.
No. 18. A watch-chain.
No. 19. A vanity-box.
No. 20. A lip-stick.
No. 21. A powder-puff.
No. 22. Keys.
No. 23. Key-ring.
No. 24. Eye-glasses.
No. 25. Eye-glass case.
No. 26. A letter.
No. 27. A wallet.
No. 28. A coin.
No. 29. A check.
No. 30. A bill, or bank note.
No. 31. A book.
No. 32. A match.

No. 33. A box of matches or match box.
No. 34. A tooth-pick.
No. 35. A collar-button.
No. 36. A note.
No. 37. A piece of string.
No. 38. A flask.
No. 39. An emblem of some order.
No. 40. A flower.
No. ... etc., etc., etc., etc., etc., etc.

Should a joker, who is often found in a gathering, suggest that the box be left empty, so possibly to trick the magician, our cunning wizard has provided for this probability, by an additional sign. The silent confederate has but to cross his feet, which is an indication of an empty chest. By the combination of numbers, herewith given, it is simple to conceive that any of them may be constructed by the use of the ten digits. Should an item in the box, however, be plural, the assistant has but to play with his watch chain, in addition to the telltale foot language. For instance, should the magician, by looking at the assistant's feet, find them to be in position 5, he at once knows that a cigarette has been locked in the box. Should he, however, observe that his confederate is likewise also playing with his watch-chain, he at once knows that they are plural; and Cagliostro, over the mystic telephone, informs him that cigarettes have been placed in the box. This idea is likewise carried out with other objects, such as key or keys, letter or letters, coin or coins, flower or flowers, tooth-pick or toothpicks, etc., etc., etc.

As considerable time is consumed during the magician's imaginary conversation with the voice over the telephone, the confederate has sufficient time to give him the desired code. As the movements of the feet are, therefore, made quite slowly, they will not become conspicuous.

Demon Decanters

THE magician exhibits two glass decanters, which to all appearances are empty, and clearly transparent. A silk handkerchief of a bright red shade is exhibited, and placed in one of the decanters. The wizard holding one in either hand, with his arms apart, as far as possible, asks the audience to observe closely an unusual magical effect. He explains that, without covering these containers in any manner what so ever, he will cause the handkerchief to vanish from the one container, and instantaneously re-appear in the other.

Very little explanation as to the modus operandi of this trick is necessary, after the reader has carefully studied the drawings accompanying this article. Two handkerchiefs of similar size and color are used. The one makes its invisible passage up the performer's

sleeve, aided by the ever-reliable and indispensable elastic-pull arrangement. The other duplicate silk has been previously concealed in the mouth of the second decanter, and at the proper moment, is pushed into view down through the mouth of the container, by the performer's index finger. The handkerchief is hidden from view before making its appearance, as the neck of the decanter has been lined with silver colored paper, which preparation, at short distance, is quite unnoticed.

In this effect, a handkerchief is made to fly from a decanter held in one hand, to another held in the other hand. The trick is accomplished by the aid of a pull and the finger. When the pull is released, the handkerchief is pushed into the other flask.

Wizardry Unusual

A deck of cards is thoroughly shuffled by the magician. This is then placed in a derby hat. The hat is covered by another and the contents again shaken by members of the audience. Meanwhile the magician is blindfolded. The hats are returned to him and he removes the top one, covers the other with a cloth, and extracting one card after another, he correctly reads them. The effect is accomplished by the aid of a prepared group of cards clipped together by a paper clip, and tossed into the hat with the shuffled cards.

THIS is rather a startling and exceptional effect, and perhaps one of the very few that has mystified some of the cleverest of present-day magicians. Tricks of this kind are exceptionally rare, and, I trust, for this reason my readers will not be misled by the simplicity of its secret; as the true value of this problem, as far as its power of mystification is concerned, will present itself only when the trick is actually executed.

A deck of cards is thoroughly shuffled, and placed in the crown of a borrowed derby hat. The magician requests the loan of another hat, which is placed upon the first, rim to rim, and the cards are thoroughly shaken up between the crowns of the two hats, by one of the spectators. This voluntary assistant is now requested to return the upper hat of the two to its owner, and cover the other hat containing the cards, with a previously examined and unprepared handkerchief. The wizard is now blindfolded by a committee of spectators; and it may be said right here, that this blindfold is genuine, and the performer actually cannot see beneath or through the binding. If desired, the magician may heighten the effect, by permitting the spectators to place short strips of court-plaster over his eyes, in addition to the bandage, so as to prove, beyond fear of contradiction, that vision, under these conditions, is quite out of question. The magician is now led to a table supporting the hat, cards, and handkerchief, and places his hand (as illustrated) under the handkerchief, and inside the crown of the hat.

Deep concentration follows. "The first card my fingers seem to touch, seems to be the ace of spades," says the wizard, as he slowly draws out from the hat the card, which is shown to the audience, and found to be correct. "The next card which comes to my mind is the four of diamonds, I believe." This is likewise displayed, and found to be correct. In this manner the magician mysteriously calls the names of ten or twelve cards, and produces them in accurate succession from out the hat. He has by this time convinced his audience of his unique "second sight," and removes the bandage from his eyes. The cards, hat and handkerchief, are again passed for thorough inspection, but there are no clues to be found that would establish an explanation to this effect.

The secret, in this case, as in other great magical mysteries, is exceptionally simple. The magician has previously memorized and placed in rotation, ten or twelve cards, which are held together with a paper clip, as illustrated. This stack, after being placed together with the balance of the deck, is freely shuffled by means of the old-fashioned shuffle, hand-to-hand in order not to disturb the stack. While blindfolded, the performer has but to reach beneath the cover of the handkerchief, and find this stack among the rest of the cards. As he calls them in memorized rotation, they are produced. A slight bend in the clip will make it possible for him to distinguish the face from the backs of the cards.

The Wizard's Bonnet

2 SHEETS OF PAPER → BLUE RED ← TEARING PAPER INTO STRIPS → POCKET IN ONE SHEET OF PAPER CONTAINING FOLDED HAT → PAPER HAT ↓ POM-POM

Two sheets of paper are torn into strips and when reopened, they will have formed a paper hat. The paper hat is concealed in one corner of the strips of paper in the pocket provided for. The torn strips are rolled up to form the pom-pom.

THIS trick, which is rather unique in effect, will be found especially valuable to conjurers favoring problems of a humerous nature. It will, however, likewise be a rather good number in anyone's program, being of an extremely impressive nature.

The magician exhibits two pieces of tissue paper, about twelve inches square, the one tinted red, the other blue. With the exception of this paper, his hands are otherwise empty, which he clearly demonstrates. The sheets are torn, and rolled into a ball. A moment later, this parcel is again unrolled, and the pieces are seen to have mystically changed in form, as the magician displays a paper hat, pretty in design, composed of the red and blue paper, with a "pom-pom" attached to its side.

The hat, which as previously stated, is of paper, has been flatly folded, and concealed in a pocket in the upper corner of the blue sheet of tissue paper. In the action of tearing the sheets, the hat is gotten possession of, and unfolded. The discarded red and blue papers are neatly rolled into a small, tight ball, and compose the "pompom" referred to. As the magician places the hat upon the young lady assistant, she smilingly walks off the stage, carrying with her not alone the hat, but the discarded pieces (pom-pom) as well. Nothing more remains for the magician to do, than to show his hands, unmistakably empty, and bow gracefully.

Enchanted Handkerchief Production

THE conjurer, who is about to present some handkerchief trick suddenly discovers that, through an oversight upon the part of his assistant, he has no silks, with which to manipulate. Being a conjurer, however, he is expected to find mystic methods for overcoming such emergencies, as he explains; so he immediately proceeds.

Looking about his stage setting for some suitable item, with which to conjure, his eyes alight upon a candelabra lamp-combination arrangement) which is brightly burning. Removing the shade, the apparatus is found to consist of nothing more than an apparently ordinary candle, standing erect in a silver candle-stick of common type. To the candle is affixed the usual wire-clip-and-frame arrangement, customarily used to hold the lamp shade in place. The innocence of the apparatus is quite apparent. The lamp-shade, made of decorated parchment paper, is passed for examination, and returned to the magician, with the approval of the spectators, who proclaim it quite unprepared. The shade is replaced

A large number of silks may be produced from a candle lamp if the apparatus here illustrated is employed. Notice that the silks are contained in the false candle, the top of which is again pushed down just before the shade is passed for the second examination.

upon the lamp, in the proper position. The wonder-worker, exhibiting his hand quite empty, reaches down into the mouth of the lampshade, and produces dozens of silks in various colors, and yards and yards of ribbons, flags, etc.

The tell-tale diagram shows clearly that the candle is not quite as innocent as its appearance indicates. It is really a metal tube, in which the ribbons and silks have been previously concealed. A plunger arrangement, operated from within, helps to carry the silks upward, so as to bring them within reach of the performer's fingers. A rod, which has been soldered to this plunger, supports a cup, into which a small piece of candle has been previously placed. This candle supplies the light, and likewise helps to give the camouflaged item a natural appearance. It also acts as a knob, which may be lifted, bringing the silks within reach, when the production is about to be made. The lampshade conceals this action entirely from view. The plunger is pushed back into place, after the production, and the shade passed for examination.

Mental Wizardry

By cutting a hole just over the index of the cards in the card case, they can be correctly named in order.

A SPECTACULAR mental effect of the rare variety that seems absolutely convincing to an audience. The magician removes a deck of fifty-two playing cards from its original case, and passes the cards about freely for complete inspection. When the audience is thoroughly convinced of their genuineness, he requests one or more of the spectators to thoroughly shuffle the deck, which, when returned to him, he replaces in the case. Holding this case of cards at arm length, he explains that by psychic force, he will with his X-ray eye, see clearly through the case and read the entire rotation of the cards, regardless of the fact that they have been thoroughly shuffled, thereby eliminating any prearrangement. One card after another is called, and the wizard immediately removes the cards in rapid succession, showing them to the audience as he does so. A small section in the lower corner of this case, has been cut away, enabling the entertainer actually to see the *index* of every card in the deck. The magician's thumb, of course, covered this opening during the necessary handling of the deck and case.

A Chinese Ball Mystery

THIS is a very unique and startling effect. It is especially adaptable for magicians presenting an Oriental magic act. The effect is as follows:

A large black ball, made entirely of metal, is shown. This sphere is about ten inches in diameter. The magician sounds this ball with a small hammer, at various parts of its surface, to convince the audience that it is actually unprepared. It may likewise be inspected. The attendant now brings forth a square box, with a lid attached. This box is sufficiently large to hold the metal ball. The magician once more proves the genuineness of the sphere, by permitting it to fall to the ground, to emphasize its weight and metal. The ball is now placed in the box, and the lid closed. The attendant fires a shot, in the direction of the box. The entertainer at once opens the lid of the box, and the ball is found to have mysteriously vanished. To prove that this is not an optical illusion, the magician at once proceeds to dissect the box. Board after board is torn apart, and the boards tossed carelessly, upon an undraped stand. No clue, as to the *modus operandi* is evident.

Explanation: Two balls are used. The one, passed for inspection is genuinely made of metal. The other, painted to resemble the first, is a rubber toy balloon. This has been blown to a size in exact correspondence with the metal ball. The box is ordinary, prepared in a way to be taken apart. The sides are held together with pin-hinges.

Presentation: An off-stage assistant, hidden in the wings, has the toy balloon in his possession. The showman passe the solid ball for inspection. As he returns to the stage, he throws the ball to the floor, to prove it is solid. He then accidentally drops it and causes it to roll slowly into the wings, and for a moment, out of sight. The wizard quickly reaches for it, but secretly exchanges it for the toy balloon. He is aided in this exchange, by the concealed attendant, who takes the solid ball in charge, and carries it off the stage. With practice, two clever men can accomplish this exchange so that the move will not be detected by the cleverest of spectators. The toy balloon is now placed in the box, the lid of which is closed. To the lid has been affixed a fine needle, with its point projecting. The needle perforates the balloon, causing its disappearance. As the box is dissected, the rubber remnant of the balloon is secretly held in the magician's hand, and disposed of.

This trick is quite suitable for either a talkative conjurer, or pantomime performer. If the wizard presents his act in the costume and make-up of an Oriental, the box should be nicely decorated in brilliant colors and design, characteristic to either the Chinaman or Hindu, as the case may be. The wizard must exercise great care to carry the balloon about, as if it were actually heavy, as careless handling of this object would in all probability, create suspicion in the minds of his audience.

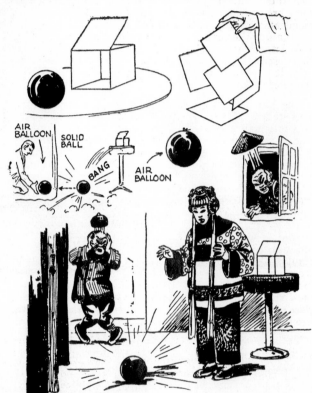

A seemingly solid ball is instantly disappeared from a wooden box which is likewise collapsible. The effect is accomplished by substituting a rubber balloon for the solid ball. The balloon is pierced by the point of a pin fitted to the cover of the box.

A Card and Flag Trick

A deck of cards can easily form a box in which a flag may be concealed and from which it is produced.

AN EXCEPTIONALLY pretty and novel effect. The wizard has been presenting a series of tricks with cards, when, suddenly, the pack is mystically transformed into a large silk American flag. The flag is laid aside, and no trace of the cards can be seen.

The flag had been concealed in a small box, painted along the edges to resemble one half of the deck. A real card had been glued to the top, and one to the bottom of this box. Several other ordinary cards, with a string passing entirely through them, are attached to the box. This contrivance, when placed upon a table, would to all appearances represent an ordinary deck. After tricks with a genuine pack have been shown, the genuine pack is exchanged secretly for this prepared one. The arrangement of this deck permits natural handling. The flag is drawn out from the deck with startling effect upon the audience. The pack, attached with a string to the back of this flag, is placed upon the table, together with the silk, quite unnoticed.

The Spirited Hat

THIS is a rather delightful trick, which is humorous, as well as puzzling. It should be welcomed by the amateur and professional alike, due to its very different qualifications.

The magician borrows a high silk hat from a member of his audience. As many present-day gatherings are not productive of silk hats, and inasmuch as those who are wearers of such evening attire do not care to take chances with their chapeaus, the conjurer may use his own, if desired. This, however, is truly unprepared, and therefore may be passed for absolute inspection. The magician shows a petcock, in fashion like one ordinarily used in pre-Volstead days, upon wine kegs and the like. This petcock has a long pin affixed to its side. The magician forces this pin through the crown of the hat, and holds it in place upon the inside, by passing it through a common cork.

The hat, so prepared, is placed upon a small stand. This stand is of light skeleton-like construction, and may be completely examined, upon any skeptic's demand. The wizard explains that the spirits seem to have no regard for our present laws, and although he is quite within the boundary of the law in permitting any prohibition officer to inspect his wares, he is still able to produce any drink the audience calls for, from this unique arrangement. "Cognac," says one. The wizard similarly takes a drinking glass from off the table, and walks toward the apparatus. Turning the petcock, the desired liquid is seen to flow merrily from the faucet into the tumbler. This is placed aside, as the magician requests that another brand be called for. A little créme-de-menthe is the choice of another. The conjurer, with a second glass, finds no difficulty in producing the spiritous green beverage from the mystic faucet. A glass of wine is requested by a lady, who chooses nothing stronger.

The magician loses no time in his desire to please the lady, and at once port is seen to flow forth into a third drinking glass, which is held in place below the faucet, to receive it. Sparkling burgundy is now requested, a bit of rye, or perhaps a little Scotch—yes—all of these are produced from out this inexhaustible hat. Bear in mind, dear reader, that the writer emphasizes that these things are produced; but, being a strict observer of the law, he does not advise that the samples be passed about. One must remember that this is a conjurer's entertainment, and not a birthday celebration, so, dear reader, be discreet. It is safe to say, however, that were these drinks to be tasted, any connoisseur would pronounce them the real thing; so the *modus operandi* of the trick is, up to this point, I am sure, quite puzzling.

If my description has led you to believe that these beverages are chemicals, you might have formed a solution in your minds. Believing that your ideas are far from right, as to the method employed, I will hold you in no further suspense, and give you the explanation. The drinks are concealed in a number of rubber bulbs, respectively, each sufficiently large to hold a good sized drink. They are concealed until wanted, upon the magician's table, behind some piece of apparatus or other. The drinking glasses are upon the same table. These rubber containers are of different colors; so the magician, beforehand, fills them accordingly, and remembers the brand of the beverage that each one of them contains.

The brand is suggested by a spectator. The wizard walks to the table for a tumbler, and secretly palms the necessary bulb. In the action of turning on the petcock, the bulb is pressed, forcing the liquid to a channel or

By means of this method it is possible to get a very original comical variation. A high hat from a reformer is removed and after being passed for examination is placed in a suitable stand. A wooden spigot is affixed to the hat by means of a needle and cork, and various kinds of liquors flow from the spigot when the magician turns this on. The secret lies in the fact that rubber bulbs contain the fluid and these are picked up under cover of picking up a glass, and attached to the spigot and then pressed.

opening, extending clear through the petcock. The empty bulb is discarded, and a new one palmed, as the conjurer steps to the table, to secure another tumbler. This action is repeated several times, until the supply is exhausted. This experiment is far more startling than cold type can possibly describe.

The nature of the trick offers many suitable opportunities for witty remarks, and good humor. This feature should not be overlooked by the wizard. Tricks of a humorous nature seem to be most favorably accepted by an average audience. The wizard must remember that the art of magic, like any other field of the theatrical profession, requires a great amount of study and practice. This trick is no exception to the average rule, and should be many times rehearsed, so that the palming and carrying of the bulbs is performed with grace and ease. Practise before a mirror, and get the movements as natural as possible, before attempting this work before an audience. Some tricks naturally are simpler than others. Many require little or no practice, whatsoever. The "Spirited Hat," however, is not one of these, and should be considered accordingly.

The Disobedient Match

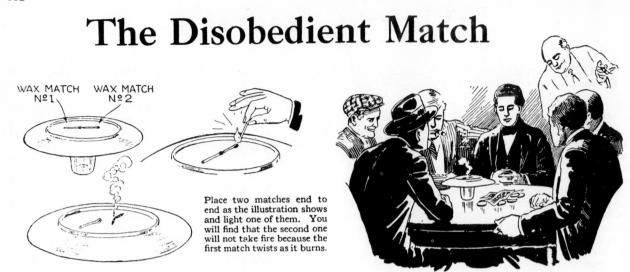

WAX MATCH Nº 1   WAX MATCH Nº 2

Place two matches end to end as the illustration shows and light one of them. You will find that the second one will not take fire because the first match twists as it burns.

TWO matches are placed, as illustrated, lengthwise, on the back of a common china plate, resting upon a glass tumbler. The magician lights the end of one, and asks his friends to guess among themselves exactly how many seconds it would take before the second one will light. Regardless of how many opinions the by-standers may have, they will most probably be wrong. The second match will not catch fire.

It will be found that when the first match burns half-way, it curls, and circles away quite a distance from the head of the second match, which will naturally remain where it was originally placed. It is important to remember that the plate must be absolutely dry, otherwise the match will not curl, and thus upset the trick. Wax matches might likewise be favorably used in this experiment.

Trick Sugar

ANOTHER really good after-dinner trick. It requires some pre-arrangement, but the effect is very good, and will more than repay the conjurer for the slight bit of trouble necessary to prepare it. A large basin of water is freely inspected. No preparation will be found by the keenest observer. A small tray, containing two or three pieces of lump sugar, is shown, and handed to a spectator. He is requested to take one of these, and drop it into this basin of water. As expected, the sugar naturally sinks to the bottom; but to the amazement of every one, it rises up again to the surface, and floats about, at the wizard's command.

Secret: The sugar is prepared beforehand. Take several lumps of ordinary sugar, and dip them quickly into some collodion. This must be done very rapidly, and the sugar should be held there for a very short space of time. It is best to do this, by holding the lumps between a candy prong. After this has been done, place them in a warm, dry place, and permit the sugar to dry for from twenty-four to thirty hours. Remember, the sugar must not be placed where it is too hot, as all that is intended, is sufficient evaporation of the collodion. After the drying, it will be absolutely impossible for any one to detect that the lumps have been prepared, as they will, to all appearances, represent the ordinary article. These lumps, when dropped into the water, will sink rapidly; but as the sugar will dissolve quickly, the framework of collodion, which remains, will come up, and float upon the surface of the water. Care must be taken that these lumps are not left about, as they may be taken for unprepared sugar, and might find their way into someone's tea or coffee cup.

If desired the lump of collodion may be removed, placed in a napkin and and crushed. It occupies such a small space that when dropped from the folds of the napkin it will not be noticed.

SUGAR

SUGAR SINKS TO BOTTOM

SUGAR REAPPEARS ON SURFACE OF COFFEE

Sugar previously dipped in collodion will sink to the bottom of a cup of coffee, but after the sugar has been dissolved, the collodion shell will float to the surface.

The Crystal Clock

THIS is a vast improvement over previous methods which have been employed by magicians to obtain a similar result. The wizard shows a large glass clock dial to his audience. This is apparently free from deception. It consists of a circular disk of glass, about twenty inches in diameter. The numbers, in gold lettering, have been painted upon the disk, in imitation of the customary manner. In the center of this dial can be found a freely-working clock hand, or indicator, in construction similar to the one illustrated. This may be freely removed at will. A handle attachment, merely for the convenience of carrying the dial about, is affixed to its top edge. This apparatus is passed among the audience, and the most rigid examination invited. The wizard explains that the transparency of the dial eliminates entirely all possibilities of concealing mechanism of any description secretly. The paraphernalia, having met with the approval of the examination committee, is now brought back to the stage, where it is placed in position, in a receiving socket, affixed to a slender nickel-plated stand. This stand is many feet above stage level, and assures the impossibility of mechanical assistance from below. The hand of this clock is now made to spin mysteriously about, in either direction, either rapidly or slowly. The hand will stop at a desired number, and will, in this fashion, answer questions, add up sums, give the total of mathematical problems, and in many other ways prove itself to be an uncanny indicator of mysterious facts.

To accomplish this startling and sensational trick, the wizard must have the assistance of a concealed assistant. This man has in his possession an additional section of concealed apparatus. This consists of a long glass rod, to the free end of which is attached a crank handle. This rod is pushed through a small opening in the curtain, and connects to a receiving joint, attached to the back of a spindle. The hidden assistant in this manner comcplently controls the action of the clock hand. Previous arrangement between him and the conjurer, as to mathematical problems, the choosing of playing cards, etc. etc., makes possible the obtaining of correct results. The crystal clock, being made entirely of glass, creates an optical illusion, of such a nature as to disguise entirely the presence of the glass rod behind it. The transparency of the rod makes it further possible for the audience to see the scenery clear through it, which likewise helps to make it quite invisible to the eye. Good patter, and a trained assistant, help greatly to make this a master magical effect. It is almost unnecessary to state that this rod is withdrawn through the hole, back behind the drop, when the clock is passed again for inspection, after its manifestations have subsided.

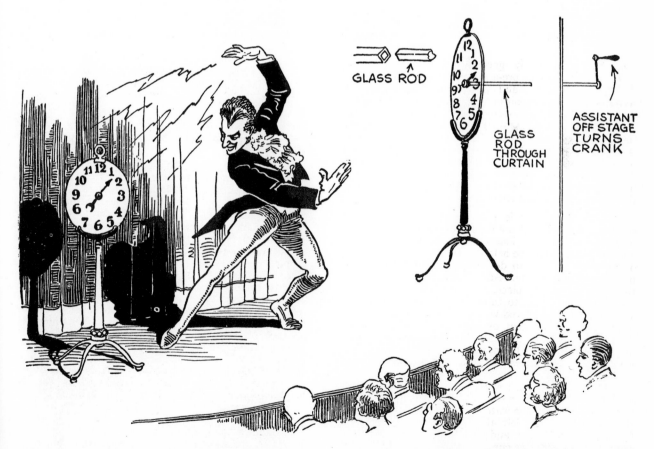

GLASS ROD

GLASS ROD THROUGH CURTAIN

ASSISTANT OFF STAGE TURNS CRANK

In the Crystal Clock effect which is explained in the diagram above, the magician passes a glass disc provided with a single hand, among the audience. This is carefully examined and then returned to the stand on the stage. The hand will point to any time requested by any member of the audience. The secret lies in the fact that a long glass rod is pushed through from the back of the stage and is coupled to an extension of the hand. The rod is pushed forward and then operated by an assistant in the back of the stage.

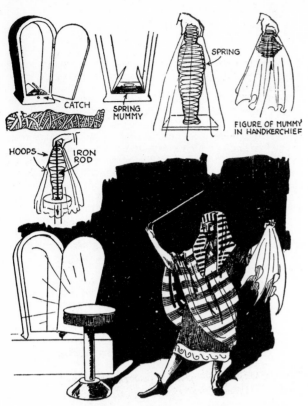

SPRING

CATCH

SPRING
MUMMY

FIGURE OF MUMMY
IN HANDKERCHIEF

HOOPS   IRON
ROD

In this effect a well wrapped mummy is exchanged for one made
of spring. This is covered with a cloth. The mummy is held in
the extended position by an iron rod and collapses as the cover
is removed and the rod slides away into the table.

King Tut's Coffin

THE recent discovery of the tomb of King Tut has
likewise spread about an air of mystery, which
echoes from out the ancient burial grounds of the
gods of old. The uncanny, creepy stories from this land
of ancient Egypt, were refreshed in the minds of many,
when the mummy of King Tut was brought face to face
with his discoverers. What could, therefore, be of greater
magical value, than a trick reflected around the sphere
of this historical finding. The writer has, therefore,
created a unique trick, in which this royal character, of
a day long passed, is rebuilt in miniature likeness.

The magician exhibits a small coffin, or sarcophagus,
about two feet high. This has been painted in stone-like
fashion, with many striking Egyptian hieroglyphics,
colored in high lights, upon its surface. The conjurer
relates some interesting story, or lecture, of a nature
such as his fancy might dictate, and then proceeds to
present the trick.

For those who choose a form of story prepared for
them, I might suggest the following. The wizard relates
that at one time this ancient ruler, who has found his
final resting place in this coffin, was considered a wizard.
In the days gone by, conspirators against the King, often
attempted his capture. He was often held prisoner by
his enemies, who took the greatest of precaution to hold
him in restraint.

Yet, unaided, apparently, by any one, he would mysteriously vanish in the night, merely to reappear at his
palace, wherefrom he would lead his army in victorious
combat, against his captors. Over and over again, his
capture would be repeated, but always a similar failure
to hold him prevailed. As the ancient legend goes, the
soldiers would often speak of seeing this phantom ruler
vanish in a cloud of smoke, before their eyes.

And so our silver-tongued orator, and master of the
mystic, explains that the mummy-like figure, which is

removed from the walls of this coffin, is likewise a spirit
of mystic flight. The soul of old King Tut, resentful of
his being brought back to earth, vanishes out of the hands
of his captors, and instantaneously reappears in his small
resting place of stone. As the small mummy is removed
from the coffin, the cover of the empty box is immediately
closed. The sarcophagus, in an upright position, is
placed upon a small, undraped side-stand, standing
innocently at one side, upon the magician's platform.
The bandaged figure of King Tut is covered with a large
silk handkerchief. The magician, holding the figure by
the head, proceeds to stand it erect, upon the top of
another undraped side-stand. He changes his mind,
however, and offers the figure to a volunteer assistant to
hold. An unusual effect now takes place. A pistol shot
is fired, to startle the audience. The handkerchief is
immediately rolled into a small ball, and tossed aside.
The mummy has apparently disappeared. The magician
walks across the stage, to the coffin that has been resting
upon the side-stand. Upon opening the cover of the box,
the mummy is discovered. There rests a doll, pictur-
esque in effect, completely filling the casket, which a
moment previous, had been entirely unoccupied.

Two figures, or mummies, similar in appearance, are
necessary. They are, however, different in construction.
The one is composed of a cloth figure, which has been
drawn over a series of rings, forming its ribs. The figure
will, therefore, fall quite flat, of its own accord, unless
held in an upright position. It is held from collapsing
and assisted in its erection, by a steel rod, which runs
clear up inside the figure, to its complete length.

This figure, so prepared, is the one originally shown,
and over whom the lecture is delivered. The handkerchief, which covers the figure, is ordinary, but sufficiently large to completely con al the mummy from
view.

In the act of placing "King Tut" upon the table, the
steel rod is permitted to slide secretly from the inside of
the doll, and into the table leg. The figure, now being
without support, can be easily crushed, within the folds
of the handkerchief. This may, therefore, be rolled in
rather small compass, and tossed aside, effecting the
"vanish" of King Tut when desired. The figure that
reappears in the coffin, is the duplicate dummy. This has
a spiral spring, likewise covered with the outer cloth.
The spring reaches from the head to the foot. The figure
may be pressed perfectly flat, bu will jump up again
and stand erect, of its own accord, when pressure is
released. This mummy has been concealed in the foot
or base, of the sarcophagus, beforehand. Occupying but
an inch or so in space in its flattened condition, its
presence there will not be suspected. As the cover of the
coffin is closed, a push-button spring arrangement, upon
the outside, releases the trap door bottom of the case, as
illustrated. The figure now extends to its complete
height, completely filling the casket. The coffin should
be ornamented, and painted in accordance with the
period of its supposed construction. This helps the trick
considerably, and assists to establish the necessary
Egyptian atmosphere. This is a good trick to carry, as
it is quite light and the figures taking up so little space
in the coffin, allow considerable for the packing of other
tricks in the box, as well. This makes it suitable as a
parlor trick, as well as an effective offering for either
Lyceum or stage.

Indian Snake Pot

APPARENTLY EMPTY

SERPENTS COILED AROUND FALSE INTERIOR

TOURISTS from European countries, who have from time to time traveled thru the mystic region of India, are usually heavy-laden with tales of occult happenings, and queer manifestations, which they claim to have seen. My readers undoubtedly know the East Indian magician operates his presentation quite differently from that of the European conjurer, inasmuch as his items of mystification, are usually presented in the wide open spaces, beneath the teeming rays of the Oriental sun.

I witnessed a fakir, several years back, offer a rather creepy and amazing magical spectacle that has never been explained in a literary way before. He exhibited a large, brass jar, of peculiar shape, (as illustrated) and showed the same to be empty. A rug was then spread upon the ground, and the jar placed in the center of it. A second cloth he freely passed about for inspection, and after it had been examined and returned to him, the Oriental threw it over the mouth of his mystic urn, completely covering the jar. Weird strains of music came from the horn of a flageolet, played by his dark-skinned assistant. A shrill cry unexpectedly came from the mouth of the wizard, with the effect of startling the bystanders. With a sharp action he drew the cloth off the urn, and tossed it high into the air, catching it as it descended, and tossed it aside into the hands of a young Hindoo boy, who stood waiting to receive it. With a second shriek of bewilderment, he pointed to the urn, and from its mouth could be seen the heads of four or five snakes, making their mystic entrance.

As to the secret. These serpents (harmless to handle) were originally in the jar, but were completely hidden from view, inasmuch as they had been curled around the sides of a cylinder. This cylinder, free-working, sliding in and out, was sufficiently large to reach from the upper edge of the jar, clear down to its bottom. My readers will easily realize that in this condition, the wizard could safely show the interior of the urn, apparently empty. (The inside had been painted a dead black, and the jar was passed about rapidly, giving the spectators but a momentary glance at the inside)

As the cloth, which for a few moments covered the urn, was removed and tossed into space, this inner cylinder was likewise removed under cover of this cloth, and the entire affair tossed to the young boy, who immedi-

A pot apparently empty is shown for examination and on removing the cover is found full of snakes. The drawings explain how affect is produced.

ately placed this bundle in a near-by wicker basket. This action, together with the slightly bulky condition of the cloth, was quite unnoticed, as the turban-covered wizard cleverly misdirected the attention of the onlookers to the mouth of the urn. The snakes, by this time, had taken advantage of their release, and were rapidly crawling out of the Oriental jar, down the sides of this container, and on to the high colored rug beneath it.

Magical Fingers

A DERBY HAT is caused to adhere magically to the magician's finger tips. He changes it about, from one hand to another; and, whether it be the back of the hand or the palm, whether the index finger or the thumb, whether using the rim of the hat or the crown, it matters not, the hat still clings, as if held to the performer's flesh by some great unknown force. The magician descends the steps of the auditorium, passes up and down the aisles, permitting the spectators from all sides to view this unusual magnetic spectacle. Both hands are thoroughly inspected, and the hat freely examined at the conclusion of the trick.

The illustrations herewith help to clear the fact that a hair, tied about the hat, makes this experiment possible. Several long, thin, hairs are tied together to form an endless loop, sufficiently large to permit the performer to place his fingers or hands between the loop and the derby. The hair is broken before passing the hat for inspection. The performer can safely pass through the aisles, as the hair cannot be detected by the naked eye at a reasonable distance.

HAIR

By the aid of a hair a derby hat will magically adhere to the finger tips.

Puppets – How to Make

WASTE of time is a sin. Keep a person busy and he is kept out of mischief. The idle person can be made to work and take an interest in things if he has a hobby. The same is true of children or boys and girls of the adolescent period. At this time they are very liable to become phlegmatic, perhaps indolent, sometimes to the impairment of their health. Something to awaken them and spur them into action, something to induce them to take an interest in work of some kind, will be of inestimable benefit to them. Get them to adopt a hobby and notice the change. Doing something as a trade might seem hard work, but doing the same thing as an avocation makes it most attractive and easy. The person with a hobby never has "nothing to do;" rather he has too little time in which to do the things he wants to do.

There is a great sense of satisfaction in being able to create something with one's own hands; when "this something" is a little out of the ordinary, the gratification is greater.

The making and operating of puppets and the giving of puppet shows is a most alluring and fascinating hobby. It is a combination of play and work. Its benefits are varied. No other hobby permits of so wide a range of expression of talent. The manufacture of the puppet develops mechanical skill. The working out of new ideas gives an opportunity for the unfoldment of inventive genius. Properly costuming the figures requires the ability for research work and helps to bring out talent for dress making and designing. Painting the scenery allows expression of the artistic. Copying, writing or dramatizing a story will make known and help to develop literary ability. Finally, presenting the play will call for, and help to improve, dramatic ability.

Children of a reasonable age should be encouraged to interest themselves in puppets and puppet plays. Material for their manufacture is inexpensive and mostly at hand. Once they make a start, there is a sort of fascination which never looses its charm. The number of stories which are dramatized and which can be used as puppet plays is almost endless. The satisfaction resulting from the successful presentation of one puppet show, and good puppet shows are always successful, will be a sufficient inducement to rehearse and present another. Thus a pastime will be developed which will be of invaluable benefit.

This article gives in a simple way the knowledge required to construct the puppets, how to string and manipulate them how to build the stage and scenery, and all information necessary for the successful production of a puppet play.

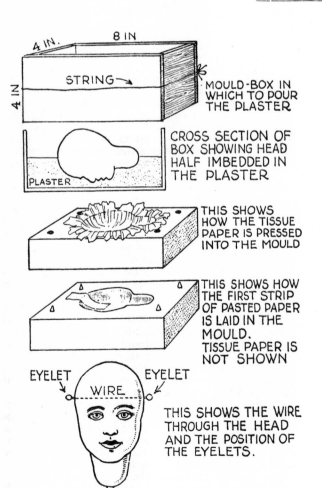

MOULD-BOX IN WHICH TO POUR THE PLASTER

CROSS SECTION OF BOX SHOWING HEAD HALF IMBEDDED IN THE PLASTER

THIS SHOWS HOW THE TISSUE PAPER IS PRESSED INTO THE MOULD

THIS SHOWS HOW THE FIRST STRIP OF PASTED PAPER IS LAID IN THE MOULD. TISSUE PAPER IS NOT SHOWN

THIS SHOWS THE WIRE THROUGH THE HEAD AND THE POSITION OF THE EYELETS.

THE HEAD

The first thing to be taken into consideration, when constructing a puppet, is the head. The beginner may use doll's heads if he does not happen to have the inclination or the ability to construct them himself. However, a great amount of pleasure and satisfaction may be had from the work required in the manufacture of the different parts of the puppet; and this fact should be taken advantage of if possible.

The heads may be carved out of wood, modelled out of papier maché; or they may be built up out of paper by the following method. Out of half-inch lumber construct a box as shown in the illustration. This box has four sides and a bottom but no top. It is not nailed, but the sides and ends are placed around the bottom and are held in place by tying a string around them. This is

---

In the illustration at the left we find the method of making the head of the puppets. The apparatus required can be easily obtained in the average person's cellar. A doll's head may be used as a model.

---

the mold box in which to pour plaster of paris, when making the mold out of this material. To prevent the plaster from adhering to the sides of the box they must be coated with an oily substance. The easiest substance to obtain and use is common soap lather, the kind that is used when shaving. Put some soap and a little water in a cup and with the aid of any small brush prepare the lather. At the drug store, or painter's supply house, purchase five pounds of commercial plaster of paris. Also obtain two ounces of shellac varnish. A large china bowl will be required, in which to mix the plaster and water.

MAKING THE MOLD

A model of the head to be manufactured will be necessary. If the reader is so fortunate as to possess suffi-

and Operate Them

cient artistic ability he may make this out of modelling wax, or a doll's head may be used. In either case the method o' procedure is the same. It is presumed a doll's head is being used. In a toy store procure a head which is suitable for a doll fifteen inches high. Select one which has a socket-neck, not the kind with the shoulders in the same piece. If the head has a wig on it, remove this and keep it for replacement later on. First it will be necessary to make a plaster of paris mold of this head. Coat the inside of the mold box with the previously prepared lather. Take sufficient plaster to more than half fill this box. Mix it with water in the china bowl till it is about the consistency of cream. Pour this into the mold box till it is half full. Quickly coat the doll's head with lather and press its face down into the soft plaster till half of it is imbedded. Allow the plaster to harden; which will require about thirty minutes of time. With the point of a pocket knife, drill several conical holes in the plaster, say one near each corner, one inch from the edge and half an inch deep. Next coat the exposed surface of the plaster, the interior of these holes and the visible half of the head, with lather. Mix some more plaster and water and pour it into the box, so that it completely covers the head. Give this half an hour's time in which to dry. If the string which holds the box is now untied, the sides and ends may be removed, the halves of the mold separated and the head taken out. The lower half of the mold will be a depression corresponding to that half of the head with the face on it, while the upper half will be a replica of the back of the head. In twenty-four hours the plaster will be thoroughly dried and the depressions, and the surface of the plaster around them may be given a coating of shellac varnish. It is obvious that if these two depressions are filled with any soft substance which is allowed to dry, a reproduction of the doll's head in halves will be the result. If these halves are glued to each other the complete head will be formed.

MAKING THE HEAD

Solid heads are too heavy for our purpose. An easier and more desirable kind are made out of paper and are hollow. To make these proceed according to the following instructions. Make some paste with flour and boiling water, or use the prepared dry paste which is manufactured and sold for the use of wall paper hangers, or use library paste. This last is the most expensive, while the flour paste is the cheapest and the kind most generally used. To make this mix two heaping tablespoons full of flour in sufficient cold water to make a creamy paste. Put a pint of water in any kind of a vessel and heat it to the boiling point. Next pour the flour paste into the boiling water and stir it till a paste is formed. When this is cool it is ready to use.

Take any newspaper and tear it into strips about three inches long and half an inch wide. Soak these in water till they are soft and pliable. Remove them from the water and press them between the palms, a few at a time, to remove as much of the water as possible. Next take either half of the mold, place a piece of tissue paper over the depression and with the fingers press it down into the mold to form a lining, the surplus tissue paper being spread over the top of the mold.

Next take a strip of moistened newspaper and laying it on a smooth board or pane of glass, coat it with paste, using a small paint brush for that purpose. Coat it on each side. Commencing at the top of the head, line the mold with these paste-covered strips of paper. The first strip should be laid in the mold so that it starts from a point past the lowest part of the depression and reaches up to and over the edge about half an inch, as shown in the illustration. Press this down so that it conforms to the shape of the mold. Place the next strip so that it overlaps the first one about a quarter of an inch. Continue in this manner till the mold is completely lined. Next repeat this process till four layers have been placed in the mold. Press the paper well down into the depression so that it will conform to the shape. The ends of the strips which are up over the edge must be turned back into the mold so that the folded edge will be just even with the flat surface. It may be necessary to put a little more paste on these turned-in ends, so that they will adhere to the larger portion of the head. This will complete the first half of the head.

Take the other mold and repeat this process, thereby forming the other half of the head. Place both molds in a warm place, and in twenty-four hours the paper shells will be dry and may be removed. Glue is now applied to the edges and the two halves cemented to each other. thus forming the complete head. When the glue is dry the uneven places along the edges may be trimmed off with a sharp knife, smoothed with sand paper and a few strips of paper pasted over the joints to help hold the halves together.

The head must now be given a coating of hot liquid glue, applying this as if it were paint. Allow it to dry. This will give strength to the head and will also form a foundation for the paint to be applied later. Through the head, from temple to temple, pass a piece of light wire. At each temple bend the wire to form a small loop or eyelet. It is to these eyelets that the head strings are fastened.

ALTERING THE FEATURES

Of course all heads made by this process from this mold will look alike; but the features may be altered by modeling them with papier maché, which may be made as follows. Tear old newspapers into small pieces, about half an inch square, till there is a quantity sufficient to half fill a ten-quart water pail or an earthen jar of the same capacity. Pour enough boiling water into the pail or jar to cover the torn paper. Allow the paper to soak for an hour; then take a hand full of the soaked mass and rub it between the palms and reduce the paper to a pulp. Keep rubbing the mass till it is about the consistency of putty, and very much like the pulp from which the paper was originally made. Next remove two handfuls of the pulp; squeeze the water out of it and shape it into a rough ball. Repeat this with the rest of the pulp. This is the foundation for the papier maché, and that portion of it which is not used immediately should be laid away to dry.

Take a lump of the pulp about the size of a fist and knead into it two tablespoons full of glue, the kind made with flake glue and water and used by cabinet makers and carpenters. Work the glue thoroughly into the pulp with the fingers and add to this two heaping tablespoons full of plaster of paris. Continue the kneading process till the pulp, glue and plaster are well mixed.

The result will be a sticky mass of the consistency of putty. This is called papier maché. With it the features of the paper head can be altered to please one's fancy, by building up on it. The nose can be made longer or wider, the chin and cheek bones may be made more prominent, the eyebrows may be arched, etc.

Take a small amount of the papier maché, model it into shape and press it on at the desired place. It will

Puppets—How To Make and Operate Them
(*Continued*)

stick to the head and may be modeled and changed till it is the desired shape. A modeling tool, or an orange-wood stick such as is used by manicurists, is useful for this purpose. When this is dry and hardened the features may be smoothed with fine sand paper. It is now ready to be painted. The unused portion of papier maché may be kept from hardening by wrapping it in a piece of dampened cloth.

PAINTING

A supply of paint and some small brushes will be required. Procure a small can of flat white paint and an assortment of artist's colors in tubes. The former can be purchased in any paint store and the latter may be procured at an artist's supply house. With the can of flat white paint mix a very small amount of red to give it a flesh tint. Give the entire head a coating of this, which will be a foundation for the detail work. When this first coat of paint is dry, the lips, eyes, eyebrows, etc., may be painted on, using a small brush and appropriate colors. Put a little red on the cheeks to give them added color.

HAIR

Doll repair shops always have wigs which have been removed from dolls which are being repaired or rebuilt. These wigs may be purchased cheaply and made to do service for the puppets. They are fastened on with glue. Long hair can be shortened by cutting off the surplus. If the figure is to wear a hat it will be necessary to put on only that part of the hair which shows.

MOVABLE MOUTHS

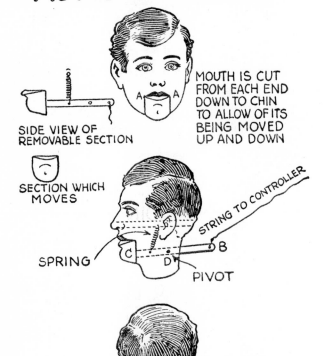

SIDE VIEW OF REMOVABLE SECTION

MOUTH IS CUT FROM EACH END DOWN TO CHIN TO ALLOW OF ITS BEING MOVED UP AND DOWN

SECTION WHICH MOVES

STRING TO CONTROLLER

SPRING

PIVOT

REAR VIEW SHOWING SLOT IN WHICH THE LEVER OPERATES.

These diagrams explain how to construct movable mouths for puppets to produce a more realistic talking act. The movements are synchronized with the voice of the speaker or operator.

MOVABLE MOUTHS

When it is desired to add a moving mouth to the puppet so that his talking may seem more realistic, the head must be carved out of soft wood and constructed as shown in the illustration. The section comprising the lower lip and chin is movable. There is a slit cut from each corner of the mouth down and under the chin (as shown at A, A), so that this section can be removed. To the rear of this is attached a wooden bar or lever B, which projects through a slot cut in the rear of the head at the neck. This bar works on a pivot, D. A spiral spring, holds the movable section in place. To the rear end of the lever, B, is attached the string which goes up and is fastened to the control stick. Pulling and releasing this string will open and close the mouth.

The person who does the talking for the puppets must synchronize the words with the mouth movements, in order to produce the proper talking effect. This movable mouth is only suitable for large puppets. With the smaller heads the construction is difficult and the movements would hardly be noticeable. When a spectator becomes interested in a puppet performance he always imagines that the mouth moves, even when it is stationary.

BODY CONSTRUCTION

The body of a puppet is constructed very much like that of a doll, the joints being more flexible. A close inspection of the illustration will show how it is made. The upper part of the body is made of ⅞-inch lumber, preferably soft pine, as it is most easily whittled. A semi-circular depression is carved in the upper portion of this to receive the neck.

The head has a hole drilled through it from the center of its top, straight down through it to the center of the bottom of the neck. A piece of heavy fish cord with a knot at the top or upper end (see cut) is passed through these holes, its purpose being to fasten the head to the body. This is done by continuing the cord through a hole which has been drilled from the center of the neck depression, through the upper part of the body in a slanting direction so that it emerges at the front of the body as shown at B. A small staple C attaches the cord securely to the wooden body. This cord acts as a pivot joint and the head can move easily in any direction, the same as the human head does.

The lower part of the body is made of ⅞-inch lumber of the size and shape indicated. Two holes are drilled through this at E, E. Two similar holes are drilled through the upper half of the body at D, D. Heavy fish cord connects the two sections of the body as shown at F. This makes the waist very flexible, which is a necessity in puppet manipulation.

The upper part of the legs are stuffed like those of a doll and at the knee are attached to half of a wooden joint made of pine, the other half of the joint being the top of the lower leg. The construction of this joint is shown in detail in the illustration. The lower part of the leg, or calf, with the foot, is whittled out of wood and is attached to the upper half of the joint by inserting a wire pin at H. The legs are fastened to the lower part of the body by tacks at G, G, G, G.

The forearm and hand are whittled out of soft pine lumber. The upper part of the arm is stuffed and the lower end of the cloth casing is slipped over the wooden forearm and tacked to it (see cut). The upper end of the complete arm is tacked to the shoulder as shown (see cut). Into each shoulder drive a small blind staple, to which the strings will be attached, as described later on. All joints must be very flexible to allow all parts of the body to move with the utmost freedom.

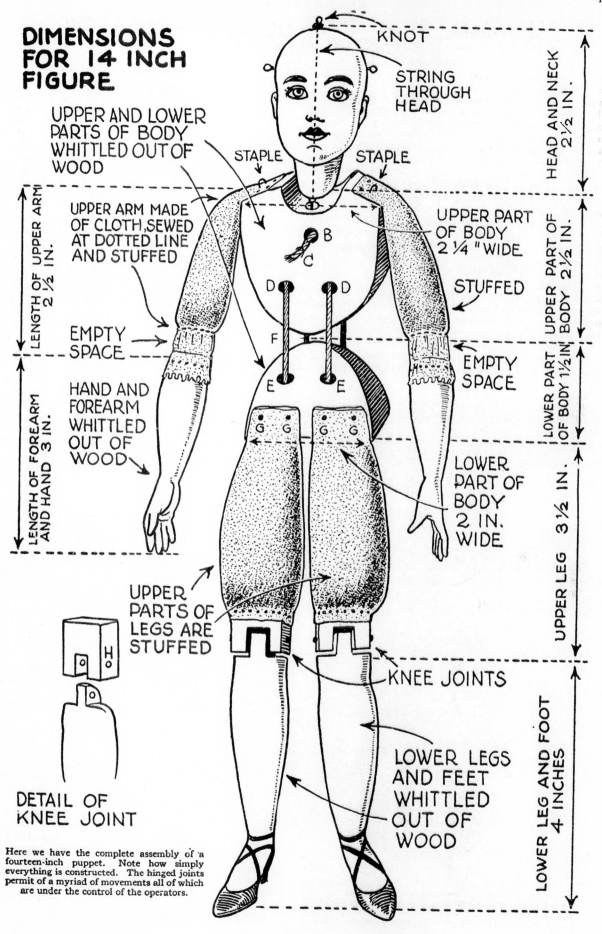

DIMENSIONS FOR 14 INCH FIGURE

KNOT

STRING THROUGH HEAD

HEAD AND NECK 2½ IN.

UPPER AND LOWER PARTS OF BODY WHITTLED OUT OF WOOD

STAPLE

STAPLE

UPPER PART OF BODY 2¼" WIDE

UPPER PART OF BODY 2½ IN.

LENGTH OF UPPER ARM 2½ IN.

UPPER ARM MADE OF CLOTH, SEWED AT DOTTED LINE AND STUFFED

STUFFED

EMPTY SPACE

LENGTH OF FOREARM AND HAND 3 IN.

HAND AND FOREARM WHITTLED OUT OF WOOD

EMPTY SPACE

LOWER PART OF BODY 1½ IN.

LOWER PART OF BODY 2 IN. WIDE

UPPER PARTS OF LEGS ARE STUFFED

UPPER LEG 3½ IN.

KNEE JOINTS

LOWER LEGS AND FEET WHITTLED OUT OF WOOD

LOWER LEG AND FOOT 4 INCHES

DETAIL OF KNEE JOINT

Here we have the complete assembly of a fourteen-inch puppet. Note how simply everything is constructed. The hinged joints permit of a myriad of movements all of which are under the control of the operators.

Puppets — How to Make
(Con

The puppet is now ready to be dressed. The procedure is the same as in dressing any doll. Bright colors should be used as a flashily-dressed puppet shows up to advantage. Dolls' slippers, procurable in toy stores, may be used to dress the feet. The character to be represented must be taken into consideration.

In the puppet plays many different characters are used and much study must be given to the proper costuming. The costume must be historically correct and representative of the period the play represents. Books on this subject can be found in every public library. These should be consulted frequently. With proper attention to all details in the costume of the characters to be represented, most interesting puppets can be made.

THE CONTROLLER

When the figure is dressed it is a doll or a puppet; but when strings are attached so that it can be controlled by an operator attending on an elevation it is more rightly named a *marionette*. With proper stringing, an expert manipulator can cause the little figure to imitate lifelike movements. It can be made to walk, bow, dance, sit on a chair, kick, gesture with its head and hands; in fact, it is capable of being made to duplicate any movement of the human body.

In order that this may be accomplished the puppet must be hung by strings and these must be fastened at their upper ends to sticks or combinations of sticks known

FRONT VIEW - PUPPET COMPLETELY STRUNG

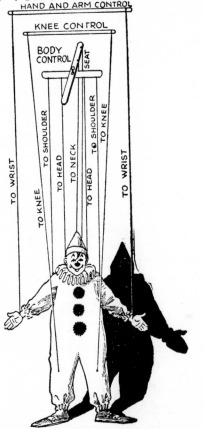

This illustration gives us an idea of what a puppet looks like when completely strung. Suppose that it is desired to raise the right arm, the operator would tip the hand and arm control. If both hands are to be raised the control is lifted. Scores of twists can be secured with the body control.

as *controllers* (see illustration). The principal controller, No. 1, is made of two pieces of light wood attached to each other at right angles by the aid of a screw-eye. The piece to which are attached the chest, back and seat strings is a little longer than the cross-piece to which are attached the head and shoulder strings. As they are attached with a screw eye, they may be turned and brought parallel with each other, this being a convenience in packing and transportation. Two other controllers are used; No. 2, for the knees, is six inches long and No. 3, for the hands or arms, is eight inches long.

STRINGING THE PUPPET

The best material to use for strings is Barbour's Linen Thread, No. 25 or No. 30. Sometimes black fish line is used. This is stronger. Black linen thread gives good results and is nearly invisible.

The length of the string from the puppet to the controller must be determined by the distance the operator is to be elevated above the stage floor on which the marionette performs. The length should be so gauged that when the operator has his elbows at his sides, and his hands holding the controller are straight in front of him, the feet of the marionette will just touch the stage floor below. Generally this length is four feet.

If four feet is the distance decided on, drive two medium-sized wire nails into the wall of the place in which the work is being done. Drive them so that the heads are slanting upwards. They should be six inches apart. Take a pair of No. 1 controller sticks and, turning the cross-piece so that it is parallel with the other lay them on the nails against the wall. Next tie one end of the linen thread to either eyelet of the puppet's head and, standing the latter on the floor, carry the thread up and pass it through the hole in the controller at X. Adjust the thread to the proper length, wind it several times around the stick, cut it off and tie it securely. Repeat this operation from the opposite side of the head.

The puppet should now be hanging with its feet squarely on the floor. Next string the shoulders in the same way, attaching the strings at the shoulders to the blind staples and passing them up and tying them to the ends of the stick No. 1. As the blind staples at the shoulders will be underneath the clothing, it will be necessary to thread the string on a small darning needle and with its aid pass it through the material of the clothing and the blind staple. One of the smaller drawings shows the figure with these four strings attached.

The longer stick of the pair is now turned at right angles to the shorter one and the cross so formed is held by another person so that the feet of the puppet are on the floor; or it may be suspended by a string from a screw hook in the ceiling. A string is now fastened to the chest of the figure, this being tied at its upper end to the front end of the longer control stick. In a similar manner a string is fastened to the center of the back near the neck, its upper end being tied to the rear end of the long controller. A similar string leads from the seat to rear end of the rear controller. The body ends of these latter strings can be sewn to the clothing of the figure. One of the small drawings shows the puppet with all body strings attached.

The legs and arms must be strung next. A string is attached to each knee. This may be done by driving a small staple into the upper part of the wooden joint and passing the string through this and tying it; or the string may be sewn on to stuffed section of the leg near the knee. The upper ends of these strings are attached to the ends of a light stick six inches long known as the knee and leg control, No. 2 in the illustration. In the same way the

and Operate Them

tinued)

wrists are strung to control stick No. 3. This stick is eight inches long. A study of the various illustrations will render these explanations more lucid.

CONTROLLERS AND METHOD OF STRINGING

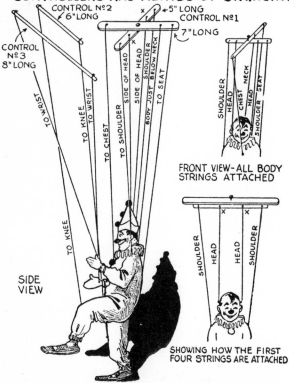

FRONT VIEW—ALL BODY
STRINGS ATTACHED

SHOWING HOW THE FIRST
FOUR STRINGS ARE ATTACHED

These diagrams give further information for stringing and controlling the puppets. While this controller varies slightly from the professional controller, the result is identical.

This is one of the many methods of stringing a puppet. Others are either simpler or more complicated, according to the motions required of the figure. The arm controller may be omitted and the strings from the wrists fastened to each end of the leg controller; or they may be tied to the front end of the No. 1 controller near the place where the chest string is fastened. If it is intended that the puppet should lift its foot to the rear, a string must be fastened to the heel, led up and fastened at any convenient place at the rear of the No. 1 controller.

THE PROFESSIONAL CONTROLLER

The simple controller just described is the kind best suited for the needs of the beginner or aspiring amateur. With it, and the special stringing that may be used with it, all the ordinary movements of the body may be reproduced in the puppet. There is, however, a more complicated form of controller used by professional operators which enables the various motions to be imparted with greater ease, and also permits the operation of a puppet with one hand, thus leaving the other hand free to operate another puppet or to be used for any other purpose. The beginner is advised to learn puppet manipulation with the simple controller before attempting to use this more difficult but very practical one.

The main part of this controller is a flat wooden stick about one and one-half inches wide and eleven inches long. At its front end is inserted, in a hole bored for that purpose, a small wooden peg projecting upwards for

one inch. The front cross-piece is five inches long and is attached underneath the longer stick by a screw so that it may be turned till it is parallel with it. In either end of this short cross-piece, and projecting downwards, is a wooden pin four inches long as shown at A, A. The second cross-piece is seven inches long and is fastened on the upper side of the cross-piece. This is permanent and does not turn as the shorter one does. At each end is a wooden pin four inches long, projecting downwards (See B, B). In the rear end of the larger stick are fastened two such pins about four inches apart (See C, D). All of the pins mentioned have a very small screw eye inserted in their lower end. The arm-and-leg controller is one piece of flat stick seven inches long with a four-inch projecting pin at each end. These also have tiny screw eyes in their ends, E, E.

The stringing of the figure to the professional controller is as shown in the illustration. The head strings are fastened to the lower ends of the long pins, A, A, being tied to the little screw eyes. As this cross-bar is pivoted, it may be turned to either the right or left, thereby imparting a similar movement to the puppet's head. This movement is impossible with the simple controller. The shoulder strings are attached to the pins, B, B, of the second cross-piece. The neck and seat pins are attached to the two rear pins, C, D. The leg strings are attached to the ends of the flat stick at F, F, while the arm strings are attached to the lower ends of the pins, E, E. This stick will enable the operator to move either the legs or the arms with the same hand and without the necessity of changing sticks as in the other method. The stick is held in the right hand. The ordinary up-and-down movements will operate the legs; but if the stick is turned to give it a quarter revolution, the pins, E, E, will describe the arc of a quarter of a circle, thereby moving the pins to position, H, H, thus pulling on the arm strings and moving those members, while the legs remain stationary. If, however, one end of the stick is elevated at the same time that it is turned, the leg and arm attached to that end will both move.

THE PROFESSIONAL CONTROLLER

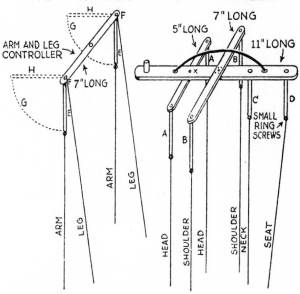

In the professional controller, both arms and legs are operated by the same stick. The stick is twisted to actuate the arms. The twist is indicated by the dotted lines in the above diagram.

Puppets – How to Make

(Con

When not in use this control stick rests on the main control stick; being held there by engaging the hole in its centre over the peg first mentioned.

The main controller is held in the left hand and by tipping it at different angles the motions are transferred to the puppet. The long pins to which the strings are attached pull these strings at an angle different to the one imparted to them by the simple controller. The method of constructing this controller is capable of variations; each operator having his pet method of constructing and stringing it to meet his particular requirements.

SPECIAL EFFECTS

Special puppets require special stringing. For instance, if a puppet is required to drop a handkerchief and pick it up, it would have to be strung, besides the regular stringing, for this particular purpose. The handkerchief would have to be attached to a string which passes through an eyelet in the palm of the hand and then up to the controller. When this string is released the handkerchief will drop to the floor. When it is desired that the puppet pick it up, the front end of the main controller should be tipped downward. This would bend the body forward till the hand reached the handkerchief. When the body is straightened up, the slack in the handkerchief string should be taken up also and the handkerchief would appear as if held in the hand. A lead weight concealed in the handkerchief would make it more positive in action. By the same method a puppet of a woman can be made to lift her skirt.

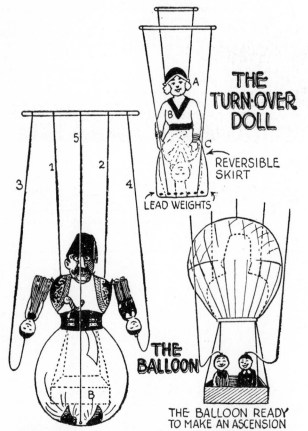

THE TURN-OVER DOLL

← REVERSIBLE SKIRT

↙ LEAD WEIGHTS

THE BALLOON

THE BALLOON READY TO MAKE AN ASCENSION

Puppets can be made to change with lightning rapidity by means of the effect here given. It will be noted that the articles are so made that the bottom of the costumes cover an entirely different object which comes into view when the bottom is raised.

THE BALLOON

This peculiar-looking puppet has nothing but its novelty to recommend it. An inspection of the illustration will show it to be an awkward looking figure. In appearance it resembles a poorly-constructed figure of a fierce Turk. It is made of thin lumber or heavy cardboard and is covered with cloth so as to give it the appearance of a dressed doll.

The puppet is divided at the waist and the parts are hinged as the cut shows. This hinging will allow the lower or skirt part to be folded up to conceal the upper part. The arms are two little dolls made of wood are hung on a hook at the shoulders, a small eyelet being fastened to the doll for this purpose. At a distance these dolls will resemble arms and hands. Behind the skirt section is suspended, by a string from each corner, a small box or wicker basket. This is shown by the dotted lines at B. The rear of the skirt is painted and striped to resemble a balloon.

The controller is one single stick and the whole is strung as shown. The strings 1 and 2 support the figure by the shoulders. The strings 3 and 4 lead to the little dolls and are fastened to their heads. String 5 passes down in front of the figure and is fastened to the lower edge of the skirt. The puppet is operated as follows.

As it has no legs or feet, it has to be jumped on in a sort of a crude dance. A jerk on strings 3 and 4 will remove the little dolls and reverse them so they can be stood on the floor. A pull on string 5 will bring up and reverse the skirt, disclosing the basket, which, with the striping on the reversed skirt, will give the whole the appearance of a balloon. With the aid of strings 3 and 4 the little dolls are danced into the basket and the balloon with its tiny passengers ascends out of sight.

THE TURN-OVER DOLL

This puppet is constructed on the principle of the turn-over toy doll: It consists of a head, trunk and skirt (A, B, C, in the illustration), the skirt presumably concealing the legs. But instead of the legs there is another trunk and a head, beneath the skirt. The hem of the skirt is heavily weighted with lead shot. If this figure is turned upside down, the skirt will be reversed, covering the visible head and body and exposing the one that had been concealed. These two dolls should be of widely different character and dress. As shown in the illustration, one is a rough-looking white girl while the other is a negress. The reversible skirt should be of a different color on each side and the two figures should be dressed in contrasting colors; so that when the change is made it will be easily perceived. Two simple control sticks are used, the figure being strung as shown in the diagram. The short stick is held high and the other held low. The figure is simply danced on with the edge of the skirt just clearing the floor. If stick No. 1 is lowered and No. 2 is raised the concealed doll will be brought up, the weights in the hem of the skirt will cause it to be reversed thus covering the figure first seen and exposing the second one. The figure may now be danced off. Do not repeat this change; as, the second time, there would be no element of surprise and the effect would be lost. This is a good comedy number.

TRICK CHANGING PUPPETS

This kind of a puppet is constructed so as to permit its being suddenly transformed into something entirely different. Some of these are very complicated and their manufacture is beyond the ability of the average amateur.

and Operate Them

tinued)

The high cost of having them made by a professional mechanic is almost prohibitive. In order that the readers of this book may have a general idea of their construction and the method of working them, a description of two of the more simple kinds has been given.

THE DANCING SKELETON

This is an articulated wooden skeleton, made in imitation of the human skeleton in miniature. The head is carved out of a block of wood or it may be modeled out of papier maché. The instructions for making this pliable pulp are given in the chapter relating to the construction of heads. In the lower part of the head, behind the jaw, there is a hole into which fits the upper end of the spine. The body section is whittled out of a piece of half-inch board and nailed on to the spine. The pelvis, is made in the same manner and is also fastened to the spine. At D, D, D, D, small holes are drilled. The bones composing the arms, legs, hands and feet are carved out of wood and are fastened together with small screw eyes. The whole is painted white and the ribs outlined with black.

The stringing of this mannikin is not as difficult as it might seem at first glance. The controller is made up of three pieces of wood, the longest being about five feet long. The lengths of the two shorter ones are five and eight inches. These two sticks lie flat on the longer one; but in the illustration they are shown slightly separated so that the method of stringing may be more easily understood. A small staple is driven into the wood at each shoulder. Strings tied to these are led up *through holes* in the long control stick No. 3 and are fastened to the ends of control stick No. 2. Strings are tied to staples driven into each side of the head at the temples, these being led up and passed *through holes* in the long control stick No. 3, then *through holes* in control stick No. 2, and are fastened to the ends of control stick No. 1.

The strings leading from the long control stick No. 3 to the arms pass through the small holes at D, D, and are fastened to a small screw eye screwed into the upper end of the arm bone. The upper portion of these strings is replaced by pieces of heavy elastic cord. If properly adjusted this elastic cord will pull the arm up against the shoulder, but if the elastic is stretched the arm will fall away. Releasing the elastic will cause it to pull the arm back to the shoulder. The legs are strung in a similar manner. The strings start at the controller, pass through the holes of the pelvis at D, D, and are fastened to the leg bones. A similar piece of elastic cord is at their upper ends. The two outer strings, which are tied to the outer ends of the long control stick No. 3 at X and led to the elbows and knees, help to pull the arms and legs away from the body when the elastic cords are stretched. The greater the length of the long control stick, the farther away the arms and legs will swing.

When swung in this manner the skeleton is ready for his performance. Dancing is his specialty. Jumping him up and down is one simple movement. Elevating the controller at the ends elevates the legs and arms. Pulling upwards on the strings at E, E, with a sharp jerk will make the leg kick and arm wave. By pulling on the lower end of one of the elastic cords, the arm or leg controlled by it will drop away from the body. A quick release will bring the member back with a bone-like click. Grasping the ends of the four pieces of elastic and pulling on them all at the same time, will cause the four members to move away from the body. Releasing the pull will bring them back. By elevating control stick No. 1 the head will be taken up and out of

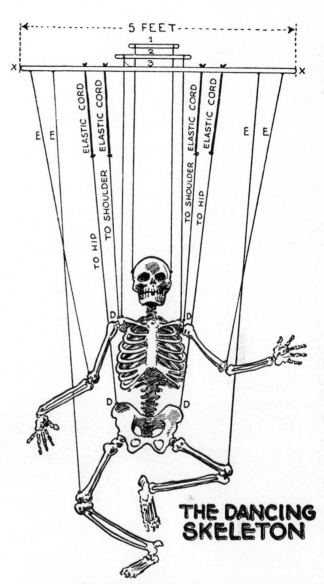

THE DANCING SKELETON

In order to greatly augment the effect of dancing, the skeleton is connected to the control sticks by means of cords which are in turn tied to short pieces of elastic bands. A slight tremble of the operator's hand gives the semblance of dancing.

sight, while the body continues its dancing. Then the head can be made to suddenly drop into place again. By elevating control sticks Nos. 1 and 2 at the same time, the head and body will go up and leave the legs dancing about. The head and body can be dropped singly or can come down together.

This is a comedy performance and is always provocative of much laughter. It is a pleasing departure from the more serious characters.

ANIMALS

In presenting puppet plays, especially those exploiting fairy tales, animals are necessary characters. Those who are lucky enough to possess a sufficient amount of artistic skill to carve these out of wood, or to model them out of modeling clay and reproduce them, loose-jointed, with papier maché, may use these methods to advantage. Very few of us are so gifted, however, and fortunately

Puppets – How to Make

(Con

THE BALL JUGGLER
ONE STICK MAIN CONTROLLER

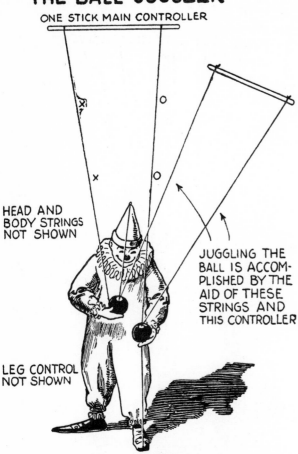

HEAD AND
BODY STRINGS
NOT SHOWN

JUGGLING THE
BALL IS ACCOM-
PLISHED BY THE
AID OF THESE
STRINGS AND
THIS CONTROLLER

LEG CONTROL
NOT SHOWN

In the diagram above only two sticks are shown. It will be observed by operating one of these that the juggler is made to toss the balls in the air and at the same time follow the movement with his head. Notice how cords XX and OO pass from the main controller to the juggling controller.

there is another method we can resort to. The animals sold in toy stores may be changed or reconstructed for this purpose. Those of solid construction, such as are made of wood or papier maché, are not desirable, as the legs must be loosened or made over to be movable. Sometimes it is impossible to do this without mutilating the animal so as to render it useless. The stuffed variety is more easy to manipulate.

Rip the seams of the legs and remove the material with which they are filled. Fill the foot with fine shot and sew up the seam, leaving the legs empty. This will allow the legs to swing, as they are composed of cloth or other woven material. The puppet is strung in a very simple manner, one control stick being used. The figure hangs from this by three strings, one from the head, one from the shoulders and one from the hips. If the ears and tail are to move an extra string must be attached to each of these appendages.

In manipulating puppets of this kind they are held so that their weighted feet rest on the stage floor. They are made to move forward in a sort of galloping motion by raising and lowering each end of the control stick alternately. The legs will swing and have the appearance of moving as in the natural walk. As they are not moving alternately and with system as they should, this will soon be observed by the spectators. This can be

overcome by moving the animal a short distance at a time and bringing it to a rest before the defective walking is noticed. There should be some reason for these stops. For instance, a dog coming into a room could make his first stop by the nearest person as though begging to be petted. From there he could be moved to whichever position it is intended that he should occupy.

THE BALL JUGGLER

As his title indicates this little fellow is a juggler. The illustration shows how he is strung. To avoid confusion the body strings are omitted. The main controller is a single stick. The wooden balls are threaded on the arm strings. On jerking upwards with one end of this arm controller, the hand corresponding to this end will throw its ball upwards and catch it when it drops. By quickly alternating these jerking movements the balls will be juggled. By turning the controller half way around the strings will be crossed like an X. The jerking movements will now impart a motion to the balls which will give them the appearance of being tossed from one hand to the other.

There is a special string which will cause the figure to toss the ball to his head. This string starts from the puppet's head or hat, passes down through the hole of the ball in the right hand and then up to the controller where it is fastened. A pull on this string at X will move the ball to the figure's head or hat. Releasing the string will drop the ball to the hand.

For another special effect a string is attached to the right toe. This string is then passed up through the hole of the ball in left hand and then up to the controller where it is fastened. A pull on this string at O will raise the left leg and the ball will be transferred to the toe and be held there. Releasing this string will bring the ball back to its original position.

THE POLE BALANCER

This performer tosses his pole up and catches it, lies on his back; and, transferring the pole to his toes, juggles it with his legs. Taking it in his hands again he places it on top of his head and balances it there. With his head he tosses it to his hands, catches it and makes his exit.

The illustration shows the modus operandi. The pole has four holes bored through it, through which to pass the arm and leg strings. In this instance the leg strings are fastened to the toes and pass through the holes Nos. 1 and 4 and up to control stick No. 2. The hand or arm strings pass through holes Nos. 2 and 3 and up to control stick No. 3. In order to avoid confusion the head and body strings are not shown in the illustration. By manipulating control stick No. 3, the figure will toss the pole up and catch it. Lay the figure on his back, raise control stick No. 2; the feet will be elevated and at the same time the pole will be transferred to the toes. The alternate raising and lowering of this control stick will cause the little man to juggle the pole with his feet. Lower stick No. 2 to the other hand and raise stick No. 3 and the pole will be transferred to the hands. If control stick No. 3 is raised high enough the pole may be placed on the head and the hands lowered. Two fine wire nails in the head for the pole to rest against will help keep it in place. Raising control stick No. 3 quickly will bring the hands up to the pole and when they are lowered the pole will go with them. On account of the leg strings being fastened to the toes the figure will walk pigeon-toed.

The diagram for the pole balancer is given on the accompanying page. The reader can see how this is operated.

and Operate Them
tinued)

THE CONTORTIONIST

This little performer goes through all the movements of the contortionist or limber man of the circus. A one-stick main control is used the cross-piece being dispensed with. In the illustration the head, shoulder and seat strings are omitted in order that the special stringing may be more easily seen. The ordinary controller and strings for the legs are also left out.

The body and all joints of the figure should be unusually flexible. The eyelets at each side of the head should be a little larger than usual, as a number of strings will have to be passed through them. A string is fastened to each toe, passed through the eyelet and fastened to the main control stick. A pull on this string will cause the figure to raise his foot to his head after the manner of a real contortionist. A string fastened to each heel, passed through the eyelets and at its upper end fastened to the main controller will enable the operator to cause the figure to bring either heel up to the back of its head. By holding on to the seat string and lowering the main controller, the figure will bend forward and downward, bringing its head to the ground. By lifting one toe, at the same time moving the figure forward and down to the floor, it will execute the trick known as "the split." A string fastened to the right hand, passed through the eyelet and attached at its upper end to the main controller will enable the operator to make the puppet to bring its right hand to the temple and salute. This is done at the finish of each trick.

THE POLE BALANCER

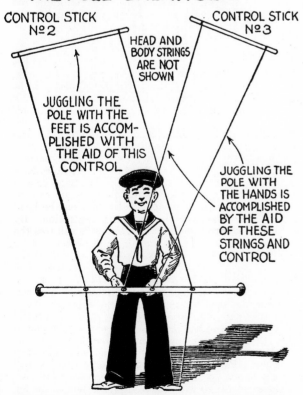

CONTROL STICK Nº 2

CONTROL STICK Nº 3

HEAD AND BODY STRINGS ARE NOT SHOWN

JUGGLING THE POLE WITH THE FEET IS ACCOMPLISHED WITH THE AID OF THIS CONTROL

JUGGLING THE POLE WITH THE HANDS IS ACCOMPLISHED BY THE AID OF THESE STRINGS AND CONTROL

The pole balancer is slightly different from the ball juggler in that juggling is accomplished by both the hands and the feet. By loosening the tension of the strings to control stick 3 the pole slides down to the feet. The other controls are not shown.

THE CONTORTIONIST
ONE STICK MAIN CONTROLLER

HEEL STRING

TOE STRING

HAND STRING FOR SALUTE

TOE STRING

HEEL STRING

BODY, ARM AND LEG CONTROLS ARE NOT SHOWN HERE

Because of the weird effects required of the contortionist this puppet is strung differently than any of the others. The strings pass through eyelets on either side of the head, enabling the feet to be brought up to the head in either a forward or backward movement.

VAUDEVILLE PUPPETS

The entertainments given by marionette shows in vaudeville theatres have puppets which perform seemingly remarkable acts. There are tight-rope walkers, ball jugglers, bar performers, trapeze acts, contortionists, acrobats, etc. Each of these requires special stringing to produce the desired results. It is not probable that the beginner in puppet manipulating will want to waste his initial efforts on one of these difficult figures. After he has learned to make and operate a walking figure, such as is used in dramatic performances, the construction and working of these more complicated kinds will not be so difficult.

SCENERY

Painted scenery is seldom used in amateur productions of puppet plays. To have the scenery painted in a professional scenic studio is rather expensive, and amateur scene painters are very rare. But if it so happens that such an amateur is available, he should be regarded as a special prize and every effort made to induce him to interest himself in the puppet plays and to paint a set of scenery for the miniature stage.

Puppets — How to Make
(*Con*

FOREST COTTAGE

The above diagram depicts a simple forest scene with a miniature bench and tree stump as additional props placed in the foreground of the stage. The back scene may be painted or inked in as indicated.

Generally only the back scene or back drop is used. Borders are not practical, as they interfere with the operators in working the strings. A small wing may be placed near the front of the stage at either side to serve as a masking; so that the spectators will not be able to see behind the scenes.

Where painted scenery is not obtainable, plain cloth drapes or curtains are the best substitutes. For a background select cloth of a color that is the same as the scene to be represented. On this are sewn or roughly painted, the details of the scene. These should be as few as possible. Additional details are secured by using small set pieces, placed in front of these backgrounds.

FOREST SCENE

This is constructed in a similar manner. The grass and background is light green. The tree trunks, B, are

FOREST SCENE

In the forest scene a stone and two tree stumps are also advantageously placed in the foreground. The puppets can sit down on these props.

made of either dark brown or black cloth. The upper section representing the foliage is a darker green than the background. The grass and leaves on this are of the lighter-green cloth. The set pieces are two stumps and a rock, as seen in the foreground. The stumps are made of cardboard covered with black cloth. The rock is made in a similar way, grey or brown cloth being used. These set pieces must be supported by a little cardboard brace, glued to their backs.

FOREST COTTAGE

In this scene the grass and background are light green. The tree trunks are black or brown and the foliage is a darker green. The log house is constructed of grey or dark brown cloth cut to a suitable shape and size and lined with black ink or paint to make it look like logs. The upper beam may be black. The window is made of grey and black cloth. The set pieces are a small bench and a stump, in front. If it is desirable to have it so, the log house may be a set piece. In this case it is constructed of cloth-covered cardboard.

SIMPLE INTERIOR

A sketch of a very simple interior is given, which can be augmented with any necessary set pieces that may

SIMPLE INTERIOR

Ordinarily puppets are rarely required to pass through a door; consequently interior scenes can be painted and aside from the fact that the curtains could be withdrawn by one of the puppets a moving door never need be employed. If desired that a puppet enter through the door he must be properly strung before the curtain is lifted.

be required for any special interior. If a drawing room is required, add set pieces consisting of chairs, table, piano and lamp, etc. If a library is required, remove the piano and add some shelves of books.

INTERIOR OF A FARM COTTAGE

To make this scene procure medium brown mercerized sateen for the back ground, using the dull or reverse side of the material. For the overhead beams, B, cut strips of cloth from the same kind of material, but of a darker shade of brown. The lines to represent the bark of the logs are put on with ink, using a very fine brush; or a pen or pointed stick of wood could be used. These strips are sewed to the back ground proper. The door, C, is made in the same way, using dark gray material, the grain of the wood, hinges, etc., being painted on the material. When finished this is also sewn to the background. The window can be made of the same material as the door and attached to the background in the same

and Operate Them

tinued)

manner. In a similar way the fireplace is constructed. For the shelf use dark grey or dark brown material. The stone work is made of dark grey, the lines of the stone being painted on. The interior of the fireplace is medium brown. The logs, kettle, etc., can be either painted or or they can be made of black cloth and sewn on. The plate and vase are made of grey cloth, the candle stick is made of black material, the candle, of course, being white. The set pieces are complete in themselves and may be set out on the stage.

In this particular scene, a table, a stool and a broom are used. These can be made of cigar-box wood and painted the proper color. The broom is made by taking enough straws from an old broom and tying them to a small stick. When these set pieces are set or placed on the stage several inches in front of the flat background, the effect is remarkably realistic.

OTHER SCENES

By using the directions for making these four scenes as a guide, other scenes may be easily constructed. The scene should first be sketched on paper and the coloring put on with crayons. This will be a guide in making the finished scene and less difficulty will be encountered in its construction.

MANIPULATING THE PUPPETS

In manipulating the puppets with the simple controller the main control stick is grasped in the eft hand as is also the arm control stick. The leg control stick is held in the right hand. Stand on an elevation, say a chair, holding the controller so that the figure's feet just touch the floor. Have the figure facing either to the right or the left. Raise one end of the leg control stick and the knee will bend, thereby elevating the foot from the floor as in walking. Lower this end of the control stick and at the same time move the main control forward so as to impart a similar movement to the body. Immediately raise and lower the other end of the leg control and the other leg will move as though walking. Alternate these leg movements, at the same time moving the whole figure forward and the puppet will walk. Be sure that the feet just touch the stage floor. If the figure is held a little too low, the knees will bend and an awkward posture will be the result. If held too high the figure will appear to be walking in the air. The leg stick may be transferred to the left hand and the arm stick taken in the right, if it is desired to cause the puppet to gesticulate with the hands.

When this walking movement has been mastered the others will be easy to learn. To make the figure bow with its head hold the neck string with the right hand and slightly lower the main control stick. This will release the strings holding the head which will fall forward. Raise the main control and the head will be brought back into position. If it is desired that the body should bow, repeat this performance with the right hand holding the seat string instead of the neck string. Tipping the main controller from side to side will cause the head to tip the same way. A quick jerk on a leg string will cause the figure to kick. Agitating the main control stick will cause the body to tremble. When these movements have been acquired, others will suggest themselves. A special string may be required for some particular movement.

CONTROLLING THE STRINGS

It is quite certain that the artistic value of a marionette performance will be much enhanced if the spectators do not perceive the strings, though very few manipulators

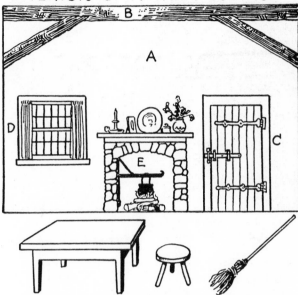

INTERIOR OF A FARM COTTAGE

A clever technician can produce a sunlight glow effect through the window D by using tissue paper and an electric lamp and the same lamp can produce the effect of flame in the fireplace if the flames are cut out and the cut is covered with red celluloid or glass. The objects in the foreground are props.

make any effort towards this end. Usually the strings are very much in evidence and this must surely detract very much rom the illusion of the performance, which is to create in the minds of the members of the audience, the temporary belief that the little figures are alive. This illusion is not a difficult one to bring about. being as easy with adults as with children. The presence of strings suggests nothing but strings and the fact that some one is pulling them; whereas if strings are not visible no impression of that kind is made.

Various methods have been used to conceal the strings as much as possible. One way is to use a black back ground for the miniature stage on which the figures are performing, and strings of the same color. At a very short distance these strings will be invisible. Dark green or dark blue back grounds may be used with the figures strung with colored thread to match. These brighter colors do not lose themselves as easily as the black. Another method is to use black thread in stringing and to use a back ground of narrow black and white vertical striped cloth. These stripes will effactually conceal the strings even when a spot light is turned on them. Still another method is to operate the figures behind a black quarter, or half-inch mesh netting. The puppets will not present as good an appearance as when the other methods are used, but the strings cannot be perceived. When scenery is used on the stage it is almost impossible to conceal the strings excepting by this latter method.

THE STAGE

The miniature stage on which the little figures give their performances and presentations may be as simple or as elaborate as one's finances will permit. A very simple method is to use a doorway for a proscenium or stage opening. On one side of this doorway build a foot-high platform, constructing it out of any available material. If lumber is to be had, this may be used, elevating it on small boxes. Or if a number of small

Puppets — How to Make

(Con

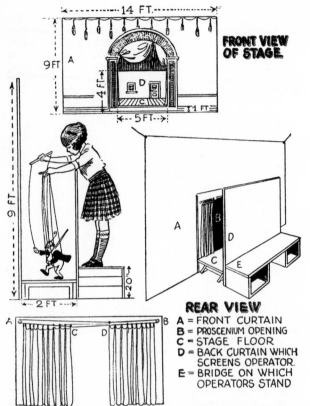

FRONT VIEW OF STAGE

14 FT.

9 FT

4 FT.

5 FT.

9 FT

2 FT

20"

REAR VIEW

A = FRONT CURTAIN
B = PROSCENIUM OPENING
C = STAGE FLOOR
D = BACK CURTAIN WHICH SCREENS OPERATOR.
E = BRIDGE ON WHICH OPERATORS STAND

The diagram shows a typical stage upon which the puppets act. They are controlled by the operators standing on platform E and working over partition D. Hooks can be affixed to D for hanging the spare puppets to be used progressively as desired.

boxes of similar size can be procured, the stage may be built up out of these. An obliging groceryman could furnish some large cardboard boxes, the kind used in shipping breakfast foods. Two of these, placed end to end, would make a stage of the size suitable for the ordinary door. Whatever the stage happens to be made of, it must be covered with a piece of cloth to give it a presentable appearance. A stage of this kind should not be more than two feet deep, the depth being the distance from front to back.

The background or back curtain should be of any dark color, preferably black. This may be hung from two upright strips of wood at each back corner of the stage. If it is not permissible to nail these uprights in place, they may be tied to two ordinary kitchen chairs placed with their backs against the stage. This will leave the seats of the chairs at the rear of the back curtain. If a board the length of the stage is laid on the chair seats it will make an admirable bridge for the operators to stand on while at work. In appearance this outfit will bear a general resemblance to the more desirable one to be described below. It is only suitable as a practice stage, for children to use in home puppet plays or for use when the larger outfit is not practical.

Professional marionette workers have a stage which is an exact duplicate in miniature of the regular full-sized stage used in theatres. The front curtain operates much the same as the regular stage curtain. There are many sets of scenery of a size to fit the small stage. There are two bridges, one over the proscenium and one at the rear. With this combination of bridges and a sufficient number of operators it is possible to obtain results which could not be had with the single bridge.

These professional stages are also equipped with their own electrical effects. They have foot, side, border and spot lights; also colored lights and rheostats for special effects.

As the average person who reads this book will not become a professional operator for some time, it is considered advisable to give a description of an outfit which can be easily constructed with a small outlay of time and money and which will meet with all the requirements of the amateur producer. An inspection of the illustration will give a general idea of the construction of the stage and curtains. The dimensions need not be strictly adhered to but may be changed as conditions or desires necessitate. The front curtain may be made of any opaque material. Heavy calico is a cheap material; but mercerized sateen, which is a little more expensive, presents a more attractive appearance. Dark green or purple has a rich looking effect. The trimmings may be of gold cord or tassels. These may be sewed on so they will always be in place or they may be omitted. If expense is no obstacle, the front curtain may be made of black or purple velvet, decorated with gold ornaments. The proscenium, or stage opening, is cut out of this curtain and decorated as shown. The upper edge of this front curtain is reinforced with a piece of heavy webbing.

If the curtain is to be a permanent one it may be supported by a framework made of light strips of wood; but if it is to be portable sew an iron ring to each upper corner and suspend it by light ropes fastened to screw-eyes placed in the side walls of the room in which the stage is being used.

The size of the stage is two feet deep and six feet across. This allows for six inches to extend past the proscenium opening on each side. The stage floor is a piece of wall board supported by small wooden horses similar to those used by carpenters. The height of the stage floor above the regular floor is one foot. A piece of green baize or other cloth covers the stage floor and is allowed to fall over the front and reach to the regular floor. This will form a drape for the front of the stage. It should be tastefully decorated to present a pleasing appearance.

The back curtain of the stage is attached to two wooden uprights made of light wood, each of these being nailed to a wooden box about twenty-four inches high. These boxes serve the double purpose of holding the uprights and furnishing a support for the "bridge." This bridge consists of a piece of 2 x 12-inch plank, six feet long. It is on this bridge that the operators stand while manipulating the marionettes. A stage constructed along these lines will be serviceable and portable, and will meet with the requirements of the average amateur.

When the play is presented in one scene it is possible to dispense with the front curtain, but when the scenery is to be changed for each act a curtain must be used. The easiest kind to construct and operate is a sliding curtain which separates in the center, the halves sliding on a wire to each side of the proscenium. The curtain is opened and closed by the aid of a thick cord and two pulleys. The illustration shows the method of operation. A frame work of light wood will be necessary to support the curtain. Curtain rings are sewn to the curtain about six inches apart. A wire is passed through these rings, and is then stretched tightly across the upper batten and fastened at A and B. A small pulley is fastened at each upper corner, or a large iron screw eye will answer the same purpose. The opening and closing of the curtains is easily accomplished by arranging a cord for this purpose as follows: First close the curtains. Tie one end

and Operate Them

cluded)

of a stout cord (heavy fish line will be found to be the most satisfactory) to the curtain ring at C. Take the cord to the left and pass it through the pulley at A. Next take it over to the right, fasten it to the curtain ring at D, take it on to the right through the pulley at B, bring it back to the left and fasten it to the curtain ring at C, this being the ring from which the cord started. There should be no slack in the cord.

The operator can take hold of this cord at any place and by its aid open and close the curtains. He can stand on the bridge and reach forward and open the curtain. This cannot be done when other methods are used. The curtains should be fastened to the battens at either side.

GIVING THE PERFORMANCE

It is the intention to give only the method of construction and operation of marionettes, in this book. However, a few words concerning the giving of a performance may not come amiss. The beginner in any line of work, who is uninstructed, is sure to make mistakes and learning by experience alone is often an unsatisfactory and expensive method of acquiring knowledge.

Almost any drama can be given through the mediumship of puppets. The beginner should select one with few characters, leaving those with more characters, and consequently more difficulties of presentation, for a later period. A good choice would be one of the well-known fairy stories which are of special interest to children. Children have a general knowledge of these and their minds will more easily grasp the various situations than they would if they were witnessing some play with which they were totally unfamiliar.

Having selected the play, a list should be made of the characters, properties and scenery required. If several persons are interested in the play, the work should be systematically divided among them. Perhaps all will want to assist in making the puppets. To one should be assigned the duty of consulting books on costumes so that the figures will be properly dressed. Books on costuming can be found in the public libraries. A lady should be appointed to make the dresses. One person should have charge of the making of the scenery and should begin work on it at the earliest opportunity, to have it completed in good time for rehearsals. Still another person should have charge of the making of the small accessories known as "properties." These are such articles as chairs, tables, etc.

While this work is in progress, study of the lines of the play should be commenced. The lines should be memorized thoroughly so that there may be no hesitation in speaking them during the public presentation. When the puppets are finished and all the scenery and properties are ready, the rehearsals should begin. Of these there cannot be too many. Constant practice makes perfect in this case. When the performers are confident that they have everything letter perfect, there is little chance of anything going wrong at a crucial moment. But if this confidence is lacking, that very fact is generally sufficient to cause nervousness with its resultant mishaps.

The most successful performers in this line practice many weeks on a new play or production before they feel that they are sufficiently proficient for a public performance. The mediocre marionette workers are the ones who present their performances in a slip-shod fashion without giving it sufficient rehearsal. If professional entertainers can afford to give many weeks of their time and work to rehearsal, surely the aspiring amateur, who is doing the work for the pleasure of it, can afford to imitate them in this respect.

The marionette drama should be presented the same as a regular kind given by human actors. A piano solo should precede the play; or if this is not possible a selection should be played on a phonograph. The operators stand on the bridge, operating the puppets and speaking the lines at the same time. The enunciation should be distinct. The words should be spoken slowly. The movements of the figures should harmonize with the spoken lines. They should be held so that their feet just touch the stage floor. By proper manipulation of the controllers they should be made to gesture with their head and hands. Care must be taken that the figures are strung with strings long enough to prevent the operators' hands from being seen by those who are sitting close to the little theatre.

Light for the miniature stage can be furnished by electric light bulbs attached to an extension cord and placed at convenient places at the side or overhead. A bridge lamp may be adjusted to throw its light on the stage, thus forming a miniature spotlight. All other lights should be extinguished. The only illumination should be that on the stage.

Properly lighted, the marionette stage with its little actors, produces a peculiar illusion. Looking at a bright object in a dark room produces a kind of partial self-hypnosis, deadening temporarily the reasoning factor of the brain. In this state the observer forgets that the puppets are small and imagines that they are life size. The persons who do the talking for the figures do not have voices which one might expect the little figures would have. The observer, while under this odd hypnotic influence does not observe this; instead he thinks the puppets to be of a size to fit the voice. To produce this illusion properly nothing but the stage and figures should be visible. If any full-sized object, say a chair, were visible near the stage, the chance for comparison would be taken advantage of and the deception would not be possible.

It is not possible to describe the sense of satisfaction which goes with the successful presentation of a puppet play. Once a single play is presented and applauded, the average person will find that there is an irresistible attraction connected with puppetdom which will cling for many years. The author has been making and operating puppets for twenty-five years; but the little people have never lost their fascination.

THE MATCH AND BOX TRICK

Can you carry matches around the room without using your hands? Lay them on the table, cover with a match box and draw the breath inward. The matches will adhere to the box as indicated.

Mental Telepathy De Luxe

*T*HIS exceptional trick in thought transference can be presented as an impromptu demonstration, with absolutely no prearranged paraphernalia. The wizard explains that he can use a radio to demonstrate the possibility of broadcasting thoughts over the ether. The loud speaker is disconnected from the set and the earphones are attached. The assistant who is to partake in this demonstration is now led to another room, and after a committee has been chosen they impart a word and the name of a playing card to this assistant, who naturally is stationed at a fair distance from the performer. The committee return to the radio chamber, and after a few moments are amazed to find that the magician is in possession of the secret name or card.

Explanation:. Anyone who has experimented with radios knows that if an electric switch be turned on or off in another room a click or sound is distinctly heard. A code is prearranged and the trick is done.

MAGIC

Wand Vanish De Luxe

*T*HE effect: The magician proves the wand that he has been using to be solid and apparently unprepared, by giving it a few violent raps upon a table top. Taking a sheet of newspaper which has been hanging across the back of a chair, he tears the paper in two and proceeds to wrap the wand snugly into one of the sections of the paper. Without any suspicious moves he nonchalantly tears this paper into small sections, the wand having completely disappeared.

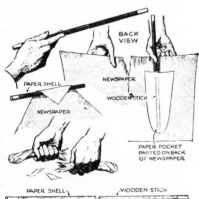

The secret: The wand consists of a wooden stick, concealed within a piece of paper tubing, which has been painted to represent the genuine article. In the act of tearing the newspaper in two, the solid stick slides from out the tube into a newspaper pocket which has been pasted in back of the paper. Thus, the paper tube which, to all appearances, is the solid wand, is rolled into the newspaper which is afterward torn to bits.

The Phantom Derby

*T*HE magician enters a room, and for a moment shocks the ladies by neglecting to remove his hat. Seeming to be somewhat embarrassed, the wizard places his finger to his mouth, and blows upon it. Instantly, the derby leaps off the magician's head, flying into the air.

An examination of the hat is sure to be called for. The spectators, however, are greatly amazed to find the derby is entirely unprepared.

Secret: Two plain pins and a piece of elastic is all that is required. A pin is tied firmly to each end of the elastic. Stretching the elastic, the pins are driven directly opposite one another into the band of the hat. The derby is then placed upon the head, as illustrated. The hat should fit rather tightly. In the act of blowing the finger, which is merely a bit of by-play, the wizard has but to frown, thereby relaxing the muscles of the forehead, which produces sufficient slack to cause the hat to fly upward, and off the conjurer's head.

All that remains to be done is to remove the pins and elastic secretly.

Enchanted Goblet

*T*HE wizard brings forth a large, transparent glass goblet. This container is seen to be filled with milk.

The magician then borrows a handkerchief, which he throws over the goblet, and places it on a table. To the amazement of the spectators, the goblet is brimfull of wine when kerchief is removed.

The goblet is a specially prepared one, with hollow stem, and an inner glass lining. Some milk is poured in through the stem, while the glass is inverted. A cork prevents the milk from leaving. The inner lining is filled with wine, concealed from view by the milk in the outer shell. When covering the goblet with the handkerchief, the cork is secretly removed, and the forefinger pressed over the hole.

The glass is placed over a trap in the magician's table, the inside of which contains a tin cup, into which the milk freely flows, while the goblet is still covered.

A Mind Reading Secret

Many dealers in magical equipment are charging exorbitant prices for this effect, claiming it is the method employed by me in my performances on the Keith circuit. To prove that it is not, I am disclosing the system herewith. Several assistants walk among the audience distributing small slips of paper. The mind reader requests that the audience write names, addresses, etc. on the slips and fold them several times so that the writing cannot be seen. He then passes envelopes among the audience, requesting that groups of slips be placed into each of them and that they be retained by the writers. Seating himself on the stage with slate and pencil, he calls names, etc. Under cover of passing the envelope down the aisles, for the slips, the magician secretly palms some of the slips, permitting the rest and blank duplicates to remain in the envelope. The contents of palmed slips are subsequently read.

Production Cylinder

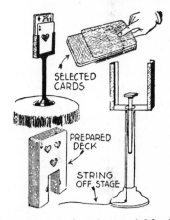

In the Chinese production cylinder shown above the compartments in the sides serve for holding the load.

HERE is an open production case, which bases its results upon the perfection of an optical illusion. As will be seen, in the illustration above, a small metal stand is placed upon an undraped table. A sheet of glass is then put upon the stand. A four-sided tube, with neither top nor bottom, after being freely shown, becomes the mysterious production apparatus. With arms bare to the elbow, the magician withdraws from the same, flags, ribbons, pigeons, etc. The tube can be shown empty several times only to be replaced again and production of more material continued. As will be observed from the illustration, the load is concealed in the four sides of the tube, the walls of which are built upon an angle and the interior lined with black velvet. A short distance from the spectators, it is quite impossible for the human eye to detect the peculiar bulge of the inner walls. A series of catches hold the lids in place while the cylinder is being held up for examination.

Ball Catching Wand

THIS trick is somewhat similar in effect to the well known coin catching wand. With the apparatus it is possible for the wizard to apparently catch four or five billiard balls upon the end of his magic wand. To all appearances, the devices consists of a nickel-tipped black stick 14" long and ½" in diameter. The mechanism consists of a metal tube which may be pushed back and forth in the wand by the thumb. The billiard ball at the end is a round red balloon affixed to the tube. At the opposite end there is a rubber bulb. By pressing the bulb and pushing the tube outwardly, the ball is made to appear at the end. A palmed solid ball is then apparently removed from the end of the wand under cover of which movement the tube is slid backward and the air released from the red rubber ball.

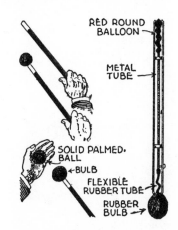

A wand fitted with a rubber bulb at one end and an inflatable ball at the other end is the mechanical requisite for the ball catching wand effect.

A Demon Houlette

A prepared deck and a special houlette assist in the production of this mysterious card rising effect.

AN unprepared deck of cards is shuffled and three or four freely chosen. The balance of the pack is placed into an ornamental houlette after the spectators signed their names across the chosen cards to identify them and returned them to the deck. Slowly and mysteriously the cards rise from the deck at one time and are then identified as originals by the signatures. The cards are freely chosen from an unprepared deck, but as they are being marked, the magician exchanges the balance of the deck for a deck especially prepared with a slot as indicated in the drawing. A perfect card rests on top of the deck to hide the cut. The piston of the houlette naturally pushes the good cards up out of the prepared deck. The piston-like arrangement is operated by an assistant off stage and as the drawings indicate, the arrangement is simple . The same effect using the little finger can be duplicated for hand manipulations.

The Rising of the Cards

A NUMBER of cards are drawn by various members of the audience, memorized and replaced into the pack.

The pack is now put into a skeleton stand which is placed on a table.

A few mystic passes with the magic wand and the selected cards are seen to slowly and majestically rise from the deck.

Of the numerous magical effects, the rising card experiment is the prettiest and the most mystifying of them all.

Here is a master trick, in simplified form, which in the hands of a magical entertainer will be the most applauded effect in his entire repertoire.

Secret:—The stand is weighted at the base so it will not tip over easily. Otherwise there is no preparation about it. The cards are

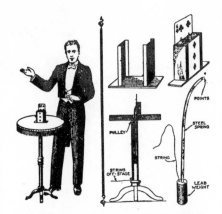

Cards placed in a small metal stand are caused to rise up one after the other by the assistant who pulls on the string which operates the weighted plunger and forces the points of the steel spring into the back of each end card, one at a time.

ordinary and will withstand examination. But the table isn't of ordinary description. This table contains a long steel spring, at the bottom of which is fastened a long, heavy, thin weight of lead. A linen thread is attached to the eyelet in the top of the lead weight and this thread runs up the center rod of the table through a minute pulley and offstage to an assistant.

When the selected cards are placed one on top of the other at the extreme back of the pack and these put into the skeleton stand, the forked sharpened end of the steel spring catches the card backs and when the assistant offstage pulls the thread, upon receiving a signal from the magician, one of the cards rise. The magician takes the cards out of the case when about half-way up and scales them into the audience.

The rising card experiment is a feature on any programme.

Anything to Please!

THE magician has a card drawn, for example we will say the King of Diamonds, and returned to the deck. A number is called and the cards are counted down on a table, one at a time. Holding up the card that appears at that number, the conjurer shows it but is told that it isn't the right card.

The magician now seems a bit puzzled, and asks the gentleman or lady who had drawn the card to count them himself or herself, as the case may be.

This is done and the card is shown. Pretending he hears a remark from some lady in the rear of the hall, he says, "What is the trouble, madam? Oh . . . you can't see the card? Well . . . how's that?" Suddenly the card becomes three times its original size. The magician continues, "Anything to please, madam!"

Secret:—The card, of course, is forced at the beginning. In this case it was the King of Diamonds. Say the number called was "ten." The King of Dia-

monds is on top of the pack now, unknown to the spectators. Naturally, when the tenth card is counted it isn't the right card as they were counted on the table with the top card counted as one. Picking them up, the magician places them back on the pack

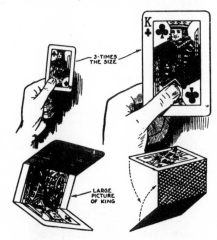

With the aid of the card made as illustrated in the diagram, it is possible for the magician to quickly change the size of the card so that those in the back of the audience can clearly see its suit and color.

and asks someone to count them for him. Again ten is counted and this time the King of Diamonds appears. This is shown and the pack is picked up with the left hand and the single card replaced with the right hand. The right hand then immediately picks up the prepared card and the magician speaks the above given lines, at the same time opening out the card to its full size.

The prepared card is made by hinging three cards together. Narrow pieces of tape are pasted on the sides so that the cards open up as one card. The large card also represents the King of Diamonds.

This can be home-made by taking an ordinary King of Diamonds and photographing it up, on a "silver print." Any photographing place will do this for you at but a slight cost. The red portions are then bleached out and painted in by hand.

This trick is sure to get a laugh.

The Idol of Han

THE conjurer unfolds a tale of a mysterious little idol which was presented to him by the court magician of Han.

The Idol of Han has the peculiar property of locating a card once human hands have selected it.

Enlarging on this tale, the entertainer takes a pack of cards and shuffling them well, steps among his spectators and asks some member of the assemblage to select a card.

This card is returned to the pack and again the conjurer shuffles the cards so the selected card is lost in the deck.

The cards are laid out in a circle within a circle, until someone calls "Stop."

The performer now picks up the little idol, and with a bit of hesitancy places it on one of the cards.

Requesting the party who had drawn the card to name it, the

The Idol in this case is merely a subterfuge. While it adds an interteresting side light to the trick and it aids in completely mystifying the audience, it is not essential to the operation of the effect.

card underneath the idol is shown to be the one selected.

Secret:—The idol is only for effect. The cards are shuffled by the entertainer, but the top card is peeked at and memorized by him. This card is kept in view and when asking someone among the spectators to select a card this is the card that is, in magician's parlance, "forced" on them.

When the cards are again shuffled, this selected and sighted card is kept track of in any way the magician thinks best and the cards are laid out in a circle within a circle on the table.

A bit of by-play and the idol is placed on top of the card known to the magician by location and name.

The trick is brought to a proper climax by asking the party selecting the card to name it, immediately after which it is turned up with a dramatic gesture by the entertainer.

* * * * *

Name My Card!

THE conjurer brings forward a small, thin wooden case and a pack of playing cards.

Placing the box down on a table, he hands the cards to a member of the gathering and requests that he allow, after shuffling the cards, several of the ladies and gentlemen to select a card apiece.

This is all done without the entertainer having the least idea what the cards are that are taken from the pack.

"Now, please hand me back the remainder of the deck," says the magic man, "and I shall allow you, sir, to place your card in this case and at the same time to form a mental picture of the card."

The spectator places the card into the case and the entertainer closes it. Holding the case to his

forehead, he concentrates intently for a second, and then says (for example), "I see a red card.

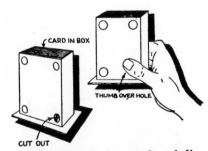

A metal box is decorated as indicated in this illustration. One of the decorations is cut away so that any card or cards put in the box can be read by looking at the index. The opening is covered by the thumb after the magician sights the index.

It is a diamond card. It has three pips on it. Yes, it is the three of

diamonds. Correct, sir? Thank you."

Card is removed from case by the entertainer and shown. Several other cards are revealed in the same way.

Secret:—The cards are of the usual kind, but the case, which the performer takes care never gets out of his hands, is doctored up a bit. At the bottom of the case, which is made of thin wood or metal, is a small hole which corresponds with the index portion of the cards. During the experiment, the magician is careful not to remove his finger from this opening. When the card is placed in the case and the cover put on, all the performer has to do is to raise the case toward his forehead and take his finger away, thus revealing to himself, via the card index, just what the card is.

*A torn card is placed into the expanded end of the magician's pistol. The magician
then aims at the target, fires a shot, and the card, intact, appears in the center thereof.
A simple piece of apparatus, illustrated in the diagram, makes this trick possible.*

Magical Marksmanship

A YOUNG lady the other day remarked that she thought magicians practised marksmanship as part of their trade.

Upon closer questioning the fact was brought out that an entertainer used as one of his feature tricks a feat of shooting a card into the center of a bull's-eye.

The young lady had watched this certain conjurer a number of times, and each time his aim was true and the selected card hit the exact center of the target.

The way he worked up this effect was to allow someone to select a card and tear it into any number of pieces.

Placing the piece into the tin cone which fitted the revolver, he took aim and fired at a target which stood on a table a considerable distance away.

He seemed to be an expert marksman, for the card that was torn to pieces was restored and shot right against the dead center of the target. It is needless to state that this exhibition of magical restoration and marksmanship won the applause of his audience.

How It All Happened:—The magician may have been an expert pistol shot, but we doubt it. So will you as you read on.

The card is torn and placed into a slit in the large tube contrivance which fits the end of the pistol. The inside of the tube was painted a dull black color. Upon looking into the tube from a distance the tube looked innocent, but if you were to subject it to closer examination you would have found the tube had a false partition into which the pieces of card were dropped.

The target was arranged with a spring rod which when not in use was held down to the table top by a piece of wire passing through two small eyelets. Fastened to one end of the wire was a length of black silk, which passed off-stage to an assistant.

The rod was so arranged that the duplicate of the torn card would come up to the exact center of the target when the wire pin was released. This was done by a sudden jerk given the thread by the man back of the scenes.

The pistol is aimed at the target, the trigger pulled and at the same moment the shot is fired the assistant pulls the thread releasing the spring and the card flies up flush with the bull's-eye.

Discovered!

THREE cards, the ace, two and three of any suit, are taken from a pack and placed on a table. Three cardboard covers, a trifle longer and wider than the cards, are handed to some member of the gathering and he is instructed by the magician to shift the cards as he will, and then cover with the pieces of cardboard and he (the magician) will always pick out the ace.

The magician now retires and the cards are moved around the table, then covered with the cardboards.

The conjurer now reenters the room, glances at the cardboard

Even though three cards, one of which is the Ace of Spades, are covered by pieces of cardboard while the magician is out of the room, he finds no difficulty in instantly locating the black Ace. A small piece of hair, glued to this card, makes the quest easy.

covers and every time picks out and turns over the ace card.

Secret:—The ace, in this case the ace of spades, has a short hair pasted to it. No matter how it is moved around, the hair pro-

jects outside of the covers when cards are hidden from view.

It is advisable to use a table cover of some sort of dark material so sharp eyes will not discover the modus operandi.

❋ ❋ ❋ ❋

A Useful Piece of Apparatus

THERE are numerous pieces of paraphernalia used in magical performances which in themselves are not tricks, but rather utility aids that prove of unusual value to the conjurer.

This tray I am going to describe may be used for the exchanging or switching of a pack of real playing cards for a deck of marked or tricked cards.

The tray is made of wood, and is stained mahogany color.

The center of the tray is securely nailed halfway between the two sides. The sides of the

tray should be about an inch and a half to two inches in diameter.

The tray is on the magician's table with a pack of marked or tricked cards underneath it.

The regular deck is handed out to be shuffled, and when returned to the magical entertainer, he places them on the tray flush up to the back ledge or rim.

While pattering, he takes from his pocket a handkerchief with which he wipes his hand preparatory, as the audience thinks, to doing a trick.

In reality, this is only a bit of

misdirection which does its part in taking the attention of the spectators from the pack just placed on the tray.

Picking up the tray for a fraction of a moment, he stands before the table, which is the most natural thing in the world to do.

During this crucial moment he turns over the tray and leaves the regular pack of cards on the table and brings the prepared deck into view. Or he may immediately, without turning his back, pick up the tray, also picking up and gripping with his fingers the pack of cards underneath.

Stepping quickly to someone in the audience, a lady preferably, he allows the deck of cards on the tray to slide into her lap. Then he goes on with whatever trick he is going to do.

Be sure, if you use the first method where the cards are left on the table, that they are well hidden from prying eyes.

During the act of switching the cards, keep up a steady line of patter, telling them all about the next trick you are about to do.

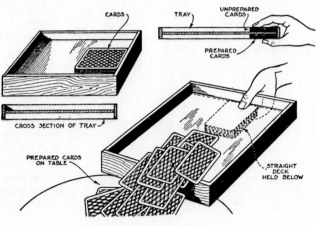

A box, made as indicated in this illustration, is very useful for switching one deck of cards shuffled and placed on the tray for another already prearranged.

Mystic Card Discovery

THE magician comes toward his audience shuffling a pack of playing cards, explaining that the cards are known as the prayer book of the devil, but nevertheless they have mystic qualities only known to students of the magic art.

He passes the cards from hand to hand and requests a member of the audience to select a card. This is done, and immediately after the card is returned to the deck, the magician locates the card, names it and hands it to the party who drew it.

Further calling attention to the fact that an experiment of this sort is all the more difficult when repeated before the same audience, he passes among his audience and has several ladies and another gentleman select cards, show them to their friends and place them back into the pack, proving to their satisfaction that the cards selected have been hopelessly lost in the deck.

Each of these three cards, which the magician positively does not know the names of, are located in the deck and drawn out and handed back, if he cares to, to the original people assisting him.

This is an excellent after-dinner trick, and when properly pre-sented leaves a marked impression on the spectators and they give the magician credit for being an adept in digital dexterity, more commonly called sleight-of-hand.

The secret:—Simple but well worth while. Many times a sim-

One of the simplest means of card location is illustrated here. A pencil line drawn across the cards and the deck is reversed when presented to the spectator for the reinsertion of his card. It is a matter of but a few moments to locate the card with the pencil line at the wrong end.

ple trick like this one gains all kinds of credit for the magician. No matter how simple a trick may be when you know the *modus operandi*, bear in mind that the spectators do not follow the ways and means of accomplishing the experiment, but are surprised by the outcome of the effect.

Now for the tearing aside of the curtain of mystery in this test. Consult the drawing and study it carefully.

You see a pack of cards squared up, and on one side of the deck near the top a pencil line drawn across the thickness of the pack.

Only the magician knows that line is there and this side of the cards should be kept away from the prying eyes of the know-it-alls.

When the cards are selected from the pack in the act of passing them from hand to hand as you have time and again seen magicians do, allow the spectators assisting to draw their cards clear of the deck and under cover of telling them what to do and warning them not to allow you to see the cards reverse the entire deck in your hands and have them immediately replace the cards drawn.

Now after the proper squaring of the deck and telling them their cards are hopelessly lost, you step back from them and turn the cards sideways in your hands, holding the side of the pack you have the pencil line drawn on away from you and sight (as in the drawing) the cards selected and replaced in the reversed deck.

The Hindu's Gift

ALTHOUGH this trick has nothing whatsoever to do with the Hindus, I attach this name to a stunt that will bring forth plenty of mystification as well as applause when presented.

Tell your spectators about a trip to the secret places in the land of many enchantments and mysteries, where you had as a guide an old Hindu who, becoming interested in your magical efforts, taught you the following experiment:

Take up a pack of cards and have them shuffled well by one of the most skeptical among your spectators. While in the audience you select some likely-looking young man or woman and ask him or her up on the stage to assist you.

Taking back the cards, you allow the assisting party to proceed ahead of you to the platform or stage.

Tell the assistant to follow your instructions carefully. "When I turn my back I want you to deal off the top two cards on this tray and step back to the audience once more and have two persons take the two cards and place them in their pockets."

This is done, and upon the assistant telling the magician every-thing is ready, Mr. Miracle Worker steps to the edge of the platform and stands there in deep thought. He then requests the parties who have the cards concealed to concentrate on their respective names.

Suddenly the magician calls the names of the two hidden cards.

Secret:—The deck is actually shuffled but on the way to the stage the magician slips, unseen by the spectators or the assisting gentlemen, two cards, of which he already knows the names, from his pocket on the top of the pack. The rest is but a matter of working the experiment up to a climax

Mystic Flying Card

A PACK of cards is shuffled and a lady is requested to select anyone she desires.

The selection is made, and while the magician turns his back she is instructed to show the card to others about her, replace it in the pack, shuffle it well and return it to the performer.

The prestidigitator takes the cards and places them on his table near the edge.

He now requests the lady to tell him the name of the card he selected, informing the spectators that he will not go near the cards, but remain where he is standing, and will call the card from the deck.

The lady names the card and the master of legerdemain commands the chosen card to fly from the shuffled pack.

To the surprise and bewilderment of all that is just what does happen.

The card is picked up and shown to be the selected one, then tossed into the audience for some-one to take home as a remembrance of the performance.

Secret:—A small pellet of chewing-gum and a piece of black silk thread about twenty inches long is required for this effect.

On your table you have the thread worked into the gum attached to a duplicate of the card you are going to have the obliging young lady select.

While shuffling the cards keep track of the card, say, for example, the seven of diamonds. After the shuffle, spread out the cards by running them from left to right hand and "force" the required card into the lady's hand.

Now that the card is "forced" on the lady, make a big show of handing the reminder of the deck to someone sitting nearby, allowing the card to remain in the drawer's hand.

Tell her to place the card back into the pack and hand the pack to someone else to have it completely shuffled.

Call attention to the fact that you do not touch the cards.

Now take back the pack and, stepping to your table, place the cards down on top of the card ready for the trick.

Turn the pack on the table over so the card to which the thread is fastened is on the top.

Pick up, without the audience suspecting your moves, the thread and walk away from the table, retaining the thread until it is played to its full length.

Now, calling attention to the fact that you are well away and will remain away from the table, ask the name of the selected card.

She calls the name of the card and you tell them you will, by magic, command the chosen card to draw itself from the deck and leave the other cards on the table.

Give the thread a sharp tug and the card will leave the top of the deck and fly on the floor. Pick it up and exhibit it.

Get rid of the small gum pellet and drop the thread to the floor. Step toward the front and scale the card into the audience.

* * * * *

The Eyes Deceive

THE three of diamonds is taken from a pack of cards and shown. The card is held between the tip of the first finger and thumb of the right hand. A slow circular motion is made by the magician and the three of diamonds magically changes to the two of diamonds right before your very eyes.

The card is now sent spinning into the audience and can be taken home as a souvenir by the one catching it.

This puzzles the many that know all about the secret of tricks.

They are all smiles when the trick starts, but when the card is actually thrown into the audience after the change is made watch their faces change and enjoy a hearty laugh.

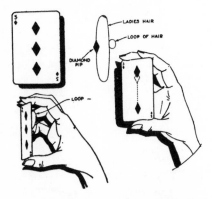

A small loop of hair to which a diamond pip is secured enables the performer to demonstrate that the three of diamonds can change to the two of diamonds before your eyes. A loop in the hair is engaged by the ring finger and manipulated by that finger to effect this mysterious change.

Secret:—The eyes deceive, is the truth as far as this trick is concerned. A diamond pip is carefully cut from a diamond suit card and glued to a piece of hair with a loop just large enough to go around the card snugly. This hair has a small loop large enough to place on the tip of the second finger of the right hand. The card is in the right hand during the experiment. Under cover of the circular motion the finger in the smaller loop of hair slides the pip around to the back of the card. The card is quickly passed into the left hand, which grasps it at the extreme fingertips and the loop of hair to which the pip is stuck is gotten rid of into a convenient pocket.

The card is now tossed into the audience.

Transferrence of Thought

READING the minds of spectators always thrills an audience.

There are a hundred different methods of accomplishing this feat which leaves the gathering or audience mystified and thoughtful.

In this experiment the magician explains to his audience that he believes in the transferrence of thought. Picking some obliging young lady or gentleman from the gathering, he asks them to be kind enough to assist him and at the same time act as a sort of go-between with the spirits that are hovering unseen all about them.

Mr. Wonderworker hands the obliging party a pack of playing cards and asks him to shuffle them well.

"Now," patters the conjurer, "I want you to take one of these cards as I run them through from hand to hand." Illustrating the talk the magician runs the cards from hand and hand, allowing the assisting party to select a card and take it out of the pack.

"Kindly hold the card up so all can see it except myself," continues the magician. "I want a number of you people out there to remember the card so there will be no error on my part.

"I have here a packet of envelopes which I wish some young lady to hold and pass to some member of the audience who will in turn kindly select one, place her initials or full name upon it and you, my dear sir (to assisting gentleman or lady, whatever the case may be) kindly step to that lady and place your card in the envelope, seal it securely and hold it in your hand high above your head so all may see it plainly.

"Remain there, please, until I call you, but keep the envelope into which you have sealed the card in full view high above your head so all may rest one eye upon you, one eye upon the envelope and the other eye affixed on me."

The magician now takes a number of blank cards (same size as the playing cards) and runs them

from hand to hand to show they are all blank cards.

He further patters: "Now, my friends, I want you to all see these slates of the ghostly visitants who hover all about us. Upon these blank and innocent cards the spirits write.

"That's right, my dear sir. Smile, but I shall convince you in a very few moments.

"Spirits must have their own writing desks and equipment so I shall use this tumbler, which one can plainly see through, for the office of the visiting spirits, and this card, as I said, will act as a slate. I place the card (places a blank card into the glass) into this house of glass and turn it around, so. I do this because being well acquainted with spirits, I know they do not want everybody to know just how they work. If you all did then you would all become magic workers and spirit mediums.

"Now, I shall ask the gentleman who has been so kindly holding the envelope to hand it to me. What, you do not trust me? I am sorry. We magicians are quite an honorable lot, I assure you. We may deal in spirits, but not the kind of spirits that gentleman over there is thinking of.

"Now I shall ask any member of the gathering to stand up and assist me. Thank you, sir. Will you kindly tell me the name of the card this gentleman showed you after he selected it from the pack? What was it, sir? The queen of hearts? Thank you, sir.

"Spirits, the name of the card the gentleman selected was the queen of hearts. Did you write that name on your spirit slate?"

Taking the blank card from the glass, the entertainer shows it, and lo and behold upon its face is clearly written "The Queen of Hearts," which was the name of the card the obliging gentleman selected.

The Secret:—Here is an effect worthy of a place in any entertainer's repertoire of magic.

It is simple to do, but if properly put over will make the audience think, and what is the worth of a magician who is unable to make his audience ponder?

Before the experiment, the performer decides upon the card he will have the voluntary assistant select. In this instance it is the queen of hearts.

This card is kept track of by the entertainer and forced in any manner convenient on the gentle-

The flap on the card here shown is responsible for this rather remarkable demonstration of thought transference. In this effect, an apparently blank card is put into a glass tumbler. When the tumbler is turned around, the magician who has allowed the flap to fall, exposes the words of the name of the card he previously forced.

man or lady who offers his or her services.

The blank card is a flap card, as illustrated in the drawing. One half of the card is hinged with a layer of thin gummed paper placed between two cards so fixed that when the top half of the card is let loose, it falls down, laying flat on the bottom half of the prepared card, thus bringing into view the name of the card written across the entire surface.

The envelopes are ordinary and the initialing of the envelope is only a matter of by-play or, as magicians call it, misdirection, which heightens the final effect of the trick.

When the card, held by fingers, is placed in the glass, the top half is let loose and falls down against the bottom of the card and exposes the written name of the card selected.

When the name of the card is called the magician takes care to hold his finger against the bottom flap of the card so the tricked card is not exposed.

Follow the illustrations carefully and you can't fail to mystify your audience.

🙙 🙙 🙙 🙙 🙙

The Glass Bowl Vanish

COINS   EMPTY

Several coins are placed into a glass bowl. This bowl is then tilted up to show the audience that the coins are actually contained therein and that there is no deception whatever. The magician then holds up a pocket handkerchief in front of the bowl in the manner indicated in the middle illustration.

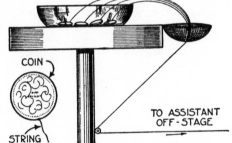

COIN

STRING

TO ASSISTANT OFF-STAGE

Without actually covering the bowl, the magician withdraws the handkerchief and demonstrates to the audience that the bowl is entirely empty. The secret lies in the fact that the assistant pulled the coins out of the bowl into a basket in the back, as the diagram indicates.

WHEN a magical entertainer uses glass properties in his act, his main worry is that the spectators can see through his tricks!

Here's one I trust will be clear to you, but I am sure, unless you read the method of working first and effect last, you will not be able to solve this problem without a bit of thinking.

Effect:—Four coins are placed in full view in an unprepared glass bowl.

A silk foulard is held, for a moment, in front of the bowl and the coins are commanded to leave their glass resting place.

Away goes the foulard and the coins have vanished!

Secret:—Like the majority of good magical effects, this one is also very simple and easily prepared for presentation.

The bowl is of ordinary description. The table is the same, but with one exception, and that is, it has a sort of bag stretched on a wire frame attached to the rear into which the coins go.

The four coins are fastened to as many pieces of strong black silk or linen thread. Each thread runs down through the bag arrangement separately, after which they are tied together. The

bag is at the back of the table. The single thread then runs through screw-eyes in the table base and then off-stage to your trusty assistant.

The performer holds the foulard in front of the coins and orders them to fly away to their happy hunting grounds or where you will. The assistant takes that as a signal and quickly draws the coin out of the glass dish into the secret bag and the vanish is complete. Having separate openings in the bag prevents the coins from clicking together when they are pulled out of the glass.

Novel Card Painting

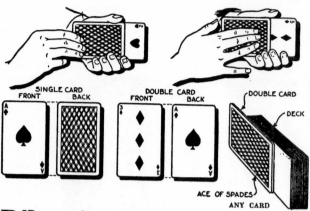

SINGLE CARD
FRONT   BACK

DOUBLE CARD
FRONT   BACK

DOUBLE CARD

DECK

ACE OF SPADES
ANY CARD

If one will prepare a card such as the Ace of Spades by pasting the three of diamonds on the back thereof, it is an easy matter to cause the spade Ace to change to the tray of diamonds.

DID you know that spirits could paint?

Well, here is an example of how it is artistically done.

Naturally, when spirits work they must either have darkness or something to hide their efforts.

In this instance, we will make use of a full deck of playing cards, using one card for the screen to hide the artistic endeavors of the spirits at least while they are at work.

Holding the pack in his hand, the entertainer shows a single card which he holds between his fingertips. This is lightly brushed across the face of the pack and the card which was on the deck changes to another. The card is once more shown.

Thus another spirit manifestation has taken place.

Now for the way the spirit painters work: You make use of a double-faced card prepared by carefully splitting a card in half. This is a duplicate of the card which is used as a screen.

The face of still another card is carefully separated from its back and these two thin-faced cards are glued together back to back and placed between the leaves of a heavy book until dry. Now you have a double-faced card.

For example, the ace of spades is the card which will act as the screen which keeps prying eyes from watching the spirits as they are at work painting the face of another card.

The double-faced card, which has on one side the duplicate ace of spades and on the opposite side the three of diamonds, is placed on top of the single card, the ace of spades.

The card is now brushed over the face of the pack and at the psychological moment the tricked card is left on the pack.

This changes the face of the card on the deck to the tray of diamonds.

The card remaining in hand, the genuine ace of spades, is now casually shown to be a card of the most ordinary description.

The spirits have done their work well.

By way of further explanation, let us assume that the deck is shown face upward to the audience. The ace of spades is on top. Immediately beneath this is the second ace of spades and tray of diamonds tricked card combination. Below this is, let us suppose, the ten of clubs. The performer picks up the ace of spades cards, both of them, as though they were one card and casually shows the face to the audience. Turning this over on its back so as to hide the spade ace and the ten of clubs, he passes the card lightly across the face of the deck, leaving the combination card behind. This changes the ten of clubs to the tray of diamonds (the other side of the tricked spade ace) and still permits examination of the one remaining ace of spades under cover of which the "painting" was done.

A Mental Test

THE performer informs his audience that he is about to introduce a magical feat which in reality is of the mental kind.

He patters about how strange it is that when three persons see the same accident happen, many times each one of the eye-witnesses will tell a different type of story.

Lifting up three cards, one at a time, from their places on a table, the entertainer asks that each one of the three persons memorize one of the cards, but to insure each one seeing and remembering a different card he will have each one, as they select their card,

turn his or her back after the selection is made.

This is done and the cards are replaced upon the table.

"Now I am going to ask each one of you folks to, in turn, tell me the name of the card you saw.

"You, sir," to the first assistant, "what is the name of the card you saw and have retained in your memory?"

Whatever card the gentleman saw he names, and much to his surprise the card is pointed out and turned up, and it is an entirely different one.

The same procedure is gone through with the other two, and

when their cards are turned up they also find they are wrong.

Explanation: — The trick is simple but baffling. There are six cards employed. Three are ordinary, but the other three are not only entirely different cards, but have dark material the same color as the table cover pasted onto the backs.

In each instance the bottom card is shown, but when the card is taken up to re-exhibit it, it is the top card that is seen by the assistants. The faked cards with cloth tops or backs are left in their places on the table cover.

Marvelous!

THIN WAND

COIN

SLIDE

COIN

COINS ON WAND

A really remarkable wand with which coins can be caught from the air.

PLACING imaginary bait at the end of a magic wand, the magician goes a-fishing in mid-air. But fish is not what he is after, for one after the other he catches three or more pieces of silver for the day's catch.

Method:—The wand is a thin steel rod, the end of which is slit as exaggeratedly shown in the drawing. This allows the coins after they are caught to be removed from the end of the stick and also answers the purpose of holding them in place when they reach the end of the wand. The wand can then be raised overhead without fear that the coins will slide down again.

To each coin is soldered a short piece of tube through which the rod or wand is slipped before the trick begins.

The coins are secreted in the hand and are allowed to slide along the rod one at a time. They are carried to the end by a slight throwing movement which carries them to the tip of the wand.

It is a very pretty sight to see the coins appear at the wand end and very puzzling, too, because the stick is so slender and the coins five or more times as wide.

Thought Foretold

A PACK of cards, well shuffled, is exhibited and three cards are taken from it and the balance of the deck is placed on the table.

The performer now shows the three cards slowly, and asks members of the audience to retain a visual impression of each card.

Taking up the deck, he calls for the assistance of some gentleman from the audience. Handing him the three cards, he asks him to place them, one at a time, into the pack.

The assistant is now handed the deck and asked to shuffle them well. The performer then takes the deck of cards and places them into his side coat pocket.

"What card of the three shall I produce first?" asks the magician.

The cards, one at a time, are called by various members of the gathering, and these cards are produced from the deck in the magician's pocket in the order they are named.

Secret:—The three cards, duplicates of which have been placed beforehand in the side coat pocket of the magician, are located on top of the deck and are kept there, even while a shuffle is made. This is easily done by separating the deck so that one half of the deck is larger than the other.

Then riffle together, but be careful that the top half always leaves at least three cards on top. These are the three which have been purposely put there.

The pack, which is now well shuffled, is placed for a moment on the table.

Next, the pack is picked up and as if at random the three top cards are taken off.

These are shown slowly to the audience and the request is made that these three cards be memorized.

The assistant is now called upon to replace these cards in the deck anywhere he chooses.

The rest is easy.

Into Thin Air

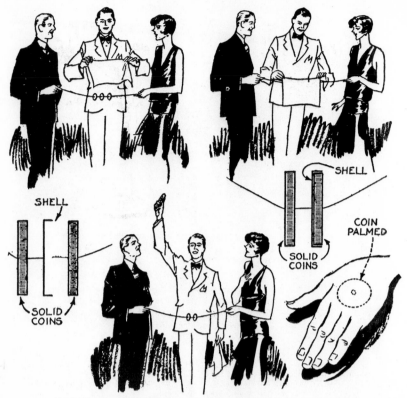

A shell coin is responsible for the effectiveness of this trick.

LADIES and gentlemen of the radio audience:

It gives me great pleasure to broadcast to you from station M-A-G-I-C a magical effect in which three coins are involved.

Sending this over the air makes me think of an appropriate title for the trick, namely, "Into Thin Air."

Listen to the various moves as I make them, and I trust my invisible audience will be able to use this little novel effect with which to mystify their friends.

I have three magical coins. (Clinks them together). They are endowed somehow or other with magical properties.

Each coin has a hole through the center to enable me to thread them on a length of string which two kind gentlemen are to hold at either end.

The three coins are now strung on the string and spaced about two inches apart.

Do you see the three coins, sir? You do? Thank you, sir.

I shall now place a colored silk handkerchief over the three coins threaded on the string. This keeps the light off them and makes the experiment more mystifying.

Pronouncing a few magical words, I take the handkerchief off and how many coins remain on the string?

Two? That is quite correct. One of the coins has by some magical means left the string. I shall take the coin out of your pocket, sir. You don't mind? There it is!

And now, my friends, I am going to explain just how you, too, can do this trick.

Later this station will broadcast by television a detailed diagram of the entire trick.

First let me make it plain that I make use of three genuine coins and a shell coin which fits snugly over any one of the real ones.

On the string I thread two real coins and the shell, placing them about two inches or so apart.

In my hand I hold another genuine coin which I slip unseen into the pocket of one of the gentlemen who so kindly steps over to assist me.

The silk handkerchief is placed over the coins on the string. Under cover of this I force the shell to slide over and fit one of the real coins.

Now all that remains to be done is to take the handkerchief away and exhibit the two remaining coins.

I next ask one of the gentlemen where the coin has disappeared to.

As he does not know, I tell him to place his hand in his pocket and hand me the coin I placed there, or I place my own hand in his pocket, if he trusts me that far, and bring into view, between my fingertips, the extra coin.

Stand by for the television transmission of the diagram to explain this trick. Tick-tick-tick!

The Sultan's Favorite

A SULTAN can have many favorites. They do not always have to be members of his harem. He often has his hobbies, even as you and I.

Magic was one sultan's favorite pastime, and so jealous was he of other conjuring enthusiasts that some years ago in a fit of frenzy and jealousy he ordered all magicians cast out of Turkey and all books relating to conjuring and kindred subjects burned.

He figured that he would have no further rivals of the art he so enjoyed.

Among the many tricks he had collected from all parts of the world and the one he performed time and again for his own amusement was the vanishing coin in a glass of water.

But his method wasn't the well-known one in which a glass disk is allowed to drop from beneath the folds of a handkerchief into a small glass of water and disappear because of its transparency. He used a method one of his former court entertainers taught him.

He would place an empty glass on a table which he used for conjuring purposes and in his right hand hold a coin. Throwing a large handkerchief over the hand and the coin, he would drop the coin into the glass. He would smile mysteriously as he heard the tinkle of the coin as it went on its downward flight.

Whisking away the handkerchief, the coin had vanished. Then smiling broadly, he would exhibit to the invisible audience his hands entirely empty. He would then produce the coin from some unthought-of place.

The Secret:—The coin and glass were unprepared. The handkerchief had a small pocket sewed into it, in which he could, under cover, slide the coin. Up his sleeve, attached to his forearm by an elastic band, was a fairly long glass tube lined on the sides

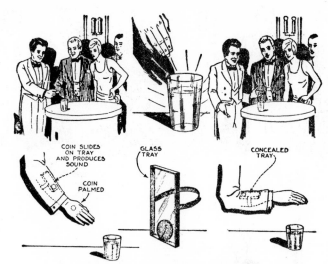

with cloth shellaced in place so the coin would not make any noise until the tube was tilted downward. This allowed the coin to hit the glass bottom and emit a sound.

When the tube is properly adjusted to the arm the illusion is perfect.

The coin was then made to reappear from any place his fancy dictated.

In this effect the performer invisibly drops a coin into a glass. The clink is distinctly heard as the coin seems to strike the bottom. Nevertheless the coin is never seen. The tray attached to the arm is responsible for the illusion.

❦ ❦ ❦ ❦ ❦

Invisible Penetration

HERE follows an unusual effect worthy of a prominent place on the magical entertainer's programme.

This is exactly what the spectators see: A glass tumbler is shown and placed on a table. A pack of cards are placed over the mouth of the tumbler.

A number of coins are shown and counted from hand to hand.

The coins are placed into the right hand one by one. Suddenly a sweeping motion of the hand is made; the hand immediately opened and the coins have vanished. At the same moment the coins are heard to pass into the glass.

The coins are then tipped out of the glass into the entertainer's hand and once again counted.

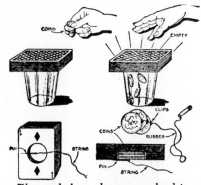

The cards here shown are glued together and provided with a suitable opening for accommodating the coins. The coins are released at the psychological moment by pulling the pin out of the way.

This is an excellent effect, and when properly practised and presented ranks second to none in the entire catagory of magic.

Secret:—The coins are vanished up the sleeve by aid of an elastic cord after being clipped together in a spring brass special clasp which holds the coins so they won't drop off when on their journey up the sleeve.

The pack of cards are all glued together with a circular opening a bit wider than the coins. The duplicate coins are placed in this compartment. These are to later make their appearance in the tumbler.

A thin piece of strong wire to which a long piece of black linen thread is attached holds the coins in place in the feked deck until the crucial moment, when the spring is pulled, either by the performer or his assistant who may be off-stage.

The Dream of King Midas.

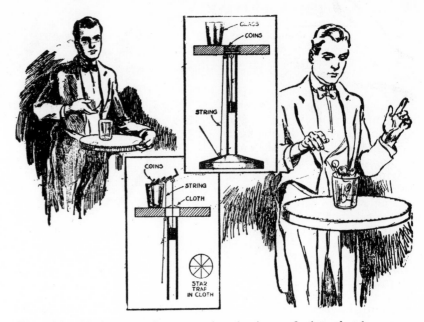

The trick table here permits a quantity of coins to fly into the glass conveniently set upon the table. Note that the string which causes the coin elevator to tip, is just the height of a glass.

REMEMBER the story of King Midas, who possessed the magical faculty of turning anything he touched to gold?

Well, this poor fellow had a dream every night, and as he lived in the days before dream books were printed, his dreams were always told to his court the next morning.

The poets and storytellers who wrote stories and made poems of everything that happened, composed poems and stories about this dream which I am about to illustrate.

King Midas, one night after worrying himself to sleep, having had a strenuous day in the stock market of that time, dreamed that he sat watching the court magician who did a trick with magical coins.

One by one these coins were tossed into air, where they disappeared, much to Midas' mystification.

A glass was shown, by the stately wonder-worker, and placed on a small table.

He asked the mighty monarch to command the coins to reappear from the air and drop into the glass at the magician's count of three.

"Are you ready, oh mighty ruler?" asked the court magician.

"Sure!" replied the King, whose touch turned all to gold.

"One — two — three!" counted the magician.

"From the air into yonder glass vessel I command the vanished coins to reappear!" ordered the King.

And suddenly the tinkling of coins was heard as the five vanished coins appeared from no-where and fell into the innocent looking-glass.

The magic man took the glass over to the King.

"Hold out your hand, your Majesty," instructed the miracle worker.

And into the outstretched hand of King Midas the magician poured the five silver coins.

The magician was a business man. He had what men of the business world call "business sense," for no sooner did the five valueless magic coins of the conjurer touch the hand of King Midas than they immediately turned to gold.

So the master of magic was richer by five golden coins.

Will someone kindly page King Midas?

The Secret:—A special type of table is required for this experiment. The drawing will clearly show how it works.

The coins are placed in a small special compartment over which is cut a small star trap in the velvet top which covers the table.

An assistant out of sight of the spectators operates the thread which in turn is connected or tied to a lead weight in the center rod of the table, enabling the hidden assistant to raise the weight which lifts the concealed plunger quickly to its highest point. A thread tied to a top piece of tin tilts the coins into the glass which has previously been placed in the proper place on the table to receive the coins.

As soon as the coins have dropped into the glass, the assistant releases the thread and the weight carries the plunger rod back to its original position through the star trap made in the cloth. The table top now looks the same as it did at the beginning of the experiment.

The five coins are vanished up the sleeve or in any manner the performer desires. One coin can be prepared by boring a hole through it and tieing a silk or wire loop to it. This loop is slipped around the thumb which can swing the prepared coin to the back or front of the right hand by a slight tossing movement. A sharp movement forward brings each coin into view where it is quickly caught at finger tips between the thumb and first finger of the right hand. Upon the passing into space of the fifth coin the looped coin may be gotten rid of in any way the performer desires.

The patter should be followed and the effect upon an audience is all that one could desire.

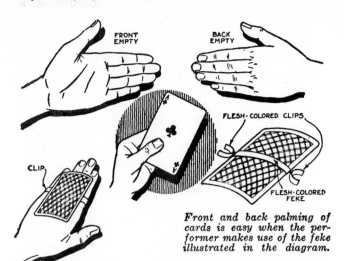

Front and back palming of cards is easy when the performer makes use of the feke illustrated in the diagram.

Card Manipulation Simplified.

SOME years ago a stage magician startled the entire magical fraternity by introducing into his act a trick wherein a card was taken into the hand and, after a series of manipulations, the card, which the spectators thought to have disappeared, suddenly made its reappearance.

This was known as the back and front pass with cards.

Magicians the world over soon copied the effect, and almost everyone spoken to among magicians claimed this sleight as their own.

The real sleight requires many years of patient practise to properly present it, so in view of this fact, I have devised a simple method which will enable the novice to do this effect.

What the audience sees: You take up a card and hold it at the fingertips of the right hand. Suddenly you seem to throw the card backward and it looks as if the hand is empty. Reversing the movement, the card is caught at the fingertips.

This time the card is thrown forward and the hand again looks to be empty.

By a continuous backward and forward movement of the hand the card seems to have vanished when suddenly the fingers seem to reach up and pluck the card right out of the air.

Employing genuine sleight-of-hand this is one of the prettiest of card manipulations, when performed by an expert.

The method we give here will quite satisfactorily bring about almost the same result.

The Simplified Way to Do It:— A flesh-colored feke made of a strip of tin about one-eighth of an inch in thickness is bent to fit the back of the hand.

To the ends of this feke is soldered two thin wire clips which enable the first and little finger to fit themselves into the same.

The feke is pasted on the back of a playing card with glue that will hold fast. This is very necessary, as the card if not properly pasted to the feke is apt to slip off and fall to the floor while the required manipulations are being made.

The illustrations will make the entire trick clear. Practise the moves before the mirror.

A double piece of metal of some springy nature can be employed for passing a group of cards, and they in turn can be produced one at a time by manipulations of the fingers in the usual way.

Egg-Straordinary

An excellent comedy trick. The magician requests the loan of a gentleman's pocket kerchief and persuades the victim to assist him with the problem. An egg is chosen from a tray, placed under cover of the pocket kerchief and struck with a hammer. The owner of the handkerchief realizes that it will never be the same, but, when the *magician shakes it by its corners it is quite intact. Secret. The Magician prepares himself with an empty egg shell and a small cloth bag attached to an elastic. Beneath cover of the kerchief the real egg is placed in the vest pocket and the blown egg and sack put under the handkerchief. It is the blown egg which is struck with the hammer.*

Magical

A cloth covered slide fits under the tray and makes possible this coin multiplying tray.

ONCE upon a time in a quiet country town lived an old banker. After amassing a huge fortune he retired and told his friends he was going to spend the rest of his days experimenting with gold and silver coins. When pressed to tell what his experiments were to be he refused to answer. "You shall see one of these days, you shall see!"

So many days passed. Weeks turned into months and months into years.

Came the dawn of a day marking on the calendars of time the passing of the fourth year of the banker's experimenting.

"Go forth and tell all my old friends, business associates and cronies that I bid them have dinner with me tomorrow evening here," ordered the banker to his faithful butler.

And so on the very next day he held a veritable feast. After cigars were lighted, the banker stood up and delivered the following speech: "Ladies and Gentlemen: I have spent the whole of my four years in a private laboratory here in this house, in this room; even the most intimate of my friends knew nothing. I have been experimenting with gold and silver coins. I have not attempted to reproduce these coins as do the makers of bogus money, but I have studied the scrolls of a number of Egyptian magicians and have learned to my satisfaction how to cause the magical duplication or multiplication of coins.

"Don't think me balmy," con-

tinued the banker, "for I am not. But that which is truth sometimes staggers the most skeptical. Now I am about to demonstrate to you my perfected method of magical multiplication. Let us go to my study."

Leading the way, the banker ushered us into a large, beautifully appointed study on the third floor of his palatial home. Seating ourselves in a semicircle, the banker continued his talk: "Now, my friends, I want you all to bear in mind that what you are about to see is but the outcome of extensive study and experimentation of many years. I have not perfected this mythical, or whatever you care to call it, device for gain. Such a thought is furthest from my mind. I have accomplished this seeming miracle only to satisfy my own curiosity. For, as psychologists tell us, the mind is the mental power house from which every vibration of thought emanates, and that furthermore, and which is more to the point, curiosity is probably a germ which has embeded itself into the brain cells of humans. The more firmly these germs cling to our brain cells the more curious the person becomes. The fairer sex must be full of these curiosity germs, eh, what?

"At any rate . . . as this is not a scientific lecture on the germs of curiosity, allow me to show you an experiment which I am pleased to call Magical Multiplication.

"I have here a small tray cut from the wood of sacred trees

which stood majestically on the high hills overlooking the sacred river of the Egyptians.

"May I ask for the loan of 6 five dollar gold pieces?"

Only two were forthcoming, so the banker went to the drawer of a nearby cabinet and took from there four other pieces of gold which were handed to various members of the gathering who were instructed to hold them until they were called for.

"Next I shall ask some one of you gentlemen to stand on the right-hand side of that table and assist me.

"Now, my dear folks, watch me very closely, as the magician always says, and the holders of the coins will kindly place them one at a time on this tray. So!

"You can all see that the six coins are on the tray. Now count them again so there will be no error after the magical multiplication takes place.

"Now you, sir, will take this handkerchief of Egyptian silk and hold two of the ends, one hand gripping each corner firmly.

"Another gentleman to assist please. You, sir. Very well. You, sir, grip fast to the other two corners.

"Now, friends, this handkerchief, held at the corners by these two gentlemen, will act as a sort of bag or hammock to hold the golden coins as I slide them off this tray into the silk.

"Now when I say go! I want you two gentlemen holding the silk handkerchief to bring your hands together so a bag is formed holding the coins. Understand?"

With these instructions the banker picked up the tray upon which rested six coins of gold and slid them off into the silk handkerchief-hammock formed by the two assisting gentlemen.

"Go!" cried the banker. Immediately the two gentlemen, following instructions, brought their hands together, thus forming a sort of bag which contained the gold coins.

The banker stepped quickly to

Multiplication

the table and, putting the tray down, picked up a thin silver rod.

Stepping to the two gentlemen he waved the rod, which in reality was the wand of King Tut's favorite court conjurer, over the contents of the handkerchief, muttering a few indistinct words of a no doubt mysterious Egyptian magical formula.

"Now, my friends, do not let your eyes play tricks with you. Originally there were how many gold coins?"

"Six," replied one of the assisting gentlemen. The other also nodded in agreement.

"Open the handkerchief," commanded the magician-banker.

This was quickly done. The remainder of the audience leaned forward in their chairs in anticipation.

"How many gold coins are there now?" asked the student of Egyptian magic.

"Twelve," exclaimed one of the startled assistants.

"The magical multiplication is complete," triumphantly cried the banker, "it is a success!"

Astonishment was clearly written across the faces of the entire company, with the exception of one man who had traveled far and wide and had seen most of the miracles one reads about in the four corners of the globe.

He was skeptical, yet puzzled.

"May I examine that tray and handkerchief?" asked the skeptical globe-trotter.

"Positively," replied the banker-magician. "Take them in your own hands, examine them well and pass them along for examination."

This was done and the globe-trotter was sorely perplexed. Said he: "I have toured this world over. I have seen the much heralded tricks of the Hindu, the Chinese and our own magicians, but I am at a loss to explain this stunt."

After the guests had ceased applauding, the two gold coins originally borrowed were returned and the banker made gifts of the remaining ten golden coins to the ladies present to prove to them that the money was genuine and not the properties of the stage magician. Thereby also proving that there are bankers who are liberal with their own funds.

Secret:—This experiment, which is simple, proves how any magical effect can be dressed up with appropriate, smooth running patter. The patter of the magical entertainer is many times his strongest asset. It isn't always the trick. It's how the trick is presented. Once you get the knack of presenting a magical problem properly, dressed in interesting patter or monologue, you have a trick that is sure to meet the approval of those before whom you have the pleasure of presenting it. The magician must learn to do two things at once. First, the trick, then to patter his way along glibly as he presents it.

This "multiplication of money" effect is simple.

Unknown to your audience, you hold a small thin wooden box covered with black velvet on all sides with one end left open. Into this box, before you start, you slide six coins. If you are a banker, use gold coins. Quarters or half dollars will do just as well.

This slide is placed beneath the tray, which in turn is covered at the bottom with black velvet or painted a dead black. The covering of the table should be of black velvet to match the covered slide. This is important.

When you borrow the six coins, or use your own as you will, you are careful not to allow the slide, which you hold pressed tightly to the under part of the tray, to be seen by the assisting party or the rest of the audience.

When the coins are placed on the tray, step to the gentlemen who hold the large silk handkerchief by the corners and allow the coins on the tray to slide into the handkerchief, together with the extra six coins contained in the hidden slide under the tray.

Have the gentlemen quickly close the handkerchief and await further orders.

Step to the table, which should be about three feet or so away from your assistants, and place the tray carefully upon it.

The necessary by-play of muttering a few magical incantations are gone through and the handkerchief is opened and the coins counted out slowly, thus proving that the magical multiplication has actually taken place.

Magnetic Hand

The illustration shows a new type of magic wand. Any ordinary magic wand may be used in constructing a device of this nature. The performer should have a good selection of magic wands, and they should all be similar in appearance, so that he can employ one or the other whenever needed, and the change in the selection of wands will be scarcely apparent. Strange as it may seem, a great many tricks may be done with wands alone. Thus we have a type of wand which defies gravity and will remain suspended in almost any position from the edge of the table, chair or book. Then there is the disappearing wand and the rising and falling

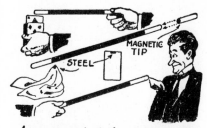

A permanent steel magnet in the wand attracts pieces of clock spring fastened to cards or to a silk kerchief. This makes a typical "magnetic" wand in name and action.

wand, and countless other styles which in themselves make a very pleasing exhibition. Here, however, we have a tip which may be added to any wand, and with which two or more interesting tricks may be added to the magician's repertoire. The metal tip of another wand can be fitted with a bar magnet of the permanent type. This causes cards specially prepared with strips of clock spring attached to their backs to cling to the wand. The magician may also put a silk handkerchief into the pocket of his assistant and withdraw it with the wand to which the silk clings. Here, affix metal to silk.

The Coin that Vanished

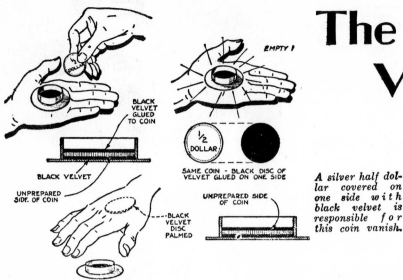

BLACK VELVET GLUED TO COIN

EMPTY!

BLACK VELVET

UNPREPARED SIDE OF COIN

1/2 DOLLAR

SAME COIN - BLACK DISC OF VELVET GLUED ON ONE SIDE

UNPREPARED SIDE OF COIN

BLACK VELVET DISC PALMED

A silver half dollar covered on one side with black velvet is responsible for this coin vanish.

A HALF dollar is borrowed from a member of the audience and placed in a small circular piece of apparatus just large enough to accomodate the coin.

A few magical words are spoken and the spectator who so kindly parted with his money is invited to look into the container and finds that his coin has vanished.

The borrowed coin is reproduced by the magical merry-maker from some unthought-of place or from the pocket of the man who assisted him and loaned him the half dollar originally.

Secret:—Some of the finest tricks in magic are simple ones. It isn't at all what the trick really is, but it does depend on how you do it.

Some magicians can take the simplest pocket trick and with the appropriate patter and misdirection make a mild sensation out of it.

The student of modern magic must learn how to present properly the effects he wishes to use in his program.

In this "Coin that Vanished" experiment, we employ a simple piece of apparatus which can very easily be made. The illustration shows a small metal circular base upon which is soldered a circle of tin about two or two-and-a-half inches in height. The circular base is covered with black velvet.

You have a half dollar, where you can get at it quickly, on one side of which is shellacked a piece of black velvet to match the circular base of the piece of apparatus.

When the coin is borrowed the date is read off to someone by the magician.

The magician exchanges the borrowed half dollar for the half dollar he possesses with the circular piece of velvet affixed to one side of it.

The borrowed coin rests near at hand for the magician, who, when he sees his chance, lets it slide into the side pocket of the gentleman assisting him.

The faked half dollar is now placed into the piece of apparatus.

Some byplay is indulged in between the assistant and the magician and finally the assistant is asked to take out his coin.

The magician then tells him that is what he gets for loaning money to people he doesn't know.

Suddenly, after the magician wants to square with him in some way the loss of the half dollar, he instructs the assistant to look in his side pocket. He does and the coin is brought to light.

The date is now verified and the assistant shakes hands with the magician, who remarks as he leads him toward his seat, "I have returned the borrowed half dollar. Would you care to sign a note for me next week?"

There is another way of doing the trick and that is to have a piece of metal just large enough to fit the apparatus, covered with velvet on one side. The coin is seen to be dropped in the box. With the disc palmed, it is a simple matter for the magician to drop it on top of the coin.

The Passing of the Phantom Coins

ONCE upon a time, so the radio announcer tells us, there was a band of counterfeiters w h o roamed the country passing out lead coins in exchange for purchases and obtaining real money in return.

The police searched high and low for these culprits but could never find out who or what they were.

One day detectives trailed them to, as they thought, their headquarters, arrested them a n d haled them into court.

On the person of one of these prisoners were found three half dollars, which, upon being tested, were found to be bogus money not manufactured by Uncle Sam's men in the mint.

These coins were held as evidence—the only bit of evidence the police could find.

Upon the day of trial the newspaper men found out that among this band was a magician who had fallen from grace . . . maybe he left the Keith time for a smaller circuit . . . at any rate nothing was said about it and the newspaper men forgot it. Proving that magicians are forgotten.

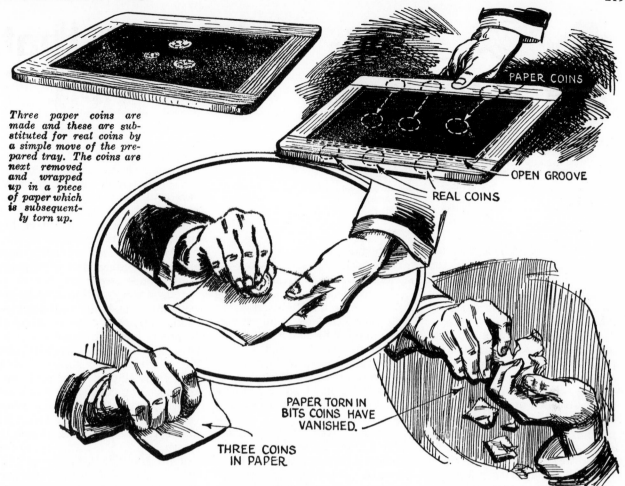

Three paper coins are made and these are substituted for real coins by a simple move of the prepared tray. The coins are next removed and wrapped up in a piece of paper which is subsequently torn up.

PAPER COINS

OPEN GROOVE

REAL COINS

PAPER TORN IN BITS COINS HAVE VANISHED.

THREE COINS IN PAPER

When the ex-magician was put on the stand, a detective told of finding the bogus coins on his person.

The magistrate, who was interested in magic, asked the man who he was and how it was he had the coins on his person. And this is the tale he told: "Your Honor . . . they found those three coins in my pocket. They are Phantom Coins. All I have to do is wrap them into a piece of paper, command them to vanish and they pass into the ether from whence they came.

"Are you sure," asked the mighty monarch of the high bench, "that you are not a passer of manufactured lead coins?"

"No, Your Honor," replied the ex-magician. "If you will allow, I will prove that we are all innocent folks, and know nothing of the charge brought against us."

"Very well," agreed the magistrate, "if you can vanish these coins as you claim I shall discharge you all."

The magistrate was a wiseacre and wanted to learn a new trick.

Borrowing a tray containing pens and pencils that was standing on the clerk's desk, the ex-magician rolled up his sleeves and asked for the loan of a piece of paper.

The judge handed him a piece torn from a pad.

The ex-magician asked an officer to hold the tray. This done, the three coins were handed him and he placed them in the center of the wooden tray.

Showing the paper on both sides he picked up the three coins with his fingertips and placed them in the paper and wrapped them up securely.

"Now, Your Honor, watch me closely, for the closer you watch the more you think!"

Holding the paper high in the air, he muttered a few magic words and thinking of his dues past due in one of the seventy-five magical societies, he quickly tore the paper into bits. The pieces torn as small as confetti fluttered to the floor—the phantom coins and his magic art had not deserted him. No trace of

the coins could be found.

"That's a great trick," applauded the magistrate, "you ought to be a traffic cop!" "That would be a wailin' job, wouldn't it?" queried the magician.

The Secret:—The tray is not what is seems. Around the edge of the tray there is an inch and a half ledge, which, when seen by the audience looks innocent enough, but to the magician this is the vital thing.

When the three coins are placed in the center of the tray, the tray is tipped to one side a trifle and from under the ledge slide three pieces of cardboard covered with silver paint. These feked coins from a short distance appear to be genuine. The real coins are tilted into the opposite ledge of the tray where they remain hidden.

The feked disks of paper are placed into the piece of paper and when this is torn into pieces, naturally you destroy the feked disks.

The coins have vanished and their passing remains a mystery.

Magical Transformation

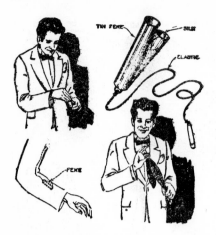

The double tin feke permits of vanishing a cigarette and appearing a silk handkerchief.

"CIGARETTES have peculiar properties," patters the magical mystifier, "Scientists tell us that the more we smoke, the more earth we dig for our final resting place.

"But be that as it may, it is with delight and satisfaction that I woo my Lady Nicotine.

"Yet . . . when one thinks of what a cigarette may contain one is ofttimes puzzled as to its contents.

"I have found thrills, satisfaction and perfect contentment in a cigarette. When I sit smoking in my den conjuring up hopes and dreams as I idly watch the smoke curl leisurely from my soothing little white paper companion, I dream of new worlds to conquer, or new modern methods of mystification with which to entertain my friends.

"The other day I discovered something very interesting."

The magician takes a cigarette from its case and lights it.

"I found that by taking a cigarette and placing it in the cupped fist of the hand (entertainer follows the various moves as he unfolds this patter) I gently move my hand so and slowly pull into view a beautiful colored silk handkerchief.

"Under cover of this movement I think of several magical phrases which makes this transformation possible.

"Upon examining my hands you can see there is nothing left of the cigarette. It has passed into the beyond smoke and all.

"You may try this on your radio when you get back home!"

Secret:—The wonderman has concealed up his sleeve a little piece of apparatus made of tin to the side of which is soldered a cone-shaped device which holds a silk handkerchief.

This apparatus is attached to the usual elastic band the other end of which is secured with a safety pin to the top of the vest armhole.

At the appropriate moment the feke is slid down into the hand. The elastic is just long enough to allow it to remain hidden until required.

It is a simple thing to get the feke into the hand and holding it in the cupped fist to push the cigarette into it and at the same time get the silk handkerchief out of the cone.

Keeping the silk bundled up in the closed or cupped fist the end is brought into view at the same time the feke containing the cigarette is allowed to slide up the sleeve.

The trick is practically all done. All that remains is to slowly, pattering all the while, bring the silk completely into view and show the hands empty . ... the magical transformation of a lighted cigarette to a silk handkerchief is completed.

Magical Jugglery

THE next effect, in itself, is not a magical experiment, although, when introduced as a bit of side play, or stage business, during the routine of a trick, is a flashy bit of jugglery with all the impression of real magic.

Take, for example, . . . a magician wishing to light a candle or a cigarette. He picks up a match and matchbox, and instead of striking the match on the side of the box, throws the box into the air and as it descends brings the match up against the box and the match ignites.

The secret is that the matchbox, although looking like the genuine article, is a solid block of wood, so camouflaged, with a label on top, and "strike" paper on the bottom and sides, that to the spectators, it looks to be all that it should be.

They never notice the fact that when you pick up the match it isn't taken from the box.

Toss the box into the air with the left hand and hold the match in the right between the fingertips.

Reach out and up toward the box as it descends in the air, striking the match against the side or bottom of the box.

The block of wood, being heavy, will give you the necessary weight, in its descent, to enable you to light the match.

Catch the box, replace it on the table, light the cigarette or candle and go on with whatever trick you were doing.

Bits of byplay, or stage business of this kind, introduced into a magical entertainment, makes it look all the more like real conjuring.

A wood block, covered to imitate a match box, makes possible this bit of jugglery.

The Cigarette from Nowhere

With this feke one can convert loose tobacco into a rolled cigarette.

FOR our next experiment in the art of magic, ladies and gentlemen . . .

We show our hands to be absolutely empty and from a tin of tobacco in the closed right hand, kept open a little to receive it, we take enough tobacco to roll a cigarette.

A few mystic words and the hand is opened, tobacco has vanished or rather magically passed into the cigarette now held between the fingers.

Where did the paper come from? Was it the work of the spirits? Who knows? But you do care . . . so we'll tell you all about this cigarette from nowhere so you can perform this trick before your friends.

Secret:—Up your sleeve (or around your waist) you have a length of elastic fastened by a safety pin to the upper edge of your vest or shirt and at the other end is attached (see drawing) a small pouch-like contrivance which acts as a bag. The top of the small pouch has a bit of whalebone to close it, or, if you would rather, use a hem arrangement inside of which is sewn a strong piece of elastic which keeps the bag closed until you are ready to use it.

On the side of the framework of the bag is a small round strip of tin or other metal to which is soldered a ring just large enough to fit and hold a cigarette.

The pouch is grasped by the right hand when you are ready to perform and the tobacco is emptied into the pouch, but to the audience it looks as if you are letting it fall into the closed fist.

Under cover of a slight rolling movement, the bag is allowed to pass up the sleeve (or around the waist) after the cigarette is slipped out of the ring and kept in the hand until the psychological moment.

Now all one has to do is to show the cigarette that came from nowhere.

Cigarette tricks are always popular and this effect to the man who knows a few tricks will prove a mystery.

Patter could be arranged around this trick using the idea that, due to so many blindfold tests, it is hard to really tell these days which cigarette is worthwhile and the best way to convince yourself, without reading the many tales which appear in the advertising columns of your local paper is to just call on the spirits to make them for you.

The Glass and Coin Trick

This is a novel way of presenting a rather simple trick which nevertheless is puzzling.

A PIECE of colored felt is placed upon an unprepared table, a drinking glass and a coin in the nature of a half dollar or other similar coin, constitute the necessary apparatus. Beneath the cover of a paper cylinder, a drinking glass is placed mouth down, and both are then put directly over the coin. The paper cylinder is removed and the coin will be found to have vanished. The cylinder of paper is again replaced, the glass once more lifted, and the coin reappears. After several demonstrations of this strange reappearance and disappearance, both coin and tumbler are passed for examination. Students of conjuring will appreciate the fact that this particular feat of inspection has been quite impossible in other forms of this trick. A disk of felt corresponding in nature and color to the felt pad used on the table, fits over the mouth of the glass. To the under side of the felt disk a needle is fixed. This needle serves to catch into the felt pad and pulls the disk away from the glass when the glass can be examined.

The Clinging Cigar

TWO men met the other day on the street and started discussing magical experiments.

One told of a magician who did all kinds of magical manipulations with cigars and cigarettes.

"I have a good stunt I'll show you one of these days," said one of the fellows.

"What's it all about?" asked his friend who was always on the lookout to learn a new trick.

"It's a trick with a cigar," replied the other. "Let's get a couple of cigars and in the store, if no one is around, I'll show the stunt to you."

So they entered a cigar store and bought cigars.

"Have a light?" asked one of them of the other.

"No. Not just yet. Here's the stunt."

So saying, he took the cigar and made a few passes over it. "Now watch this one closely."

The cigar was placed, before the magician made his hypnotic passes, on the palm of the hand. The hand was held with the palm upward. Slowly he turned his hand around and the cigar remained clinging to the palm of the hand.

Turning back his hand, he took the cigar, and tore the band

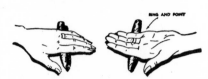

A small pin secured to a ring causes the cigar to cling to the fingers.

off. Turning his hand over with the palm toward the ground he balanced the cigar carefully on the back of his fingers.

Slowly he turned the hand over and the cigar remained on the back of the fingers, much to the surprise of the onlooker.

"That's great," exclaimed his friend, "how do you do it?"

"Very simple," replied the other, "all you have to do is to make a few mesmeric passes over the cigar . . ."

The two left the cigar store and walked up the street.

"How did he do that trick?" asked one of the clerks.

"Don't know, but it was a good one, all right!" answered the proprietor.

And again an exceedingly in-

teresting yet simple effect in legerdemain aroused interest.

Secret:—The cigar is ordinary, but what they did not notice was the plain ring the conjurer wore.

This ring had a needle point, projecting about a quarter of an inch, soldered to the center of the ring.

This could be switched by the fingers from the front to the back of the hand with very little trouble.

When the cigar was first placed on the palm of the hand it was placed on the projecting needle and pressed home. Slowly the passes were made, and without haste the hand was turned over. Naturally the cigar remained in place.

The ring was next moved around the finger so the needle point was in the back. Quickly the cigar was pressed home and more passes were made in true hypnotic style. The hand was once more slowly turned over. Again the cigar exhibited the uncanny power of clinging to the fingers of the back of the hand.

It was mystifying, because the fellow who did the trick knew how to present it.

Make up a finger ring with the needle point and try this effect on your friends.

Pigeons from Hat

STRING

LOAD

In this production the hat, unprepared and borrowed, is placed upon the table as indicated by the dotted lines. During the act the string from the load is attached to the rim of the hat. The hat is then tipped to show its inside, which, of course, is empty. Then the hat is rested upon its rim and again tipped, but in the reverse direction showing the crown. This in-

nocent movement carries the load into the hat automatically and now the production can be made. Live birds are easily carried in a dull-black silk-bag with a draw-string top. The bag is easily gotten rid of by dropping it into a servante. Loads may be picked up from different parts of the stage by duplicating the movement with the same hat.

Out of the Air

IN this effect, the atmosphere plays an important part and the "spirits" make a cigarette which proves to be not of phantom variety but of your favorite brand and needs no blindfold to enjoy.

The magician calls attention to the fact that there are many more brands of cigarettes manufactured this year than last.

No matter what your tastes are there are as many different kinds of cigarettes as there are different brands of perfume for milady's use.

"It is so simple to conjure a cigarette from the air when one wishes to indulge in a smoke," says the magician.

"I invented this idea because my lady friend who would rather reach for a cigarette than a sweet, is rather forgetful, and leaves her cigarette case filled with her favorite brand of smokes at home, on the table, when she goes out with me. She declines one of mine even though they are named after that illustrious young flier Lucky . . . but you know all about that.

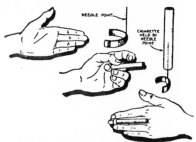

A flesh colored feke with pin soldered to it will hold a cigarette until ready for production

"I invented this trick because the brand she smokes is hard to get in the average store.

"Now when she wants a cigarette I just do so and so and there I have the brand milady loves to smoke!"

Saying this, the magician reaches out and grasps a cigarette out of the air. This he throws to some charming lady member of the gathering.

The secret:—It is so simple that it cannot fail. You can catch a cigarette out of the air, on the platform, stage, or in a drawing room.

And this is the way in which it is done. The drawing shows

a small half-ring piece of tin, painted flesh color, to which is soldered a needle or pin.

This feked piece of property is placed around the top of the finger of the right hand with the pin at the back of the finger.

The hand is held straight out with the palm toward the gathering, and when the actions of catch are gone through, the feke is brought toward the front by bending the finger to which the feke is attached. The other fingers of the hand then grip the cigarette.

This is done so quickly the eye cannot follow it. It really looks as if the cigarette was actually picked out of the air.

In these tricks you must bear in mind the fact that the audience are always held in a state of suspense, because you as the magician have an advantage over them, due to the fact that they do not know what you are going to do.

When you arrive at the climax of a trick it heightens their suspense and turns it into surprise if you do the trick right.

The Disappearing Lady

BELOW we see a very interesting method of making your female assistant disappear. The effect is as follows. A cloth is laid over an undraped table and the

lady lies down upon the same. The front and back ends of the cloth are then raised clear of the stage and the outline of the girl's body can still be seen through the

cloth. A shot is fired and the cloth collapses and drops to the stage floor, the girl having completely disappeared from mid-air. The girl rolls into a trap.

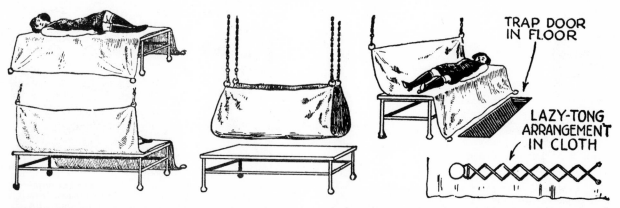

The girl lies down on an undraped couch which has been covered with a cloth provided with rings as shown. The front is raised and then the back follows. Apparently the girl is still within the cloth. As a matter of fact she

disappeared into the trap. The lazy-tong arrangement in the cloth makes the audience believe that the girl is still concealed within the suspended sack. This tong is collapsed when the cloth is permitted to fall.

A group of matches glued together on the bottom of a box, permits this change from a full to empty box.

The Demon's Matches

THERE are many tricks with matches. When you are about to do a trick in which the use of matches is concerned, the people watching you seldom if ever suspect that there is any sort of trickery connected with the experiment. This is caused by the many tricks they have either read in other issues of Popular Magic or have seen demonstrated by acquaintances.

This leaves the magician with a sort of open field. His friends do not expect another match trick so are quite unprepared for the effect they are about to witness.

But no matter how much things are on your side, be sure and always have uppermost in your mind the magical caution, that whatever you do, do it well!

Effect:—The entertainer offers a cigarette to a friend and then places a cigarette in his mouth and lights it with a match he takes from an ordinary (so they believe) penny match box. Casually exhibiting the box, the spectator sees it is of the ordinary sort and full of matches.

Closing the box, the entertainer excuses himself for not offering the other fellow a light. So he naturally re-opens the box and offers it to the spectator who in turn is about to take a match when to his surprise he sees that the box is empty.

Pretending he doesn't know why his friend is looking so astonished he closes the box and asks the fellow what is wrong.

When told there are no matches in the box he but a moment ago saw filled, the entertainer once more opens the box and hands the spectator a match from what the spectator can see is a full box of matches.

Nonchalantly the entertainer replaces the box of matches in his pocket and the talk drifts off into other channels, but the victim of the trick doesn't forget so easily. He asks for the match box, which the entertainer hands him and tells him he may keep it if he cares to.

Then watch the facial expression of the other fellow while he gets busy examining the box of matches!

The secret:—Prepare a match box by placing a false bottom in it. To this false bottom is pasted a number of matches to make it look as if the box was filled with matches.

One or two real matches are placed beside those pasted in so they can be used when the opportunity presents itself.

On both sides of this box (top and bottom of the flat sides) labels corresponding with one another are pasted.

In your pocket you have a duplicate box filled with matches.

You open the box and allow the gentleman to catch sight of the matches. Offer him a cigarette and place your own cigarette in your mouth. Take a match from the tricked box and absent-mindedly light your own cigarette. He will not overlook the fact that you did not proffer him a light first.

Now close the box and under cover of your remark, "I am sorry," reverse the box in your hand and open same and hold it out to him so he can, as he thinks, take a match.

Notice his expression when he sees that the box is empty, nonchalantly close and reverse the box, then reopen it under cover of the remark, "What is the trouble?"

Take out a match, which you light on the box, and hand to him, quickly placing the box back into your pocket, immediately bringing into view the real box which you hand him with the remark, "Here, keep these, if you care to!"

Shooting Through a Glass

HERE is illustrated a new method of apparently shooting through a sheet of plate glass, and breaking a tumbler on the other side of it. It will be noticed that on the table an ordinary drinking glass is to be seen. In front of this a sheet of plate glass is held by a suitable holder. The magician picks up an automatic revolver and fires directly at the tumbler, which is seen to burst.

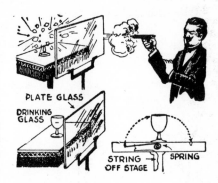

PLATE GLASS

DRINKING GLASS

STRING OFF STAGE   SPRING

The plate glass remains undamaged. The effect is produced by table arranged with a spring trigger as illustrated. At the end of the spring a pointed weight is found, which springs when released by the assistant, comes up and breaks the glass tumbler. The revolver is loaded with blank cartridges. The spring flies into a groove provided for it in the top of the table.

A resined string passing through a keyhole to the hand of another assistant is put across the strings of the violin and produces the wierd music. Note weight at free end of string.

Ghostly Music

SO-CALLED spiritualistic effects are always of interest. Many are the tricks of the fraudulent mediums.

You have heard of tambourines playing, bells being rung, and horns being blown by unseen hands. Spirit hands are the explanations of the mediums.

In my travels I have been present at sittings given by the best of them, and have sat and held hands in the circles of the worst of them. They are all of one ilk. The cleverest are but little better than the crudest.

Not so long ago I demonstrated to members of the New York press, at a séance held in the office of the *Science and Invention* magazine, that the main tricks of the mediums could be duplicated by the aid of wireless. I attended a seance several weeks thereafter in which the following trick was used to convince the believers that there *was* such a thing as ghostly music.

A plain wooden table was standing in a small bare room. An old violin was handed around for inspection and was placed near the center of the table. We were now ushered to another part of the room where we were to listen for the manifestations of musical spirits.

Listening carefully, we soon heard strains of ghostly music.

The ghostly strain seemed to impress the followers of the medium greatly.

On word from the medium, a number of us rushed to the table, but a quick glance convinced me that the violin had not been disturbed from its resting place and, as far as the spirits were concerned, that naturally was laughable. Now let me tell you how to get ghostly music:

Any kind of string instrument will do for this experiment, but a violin will be most suitable. Secure also a well-resined thread.

On one end of the thread tie a small lead weight just heavy enough to allow it to be easily raised by the thread when pulled by the hand of a hidden assistant. The weight must carry the thread downward and across the strings of the violin without disturbing the violin from its resting place.

The end of the thread is carried across the room to a doorway opposite, and then through the keyhole of this door.

Upon entering the room the thread with weighted end is secretly held in the hand of the medium. He is the last to leave the room, and during his brief stay places the thread across the strings of the violin.

When all have retired to the far end of the room and are intently listening, the assistant, who has watched the proceedings through the keyhole, slowly draws up the string and gradually lowers it. This is what causes the ghostly hands to mysteriously swing a soft bow lightly across the strings!

Upon returning to the table the medium gets the weight and thread out of the way.

Psychic Messages

In this effect, the trick known as the "one ahead" method of reading is described.

"I AM not so fortunate as to be able to collect for this next effect five dollars a minute from gullible, misguided people who believe in spirits," patters the psuedo medium, "but I will try and give you, ladies and gentlemen, my conception of how spirit message readers work.

"There are many different methods, and as I am unable to depend upon twenty or more confederates who mix with you and pump information from the writers of messages, I will demonstrate that I am able to read the messages you will write as well as give answers in keeping with your thoughts.

"I do not hear spirit voices here and there because you are not spiritualists who would believe such ordinary commonplace impositions, nor do I claim any supernatural powers.

"You would laugh at me if I were to claim any sort of spirit aid, for which I wouldn't blame you. But bear this cold fact in mind, there are thousands of intelligent people who sit in large halls for hours listening to the smooth voice of a spirit message giver who offers tidy sums of money to anyone proving he is either a guesser or tampers in any way with the messages.

"Truth is, these faking clowns use the most simple of systems, an assistant gathering the messages and giving the required information to the 'spirit reader' via notes in lead pencil on the ends of envelopes.

"I use no such methods. I haven't the time nor the staff necessary. I do this message reading in a spirit of mystification and fun. I am not a spiritualist, but a performer who will do my best to mystify and entertain you.

"I shall proceed first to distribute a number of slips of paper among you." (This is done.)

"I wish you to write any short message you desire answered or the name of some friend or relative who has passed away on your slips; sign them with either your full name or initials, fold them any way you care to, and place them into this hat as I pass among you.

"Now, sir, will you kindly mix these billets or messages in this hat I hold? Thank you, sir."

Taking a slip from the hat, he holds it unopened to his forehead, reads what is written thereon and gives a suitable answer to it.

The spectator who wrote the question in each instance admits, upon being questioned by the entertainer, that the medium is right.

After each question the medium says: "You do not know me, sir. Nor could I have received from anyone else that thought."

The entertainer continues to read each of the messages in the same manner, leaving an audience completely mystified and badly puzzled as to the way and means employed.

Secret:—This is an excellent effect and much in use by so-called spirit message reading mediums who falsely lay claim to supernatural means of accomplishing an effect which is nothing more than a simple conjuring trick.

The entertainer has a secret assistant seated among the spectators who writes a certain name and message, as prearranged between them, before the entertainment begins.

This "planted" message is so folded by the assistant that the performer will have no difficulty in locating it among the rest of the messages in the hat.

The medium begins by placing the hat containing the messages on a small table which stands in front of him. He takes out one of the folded slips which he knows to have been written by a member of the audience. This he pretends to mentally read, but in reality he reads the prearranged message and name from the slip the assistant wrote.

He does not open the message in his hand until after he has read it, and after he has given a suitable answer.

He then opens the message he held in his hand as if to verify that he was right, but in reality to read and memorize the question actually written on that slip of paper.

Taking the next slip from the hat he pretends to read that one, but mentally again he is reciting from memory the message and name he has just learned.

The remaining messages are read in this same way, leaving the original prepared message, written by the assistant, until the last. This trick is also known as the "one ahead" method of sealed message reading, and is a most worthy effect when properly presented.

At the end of the question reading the entertainer passes out the hat containing the messages, as there is no evidence now remaining to give away the trick.

In the hands of a capable performer this is one of the most mystifying spirit effects known; for its very simplicity it is unfathomable by the average audience.

In my forthcoming work of Spirit Exposés I shall expose a number of other methods, including the *modus operandi* of seeming later-day miracles that have mystified scientific investigators the world over.

Spirit World Messages

Unique tricked envelope gives "spirit" answer to question sealed in it.

SEVERAL persons of your audience are handed blank visiting cards and pencils and asked to write some kind of a message to someone who has passed into the Spirit World.

This is done and the cards are placed in envelopes and sealed.

The spirits are called upon to answer the questions and when the envelopes are cut open with a pair of shears the answers are found, written in a shaky handwriting, in reply to each of the questions asked.

The secret:—The envelopes are double—*i. e.*, a front or face of another envelope is carefully trimmed and pasted to the face of a whole one. Between the faces, the answer, written on a card, has been placed. The real card the spectators wrote upon, is securely sealed in the envelope and when the side of the tricked envelope is cut open by the entertainer he takes care that the card with the answer is taken out.

The envelopes are tossed aside out of reach of the folks present.

Work this effect up well with

The lower left hand illustration shows how the envelope is prepared to produce this unique spirit message.

appropriate pattering of the spirit message about which one hears and about fraudulent spirit mediums and so on.

* * * * *

The Hypnotic Cane

A WALKING-STICK is mesmerized and placed on the underpart of the hand where it remains levitated.

A member of the audience is requested to step up and take the cane from the hand.

Secret:—This effect is not a trick in itself but one of those little bits of byplay introduced into the performance of a magical entertainer.

The secret lies in the use of a finger-ring which has a small

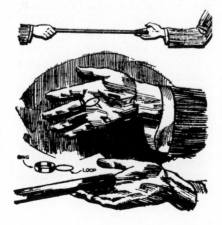

loop of thin wire attached to it.

The illustrations will make clear just how the cane is placed through the wire loop and how it remains suspended from the hand. Leverage plays a part in this interlude.

It is only for effect that the magician asks some member of the audience to step up and take the cane from his hand.

The loop attached to a ring is for the insertion of a wand or cane to produce levitation.

By a series of jerks on the silk thread, the assistant off stage codes the name of the color of the handkerchief to the performer's assistant on the stage. She, even though blindfolded correctly calls the name of the color held up.

Color Telep-athy

MIND reading in all its many forms and branches will remain as the highest and most sensational type of stage, club or parlor entertainment ever presented.

It is sensational and mystifying to watch and ponder over the ways and means by which the stage performer and his charming assistant are able to read your messages or thoughts and give your name and address.

Scientific minds have agreed that it is by far more thrilling, sensational, mystifying and puzzling when the mind reader steps before his audience and without the aid of the thousand-and-one devices, signals and means the mind reader and his assistant can resort to, and single-handed read the innermost thoughts of people he has never before laid eyes on. But *a la* Kipling, that is another story.

Simplified methods of presenting mind reading, thought transmission, and mental telepathic effects before audiences which have appeared in my other two volumes of *Popular Magic* have been used time and again by various professionals as well as hundreds of amateur performers.

In this book I give several methods of mind reading, which anyone with but little if any practise can do.

This is an effect that when properly put over will mystify a gathering anywhere, and it is one of the simplest of effects possible.

What the audience sees: The performer steps to the footlights or toward the audience and tells of the miracles performed by mental telepathy, stressing the point that when two minds are in complete sympathy, the results obtained have astounded and baffled the most scientific minds the country over.

After his brief talk his charming assistant is introduced

The lady is securely blindfolded and is led by the performer to a chair a few feet back of the footlights.

"I have here a number of colored silk handkerchiefs," says the mind reader. "Madame Marion is securely blindfolded and it is impossible for her to see. Yet by transmission of thought she will be able to call the colors of the various handkerchiefs as I hold them up."

He now mixes the silk handkerchiefs up and lays them on the table and slowly, one by one, holds them up, skipping from here to there and several times trying to catch the madame, he repeats on the color he holds up.

The madame is absolutely unable to see, and as there is no spoken or verbal code employed, how does this miracle lady tell the different colors? Does she sense them? The magician can permit any member of the audience to hold the kerchiefs.

The Secret:—Mystifying as it may seem, it is one of the simplest of mind-reading effects.

There is a hidden assistant in the wings. He not only carefully watches what goes on at the table where the magician stands, but holds a black thread which, invisible to the eyes of the spectators out front, is tied to the thumb of the lady on the stage. They have a prearranged set of signals. For example: One jerk of the thread means a red handkerchief is held up; two tugs, a blue handkerchief; no jerk, none, and so on. Say six silk handkerchiefs are used. There must be six colors to correspond with the six tugs on the thread. The medium does not have to immediately answer, for a slight hesitation impresses the audience with the difficulty of the experiment which can only be explained (?) by mind reading or mental telepathy!

Hark Ye, Spirits!

SPIRITS play many pranks. Some folks have the nerve to claim they can communicate with them, at so much a minute in real money. The laughable part is that other folks believe them. Sensible people laugh at them.

Spirits are blamed for the pranks and so-called phenomena some of our wooden-headed scientists claim they have witnessed and cannot explain.

Be that as it may, here's a stunt the folks may attribute to members of the spirit world.

Draw four marks with a piece of chalk on a table. Show both your hands and explain to the spectators that you will try and pass the chalk marks through the table, to, if the experiment is a success, your right hand palm.

Show both of your hands once more and have someone act as a committee and examine the underside of the table to assure the spectators that there are no marks or clues there.

Place your right hand under the table, with your palm open.

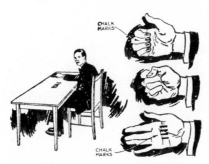

Note how chalk marks are transferred to the palm when hand is closed.

Wait a second for effect, and then strike the chalk marks on the top of the table three times. Bring up your hand from under the table and exhibit it to the audience, who discover the three spirit marks thereon.

This can be repeated several times, but after each spirit marking clean your hand with a handkerchief and have the under portion of the table examined to convince the skeptical ones.

The Secret:—Take a piece of fine-grained sandpaper or a nail file and run it across the fingernails of the right hand. You can use either hand you choose. Put a chalk mark lengthwise on each of the fingernails.

When you place your hand underneath the table close it tightly into a fist, bringing a bit of pressure to bear on the fingers. This transfers the chalk marks to the fleshy part of the hand similar to the marks already put on the table-top. All there is left to do is to bring the hand up from under the table.

Second Sight

THE entertainer leaves the room after asking someone to hide an object.

The entertainer is now recalled and, picking one of the guests to mentally guide him, he starts around the room in a wide circle. Slowly the circle narrows circle, finally locating the article.

Muscle readers have successfully accomplished this test, but that kind of work takes time and practise. Here is the way to do this stunt quickly: Attach to the hand of one of the guests, who is a confederate, a short piece of black silk. As soon as the entertainer comes into the room he grasps the other end of the thread and after a bit of byplay seems to lead the fellow to the hidden or selected object. But in reality the performer is following the lead of the confederate, who leads the entertainer by a series of prearranged jerks of the thread.

Hat of Mystery

'YOU have all heard of the house that Jack built. Well, this is the hat that - mystery built. And I am going to tell you how.

his daily stroll around the house.

"One day one of the shopkeepers in the village asked the servant who he was and where he came from.

with his servant and they erected on the village green several nickel-plated tables and demonstrated magic.

I purchased the best trick from the mystery maker's servant after the master had passed across the border."

So speaks the magician and here is the effect of the trick: A high hat is shown to be empty and placed on a small table quite close to the spectators.

The magical entertainer continues to patter about magic seeds and pretends to sprinkle some of these into the hat.

Soon, from the interior of the hat, into which his hand reaches, he takes out one or two live pigeons or doves, followed by a number of colored silk handkerchiefs and yards and yards of ribbon.

Again the hat is shown to be empty, and more magic seeds are sprinkled in it, and out comes hundreds of yards of various colored paper until the table is piled high with it.

Secret:—The hat is not as innocent as it looks. About four or five inches from the lid is a black painted tin false bottom which has a label pasted on and looks, from a short distance, like the genuine thing. The tin feke has a loose-flap arrangement which is kept in place by a small hinge. In the hat is loaded or placed the doves, the ribbon and the paper streamers which make their appearance in good time.

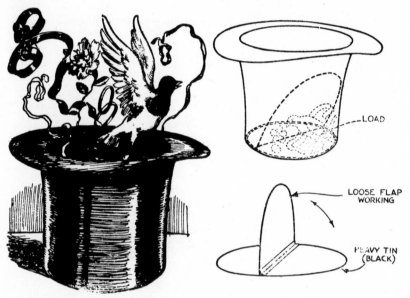

A loosely working flap in a hat enables the performer to repeatedly show the hat empty and in the interim between such demonstrations, produce a varied load.

"Once upon a time, as the fairy tales of old would begin, there lived a mysterious old man in a ramshackle house high up on the top of a hill. Folks wondered who he was and what he did for a living. He had an old servant who used to hobble to the nearby village every day for supplies; but the master was seen only now and then when he could be observed by anyone with a pair of good eyes, taking

"The servant told him that his master was an old-time conjurer who lived among his magical treasures and mysteries.

"Soon after this a fete was to be held in the village square and the shopkeeper who was on the entertainment committee sent word to the old magic master inviting him to come down and do a few tricks for them.

"In the afternoon of the celebration the old man appeared

The Sphere Dissolves!

A SMALL red ball is shown and tossed into the air a few times, when suddenly the performer shows his hands to be empty—the little red sphere has mysteriously melted into the atmosphere!

Secret:—Get a small red, or any other colored, wooden ball. Push a pin about two-thirds of the way into the side, then with a pair of cutting pliers cut off

the head of the pin and file it to a point. Bend the pin over until it almost lies flush with the ball itself.

Tossing the ball upward into the air several times misdirects the eyes on the third tossing movement, which to the spectators seems as if the ball is tossed again, but what really happens is the ball is hooked to the right trouser leg and the

hands make the upward movement.

This move is very deceptive and the impression is created that the ball has disappeared.

A sudden downward sweep, unhitching the ball quickly, bringing the hand with the ball up. Now allow the sphere to slide to the fingertips and the ball has reappeared! It only takes a moment to construct this trick.

The Mystery Box

A BOX about ten inches square is shown to be empty and placed on a small skeleton stand table upon which rests a large silk handkerchief, a magic wand and a large carpet needle, through the eye of which runs a length of ribbon about twenty inches long.

A lady's ring is borrowed and shown around.

A handkerchief is now placed over the left hand of the magician and the ring is placed on it. The handkerchief is folded up and placed in the keeping of a member of the gathering for safekeeping.

The assistant then carries the table down close to the footlights and retires.

The performer asks if some one in the audience happens to have several oranges or lemons with them, remarking: "Other magicians try to borrow money. I only want to borrow several oranges or lemons."

Finally, unable to make the necessary loan of fruit, he calls to his assistant to bring out a tray of lemons or oranges.

The assistant comes out carrying a tray on which are several oranges or lemons.

Picking up one of the lemons, he holds it at the extreme fingertips after showing it all around.

Taking the carpet needle, he passes it through the fruit and removing the needle, he draws the string on either side to equal lengths.

Next, placing the fruit in the box, which he once more shows to be empty, he threads the two ends of the string (the fruit at the center) through two holes on either side of the box.

Requesting the assistance of two charming young ladies, he allows each one of them to stand on the platform or stage holding the ends of the string which passes through the holes in the box.

Stepping to the spectator holding the ring in the handkerchief,

he asks that party if the ring is still safe.

Upon the spectator assuring him it is, he grasps one corner

The slit cut in the lemon allows for the insertion of the ring. The fruit is then threaded and the ring found within the fruit when this is cut open.

of the handkerchief and whisks it out of the assistant's hand.

The handkerchief is empty and the ring has disappeared.

Picking up the lemon from the box, the ends of string still held by the assistants, he cuts the lemon in half and the borrowed ring is found to be strung on the string.

Pulling the ends of the string through the box, he holds them and carries the ring to the owner, requesting that he or she kindly take the ring from the string.

Explanation:—This is a pretty effect and will puzzle your audience. Keep in mind the fact that the magician must act the part he is playing.

The secret is simple. Follow the moves carefully and you will grasp it quickly.

The handkerchief used has a ring sewn into either a corner or the hem. This is the ring the spectator holds. The other ring is dropped on the table where

your assistant gets it when he carries the table down toward the footlights or edge of the platform. He then walks off stage.

Back-stage he has a lemon or orange with a slit already made of about half the width of the fruit. Into this slit he slips the borrowed ring.

Bringing out the tray of lemons or oranges (it is a good idea to one time use lemons and the next time oranges) the prepared one is on top for the magician to grasp.

Knowing the slit is half-way through, the magician passes the needle through the center where the assistant has, on the outside of the fruit placed a small mark, thus threading the ring on the string.

All there is left to do is to play the trick up, vanish the ring by jerking the handkerchief out of the spectator's hand, and finding the ring on the string upon cutting the fruit.

Follow the effect carefully and you will have no trouble in presenting another baffler for the folks out front.

"Goodness Gracious Me!"

INVITING his friends into his den of magic, a magician friend of mine puzzled the guests with the following effect.

Here is a picture which changes its scenes whenever you desire.

On the walls were a number of paintings. But he called particular attention to a beautifully hand-painted seascape which had the place of honor on a side wall.

One young lady with artistic talent would not take her eyes off the seascape.

"I'm going to paint things like that this summer," remarked the lady, "while I am on my vacation."

"Study it well," answered the magician, attracting her attention from the frame for a second, "that was painted with a magical brush."

"Tut, tut," replied the young lady, "who did paint it, anyway? Turning once again to the painting, she was heard to sharply ejaculate: "Goodness gracious me!"

The guests turned and looked at her in surprise. What had happened?

Crowding about her, they asked question after question. She was speechless and the more questions the blanker grew the expression on her face. Finally she pointed a shaking finger at the frame which a moment ago held the seascape she had admired.

The guests, too, were puzzled. Did their eyes deceive them or what?

"Look!" cried the magician, pointing out of the window.

They looked, but saw nothing except the trees swaying in a gentle breeze. Looking back at the painting on the wall, the seascape was back in its frame.

The picture of the high mountain country had vanished.

Suddenly they all broke out into laughter.

Anything was to be expected in this den. For the moment they had forgotten their host was a magician, and they were in his den of mystery.

Secret:—Behind the frame and picture the mystery monger had rigged up a roller curtain contrivance. Upon pulling a string the seascape in the frame rolled down and out of view and a painting of the mountainous country made its appearance. Again releasing the catch on the framework, the mountains disappeared and the sea view once more came into view.

The mystery picture is well worth the time and trouble it takes to build it. Work it on your friends and watch the mystified expression that comes over their faces.

As Ye Sow!

THE performer brings forward two large pieces of stiff colored cardboard and a box with glass sides.

His charming assistant stands in the audience and is handed the glass box to hold. Stepping up the aisle a bit, the magician hands the blue piece of cardboard to one of the spectators and requests him to roll it into a cornucopia as he is doing. The magician, who has retained, say, the red piece of cardboard, rolls his into a cone and, stepping quickly down to his assistant, taps the cornucopia and a shower of red confetti falls from the cardboard cone into the glass receptacle.

Opening the red cornucopia, he shows it to be entirely empty.

Stepping to the gentleman who holds the blue cardboard cone, he takes it from him and holds it in his hand, and pretends to scatter magic seeds into the cone on his way to where the assistant stands.

Gently tapping the cone, a shower of blue confetti is emptied into the glass box held by the assistant. Blue cardboard is unrolled and shown empty.

Secret:—When rolling the red cardboard into a cornucopia the conjurer secretly introduces a packet of red confetti from the special pocket in the left side of his coat.

When he takes the blue cornucopia rolled into shape by the obliging gentleman on the way toward the assistant he quickly loads the packet of blue confetti.

The confetti, being done up in tissue paper, only a slight pressure is necessary to break the paper and pour the confetti.

In pouring the confetti from the cones, the paper falls into the receptacle, where it may be crumpled up by the assistant.

It is optional with the entertainer whether he uses one or two packets of confetti in this experiment. If cleverly done, this trick is spectacular.

The Bell and Box Seance

THE talk turns to the spirit worker and spiritualistic experiments. The entertainer tells of some of the effects which fraudulent mediums offer to believers as genuine spirit phenomena.

"To prove there are no such things as genuine spirit mediums and the so-called phenomena they may claim to, I shall introduce what a certain spirit worker claims is a test to prove he is possessed with supernatural powers." So saying, the entertainer starts by exhibiting a small wooden box about fourteen inches in depth, with a cover hinged to the back.

He then shows a small bell with a handle of black wood.

The patter of the magic man continues: "As the spirits always work better in the dark, I shall place this bell in the box and stand the box on this chair.

"The lights will be dimmed a bit so that you, ladies and gentlemen, will be able to watch for the spirits who may not appear if this stage is too well lighted.

"Now I want to introduce you to my spirit code. One for 'yes,' two for 'no,' and no commotion in the box for doubtful."

As the magician explains the one for "yes," the bell in the box sounds once, for "no" the bell becomes agitated twice.

"I am ready for the question," states the pseudo medium. "Call them out to me one at a time, please."

One lady wants to know if she will go to Europe this summer. The bell in the box answers "yes." In this manner a number of questions are asked and answered, spirit-like, by the bell in the box.

Finishing the performance, the bell is taken out of the box and shown, together with the box itself.

Secret:—The box is quite unprepared, and the only preparation the bell requires is that a black wire hook extends about half an inch halfway down the wooden handle.

Across the stage is extended a thin, strong piece of silk thread, one end fastened to the right of the stage about six feet up on the wall, and the other end of the thread is passed through a small screw eye on the opposite end of the off-stage portion with the end trailing down and hooked to the right-hand pocket of the magician's trousers.

When the manifestations are about to begin the magician's hand is brought into contact with the thread and he does the work of the spirits.

When the bell is shown it is quickly hooked to the thread extending across the stage, and the trick is ready.

The cover of the box should work loosely and will not interfere with the spirits, who are given more or less credit for the answers. The thread can later be removed.

Invisible Transportation

In the diagram above the method of making an object pass from one hat on one side of the stage, to another hat on the opposite side of the stage, is clearly illustrated. The magician drops a watch or other object into one hat, taking care that it is hooked to the thread. Under cover or his body the watch is then transported to the other hat.

Handkerchief Production

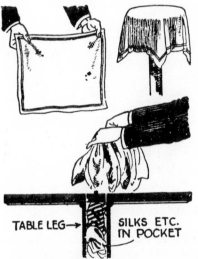

In the diagram illustrated above the magician employs a unique end table, which contains a pocket in its single supporting leg. Silks are pushed down covering the hole. Then he places one silk kerchief over the table and grasps it in the center, he pulls the load away with him and produces it.

Water Pitcher Load

A pitcher of water is seen standing in a wash basin as illustrated above. Water is poured from the pitcher and immediately thereafter a rabbit, flags and silks are produced from the basin. No table traps are used. Notice that the pitcher contains a compartment in the bottom which houses the load. The water is poured outside of the compartment.

Silence and Numbers

THIS is a mind reading experiment which is simplicity itself, yet very mystifying to those who do not know it.

This is another effect in which the histrionic ability of the entertainer will count.

"I shall endeavor, ladies and gentleman, to attune my mind with yours. I shall be the medium, who, through the transmission of thought waves and with not a word spoken after the experiment is once started, will receive a mental impression of the thought that will be uppermost in the minds of you all," explains the mentalist.

"All I ask is that fair play be uppermost in your minds and kindly bear in mind that if you do not help me by concentration I shall not be able to carry this experiment in mentalism or telepathy to a successful conclusion.

"I shall ask a number of you to kindly act as a committee. Just stand in a group out in the aisle, please, and decide upon any two numbers or initials.

"While this is going on I shall step to the stage out of hearing and when you have decided kindly call me."

So saying, the mentalist steps upon the platform upon which rests a small blackboard on a stand which he turns back to the spectators after erasing whatever might be on the board.

One of the committee, either a lady or a gentleman, calls the entertainer into the audience.

Taking the hand of each of the committee, he concentrates a bit, then passes to the next one. After three or four have been placed *en rapport*, the entertainer steps upon the platform, picks up a piece of chalk and writes something upon the blackboard. Back he goes into the aisle and continues to concentrate, with severe mental strain, with the remaining members of the committee.

Again he steps upon the platform and, covering his eyes with his hands, dramatically exclaims: "You have thought of the initials (or numbers) suggested to you by some person absolutely unknown to me. Is that right? It is? Thank you. Now without laying claim to any supernatural means I shall write on this blackboard the initials (or numbers) that seem to come to me."

This he does, and then: "What were the initials (or numbers) you, ladies and gentlemen, thought of?"

Upon one of the committee calling either the initials or numbers, whichever the case may be, the mental marvel dramatically turns the blackboard facing the audience upon which is written either the numbers or the initials selected.

A deep bow and the entertainer has scored another hit during the evening performance.

The Secret:—Read the effect again before you seek the solution. Can't you imagine the dramatic results of a startling problem of this type? Can't

you almost hear, in your mind's fancy, the murmur of the mystified spectators?

The *modus operandi* which makes this effect possible is simple. You have an assistant among the audience who becomes one of the committee. He, knowing whether or not it is initials or numbers they decide upon, gives you the cue by taking out his handkerchief and using it, if initials are selected, and if numbers have been the choice he simply replaces the handkerchief without using it at all. That much learned, the rest is just as simple.

There are twenty-six letters in the alphabet, so the transmission of the letters are easy; cueing the numbers more simple.

The second party you work with is your assistant naturally unknown to the rest of the committee.

Here's how he codes the initials or numbers to you: When you hold the assistant's hand (and you repeat this with all of them, taking a bit of time with each one) he presses the index or first finger the required number of times against your palm, with a slightly longer pause between signaling the first and second letter or initial.

Holding the hands of the rest of the committee is for effect.

If this trick goes into the hands of a natural born actor he will make it the feature effect in every programme. It is an excellent impromptu effect.

The Mystic Block

ON the magician's table stands a solid looking cylinder about seven inches high. In back of this rests a tin cover about ten inches in height.

The cylinder is shown and a cover is placed over the same. A large colored handkerchief is put over the cover.

A few magic words and the handkerchief is whisked away and the forearm of the magician is thrust completely through the cover, proving that the solid cylinder which was there but a few moments ago has vanished.

Secret:—The solid looking cylinder is not as innocent as it looks. This consists of a center tube with a top and bottom which can be easily slid out of the cylinder.

When the handkerchief is placed over the cover, which, in turn, has been placed over the cylinder, the hand pushes the top and bottom of the cylinder into the handkerchief and the handkerchief covers up the move wherein the two disks, which acted as the top and bottom of the cylinder, are removed.

All that remains to be done is for the performer to pass his forearm through the tube indicating it is not solid.

Startling Reproduction Effect

HERE is the ideal sort of trick with which to bring a magical performance to a close when illusions are not used.

The entertainer in this instance requires an assistant to properly put it over, but it can also be done with the single performer, so I shall give the two simplified methods.

Effect:—A box is picked up from the table and shown to be empty as well as free from trickery of any description.

The cover is next exhibited and tapped with the wand to prove all is well.

The cover is now placed on the box, which is held at arm's-length by the assistant, or may be placed on a small skeleton-topped table as near to the footlights or edge of the platform as possible.

The magician now waves his wand over the box, throws aside the cover, after showing it from all sides, and proceeds to extract from the interior yards and yards of colored silks, flags of every nation, a large heap of

---
Showing one of the methods of loading the box. Others described in the text.

---

colored paper and streamers, and finally either a guinea pig or a fair-sized rabbit.

Again the box is shown and, if you care to, pass it, together with the cover, for examination.

Secret:—It's a really spectacular trick if properly played up, but an exceedingly simple one as well.

The box is ordinary and of a size to suit the performer's fancy. I would suggest it be painted in Oriental or Egyptian style. The load is introduced by the assistant from under his coat while the performer steps for a moment in front of him with the cover, which he shows to be quite ordinary. The loading of the box must be done very quickly. Tilting the box toward the person will help in introducing the load.

If the performer is working single-handed he introduces the load from a special left-hand pocket under cover of turning to the table to get his wand. The load can also be introduced into the box by placing the box on the table and covering it with a large colored foulard. But I prefer the use of an assistant in this effect.

When the load is in the box, using the assistant method, the cover is placed on and the rest of the wand-waving stuff is only for effect.

Take the articles slowly from the box, and finally the animal. It makes a great showing to those out front and the applause will be sweet music.

Where Is the Ring?

A LADY'S ring is borrowed and placed in a handkerchief. The handkerchief is next placed into a glass which stands in full view of all. Suddenly the handkerchief, after a few appropriate remarks, is whisked out of the glass and the ring is gone.

The assistant brings forward a tray of potatoes. One is selected and cut in half. Done up carefully in colored tissue paper or in a small ring box is found the borrowed piece of jewelry.

The Secret: — The ring is palmed or concealed in the hand. The assistant hands the performer the glass, into which the handkerchief is placed, at the same time he takes the ring from the magician and leaves the platform.

A few remarks and the handkerchief is shown to be empty.

Back of the stage the assistant has a potato from the side of which a piece is cut out, but easily about a third of the cut portion can be replaced and the potato looks like the real thing.

Out walks Mr. Assistant with several potatoes on a tray with the one to be used on top so there will be no mishap.

A knife is brought into action, potato cut in half and the ring (previously wrapped in paper or placed in a ring box) is found and returned to the owner with the magician's many thanks and profuse apologies.

Find the Lemon

A SMALL lemon is shown and under a waving movement of the magi's hands is seen to become smaller and smaller until it is no longer visible, but from are seen to be balancing the magic fruit!

Secret:—This is a fine effect and should be given a few trial showings before a mirror so you and make it look as if the genuine article is in there. When picking up the bag, drop the lemon behind a handkerchief or several books, but pretend to place the fruit in the bag.

This is a very unusual lemon vanish that remains a mystery. The paper lemon solves the secret.

the hands of the wonder-worker emerges a silk handkerchief the same color as the fruit that has vanished.

Once more the waving motions, and the silk is gathered into the hands and when the handkerchief disappears in its place is the lemon.

The lemon is next dropped into a paper bag and to prove the fruit is still there, a candle is lighted and held behind it. The spectators can clearly see the lemon. The candle is extinguished, the bag crushed or torn to pieces, and the lemon gone.

Reaching into the air suddenly the fingertips of the magician can properly execute the necessary moves without haste and rehearse your gestures and facial changes, as a neat bit of acting will help you to present this experiment in a telling and enjoyable manner.

The lemon is really a skin with an opening at the bottom into which to push the silk handkerchief. The transmission of the silk and lemon needs no detailed explanation. Act the part and express surprise at the proper time. It all helps.

The bag is feked by pasting a piece of thick paper on one side close to the bottom. The candle will throw this feke into sight

When you tear the bag place the pieces in the left hand standing with your left side toward the spectators. Throw the pieces to your assistant or toss them on the table at the same time that your right hand goes into your right-hand pocket and brings out a lemon the same size and shape as the tricked fruit.

Make a quick grab in the air, and roll the lemon between your fingertips and look surprised at the sudden appearance of the magic fruit.

The good magical entertainer is always an actor. To him no matter how many times he has presented the trick it is always, so his gestures seem, something he has seen for the first time. He is startled, surprised and sorry for whatever happens, and plays the part or rôle of the magician from the rise to the fall of the curtain.

Many bits of misdirection, which are very necessary in a number of tricks, are what really aid the magical worker in putting the experiment across.

The student should always bear in mind that it is possible to inject humor in many of the items in the programme and the audience will appreciate the trick more, but above all, avoid and shun forced humor and learn to patter in a smooth, easy style which makes your audience think you are making up your talk as you go along. Also create your own style.

The Mesmerized Knife

HERE is an interesting little parlor trick which may be performed around the dining table. The amateur picks up a knife, rubs it briskly on the palm of his hand and then suspends it from the finger tips, from the palm or from the back of the hand in a very mysterious manner. A very weak solution of sec- cotine and water is applied to the palms and fingers and allowed to dry. This is sticky enough to cause the knife to stay in any prescribed position.

The Miracle Tube

DISCLOSED at the rise of the curtain is a small skeleton table upon which stands a box of colored confetti and a nickeled tube about ten or twelve inches in height.

The entertainer enters carrying two small squares of colored tissue paper and immediately picks up the tube and shows it to be entirely empty.

Next he places a square of the colored tissue on one end and seals it with a ring of nickel to hold the paper in place.

From the box he picks up a quantity of confetti and pours it into the tube.

Taking another square of paper and a duplicate ring of nickel, he seals the opposite end of the tube.

The magician now calls attention to the fact that if he attempts to place anything into the tube the tissue paper at either end will break and that would be the end of the trick.

So he will call upon the spirits to render him the necessary aid in turning the sealed cylinder into a miracle tube.

Passing his hand over the top of the tube several times, he finally breaks the tissue end and takes from the tube several pigeons much to the mystification of the spectators.

The Secret:—The tube is only a nickeled cylinder with two rings which fit over both ends after the tissue paper squares are placed on, sealing the tube. The box contains confetti and nothing else.

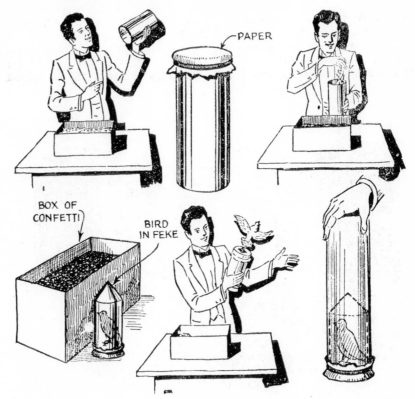

This effect is also represented on the cover where this tube is portrayed. Note how bird is made to enter with the feke.

But, when the magician seals one end of the tube and places it down on the table for the fraction of a second while his hand goes into the box of confetti the tube is brought down over a feke cup-like arrangement which tapers into a point. In this are two pigeons, the end of which is fastened with still another band of nickel and a piece of tissue paper.

Even if this end is pointed toward the audience they believe all is well, as it looks just like the other end of the tube.

All that remains is to break the paper of the tube and release the pigeons.

This miracle tube can be worked up into a very pretty effect, as it is a bit startling to the spectators when they find the confetti has changed into the pigeons, because they never expected that to happen.

A New Card Box

A BOX of the drawer type sufficiently large to hold a deck of cards is shown. The cards are removed and offered for inspection and the request is made that they shall be shuffled. The empty box is closed and set aside in full view of the audience. A card from the shuffled deck is then caused to vanish and upon opening the box the vanished card will be found in the drawer. This

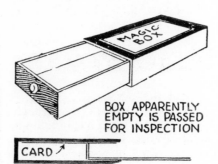

box has a decided advantage over the other forms of mechanical card boxes, in that it is truly unprepared. It will be seen that a duplicate in suite to the card that is forced upon the audience has been previously concealed in the box. The card is held captive between the top of the box proper and the edge of the sliding drawer. On closing the drawer, the card drops in place.

One needs the hollow wand here illustrated to present this paper problem.

The Paper Problem

A LONG strip of colored paper one-half inch in width and fifteen inches in length is placed between the extreme fingertips and slowly torn into many pieces.

The pieces are touched with the magic wand, the wand placed under the arm, and the paper is slowly pulled from between the fingertips, fully restored.

The Secret:—This is another very pretty effect. Two pieces or lengths of paper of the same color are used.

The wand is hollow at one end and into this is placed the rolled duplicate piece of colored paper.

The wand should be only large enough to accommodate the paper roll and a movable bottom arranged with a small iron pin keeps this securely in place until the proper moment.

The pieces are torn and exchanged for the whole piece while manipulating the pieces in the hand and after the exchange is quickly and secretly made the bottom of the wand when pushed in place keeps the torn pieces from falling out.

The stunt is not a bit difficult and in the proper hands produces a very mystifying effect.

Accidents Will Happen

THE magician borrows a handkerchief from a member of the audience and proceeds to brag about the success he has had with this trick inasmuch as he has been presenting it in his programmes for five years and has never destroyed or burnt a handkerchief yet.

Proceeding with his braggadocia, he takes the handkerchief in one hand and a match is lighted with the other. Carelessly bringing his hand in contact with the handkerchief, the match, unseen by the man of mystery, ignites the handkerchief.

Naturally the spectators start to laugh, all but the party who owns the handkerchief. The magician is at a loss to know why the spectators are laughing, but to his apparent sorrow he soon finds out.

Nonplussed for the moment,

he weakly attempts to laugh it off by saying he is sorry that it has happened. Pretending he sees the face of the angry owner of the loaned handkerchief he makes jest of the whole matter and remarks that accidents will happen.

Rubbing the handkerchief together in his hands, he says a few magical mending words over it, and behold the handkerchief is restored and returned, with thanks, to the owner.

Secret:—Before the trick begins the magician conceals a piece of cloth in his hand. When the handkerchief is borrowed the handkerchief itself is crumpled in his hand. The end of the cloth projects from his closed fist. Naturally the piece of cloth is what is really brought in contact with the flame. Being careful not to have the burnt pieces come in contact with the

real handkerchief in his hand, he waves his hands up and down, thus dropping the burnt piece. Immediately he comes forward and returns the handkerchief to its owner.

Showing how the piece of cloth instead of the kerchief is burned.

Unique Handcuff

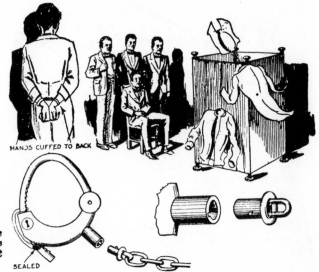

The chain of these handcuffs can be released for spirit effects.

THE tricked handcuff herein explained may be used in many tricks. It can also be used as a straight handcuff escape or used in a seance, as follows:

Effect: The curtain rises disclosing a stage with a cabinet made of wooden or iron standards and three sides of dark curtain material. The front of the cabinet has the drapes divided into two parts so that entrance to the cabinet can be made by the entertainer.

A committee is called upon the stage and asked to place the handcuffs on the performer's wrists. This done they are securely locked and the locks sealed.

The key is placed in the keeping of one of the voluntary assistants.

The performer now enters the cabinet. If he has an assistant he closes the cabinet curtains.

The assistant borrows the coat of one of the committee and tosses it over the top of the cabinet. The cabinet top is not covered.

Almost immediately the performer's coat flies over the top of the cabinet and the performer makes his appearance wearing the coat of the gentleman. Upon examination the handcuffs are still locked on the entertainer's wrists.

He once more goes into the cabinet and in a second emerges this time with the cuffs in his hands.

Method:—The handcuffs are feked near one of the circlets that go over the wrist. This is a piece of bar with a socket-like arrangement with a slight projection at either side.

When this socket is pressed home and a slight turn is made the cuff is locked and all looks fair, but a slight twist of this feked part allows the circlet of steel to separate itself from the chain of the cuff.

This is a very useful piece of utility apparatus and can be used in many effects necessitating the handcuffing of either the performer or his assistant. The cuff is opened with duplicate key.

The Mat of Cagliostro

The concealed pocket in this mat contains the load.

"WHILE abroad I purchased this mat, which is said to have been the property of the greatest magician of his time, Count Cagliostro," lectures the magician.

"This mat has magical properties. I have mastered the art of producing various articles from it, thanks to a rare little brochure written by Cagliostro himself."

Continuing on in this strain, the magician rolls the mat into a cylinder and, placing his hand in one end, extracts flowers, silks, flags and what not.

Again he shows the mat from all sides and once more rolls it up and places his hand into the opposite end of the mat and from the interior produces more silks, yards of paper ribbons and finally a dove or two.

The mat is unrolled and shown from all sides.

The Secret:—The picture of a devil's mask is painted on the mat, but this is really to hide the slit at the side. Into this slit the entertainer thrusts his hand after it has been placed into the cylinder formed by rolling the mat, and from a special pocket on his right makes the first series of productions. The second time he takes the silks, paper ribbons and doves from the special pocket of his coat on his left side. The hand entering the rug or mat looks to the spectators as if the loads are really taken from there. This is an excellent production trick when the moves are carefully made.

Something to Think About

TRICKS with thimbles are very popular with the magical fraternity. The only fault to find with their use is that they are small and in a large hall or theatre are almost invisible to spectators seated ten or twelve rows back.

Some exceedingly clever routines of manipulations can be arranged with this little housewives' friend and for impromptu magic various clever moves can be quickly appreciated.

The effect I am about to describe is very good for closeup work, and should be mastered by the novice and carried around in his pocket, so when he is asked to do a trick he is ready.

Effect:—A thimble is shown and a handkerchief, preferably a silk one, is borrowed. The thimble is placed on the finger of the right hand and pushed half-way through the handkerchief. You now show the thimble from all sides. Once more the pushing through process is repeated, when suddenly the spectators see the entire thimble has passed through the borrowed silk handkerchief. Upon returning the handkerchief to its owner he is puzzled to find it is fully restored and the penetration of the thimble has done no harm.

Secret:—You must have a genuine thimble and a top of another thimble. The feked cap is nothing more than a thimble the duplicate of the genuine ar-

If one will take care to prepare a thimble as shown in the illustration, the penetration of a handkerchief can be demonstrated.

ticle cut off just above the rim about a half inch or less from the part of the accessory where the finger enters.

This top must fit neatly over the other thimble so it will look like one when slipped into place.

When the thimble is first placed on the hand the real thimble is on the finger, but the feked end is kept concealed in the other hand.

The handkerchief is thrown over the real thimble and the hand containing the feke is brought quickly up and in the act of pushing the thimble through the feke is slipped on the top of the real thimble over the handkerchief. This looks as if the thimble has penetrated half-way through. This can be shown from all sides.

Taking the end off quickly and concealing it again in your hand, immediately pull the handkerchief from the thimble. When they see the real thimble still on the finger they believe it was pulled back. Now the feked thimble tip is quickly placed over the real one and when the handkerchief is placed once more over the finger the thimble and tip is in the other hand. Now all you have to do is to slip the real thimble with feke over the handkerchief on the fingertip. Take it off, palm or conceal the feke tip and under cover of showing the real thimble around slip the feke into your pocket.

This is a very neat effect and a startler when presented in impromptu fashion.

Circlets of Steel

THE entertainer shows a long piece of string and five rings of steel. Around each of the rings exhibited are short lengths of colored yarns wound tightly. This, explains the glib man of mystery, is to distinguish the various rings.

The gentlemen are now asked upon the platform to aid in the experiment.

Each end of the string is handed the gentlemen, who are told to pull it tightly. This proves the string is all right.

The five circlets of steel are next threaded upon the string and again the ends are passed to the gentlemen to grasp firmly.

A handkerchief is thrown over the rings and the performer requests the audience to call for the color they wish.

As each color is called, the circlet of steel is taken from the tightly held string and shown to spectators.

Finally the handkerchief is withdrawn and the string is proven to be intact.

Secret:—Each of the five rings have a small opening in them over which the length of colored yarn is wound. This covers the opening. When the color is called and the ring is to be taken from the string, the fingernail is used to push aside the yarn and the ring is slipped off the string through the opening. When rings are held up to show the various colors, as called for, the fingers cover the opening so it cannot be seen. The yarn also serves to conceal the slit.

Cabinet of Transformations

"I HAVE here a mystical cabinet which upon repeating a certain magical formula will transform anything placed inside.

"This was invented and perfected in 1493 by the Great Bosh-Bosho in honor of the celebration held by the creditors of Christopher Columbus before he returned from his accidental discovery of the Bronx!

"The Great Bosh-Bosho was the father of the first sane radio announcer since radios kept housewives away from their washtubs.

"I purchased this masterpiece for the enormous sum of eight plugged coins.

"I might say, before continuing with this miracle of modern witchcraft, I have had the extreme pleasure of performing this trick before President Hoover . . . became President.

"But to get back to the trick.

"First I show you the cabinet. Entirely empty. Now I roll up my sleeves and exhibit my beautiful arms . . . both of them . . . just like a real magician.

"Here are a pair of turtle doves. They bill and coo all day in their little love nest. . . . She does the cooing and their feed man does the billing.

"I might state that only the greatest magicians in this world do this trick . . . but I won't. I am great, but I blush when I admit it!

"Now, turtle doves, you shall move from your love nest to this mystic cabinet so we can show the customers how the law of averages allows one man nowadays six or seven lady friends.

"Placing the doves into the

cavern of the empty cabinet, I close the lid so the spirits can get to work.

"Saying the magic words Abra Cabra Senselessitis . . . I open

A special box construction allows for the conversion of two doves into white rats.

the side door or family entrance and behold the turtle doves have been transformed into a couple of white mice."

The diagram explains the entire construction of the cabinet.

The Miracle Slate

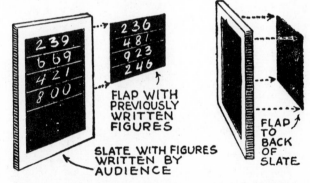

Here is one of those tricks so easy to explain, and yet so remarkable that the audience fairly gasps when they see it. The magician asks four different members of the audience to write down four numbers on a slate. While they are doing this, the magician back on the stage writes a figure on a slate. When the spectators' figures are added up, the sum is found to be identical with the

number previously written on the magician's slate. The effect is produced by the aid of a thin flap originally concealed in the back of the slate. After four spectators have written their numbers, the fifth is requested to add them up, but he adds up the figures on false flap which is slipped into place before he gets the slate. Naturally the two totals agree.

Trunk Escape

Double Trunk Escape
Thrills Audience

Assistant Handcuffed and Placed In Two Trunks, Securely Locked and Bound, Escapes, Leaving No Trace As to Solution.

Furnishes Food For Active Minds Who Attend Local Theatre.

During the performance of mirth, music and mystery of the Great So and So at the Local theatre this week a most sensational experiment in escapeology is exhibited.

The illusionist places one of his assistants into a fair size trunk, which is securely locked by members of the audience who are invited upon the stage to act as a committee.

This trunk is lifted and placed inside of a larger one which in turn is locked and bound with rope. There seems to be no logical solution as to how the assistant makes his escape, which is effected when the performer fires a revolver.

This double trunk sensation is a true example of the illusionist's art and a problem that makes the spectators think deeply.

IF you read the above in your favorite newspaper wouldn't you be anxious to witness a performance of this description?

Wouldn't you start figuring out just how and when the imprisoned assistant makes his escape?

You certainly would, and while viewing this trick you would get a great thrill out of it, especially if you were a student of the magician's art.

The most simple one is as follows:

The assistant is really handcuffed (the trick handcuff can be used here), placed in a trunk which is locked by some member of the committee from the audience and the key is retained by that committeeman.

The assistants now lift the trunk and put it into a larger one, which in turn is locked, and to make the trick more sensational and more difficult from the audience's point of view, a long rope is tied around the box, securely knotted by the assisting gentlemen from the audience. The rope knots may be sealed if you care to take the time and trouble to do it.

A screen is placed in front of the trunk and after a short monologue by the entertainer telling of the wonders of escape artists and how, according to spirit workers, a body may become, under proper conditions, so small that it can slip through the most minute crevice, a shot is fired, the screen falls over and upon quickly untying the ropes and unlocking the trunks they

are found to be empty. The assistant may come running down the aisle of the theatre or appear from back of the scenes.

Explanation:—The trunks are fitted, on the sides, with movable panels kept securely in place by catches at the sides, but on the outside. See and follow the illustrations carefully. The rope which is placed around the outer trunk and tied does not in the least interfere with the assistant while making his escape.

Once outside of the trunks, he uses the flat-bladed screw-driver to push the side clips into place. Naturally, he, while inside of the trunks, pushes the flat blade through the side crevice and slips the bolts down so the panels will move, making the opening through which he gets out.

He makes his way quickly and carefully through a slit in the back drop or center door in the scenery and either runs around to the front of the hall or theatre ready to make his appearance when the time comes or stands back stage, out of sight of the committemen, until the cue is given for him to make his entrance.

The screen is toppled over by a length of strong linen thread.

Chinese Box Trick

RIBBON   SHELLS

POINT OF VISION

A small box about six inches square without top or bottom is shown and a ribbon passed through holes in the sides of the box. The ends of the ribbon are held by two spectators, the box is covered for an instant by a handkerchief, and a billiard ball with a hole bored through it is caused to appear on the ribbon. The secret lies in the construction of the box, which contains two metal hemispheres, through which the ribbon must pass in being threaded through the box. Under cover of the cloth, the shells are brought together at the centre.

CLOSED

OPEN

The assistant is first locked into a trunk. This is placed into a still larger trunk, which is also locked and bound. Nevertheless the assistant effects his escape. (Note construction of the trunk.)

SILK LOOP

WHITE PAPER PATCH

FILLED WITH CONFETTI

EMPTY

EGG

This is one of the prettiest and cleanest tricks which the amateur or professional can perform. An ordinary egg is first produced at the finger tips. Under a crushing movement of the hands, this is converted into a hand full of confetti and the egg vanishes.

Japanese Magic

CONJURERS of Japan take great delight in mystifying their audiences with magical experiments in which eggs, fans, silks, water or confetti play a prominent part.

They always accompany their tricks, when appearing before Japanese audiences, with what sounds to us like a sing-song monotonous monologue.

While visiting Japan I saw several native prestidigitators giving their entertainments.

They are very clever in their manipulations and their sleight-of-hand very dexterous.

One Japanese magician in particular, whose performance I witnessed several times, seemed to take pleasure in presenting a trick somewhat on the following order.

Turning back his sleeve (which was large enough to hold, so it seemed to me, anything from the Brooklyn Bridge to the Statue of Liberty) he slowly lifted his right hand, which was cupped into a fist, and opened his fingers one at a time to show that his hand was entirely empty.

With his left hand he picked up a small, beautiful hand-painted silk fan and again closing his fist gently fanned his right hand which he suddenly opened and at the finger tips appeared an egg.

Tossing the egg into the air several times, he caught it in his hand.

Again manipulating the fan as only the Japanese can, he closed his right hand over the egg and

as he continued fanning the hand there descended slowly a shower of colored confetti.

The shower ceased, the fanning continued, the hand was slowly reopened and was gracefully shown, back and front, entirely empty.

Taking you back of the scenes:—In performing this magical experiment from the Land of the Cherry Blossoms, the more gracefully one presents the trick the prettier and more effective it will be to the audience.

A little preparation beforehand is necessary. Take a rather large-size egg and with a hatpin puncture the shell top and bottom. Hold the egg over a saucer and blow through one end and the contents of the egg will come out. Again the hatpin is brought into use and makes another hole about a quarter of an inch from the top of the egg. Do not try to bore through the shell, but a sharp puncture should be made and if properly done will not crack the shell. A small loop of silk thread is tied through the two small holes at the top of the eggshell. This is for the manipulations which are to follow.

Now a bit of delicate work is in order. On the side of the egg a small hole is made l a r g e enough to force in as much colored confetti as the empty shell will hold. This is covered up with a piece of thin white paper as nearly the color of the shell itself as possible. This piece of paper is pasted to the outside of the shell.

At the beginning of the trick the loop of the eggshell is slipped around the first finger or the thumb of the right hand, where it is allowed to lay on the back of the hand. If the length of silk is right, the shell will hang behind the fingers and remain unseen by the spectators.

Now follow the various manipulations carefully: The r i g h t hand is brought up and tilted a bit upward, the fist is closed and the shell hanging in back of the hand is not visible.

The fingers of the right hand are slowly opened, one at a time.

You now pick up the fan, which lies on a nearby table. Then open the fan with a quick movement and at the same time the fan is momentarily brought before the closed hand, a quick movement is made which brings the eggshell from the back of the hand to the front, where it is caught at the fingertips. This movement should be practised before a mirror, for the entire "eggsperiment"— beg your pardon, I meant experiment—depends on this move.

The egg is allowed to slide from the fingertips to the palm of the hand. Continue the fanning, while you crush the shell and with the fingertips break it up and slowly allow the confetti to fall to the table or floor, getting rid of the pieces of crushed shell at the same time.

When all of the shell and confetti have fallen from the hand, still continue to fan, and again slowly open the fist and turn the hand around to the back and reverse this movement. The silk thread will remain invisible at a distance of a few feet.

Improved
Spirit Clock

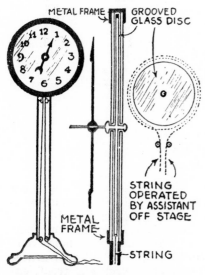

Above is a diagram of the improved spirit clock in which the hand may be commanded to rotate.

IN this version of the spirit clock a large glass dial such as illustrated, is seen resting in a metal frame supported upon a stand. A pointer is examined and fixed to a pin leading from the center of the glass disk. Under mesmeric passes, the hand begins to spin in either direction, stopping at will at any given number. In this way the clock can be made to tell a person's age, pick out cards, and answer questions. The arrangement really consists of three dials of glass, the inner or middle one being in the form of a large pulley, rotated by a string around the periphery which trails off to the assistant.

The
Phantom Cigarette

IN this effect, the wizard or amateur entertainer can enter upon the scene smoking a cigarette held in a rubber or amber holder. Encircling his fingers around the cigarette, even though it is lit, he apparently removes it from the holder and on opening his fist, the cigarette will have mysteriously vanished. Immediately thereafter, closing his hand in the air and drawing it across the holder, he is able to make the cigarette reappear. The effect is accomplished by having the cigarette attached to a sliding cup, which moves in and out of the holder. By sucking on the holder, the cigarette rides in. It can be blown out again.

The construction of the cigarette holder enables the wizard to vanish the cigarette or restore it again at will.

Multiplying Matches

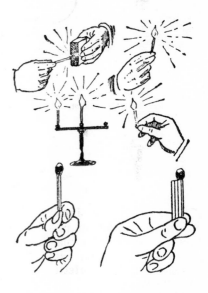

A match is struck on the side of a match box held between the fingers, then apparently split and made up into three matches, which individual splints are put in a suitable holder.

HERE is a simple effect which nevertheless possesses considerable novelty. The magician removes a wooden match from a matchbox and strikes it on the side in a perfectly natural manner. Showing both sides of the hand, he proceeds to grasp the first match which, under his magic touch, multiplies into two. He takes one of these matches, and waving his hand through the air, he again multiplies the match. The trick is worked by having three matches stuck together with bee's wax; two of these have their heads cut off.

Enchanted Oranges

SEVERAL men of magic were discussing ways and means of creating a series of new experiments for a new mystery show.

Each one suggested several effects with commonplace articles familiar to everyone.

"Great," one of these mystic learned men remarked, "but what we need is some sort of a trick using fruit. Oranges, for example."

"Sure," replied his friend, "but let it be a trick where the fruit isn't prepared in any way. Buy the oranges, allow the assistants to place them on a table and then go to work doing the trick."

The other pondered a while and then suggested, "I think I have just the idea."

Going to his study, he browsed around a while looking through his many scrapbooks and finally picking the one he wanted, took it to his friend and opening the book to a certain page, placed it so they both could read it.

Here is what the page contained: Effect:—Magician displays a silver tray upon which rests five or six oranges. Calling an assistant, he explains to the audience that he wishes some lady or gentleman to select one

of the pieces of fruit while the assistant passes through the audience. This is done.

The selected orange is now tossed upon the stage and caught by the magician, who immediately takes a knife and cuts a triangular piece out of it. From the

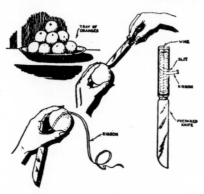

Cutting a hole in a previously examined orange, the performer removes yards of colored ribbon. The hollow handled knife is responsible.

opening made is pulled many yards of vari-colored ribbon.

The orange is next cut in two, placed on a plate and the assistant once more passes through the audience showing that the orange was of the most ordinary description and not prepared in any way whatsoever.

Secret:—The oranges are the

real things. When the selection is made any one of them may be picked.

The trick is made possible by the knife, which is constructed with a feked handle. In the handle is a sort of roller with two thin wire ends fastened into the top and bottom of the knife so that when pulled slowly this roller arrangement revolves, allowing the colored ribbon to unroll.

The knife is held in the same hand as the orange after the performer cuts a piece from the same. Now the blade end of the knife is held downward in the hand so that the handle of the knife rests against the top portion of the orange.

When end of ribbon is slowly pulled, the ribbon unrolls from the knife handle and to the audience seems as if the ribbon were being extracted from the orange.

Patter can be arranged to suit the entertainer's fancy elaborating on the beginning of this article and winding up with the remark that "All oranges seem nowadays to be sunkist, but here is one ribbon-kist and which must have been plucked after a storm when the rainbow was at its best."

Mystic Materialization

THE conjurer has on his table three pieces of various colored paper. Taking a yellow piece into his hand, he crumples it into a ball and slowly out of the crushed paper a yellow silk handkerchief is materialized.

Forming a green piece of paper into a cone, he evolves a green silk handkerchief.

Picking up a black piece of paper, he causes a black silk handkerchief to materialize. Not liking the color of this handkerchief, he waves it slowly to and fro between his hands and the black silk changes into a white one.

Secret:—The yellow and green silk handkerchiefs are rolled up as small as possible and placed in paper packets of the same color as the paper. The white handkerchief is tied to the end of the black silk and after rolling it up the white silk is tucked in the corner of the black. The black is now rolled up into as small a compass as possible and placed in the black paper pocket of the black sheet.

With the yellow and green sheet of paper a slight tear is made in the paper pocket and the remainder of the sheets are thrown away after the material-

ization of the handkerchiefs. When the black silk makes its appearance be sure to hold firmly in the hand the balled-up white handkerchief so the audience does not see it. When the magician makes the remark that he does not care for the color as he produces the handkerchief, he crumples up the black handkerchief slowly, allowing the white one to come into view, then conceals the black handkerchief in the palm of his hand as he exhibits the white one.

Numerous mystifying variations of this simple trick will readily suggest themselves.

The Flower That Colors

THE flower that magically colors itself is an appropriate opening trick for the amateur magician's drawing room or parlor entertainment.

It is worked rather fast and proves food for thought to the spectators.

A few bars of introductory music brings you before your audience. You bow and, without talking, point, with your wand to the red flower in your buttonhole.

Wave your wand a bit around the flower, and suddenly, as if by magic, the red flower becomes a white one.

Then go right into your next effect without a moment's hesitation.

The secret:—Over the white flower is a red silk covering to which is attached a piece of linen thread which runs down into your top pocket, through the lining of the coat down to your left hand, which remains at your side. This hand grasps the thread ready to pull it quickly and smartly when the color change of the flower is to be accomplished.

A sharp pull and the red silk covering, which is made to represent the duplicate of the white flower, comes off of the flower and is drawn snugly into the top pocket of your coat.

Don't wait a moment, but go right into the following trick.

This is a startling transformation when smartly done.

The same sort of trick might be employed to cause your necktie to change its color, or perchance the color of a kerchief in your coat pocket.

A tug on the string pulls the cover of the flower into the top pocket and produces the color change here suggested.

Thought Waves

THE medium in this experiment is the young lady assistant of the entertainer who by a simple method of thought transference, unusually baffling and startling, reads the minds of several of the spectators who make up the spirit circle.

After a short introductory talk on the transmission of thought, the medium is introduced and a committee of two or more are asked to accompany the medium into another room where it is impossible for the lady to know or hear whatever may be transpiring.

While the medium is out of the room, a spectator is asked to select any object or article in the room.

The medium, still accompanied by the committee, is now recalled. A blindfold, made with a large pocket handkerchief, is now adjusted over the eyes of the medium and she is led to a chair in which she seats herself.

The spectator, by silently pointing, calls attention to various articles in the room, one at a time. As the various objects are pointed out, the entertainer, without speaking a word, also touches them one at a time.

The medium sits quietly and silently, until the selected object is touched, whereupon she immediately names it.

At no time beforehand does the medium know the object that has been selected.

The secret:—In a quiet room it will be found upon experimenting that if the entertainer takes several heavy steps, a bit heavier than he would ordinarily take, the change in sound is easily detected by anyone listening for it. Upon this simple principle depends this experiment.

For effect the medium may be blindfolded while she is still out of the room by the committee.

The entertainer reels off a yarn about the psychic thought waves that pass between the medium and himself. This he does in a convincing and serious manner to further heighten the effect.

He further asks the spectators to remain as quiet as possible during the experiment or test so that the mind of the lady will become perfectly attuned to his own.

The medium, when seated in the chair blindfolded with her back toward the spectators, places her feet firmly on the floor and rests her hands either against the sides of the chair or on the arms of the same. This enables her to also plainly feel the vibrations of the room when the performer walks from one object to another.

The committee may stand before the medium and carefully watch every move. This also helps to build the effect.

Different objects are now pointed out by a spectator, and each time the performer walks up to that object with a light step and touches it.

He then walks back to the center of the room.

This is repeated until the chosen object is pointed out, whereupon the entertainer takes two or three heavy steps toward the object and after a short pause the medium calls out: "That is the selected object!"

A Possible Impossibility

MAGIC is an art that stands the test of making t h a t which is impossible possible.

The Hindu has his rope trick, which seldom if ever has been witnessed in the forms we read about.

The Chinese have their water

spectators by the lack of flowing robes but seldom use large pieces of cumbersome apparatus, that look beautiful but arouse the suspicion of the people, as we say in the show business, "out front."

The more simple the effect, the

He also has a piece of top string and a red ball through the center of which a hole has been bored from end to end.

A large handkerchief with a circular hole through its center completes the paraphernalia necessary.

All these requisites may be passed to the audience for examination, as t h e y are not tricked or feked in any way. Everything is g e n u i n e and aboveboard.

Several discs of wood are threaded on a double string after a woden ball has been fastened to the end thereof. It seems impossible for anyone to remove the discs. Under cover of a handkerchief, the performer removes any of the discs requested. At the termination of the trick, even the wooden ball is removed. The manner in which the ball is threaded is responsible for the effect.

tricks, which are very spectacular to the lay audience who marvel at their dexterity and seeming miracles.

The Egyptian has his mammoth rolling ball, which defies all the laws of gravitation by rolling, upon word of command, up and down an innocent looking inclined board.

But the American magician is the modern day miracle worker, for he needs not the flowing robes and the gigantic pieces of apparatus that the foreign wonderworker seems to be at a loss without.

Americans of the magic cult step forth in either a tuxedo or evening suit and perform all sorts of magical m y s t e r i e s which not a l o n e astonish our

m o r e mystifying it becomes u p o n presentation to an audience.

The following is a simple little experiment which has always seemed excellent as far as an audience is concerned.

Naturally, I am offering a simple way to do this effect. On the stage from six to eight disks are employed, and the procedure is somewhat different.

I call this trick the Possible Impossibility.

On with the trick:

The entertainer comes forward with a small, light parlor or hallway table upon which rests four different colored circular pieces of wood.

They are colored red, blue, brown and white.

The string is doubled and passed through the circumference of the ball and tied so the ball hangs at the end of the string.

The colored disks, which may be square, round or made in any shape to suit the fancy of the performer . . . are then threaded on the string.

When the disks are on the s t r i n g, the handkerchief is placed over them and the string is carried up through the circular cut in handkerchief, so the string can be readily seen to be above the cover.

The entertainer now asks for the assistance of a strong young man.

"Kindly grasp the end of the string through the handkerchief," the magician directs the young man; "hold it tight with your right hand and feel through this cover and tell me if the disks are still there."

"They are," replies the assisting party, upon examination.

"Now I want to ask you a few questions. May I?" requests the miracle man.

"Yes," replies the assistant, wondering what is coming next.

"Do you believe it is possible to make an impossible t h i n g possible?"

"Maybe," answers the gentleman.

"Very well, then," continues the magician, "I am going to convince you before long. You must remember that the hand is quicker than the eye, and things not always what they seem."

"I am going to prove to you that no matter how impossible a thing may seem to you I will make it possible.

"The disks are threaded completely and s e c u r e l y on the string you hold, right?"

"Yes," mutters the embarrassed one, who feels the eyes of the audience on him.

"By placing my hand under this handkerchief or covering, I shall take off as many disks as you may ask of me.

"How many shall I take away from here?"

"Five," replies the assisting young man, repeating what the magician has whispered to him.

"How can I take away five when there are only four in all?" asks the magician.

After the laugh has died down the magician continues: "Now give me another number."

"Two," replies the y o u n g fellow.

The magician takes two of the disks from the string and hands them to the surprised assistant, who immediately takes a firmer hold on the string, both ends of which he holds in his hand.

Finally the last disk is handed to the assistant, the ball is given h i m and the handkerchief is thrown up over the assistant's hand and the spectators see the string loop hanging downward innocent and whole.

The assistant is thanked for his help and returns to his seat while the entertainer bows to the applause.

The secret:—The illustrations will make clear the v a r i o u s moves and method of looping the string around the ball. Study it carefully.

The string is doubled a n d passed through the hole in the ball and looped a r o u n d the bottom so a slight pressure of the string unloops it and the

disks and ball are free for the magician to do with as he sees fit.

The surprising thing to the assistant and the audience is that they cannot seem to figure out how the string can be unfastened from the ball as they believe, and the magician must make it a point to impress upon them the fact that he has fastened the string firmly at the top after threading the string through the ball.

Another angle that could be worked is, that when the magician asks the voluntary assistant how many disks he wants, he can also request the assistant to call the colors he wants. This can be done by the entertainer memorizing the order in which the colored disks are placed on the thread and it is an easy matter for the magician to hand out the disks as they were called for.

The Vanishing Lamp

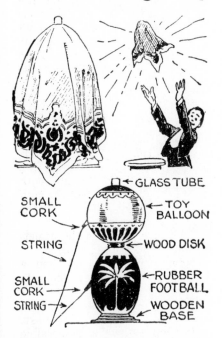

SMALL CORK

STRING

SMALL CORK
STRING

GLASS TUBE

TOY BALLOON

WOOD DISK

RUBBER FOOTBALL

WOODEN BASE

Whenever the magician attempts to vanish bulky objects, and manages to vanish them successfully, he is sure to be greeted with great applause. . The trick illustrated in the diagram above is one of those large mid-air vanishes. A lamp is covered with a cloth, the covered affair lifted and tossed into space, the lamp vanishes instantly. The construction is merely rubber inflated and composed of a toy balloon and a football. The string pulls out both plugs, permitting the air to escape.

The Enchanted Lemon

Tricks in which articles borrowed from spectators become the subjects of manipulation are always considered novel. In the above trick a handkerchief is borrowed, vanished and then found in an unprepared lemon. The vanished silk may easily be loaded into the hollow handle of a knife, and after the lemon is cut and knife and lemon held as illustrated, the silk piece can be apparently pulled out of the lemon. The silk is dry when produced.

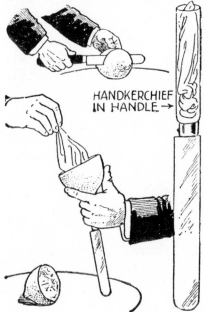

HANDKERCHIEF IN HANDLE

Cut and Restored Ribbon

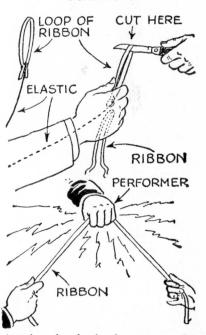

LOOP OF RIBBON

CUT HERE

ELASTIC

RIBBON

PERFORMER

RIBBON

A string after having been measured is cut in half, a knot made and by passing the hand over the cut portions, the ribbon again repairs itself. The secret lies in the fact that another duplicate ribbon attached to a rubber band is the one actually cut. When this cut ribbon is tied, the performer places his hand over the knot and manipulating it, releases it, permitting the elastic band to draw the small piece up his coat sleeve.

The Dream of Fu Chong

ON the outskirts of a town in China lived a dreamer named Fu Chong.

Fu Chong didn't believe in hard work, and as he had an income of a few pennies a day, from some rice fields he rented out, all he had to do was to sit before his humble hut and create the most fantastic dreams.

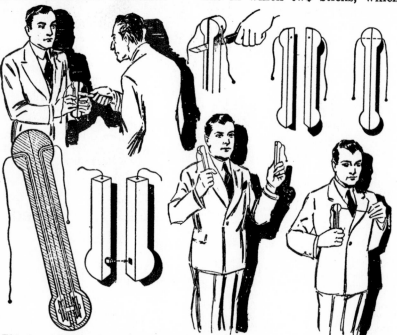

This is an improved version of the chinese blocks which are threaded with a piece of string. The string is then cut, the blocks separated, but when again placed side by side the string is found to be whole.

He would weave the quaintest sort of meanings into his dreams, and when among his brothers and the townsfolks, he would delight in spinning dream yarns, which soon earned him queer looks when he passed along his happy way to his home, where in peace and contentment he would sit and dream the whole day long.

One day a passing peddler of miscellaneous wares wandered his way, and finding the dreaming Fu Chong idling away the time sat down and held conversation with this happy son of China.

Upon parting, the wandering peddler gave Chong a trick book in Chinese and bidding him peace and good luck continued along the road.

Several days passed and Fu Chong changed his mode of living. Now he only spent half the day dreaming, and the rest of the day he devoted in practising magic, from the trick book.

One trick in particular struck this dreamer's fancy. This was one in which two sticks, which he fashioned out of wood, were held together with a piece of string.

Puzzle as he would, he couldn't for some time understand the working principle of the trick. Finally after several weeks had passed and much incense was burned before his favorite Joss God, Fu Chong's mind started to work. He found he didn't have the trick made properly. So when collection day came round he took his few pennies and hied himself forth to call upon the royal court magician.

After a short wait he was ushered into the presence of the Magi Supreme of the Land of Poppies.

Chong told him he wanted to learn the trick with the magic sticks. Upon showing the magic

man the book he had, and the trick he tried to make, the great dealer in magical powers threw the sticks away and said to Fu Chong, "They are not fashioned properly. I shall show you the trick and do it for you. If you care to, I will teach you the trick, and then present you with my own sticks if you who are a dreamer will weave from out your dreams a fitting tale which I may spin while doing this trick when I visit the mystic shrine."

"Agreed!" came from the awestricken Fu Chong.

Whereupon the great Chinese wonderworker took the two sticks and drew the string which passed through both sticks this way and that. The long end became the short and the short end became the long one, much to the bewilderment of the heathen Fu Chong.

Finally the great man told Fu Chong to cut the string in the center. This done, the two sticks were separated and Fu Chong was seized with panic. Had he spoiled the trick of the great miracle man?

Seeing the fear of Fu Chong, the wonderworker smiled and placing the two sticks together, waved his hand over them and then pulled the string slowly from side to side, and lo and behold, a miracle was taking place! The sticks of enchantment worked. The trick was restored to its original working condition. Completely mystified, Fu Chong told the great man a story he wove around the sticks as he sat and dreamed before his humble abode.

So impressed was the court magician that he had a secretary take down Fu Chong's dream story, showered him with gifts and taught him how to do the trick properly.

Fu Chong, the happiest man in all China, took the gift trick and singing Chinese songs of praise of the great man, hied himself along the dusty road to his home.

And if you, dear folks, ever have the good fortune to travel and visit China you will perchance pass by the humble home of that weaver of dreams and doer of magic, Fu Chong, and if you wish to make him happy, just step right up to him and ask him to do this trick for you and you will wonder at this quaint heathen Chinese and unconsciously you will mutter as you pass, "Very clever, t h e s e Chinese!"

The secret:—The drawing will explain the detailed workings of this experiment which I am sure you will enjoy presenting whenever the opportunity avails itself.

Keep the story of Fu Chong in your mind and spin this tale.

The Mystery Rose

THE magician holds in his hand a large red silk handkerchief. As he waves it up and down between his hands the handkerchief becomes smaller and smaller, until finally it vanishes altogether and in its place he holds a beautiful red rose.

If he wishes to reverse the process, he once more starts to slowly wave his hands up and down and as the rose grows smaller and fades from view the handkerchief once more makes its appearance.

The Secret:—The rose is a hollow one. While the hands are slowly waved up and down the fingers push the handkerchief into the prepared artificial flower. The handkerchief soon vanishes, leaving the rose in its place.

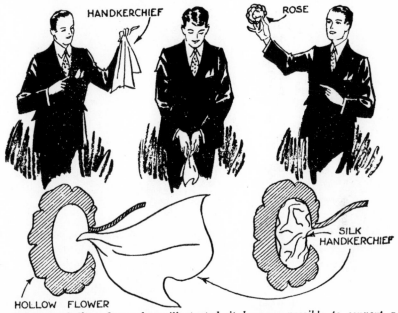

With the hollow flower here illustrated, it becomes possible to convert a flower into a handkerchief and the handkerchief into a flower again.

A String Problem

THE patter of the prestidigitator runs something like this: "Everybody doing magic these days does a trick in which a string is cut in two parts and magically made whole again. I shall go that trick one better. Will some obliging gentleman kindly step up here and assist me? You, sir. Thank you. Don't feel nervous, my friend; there isn't any danger in coming up here. The dangerous part is as you leave. That is the time I finish my trick, and no one knows just what may happen then. But no matter, I shall ask you to hold this piece of colored string so all the people can see it.

"Taking these shears in my hand I shall proceed, aided by some cutting music—now wasn't that a rather sharp remark?— to cut this piece of string into a number of parts. How many pieces do you see, sir? Twenty is right.

"Placing them in this piece of newspaper—no, sir, there is nothing in that paper, it is the (localize) paper which never does contain anything—I wrap them up so and ask you to hold the parcel until I get my wand.

"A slight tap on the package— and—why, I am so sorry, I have broken the paper. I guess the So-and-So paper isn't such a strong one, after all, eh?

"But never mind, we will extract the string from the sheet nevertheless, and no one can say that one doesn't get something from that paper after all."

Secret: — Take a sheet of newspaper and lay it flat on a table. Cut out another piece about twelve inches square and paste it on the flat sheet along three edges, forming a sort of pocket. Now roll up a piece of colored cord about thirty inches in length and lay it flat in the paper pocket and paste the fourth edge down firmly. Now you have the coil of string sealed in the newspaper.

Place this into a large book so it will be pressed down firmly by the time you are ready to make use of it.

All that remains to be done is to work up the effect, cut up the duplicate length of string and roll it into a bundle in the prepared piece of paper. When you tap the parcel do so sharply, breaking the prepared pocket and slowly uncoil the string—the pieces have been mysteriously restored. Get rid of the piece of paper by placing it aside out of reach or toss it carelessly to your assistant.

Handkerchief Pencil

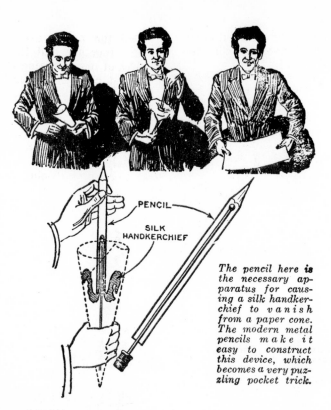

PENCIL

SILK
HANDKERCHIEF

The pencil here is the necessary apparatus for causing a silk handkerchief to vanish from a paper cone. The modern metal pencils make it easy to construct this device, which becomes a very puzzling pocket trick.

HAVE you ever attended a magical entertainment and, try as you would, never could quite solve to your own satisfaction just where the handkerchief that was vanished went?

I remember when, as a small boy, I sat time and time again watching the Great Herrmann perform, and the trick I enjoyed most was one in which this master of the magic art vanished a borrowed handkerchief. A dozen solutions used to pop into my mind after I had left the theatre, but upon seeing him do that trick over again I gave it up as an impossible problem, for watch as I would, I never could seem to figure it out. In later years when I learned that trick, I practised night and day, for no matter how well my friends thought I did it, I wanted to do it as well as the Great Herrmann did. But there was only one Herrmann, which experience quickly taught me.

Now there are many ways of making a borrowed or your own handkerchief, be it made of silk or linen, vanish into thin air.

For your approval I offer the following trick with a silk handkerchief under the title of "Where Does the Handkerchief Go?"

Silk handkerchiefs are best to use in magical performances, as they are more pliable, can be packed into a comparatively small space without much trouble, and when reproduced have a tendency, due to the material, to spring up at the proper time, thus adding a bit to the general effect.

Effect:—A silk handkerchief is shown and placed on a table. A sheet of paper is rolled into a cornucopia. Next a pencil is taken from the entertainer's pocket or from the table and pushed down into the paper cone to prove there is nothing there.

The silk is next thrown over the top of the cone and pushed down into the open part by the pencil. The magician's hands never once closely approach the paper.

The pencil is now placed aside or returned to the pocket and the paper cornucopia is turned down at the top and either placed into the hands of a spectator for safe keeping or laid on the table.

The performer shows his hands empty, and suddenly brings them together, at the same time making an up and down movement.

The hands now are fisted while being held together, and slowly a piece of silk, the same

color as the vanished handkerchief, appears at his fingertips.

Continuing the movements, the vanished handkerchief is materialized from between the performer's hands.

But what about the cornucopia?

The performer now either takes the paper cone from the table or from the party holding it and, opening it slowly, shows that the paper is empty.

The Secret:—The piece of paper rolled into a cornucopia is quite innocent. There is no trick about it in any way. But the pencil which looks to the spectators as just an innocent little pencil that must be lead, is used in this instance for quite a different purpose than writing.

This pencil is in reality a piece of brass tubing not much thicker than a pencil, but on the top where there should be an eraser we find an eraser glued or fastened in some way to the end of the rod which is just long enough to fit the brass, black-painted tube. This tube must be painted so it looks as much like a pencil as possible. This piece of handy apparatus can also be made in the form of a fountain pen.

Now follow the routine carefully and you will at once grasp the idea.

After the paper is rolled into a cornucopia and held in the magician's hand, the pencil is poked into it to prove it to be empty, so the spectators believe, but in reality when the pencil, eraser side downward, is pushed into the paper, the fingers of the hand gripping the end of the cone also grip the inner rod of the pencil, and when the pencil is drawn forth, the rod remains in the paper, firmly gripped.

The silk handkerchief is now placed across the top of the paper cone and the pencil is once more brought into play. This time it aids in pushing the silk down into the paper, but answers a double purpose—*i. e.*, the tube-pencil is brought down carefully over the handkerchief which now rests upon the rod held in the paper cone and the rod and handkerchief slide into the pencil. The pencil is now taken away and placed aside or in the performer's pocket.

The paper is now folded down at the top and given someone for safe keeping.

The hands are shown empty, and while the right hand is being shown to contain nothing, the left hand is busy getting hold of a duplicate colored handkerchief of silk which has beforehand been placed in the left vest pocket.

As soon as the handkerchief is

grasped the hands are quickly brought together and the stage business of materializing the silk is carried out in as convincing a manner as possible.

All that now remains to be done is to take the cornucopia from the gentleman or lady who has been so kind as to hold it and slowly open it and show the paper to contain absolutely nothing.

A Winged Ring

BIRDS and aeroplanes fly but do rings fly? They certainly do . . . and how! This experiment is correctly titled, "A Winged Ring," because that is just what happens. The ring under the cover of a handkerchief takes wings and flies away.

A ring is placed on the performer's finger and someone in the gathering is invited to assist, by holding the finger on which the ring is placed.

This is done. There isn't a possibility of the ring being taken from the finger unless the voluntary assistant releases his hold. But he is instructed not to let go, and he doesn't, but strange as it may seem, suddenly the magician's other hand comes from beneath the handkerchief holding the ring between his fingers.

They puzzle and ponder, but it happened and the ring is passed along for examination and proves to be the genuine article.

The secret:—The illustration will make everything clear. You can see that the ring that is first shown on the magician's finger is only half a ring but from a

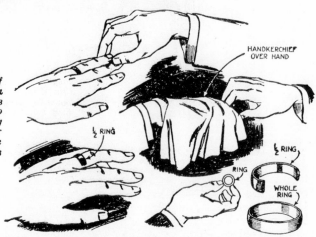

The substitution of a half ring for a whole ring allows the performer to remove the ring from his finger even though the end of the finger is securely held.

few feet it looks just like the real article. Palmed in his right hand, which also holds the handkerchief, the magician holds the genuine ring. It is a simple matter to throw the handkerchief over the hand with the ring still on the finger and ask the assistant to tightly hold the finger and under no circumstances let go. This is done to the letter. But Mr. Magician brings his right hand with the real ring up under the handkerchief and under cover of the real ring which he holds at his fingertips

while exhibiting it he conceals the half or feked ring in his palm.

The assistant still clings to the ring finger under cover of the handkerchief.

After a bit of misdirection, during which the magician asks him if he felt the ring leave the finger, the magician nonchalantly drops the feked or half ring into his pocket.

Suddenly with his right hand the magician pulls the handkerchief clear of the hand and the ring has vanished.

A Clever Pocket Trick

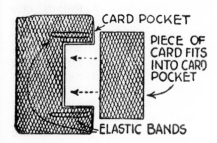

This is an excellent pocket trick. The performer apparently saws a match box in half with a playing card. Upon removing the playing card, the match box is found whole. The match box is unprepared, but the card is not innocent.

It will be observed that the playing card is really made of two cards, partially glued together and so arranged that a pocket is formed between them. Another piece of card fits into the pocket thus formed.

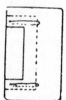

A Matter of Fancy

MAGICAL effects are created around nearly every sort of object. We have illusions where men and women vanish and re-appear, automobiles vanish into thin air, statues come to life and what not.

A short time ago watch and clock tricks were in vogue. Many excellent effects are ac-complished by aid of an innocent looking watch. But some folks object to tricks of this sort for they claimed that the watch, be-ing a comparatively small object,

"The French police claim that whenever a crime is committed one must seek out and find the woman. Everything seems to be blamed on women these days.

"But be that as it may logic is logic and it is staple reliable logic, which says that time flies even without lessons in aviation.

"I became my grandfather's heir not so many years ago.

"Among his many effects I discovered what is known as an odd sort of mantel clock. Here it is. Have you ever seen a

secret phrase several times and upon lifting the cover so I find that the years have flown on magic wings and here we have our friend the alarm clock.

"Upon showing the mysterious cover you can see right through it . . . not through the trick, I hope."

This effect is really startling to an audience as everything looks and seems so absolutely in-nocent that they cannot figure out how the transformation could be accomplished. Natur-ally were a trick of this sort presented upon the stage, the folk out front would believe that a special table or hidden assist-ant had done the trick.

The secret:—This trick can easily be made at home. It will repay the entertainer many times over to make it and use it as a sort of feature trick in his program. The illustrations show a mantel clock standing on a table. In the magician's hand is a cover which is made of card-board or tin decorated with some sort of design. This cover is not tricked or prepared in any way. It is simply a cover, but the mantel clock that seems so in-nocent isn't so by any means. This is a four sided box-like case painted to represent, as near as possible, a typical mantel clock. This clock has no bottom to it and the upper part or top of it is hinged in two pieces with a spring and catch so arranged that when the spring is released by a slight pressure of the ma-gician's fingers the cover opens up in two parts and lays flat against the sides of the unpre-pared cover which is placed over it.

Quite a startling trick is exhibited here. It consists of changing a square clock into an ordinary alarm clock under cover of a square shield and showing the shield empty.

can be manipulated in a hundred-and-one ways and the expert magical entertainer can do as his mind dictates with a watch. Then someone else remarked that if watches were so popular in magic, why couldn't clocks of the mantel and alarm variety be adapted to magical effects.

Not a bad idea, thought I, so I got busy and evolved a mild sort of sensation, as follows:

Mr. Magician starts a-patter-ing: "Time flies, and time, like the tide, awaits no man. He who said these lines never con-sidered woman, because woman makes time fly and also lets the time fly (when one awaits the woman).

clock like this one before? No? Neither did I. But I assure you that this simple looking mantel timepiece has magical qualities.

"The other day it struck thir-teen and I was puzzled. I took a stroll to a watchmaker's shop and asked him what time it was when a clock struck thirteen. He replied, 'Time to have it fixed.'

"Well . . . on with the work. So I will. I found out that my grandfather had built an odd looking cover for the clock. Here it is. (Show cover.) It fits the mantel clock snugly and by plac-ing a few invisible travel seeds into the cover after covering the clock . . . I repeat a certain

When the sides spring up the magician grasps the feked clock by the sides with fingers down a bit into the cover, thus holding the feked clock inside of the cover and he lifts it off the gen-uine alarm clock left standing on the table.

The cover, with the feked mantel clock inside, is shown to be empty (?) and placed aside.

A Timely Bill Trick

HERE is a timely trick with a $10 bill which will prove of unusual interest when presented in the club or drawing room as an impromptu effect.

Effect:—A large $10 bill is exhibited and held at the extreme fingertips.

The magician patters along the lines that he has a magic mint of his own. He says that although he is unable to turn out bills that will pass critical eyes, he will demonstrate the fact that by folding this large-sized bill into halves, quarters and eighths, he will, by his own original reducing method, change the large bill into a new style, small-sized ten dollar bill.

Continuing to manipulate the bill, he slowly unfolds same and the bill is seen to have visibly changed itself from a large-sized $10 note to the size now in use.

There are several methods by employing sleight-of-hand to reduce the bill, but I am giving here a simple yet practical method which, if carefully done, will even mystify the average magical enthusiast.

Method:—For this experiment you require two ten dollar bills. One a large bill and the other a smaller bill. These small bills are now in circulation. The small bill is folded in half, then into quarters and tightly pressed down, next a little paste is applied to one of the folded sides so that after it is pasted to about the center of the larger bill, it can easily be opened when the psychological moment presents itself.

The large bill is exhibited and as the magician continues with his patter, he folds the bill smaller and smaller, Making a few passes over the hand which holds the bill, he now in turn slowly opens the smaller bill behind which is now concealed the larger ten dollar bill folded as small as possible and held in place by the pasted side of the small bill.

Care must be taken when presenting this trick and a running line of patter should be kept up to misdirect the spectators from the actual necessary manipulations.

The patter can also be arranged around the fact that to-

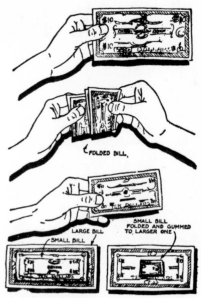

Here is a simple way to transform a large dollar bill into a smaller one.

day even the mint in Washington, aided and abetted by the high cost of living, is making a ten dollar bill look mighty small.

You may have a duplicate small ten dollar bill in your pocket and after finishing the diminishing of the bill casually place the bill in your pocket, leaving the prepared bill there and immediately bringing out the unprepared bill, remark, "Have you seen these new bills?"

The Hand Stocks

SMALL stocks to encircle just the wrists, and made of wood, are offered for examination. They are then securely locked by means of a hasp and staple arrangement, with two borrowed or unprepared padlocks, and the performer can at once release his hands for spirit manifestations, and can immediately afterwards show them still locked. The performer cannot slip his hands through the wrist holes when they are locked, as illustrated in the first diagram.

By way of further description concerning the hand stocks, we would say that the wrist holes which encircle the performer's wrist, are small enough to prevent the performer from slipping his hand through them when they are locked, as illustrated in the first diagram. However, when the top section is reversed, as illustrated in the second diagram, one of the wrist holes becomes larger while the other becomes smaller. The larger one then permits the hand to be easily freed and allows for the manipulation of various things while the performer is seemingly securely locked. When the wrist cuffs are removed from the wrist, the performer takes care to again reverse the position of the cuff sections before he passes them out for examination. It is evident that unprepared locks may be used.

Watch the Watch!

TIME flies! How often have you heard those familiar words! But it is truly a fact.

The magical worker patters: "I shall take pleasure in demonstrating the fact that here is a watch that you cannot watch and the closer you watch, the less you'll see of the watch . . . so, my friends, take advice and watch the watch!"

So saying, the wonderman shows a watch he takes from his pocket and tearing a piece of paper from a newspaper, he once again exhibits the watch for all to see and wraps it in the paper.

Continuing to patter: "Now this watch has a number of peculiar idiosyncrasies . . . whatever that may mean. One thing it does is to keep the most incorrect time of any timepiece it has been my misfortune to have in my time.

"If it is eight o'clock by someone else's watch it is nine by this one. Which proves that it is a fast watch and goes fast at every opportunity.

"I can hear the ticking. (Holds it to his ear.) Even the ticking is fast. And now let us see if it can do a transatlantic flight without a stowaway getting into the case!

"One, two, two-and-a-half! I fooled you, didn't I? Well . . . maybe you thought I did but I didn't. The watch fooled all of us.

"Keep your eyes on the watch. It has some quick movement. It goes and goes and goes and suddenly it is GONE!"

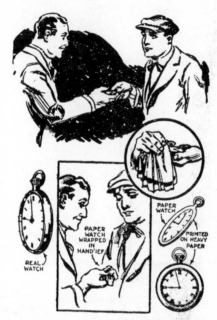

A paper disc is substituted for a watch and the disc vanished in an interesting way.

Upon saying this the magician swings the paper containing the watch about a bit and suddenly exclaims, "Watch the watch. The watch was, but now the watch isn't!"

Suddenly with a dramatic gesture he tears the paper containing the watch into small bits and scatters them.

The watch has disappeared!

The secret:—When the entertainer takes the watch from his pocket it is a real watch with a photographic or a printed reproduction of the watch over a real one.

From a few feet the feked front is not noticeable.

Under cover of wrapping the watch into the piece of newspaper the real watch is retained in the hand and while pattering the real watch is placed, unseen by the spectators, into his pocket.

In the act of continuing to wrap up the watch he makes believe he hears some remark that the watch has gone.

Looking hurt at the lack of confidence displayed, he shows the watch still in the paper by lifting a corner of the paper and showing the picture of the watch which is printed on the stiff paper.

Again the wrapping business is carried out.

Now all that remains for the entertainer to do is to work the trick up into a climax and dramatically tear the paper to pieces.

Naturally the watch has disappeared. It's a real baffler and I have made use of it time and again when called upon to do something of an impromptu nature before a gathering of friends.

Bill and Pencil Mystery.

THERE is no mystery about breaking a dollar bill but there is a bit of mystery and a lot of astonishment for mystery lovers when a dollar bill is used as an axe to break a wooden pencil.

Try as you will it will be found utterly impossible to fold a dollar bill in such a fashion that it could be used as an improvised axe to cut a lead pencil in half unless one is in on the secret.

First let me give the effect of this puzzling little impromptu stunt.

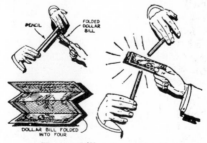

How a bill cuts a pencil.

A bill is taken and folded in lengthwise half and then in quarters.

An obliging gentleman happens to have a long lead pencil which he offers for the experiment.

The pencil is held firmly in the hands of some other gentleman and the bill in its folded state is held rather firmly between the thumb and first finger of the right hand.

The bill is brought down

smartly against the pencil several times and upon the third trial breaks the pencil in half.

I most always square the kind gentleman who loans me his pencil with a cigar.

Here is a little story of an amusing incident yet rather painful to the magician I saw not so long ago.

Having shown the trick I will soon disclose to a magician friend of mine, he went around doing it whenever the opportunity presented itself. He happened across a mutual friend of ours to whom I had shown the trick and how to do it. The practical joker asked the magi if he knew any new tricks. Glad to have the chance of showing his favorite effect, the other bor-

rowed a pencil and instructed his brother wonderworker just how to hold it. He next borrowed a dollar bill.

Finally he folded up the dollar bill and upon the third striking he brought the bill down smartly and immediately let out a howl of pain.

Upon examination the magician found that the pencil he had borrowed from the magician friend was a metal one. So he kept the bill and nursed his finger for several days.

The secret:—The bill is borrowed and folded up as previously explained. A friend is told to take a pencil from his pocket and grip it tightly between his two hands. The bill is brought down against the pencil twice as

if trying to get a straight aim. The final time the bill hits the pencil the forefinger straightens out quickly and strikes the pencil which is being held firmly. This breaks the pencil in half. The move of straightening the finger is not visible to the eye as not only is it done quickly and smartly but the folded bill hides the manoeuvering of the finger.

But be on the cautious side and examine the pencil loaned you before undertaking the experiment.

Beware of the practical joker. He likes to play his foolish pranks on the other fellow and laugh at the discomfiture which follows, but when the tables are reversed he seldom enjoys the laugh.

✿ ✿ ✿ ✿ ✿

Levitation of Crystal

"Once upon a time," states the conjurer, "deep in the forbidding stone monasteries of Tibet, there lived a group of men who had forsaken the world. These men were scholars and students of the occult and had delved deeply into the many hidden mysteries of metaphysics.

"Prayers and meditations were the larger portion of their daily routine, but many hours were spent in research.

"Hypnotism and mesmerism were practised, so the story tellers tell us, and many are the unthought-of seeming miracles these men of the hills brought to light.

"One of the monks used to sit for hours at a time looking into a tumbler or glass like this." (Show an ordinary glass tumbler.)

"It was his crystal. He used this glass much as the crystal gazer or seer of today does—to seek hidden mysteries of the past, the present and the future.

"In the glass, partly filled with water drawn from a secret well, he looked for things that were to happen. It was the belief of many of his brothers that he could foretell destinies.

"One day after unfolding to one of his colleagues a series of past events, the other monk told him of a number of startling experiments he had made while in-

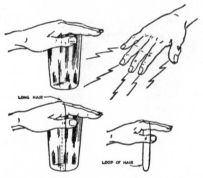

Levitating a glass of water is simple if you use a loop of hair as shown.

vestigating and studying suspended animation.

"He also told a fantastic tale of how he had levitated a large stone in front of the door of one of the cells a monk occupied.

"The other monk asked him if he couldn't see a demonstration of levitation.

"Agreeing, the monk took the glass and, placing it on a stone table, repeated some sort of weird incantation. At the same time he passed his hand so

(make passes over the glass) over the glass. Slowly he raised his hand which was still held above the glass and slowly the glass was seen to rise under some mysterious power. The higher the monk raised the hand the higher rose the glass.

"Awed, the other monk grabbed for the glass. The spell was broken."

Hand the glass out for someone among the spectators to examine. Then show your hands empty.

The Secret:—The glass is placed on the table. A number of passes are made over it. As the passes continue the hand is lowered above the glass and slipped through a piece of thread which extends around the glass. See drawing.

Slowly the glass is seen by the spectators to levitate below the hand. The other hand is then brought forward and grasps the glass, freeing it of the thread.

The thread drops unseen to the floor and the glass is handed for inspection to the surprised spectators.

Note: By using a lady's long, black hair instead of the thread the trick can be presented at closer quarters.

Hindu Sand Mystery

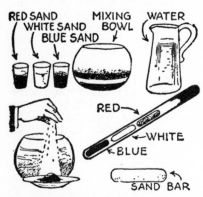

The accompanying article explains how it is possible to mix red, white and blue sand with water and then remove a handful of the particular color asked for. The bowl is not faked.

THREE sands of different colors are mixed into a container of water, the contents completely stirred with a rod. Any color is now called for for and the magician, placing his hand into the container, removes a handful of the sand, corresponding to the requested color, perfectly repeated, until a handful of each respective color has been removed from the water. Cakes of sand, previously made by mixing a small portion of paraffin with the sand, are concealed in the hollow mixing rod and are secretly dropped out of this rod, while stirring the contents of the container. As they are respectively removed, slight pressure will break the cake, permitting the sand to flow freely through the fingers. It is preferable to use a mixing bowl which is not transparent and yet which is not entirely opaque, as in the latter case there would always be a suspicion of a feked bowl.

The Enchanted Cigar

A MAGICIAN offers a cigar to his friend who states his preference for a cigarette. Instantly, the cigar transforms itself into the desired smoke. This surprising trick is easily accomplished when one realizes that the cigar is drawn into the magician's sleeve by the usual pull arrangement. Most of the modern pulls operate from the waist. Consequently the one alert to this type of pull will never suspect that the old system is being used. The cigarette makes its appearance by dropping from the interior of a prepared cigar while the same passes up the sleeve. An ordinary cigar may be hollowed out to conceal the cigarette or a wooden plug covered with tobacco leaf may be used instead.

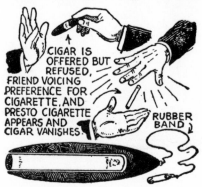

A friend offers you a cigar, knowing full well that you only smoke cigarettes, and instantly the cigar changes into your favorite smoke.

Chinese Plate Problem

Your own mark placed on a China plate which is subsequently ground into powder mysteriously appears on the palm of your hand. The method is explained herewith.

A CHINA plate which has been inspected is broken into many pieces with a hammer. A spectator selects one piece which he marks with his initial or some other insignia, using a brush and India ink. The piece of plate is now ground into a powder and the powder emptied upon the spectator's hand. This is blown from the palm a moment later, whence the identical mark will be found to have been mystically imprinted in the center of his palm. The explanation is quite simple. The spectator smashes a plate with a hammer and marks one of the pieces. Thereupon the magician picks up this piece and hands it to the spectator to grind it up. While doing so an impression is carried off on the magician's thumb, which is transferred to the spectator's palm.

A Barrel of Plenty

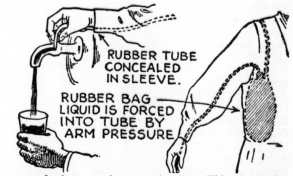

A small barrel made entirely of glass is passed for inspection. A committee is invited upon the stage and requested to suspend the barrel in mid-air, assisted by four unprepared strings or chains. The Egyptian-clad wizard opens the faucet and fills glass after glass with wine, yet the transparency of the barrel shows the structure free from any liquid content. At any moment the action may *be repeated after complete examination. This clever effect is merely an illusion, inasmuch as the liquid is contained in a rubber-bag arrangement concealed beneath the wizard's cloak. The liquid is forced by arm pressure through the tubing and faucet of the barrel as illustrated. It may be advisable to place the bag under the left arm while manipulating the faucet with the right hand.*

New Rising Card

MAGICIANS desirous of improving their programs by adding a piece of mechanical apparatus to their outfit, will find the effect about to be described well worthy of the trouble that will be necessary to build this clever piece of paraphernalia. In the illustration one sees a nickel-plated stand large enough to contain a deck of cards. An ordinary deck of cards is freely passed for examination, and then placed in the houlette. At command, any number of cards will rise in rotation, or if desired the entire deck will leave the houlette one at a time in a most mysterious manner.

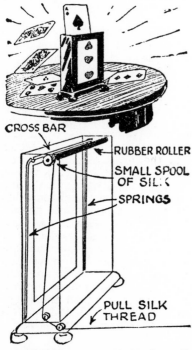

The diagram will disclose the fact that a rubber roller to which a small spool has been attached, is mounted within the houlette. The spool itself has been previously wound with a thin black silk thread and it is this thread which is chiefly responsible for the weird effect. As the roller revolves when the thread is pulled, the card pressed to its edge is first caused to rise, due to the friction exercised by the roller upon the back of the card. The entire deck is constantly pressed against the roller by means of a double spring arrangement across which springs a cross bar is attached. The springs maintain a constant friction against the roller, and for this reason the entire deck may

be made to leave the houlette one at a time. The rapidity of their departure from the holder may be increased or decreased by pulling the thread more rapidly or slowly.

A Mystic Smoke

This trick may be easily performed. An ordinary cigar box is constructed as illustrated in the above diagram. The male members in the audience first select a few cigars. The performer then starts to return to the stage but remembers that there are also ladies in the audience. In turning over the cigar box and opening the same the doves in the lower compartment fly out.

The Ghost Flame

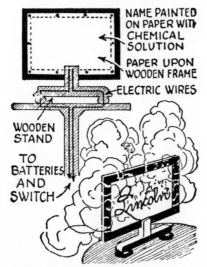

Some member in the audience is requested to mention the name of one of the great men in history. The name selected mysteriously appears in the form of a small traveling flame. A small piece of fuse wire connected across the cables leading to the batteries ignites the mixture with which the sheets have been prepared. The name is written with a solution of six parts of potassium nitrate and one-half part of gum-Arabic dissolved in four tablespoonsful of water.

A Spirit Slate

PERHAPS one of the most impressive forms of mystification are those wherein apparently unknown psychical powers are brought into play. In the particular device here described a new principle is employed which the writer feels will meet with the approval by those who desire to perform this trick before an audience. An unprepared slate is passed for examination. A member of the audience is then

requested to write a series of sentences or questions upon the slate. This is then placed upon a tray with the writing facing the tray so that the performer could not possibly have obtained a glimpse of the questions written upon the slate. The performer then holds both the slate and the tray in an upright position and walks back upon the stage. He may then go into a seeming trance, during which he will answer the questions written upon the slate. In this effect, as in many others, "all things are not what they seem." Of course the writing cannot be perceived while it is held on the slate in a horizontal position, but the instant both slate and tray are raised to a vertical position, the performer may secretly let down the flap in the tray which will reveal to him all the writing upon the slate. The tray is never passed for examination.

The X-ray Eye

An interesting stunt performed with the aid of three wooden blocks numbered as shown is here illustrated. One of the blocks is put into the box and the performer without opening the box tells the number of the block.

IN performing this stunt the magician passes an empty box and cover and three wooden slabs for examination. During his absence from the room, one of the spectators places one of the slabs into the box, and the other two are secreted in his pocket. The wizard enters and demonstrates that his X-ray eye can "see through the cover of the box," by correctly calling the number of the slab contained in the receptacle. The secret lies in the fact that the blocks are weighted as indicated by the dotted lines. The string which is used to tie the cover in place really acts as a pivot, and by holding the box between the fingers at the knot, it tips, correctly indicating the slab which it contains.

Card Mind Reading Extraordinary

THE most unusual and extraordinary method of apparent mind reading is described. A young lady psychic is introduced when she comes forth in a costume of oriental splendor. She sits herself upon a chair in the middle of the platform facing the audience. The magician walks down among the audience, exhibits a package of cards and has them freely shuffled. On returning to the stage, he blindfolds the lady, and then stepping considerably toward the rear, she reads the exact order of the cards. This effect is accomplished by substituting the shuffled deck for a prearranged deck under cover of the blindfolding operation. The lady has memorized the prearranged order of cards.

The diagram above shows the position of the prearranged deck and the position assumed by the magician in performing this trick.

Mind Reading Calculator

The illustration here shows position of assistant behind a gauze screen for producing an interesting, yet simple effect in mind reading.

A blindfolded mind reader seated upon a stage calls totals aloud of a series of numbers on the blackboard in back of her. She also describes objects picked by the magician in his journey through the audience. The secret lies in the fact that an assistant behind a gauze screen manipulates a string attached to her ankle and codes the mesage to her. Field glasses are used for auditorium observation. If the unseen assistant is located in back of a screen with no light behind him, his position will not be observed by the audience, yet he himself can look out from in back of the screen without very much difficulty.

Watch in Balloon

Effects of an unusual nature are scarce in conjuring, but the readers will agree that this one is an item of unusual interest. A tray of toy rubber balloons is offered for inspection and one is selected which is blown up to its fullest extent, and the air valve is tied. The balloon is then rested on a nickel stand. A borrowed watch is apparently smashed and its demolished pieces placed into a magician's pistol, and fired at the balloon. The balloon bursts and the watch is found hanging from a thin wire on the pedestal. The secret lies in substituting a duplicate watch for the borrowed watch, smashing the duplicate and fastening the borrowed watch to the spring. A needlepoint pierces balloon.

New Pipe Trick

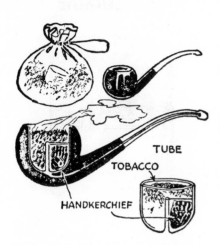

From a seemingly unprepared pipe which is smoked by the performer, a colored handkerchief is removed.

TRICKS with seemingly unprepared articles always are the most mystifying. In this one the wizard passes his pipe for inspection and fills the same with tobacco from his pouch. He lights the pipe and puffs away. A small silk handkerchief is now vanished by any of the popular methods and is immediately reproduced out of the bowl of the pipe. This silk of course is a duplicate of the one originally disappeared and is contained within a cup previously concealed in the tobacco pouch and introduced into the mouth of the pipe during the innocent action of filling the same.

Jumping Peg Pencil

THIS trick differs from the usual and impractical method (in which the pencil could not be passed for inspection) inasmuch as the holes in the present offering actually penetrate the wood. The end of the pencil which is examined, however, is secreted in a brass sliding pencil cap of the ordinary type. This action brings to view the holes of the pencil constructed as indicated in our diagram, which holes are primarily responsible for the effectiveness of the trick. Notice that the two end holes are only bored halfway through the pencil.

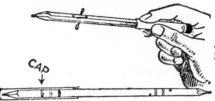

In the jumping peg pencil illustrated above care should be taken in drilling the holes properly. The cap should also fit this pencil tightly so that it will not be removed during cursory examination.

Placing the peg in the center hole on one side of the pencil makes the other side of the peg appear to be in the end hole. In presenting the trick both sides of the pencil are seemingly shown, but during the wafting movement the pencil is twisted between the fingers, showing the same side again. To make the peg jump the pencil is not twisted under cover of one of these movements.

Rubber Band Palm

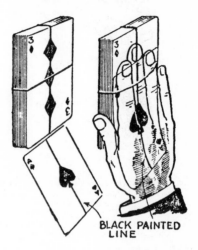

At first glance the above trick will appear very ineffective, yet it is actually an interesting stunt.

AFTER the magician has been changing cards by any of the well-known sleight-of-hand methods, he places a rubber band crosswise around the entire deck, thereby "preventing the possibility of card palming," yet in passing his hand over the surface of the card, its suit mysteriously changes. The effect is accomplished by painting a black line longitudinally down the face of two or more cards, producing the illusion of a rubber band being strapped across the face in two directions. When the cards are passed for examination, those on top which are marked are palmed off from beneath the band.

The Patriotic Liquids

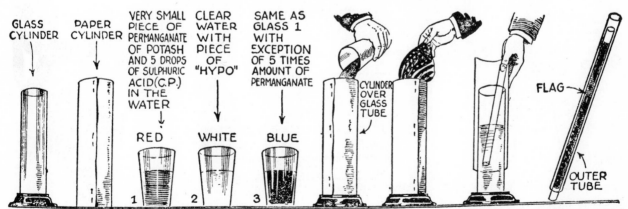

A transparent glass cylinder is covered by an opaque paper cylinder and red, white and blue liquids from three glasses are poured into the cylinder. The contents are stirred and on removing the rod, an American flag is taken from the cylinder and the solutions become transparent. Formulae for making these solutions are given in the diagram which also shows that the stirring rod really consists of two tubes the outer one being first removed and the inner one being extracted at the time the paper cylinder is lifted. The flag is concealed in the stirring rod.

Boxes of Plenty

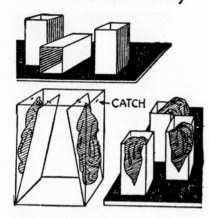

Three apparently empty boxes are shown, the performer looking through them and the audience seeing his face on the other side. Due to false sides, a large quantity of silks can be produced from the interiors.

IN this particular effect the performer shows three boxes opened at both ends. He looks through them to show that they are empty. On setting them down on a thin tray, he removes great quantities of silks from the inside of the boxes. The diagram explains how the effect is produced. It will be noted that two of the sides of the boxes are false and behind these the handkerchiefs are nested. On setting them down on the table, the performer merely releases the catches permitting of access to the kerchiefs.

Miraculous Eggs

AFTER vanishing a ring, the performer requests that anyone bring an egg to the stage. This egg is passed for examination, proving that it is absolutely intact and is the genuine article. The egg is marked for identification at the bottom and then struck a blow with a small hammer. An examined probe is dipped down into the contents of the egg, the ring removed, washed and returned to its owner. It will be observed that the hammer itself serves to drive the ring into the egg under cover of the blow. This is one of the most unique tricks which has as yet been produced.

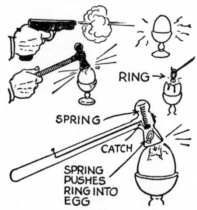

A hammer provided with a spring and catch precipitates a borrowed ring into the interior of an unprepared egg as indicated.

The Obedient Ball

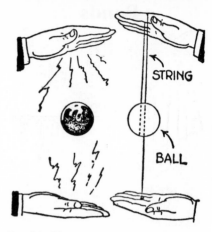

By the aid of a string passing between the hands as the diagram indicates, a ball may be made to raise vertically in the air.

A WOODEN croquet ball has a small hole drilled clear through it through which a string passes. This string is free at one end and is opened in the form of a loop at the other and again affixed to the ball itself as the diagram indicates. The performer on picking up the ball, passes his hand through the loop and affixes the other end of the string to his left hand. By bringing the hands apart, the ball may be made to rise and again on bringing them closer together, the ball will be found to settle into the left hand.

The Puzzle Blocks

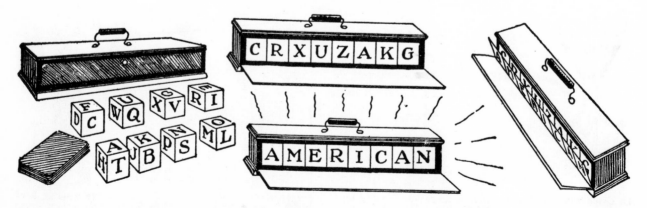

A number of blocks are passed for examination and these are then placed in a wooden case so as to form no word in particular. A member of the audience, generally a "plant" is asked for a word with eight letters. He thinks of the word American, the cover of the box is closed and when opened, the blocks are found to have rearranged themselves to form the word. The stunt is produced through the agency of a thin metal flap which covers the blocks. This is indicated at the extreme right of our drawing. The cover may be closed and blocks removed for examination.

The Chameleon Bands

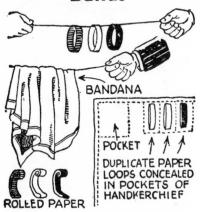

Endless paper bands of different colors are placed on a string, the ends of which are held by a spectator. The magician can remove any of the bands requested.

THREE endless loops of differently colored paper are arranged on a string as illustrated and two spectators are requested to hold the opposite ends of the string. A large bandana is displayed and the hands are covered with it. One of the spectators suggests a color and the performer reaching beneath the handkerchief mystically removes the chosen colored band from the string, the band itself being intact. The diagram explains the secret of the stunt. When one of the bands is to be removed, it is torn, placed into the empty pocket and a corresponding duplicate is removed from the kerchief and displayed.

The Mystic Bread

A LOAF of bread through which a ribbon has been passed and which projects from either end is displayed. A magician takes a knife and divides the loaf in half with a cut through the center thereby apparently also cutting the ribbon. The pieces of bread are separated slightly to show that the ribbon has been cut, then they are joined together and the ribbon withdrawn intact.

Two pieces of ribbon are used. One was tucked into one end of the bread and the other is attached to a piece of string working down into the table leg and into the hands of the assistant off-stage. As the ribbon is drawn from the bread after the cut the assistant gradually pulls the other end down into the table leg and causes it to disappear.

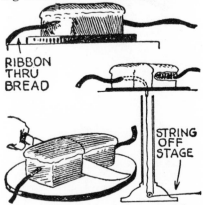

To cut through a loaf of bread without cutting the ribbon, prepare articles as shown.

The Paper Birds

By this system the magician can convert two paper birds placed in the pages of a book into real live birds which fly out from between the pages.

A LARGE book is brought by wizard and a page or two is torn out of this book and handed to a spectator who is requested to cut two birds out of paper. These cut birds are placed in pages of the volume from which they were originally removed and a few words of enchantment uttered. A moment later the book is opened and two live doves fly out of the book itself. The pages of the book can be shown to be whole so that the spectators will not suspect that a box is found within the pages. The book although of innocent appearance has a special compartment arranged at the back. When opened at the proper page the compartment is opened.

Colored Liquids

An Orientally-clad Hindu passes a large ornamental bowl for inspection and then places the same in position upon a thin skeleton stand designed to receive it and resembling the stand found in our illustration. The bowl itself may be semi-transparent or perfectly transparent, depending on whether or not the magician desires to cover it while it mysteriously fills itself. Making a few passes over the bowl it is found to be brim full of water which is poured into transparent containers. Each time that the bowl is filled it contains a differently colored solution, the colors being requested by members in the audience. The illustration clearly shows the method of operation. Beneath the stage an attendant operates one of the pumps forcing the previously prepared colored solution through the legs of the stand and into the bowl. For lyceum entertainment the method illustrated at the right may be employed.

A New Coin Box

WAX
COIN
COVER
PAPER DISK

PAPER DISK ON LOWER SIDE OF COIN

EMPTY

It will be observed above that a coin is held to the cover with a bit of wax. The bottom of the coin is concealed by a disk of black paper. A second coin is vanished and apparently made to appear in the box.

THIS is an excellent parlor trick, absolutely new in principle, and has not yet appeared in its present form either in another book or on the market. A small box similar to the one in the illustration above has an inside diameter slightly larger than either a silver half-dollar or a dollar. The coin is covered on one side with a piece of black paper and then held in position by a pellet of wax. The inside of the box itself is painted a dull black. A duplicate coin is made to disappear by any of the regular methods and is found to appear in the box. Setting the box down sharply on the table releases the coin.

Hindu Rice Trick

HERE is a spectacular mystery credited to the wise men of the East. A brass bowl is displayed and passed for examination. A bag of rice is also shown and likewise examined and, lastly, a shining dagger is thoroughly inspected. The Orientalist pours the rice into the jar, inserts the dagger into the center of the rice and lifts both rice and bowl, using the dagger as a handle. Immediately thereafter everything is passed for examination. When pouring the rice into the bowl, the jar is tapped, causing the rice to adhere firmly to the sides of the jar and producing a very hard gripping filling, which will firmly hold the knife.

RICE

DAGGER

A bowl full of rice may be raised from the table if a dagger is plunged into the rice previously firmly packed in the bowl.

Columbus Outdone

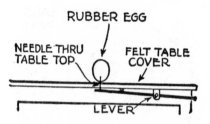

RUBBER EGG

NEEDLE THRU TABLE TOP

FELT TABLE COVER

LEVER

A rubber egg may be balanced on the surface of the magician's table if the table has been provided with a lever and needle as this illustration clearly shows.

THE reader will undoubtedly remember the story of Columbus and the egg. This discoverer must undoubtedly have been an amateur conjurer, otherwise nothing would have induced him to show this trick to the Queen of Spain. He found it necessary however, to break the shell to balance the egg. In this stunt a rubber egg is used, which can neither be broken nor balanced, except by the magician. He is able to accomplish this by the aid of a lever, to which is secured a needle point, as indicated in the diagram above. The lever is operated by hand.

The Enchanted Aquarium

EMPTY

FULL OF FISH

CATCH

FISH UNDER FLAP

A fair-sized fish aquarium is exhibited. It is filled with clear water. The magician standing at a distance loads a pistol with fish eggs, fires at the tank, and instantaneously it will be found to be filled with hundreds of fish swimming about. The effect is very impressive upon an audience. It is one of the few which can be presented without covering the tank with any cloth. The fish themselves are found in the bottom of the tank concealed beneath a flap operating over a spring pulley. When the shot is fired, a string releasing the catch is pulled. The noise of the shot drowns the sound of the movement of the flap. Several large fish and a great many smaller fish are held in the bottom of the aquarium. They are kept alive by a sufficient quantity of water under the roller blind-like arrangement.

Handkerchief and Confetti Trick

PAPER BAGS WITH CONFETTI

As indicated above, two kerchiefs are placed in two glasses mounted on the table. A cloth is held in front of them and the kerchiefs change into confetti.

THE conjurer exhibits two ordinary drinking glasses, which may be passed for examination, and then places them on an undraped side stand. He puts a blue silk kerchief in one and a red kerchief in the other. The wizard now holds a borrowed linen handkerchief momentarily in front of the glasses. When it is removed, red and blue confetti will be found in the glasses. The kerchiefs have disappeared. The trick is accomplished with the aid of a trick table, having a lever working on hinges and carrying two metal envelopes for the confetti. The lever is lifted under cover of the linen kerchief.

Mystic Knife Trick

HERE is another original problem which will be found effective. It should be presented a short distance from an audience in order to protect the illusion. A pocket knife is passed for inspection and then a playing card is selected from an ordinary deck. The magician, picking up the card, proceeds to cut it as illustrated. A moment later, both card and knife are again passed and the card will be found in no way injured. The trick is accomplished by the aid of a duplicate knife blade a little shorter than the original, to which a piece of steel wire, bent as illustrated, has been soldered. The loop fits the index finger of the hand, and encircles the card so that the knife blade apparently projects.

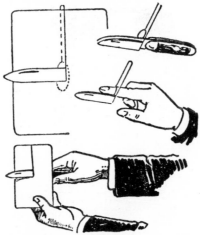

By the aid of a blade of a knife fastened to a thin wire and the wire looped to fit the finger, one can apparently cut a card and immediately restore it again.

Gold and Silver

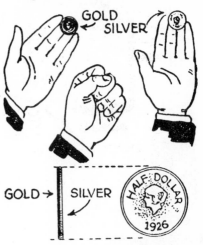

GOLD
SILVER

GOLD → SILVER

HALF DOLLAR 1926

A gold coin held in one hand and a silver coin held in the other mysteriously change their places when the hand is closed. The coins are made in halves, fastened together as the diagram above indicates.

TWO coins are shown. In size they resemble the American half-dollar, but one is of gold and the other of silver. One of these is placed in the right hand and the other in the left. With the hands quite a distance apart and away from the performer's body, the magician closes his fist upon the respective coins. When the hands are opened, the pocket pieces are found to have mysteriously changed places. As an explanation, it would be advisable to state that the coins are prearranged. Half of the coin is gold and the other half silver. When placed on the ends of the fingers, it is natural that in closing the hand, the coins are turned over.

The Obedient Spools

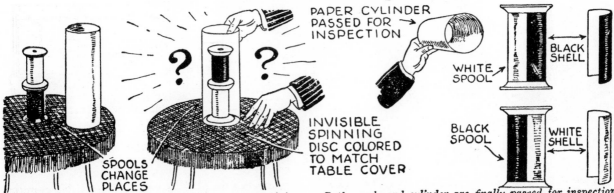

SPOOLS CHANGE PLACES

PAPER CYLINDER PASSED FOR INSPECTION

INVISIBLE SPINNING DISC COLORED TO MATCH TABLE COVER

WHITE SPOOL

BLACK SHELL

BLACK SPOOL

WHITE SHELL

Two spools of silk thread are shown. The one containing black thread and the other white. They are now stacked upon the table, the white one upon the black. A paper cylinder having neither top or bottom is passed for inspection and is then placed over the spools. On being removed the spools will be found to have changed positions.

Both spools and cylinder are finally passed for inspection. This trick is performed by the aid of two half shells made of metal, painted white and black respectively. These fit over the spools as shown. The revolving disk on which the spools stand is rotated while the cylinder is being slowly lowered over the spools. The shells are palmed.

The Yogi Coin Illusion

A Hindu fakir displays a coin and an egg. These are placed upon the ground. At the mystic's command the coin jumps from this position and secretes itself below the egg. The secret lies in the fact that a small black thread is tied to the toe, buried a fraction of an inch in the ground, and a pellet of wax is affixed to its far end. The coin is attached to the wax pellet. Moving the toe moves the coin. This makes a good demonstration at a bathing beach.

The Crystal Houlette

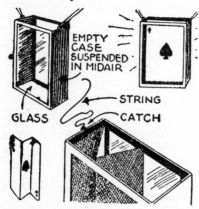

In an empty crystal case suspended from two ribbons a card can be made to mysterious appear after it has been caused to disappear. It will be observed that the card itself is folded at one end of the houlette.

THIS is a new system for the reappearance of a previously chosen and vanished card. A deck of cards is seen in the case which is suspended by two ribbons and hangs in mid-air. The deck is removed and a card is chosen. This card is destroyed and placed in the magician's pistol, who fires at the now empty transparent case. The card magically makes its reappearance completely restored in the box. The sides of the houlette are made of brass and front and back of the holder are of glass. The chosen card is forced upon the spectator and then destroyed. A duplicate card divided into three parts hinged together with pices of rubber and concealed alongside of one of the sides is released when the string is pulled. A catch holds the folded card in place.

Second Sight Mystery

HERE is an impromptu trick which any amateur magician can present with an assistant and which requires no practice whatever. In the hands of a clever showman, the offering is little short of miraculous. The wizard sends the medium out of the room and during her absence the spectators decide upon some object which is pointed out to the magician. Upon the magician's request, a committee asks the medium to re-enter. The magician then, without saying a word, points to many objects in the room and the moment the proper one is pointed out, the medium calls out that it is the selected article. The spectators can decide beforehand at what number the magician is to point to the object. Extension of the finger alongside of the wand is the code.

This is a very ingenious stunt and incidentally an excellent impromptu parlor trick in which the code to the medium is indicated by the manner in which the wand is held.

Silks From Nowhere

A sheet of cardboard is rolled into a cylinder and then held in position by means of paper clips. It is slipped upon the arm to show that it is empty, but on being removed is found to be full of silks.

HERE is an excellent magical diversion quite simple to perform. The wizard presents a large sheet of cardboard to his spectators for their examination. The inspection having been made, he rolls the cardboard into a cylinder which is held in this position by a number of paper clips. He proves the tube empty by looking through it and pushing his hand and arm into the cylinder. The tube is then placed on an undraped side stand, after which the magician bares his arms to his elbows and proceeds to withdraw many silk kerchiefs from the interior of the tube. The paper clips are then removed and the tube is unfolded, both sides of the paper being again shown. The silks are introduced into the tube via the coat sleeve as illustrated.

An Annoying Telephone

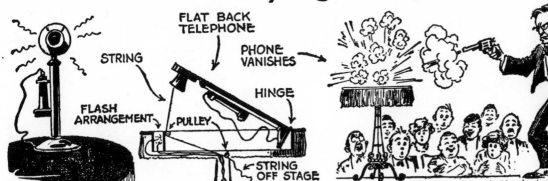

Upon the performer's entrance at the opening of his act, he is repeatedly annoyed by the ringing of the telephone, but gets no answer when he lifts the receiver. While addressing his audience, the telephone bell again sounds. Enraged, he removes a revolver from his pocket, fires at the telephone, which vanishes with a flash and puff of smoke.

The telephone itself is really a half telephone. It is made of wood, the back of which is covered with black velvet. The inside of a table is similarly lined. Both the telephone and the flash powder are operated by an assistant off-stage. He pulls on a string, pulling the telephone down into the table, and operates a spark coil which ignites the powder.

The Diabolic Handkerchief

A HANDKERCHIEF which has been marked for identification is forced into the mouth of an ink bottle with a wand as illustrated. A moment later the ink is emptied from the bottle and the handkerchief is found to have mysteriously vanished. It is later located at the center of a large apple. In reality the kerchief is pushed into a small receptacle which is hidden in the table leg, making its entrance via the special opening in the bottle. When an apple with a prepared cavity is placed over the piston arrangement, the reverse action takes place.

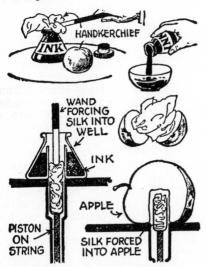

The diagram above illustrates how the handkerchief is pushed through the well in a special ink bottle and is later forced into a prepared apple by the piston-like arrangement in the table.

A Candle Transformation

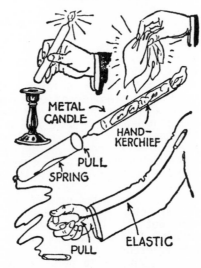

This diagram illustrates how a handkerchief concealed in a candle can be made to appear in the performer's hand, the candle itself vanishing by means of a special pull which grips the metal candle.

IN this stunt a lighted candle is removed from its holder and visibly disappears leaving in its place a handkerchief that may have been previously vanished. The candle in this particular trick is made of a piece of metal tubing, in the end of which a real piece of candle is placed. The handkerchief itself is concealed in the metal tube. The performer drawing the pull down into his hand pushes the lighted end of the candle into it. At the same time he grasps hold of a handkerchief and releases the pull, retaining the handkerchief.

A Tumbler Trick

A LARGE glass tumbler is visibly filled with wine and then a gummed label is attached to it marked by some spectator for identification. A cylinder is now passed for examination and is then placed over the glass. A moment later it is removed and the glass is found empty. The secret lies in the fact that the liquid is actually poured into a celluloid lining in the glass. When the cover is placed over the glass filled with wine, the celluloid lining is lifted out of it by the aid of a wire loop and is carried off.

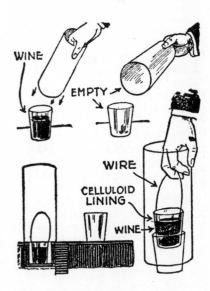

Here we see how the celluloid lining filled with wine is lifted out of the glass and carried away to be deposited in a table receptacle. The celluloid is invisible when placed in the glass.

The Tube of Plenty

A cylinder with a bottom but no top is filled with confetti, covered, and on being opened is found to contain ribbons and kerchiefs. The effect is produced by having a cylinder with a sliding bottom. This cylinder is stood up in the middle of a box of confetti and pushed down into it. This motion causes a feke to be pushed into the cylinder. The feke contains the kerchiefs. After being filled with as much confetti as it will hold and then covered, the cylinder is reversed. A few mystic passes are then made, the cover removed and the handkerchiefs are withdrawn.

The Yogi Bottle

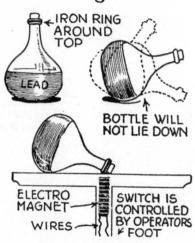

This trick in effect is similar to the imp bottle trick except that the bottle has a cork in the top and consequently cannot be weighted. It responds to the master's command because of the electro-magnet.

UNDOUBTEDLY the readers are familiar with the old imp bottle trick. When the performer took the bottle, he could lay it flat with comparative ease. Others could not. These bottles were weighted at the bottom. When grasped by the performer, he permitted a small piece of lead to drop down into the neck of the bottle, thus counterbalancing the weight in the base. In the present version, a much larger bottle is employed, the mouth of which is closed by a cork stopper. The performer steps on a button controlling a source of electric supply to the electro-magnet which attracts the iron ring around the mouth.

Mind Reading

THE wizard requests the spectator to write a question upon a small piece of note paper, roll it into a ball and drop it in a small tubular container. The ball is forced into the bottom of the container with the magician's wand. The wizard invites the spectator to assure himself that the paper is in full view at all times. While the examination is taking place the question is answered. The effect is produced by the aid of a double wand tip. The real message is removed from the container with the wand and another piece of paper rolled up and previously placed in the false bottom of the container is the one which is held in full view of the spectator.

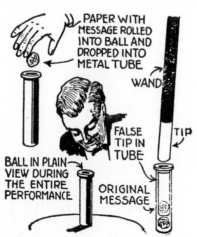

A double container, the bottom half of which contains a piece of paper and the upper half of which hold the message is the secret for performing the mind-reading experiment here described.

The Demon Billiard Ball

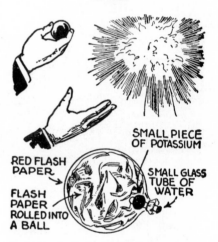

A ball of flash paper containing a small vial of water and a bit of potassium bursts into a flame when the ball is tossed into the air. This produces spectacular closing stunt for the billiard ball trick.

AFTER presenting a series of tricks with billiard balls, the magician tosses one of the balls into the air. In mid-air it bursts into flame and vanishes completely. In preparing for this trick the magician rolls a sheet of flash paper into a tight ball and then covers this with another sheet of paper colored red and as nearly like the color of the billiard ball as he can secure. A small, thin glass tube with water is then inserted into the ball and a relatively large piece of potassium is so placed that the water from the bottle will act on it. The bottle is broken as the ball is tossed in the air.

The Glass Chimney

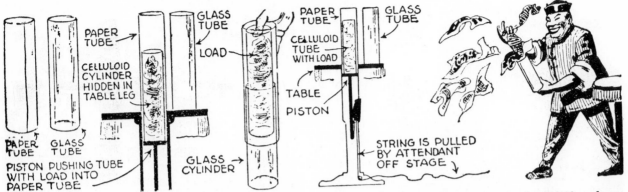

The conjurer presents a glass chimney and a paper tube for examination. They are returned to the table, meanwhile the conjurer bares his arms. Nesting the glass cylinder within the paper cover, he proceeds to draw yards of silks and ribbons from the glass chimney. The load in this effect is placed in a container made of celluloid, and concealed in the leg of the magician's side stand. While baring his sleeves, an attendant pulls on a string, operating the piston which pushes the load into the cardboard tube. The paper tube and load are then taken from the cylinder.

❈ ❈ ❈ ❈ ❈

New Card Mystery

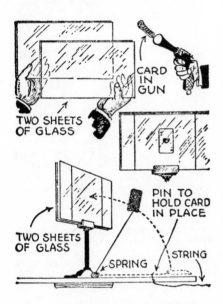

Two sheets of glass mounted on a stand are later found to frame a playing card fired at them from a pistol.

TWO sheets of glass are held together with two elastic bands and then placed in a stand. A selected playing card is then loaded into the barrel of the magician's pistol who, firing at the glass, causes the card to mysteriously appear, apparently between the glasses. Actually the card is carried up in back of the glass and held there by a spring arm. Manipulating the glasses makes it appear that the card is removed from between them.

Living or Dead

THE magician supplies his spectators with eight or nine small visiting cards. He requests all of them to write the name of living persons whom he does not know upon the cards, except one spectator, who is requested to write the name of a dead person on the card. The cards are dropped into a hat, and the magician on picking them out announces the name of the dead person. The penciled writings give him the clue. The magician gives the spectator writing the name of the dead person a hard lead pencil; all the others get soft pencils.

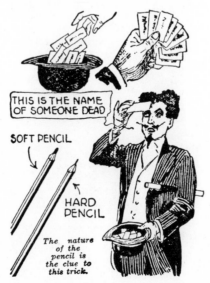

THIS IS THE NAME OF SOMEONE DEAD

SOFT PENCIL

HARD PENCIL

The nature of the pencil is the clue to this trick.

A Sponge Trick

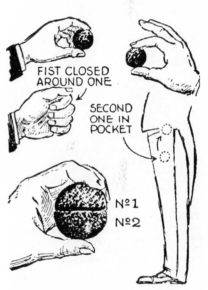

FIST CLOSED AROUND ONE

SECOND ONE IN POCKET

Nº1
Nº2

A sponge ball is put in the pocket, another is held in the hand, and a moment later, the one in the hand becomes two, whereas the one in the pocket has disappeared.

IN performing the trick illustrated above, three balls are actually used. Two of them are held between the forefinger and thumb as illustrated. They appear as one. A third is pushed into the pocket and by the aid of the thumb, secretly moved upward in the corner of the pocket toward the waistband. Turning the pocket inside-out will not reveal the third ball.

Devil's Finger Ring

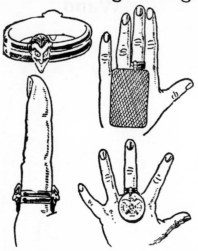

As is indicated in the illustration above, the magician provides the middle finger of his hand with a finger ring having two devil heads. These permit of palming cards or coins as shown.

SLEIGHT of hand artists, only through many years of practice, are able to manipulate their fingers in such a manner as to conceal coins, playing cards, or other like small objects with any degree of perfection. This ring eliminates many years of practice and gives the amateur an opportunity of presenting seemingly impossible feats in sleight of hand which have heretofore been creditable to skilled professionals. A finger ring of the necessary design is illustrated. This can be made of any metal the performer chooses. The coins or cards are pushed under the projecting chin of the demon head where they hold the objects in tight contact with the skin.

Hypnotized Objects

NOW that spiritual effects and illusions bordering upon the psychic are in vogue, this illusion is bound to meet with the approval of the conjurer. A large table of simple design is standing upon the center of the stage and a box or bottle is placed upon the extreme edge of the table. Standing at a considerable distance from the table, the m a g i c i a n makes mysterious passes over the object and then drawing his hand away, the object will be seen to slowly and mysteriously travel toward the hand. Two rollers are concealed at the opposite ends of the table and over these a liberal length of black cloth is wound. This forms the table top proper. The rollers are worked by assistants beneath the stage, who, pulling upon a string, winds up either one roll or the other.

The mechanical table, by the aid of which it is possible to make objects move from one end to the opposite end.

Rising Cards from Hat

In this effect a deck of shuffled cards is dropped into a hat and any one of the cards or a whole series can be made to rise. An extra pocket and deck of cards are required.

PRACTICALLY every magician understands the o l d rising card trick in which a houlette and string were employed. This effect is slightly different, but its presentation is far more spectacular and impressive. A deck of cards are shuffled and thrown into a hat, after a spectator had selected one and returned it to the deck. At the word of command, the chosen card is first made to rise and then immediately thereafter, cards in respective order come out of the deck. The selected card is forced. A duplicate deck, threaded as indicated, is used. The string tied to a shirt stud, serves to raise the cards up when stretched.

A Phantom Treat

Here is a splendid illusion for a wizard's home. Upon a server one can plainly see a large box of cigars and a bottle of wine. The wizard invites his guests to help themselves, but much to the amazement of the onlookers, the articles prove to be but phantoms as the fingers of the disappointed guests pass through them in ghost-like fashion. By arrangement of a concave mirror, a hole in the server and an ordinary mirror, this effect is produced. When standing directly in front of the server, the articles apparently rest on the tray. The objects are located in the server.

Hercules' Fingers

HOLE STUFFED WITH TIN-FOIL

PALMED

An unprepared coin is passed for examination. When it is returned to the wizard he takes an ordinary pin and pushes it through the center of the coin. On removing the pin, the coin is again passed out. A second coin helps in the deception.

THE wizard passes an unprepared common steel pin together with a silver half dollar for minute inspection. Both are returned to him, having been found intact. The magician then explains that he has the most remarkable and uncanny amount of strength in his fingers and after centering the pin, he pushes it clear through the coin. Grasping both ends of the pin, he then spins the coin. Two coins are necessary for the trick; one has a small hole drilled through the center and stuffed with tin-foil. This is palmed while duplicate is being examined.

The Vanishing Bird

TRICKS with livestock are always a favorite with the average audience. In this novel creation the wizard holds a small fluttering bird between his fingers. Gently placing his hands around it so as to completely cover the bird, his palms are brought gradually together. The fingers are opened a moment later one at a time, when much to the amazement of the audience the bird has completely vanished. The canary finds its way safely into the mouth of a small metal feke, which is drawn up into the magician's sleeve by the usual elastic arrangement. A pivoted cap prevents the bird's escape, while holes in the metal case allow the bird to breathe freely.

COVER

ELASTIC

By the aid of the feke illustrated in the diagram above, a bird can be made to vanish from the hand.

The Magnetized Wand

WAX PELLET

FINE SILK THREAD

WEIGHT

An ordinary wand is passed for examination. On its return it can be made to mysteriously adhere to the fingertips or to the palm. A piece of wax, a thread, and a weight are required to produce this trick. Notice the weight in the trouser leg.

IN this unique experiment the conjurer, after passing his wand for examination, causes it to adhere to the fingertips, to the palm or back of the hand in a series of mysterious positions. At any moment he can pass the wand for examination. A fine silk thread, and a pellet of wax are responsible. The thread leads down through the magician's shirt front into the leg of his trousers where a small weight is affixed. The weight holds the thread under constant tension, yet it is possible to move the wand away from or toward the body.

The Hindu Sacrifice

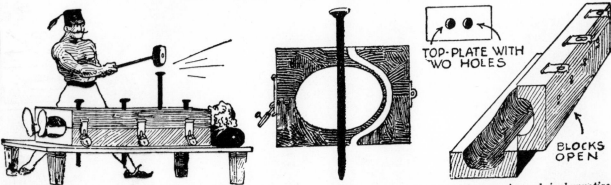

TOP-PLATE WITH TWO HOLES

BLOCKS OPEN

In this novel illusion several attendants drive a number of spikes through a casket which is just large enough to hold a young lady. She watches the procedure with evident interest. The casket is turned in such a way that the audience can observe the spikes being actually driven through the box. They are removed with the aid of a crow-bar.

The box is opened, the girl steps in and is hypnotized, whereupon the box is locked. The spikes now are again driven through the box. The deception is perfect. In reality, however, the nails pass through a steel tubular guide which circles around the body of the hypnotized maiden. The spikes may be made of any flexible alloy.

Mysterious Marksmanship

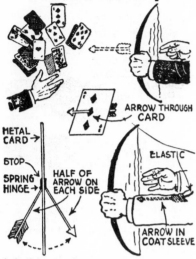

A balloon is placed in an empty card-into the deck, the deck shuffled, tossed into the air, and while the cards are flying, the magician shoots an arrow through them. The selected card is found pierced with an arrow.

THE magician permits any member of the audience to select a card from a pack, return it and shuffle the deck. Standing a short distance away from his assistant, he aims a small bow and arrow in the assistant's direction. At a signal, the assistant tosses the cards into the air as the wizard releases the arrow. The selected card is found with the arrow clear through its center. In the operation of the effect, the card is forced. A duplicate made of tin has two sections of an arrow hinged to the center. The real arrow disappears up the sleeve.

A Hindu Phenomenon

IF the wizard is presenting an Oriental performance, this effect will be of unusual interest to him. He first displays the cylinder, allowing the spectators to see through it. This cylinder is placed over the head of an assistant; paper, wood and coal added and a fire is started. Eggs are then fried in a pan over the flame. The tube is so arranged that a star trap is contained within it. As it is placed on the head of the assistant, the star trap is released and it folds down, to make a fire bed. The trick must be presented quickly so the mechanism does not get hot. The pan puts the fire out.

After displaying a cylinder, it is placed on the head of the magician's assistant and coal, wood, and other inflammable materials are thrown into the open end of the tube. A fire is then started.

The Enchanted Balloon

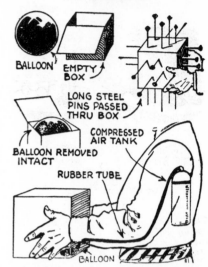

A balloon is placed in an empty cardboard box, the cover closed, and the box pierced with long hat-pins. After the hat-pins are removed, the balloon is shown intact.

A TOY balloon fully inflated, is placed in an empty cardboard box. This box is just large enough to hold the balloon firmly. The lid is closed, and a number of large steel hat-pins are passed through the box, apparently piercing the balloon. The hat-pins are then removed, and the balloon will be found intact. The secret lies in the fact that two balloons of identical appearance are employed, both being equipped with valves. The first is pierced when the steel pin is thrust through it. The second in the box is inflated as the pins are being removed.

Second Sight

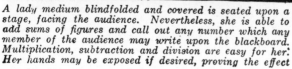

A lady medium blindfolded and covered is seated upon a stage, facing the audience. Nevertheless, she is able to add sums of figures and call out any number which any member of the audience may write upon the blackboard. Multiplication, subtraction and division are easy for her. Her hands may be exposed if desired, proving the effect mental. *Actually, the system is operated from the wings where an assistant with a comptometer performs the necessary operations in addition, subtraction and division. In front of him are a series of switches or preferably push-buttons, which operate miniature lights, coverable by a flap and set in the arm of a chair.*

The Cylinder from Olympus

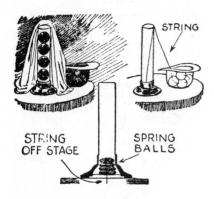

The above illustrations show how spring balls which have been substituted for solid billiard balls are made to disappear from a glass cylinder.

LET us say that the magician had been doing some trick with the multiplying billiard balls. He tosses these into a hat. He now produces a glass cylinder supported on a metal base. He now removes the billiard balls from the hat and places them in the cylinder, and covers it with an unprepared handkerchief, and, presto!—on removing the handkerchief the balls have vanished. The secret lies in the fact that the spring balls substituted for the solid balls, are put into the cylinder. A string passing from the upper spring ball terminates in the hand of an assistant, who by pulling the string crushes the balls into the base of the cylinder.

Mephistopheles' Glass Plate

A PLATE of glass measuring 12x14 inches is suspended in mid-air by means of two ribbons hanging from the flies. In the center of the transparent plate one will find a hole about 2½ inches in diameter. A handkerchief is shown and loaded in the funnel arrangement at the end of the performer's pistol. Standing at a distance of some twenty odd feet, the performer fires the gun and the handkerchief is seen to mystically find its way through the hole in the plate. Secret: Two identical handkerchiefs are employed. One of these remains in the gun, and the other is loaded in a metal tube arrangement on the lower end of the ribbon. A string is attached to this handkerchief, passes through the hole in the glass and to an assistant.

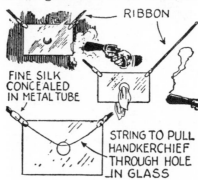

The assistant pulling on the string causes the kerchief loaded in the small metal tube to be drawn through the hole in the glass plate.

Rising Cards Improved

CARD LIFTED WITH INDEX FINGER

With the use of the prepared deck made as illustrated above a very pretty rising card effect can be produced.

AN unprepared pack of playing cards is passed around playing cards is passed around for inspection. Three or four cards are selected and withdrawn by some of the audience and the rest of the pack returned to the magician who, holding it at arm's length, asks that the selected cards be reinserted and one by one they are made to rise from the deck. To accomplish this the magician has provided himself with two decks of cards of an identical nature, in one of which fifty of the cards are cut out in the center, one is partially cut out so as to form a flap, and the other uncut one is placed on the face of the pack. It becomes a simple matter to raise unprepared cards by pushing finger into the hole.

A Temple Buddha Mystery

Here is an original illusion, inexpensive to construct and mystifying to the extreme. An East Indian Buddha is seen sitting on a platform. The figure on the magician's command sings, whistles, speaks and answers whatever question the wizard asks. In order to illustrate that the figure is simply mechanical, the wonderworker proceeds to run a number of sharp-edged swords through the body of the Buddha. One of these passes through the neck, two through the chest, one through each leg and one through the stomach. nl spite of these the automaton continues his conversation. The secret lies in the fact that a small midget is concealed in the figure which is made of metal. The figures has a mechanical moving face, operated from strings on the inside, similar to that of the ventriloquial figure. Tubes leading around the body, legs and neck permit the swords to pass around the body of the midget.

Enchantment

A SHEET of cartridge paper, about 12" x 16" or square, either 12" or 16" on a side, is rolled into a tube. Some water is poured into the upper end of this tube, but contrary to general expectations, the water does not come through, the magician puts his finger into the bottom end of the rolled form, and starts to withdraw dozens of yards of paper ribbon. After the supply of paper ribbon has failed, he unrolls the paper tube to indicate that no water is present.

In producing this effect, a metal fake is used, as indicated in the diagram. This receives the water and at the same time serves as the hiding place for the roll of paper ribbon. The metal fake is rolled into the cartridge paper, is filled with water, the ribbon then removed, and while bundling the paper ribbon into the hand, the performer drops the fake containing the water into the folds of the ribbon. Thus, when he tosses the ribbon away, the fake is simultaneously thrown away in the bundle, whereupon the paper tube can be unrolled, proving it to be entirely empty.

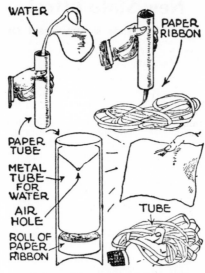

A piece of paper is rolled up in the form of a tube and water poured into it. A paper ribbon is produced from the tube which is then opened and shown empty. The secret is given in the accompanying story.

The Board of Plenty

THE diagram below illustrates quite an effective trick known as the board of plenty. First, a board about 20" square and 1" thick is passed for examination. This is ordinary save for a hole approximately 6" in diameter cut out of the center. On being returned, an assistant is told to hold the board firmly between his two hands and at a considerable distance from his body. Reaching into the hole, the magician pulls forth yard upon yard of colored silk cloth, bunting, kerchiefs, flags, rabbits and any other articles desired.

The secret lies in the fact that the performer's assistant is very well loaded. In a deep pouch concealed beneath his vest, and extending well into the trousers, the various articles for the production are concealed.

The magician himself cannot get at them without the audience getting unduly suspicious, so the assistant withdraws them from the pouch and holds them in readiness for the wizard. In order to hide the operation, a false hand is attached to the end of the board, leaving the assistant's hand and arm free.

BLACK BAG CONCEALED IN VEST OF ASSISTANT

FALSE HAND

This trick is known as the board of plenty. A board with a hole about six inches in diameter is passed for examination, and upon being returned, is held by an assistant. Through *the hole, the magician takes yards and yards of cloth, flags, rabbits and other incidental magic paraphernalia. Actually the assistant does the work with the aid of a false hand.*

A red, a white or a blue block is put in a small box and then the cover is locked in place. Holding the box behind his back, the performer can instantly tell the color

Mystic Box Trick

A SMALL metal box is passed for examination and, while the magician is absent, a wooden block is locked securely in the box. When he returns, the wizard holds the box behind his back and immediately calls the color of the concealed block. The answer to the problem, while entirely new to wizardry, is quite simple. The block can enter the box in but one position. This position causes a hole in the bottom of the block to come in conjunction with another hole in the box. Inserting a thin pin, the magician can tell as to whether the block is red or white, because the pin can be pushed into the hole to different depths.

Passe-Passe Boxes

TWO match boxes are shown, one with a blue and the other a red label. These are carefully wrapped in small squares of paper, and when unwrapped they will have changed their positions. The effect is produced by having duplicate tops of different colors attached to the boxes with beeswax. The tops are removed and palmed in the act of wrapping the boxes in paper.

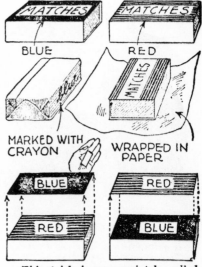

MARKED WITH CRAYON

WRAPPED IN PAPER

This trick is appropriately called the passe-passe match boxes. One of them has a red label, and the other a blue. When wrapped in paper and given to two assistants to hold, they exchange places.

Vanishing Handkerchief

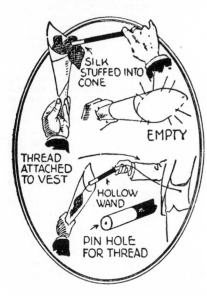

By the aid of the wand shown, a kerchief can be pushed into a paper cornucopia and made to disappear.

HERE is a new and effective method of performing the ever-popular vanishing of a handkerchief from a cornucopia trick. In this method, a fine silk thread is tied to the magician's waist-coat button which leads through the tube, and is then attached to the handkerchief . In the act of tucking the silk into the paper, the movement of the hand forward draws the silk into the interior of the wand. The thread is broken before the wand is laid down

New Slate Effect

A SCHOOL slate is first passed for examination and may even be marked for identification, if desired. It is placed flat upon an apparently unprepared table and then fantastic passes are made over it. On being lifted, a complete message is found.

A slate flap is employed, but the method of its use is quite unlike anything heretofore published. The spirit message is previously written upon the surface of this flap and then concealed in the pocket of a table top. This pocket is covered with strips of gold braid in a design similar to the one indicated. Two small hooks are attached to the edge of the flap to engage the slate as it is being lifted in the act of picking it off the table.

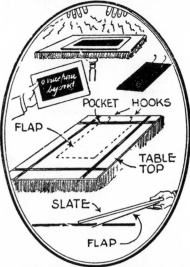

A slate is passed for examination, placed on the table and when again lifted, contains a message.

Enchanted Ballot Box

The magician locates any one of three colored balls put into the ballot box.

A WOODEN box, provided with a handle, is made just large enough to receive one of three differently colored balls. The cover of the box can be closed tightly and locked in place. It is handed to the magician as he enters the room, and he is able to tell instantly the nature of the ball it contains. Shaking produces the same sound with each ball. The effect is obtained by having the balls of three different sizes, varying but slightly. A nail secretly pushes the wall of the box against the ball and the depth of push determines the color.

Spirit Raps in Broad Daylight

Mystic table rappings in broad daylight and messages in wireless code are obtainable with the device indicated. Due to the position occupied by the magician or medium, it is quite impossible to tell from whence the sounds come. This is particularly true if the magician leans against

IN ORDER to produce the spirit raps here indicated, a belt is especially prepared with two small flashlight batteries; a single pole double-throw switch and a buzzer and tap box, or gong-less bell. The heel plate is made of two pieces of metal, separated by a thin piece of fiber and is placed under the heel and inside the shoe of the wearer.

the table and causes the tap box of the buzzer to actually touch any portion of the wood of the table. When this is done, the sound seems to come from a different point, entirely dependent upon the position of the spectator and his ability to argue the point out convincingly.

By depressing this plate, either the buzzer or the tap box will sound at the will of the operator. If he can manage to press either element against the table-top, the sound apparently comes from within the very fiber of the wood. This is ideal for spirit seances and the amateur will find many other ways of utilizing this idea.

Enchanted Serpent Skull

THE illusion below purports to be of East Indian origin and it has been claimed that it is quite common in India. One sees a dark-skinned mystic reach into a woven wicker basket, from which he extracts a small skull. Upon examination, this is found to be the genuine bony substance which at one time constituted the frame-work in the head of a serpent. This snake skull is placed upon the ground directly in front of the seated turban-headed magician. Mystic passes are then made over the skull, the jaw of which is seen to move. The mystified spectators are not aware of the presence of a small boy concealed in the hollow of a tree. A tube leading from this tree serves as a channel for a piece of thread or thin cord. The free end of this cord hooks to one portion of the skull, and permits the bony structure to rock back and forth on the lower jaw. The lower jaw must be hinged to the upper and springs added to close them after they are pulled open.

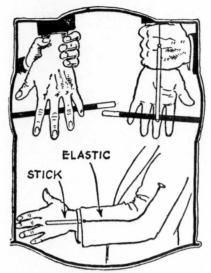

A wand can be suspended from the finger-tips by the aid of a stick as indicated in the diagrams above. The stick slides into the sleeve when not in use.

Magnetism

MANY of the readers have undoubtedly witnessed the clever little trick popularly known as magnetism. In this illusion, the magician apparently causes a pencil, ruler, table-knife, or his wand to mysteriously cling to the finger-tips. In the old version of this trick, the wrist of the hand is apparently held for support, but actually, an extended finger of that same hand also holds the article close to the palm. In another form of the trick, a similar effect is obtained by holding a pencil beneath the palm of the hand in such a manner that the pencil presses the object against the palm. This trick has a slight advantage over the first one mentioned, in that the spectators see all five fingers. The disadvantage lies in getting rid of the pencil after the trick has been performed. This new version employs a stick, but the stick itself is attached to an elastic band, terminating at a safety pin fastened to the sleeve. The methods are just as mystifying and it possesses the additional advantage of permitting the performer to show his hands empty at any moment.

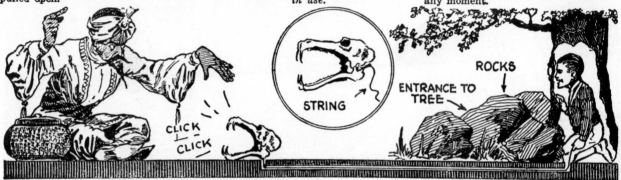

A boy in a hollow tree several hundred feet away from the scene of the demonstration controls the movements of the skull supposedly previously mesmerized by a Hindu mystic. The cord operating the skull is run through a buried rubber tube.

Chameleon

The wizard displays a four-sided tube, open at both ends. A white billiard ball, about 2½ inches in diameter is then passed for inspection. It is dropped into the upper end of the cylinder and falls completely through, but the strange feature is that in falling, it is mystically changed in color, becoming a polished black sphere. This ball is again immediately passed for inspection, and the cylinder held so as to enable the spectators to see through it. The diagram explains the mystery. A flap on one side of the tube falls down, causing the white ball to remain above it and release of pressure of the hand permits the black ball to fall.

Find the Ace

Three blocks, with cards on their faces, are placed into a three-compartment box. The doors are closed, and the audience is asked to find the ace. On opening the doors again, it will be found that the blocks have changed places. The effect is produced by having two flaps of tin painted to represent the other two cards not in the compartment. Movement of the handle either way will permit either one or both of the tin flaps to remain behind.

By aid of the tube indicated, a white ball can be instantly converted into a black ball. The white ball previously examined is palmed, and the black one released.

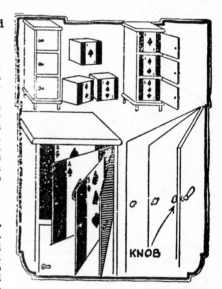

Two metal flaps hinged to the door of each of the three compartments permit of a multiplicity of card changes of the card blocks

Flying Gold Fish

THE magician holds up a glass container, three-quarters full of water in which several gold fish are seen to be swimming. A cloth is then passed for examination and the aquarium is covered with it. The jar under cover of the cloth is placed into a hat, after which the magician explains his intention of vanishing the aquarium from his fingertips. He apparently removes the container together with the cloth, and a moment later tosses the cloth into the audience. Fish, water and jar have disappeared. Thereafter the liquid-filled aquarium is removed from hat.

Explanation. The aquarium is surrounded with an outer shell made of thin transparent celluloid. Both articles are placed into the hat. The aquarium is left there and the transparent shell removed beneath the cover of the cloth whereupon the magician, inserting his hand under the cloth, slides the celluloid over the arm and under his coat sleeve.

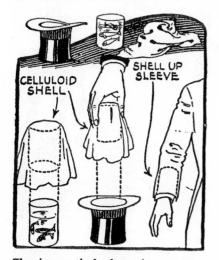

Showing method of causing an aquarium full of gold fish to vanish from the hands and reappear in a hat.

New Rising Cards

RISING cards have for years been considered to be one of the most spectacular and mystifying of conjur-

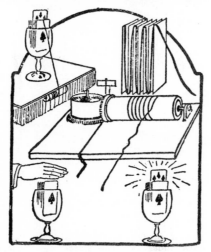

The above illustration indicates the new rising card effect which does not require an assistant.

ing effects. Magicians have discarded the trick, due to the fact that in nearly every case, cumbersome unreliable methods had to be resorted to in producing the effect. The present system is a vast improvement over the others, because it is a non-assistant trick which will continue to operate, regardless of the magician's position on the platform.

Explanation. The cards for this trick are threaded in the usual way and three cards are forced as usual and returned to the pack. Now, standing several feet away from the deck, the magician commands the cards to rise up one by one, which they do. In order to produce the slow rise, use the mechanism found in music boxes. Merely remove the reeds and the small metal pins on the revolving drum and substitute a thread for the pins.

Flying Cigarettes

IN this effect the magician after apparently showing both hands empty, reaches into space and produces a cigarette at his fingertips. Placing this one upon the table, he again extracts another from the air in a similar manner. He repeats this action until four cigarettes have been produced, and then again shows both hands completely empty. Similarly he can reverse the procedure and vanish the cigarettes.

Explanation. The secret consists in a small piece of apparatus made of quite thin metal, and shaped as indicated in the diagram. To each side a clip is soldered which serves as an aid in palming the small spread clip, making it possible to hold the cigarettes in either hand, switching them rapidly from one to the other so that both hands are apparently shown empty. After one cigarette has made its appearance, the hands are again shown empty, and then a second is produced.

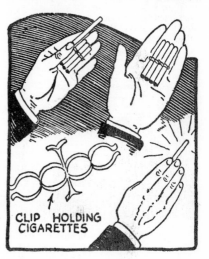

A cigarette-holding clip which enables the magician to make cigarettes appear at the fingertips.

The Mystic Hand of Dante

A glass hand of the feminine type is exhibited, examined and returned. It is placed in an upright position on a stand made to receive it. A lady's finger-ring is then loaded into the magician's ever ready pistol and the shot fired directly at the artificial hand where the ring appears. The magician removes the hand and presents it to the lady, who takes her ring from the glass finger The effect is produced by affixing the borrowed ring to a lever of thin wire, arranged in back of the magician's stand. The assistant does this, or the magician may do so while looking for another piece of apparatus. When the spring is released, the ring flies upward above the finger where, because the rod is made in two sections, the top one slides down, leaving the ring on the finger itself. Note detail and method of attaching ring.

Improved Obedient Ball

FOR a number of years the so-called obedient ball trick has been a favorite deception, particularly among amateur magicians. Its operation being

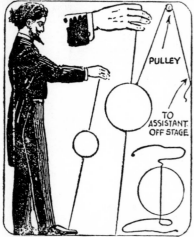

A celluloid ball moves up and down on a string, held between the performer's foot and his hand. Its operation is controlled by another string attached to the ball by a wax pellet.

generally known, it has been discarded from the programs of magical newcomers. In the present method, the possibility of passing the paraphernalia for examination is greatly increased, hence the trick much improved. In effect, a large celluloid ball with a hole drilled through it is shown and then a string is passed through the hole. One end of the string is caught beneath the foot, the other end held in the hand. At the magician's command, the ball will be seen to fall, stop, or rise again.

Explanation: There is nothing about the ball or the string which will not pass an examination. The secret lies in the fact that a very thin thread, passing over a pulley overhead and to an assistant in the wings, is affixed to the ball by a pellet of wax.

An X-Ray Eye

THE magician passes a small pill box, about 4 inches in diameter and 1 inch high to any one of his spectators. Upon turning the lid, the spectator will observe a pointer similar to a clock hand, and the dial of a clock. The spectator turns the hand to any of the twelve numbers he desires, closes the cover, and returns the box to the magician. The latter, without even opening the cover, tells the hour to which the hand has been set. The conjurer may even be blindfolded if the spectators so desire. The illustration below shows why this trick is so relatively simple. An axle runs clear through the box from the hand to a gear in the back. This gear in turn communicates the motion to two others, the last of which is connected directly to what seems to be a manufacturer's trademark. The position of this manufacturer's trade-mark with reference to the box, or with relation to another mark on the box indicates the time. Magician has but to look at the direction in which the stamp is pointing to tell the time. When blindfolded the magician looks beneath the blindfold, or resorts to touch.

The arrangement of the gears for performing the X-ray eye effect is indicated above.

The Vanishing Table

HERE is an excellent finale to a stage presentation of a magical performance. After the presentation of a series of tricks, the wizard's assistant

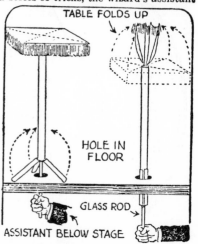

A folding table made as indicated, can be vanished at the end of the performance.

clears the side-table which the magician has been using during the performance. The conjurer displays a large cloth, holds it in front of the table for but a fraction of a second, jerks the cloth away and tosses it out toward the audience, who see at the same time that the entire table has been mystically vanished in thin air.

Explanation: The table itself is mechanical. The top consists of four ribs, which close up umbrella fashion. These are covered with silk and fringe. The table legs are three metal shells, supporting the metal stand. These shells, when folded to the sides of the table, lie perfectly flat. The stand is held in place by the assistance of a glass rod, reaching up from beneath the stage through a small floor hole no more than 2 inches in diameter. The assistant pulls down on the glass rod, to collapse the table.

The Coin in the Egg

This is quite an effective parlor trick, very easily mastered. A coin is borrowed from anyone in the audience and is marked for identification. An aluminum egg cup, together with an unprepared egg, is then examined. This egg had previously been chosen by someone in the audience. The egg is put in the cup and the whole presented to some member to hold. The coin is then mysteriously vanished, and on breaking the eggshell is drawn from the center of the egg with the assistance of an examined pair of tweezers. By way of explanation, it might be mentioned that the original coin is secretly placed in a groove in the egg cup made to receive it. A duplicate is vanished, by any of the various methods previously suggested in this publication. As the egg is placed into the cup, the thin shell is broken by the edge of the coin. The coin thus lies in the center of the egg and near the bottom until removal.

Mesmerized Salt-Cellar

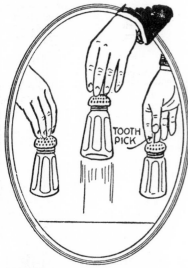

A salt-cellar can be mystically raised by what appears to be the finger tips, if a toothpick is inserted into one of the holes as shown in the diagram above.

HERE is an effective impromptu after-dinner trick which may be performed anywhere. No previous preparation is necessary. In effect, the wizard is seen to place his finger tips upon the cap of a salt-cellar, and then slowly raise it into the air.

Explanation: The magician, during the course of the meal, finds an opportunity to secrete a toothpick beneath his finger ring. Calling attention to the salt-cellar he secretly introduces the toothpick in a hole in the top. To free the salt-cellar, it is only necessary that the pick be held firmly and the finger tips stretched a bit, forcing the object off the wood splint.

Rope Comedy Trick

PRESENT-DAY magicians so often have occasion to call up a volunteer assistant from their audience, that it is often well to take advantage of these opportunities, by introducing some comedy effect or other. In this trick the magician asks his assistant to seat himself on a chair which the wizard provides. During the course of the performance and while doing some trick, the magician sees a piece of rope protruding from the assistant's coat. Reaching down, the conjurer grasps the rope and pulls it forth.

Explanation: The diagram explains all. The rope will be seen to be coiled under the seat of the chair, which has been especially prepared for that purpose. The free end of the rope comes up through the wood of the chair.

For comedy effect, the trick shown above is a good one to try on a volunteer assistant.

A New Thumb-Tie

In this thum-tie it is not necessary that both thumbs be tied, yet the effect of both being tied is present and completely fools the audience.

THE writer's original rope tie for amateurs is herewith described. Sash cord, such as that to be used, is wound around the thumb, tied or sewed, and the ends are then cut short. This hand is then kept out of sight until the moment of presentation. At the proper time, the hand with the tied finger is brought up under cover of the other hand. The spectator now proceeds as usual. He takes a piece of string, about fourteen inches long, and places it about the thumbs. By a slight movement, the magician frees the tied thumb and permits the loop to remain around the ropeless finger only. To the spectators, the binding seems to effect both hands. After presentation, both strings are cut with the blade of a knife.

Death-Defying Casket

A sensational casket illusion. A large steel coffin-shaped box stands high above stage level, upon a small platform. A committee is invited upon the stage to inspect the apparatus. The wizard introduces a young lady assistant, who enters the casket. The door is closed upon the cabinet, and very many swords are thrust clear through the box, through cavities made to receive them. To the spectators, it seems an utter impossibility for the young lady to escape death, under these conditions. Yet, when the swords are removed, the door is again opened, and out steps the damsel, none the worse for her "terrifying" experience.

Secret. The cabinet is unprepared. Not so, however, with the swords. These are so constructed as to enable the young lady upon the inside of the box to remove a section thereof, while they are apparently passing through the box. To complete the illusion, a number of sword points, which have been nested and concealed in her clothing, come into action. These points are inserted into corresponding cavities in the casket, in proper angle with the swords. In removing these swords, the points are likewise removed from the interior of the box, renested, and again concealed. Only those in her path need be prepared. The others are real and may be passed for examination. Many other variations of this trick will suggest themselves to the magician.

READING BURNED CARD

The razor blade, attached to the false thumb, enables the magician to cut the envelope in such a fashion that its contents will be disclosed.

● THE first effect described here is, unquestionably, one of the simplest and most effective for secretly obtaining information, written upon a card, previously sealed securely in an envelope. The effect of its presentation consists of requesting a subject to write a sentence, a series of names, a date of birth, or similar subject, upon a small card, which he is requested to seal inside an unprepared envelope. The magician collects the envelope, and together with its contents, burns it. The ashes are permitted to drop upon a common china plate; and the psychic, with an utterance of the mystic abracadabra, proceeds to "psychomotrize" the ashes. Mysteriously enough, he reads aloud the name or message, which was originally written upon the visiting card.

Explanation: The magician has provided himself with the ever-useful false thumb (made of aluminum or other thin material, painted flesh color and fitting the natural thumb, like a thimble). To this has been affixed the corner of a sharp razor blade. In the act of returning to the platform, with the envelope in his hand, the performer secretly cuts a section of the envelope, enabling him to read what has been written upon the card, as shown in the illustration. In the act of lighting the envelope, ample time is provided for him to read the message.

Chinese Lantern

A folded Chinese lantern is filled with water after being opened. The magician then plunges his hand into the interior of the lantern and withdraws large quantities of silks, pours out the water and collapses the lantern. It is apparent from the drawings that the telescopic Chinese lantern contains a rubber bag affixed to half of the lantern and extending halfway across the top. This serves to hold the water.

The Mystic Box

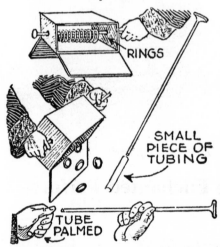

A SMALL box is exhibited. The box has two holes in opposite sides. A rod, and four or five small endless brass rings are shown. The stick has a projecting knob upon the one end larger than the holes in the sides of the box. The stick is run through these holes so as to permit the rings to slide over same upon the interior of the box, and the two doors closed. The magician explains that the rings cannot be removed from the stick because he holds the end firmly in his hand. Yet, at command, the rings drop off. The secret—A small piece of tubing corresponding in color with the stick, slides over one end of the stick. This tubing, projecting from the hole, gives the impression that the stick is held firmly in place, whereas in reality, the knob at the opposite end is pulled out slightly, so as to permit the rings to slide off the rod and drop into the box.

The Mystic Bottle

In the trick illustrated below a bottle seemingly inverts itself under a cover.

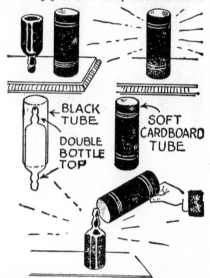

A quart bottle and a flexible cylinder are shown. The bottle is placed on the table in an inverted position. When sliding the cardboard tube down upon the table, the extra section of the bottle slides down flush with the table and causes the illusion of inverting the bottle.

Paper Magic

By tearing three sheets of paper colored red, white and blue respectively, the magician forms an American flag therefrom.

THE wizard with bared arms shows both hands decidedly empty. He now walks to the table and picks up three sheets of tissue paper each about 12 inches square. These to all appearances differ from one another in color only, one is red, another white, and a third blue. Holding three together, he proceeds to tear them into strips which are then rolled into a ball between the palms of his hands. The papers are again unrolled to form a large American flag of tissue paper. The diagram discloses the fact that the blue paper is not quite as innocent as it seems. In one corner a pocket of a duplicate sheet of paper is formed which houses the folded American flag. Torn sheets are disposed of after the flag is opened.

The Penetrating Eye

The magician is seated on a platform covered with a metal barrel, previously examined, and then with a cloth. In spite of this, the wizard reads sets of numbers and totals up columns of figures. The periscope aids him.

THE wizard takes a position on a small platform. A metal barrel carefully examined is then placed over him and the barrel is draped with cloth, to further assure the audience that it is quite impossible for the entertainer to see anything that is taking place about him. A blackboard is then arranged and figures are written upon it by anyone in the audience. Notwithstanding all this preparation, the wizard calls aloud the total of rows of figures that are written on the blackboard, and any or all figures which may be pointed out at random by a freely chosen spectator.

Explanation: This apparent second sight is performed by the aid of a telescopic periscope concealed beforehand in the performer's clothing.

Another Vanishing Handkerchief

THE magician takes a small silk handkerchief of brilliant color and fine texture and places it on the tip of his magic wand. Forming his fingers fist fashion, he proceeds to push the handkerchief slowly into his closed hand. As the wand emerges from the opposite end of the hand, it will be found that the handkerchief is no longer over the end, and when the magician slowly opens his hand, the kerchief will have been found to have completely disappeared. Insofar as the effect is concerned, the trick is not entirely new, but the modus operandi is distinctive.

Explanation: In this effect, a small weight fitted with a barbless fishhook, slides easily within the wand. When placing the kerchief at the end of the wand, it can quickly be hooked to the weight and, of course, under cover of the hand, the handkerchief is pulled down into the metal wand.

A silk kerchief, having been placed over the end of a wand, disappears.

A Hindu Mystery

With the aid of a paper shell made in the form of an imitation bamboo stick, the stick can be apparently converted into a snake; the bamboo disappears under cover of the cloth.

IN the land of the Far East, it has frequently been said that a Hindu can throw his cane on the ground and convert it into a snake. Some writers claim that the snake is paralyzed by holding it just in back of the head and exerting considerable pressure there. However, here is a trick which has also originated in the East. A bamboo stick is tapped against the side of a long glass jar. The stick is then placed in the jar, and the whole covered with a cloth. On removing the cloth, a snake is found, the stick having disappeared.

Explanation: This effect is performed by a paper imitation bamboo shell in which the snake is placed. A wooden plug is mounted in the end so that when the shell taps the glass jar, a genuine ring will be produced. The paper shell is crumbled with the cloth and tossed aside.

The Enchanted Perfume Vial

In this effect, the conjurer exhibits a small vial of highly-scented fine Oriental perfume. He permits many of those in the room to smell of its contents, and to enjoy its rare fragrance. Placing the stopper in the vial; he puts it carefully aside. Inasmuch as several of the company have been overlooked, someone is sure to remark about it. On *uncorking the bottle, this party will find that the fragrant perfume has changed to ammonia or some unpleasant smelling fluid. As the diagram indicates, the vial has a secret cup which holds a small quantity of perfume. When the stopper is placed firmly down in the neck, this vial will be removed with the next attempt to uncork the bottle.*

Popular Ventriloquial
Entertainer

VENTRILOQUISM can be mastered by anyone possessing good vocal organs who will devote the necessary amount of time, patience and practice to its study.

Ventriloquism is an art and one of the most entertaining and amusing forms of entertainment known.

Ventriloquists are not born. If they were, they could start giving ventriloquial entertainments while still in their cradles. We are forced to admit, though, that the lusty shouting of some infants does strengthen their lungs and the parents of a shouting juvenile entertainer should by all means teach them ventriloquism when they grow older.

Ventriloquial entertainers on the vaudeville stage or when appearing at amateur entertainments are well liked and their efforts usually well rewarded.

When the clever ventriloquial entertainer has the right kind of an act or dialogue, he is sure to meet with the approval of an audience. There are many novel ways of presenting an act of this type.

The deceptiveness of sound when unexpected is great. When the entertainer holds a figure or a doll on his knee and speaks to it in one voice and the figure seems to answer in another while moving its mouth in a perfectly natural manner from the audiences' viewpoint, it looks as if the words were actually issuing from the lips of the figure.

A good ventriloquial performer handles his ventriloquial figure in such manner that the figure seems to an audience to be a human being. The ventriloquist must be somewhat of an actor. He must speak to the figure, as he manipulates it, as if it were a human being and in turn listen to the doll when it speaks, just as if the figure did actually speak and the words

were being heard for the first time.

Ventriloquism, as most people understand it, is a trick in which the performer moves his lips when talking and when the figure answers the ventriloquist speaks with his lips tightly closed. This is not so.

The ventriloquist's lips are kept slightly open and most ventriloquists during their acts smoke cigarettes or a cigar. This aids in keeping the lips a bit apart. The cigarette is usually held in the center of the mouth and ventriloquial sounds are allowed to issue forth from the side of the mouth nearest the figure. A cigar can be used in the same way, keeping it in the side of the mouth farthest from the figure and allowing the ventriloquist's voice to issue from the side of the mouth nearest the ventriloquial figure.

Ventriloquism is one of the easiest yet amusing and mysterious of the arts of entertaining, but requires practice and patience. You cannot expect to play a violin in a day or week. Neither can you expect to become a ventriloquist in a few days.

It is a foolish belief that one must be superhuman vocally and have an abnormally developed throat or use some sort of mechanical appliance to entertain with ventriloquism.

If you should decide to go deeper into the fascinating study of ventriloquism and take up the art for professional work, I would suggest you secure a copy of "Vaudeville Ventriloquism" and by doing this save many dollars you may spend on worthless courses.

Learn to use your voice correctly. When using a ventriloquial figure, speak a pitch lower than your real voice when speaking to the figure, and raise your voice a pitch higher than your

natural voice when having the dummy answer you. If you can't do this successfully, use your regular speaking voice when addressing figure and for the figure's or ventriloquial voice pitch your voice higher.

The voice you use while speaking naturally to the figure must be distinctly different from the figure's, otherwise the illusion of two people talking is lost.

When speaking to the figure in your natural voice, move your lips quite a bit but don't overdo it. When speaking for the figure, keep your lips as still as possible and a bit open. This requires a lot of practice, as we have been taught from childhood to speak with lips in motion so as to pronounce words distinctly.

Practice the alphabet time and again, before a mirror, keeping the lips as still as possible. While going over the letters you will find you can say A, C, D, without much lip movement. Omit, for the time being, B, F, M, P, V, W. Go on through the rest of the letters and then come back to the more difficult ones. Don't try to go ahead too quickly.

Now try and pronounce B, F, M, P, V and W with your lips quite still. One finds that it is almost impossible. When any of these consonants appear in the words to be spoken in the ventriloquial voice, a slight change has to be made.

For instance, "Tell me what you are talking about." The figure would repeat it as "Tell nee what you're talking agout." The professional ventriloquial entertainer, due to constant practice, is able to use any word in the ventriloquial voice. A good way out of this difficulty is to have a cigarette or cigar in your mouth and when you come to a word with any of the above letters, you can put your hand up to your mouth to remove cigarette or cigar and at the same time pronounce the words with ease under cover of the hand.

After mastering to talk with jaws held rigid, commence saying, 'Hello' in a high key, straining the back of the throat *slightly*, and after a little practice it will sound as if coming from a distance. When you can do this, try longer sentences, such as, "Are you there?" "Hurry up," etc. Do not strain your throat too much till it becomes used to this sort of exercise.

After a time, you will be able to speak in your ventriloquial voice almost as easily as in your own voice. The place f r o m which you wish to make your voice appear to come must be suggested by your acting. For instance, when addressing an imaginary person on the roof, look at the ceiling and reply in your distant voice and the audience will think it comes from above.

The same when addressing the figure in the trunk or a box, when replying, place your ear close to box as if you were listening for the voice and reply in the distant voice, the result of which will seem as if the voice really does issue from the trunk or box. In ventriloquism it is absolutely necessary to breathe through the nose.

Bear in mind the ventriloquist's art consists in imitating the human voice of a child, fresh boy, old man, etc.

Acquire a f u l l and regular breathing. Correct breathing is just as important in the study of ventriloquism as it is in singing. The correct way to breathe at all times is through the nose. Acquire a full and r e g u l a r breathing, learning to inflate the lungs to their fullest capacity without strain.

Learn to keep the air in the lungs as long as possible, avoiding straining, and exhale slowly, making as little air go as far as possible. Twenty minutes a day spent in inflating the lungs fully and retaining the breath as long as possible will make quite a difference in your ability to make a very little air go a very long way without inconvenience. This must be practiced continually . . . as it is most important.

The various placings of the tongue for various voice throwing bits will be easily acquired by continued practice. Imitate from life. How did the child's voice sound from the roof? How did the man's voice sound from the cellar when he asked which was the electric meter? Figure it out and have a friend go into a closet and speak to you, etc. Study well; you won't regret it.

In the distant v o i c e work, more breath must be held back and the tongue should be placed and kept forward in the mouth and the various sounds thrown back into the throat. The nearer the sound to be given, the more air is allowed to escape with the tongue placed more to the back of the mouth.

The ventriloquist moderates his voice to suit the figure he works with in his specialty.

The fresh kid figure, usually a red-headed boy, is the kind of f i g u r e the single-figure performer can get the most fun out of. My ventriloquial figure smiles, moves his eyes, winks, moves his mouth, spits, smokes and moves his arms. Special movements can be made in figure if built by an expert. Personally, I like the natural mouth movement rather than the mechanical sliding movement with which some ventriloquial figures are equipped.

The kid's voice should be a tone higher than your own natural voice and the voice used to speak to the figure should be pitched a tone lower than your natural speaking voice, as mentioned before. Keep this important point well in mind at all times.

When you have practiced and mastered the first s t a g e s of speaking in the ventriloquial voice, practice holding s h o r t conversations with an imaginary figure. Address the figure in your ordinary voice, only in a slightly deeper tone. The reply, in a tone higher, with your teeth nearly touching and the voice will appear to come from an imaginary figure.

A little girl's voice is much higher in tone and should be pronounced more slowly and deliberately. Listen to a c h i l d

about 6 years old and try with your lips still to imitate t h e voice. If it is a girl you should speak through your nose. Imitate from life. Life is the best teacher in all things.

The little girl's voice is slightly more nasal than the boy's, as it is in a much higher key.

An old man's voice is gruff, deep-toned and s p o k e n deep down in the throat. Practice this slowly and when you have mastered it, hold a conversation, commencing in your ordinary voice and reply in the old man's voice, just as if the figure was beside you.

The old woman's voice is very much like the little girl's only not in quite so high a key. This is spoken more in the back of the throat. Practice how to manipulate the dummy's mouth in front of a mirror before presenting a specialty.

A more detailed and thorough study of this art can be more fully learned from books on "Vaudeville Ventriloquism."

I would advise the novice to purchase an inexpensive figure and practice with it, as this not only familiarizes one with the figure but makes the study more interesting.

There follows a ventriloquial dialogue or specialty which the student can study and use for his forthcoming entertainments.

BROADCASTING
A Ventriloquial Specialty

Few bars of a catchy musical number opens act.

The ventriloquist walks onto stage, without figure, sings one verse and chorus of a popular song. If entertainer h a s a strong singing voice, the act may be opened with a ballad.

During song voice from right of stage, calls "Hey!" T h i s voice calls at intervals while the song is being sung. Ventriloquist must make it seem to audience that it is his powers of Ventriloquism which cause the voice to appear from distance. This is done by a little acting and a bit of showmanship. (In reality:—a friend standing off-stage, in a disguised voice, whispers the "Hey." In dialogue:

Vent:—Ventriloquist; Fig:—Figure.)

After Song is Sung

VENT:—(*Speaking to someone offstage*) . . . I'll fix you for interrupting my singing. (*Starts R.*)

VOICE:—(*Offstage*) Was that singing?

VENT:—Certainly it was.

VOICE:—Then . . . DANCE!

VENT:—(*Goes to side of stage, comes back carrying figure.*) The idea! You sure are as rude as can be. I am surprised at you!

FIG:—(*Is made to squirm.*)

VENT:—What's wrong?

FIG:—(*Wails*) I want to go home!

VENT:—Don't be nervous. All these people out there will be your friends if you behave.

FIG:—My friends?

VENT:—Yes . . . your friends.

FIG:—Will they loan you money?

VENT:—Certainly.

FIG:—Will they ever get it back?

VENT:—Never mind . . . behave yourself, please!

FIG:—Will they loan me money too?

VENT:—Certainly not!

FIG:—(*Howls*) I want to go home!!!

VENT:—Tell me . . . do you like (*localize the city*)?

FIG:—It's great!

VENT:—How are you getting along in school here?

FIG:—The teacher told me I knew more than she did.

VENT:—And what did you say?

FIG:—I agreed with her.

VENT:—I want to ask you a question . . .

FIG:—What's the answer?

VENT:—You cost me my patience!

FIG:—That's about all.

VENT.—Do you mean to insinuate I am a miser?

FIG:—I never insinuate . . .

VENT:—I'm ashamed of you!

FIG:—So am I!

VENT:—If you'll behave I'll take you out later.

FIG:—Yes you will!

VENT:—I certainly will. What would you like to do most?

FIG:—Make whoopee!

VENT:—Your last night's home study was arithmetic. Let us see if you have studied it. How much is 3 and 4?

FIG:—Seven.

VENT:—Correct! How much is 6 and 4?

FIG:—Ten.

VENT:—Correct! What is the total of 14 and 12?

FIG:—Twenty-nine!

VENT:—All wrong. I can see you didn't study.

FIG:—Do you know arithmetic?

VENT:—I can answer any question you care to put to me.

FIG:—Dunninger the second!

VENT:—Go ahead and try me.

FIG:—How much is 8 and 10?

VENT:—Eighteen!

FIG:—(*Hesitates a bit*) Correct! 12 and 9?

VENT:—Twenty-one.

FIG:—(*Hesitates*) Right! (*To audience*) He's smart! 45 and 65 is how much?

VENT:—One hundred and seven!

FIG:—(*Whistles*) (*Hesitates*)

VENT:—Isn't that correct?

FIG:—Right! How much is eight thousand and ninety-six plus three hundred thousand nine hundred and ninety-nine and two-thirds?

VENT:—See here . . . do you think I'm stupid?

FIG:—Right!!

VENT:—(*Hits figure*)

FIG:—(*Yells*) I want to go home!

VENT:—Now see here. I don't want to quarrel with you. Let us be friends. What was that song you were singing in the dressing room?

FIG:—(*Title*) "I Don't Know."

VENT:—Have you already forgotten it?

FIG:—I don't know.

VENT:—Too bad. Can't you recall it?

FIG:—I don't know.

VENT:—(*Angrily*) Are you trying to make a clown out of me?

FIG:—Too late!

VENT:—Now stop this! Tell me the name of that song immediately . . .

FIG:—"I Don't Know."

VENT:—You know but you don't know. Is that it?

FIG:—I Don't Know.

VENT:—You blockhead! You have no brains . . . I forgot!

FIG:—So did I!

VENT:—Please sing that song for me.

FIG:—Right now?

VENT:—Yes, right here and now.

FIG:—I'd rather make whoopee!

VENT:—(*Hits him*)

FIG:—(*Yells*) I want to go home!!

(*Man walks onto the stage, gives letter to ventriloquist and exits.*)

VENT:—(*Fingers letter before opening it*)

FIG:—(*Stops crying, gets inquisitive*) Who's it from . . . the the tailor?

VENT:—That's not a bill! (*Opens it, reads to himself*)

FIG:—That letter must come from the polar regions.

VENT:—What makes you think so?

FIG:—There's a seal on the envelope.

VENT:—This letter is from a spirit medium I know. (*Continues reading letter to himself*)

FIG:—Yeh!

VENT:—Yes!

FIG:—(*Mimicing*) A spirit voice over here tells me—

VENT:—Be still—

FIG:—My fluttering heart!

VENT:—I am so happy—

FIG:—Old Slater mixing with spirits again—

VENT:—Don't you believe in spirit messages?

FIG:—I may be wood . . . but I am not dumb!

VENT:—All about us hover spirits . . . spirits of dear departed souls—

FIG:—I WANT TO GO HOME!!

VENT:—Don't be afraid. They never hurt anyone.

FIG:—Change your cigarettes!

VENT:—Do you doubt spirits can deliver messages?

FIG:—Have they a Western Union?

VENT:—I'm only wasting time with you—

FIG:—(*interrupting*) Who asked you to?

VENT:—You're too snappy to suit me!

FIG:—Says you!

VENT:—By the way . . . I almost forgot. I was supposed to bring something home to my wife. Goodness . . . I've forgotten what it is!

FIG:—I know. I heard her ask you. It's wallpaper.

VENT:—Wallpaper?

FIG:—Yeh.

VENT:—Whatever put that idea into your head? Why, you blockhead, what can we do with wallpaper? Our rooms are papered . . . see here . . . you don't even know what wall paper is.

FIG:—I don't?

VENT:—No, you don't.

FIG:—Says you!

VENT:—Listen here . . . what is wallpaper? (*Winks at audience*)

FIG:—Sticky paper to catch flies on.

VENT:—I told you you didn't know.

FIG:—What is it, then?

VENT:—What is it one sticks on the wall of a room?

FIG:—Chewing gum!

VENT:—By the way, I bought a new automobile this morning.

FIG:—Pay for it?

VENT:—Nobody asked you.

FIG:—No . . . but I asked you!

VENT:—I believe you are jealous of my buying a new car.

FIG:—I'm tickled silly!

VENT:—Then why don't you wish me luck with it?

FIG:—I'm waiting to find out what kind it is.

VENT:—Why are you waiting to find out what kind it is?

FIG:—So I'll know whether to laugh or syn.pathize!

VENT:—I think I will sing, professor.

FIG:—Why spoil the evening.

VENT:—I suppose you think I can't sing?

FIG:—I don't think.

VENT:—Is that so? You needn't get so wise, young man! (*Pushes figure*)

FIG:—(*To musical director*) Look, he wants to play with me!

VENT:—(*To leader*) Will you kindly strike a chord for me? (*Chord is struck*) Me . . me . . me . . e . . e!

FIG:—(*Places head on ventriloquist's shoulder*)

VENT:—Now I shall sing!

FIG:—Take me home!

VENT:—Why, I have a fine voice—

FIG:—Says you!

VENT:—I sing with feeling!

FIG:—If you had any feeling you wouldn't sing!

VENT:—You can sleep, if you want to, but I'll sing.

FIG:—You would!

(*Ventriloquist sings a chorus of a popular song. Figure at the end of each line emits a snore.*

VENT:—Now that he's asleep I can sing some more. (*Sings this line*) "There's a rainbow 'round my shoulder—

FIG:—(*Loudly emits a snore*)

VENT:—(*Singing*) . . . and it fits me like a glove—

FIG:—(*Sings*) If I had wings of an angel—

VENT:—(*Looks at figure.*) I thought you were asleep.

FIG:—How can anyone sleep with that noise?

VENT:—I shall now recite!

FIG:—Is it absolutely necessary?

VENT:—(*Ignoring him*) (*recites*) Dark and cloudy was the night . . . and what a night . . . what a night . . . and suddenly from out of the din and the glare stumbled—

FIG:—Julius Caesar—

VENT:—Stumbled Julius Caesar . . . a . . . no it wasn't Julius Caesar—

FIG:—Must have been another fellow—

VENT:—The man was a mighty statesman and he well knew—

FIG:—Death has no sting—

VENT:—See here . . . who is reciting this thing anyway?

FIG:—The pleasure is all yours.

VENT:—Then why do you interrupt me?

FIG:—To save your life!

VENT:—Say, Johnny, you are a smart boy. Where do you live?

FIG:—How did you know my name?

VENT:—Guessed it.

FIG:—Then guess where I live.

VENT:—Did I tell you that on the way to the theatre tonight I was half killed—

FIG:—Why do you always do things by halves?

VENT:—I overheard a lady ask you about the talking pictures the other night . . . and what did you say?

FIG:—What did I say?

VENT:—You told her they kept you awake!

FIG:—They do. Since the talkies a fellow can't even get a decent sleep in a theatre.

VENT:—Do you realize that the talking pictures are revolutionizing screen entertainment?

FIG:—How about daylight pictures?

VENT:—I'm speaking of talking pictures now.

FIG:—I don't like 'em. Most of the actors must have asthma.

VENT:—What do you mean?

FIG:—Have you ever heard a talkie?

VENT:—I have and I like them very much.

FIG:—You would!

VENT:—I go to see every talking picture I can and I take my wife along with me.

FIG.—Oh, I see now. She has to keep quiet to see the show, eh?

VENT:—I had mackerel for supper.

FIG:—I had some radio fish.

VENT:—Radio fish?

FIG:—Yeh . . . Tuna!

Vent:—I had my life insured for twelve thousand dollars last week.

FIG:—Twelve thousand of you aren't worth half that sum!

VENT:—(*Hits figure*)

FIG:—(*Yells*) I want to go home!!

VENT:—And when I die one half of my fortune goes to charity.

FIG:—Who gets the other dollar?

VENT:—(*Looks at watch*) It's time to broadcast . . . (*Arranges "mike", and turns on switch*) Good evening . . . my good friends of the radio audience. . . .

FIG:—(*Interrupts*) You should be thankful you can't see him.

VENT:—Don't you folks recognize that mysterious voice—

FIG:—The masked tenor will now recite—

VENT:—This evening we have a program I am sure you will all enjoy—

FIG:—If it ever gets started.

VENT:—First allow me to introduce a charming little lady from Spotless Town known as—

FIG:—The Ink Stain herself.

VENT:—This little lady is here this evening in person—

FIG:—Not in the mood.

VENT:—So while you are waiting—

FIG:—(Sings) Climb upon my knee, Sonny Boy!

VENT:—(Interrupts) The next number on this evening's—

FIG:—Riot.

VENT:—Program is a solo by Blockhead Johnny entitled—

FIG:—He Claims He is a Self-Made Man, But He Did Waste a Lot of Good Material.

FIGURE SINGS A SONG . . .

TOWARD END VENTRILOQUIST CARRIES FIGURE TOWARD RIGHT SIDE OF STAGE AND WALKS OFF.

Spirit Pictures

THE magician playing the role of a medium sits before a large canvas covered frame placed on an easel. A lamp with a powerful light is fixed directly behind the canvas, rendering it transparent. As the medium goes into a trance and the lights are lowered, a picture in colors gradually forms. This effect is produced by an assistant below the stage, who holds in his hand a bottle containing a solution of potassium prussiate. A tube leading from the bottle runs through the light stand through which the solution is sprayed upon the canvas. The canvas itself has been previously painted with solutions of iron sulphate, bismuth nitrate and copper sulphate for blue, yellow and brown colors respectively. When these solutions dry they are invisible. It is preferable to lightly outline the picture to be painted with a pencil before applying the solutions.

SPRAY IN LAMP SHIELD

SOLUTION OF POTASSIUM PRUSSIATE

ATOMIZER

BELOW STAGE

TRAY

RING IN HANDKERCHIEF

HINGE

Magic Tumbler

THE effect of this mysterious trick is attained by very simple apparatus. The magician's assistant comes forth with a thin metal tray holding a large tumbler of wine. The conjuror covers the glass with a silk handkerchief and removes it from the tray. Tossing the kerchief into the air the glass and its liquid contents have apparently vanished. The telltale diagrams accompanying disclose the secret. The glass itself is nothing more than a sheet of celluloid held in position as here illustrated in a semi-circular form by means of a thread. The celluloid is painted to resemble wine. When the thread is released the piece of celluloid falls flat upon the tray and is invisible. A metal ring placed in a pocket in a handkerchief of the same size as the supposed glass enhances the illusion.

The Ghost Frame

THIS particular offering has been used by the author for a number of years and holds the distinction of having mystified some of the cleverest and best posted magicians in the country. It consists of a large wooded frame in which is fixed a sheet of glass. A flap which opens up as illustrated is hinged to the affair. The flap being shown empty and the glass frame being exhibited, the affair is closed and placed face down upon the table, but in the act of closing, the "flap" is permitted to fall, exposing the secret contents. With a little practice the magician can manipulate the apparatus with such dexterity that the action of causing the second flap to fall is unobserved by the spectators.

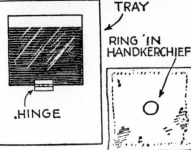

GLASS FRAME

Do the Spirits return? Use your own Judgement

SMALL MIRROR DISK

Twentieth Century Mind Reading

IN THIS particular experiment an unprepared deck of cards bearing the closest of inspection is freely shuffled and placed into a glass tumbler, which is held at arm's length by the magician. In spite of the fact that the cards face the audience with their back to the performer, he mysteriously calls the exact rotation of the entire deck reading the cards in front first, and removing one at a time as he reads them. The magician does not have to have his own deck for this experiment as any deck will serve the purpose. Like most good effects the trick is extremely simple, the magician having merely provided himself with a small mirror disk, attached to a flesh colored band or a ring. The small dental mirrors serve the purpose admirably. One need merely look at the index of the card and name it.

"Dunninger"— *An Autobiography*

I have been asked to write a short autobiography. I want to say, as a preface, that I lay no claim to being born in Russia, France, or Budapest. Nor was I brought up in the shadow of the Pyramids. I am a native New Yorker. I was not born of humble parentage, nor was I an infant prodigy. I never realized that I possessed the remarkable ability of extracting the thoughts from the brains of the other fellow, until I was well past the tender age.

My magical ability and digital dexterity, I mastered only after tireless practice and acute observation, finding that I have rather an uncanny mind for developing and solving mechanics of the craft. I have made the word "originality" a foundation for my magical doings.

Biographies, as a rule, are always a trifle egotistical, and as I have been requested to do this, I trust that my readers will pardon my plain statement of facts; as they are all real and have actually happened, and I ask to be pardoned for the privilege of using the personal pronoun.

When I was quite young and occupied in the general activities invented in the mind of a youth, it seemed that my foremost craving was for things mysterious and unexplainable. I was between 8 and 10 years of age when I visited a theatre and witnessed the performance of Professor Kellar (at that time the world's greatest conjuror). Amazed and open-mouthed, I sat bewildered at the many marvelous things presented by this Master Wizard—the disappearing rabbits, the mysterious silks, the bowls of water produced out of thin air, and many other mystifying and equally impressive wonders. All were miraculous to me, and at once I felt within myself the desire to look into the pages of the secret volumes of magic, to learn how it was all done.

True, as time progressed, I realized that many of the things I saw were rather simple to explain, but hard to do. I learned that long and tiresome practice, absolute, constant and forceful endeavor are the only qualities which would bring forth the power of successfully mystifying my many friends.

A large tool chest which had been given to me as a Christmas present by my father, served as a godsend with which I manufactured many of the tricks which produced my program. A few pennies' admission from the boys, who were constant spectators of my uncanny seances, helped to build the fund which, in turn supplied me with more building material. And, incidentally, more tricks were produced.

As the years passed on and I found myself more progressive in the fields of mysticism, I decided to follow the work as a profession; but to my sad disappointment, I realized that there seemed to be more magicians than engagements warranted. Competition seemed strong and the overcrowded field of wonder-workers was rather discouraging to me. I had, however, learned one very important factor, and that was the power of originality. I did not seek to copy the ideas of the other fellow, nor did I try to do the tricks with which conjurors had identified themselves; as I realized that there was much that could be done, without literally stepping on the other fellow's toes. I cannot impress too strongly on the minds of my magical readers, the importance of bearing this one fact as a foremost guide in their minds: "Create your own ideas. Leave the other fellow's tricks alone."

I studied the various branches of the profession, which involved the ever-famous jail-breaking act; and although I can ponder over the pages of many of my ancient scrapbooks to look upon the memories of some 200 jail-breaks and handcuff releases which I have effected, I realized that the many upper lights in this particular form of entertainment were too strong for successful competition.

Sleight-of-hand performances were likewise plentiful. A King of Cards at this time was a vaudeville favorite and a King of Coins. Much to my chagrin, professional magic seemed an impossible ladder to climb.

Although many of my competitors in writing advised readers to consider Magic only from the standard of a pastime or entertainment, I wish to go on record here as stating that were I asked to give up my profession for Rockefeller's money, I sincerely believe I would flatly refuse. When a man finds his vocation and feels he likes his work, truly there are few obstacles that can prevent his going to the top. In order to show what can be done in Magic, I am proud to state that, within a period of eight years, I found I could advance my salary from $8.00 a performance to the sum of $1,500 for a single night's demonstration. Financially, my readers will concede that this is good business; and I wish to impress upon your minds that it is not the work itself that counts or makes a man worth a higher price than his fellow conjuror, but the way one sells the tricks he uses. In other words, it is the showmanship involved that counts. I am pleased to say that at this writing I am at the head of my own two-and-a-half-hour performance, giving a series of absolutely new and original illusions, together with an array of effects in spiritualism and East Indian conjuring, and am traveling at the head of my own company, playing the largest theatres throughout the world.

I have had the honor of entertaining and mystifying such men as Theodore Roosevelt, William H. Taft, Woodrow Wilson and Calvin Coolidge; as well as Thomas A. Edison on five different occasions, and H. R. H. the Prince of Wales. It is creditable to find that such minds as these have accepted my work with interest, and that it is possible and probable for a magician to create for himself a reputation for high standards in our present form of social civilization.

Known as I am as a mind-reader, I would like my readers to know that although I do not claim to accomplish the impossible or the supernatural, this particular field of my profession consists of work different from that of the other fellow, and a gift of development which, to my belief, is rare. But, in all, I have been presenting a series of problems in mind-reading and mental telepathy for the past period of fourteen years; and I trust I shall not be misunderstood when I state that I am proud to claim that my work has never been duplicated by any of my fellow conjurors. Again my readers will appreciate the value of originality. Of course, conjurors follow certain lines of thought and, inasmuch as there are but a few principles that magicians can actually follow, I have often heard explanations of how my work might be accomplished. But—"The proof of the pudding is in the eating"—and it has never been done by any one else; which only emphasizes the fact that there is a vast and varied difference between knowing how a thing is done and doing it.

It is with great pleasure that I find that men, at the head of the business and professional worlds, have a keen and pronounced desire to present a trick or two for the entertainment of their friends. There is no finer field of entertaining, nor one as impressive, as conjuring. When one goes to the theatre and enjoys a good evening's performance, it is, of course, probable that one hears many good jokes or stories rendered that produce a good laugh, or listens to songs well-rendered by some artist, which are pleasing to the ear and soothing to the soul. But these forms of entertainment are soon forgotten, as there is no substance that leaves a lasting impression. But I am quite sure my reader can look back during the reading of this biography and recall the days when some magician presented a mystification which left an everlasting impression upon his mind.

For many years I have been identified as a social enter-

288

tainer, and have entertained, in addition to the "400," many professors of the various universities; and I have learned by these experiences that there are not many—in any walks or talks of life—who do not enjoy seeing a good trick well-rendered. In my private interviews with these people, after my performances have been completed, there has rarely been an evening when someone does not tell me of something or other that he has seen Kellar or Hermann produce when these magicians were in their palmiest days. Or possibly some one will tell me of a mystery that he has witnessed in the Himalaya Mountains, or in the streets of Calcutta.

At this moment, in my program of entertainment, I am reproducing the phenomenal feats of the many spiritistic mediums whose works I have treated. I am not laying bare the *modus operandi* which they employ to bring about these effects; as I do not believe in exposing the principles used by magicians to others not interested in the art; and I fully realize that the principles employed by mediums have been borrowed from those which magicians have been using in a form of good clean entertainment.

Young magicians who are choosing for themselves a professional standing with which to obtain a livelihood, cannot realize the number of interesting experiences that their travels will produce. I can look back with pleasant memories upon many happenings in various parts of the world, of so unique and odd a nature as to be seemingly the product of fiction.

While entertaining in China, for instance, I employed an illusion which consisted of a large glass tank of water from which I produced a young lady in full view of the audience. When this production was made, my audience practically went frantic, as it seems that I had overstepped the boundary of their religious law which forbids a woman to appear on their stage. My interpreter at once notified me of this grievous error, and I overcame the situation by placing her at once in another piece of apparatus and causing her immediate disappearance. My interpreter helped considerably by explaining to my spectators that what they saw was not truly a breathing, living girl, but an illusionary image. Inasmuch as the trick was a perfect one and the illusion complete, my audience accepted this explanation, but I did not feel at ease until I was safely upon my way to San Francisco.

My readers will undoubtedly learn, with their progress in the art of conjuring, that development of *salesmanship plus personality* is the greatest asset in this work. To be able to render an effect or illusion *perfectly* is half of the battle won. Good "patter," speeches well studied, and a smiling personality, spell success in magical performances.

You must, however, prepare yourself well for emergencies; as in this tricky business of magic the outcome of a trick may not always be what the wizard has planned, and the essential addition to one's training is a quick mind, plus quick fingers. I have seen one of our foremost conjurors obliged to pass up two illusions which had failed to operate correctly, without trying to overcome this embarrassing condition by some form of explanation that would have satisfied his audience. This, to my thinking, shows a lack of complete training, regardless of the man's magical standing, inasmuch as the audience lost considerable interest in the balance of his work, as they realized his inability to overcome a mishap.

It is important that the students of magic likewise study psychology, as there is no field of the theatrical profession which requires as much intimacy with the audience as entertaining by magic. Certain classes of people are skeptical and at times become annoying. Unless my readers are equipped with the knowledge of human nature, so as to read the facial expressions of those that present themselves as voluntary assistants, they will find themselves facing embarrassing questions, and situations which will prove not only troublesome, but often injurious to a successful mystical entertainment.

Physics, electricity, science and general mechanics, all are subjects essential and important to the education of an original magician. With the wonders of the radio, the miraculous achievement of sending pictures by wireless, and the evergrowing achievements of the seemingly impossible, it is difficult for the conjuror to keep up with the times; and the tricks for the magician of the future must be still more sensational, and surpass those which have satisfied in the past. We have so many things subject to our acceptance at the present time, which are uncanny, yet universally possible, however, that many sensational thoughts and extreme creations are brought to the mind of a conjuring entertainer.

I have found from experience that sensational illusions seem to be the most mystifying. Vaudeville managers realize this situation by headlining, and using striking titled tricks. So, let me say in conclusion of this biography, that my readers, to be successful magicians, must be apt students. Keep up with the times, read all, know all, go the other fellow one better, stop nowhere, aim high, and you must win!

JOSEPH DUNNINGER